BUSINESS
DATA COMMUNICATIONS

BUSINESS DATA COMMUNICATIONS

FOURTH EDITION

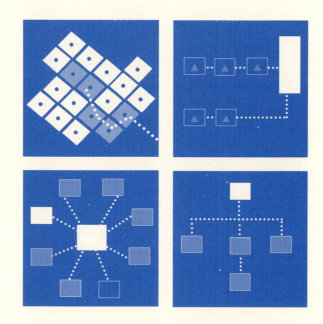

DAVID A. STAMPER

THE BENJAMIN/CUMMINGS PUBLISHING COMPANY, INC.

Redwood City, California • Menlo Park, California
Reading, Massachusetts • New York • Don Mills, Ontario • Wokingham, U.K.
Amsterdam • Bonn • Sydney • Singapore • Tokyo • Madrid • San Juan

To Virginia

Executive Editor: Larry Alexander
Associate Editor: Kathy Galinac
Editorial Assistant: Krista Reid-McLaughlin
Freelance Production Editor: Cathy Lewis
Text Design: Richard Kharibian & Associates
Cover Management: Yvo Riezebos
Cover Design: Yvo Riezebos
Art Supervisor: Becky Hainz-Baxter
Illustrator: Abigail Rudner — On the Wave
Copy Editor: Anna Huff
Proofreader: Eleanor Renner Brown
Manufacturing Supervisor: Jenny Rossi
Composition: Thompson Type
Cover Photo: ©Andy Washnik/The Stock Market.
Photo Credits: p. 52, Courtesy of Gabriel Electronics Inc.; p. 71, Courtesy of Supra Corporation.; p. 261, Photo courtesy of Wyse Technology.; p. 262, Courtesy of International Business Machines Corporation., p. 281, Courtesy of Atlantic Research Corporation.; p. 283, Courtesy of Electrodata, Inc.

Library of Congress Cataloging-in-Publication Data
Stamper, David A.
    Business data communications / David A. Stamper. — 4th ed.
      p. cm.
    Includes bibliographical references and index.
    ISBN 0-8053-7715-8
    1. Data transmission systems.   2. Computer networks.   I. Title.
TK5105.S734   1994
004.6 — dc20   94-3572
                                                      CIP

ISBN 0-8053-7715-8
      4 5 6 7 8 9 10 – DOW – 98 97 96

The Benjamin/Cummings Publishing Company, Inc.
390 Bridge Parkway
Redwood City, CA 94065

Preface

*B*usiness Data Communications, Fourth Edition, is designed for an introductory course in data communications, a required course within the Information Systems curriculum. The text provides a balanced approach, emphasizing both the managerial issues as well as the supporting technical knowledge needed to plan and manage today's communications systems.

The field of data communications continues to be one of the most dynamic in the computer industry. From client/server computing to the construction of the "Information Superhighway," hardly a month goes by without the introduction of a new hardware or software capability which extends the technology beyond its current limitations.

In recognition of these extensive changes, the fourth edition of *Business Data Communications* has been substantially reorganized. Complete coverage of the seven-layer Open Systems Interconnection (OSI), model is retained with each layer now discussed within the appropriate topic. This organizational change reflects the growing role of networking as the core of the data communications industry.

WHAT'S NEW IN THE FOURTH EDITION?

Expanded Coverage of Local Area Networks (LANs) and Wide Area Networks (WANs)

With the new organization, this edition places increased emphasis on internetworking as an important part of data communications. Thorough coverage of LANs and WANs is provided by:

- three general networking chapters (Introduction, Chapter 3, and Chapter 12)
- four LAN chapters (Chapters 4-7)
- four WAN chapters (Chapters 8-11)
- a discussion of LAN selection criteria (Chapter 7)
- expanded coverage of network management (Chapters 13-14)
- a chapter on software licensing (Chapter 6)
- examination of security issues, including coverage of encryption and virus protection (Chapter 15)
- a description of popular network systems, including Novell Netware, Microsoft Windows NT, Banyan Vines, and IBM's LAN Server and Network Management System.

Coverage of Current and Evolving Technologies

This edition includes coverage of emerging technologies that are transforming data communications. The following topics are new or expanded in this edition:

- multimedia on LANs (Chapter 3)
- the Internet (Chapter 11)
- the Information Superhighway (Chapter 11)
- international networking (Chapter 11)
- groupware, including E-mail and group decision support (Chapter 3 and 15)
- client/server Computing (Chapter 17)

New Pedagogical Feature

The numerous terms and acronyms associated with data communications can be overwhelming to students. In this edition a "running glossary" in the text margin has been added to assist students in learning and reviewing key terms as they are introduced.

Reorganization

The organization around the OSI Model used in the previous three editions has been changed to reflect the growing significance of networking and network interconnection within the field of data communications. To facilitate a logical flow of ideas and discussion, this edition has been restructured according to topic, and the OSI model is now covered where appropriate.

ORGANIZATION

Introduction to Data Communications
The introductory chapter provides a brief historical overview of data communications, establishes the needs and objectives of data communications, and introduces the OSI reference model.

Part I: Media and the Physical Layer
Part I introduces several commonly used media types and explores the advantages and disadvantages of each.

Part II: Local Area Networks
Part II considers the rationale for using networks and outlines the considerations to be evaluated in successfully integrating hardware, software, topologies, and protocols to form a local area network system.

Part III: Wide Area Networks
Building upon the discussion of LAN issues, Part III explores WAN hardware, software, topologies, and protocols, including special WAN topics such as the Internet and international networks.

Part IV: Network Interconnections and Management
Part IV explores the way in which different types of LANs and WANs can work together, and the role of network management in the successful implementation of network interconnection.

LEARNING AIDS

Part Openers   Each of the four parts of the text opens with a business or technology vignette to motivate students' interest regarding the most dynamic uses of the technology covered in the following part. The Instructor's Manual contains additional questions related to these vignettes to help facilitate class discussion and application of the concepts covered in the chapters of each part.

Learning Objectives   Each chapter begins with a set of learning objectives, that help students focus on and review the core concepts discussed in the chapter before proceeding to the next chapter.

Running Glossary   In this edition, key terms are defined in the margin as they are introduced to make them more accessible and easier for students to review.

Case Study ❖   This icon identifies a realistic case study based on the fictional Syncrasy Corporation. The case study chronicles a vigorous young company as it grows and diversifies, providing students a business context for applying the different technologies described in the text to the changing communications needs of a realistic situation.

Summary   Each chapter concludes with a summary of the key concepts discussed in the chapter.

Key Terms   Key terms are highlighted in bold throughout the text for easy identification and review. These terms are also listed at the end of each chapter with corresponding page references.

Review Questions   Review Questions at the end of each chapter stimulate discussion and encourage reflection on key points.

Problems and Exercises   Problems and Exercises provide specific research projects or situational problem-solving to augment each chapter.

References   Each chapter concludes with a bibliography which can be used as a valuable resource for independent exploration or group projects.

SUPPLEMENTS

Instructor's Manual *with Test Bank and Transparency Masters*   The accompanying Instructor's Manual includes the following features for each chapter in the text:

- objectives and teaching suggestions
- answers to selected Review Questions and Problems and Exercises
- discussion questions keyed to the part opening scenarios stimulate class discussion and encourage students to apply their knowledge of the key concepts
- over 600 multiple choice and true/false test questions and answers
- more than 100 Transparency Masters illustrate key figures and concepts from the text

Instructor's Manual (disk version)   The Instructor's Manual is also available on 3.5″ disk to adopters wanting a flexible version of this resource that they can customize with their own lecture notes or test questions.

Casebook (printed or disk version)   The six realistic cases in the Casebook help test analytical skills by relating data communications concepts to real-life business applications. The cases are designed to provide both flexible focus and solutions. The six cases explore the following topics:

Case 1   LANs and LAN Alternatives

Case 2   Network Interconnection

Case 3   Distributed Computing

Case 4   International Networks

Case 5   Network Configuration

Case 6   LAN Management

For more information about the fourth edition of *Business Data Communications* and its supplements, please contact your Benjamin/Cummings Sales and Marketing Representative, or call the publisher directly at (800) 950-BOOK.

ACKNOWLEDGMENTS

I am grateful to the numerous individuals who contributed to the fourth edition of this textbook. First, I wish to thank the following reviewers for their valuable comments and suggestions. Because of the extensive development of this text from prior editions of *Business Data Communications*, the analysis of topics and depth of coverage provided by the reviewers were crucial.

Lynda Armbruster
Rancho Santiago Community College

Mary Ann Dase
California State University,
Long Beach

David Doss
Illinois State University

Linda Eriksen
Umpaqua Community College

Dan Flynn
Shoreline Community College

Darrell Gobell
Cantonsville Community College

David Haglin
Mankato State University

Jamal Munshi
Sonoma State University

Sudha Ram
University of Arizona

Sachi Sakthivel
Bowling Green University

Clive Sanford
University of North Texas

Ward Testerman
California State Polytechnic University

Gary Turnquist
Eastern Michigan University

A special thanks to all the people at Benjamin/Cummings Publishing who contributed to the success of this project. In particular, I thank Michelle Baxter, Sr. Acquisitions Editor, for her insight over the years; Larry Alexander, Executive Editor, for his support and encouragement; Kathy Galinac, Associate Editor, for her direction and enthusiasm in guiding the content and feature development of this edition; Cathy Lewis, Production Editor, for coordinating the timely efforts of numerous people under an ambitious schedule; Becky Hainz-Baxter, Art Supervisor, for coordinating the art program; and Krista Reid-McLaughlin, Editorial Assistant, for her work on the supplements package.

Last, but not least, I wish to thank all of you—faculty, students and business professionals—who have used this book. I have received many comments and suggestions over the course of the previous three editions and your feedback has been sincerely appreciated.

David A. Stamper
October, 1994

Research Participants
FOURTH EDITION

CONTENT SURVEY

Lynda Armbruster
Rancho Santiago Community College

Cathy Bakes
Kent State University

Richard Born
Northern Illinois University

Maurice Chandra
Hofstra University

Michael Chung
Texas A & M

Dan Flynn
Shoreline Community College

Darrell Gobell
Cantonsville CC

David Haglin
Mankato State University

Sudha Ram
University of Arizona

Sachi Sakthivel
Bowling Green University

Norman Schneidewind
US Naval Post Graduate School

Eugene Stafford
Iona College

Gary Turnquist
Eastern Michigan University

Ray Tsai
St. Cloud State University

James Van Spreybroeck
St. Ambrose University

FEATURE SURVEY

Cathy Bakes
Kent State University

Mary Ann Dase
*California State University,
Long Beach*

Linda Eriksen
Umpaqua Community College

Dan Flynn
Shoreline Community College

David Haglin
Mankato State University

Sudha Ram
University of Arizona

Sachi Sakthivel
Bowling Green University

Clive Sanford
University of North Texas

Eugene Stafford
Iona College

Gary Turnquist
Eastern Michigan University

James Van Spreybroeck
St. Ambrose University

Brief Contents

Detailed Contents

PART I

CHAPTER 1

MEDIA AND THE PHYSICAL LAYER   41

Physical Aspects of Data Communications: Media   43

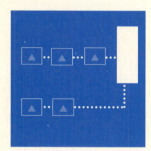

PART II

CHAPTER 3

LOCAL AREA NETWORKS   *125*

Introduction to Networks   *127*

PART III   **WIDE AREA NETWORKS**   *257*
CHAPTER 8   WAN Hardware   *259*

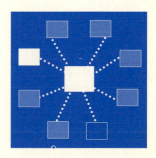

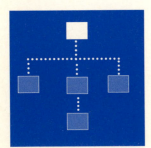

PART IV   **NETWORK INTERCONNECTIONS AND MANAGEMENT 387**

Introduction to Data Communications

After studying this chapter you should be able to:

- Differentiate between telecommunications and data communications
- Discuss several significant data communications historical events
- Identify the essential elements of communication
- Describe different types of data communications applications
- Discuss the requirements of an online system
- List the seven layers of the OSI reference model
- Define some functions for each of the seven layers of the OSI reference model
- Describe the way in which a message is passed from one application to another using the OSI reference model

A data-processing system may be viewed as an integration of subsystems that aid in solving business or scientific problems. Common subsystems include the operating system, database management system, languages, applications, and data communications. Each subsystem is implemented as a combination of software and/or hardware. This text discusses one part of the data processing system, the data communications subsystem, along with its interfaces with the other subsystems.

What is meant in this text by the term *data communications*? Although the terms *telecommunications* and *data communications* have become almost synonymous in some circles, they have distinct meanings. James Martin (1972, p. 654) gives a broad definition of telecommunications:

1

Any process that permits the passage from a sender to one or more receivers of information of any nature delivered in any easy to use form (printed copy, fixed or moving pictures, visible or audible signals, etc.) by any electromagnetic system (electrical transmission by wire, radio, optical transmission, guided waves, etc.). Includes telegraphy, telephony, video-telephony, data transmission, etc.

data communications The transmission of data to and from computers and components of computer systems.

This definition is too broad for the scope of this book. We define **data communications** as the subset of telecommunications involving the transmission of data to and from computers and components of computer systems. More specifically, data communications is the transmission of data through a conducted medium such as wires, coaxial cables, or fiber optic cables or by the use of radiated electromagnetic waves such as broadcast radio, infrared light, and microwaves. We discuss other facets of telecommunications such as telephone systems and broadcast radio only as they pertain to the transmission of computer data.

In reading this book, be aware that the field of data communications is so extensive that entire books are devoted to each chapter topic presented here. This text is intended to provide an overview of the entire field of data communications and to familiarize you with the terminology and capabilities of data communications systems. Your mastery of this material will enable you to participate in discussions about how to configure data communications components.

Based on the belief that a knowledge of history helps provide a perspective for the events of today, we start our discussion of data communications with a historical overview of the telecommunications industry and key data communications events.

HISTORY OF THE TELECOMMUNICATIONS INDUSTRY

The history of data communications differs significantly from that of other computer technologies, such as languages, hardware, database management, and applications. Because data communications development is a joint venture between the communications industry and the computer industry, development has been a combined effort. Because the telephone companies have been the primary source of long-distance communication circuits, this history begins with the state of telephone companies at the start of the computer era.

At the beginning of the computer era the communications industry was already well established. Telephone and telegraph companies had developed a network of communications facilities throughout the industrialized world. In the United States and many other countries, telephone companies had been given exclusive rights to install lines and to provide services in specific geographical areas, with government agencies exercising control over tariffs and the services provided. This situation appeared to benefit both the telephone companies and consumers. The goal of the system was to provide affordable service. However, some users paid less than the actual cost of service whereas others paid more, due to the following pricing structure.

Every individual was to have access to telephone service at a reasonable cost. Service was to be provided to all geographical areas, regardless of remoteness or population density. Small remote towns were to have the same type of service as large metropolitan communities, at about the same rates. If the total cost of installing lines and switching equipment in a small town had actually been borne entirely by users in that town, the cost of service would have been prohibitive to most residents. Therefore, losses incurred in such a town were offset by profits from other geographical areas. The three major sources of profit in the United States were the major metropolitan areas, businesses, and long-distance service. The large metropolitan areas were profitable because of economies of scale and density of installations. Business rates were much higher than rates for individuals because the value received was ostensibly greater (because the telephone was being used to generate income) and because businesses ostensibly could afford to pay more. Long-distance tariffs were set high to subsidize those portions of the system operating at a loss. In this way, the service provided was generally good and prices were reasonable for each class of user. (Note that two of these profitable segments — business and long distance — also pertain to data communications.)

In addition to having exclusive rights to transmission facilities, the telephone companies in the United States and numerous other countries had exclusive rights to attach any equipment to the telephone networks. This gave them a monopoly on the equipment needed to transmit and receive data, such as modems. (A modem changes a computer signal from digital to analog format for transmission along a **medium** such as telephone lines, and another modem converts the signal back to digital format at the receiving end. Modems are discussed further in Chapter 1.) These exclusive rights allowed telephone companies to turn the sale or lease of such equipment to profit, which is what U.S. telephone companies did.

In the United States, telephone companies were viewed as "natural" monopolies, meaning that it was considered wasteful to have two or more telephone companies servicing the same location. The "price" attached to the monopoly was that telephone companies such as AT&T were prohibited from involvement in certain business segments, such as the computer industry. Partly because of this monopoly on equipment, as well as the special status given providers of data transmission facilities, the growth of data communications was somewhat slower than that of other computer-related technologies. The development of databases, languages, operating systems, and hardware components was strong from the 1950s through the early 1970s, but large-scale expansion of data communications systems really did not occur until the 1970s. The growth experienced then was primarily the result of three developments:

1. Large-scale integration of circuits reduced the cost and size of terminals and communications equipment.

2. Development of software systems made the establishment of data communications networks relatively easy.

3. Competition among providers of transmission facilities reduced the cost for data circuits.

medium   In data communications, the carrier of data signals. Twisted-pair wires, coaxial cables, and fiber optic cables are the most common LAN media.

Without these developments, data communications systems would have been financially unfeasible for many computer users. Consider the transmission costs in 1968 and 1973, just before and just after competition appeared. In 1968, American Telephone and Telegraph Company (AT&T) charged an average of $315 for 100 miles of leased telephone line. In 1973, the average cost of the same line was as low as $85. A simple teletypewriter terminal (TTY) that sold for $2595 in 1971 could be replaced in 1975 for $750, and the 1975 terminal had more features than the older model.

HISTORY OF DATA COMMUNICATIONS

Significant data communications events are shown on the timeline in Table 1. The most significant of these are discussed below.

The Hush-a-Phone Case

Hush-a-Phone case A U.S. case that set a precedent regarding attaching equipment to telephone networks.

A 1948 court case not specifically related to data communications eventually had a significant impact on that industry: the **Hush-a-Phone case**. Recall that telephone companies in the United States had a legal monopoly over all equipment attached to their networks, to keep anyone from attaching devices that might interfere with or destroy signals and equipment in the network. The Hush-a-Phone Company developed and marketed a passive device (no electrical or magnetic components) that could be installed over the transmitting telephone handset to block out background noise and provide more privacy; AT&T threatened to suspend service for users and distributors of the device. Hush-a-Phone appealed to the Federal Communications Commission (FCC). After several hearings, the FCC decided in favor of AT&T. In 1956, however, an appeals court overturned the FCC ruling and decided in favor of the Hush-a-Phone Company, holding that no harm to the AT&T network would result from use of such a device. This precedent opened the door for other companies to attach equipment to the telephone networks. The telephone regulations as modified by this decision stated that the telephone company would not prohibit a customer from using a device for his or her convenience so long as the devices did not injure the telephone system, involve direct electrical connection to the system, provide a recording device on the line, or connect the telephone company line with any other communication device.

Competition for Long-Distance Transmission

In 1963, Microwave Communications Incorporated (MCI) filed with the FCC to provide microwave communications services between Chicago and St. Louis, their goal being to sell data transmission circuits to private industry. AT&T objected to MCI's petition because MCI could operate at much lower overhead than AT&T, because MCI — unlike AT&T — would not have to serve the lower volume markets, such as Montana, Wyoming, Idaho, and Kansas. Despite AT&T's objections, MCI received approval for the communications link in

TABLE 1   History of Data Communications

1939 — ABC computer operational

1940 — Data communications performed using COMPLEX computer

1944 — MARK I computer operational

1946 — ENIAC computer operational

1948 — First commercial computer installed, the UNIVAC I

1953 — First private commercial computer installed, UNIVAC at General Electric Corporation

1954 — IBM introduces remote job entry (RJE)

1956 — Hush-a-Phone decision in favor of Hush-a-Phone Company

1958 — First U.S. communications satellite sent into orbit Start of SAGE radar early warning system

1959 — FCC approves private microwave communications networks

1963 — First geosynchronous orbiting satellite, SYNCOM II
MCI files with FCC to provide communications services

1964 — SABRE airline reservation system completed
Packet switching network concept proposed by the Rand Corporation

1966 — IBM's binary synchronous (BISYNC or BSC) protocol announced

1968 — Carterphone case concludes in favor of Carter Electronics

1969 — ARPANET, first packet switching network, begins operation

1972 — Ethernet local area network specifications formulated
IBM's synchronous data link control (SDLC) protocol announced

1974 — IBM announces its systems network architecture (SNA)

1975 — General Telephone and Electronics' Telenet public packet distribution network (PDN) becomes operational

1975 — Personal computers introduced, the Altaire 8800

1981 — IBM PC introduced

1982 — Microcomputer local area networks appear

1984 — AT&T divestiture

1970. Since then, MCI has expanded into other major metropolitan areas. It added an individual telephone service (Execunet) in 1975, by which date MCI had service to 24 cities. This era of heavy competition for data transmission circuits in the United States has led to lower rates for data communications users.

The Carterphone Case

Another court case that helped open data communications to competition occurred in 1966: the **Carterphone case**. Carter Electronics Company had been marketing a radio telephone system that allowed for communication

Carterphone (or Carterfone) case   A U.S. case regarding attaching devices to a telephone company's network.

between a moving vehicle and a base station via radio-wave transmission. Because the original Carterphone was unable to forward a mobile call to another location, the company introduced a device that could pass on the radio transmission through a telephone network. AT&T objected to attaching the Carterphone to its network on the grounds of potential harm to the network and violation of the FCC prohibition against connecting an outsider's communications device to AT&T's telephone line. The 1968 ruling was in favor of Carter Electronics. As an outgrowth of the decision, it became legal for any device to be attached to the telephone network provided the telephone companies were allowed to install a protective device between the "foreign" equipment and the network. This provision later was changed to allow connection of FCC-approved equipment without any protective devices, which made it legal to attach other manufacturers' communications equipment to the network and led to improved products at lower prices. As another side effect of the Carterphone decision, individuals were allowed to purchase and install their own telephone sets.

Local Area Network (LAN) A communications network in which all of the components are located within several kilometers of each other and that uses high transmission speeds—generally one million bits per second or higher.

Wide Area Network (WAN) A network that typically covers a wide geographical area and operates at speeds lower than LAN speeds.

Local Area Networks

A **Local Area Network (LAN)**, like the example shown in Figure 1, is a communications network whose components are all located within several kilometers of each other. LANs differ from the oldest type of network, a **Wide Area Network (WAN)**. A WAN typically covers a wide geographical area and operates at speeds lower than those of a LAN. Major uses of LANs include exchange of data at high speed between computers within a local area, factory or production control, office automation, and financial systems. The original specifications for Ethernet, one of the most publicized LANs, were published by the Xerox Corporation in 1972. Later, Digital Equipment Corporation

Figure 1

A Local Area Network

Network Server

(DEC) and Intel joined Xerox in developing Ethernet further. In the early 1980s microcomputer and LAN technologies were merged. Today, microcomputer LANs form a significant portion of government, academic, and corporate computing power. LANs are discussed in greater detail in Chapters 3 through 7.

Data Link Protocols

A **data link protocol** governs the flow of data between sending and receiving stations. The original data communications protocols were borrowed from the telegraph and telephone industries. In 1967, IBM introduced the binary synchronous (BISYNC or BSC) protocol for use in remote job entry applications, and it was later expanded for use in other applications. In 1972, IBM introduced the synchronous data link control (SDLC) protocol, which has become the prototype for many current data link protocols. Data link protocols are discussed in more detail in Chapters 5 and 9.

data link protocol Convention that governs the flow of data between a sending and a receiving station.

Microcomputers

Microcomputers were introduced in 1975 with the Altaire 8800. Microcomputer technology proliferated in the 1980s and is continuing in the 1990s. A wide variety of microcomputer software and hardware, coupled with increased processing and storage capacity and low costs, have made microcomputers an important element in data communications networks. In many installations they have replaced terminals. In addition, the introduction of local area networks with microcomputers as workstations has created many changes in the ways offices process data.

ESSENTIAL FEATURES OF COMMUNICATION

Data communication has several important features. Communication of any type requires a message, a sender, a receiver, and a medium. In addition, the message should be understandable and there should be some means of error detection. Figure 2 illustrates the sender, receiver, medium, and message in a telephone connection.

Message

For two entities to communicate, there must be a message, which can assume several forms and be of varying length. Types of data communications messages include a file, a request, a response, status, control, and correspondence. These are illustrated in Figure 3. Let us briefly look at each of them.

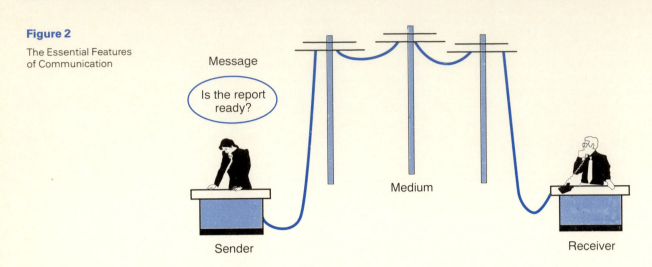

Figure 2

The Essential Features
of Communication

Message

Is the report
ready?

Medium

Sender

Receiver

Figure 3

Types of Messages

File

Any tickets for the
driver of this Maserati?

Requests

Response   Yes, lots.

Status   The system is going down in 5 minutes.

Control   Don't send me any more data—I am currently busy.

MEMO
Company Party

Correspondence

**Remote Job Entry
(RJE)** An application
of data communications.
Batches of data are collected
at a remote site and transmitted to a host for processing. In early implemen-
tations the input was card
format and the output was
printer format (between the
remote terminals and the
host processor).

A File   With **remote job entry (RJE)**, one of the first applications of data
communications, messages were transmitted from a remote location to a
processor. The message was the entire card file. In computer networks, where
several processors are connected, it is not unusual for complete or partial files
to be transferred between processing units.

A Request   In online transaction processing, a user may request that the
computer processor(s) take some type of action, such as display information,
update the database, or "logon" or "logoff."

A Response   A request ordinarily receives a return message or response.
For an information inquiry, the response is either the information requested
or an error message saying why the data was not returned (such as "security
violation," "information not on file," or "hardware failure"). For a database

update transaction, the response could be either an explicit message that the action was performed, an error message, or an implicit acknowledgment that the transaction has been performed successfully, such as "progressing to the next transaction."

Status　A status message, which can be sent to either all users or only selected users, reveals the functional status of the system. If a system must be halted for scheduled maintenance, a status message might be broadcast to all users, enabling them to bring their work to an orderly halt.

Control　Control messages are transmitted between system components. An automatic teller machine (ATM) might indicate to the controlling computer that it is out of cash; a printer might indicate that its buffer, or information storage area, is full and cannot receive additional data; or a network computer might notify other computers that a new computer has been added to the network and is available to accept and send messages.

Correspondence　Correspondence involves messages sent from user to user. Such messages include those sent on electronic mail systems, where memos and correspondence may be routed between employees of a company. Some systems transmit document images, provide bulletin-board message posting, or enable telephone-like interactive communication.

Sender

The sender is the transmitter of the message—either a person or a machine. Frequently the sender is a computer or terminal with enough intelligence to originate a message or response without human intervention. The sender can also be a system user, sensor, badge reader, or other input device.

Receiver

Receivers include computers, terminals, remote printers, people, and devices such as drill presses, furnaces, and air conditioners. A message and a sender can exist without a receiver; however, without a receiver, no communication takes place. For example, signals have been beamed into space in an attempt to contact other intelligent life forms, but until these signals are received, no communication has occurred. In a computer system, a message could be sent to all terminals saying that a new system feature is available, but if all terminals happen to be turned off at that time, no communication will have occurred.

Medium

Messages are carried from sender to receiver through some medium of communication. In oral communication, sound waves are transmitted through air (the medium). Data communications uses several media to transmit data, including wires, radio waves, and light pulses. Media are discussed more thoroughly in Chapter 1.

Understandability

Even if all the components discussed above are present, if the message is not understood correctly, then accurate communication has not taken place. In human communication the most obvious obstacle is language differences, for which a translator or interpreter may be necessary. Computer systems have similar obstacles to communication. For instance, data can be represented by any of several different codes, the two most common being the American Standard Code for Information Interchange (ASCII) and the Extended Binary Coded Decimal Interchange Code (EBCDIC). Sometimes it is necessary to translate from one code to another to be sure that data is interpreted correctly.

Error Detection

In human communication, receivers can frequently detect errors because humans have the ability to reason and interpret. Grammatical errors, misspellings, and even some misstatements can usually be corrected by a human receiver. (If a teacher mistakenly gives the distance between the earth and the sun as 93 million light years rather than 93 million miles, we would probably realize the error and, presumably, even correct it.) But computer networks do not reason. Even when a human computer operator realizes that a received message is erroneous, that operator may be unable to correct the error. When the receiver is a piece of hardware, incapable of reasoning and unable to detect or correct errors, it becomes necessary to employ special schemes for determining whether an original message has been distorted during transmission. All such schemes involve transmitting additional information along with the data, which increases the chances of detecting errors without eliminating the possibility that the received data actually may be erroneous. Error detection is discussed in Chapter 2.

DATA COMMUNICATIONS APPLICATIONS

There are several broad classes of data communications applications: **batch, data entry, distributed, inquiry/response, interactive,** and **sensor-based.** Note that the classes are not mutually exclusive; some transactions may fall into more than one class.

Batch Applications

Batch applications, including RJE, are characterized by large data transfers in two directions. Information from a batch of inventory cards might be transferred from a warehouse to a remote computer center, and in return the

batch   Typically, large data transfers in two directions.

data entry   Applications that consist of lengthy inputs with short responses.

distributed   Applications in which the data or the processing or both are distributed among a number of processing units.

inquiry/response   Applications in which inputs generally have only a few characters and output responses have many.

interactive   Applications characterized by relatively short inputs and outputs.

sensor-based   The processor receives data from sensors and if necessary acts upon that data.

warehouse would receive an updated inventory list. In some batch applications, large amounts of data flow in one direction only. When a sales representative records sales on a portable computer terminal but waits until the end of the workday to transmit the entire day's orders, a large amount of data flows in one direction and little or no data flows in the other direction.

Data Entry Applications

Data entry applications consist of lengthy inputs with short responses. In a credit authorization system in Australia, input for a "batch" of receipts consists of credit card number, merchant number, and charge amount, plus the batch total. The system then calculates its own batch total and compares it with the input total; if the figures agree, the only response is a prompt to continue entering the next batch.

Distributed Applications

Distributed applications are characterized not so much by input and output size as by whether data or processing or both are distributed among several processing units. Thus, requests as well as data flow between several system components, with possibly some parallelism in data access and processing. Order entry is an example of this type of processing. When an order for an item is entered, the system tries to determine whether the item is in stock in any of its several regionally located warehouses. Because each warehouse has a computer system and maintains its local inventory, the system inquires into these remote databases to find a location with enough stock to fill the order. The system then updates the inventory at the location(s) from which the order is to be filled, updates the invoicing and accounts receivable at the accounting location, and supplies the ordering location with a shipment date and other relevant data.

Office automation systems are a special case of distributed systems, with both data and processing distributed among several different components. Applications include word processing, communications between members of the corporation via electronic mail, spreadsheet analysis, graphics, desktop publishing, and facsimile generation for presentations, reports, and contracts.

office automation system A special case of a distributed system, with both data and processing distributed among several different components.

Inquiry/Response Applications

In this type of application, inputs generally have only a few characters and output responses have many. Inquiry/response applications involve requests to display information. For example, a police inquiry might consist of a driver's license number and the response could be several thousand characters of information detailing the driver's name, address, driving record, and so on. In a hospital application, a nurse might enter the nurse's station number (relatively few characters) and the output would likely consist of several thousand characters giving each patient's name, status, medical requirements, and so on.

Interactive Applications

The interactive type of application is characterized by relatively short inputs and outputs. The computer system prompts the user for an input, eliciting a short response. Because the sender and receiver are essentially conversing with each other, this application is sometimes referred to as conversational. Interactive applications are frequently used for online transaction processing with terminals that cannot accept an entire screenful of information. Applications in which the user's response dictates the next prompt, such as certain computerized games, are also interactive.

Sensor-Based Applications

Sensor-based applications involve special data collection devices for such uses as controlling temperature in buildings, monitoring and maintaining patient condition in hospitals, and controlling a manufacturing process. The processor receives data from the sensors and, if necessary, takes control action.

Combined Applications

The typical computer in a network of large systems supports more than one type of activity. It might have a batch processing requirement and one or more types of data communications applications. One task in designing a data communications system is to balance the workload to assure effective and efficient use. Effective use means minimizing idle time for system components. It is not effective to have a data communications line idle for long periods and then have many users attempting to use it at once. Efficient use means using the components in an optimal manner. Efficient uses of a data communications line include compressing the data before transmitting it or eliminating sources of data errors. These goals can be reached through good design and management, and we discuss techniques for reaching these goals in Chapters 12–14.

Good management often requires that tradeoffs be made. If batch jobs must run concurrently with data communications applications, a manager may configure a computer system so batch applications do not run as efficiently as possible so that transaction-oriented applications are optimized.

REQUIREMENTS OF AN ONLINE SYSTEM

Although data communications applications are diverse, most have certain basic requirements: *performance, consistency, flexibility, availability, reliability, recovery,* and *security*.

Performance

System performance can be measured in several ways. Two very common measures are response time and transaction rate (or throughput). **Response time** is the interval between entering a message and getting the response. Some define the measurement interval as being from the end of the entry to the appearance of the first response character; others define it as the interval from the end of the entry to receipt of the final response character. The difference between the two can be significant. For example, if the speed of the communications circuit is 30 characters per second and the response consists of 1200 characters, the response time by the first definition is 40 seconds less than that by the second definition. Response time has two major components: the time required for data transmission and the time required for processing. (Each component has subcomponents.) This text deals only with data transmission time.

Response times are quoted for transactions of a given type. In a hospital application there are response times for each of the following transactions:

- patient admission
- patient discharge
- patient lookup
- room occupants

In addition to each transaction having a response time, one transaction type may have different response times in different systems. This happens because of hardware differences or because the transactions are implemented in different ways. Table 2 illustrates the work Transaction A may do to admit a patient at one hospital and Table 3 shows the work a patient admission transaction, Transaction B, does at another hospital. The work accomplished by these two transactions is different; therefore, their response times differ. When comparing or evaluating transaction response times, you also need to evaluate the work done by those transactions.

Throughput, or transaction rate, is the amount of work performed by the system per unit of time. It may appear that fast response time and high throughput are equivalent. Actually, the opposite is sometimes true. For example, transactions in which customers are involved need quick response

response time   The amount of time required for a user to receive a reply to a request. Usually the time elapsed between the user pressing the Enter key to send the request (or the equivalent) and the return of the first character of the response.

throughput   The amount of work performed by a system per unit of time.

TABLE 2   Activities for Transaction A

Obtain vacant room list header from memory location

Read vacant room record

Read patient record

Update vacant room list header in memory from room record

Rewrite room record linked to patient record

Rewrite patient record

TABLE 3   Activities for Transaction B

Obtain vacant room header from memory

Read vacant room record

Read patient record

Update vacant room header from room record

Rewrite room record linked to patient record

Read related charge record for room

Write charge record for patient

Read standard patient issue record

Write patient charge record for issue of supplies

Rewrite patient record

time. Optimizing the speed of such transactions might slow down other processing activity, such as batch reporting. Although response time in customer transactions might be reduced, the total amount of work accomplished may decline. In a truly successful system, both response time and throughput are optimal.

Consistency

consistency A consistent system is one that works predictably with respect both to the people who use the system and to response times.

Consistency describes a system that works predictably both with respect to the people who use the system and with respect to response times. Inconsistent response time is extremely annoying to system users and in fact is sometimes worse than a slow but consistent response time. Of course, complete consistency is difficult to achieve because of occasional periods of heavy processing. One common system design objective is for the response time of most transactions of a given type, such as 95%, to be lower than a certain threshold, such as 3 seconds. It would be quite disconcerting if 50% of these transactions took 3 seconds, 20% took 10 seconds, 15% took 30 seconds, 10% took 1 minute, and 5% took more than a minute. Such inconsistency is not only frustrating but also limits the effectiveness of the system.

Flexibility

flexibility The ability to have both growth and change having minimal impact on existing applications and users.

One common aspect of online systems is that they change. Users might want to alter the types of transactions available, change the data format, expand an application, or add new applications. **Flexibility** means that both growth and change must be accommodated with minimal impact on existing applications and users. The ability to increase processing power, terminals, communication circuits, and database capacity is critical to the long-term success of a system, and the network implementation ought to accommodate such changes. One of the best ways to ensure this ability is to use industry-standard network architectures and protocols. This method also helps when adding or upgrading nodes and gives users a wider variety of options from which to choose.

Availability

Availability requires that an online system be continuously available to the user community during the workday. In some cases this means 24 hours a day, every day of the year. In certain applications, if the online system is unavailable it can result in significant financial loss to a business. For example, an airline might be unable to sell seats on a flight if the reservation system is down, or it may overbook a flight, which will cause extra work for the employees and possible penalty payments to travelers for their inconvenience.

availability A system is available when all components a user needs to satisfy the request are usable.

Reliability

Reliability, an important system attribute, is a measure of the frequency of system failure and in some ways combines consistency and availability. A system failure is any event that prohibits users from processing transactions. This includes any hardware breakdown, such as a processor failure in a system that is not fault-tolerant, as well as an application or system software failure or the failure of the medium (such as a faulty data communications line). **Mean Time Between Failure (MTBF)** is a measure of the average time until a given component may be expected to fail, and **Mean Time To Repair (MTTR)** is the average time required to fix a failed component. Both figures are important in determining the frequency of failure and the time required to return the system to successful operation.

One way to improve the reliability of data communications systems is **fault tolerance**, which is the ability to continue processing despite component failure. In a fault-tolerant system, single points of failure do not cause system failure because every component in the system has a backup component that takes over if a failure occurs. Fault-tolerant WANs are formed by combining fault-tolerant hardware with fault-tolerant software, and fault tolerance is also available for LANs. Fault tolerance is usually confined to a LAN's file servers.

reliability The probability that the system will continue to function over a given time period.

Mean Time Between Failure (MTBF) A measure of the average amount of time a given component may be expected to operate before failing.

Mean Time To Repair (MTTR) The average time required to fix a failed component.

fault tolerance A combination of hardware and software techniques that improve the reliability of a system.

Recovery

Recovery addresses the fact that all systems, even those built for continuous operation, can fail. In some cases it may not be the system that fails but either the source of power or the people who operate the system. Regardless of the cause, the system must be able to recover to a consistent point — a point where the database has no partially updated transactions, no transactions have been processed twice, and no transactions have been lost. System users also should be advised of the state of all work they had in progress at the time of

recovery The act of restoring a system to operational status following a failure.

failure, to keep them from submitting a duplicate transaction or failing to reenter a transaction not received before the failure.

Security

security   Security is a delaying tactic. Physical security is intended to deny access to a facility. Transmission and data security are intended to restrict access to authorized users. Typical security measures include identification and authentication (passwords), data encryption, user profiles, and so on. Security does not prevent unauthorized access to a system but simply makes it more difficult.

Security has become increasingly important as the microcomputer has made computer networks accessible to almost everyone. As more businesses use data communications, the number of accessible computer systems continues to grow, thus making a vast amount of sensitive information available, including financial data and classified military information. Unfortunately, security has not always received a high priority in system and network design, so making up for these deficiencies is a necessity in the development of future systems and in the enhancement of existing ones. Systems security is discussed in more detail in Chapter 15.

INTRODUCTION TO NETWORKS

This section discusses two definitions of computer networks and some functions common to them. The functions described are the bases for later chapters.

Figure 4

A Simple Data
Communications System

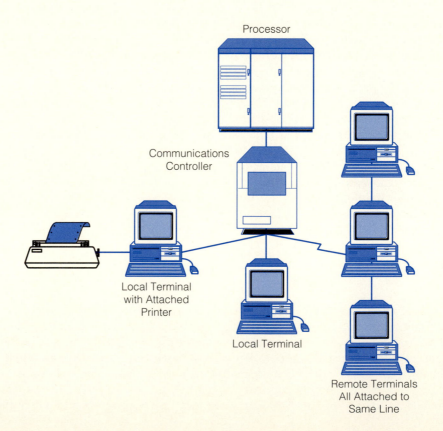

Processor

Communications
Controller

Local Terminal
with Attached
Printer

Local Terminal

Remote Terminals
All Attached to
Same Line

Computer Networks

What exactly is a computer network? First, a computer network can be defined as a single computer, called a host, together with communications circuits, communications equipment, and terminals (see Figure 4). A network can also be defined as two or more computers connected via a communications medium, together with associated communications links, terminals, and communications equipment (see Figures 5 and 6). In these cases the computers are referred to as nodes. In Figures 4 and 5, the communications links are depicted by lines attached to the nodes. These are sample configurations only; actually, a wide variety of configurations is in use, and several viable configurations may exist for one application. In addition, an entity may have several networks, such as several LANs and a WAN. It is common to interconnect networks to provide communications among all network users, such as between LAN users on one LAN and LAN users on another LAN or between a LAN user and a WAN user. Such a network of networks is illustrated in Figure 6 and by the Internet, which connects several regional networks into one large supernetwork. The Internet is discussed in Chapter 11.

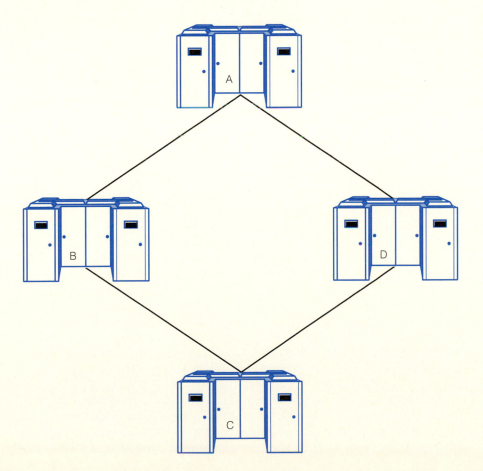

Figure 5

A Network of Computers

Figure 6

Interconnected Networks

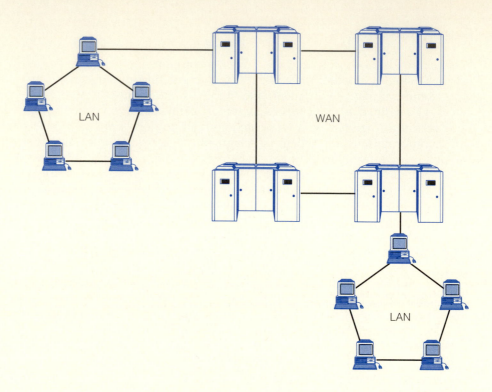

Data Communications Applications and Configurations

The following discusses several different applications and configurations of computer equipment. The sections covering local and wide area networks provide details on network configurations and where they are used.

Company A This company is an attorney's office with 12 partners and 22 support staff. The partnership maintains most of its documentation on a LAN. Each attorney and administrative support person has a microcomputer workstation that is attached to the network. Documents of a personal nature are stored on individuals' local disks whereas documents that are subject to sharing are stored on the network's file server. The file server is a repository for shared files such as completed contracts and wills, templates for legal documents and spreadsheets, and program files including word processors, spreadsheets, and desktop publishing. The file server also provides sharing of other resources such as printers, fax machines, and modems to be shared among the LAN users. Company A's network is represented by Figure 7.

Company B This company provides a service to trucking companies that enables their drivers to cash script at truck stops throughout the country. The advantages are that drivers do not need to carry large amounts of cash for long trips, truck-stop owners are guaranteed against losses from bad

Figure 7

Company A's Network

Server

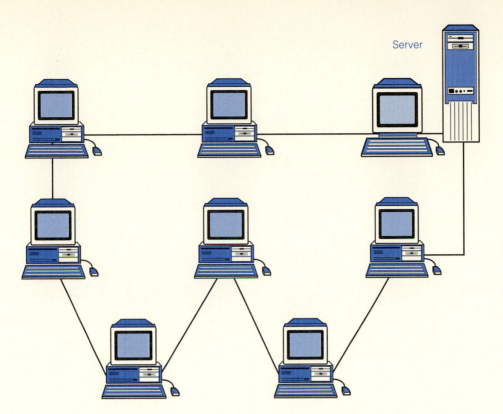

checks, and the trucking companies need not provide significant cash advances to their drivers. The communications network consists of approximately 50 terminals located in the same building as the host computer in Company B's office. Truck-stop employees can telephone data entry personnel on a toll-free number to receive authorization to pay the driver (or advice to call the police). The total amount of money allocated to the driver is updated after each transaction. All links between computer and terminals are local and are controlled by Company B, rather than being leased or purchased from a common carrier such as a telephone company. The Company B configuration is generally represented by Figure 8.

Company C   This service company is involved in the automated preparation of tax returns. Its clients are accounting firms who contract to use Company C's computer facilities and software. Depending on the size of the accounting firm, clients may choose to have a private, dedicated communications link to the host computer, or they can share a communications link with other users. Clients who share a telephone link compete with each other for access to the available telephone lines. Suppose 50 lines are shared by 150 clients and each client typically uses the connection fewer than 2 hours per day. Because of time zone differences, the workday is 12 hours long and the average use of the facility is 50% (300 hours of the 600 available connection hours). Ordinarily, there will not be much competition for these shared lines. But just

Figure 8

Company B's Network

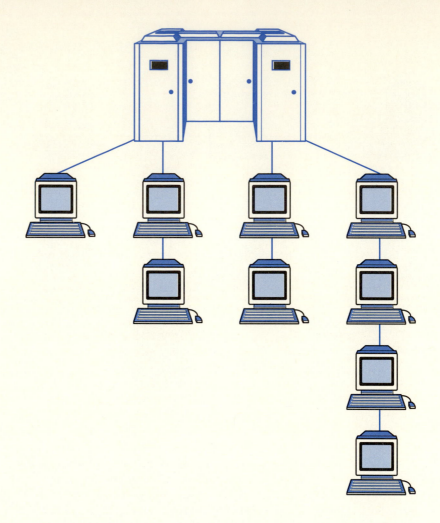

coaxial cable   A transmission medium consisting of one or two central data transmission wires surrounded by an insulating layer, a shielding layer, and an outer jacket. Coaxial cable has a high data-carrying capacity and low error rates.

fiber optic cable   A transmission medium that provides high data rates and low errors. One or more glass or plastic fibers are woven together to form the core of the cable. This core is surrounded by a glass or plastic layer called the cladding. The cladding in turn is covered with plastic or other material for protection. The cable requires a light source, most commonly laser and light-emitting diodes.

before the April 15 income tax filing deadline, clients may dramatically increase their use of the system, so availability of the communications links might become a problem. For a client who needs a line more than 2 hours per day, it is probably more economical to use a dedicated line. The Company C configuration is depicted in Figure 9.

Company D   This multinational company manufactures and markets large computer systems. Every large sales office has a LAN and a demonstration computer, and all of these LANs and demonstration computers as well as the computers in the software development facility, home office, and manufacturing plants are linked in one large network, consisting of more than 200 WAN nodes, 3000 LAN nodes, and 1500 terminals. In addition to long-distance telephone lines and local, private lines, Company D uses **coaxial cable** and **fiber optic cable** for the LAN media and satellite communications, for long-distance, high-volume transmissions between manufacturing plants

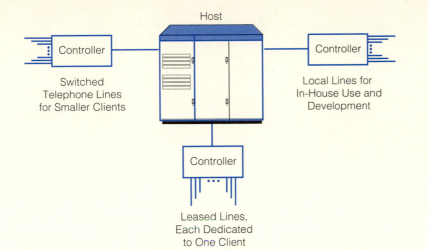

Figure 9

Company C's Network

and divisional offices. The Company D configuration is generally represented by Figure 10.

These four companies have greatly different network configurations, yet each network is effective and cost efficient for the business that uses it. Companies A, B, and C could have installed a network similar to that of Company D. Unfortunately, by doing so they would have to spend considerably more for their networks and thus might lose their competitive edge.

Many alternatives are available to a network designer, and several configurations will probably solve the communications requirements. A few such alternatives might be highly cost-effective, some may be only mediocre, and a few might drive the company into bankruptcy. It is important to realize that several "right" approaches usually exist.

System Complexity

Data communications systems may be simple or complex. A simple system might be composed of a single processor and some terminals, all located within a single building or a small local area network (LAN). Figure 4 illustrates the hardware components of a processor with terminals that are connected with user-provided wiring. Figure 11 illustrates a microcomputer LAN with a dedicated file server and five workstations. A **file server** allows the microcomputers to share resources such as data, programs, and printers. A more elaborate system might consist of several LANs each of which is attached to a mainframe or minicomputer which in turn is connected in a wide area network (WAN). Also attached to the WAN processors are terminals that are distributed both locally and remotely. A network of this type is commonly called an **enterprise network**, which is two or more LANs connected to each other or one or more LANs connected to a WAN or to each other. Figure 6 depicts a system that meets this description. The computers and terminals in

file server   A computer that allows microcomputers on a network to share resources such as data, programs, and printers. The file server's software controls access to shared files, as opposed to the operating system of the microcomputer.

enterprise network   A network of two or more LANs connected to each other, or one or more LANs connected to a WAN.

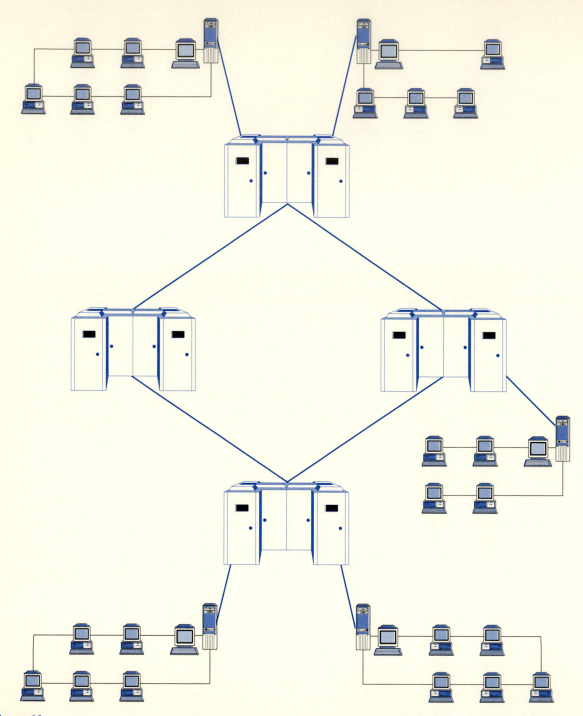

Figure 10

Company D's Network

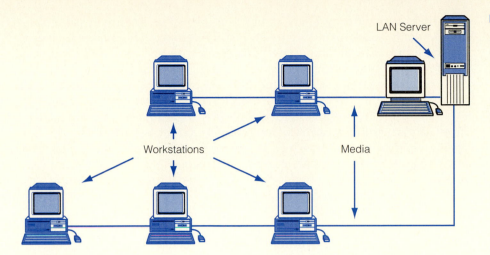

Figure 11

A LAN with File Server
and Five Workstations

LAN Server

Workstations

Media

this figure are connected via an assortment of private wires, communications lines leased from a **common carrier** (such as a telephone company), and microwave and satellite transmission. These three figures indicate the variety and complexity of communication systems. The illustrated components are discussed in detail in later chapters.

common carrier A public utility that provides public transmission media, such as the telephone companies and satellite companies.

Hierarchy of Functions

Regardless of the scope of a network and the equipment and media used, all networks share common functions. To contend with the growing number of different computer networks being developed, and in the belief that these diverse systems eventually need to be connected, the **International Standards Organization (ISO)** has identified and stratified the functions that every network must fulfill. This model makes it easier to develop interfaces among these different networks.

The ISO recommendation is called the **Open Systems Interconnection (OSI) reference model**, or the OSI reference model. The reference model does more than describe network interconnections; it also defines a network architecture. Many ISO standards relating to the reference model have been established and more are being formulated. When the standards process is completed, network developers will have an alternative to proprietary corporate network architectures such as IBM's systems network architecture (SNA). Details and examples of this reference model are found in many of the following chapters. A brief description is provided here because the OSI reference model in general and standards arising from it are used for the development of networks. This discussion also provides an overview of communications systems.

The basic objective of a network of computers is for an application on one node to communicate with an application or device on another node. Although this may sound simple, some complexities are involved. You have just

International Standards Organization (ISO) An organization that is active in setting communications standards.

Open Systems Interconnection (OSI) reference model A seven-layered set of functions for transmitting data from one user to another. Specified by the International Standards Organization to facilitate interconnection of networks.

seen that many different WAN and LAN implementations are possible and, consequently, so are many different types of interfaces. This means you need one type of hardware and software to connect to one type of LAN and a different set of hardware and software to connect to a different type of LAN or to a particular WAN. Because of the variety of network types available and the frequent need to interconnect them, a thriving business has been created for establishing connections among networks. Building network interfaces is much simpler if the network is designed around an open architecture. An **open architecture** is one in which the network specifications are available to any company. This allows a variety of companies to design hardware and software components that can easily be integrated into new and existing networks based on the open architecture.

open architecture   Architecture whose network specifications are available to any company. This allows a variety of companies to design hardware and software components that can be easily integrated into new and existing networks.

The Functions of Communications

To help motivate an understanding of the OSI reference model, consider how a worker might send a message from his or her office to a colleague in another location. This simple act can closely resemble sending a message in an OSI network. A possible scenario for this transmission might be as follows:

1. The worker writes a message on a tablet and delivers it to her or his administrative assistant.

2. The administrative assistant makes the memo presentable by typing it, correcting grammatical mistakes, and so on. The administrative assistant places the memo in an interoffice envelope and places the envelope in the outgoing mailbox.

3. The mail-room clerk picks up the mail, takes it to the mail room, sorts it, and determines a route for the message. Possible routings are internal mail, postal mail, and private express mail carriers. Because this message must go to a distant office and no priority is assigned, the clerk places the interoffice envelope in an external mailing envelope, possibly with other correspondence for that office, addresses it, and deposits the envelope in the external mailbox.

4. The mail carrier picks up the mail, including the worker's message, and takes it to the post office, where it is sorted and placed on an outgoing mail truck.

5. The post office physically delivers the mail to the mail room of the destination office. That mail-room clerk opens the outer envelope and sorts its contents.

6. The mail-room clerk delivers the memo in its interoffice envelope to the recipient's administrative assistant.

7. The recipient's administrative assistant takes the memo out of the envelope and prepares the memo for the recipient. The administrative assistant may time-stamp the memo, summarize it, make comments, set a priority for the recipient's reading it, and so on.

8. The recipient receives the memo, reads it, and reacts to the worker's message.

The preceding scenario describes a variety of different functions necessary to move a message from the sender's desk to the recipient's desk. The functions consist of message composition, presentation services, address determination, enveloping, selecting transmission routes, physical transmission, and so on. In general, these same functions must be performed when transmitting a message between computers in a network. The OSI reference model explicitly identifies seven layers of functions that must be performed in network interconnections: application, presentation, session, transport, network, data link, and physical. Figure 12 represents the OSI layers in two network nodes, a sending and a receiving node.

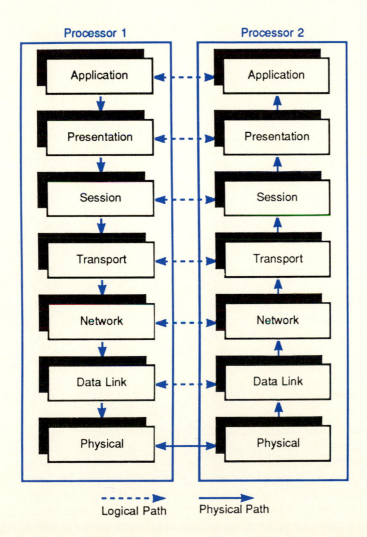

Figure 12

OSI Peer Layer Communication

Processor 1 | Processor 2

Application	Application
Presentation	Presentation
Session	Session
Transport	Transport
Network	Network
Data Link	Data Link
Physical	Physical

- - - - ▶ Logical Path

───────▶ Physical Path

In the letter-routing example, each functional layer on the sending side performed a specific set of functions, and each function was performed for a peer layer on the receiving side. Placing the correspondence in the interoffice envelope was done by the sending administrative assistant and undone by the receiving administrative assistant. In the OSI reference model, each layer in the sending network node is designed to perform a particular set of functions for its corresponding (peer) layer in the receiving network node. The application layer in the sending node prepares the data for the application layer in the receiving node. The application layer then passes the message to the presentation layer. The presentation layer formats the message properly for the presentation layer on the receiving node, passes the data to the session layer, and so on. In Figure 12 the solid line shows the physical route of the message, and the dotted lines show the logical route, from peer layer to peer layer. Also notice that each layer has a well-defined interface through which it communicates with adjacent layers.

Functions of OSI Layers

The functions of each OSI layer are briefly described below. More extensive explanations of several of these layers are given later as needed.

application layer One of the layers of the International Standards Organization's (OSI) reference model. The functions of this layer are application dependent.

Application The **application layer** is functionally defined by the user. Sometimes application programs must communicate with each other. The content and format of the data being exchanged are dictated by the needs of the organization. The application determines which data is to be transmitted, the message or record format for the data, and the transaction codes that identify the data to the receiver. Suppose an order entry transaction started on a sales node needs to pass product shipping information to a warehouse node. In this application, the message contains the ship-to address, part identifiers, quantities to be shipped, and a message code showing the action to be taken by the receiving application.

presentation layer One of the layers of the International Standards Organization's (OSI) reference model. The presentation layer addresses message formats.

Presentation The **presentation layer** formats the data it receives from the application layer. If certain data preparation functions are common to several applications, they can be resolved by the presentation services rather than being embedded in each application. The types of functions performed at the presentation level are encryption, compression, terminal screen formatting, and conversion from one transmission code to another (such as EBCDIC to ASCII).

session layer One of the layers of the International Standards Organization's (OSI) reference model. The session layer is responsible for establishing a dialogue between applications.

Session The **session layer** establishes the connection between applications, enforces the rules for carrying on the dialogue, and tries to reestablish the connection if a failure occurs. The dialogue rules specify both the order in which the applications are allowed to communicate and the pacing of information so as not to overload the recipient. If an application is sending data to a printer with a limited buffer size, the agreed-upon dialogue may be to send a buffer-size block to the printer, wait for the printer to signal that its buffer has been emptied, and then send the next block of data. The session layer must control this flow to avoid buffer overflow at the printer.

Transport The **transport layer** is the first layer concerned with the world external to its processor. It generates the address of the end user and ensures that all blocks or packets of data have been received, that there are no duplicate blocks, and that blocks have not been lost in transmission.

Network The **network layer** does end-to-end routing of packets or blocks of information, collects billing and accounting information, and routes messages.

Data Link The **data link layer** must establish and control the physical path of communication to the next node. This includes error detection and correction, defining the beginning and end of the data field, resolving competing requests for a shared communications link (deciding who can use the circuit and when), and ensuring that all forms of data can be sent across the circuit. The conventions used to accomplish these data link functions are known as **protocols**.

Physical The **physical layer** specifies the electrical connections between the transmission medium and the computer system. It describes how many wires are used to carry the signals; which wires carry specific signals; the size and shape of the connectors or adapters between the transmission medium and the communications circuit; the speed at which data is transmitted; and whether data (represented by voltages on a line, modification of radio waves, or light pulses) is allowed to flow in both directions and, if so, whether the flow can be in both directions simultaneously.

OSI Reference Model Example

Let us look at an example of activities that might occur at each level of the reference model as an application on one network node transmits a message to an application on another network node. Consider a financial application running on the network illustrated in Figure 13. Suppose that a bank customer uses an ATM attached to Node A and that the customer's account is located on Node X. An application on Node A sends a message to Node X requesting that the customer's account record be updated by an application running at Node X. To reach Node X, the message must pass through Node M.

Application Layer The application on Node A builds a record with a transaction identifier, the number of the account to be updated, the date and time of the transaction, and the amount to be deducted or added. The transaction identifier tells the message recipient what to do with the record: Insert it, update it, and so on. The message is illustrated in Figure 14(a). The application then invokes a procedure call to send the message to the recipient.

transport layer One of the layers of the International Standards Organization's (OSI) reference model. The transport layer is responsible for generating the end user's address and for the integrity of the receipt of message blocks.

network layer One of the layers of the International Standards Organization's (OSI) reference model. The network layer is responsible for end-to-end message routing.

data link layer One of the layers of the International Standards Organization's (OSI) reference model. The data link layer governs the establishment and control of the communications link.

protocol Convention used for establishing transmission rules. Protocols are used to establish rules for delineation of data, error detection, control sequences, message lengths, media access, and so on.

physical layer One of the layers of the International Standards Organization's (OSI) reference model. The physical layer specifies the electrical connections between the transmission medium and the computing system.

Figure 13

Application-to-Application
Communication in a Network

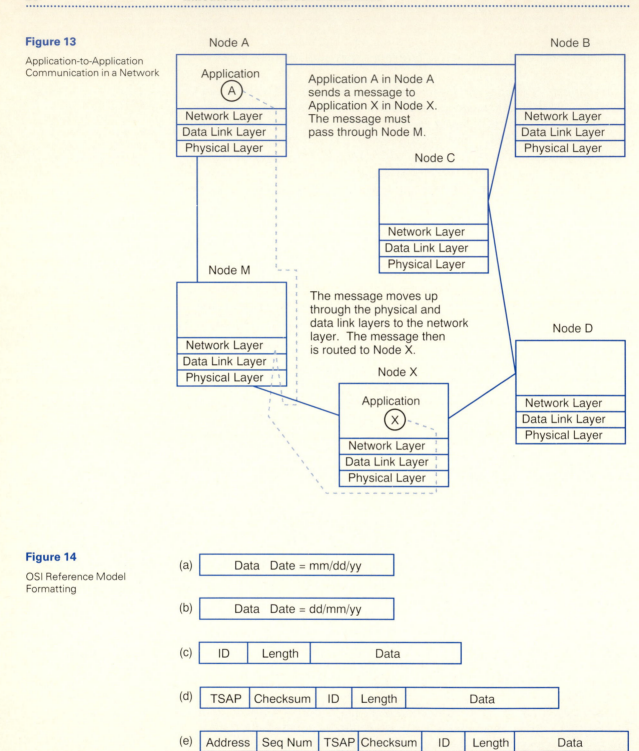

Node A

Application
(A)

Network Layer
Data Link Layer
Physical Layer

Application A in Node A
sends a message to
Application X in Node X.
The message must
pass through Node M.

Node B

Network Layer
Data Link Layer
Physical Layer

Node C

Network Layer
Data Link Layer
Physical Layer

Node M

Network Layer
Data Link Layer
Physical Layer

The message moves up
through the physical and
data link layers to the network
layer. The message then
is routed to Node X.

Node D

Network Layer
Data Link Layer
Physical Layer

Node X

Application
(X)

Network Layer
Data Link Layer
Physical Layer

Figure 14

OSI Reference Model
Formatting

(a) | Data   Date = mm/dd/yy |

(b) | Data   Date = dd/mm/yy |

(c) | ID | Length | Data |

(d) | TSAP | Checksum | ID | Length | Data |

(e) | Address | Seq Num | TSAP | Checksum | ID | Length | Data |

(f) | Header | Address | Seq Num | TSAP | Checksum | ID | Length | Data | Trailer |

Presentation Layer   The application layer formatted each field in the record being transmitted according to its own format rules. The receiving application may have a different set of format conventions. For example, the sending application may view a date in one format whereas the receiving application uses a different date format. The presentation layer is responsible for translating from one format to another. It can do this by changing to a standard transmission format, which is converted by its peer layer, or it can convert directly to the format expected by the receiving application. The message after such translation has taken place appears in Figure 14(b). The presentation layer then sends the message down to the session layer by requesting the establishment of a session.

Session Layer   The session layer's major functions are to set up, and perhaps monitor, a set of dialogue rules by which the two applications communicate and to bring a session to an orderly conclusion. A session dialogue can be one-way (simplex) or bidirectional. In **simplex transmission**, one application sends messages to another but receives no messages in return. Bidirectional sessions can allow messages to flow in both directions simultaneously (**full duplex** mode) or in both directions but in only one direction at a time (**half duplex** mode). Setting up how messages are transferred is called flow control. Once the connection has been made, data transfer can occur. The session layer appends an identifier and length indicator at the beginning of the data block, as illustrated in Figure 14(c). These two fields are used to identify the function of the message, such as whether it contains user data as opposed to control functions such as session establishment or termination.

Transport Layer   The transport layer is the first OSI layer responsible for actually transmitting the data. The higher layers described above are oriented toward the data and application interfaces, not toward data transmission. The transport layer uses an address called a **Transport Service Access Point (TSAP)** to uniquely identify session entities. TSAPs of the source and destination session entity, together with a checksum to detect errors, are appended to the message received from the session layer. A **checksum** is used to help detect transmission errors. It is created by the sender according to some algorithm. The receiver also creates the checksum using the same algorithm. If the sender's checksum and receiver's checksum agree, the data is assumed to be correct. This step is shown in Figure 14(d).

Network Layer   The network layer provides accounting, addressing, and routing functions. Upon receiving a message from the transport layer, the network layer logs the event to the accounting system and then prepares the message for transmission to the next node on the path to the destination (Node M in our example). It looks up the destination address in its **network routing table** to find the next address along that path. (A routing table for a node in a small network is shown in Figure 15.) If the message is lengthy, the network layer divides it into transmission units, appends a transmission sequence number to each unit, and sends the units across the link. This is illustrated in Figure 14(e).

simplex transmission   A mode of data transmission in which data may flow in only one direction. One station is always a sender and another is always a receiver over a simplex link.

full duplex   A data transmission mode in which data is transmitted over a link in both directions simultaneously.

half duplex   A data transmission mode in which data can travel in both directions over a link but in only one direction at a time.

Transport Service Access Point (TSAP)   An address used by the transport layer to uniquely identify session entities.

checksum   A technique used to check for errors in data. The sending application generates the checksum from the data being transmitted. The receiving application computes the checksum and compares it to the value computed and sent by the sending station.

network routing table   In the process of message transmission, a table in which the network layer looks up the destination address to find the next address along the path.

Figure 15

Network Showing a Network
Routing Table

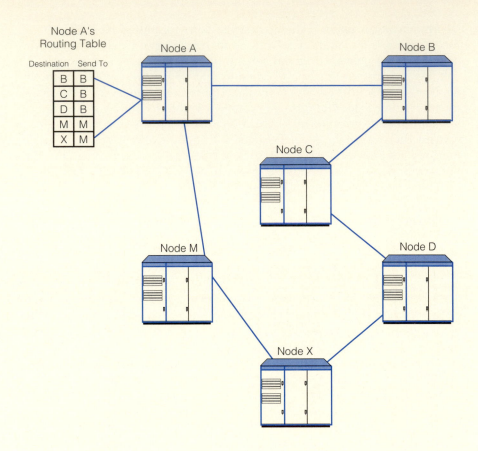

Node A's
Routing Table

Destination	Send To
B	B
C	B
D	B
M	M
X	M

Data Link Layer   The data link layer is responsible for data delineation, error detection, and logical control of the link. Logical link control consists of determining how and when a station can transmit, connecting and disconnecting nodes on the link, and controlling flow between data link entities. Thus, the data link layer facilitates flow control between Nodes A and M and between Nodes M and X. Note that data link flow control is for a link, whereas session flow control is end-to-end (between source and destination applications). To fulfill its function, the data link layer appends a header and a trailer to the message. The header contains a flag that indicates the beginning of the message, the address of the recipient, message sequence numbers, and the message type (data or control). The trailer contains a checksum for the data link block and a frame-ending flag. Headers and trailers are illustrated in Figure 14(f).

Physical Layer   The physical layer does not append anything to the message. It simply accepts the message from the data link layer and translates the bits into signals on the medium.

In the example, the message arrives at Node M and percolates up to the network layer. The network layer services recognize that the message is destined for Node X and send the message down to the data link layer for delivery to the next (and final) node. This is illustrated in Figure 13. The discussion in subsequent chapters starts from the bottom up, beginning with the physical layer (together with hardware components used in configuring a data communications network).

THE SOFTWARE ENVIRONMENT

Before beginning the technical discussion of the data communications system, an explanation of how it supports applications is worthwhile. Let us take a brief look at the application environment of a data communications system. Within the central processing system resides an operating system, together with data communications, database, and application software. This is illustrated in Figure 16. These software subsystems perform the following functions.

Application Programs

Application programs are the heart of the system. They are the sole reason for having a computer and associated software and hardware. Application software may be purchased from the computer vendor or a third party or developed locally. There are many varieties of application programs. For example, an inventory system has many programs, each of which performs one or more inventory functions, such as inventory update, inventory listings, printing packing lists, and so on. A banking system consists of many programs that provide functions such as creating new accounts, deleting accounts, updating accounts, reporting account statuses, and so on.

To make the development process efficient, programmers should not have to concern themselves with the intricacies of data communication and data storage. This is why application support software, such as the operating system, data communications system, and database system, is used. The purpose of these systems is to allow application developers to concentrate on solving business problems rather than on the specifics of devices such as terminals and disk drives. By isolating applications at this level of detail, a company can also introduce devices into a system with minimal or no impact on existing application programs.

For example, it is typical to have a variety of terminals within a computer network. The way data is displayed on these devices often differs from one terminal to the next. The capabilities supported by the devices also may differ. One terminal may have a color display, and another, a monochrome display. Requiring each application to keep track of these differences would place a heavy, unnecessary burden upon the application programmer. The data communications system accommodates device differences and provides a standard interface that allows an application to deal with any type of terminal.

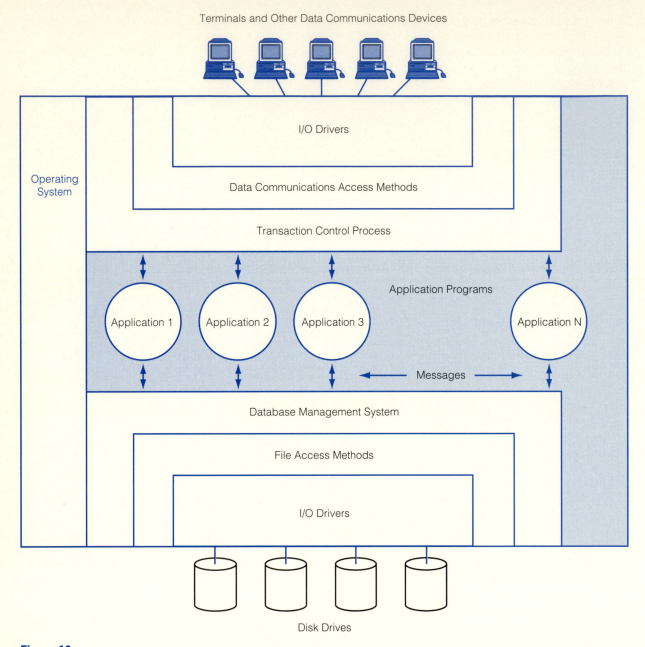

Figure 16

An Applications Environment

Operating System

The operating system manages the resources of the computer. It manages memory; controls access to the processor(s); and provides interfaces to users, the input/output (I/O) subsystems, and the file system.

Data Communications

The data communications subsystem is responsible for interfacing to terminals and other devices that are attached via communications lines. These devices are distinguished from locally attached peripherals such as disk drives, printers, and tape drives. In addition to the function defined above, the data communications system provides a bridge between applications and the devices with which they must communicate. In this capacity, it switches messages between terminals and applications and becomes involved in recovery in the event of a system failure. The data communications component that provides this service is called a **Transaction Control Process (TCP)**.

Database Management System (DBMS)

The DBMS serves as an interface between the application programs and the data they need to resolve business problems. The functions provided by the DBMS are data definition, data manipulation, and data management and control. Data definition provides the ability to define fields; to combine fields into records; and to define files, data access methods, and associations. Data manipulation allows users to retrieve, insert, delete, and modify data in the database. Data management and control allows the database administrator and operations personnel to start, stop, monitor, and reorganize the database.

We can see how these software components work together by tracing a transaction through the system. A **transaction** is a user-defined piece of work that, from the perspective of the database, performs a series of operations that leaves the database in a consistent state. Either the entire transaction must be completed or the database must be left in the state it was in before the transaction started. For a transaction that transfers money between two accounts, there are three database states: (1) at the start of the transaction, (2) after taking money from one account, and (3) after placing the money in the second account, or the end of the transaction. The database is inconsistent in the second state.

Transaction Processing

A particular example of a transaction would be adding a new employee to the database. This process consists of inserting two records into the database, an employee record and a payroll record. The transaction starts at a terminal in the personnel department; the activity is shown in Table 4.

From an opening menu displayed on the terminal, the operator selects an option for adding a new employee. This selection is transmitted to the data communications system, which determines that an employee input form is required. This screen template or input form is transmitted to the terminal, where the operator enters the required information. The terminal access method is responsible for ensuring that the proper control characters are inserted to format the data for the type of terminal being used. The lower

Transaction Control Process (TCP)   A process that receives inputs from terminals and routes them to the proper application processes. TCPs also may edit input data, format data to and from a terminal, log messages, and provide terminal job sequencing. Examples include IBM's CICS and Tandem's Pathway. Also called a teleprocessing monitor or message control system.

transaction   A user-specified group of processing activities that either are entirely completed or, if not completed, leave the database and processing system in a consistent state.

TABLE 4   User Interaction

Transaction control process (TCP) displays menu on terminal

User selects "add employee" activity and sends to TCP

TCP responds to terminal with data entry screen

User fills out screen and sends to TCP

TCP checks data for consistency and writes data to transaction log

TCP begins transaction

TCP sends message to application to process transaction

Application formats data and calls DBMS routine to add employee record to database

DBMS processes application request and returns completion status to application

Application formats data and calls DBMS routine to add payroll record to database

DBMS processes application request and returns completion status to application

Application sends completion status to TCP

TCP ends transaction

TCP sends completion status to user at terminal

---

levels of the data communications system provide the logic to properly place the data on the communications line, to detect transmission errors, and to provide the proper electrical signals for transmission.

The operator enters the data pertaining to the new employee and transmits it back to the computer, where it is received by the data communications system. The TCP checks the message for transmission errors, logs the message to a transaction log file, and determines the transaction type. Because this transaction updates the database, the TCP formally begins a transaction for recovery purposes. The TCP recognizes that it is a message for an application, determines which application should process the transaction, and sends the message to the proper application.

The application program receives the message — to insert two new records into the database — from the data communications system and begins to process it. It formats the records and makes the DBMS request to insert them.

The DBMS accepts the records and inserts them into the database. Before inserting the records, however, the DBMS logs the record images, both before and after making the changes. These before and after images can be used for recovery if a failure occurs. All necessary associations and access methods are established as well. Upon successful completion of the record insertions, the DBMS returns a successful completion status to the application program. The application program then responds to the data communications system that the transaction has been successfully processed. The TCP ends the transaction and sends the completion status back to the terminal operator.

Throughout the transaction the operating system is actively involved, transferring control from one software subsystem to another, interfacing with the peripheral devices, and managing memory. Through the interaction of all the software systems, the transaction is completed. The operating system, the data communications system, and the DBMS support the application process in performing its work.

The preceding example was presented in the context of a network using a single host processor. With only minor modifications the discussion may also be applied to a LAN configuration or a WAN. Let us briefly look at the way in which these activities would occur on a LAN.

A user at a LAN workstation may begin by running a database program located on the file server. The database program will be transferred over the LAN medium into the workstation's memory. From the user's perspective the file server appears to be a disk drive because the application issues a read or write request for a record, and the request is handled by the file server. The database processing logic will thus be carried out by the workstation's processor. The database application will periodically need access to records stored in a shared database on the file server. A request is sent from the workstation to the file server asking the file server to access the desired record. The file server accepts the request, accesses the records from its disks, and transmits the records to the requesting workstation. In this example, the file server responds to requests by simply providing the workstation with the requested records. The file server does not participate in processing database records. In a different LAN scenario we may find a **database server** that cooperates with the workstation in carrying out database requests. With this alternative the workstation sends the database server a request for database processing rather than a request for individual records. The request might be something like "Give me the total sales for the Northwest Region." The database server will act on the request and return the single figure answer rather than the set of records essential to deriving the answer. In this scenario the database server cooperates with the workstation in processing the data.

database server A computer that allows microcomputers on a network to request database processing of records, returning a single figure answer rather than the set of records essential to determining the answer.

There is a common thread in each of the above examples: A user or program made a request that was acted on by one or more other processes. In one example, all of the cooperating processes were running in one processor. In the LAN examples the software was resident in two different processors. The networking trend, particularly for LANs, is to distribute the processing for a single application over two or more network nodes. An application at one node makes requests that software on other nodes process. The requester is called a client process and the processes that act on those requests are called server processes. This general concept is called client/server computing. With client/server computing, the network is called upon to solve application problems rather than having a single node responsible for all application requirements. In essence, then, the network becomes the computer! We discuss client/server computing more extensively in Chapter 17.

CASE STUDY

To make the discussions more understandable and relevant, examples are cited throughout this book. A common case study is carried from chapter to chapter, where applicable. This case study is adapted from actual situations.

Syncrasy Corporation is a startup company in Kansas City, Missouri. The president and two founders decided to capitalize on the boom in the microcomputer marketplace by becoming a mail-order discount outlet for microcomputer hardware, software, and supplies. They have just opened their offices and warehouse and have begun taking orders. All their data-processing requirements are met by a microcomputer and there is no need for data communications. As subsequent chapters illustrate, Syncrasy will become a high-growth company whose needs for computing power and data communications change rapidly as they grow and extend the enterprise. ❖

SUMMARY

Data communications is the electronic transmission of computer-readable data. For two entities to communicate, four essential elements—message, sender, receiver, and medium—must be present. The message also must be understood by the receiver and there ought to be a means for detecting transmission errors.

The data communications industry experienced tremendous expansion during the 1970s and 1980s, largely as the result of lower prices for both equipment and transmission media. During these two decades network hardware and software became faster and more sophisticated to meet the requirements of an online system: performance, consistency, reliability, flexibility, recovery, availability, and security.

As networks proliferated, so did the ways in which they were built. In many cases this resulted in the inability of computers on one network to communicate with computers on another network. The International Standards Organization developed the OSI reference model to remedy this. The OSI reference model describes seven functional layers—application, presentation, session, transport, network, data link, and physical—for moving data from an application in one network node to an application in another node. Many standards have been developed based on the OSI reference model. The key to the model is that the interfaces and protocols are open to all, and networks designed around the model and standards can be more easily interconnected.

KEY TERMS

application layer, *26*

availability, *15*

batch, *10*

Carterphone case, *5*

checksum, *29*

coaxial cable, *20*

common carrier, *23*

consistency, *14*

data communications, *2*

data entry, *10*

data link layer, *27*

data link protocol, *7*

REVIEW QUESTIONS

1. What is the distinction between telecommunications and data communications?

2. Why did the data communications industry grow so rapidly during the 1970s and 1980s?

3. Explain the significance to the data-processing industry of each of the following:
   a. the Hush-a-Phone decision
   b. the Carterphone decision
   c. MCI

4. Characterize each of the following types of application:
   a. inquiry/response
   b. interactive
   c. batch
   d. data entry
   e. distributed
   f. sensor based

5. What are the requirements of an online system?

6. What is a fault-tolerant data communications network? How does fault tolerance improve the reliability of a network?

7. List the seven layers of the OSI reference model.

8. List two functions of each layer in the OSI reference model.

PROBLEMS AND EXERCISES

1. How does the history of data communications differ from that of database development?

2. Investigate in detail two data communications applications. Note specifically the hardware used. Determine the categories of data communications into which the applications fall.

3. Select a specific application of data communications and identify the functions that would be required in the application, presentation, and session layers of the OSI reference model.

4. Discuss the history of telephone companies in the United States or your country as that history relates to the data communications industry.

5. How do U.S. telephone companies differ from their counterparts in Great Britain, France, Germany, Japan, and Australia? In what respects are they the same?

6. How might data communications systems be used in the home?

7. Which components (if any) can be deleted from Table 4? Support your answer.

8. Do all transactions require database services? Give an example to support your answer.

9. In the section on performance (see "Requirements of an Online System"), two different definitions were given for response time. Using each definition, calculate the response time for a response of 1200 characters transmitted over a 240-character per second data communications line.

10. Syncrasy has only one microcomputer and the company does not use data communications. Explain how Syncrasy could use data communications to help run its business. For example, how could Syncrasy use information utilities such as CompuServe and Prodigy?

11. Suppose Syncrasy has several microcomputers rather than just one. Can Syncrasy use data communications effectively? Explain your answer.

REFERENCES

Bell Laboratories. *A History of Engineering and Science in the Bell System; National Service in War and Peace (1925–1975)*. Murray Hill, NJ: Bell Laboratories, 1982.

Martin, James. *Introduction to Teleprocessing*. Englewood Cliffs, NJ: Prentice Hall, 1972.

Metropolis, N., H. Howlett, and Gian-Carlo Rota, eds. *A History of Computing in the Twentieth Century*. New York: Academic Press, 1980.

Stallings, William. *Handbook of Computer Communications Standards: The Open Systems Interconnection (OSI) Model and OSI-Related Standards*, Volume 1. New York: Macmillan, 1987.

*I*n the Introduction you read that an essential element of data communication is a medium. In the best of all worlds, one medium will support high data transfer rates, be economical, be resistant to outside disturbances that might cause transmission errors, and easily extend to multiple locations. Because the ideal does not exist, you should understand the advantages and disadvantages of each of the several commonly used media types. Two situations may help illustrate this point.

Rachel is director of data processing for Tulane Industries, a company that manufactures cellular telephones. Her company has manufacturing plants in Europe, the Far East, and North America, with corporate offices in Austin, Texas. In a move to make the manufacture and distribution of cellular telephones more cost-effective, Rachel has undertaken the task of setting up a computer network that will link all manufacturing plants, distribution warehouses, and the corporate offices. This network will allow orders to be matched with manufacturing plants that are best able to meet the production schedules and make order processing, shipping, inventory management, and corporate communications more efficient. Tulane Industries does not intend to build the communications facilities that will carry its data. Instead, Rachel must work with communications companies to obtain the transmission services that will enable Tulane to transmit its data to all necessary locations at the needed data rates and within corporate budget constraints.

Manuel is the computer administrator for Stearns, Perales, and Gonzales (SPG), an accounting firm in a major southwestern city. The firm leases 2 floors in a 10-story office building in the city's business district. The office has 35 accountants and 15 administrative support staff. The company has been a user of microcomputers for 8 years. SPG has begun the process of upgrading some of its older computers and intends to connect all microcomputers on a local area network. Unlike Rachel's, in the next situation, Manuel also will install the medium necessary for implementing the network. He must choose a medium that meets the corporate speed and cost requirements and is able to reach all offices in their leased space.

In this part we explore the alternatives available to Rachel and Manuel. Following that, we show how errors can affect data and be rectified, how services are provided by communications companies, and how data can be represented on a medium. ■

Part I

....

MEDIA AND THE PHYSICAL LAYER

....

CHAPTER 1
Physical Aspects of Data Communications: Media
CHAPTER 2
Physical Aspects of Data Communications: Data Transmission

Physical Aspects of Data Communications: Media

· ·

CHAPTER OBJECTIVES

After studying this chapter you should be able to:

- Describe the major data communications media
- Compare and contrast selected data communications media
- Select media appropriate to a specific application
- Describe how signals are represented
- Explain the functions of a modem

*I*n the introduction we examined the essential features of communication, one of which was a medium. We also briefly discussed the OSI reference model, including the physical layer. In this chapter we examine the various media available for transporting information, the strengths and weaknesses of each medium, and the ways to represent data during its transmission.

The transmission media commonly used in today's data communications networks can be broken down into two major classes: conducted and radiated. **Conducted media** use a conductor such as a wire or a fiber optic cable to move the signal from sender to receiver. Conducted media include telephone and telegraph wires, private wires, coaxial cables, and fiber optic cables. **Radiated media** use radio waves of different frequencies or infrared light broadcast through the air or space and hence do not need a wire or cable conductor to transmit signals. Radiated media include broadcast radio, microwave radio, satellite radio, spread spectrum radio, and infrared light. These options are listed in Table 1-1. Each medium, together with its necessary transmission facilities, is discussed below. The discussion focuses on those

conducted media Media that use a conductor such as a wire or fiber optic cable to move a signal from sender to receiver.

radiated media Media that use radio waves of different frequencies or infrared light to broadcast through air or space and accordingly do not need a wire or cable conductor to transmit signals.

43

TABLE 1-1   Transmission Media

Conducted Media	Radiated Media
Electrical Conductors	Radio Frequency
Wires	Broadcast
Coaxial cable	Microwave
Light Conductors	Satellite
Fiber optics	Light Frequency
	Infrared

characteristics that make each medium desirable or undesirable in different situations, including speed, security, distance, susceptibility to error, and cost. These attributes form the basis of the selection criteria discussed later in the chapter.

CONDUCTED MEDIA

Wires

Wires are the earliest and currently the most commonly used data transmission medium. Much of the terminology and technology regarding this communications medium derive from telephony and telegraphy because, in setting up its own data communications networks, the computer industry used the existing network of telephone and telegraph lines. The advantages of wires are their availability and relatively low cost. Their disadvantages include susceptibility to signal distortion or error and the relatively low transmission rates they provide for long-distance links.

Private Versus Public Lines   Wires employed in data communications are either private or public. Private lines are those deployed by the user, and public lines are those provided by a common carrier such as a telephone company. Public lines are generally in use where distances are great or the terrain or other environmental factors prohibit the use of private wires.

Transmission Speed and Frequency Range   Theoretically, the maximum transmission speed along wire links is more than 10 million **bits per second (bps)**. The speed is a function of the distance spanned, the diameter of the wire, and—for the twisted-pair wires used by telephone companies—the mutual capacitance of the wires in the pair. Local or private wire links typically operate at speeds up to 80,000 bps and long-distance connections operate at up to 56,000 bps, with commonly used speeds of 9600 and 19,200 bps. Higher

bits per second (bps)   The number of bits that can be transferred over a medium in one second. Bps is a measure of data transmission speed.

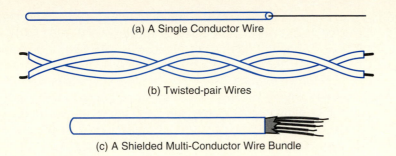

(a) A Single Conductor Wire

(b) Twisted-pair Wires

(c) A Shielded Multi-Conductor Wire Bundle

Figure 1-1

Types of Wires

speed long-distance circuits are also available for applications with high-volume data transfer requirements. Recent technology improvements have produced very high transmission rates over twisted-pair wires for local area networks (LANs). In 1987 several companies released LAN implementations running at speeds up to 16 million bps over unshielded twisted-pair wires, and in the early 1990s speeds of 100 Mbps over twisted-pair wires were achieved. This enables users to employ low-cost telephone wires for high-speed LANs.

Cable Cost, Gauge, and Types   Private cable ranges in cost from 8 cents per foot to more than $1 per foot, depending on the shielding, gauge, and number of conducting wires in the cable. The type of wire most commonly used for private lines is stranded copper, of American Wire Gauges 19, 22, 24, 26, and 28. Figure 1-1(a) shows a single conductor wire. Private wires are usually bundled, providing multiple conductors inside one insulating sheath. The number of conducting strands in such a cable varies, with 4, 7, 8, 10, 12, 15, and 25 conductors being the most common. Figure 1-1(c) shows a wire bundle with multiple conductors.

Ordinary telephone wire consists of a twisted pair of wires. Bundles of these wire pairs from telephones in a given area are sheathed together. Each pair of wires is twisted together to minimize signal distortion from adjacent wire pairs in the sheath. Figure 1-1(b) depicts an individual twisted-pair wire. Twisted-pair wires are one of the most common media in LANs. The two basic types of twisted-pair wires are unshielded (UTP) and shielded. Shielded twisted-pair wires have an extra foil cladding that protects the wires from external interference. When used in LANs, twisted-pair wires commonly operate at speeds of 1, 10, 16, and 20 million bits per second (Mbps), and they are now being used on higher speed LANs operating at 100 Mbps.

Switched Connections Versus Leased Lines   Data communications over long distances can use either switched or leased line connections. **Switched connections** use the same equipment as a standard voice telephone call. One of the two devices to be connected dials the telephone number of the other device's line. Because the telephone company cannot guarantee exactly which path or switching equipment such a connection will use, the speed and quality of the switched connection is limited by the equipment used to set up the circuit. It is possible that lower quality equipment may be

switched connection   A communications link established when one station dials a telephone number to connect to another station. A switched connection uses voice circuits. The circuit exists for the duration of the session.

used to establish the call because the circuit may be routed in a variety of ways. Most switched connections operate at speeds of 300, 1200, 2400, 4800, 9600, 19,200, or 38,400 bps. Higher speeds are possible, but the potential for error and the cost of the extra equipment necessary currently make such speeds cost prohibitive for most users. This limit on speed is being increased in certain areas as telephone companies implement digital data transmission technology, which allows speeds of up to 56,000 bps with switched connections. In the next chapter you will read about digital data transmission.

Because they are more expensive for dedicated use than leased lines, switched lines are used when the amount of transmitted data is small or when many locations must be contacted for relatively short periods. Two examples are (1) a team of salespeople entering information on their portable terminals and (2) a central host computer for a retail organization that contacts each retail outlet at the close of the business day to collect sales and inventory data. In both these situations the amount of data to be transferred is small, and the number of locations may be large or changeable. Switched lines become more expensive as the connection time increases, and their cost-effectiveness may depend on their location, the hour of transmission, and the number of required connections. Chapter 11 discusses an alternative to switched lines — packet distribution networks.

leased lines   Lines leased from common carriers. Lines are leased when the connection time between locations is long enough to cover the cost of leasing or if speeds higher than those available with switched lines must be attained.

Leased lines are used if the connection time between locations is long enough to cover the cost of leasing or if speeds higher than those available with switched lines must be attained. The cost of a leased line is a function of the distance covered, the transmission speed of the line, and the line's susceptibility to error. Common carriers provide a wide variety of options to satisfy diverse needs. For example, a leased line would enable terminals in a sales office in Seattle to communicate with a host computer in San Francisco. For this application the data volume is relatively low and a low transmission speed is adequate but the connection is maintained throughout the day, which makes the leased line cost-effective. An application in which a leased line would be used for both economy and speed is when two distant computers — in Chicago and Los Angeles, for example — must exchange high volumes of information in a timely manner. (For now, only the medium of wires is being considered, and alternatives are being ignored.)

conditioning   A service provided by telephone companies for leased lines. It reduces the amount of noise on the line, providing lower error rates and increased speed.

The telephone companies can provide **conditioning** for leased telephone lines to reduce error rates and increase transmission speeds. One example of conditioning is the use of special equipment that equalizes the signal delay for all frequencies. The five levels of conditioning are C1 through C5, with level C3 not commercially available. Conditioned leased lines typically operate at speeds up to 64,000 bps. Again, digital data transmission may be considerably faster.

Very high speed connections are also available. Although such high-speed links may utilize other media, such as fiber optics and microwaves, they are included in this discussion of wires because of their association with telephone lines. These high-speed services are designated T-1, T-2, T-3, and T-4 and offer transmission rates of 1.5, 6.3, 46, and 281 million bits per second (Mbps), respectively. T-2 service is not commonly available. More detail about these services may be found in Chapter 2 in the section about common carrier services. The cost of leased lines has continually changed as a result of new technologies and industry competition.

Coaxial Cable

Coaxial cable is primarily used in LANs or over relatively short distances, generally fewer than 10 miles (except for use by common carriers). Most LANs are privately owned and are restricted to a relatively small geographical area such as an office building or complex of buildings. LANs are discussed in more detail in Chapters 3 through 7. Coaxial cable is also used to connect terminals with terminal controller units (see Chapter 8 for information about communications controllers). Data transmission rates of up to 100 Mbps are not uncommon, and the theoretical bit rate is more than 400 Mbps.

Technology   Coaxial cable comes packaged in a variety of ways, but essentially it consists of one or two central data transmission wires surrounded by an insulating layer, a shielding layer, and an outer jacket, as depicted in Figure 1-2. Coaxial cable transmission involves two basic techniques: baseband and broadband. In **broadband transmission** the data is carried on high-frequency carrier waves; thus, several channels may be transmitted over a single cable. Frequency separation, referred to as **guardbands**, helps keep one signal from interfering with another. Broadband technology allows one medium to be used for a variety of transmission needs, so that voice, video, and multiple data channels of varying transmission speeds could all exist on one cable. A subchannel with frequencies between 200 and 250 million hertz (Mhz) might be used to carry video data, a subchannel operating between 175 and 200 Mhz could be used for a LAN, voice data could be carried on a subchannel operating between 50 and 75 Mhz, and so on.

Baseband transmission, on the other hand, does not use a carrier wave but sends the data along the channel by voltage fluctuations. Baseband technology cannot transmit multiple channels on one cable, but it is less expensive than broadband because it can use less expensive cable and connectors. Some coaxial cable can be used for either baseband or broadband. Baseband and broadband transmission are illustrated in Figure 1-3.

Advantages and Disadvantages   The television industry has helped develop coaxial cable technology, including the capabilities to add stations or tap into a line without interrupting existing service. In an environment where

baseband transmission
Sends the data along the channel by means of voltage fluctuations. The entire bandwidth of the cable is used to carry data.

broadband transmission
A form of data transmission where data is carried on high-frequency carrier waves; the carrying capacity of the medium is divided into a number of subchannels, such as video, low-speed data, high-speed data, voice, and so on, allowing the medium to satisfy several communication needs.

guardband   Frequency separation that helps to keep one signal from interfering with another.

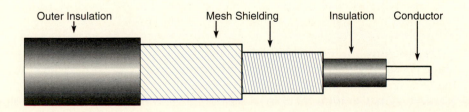

Outer Insulation   Mesh Shielding   Insulation   Conductor

Figure 1-2

A Single Conductor Coaxial Cable

Figure 1-3

Baseband and Broadband
Transmission

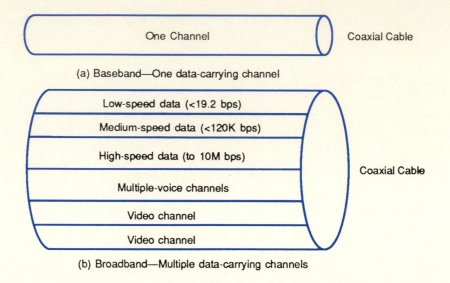

(a) Baseband—One data-carrying channel

(b) Broadband—Multiple data-carrying channels

attenuation   A weakening
of a signal as a result of distance and characteristics of
the medium.

workstations are regularly added, moved, or deleted, the ability to alter the
equipment configuration without disruption to existing users is significant.
However, the ability to tap into the cable without disrupting service is a
disadvantage if a high degree of security is required. Coaxial cable shielding
provides a high degree of immunity to externally caused signal distortion. In
local area networks of less than a half-mile range (the distance varies with
specific implementations), signal loss or **attenuation** is not a concern; for
longer distances, repeaters that enhance the signals are necessary.

Security may be considered both an advantage and a disadvantage of
coaxial cable. If a very secure medium is required, with taps being difficult to
make and easy to detect, coaxial cable presents a serious problem. Whenever
distances are great, attenuation becomes a problem, as does the cost of the
greater amount of cable and the repeaters that must be installed to enhance
the signals over long distances. The advantages of coaxial cable include its
high data transmission rates, its immunity to noise or signal distortion (compared with twisted-pair wires), its capability for adding stations, and its reasonable cost over short distances.

Fiber Optic Cable

Fiber optic cable is a relatively new communications medium used by telephone companies in place of long-distance wires. It is also used by private
companies in implementing local data communications networks.

Technology   Fiber optic cables come in three varieties, each with a different way of guiding the light pulses from source to destination, that all have
the same form and characteristics. One or more glass or plastic fibers are
woven together to form the core of the cable. This core is surrounded by a

Figure 1-4

Views of a Fiber Optic Cable

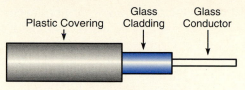

(a) A Side View of a Fiber Optic Cable

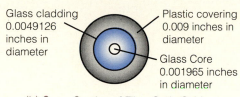

(b) Cross-Section of Fiber Optic Cable

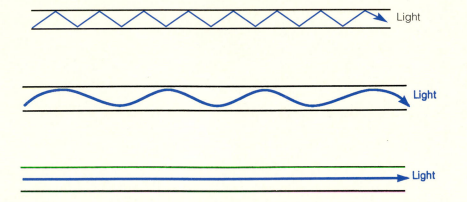

Figure 1-5

Fiber Optic Multimode Step-Index

Figure 1-6

Fiber Optic Multimode Graded-Index

Figure 1-7

Fiber Optic Single Mode

glass or plastic layer called the cladding. The cladding is covered with plastic or some other material for protection. Figure 1-4 shows both a side view and a cross-section of a fiber optic cable. All three cable varieties require a light source, with laser and light-emitting diodes (LED) being those most commonly used.

The oldest of the three fiber optic technologies uses **multimode step-index fiber**, in which the reflective walls of the fiber move the light pulses to the receiver. Figure 1-5 illustrates multimode step-index transmission. **Multimode graded-index fiber** acts to refract the light toward the center of the fiber by variations in the density of the core. Figure 1-6 depicts the movement of light in a multimode graded-index fiber. The third and fastest fiber optic technique is **single mode transmission**. With single mode transmission, light is guided down the center of an extremely narrow core. Single mode transmission is depicted in Figure 1-7. Fiber optic transmission rates currently available range up to approximately 2 billion bps (Gbps), and speeds in excess of that are possible.

multimode step-index fiber   The oldest of the fiber optic technologies, in which the reflective walls of the fiber move the light pulses to the receiver.

multimode graded-index fiber   Acts to refract the light toward the center of the fiber by variations in the density of the core.

single mode transmission   The fastest fiber optic technique, in which the light is guided down the center of an extremely narrow core.

Benefits and Cost One shortcoming of fiber optics is the inability to add new nodes while other nodes are active. Although it is now relatively easy to splice the fiber optic cable and add new stations, the network or a portion of the network must be down while the splice is being prepared. Fiber optic links for very short distances cost more than wires, but as distance or the required transmission rate increases, fiber optics becomes cost-effective. The breakeven point generally occurs when the distance is so great that coaxial cable or wires would require expensive signal-enhancing equipment. A significant advantage that fiber optics has over copper wires is its reduced size and weight—about 20 times lighter and 5 times smaller than equivalent copper wire (either coaxial or twisted-pair). Very low error rates and immunity to environmental interference are additional benefits.

RADIATED MEDIA

Broadcast Radio

broadcast radio Employs AM, FM, and shortwave radio frequencies, with a total frequency range from 500,000 to 108 million cycles per second. Its primary applications include paging terminals, cellular radio telephones, and wireless local area networks.

Broadcast radio employs not only the radio frequencies typical of AM and FM radio stations, but short-wave or short-distance radio frequencies as well, with a total frequency range from 500,000 to 108 million cycles per second. Broadcast radio's primary applications are in paging terminals, the devices carried by people (such as doctors) who are on call; for cellular radio telephones; and in wireless local area networks. A good example of radio broadcast for data communications is in the AlohaNet at the University of Hawaii. Broadcast radio was chosen to overcome the difficulty of setting up wire links in the islands, and it proved quite effective when the number of stations was relatively small. As more stations were added, however, contention between broadcasting stations increased, collisions or interference became more frequent, and effective utilization dropped. The medium also proved to be susceptible to interference from other radio broadcast sources. The AlohaNet transmission rate was 9600 bps. When broadcast radio is used with local area networks, cables connecting each microcomputer are eliminated. The elimination of cables makes installation and changing of workstations easier and reduces the problems of loose connections that can occur as a result of people walking or pulling on cables.

mobile computing Has expanded the role of broadcast radio in data communications. It requires a wireless medium such as cellular radio, radio nets, and low orbit satellites. It makes installation and changing workstations easier.

Mobile computing has expanded the role of broadcast radio in data communications. The importance of mobile computing and communications is such that major evaluation and reallocation of the available radio frequencies may result. Mobile computing, of course, requires a wireless medium and broadcast radio is being increasingly used in this manner. This new application of radio transmission is placing ever higher demands on a limited range of broadcast frequencies. The demand is reaching the point where some experts suggest that countries need to reevaluate the entire use of the frequency spectrum and use radio frequency transmission only for mobile communications. Nonmobile communications such as television would be delivered exclusively by conducted media, thus freeing those frequencies for mobile communication devices such as portable computers and personal communicators.

The most common media for mobile computing communications are cellular radio, radio nets, and low-orbit satellites. Cellular radio as currently implemented tends to be costly and operates at low speeds, typically 19,200 bps or lower. This makes cellular radio primarily suitable for transfers of small amounts of data such as electronic mail messages. Cellular radio transmission for data is also subject to high error rates.

Radio nets using dedicated frequencies over large areas are also used for mobile computing. These networks require the use of a radio modem to send and receive data. Currently radio nets operate at speeds up to 19,200 bps, but higher speeds are likely as this technology expands. Low orbiting satellites offer another communication alternative. Unlike the geosynchronous satellites, low-orbit satellites do not remain in a fixed position relative to the earth. However, by using several low-orbit satellites, you can assure that at least one is always in position to accept and relay signals. Use of this technology for commercial mobile computing is still in its infancy. Each of these three technologies has the disadvantages of low speed, possibility of signal interference, and lack of security.

Microwave Radio

It was MCI's proposal for a **microwave radio** linkage between Chicago and St. Louis that first stimulated competition for long-distance telephone service. The first commercially implemented digital microwave radio system was installed in Japan by Nippon Electric Company in 1968.

Microwaves are being used as a medium for wireless LANs. For networks where installation of conducted media is difficult or too expensive, microwaves provide a high-speed media alternative. The microwaves are generated at a low power to minimize the affects on humans but the waves are able to penetrate through walls. Microwaves as a LAN medium provide transmission speeds of 10 Mbps and higher speeds are inevitable.

microwave radio   A method of transmitting data using high-frequency radio waves. It requires a line of sight between sending and receiving stations. Capable of high data rates, microwave is used for wide area networks and wireless LANs.

Technology   Microwave transmission rates range up to 45 Mbps. Because microwave signals travel in a straight line, both transmitter and receiver must be in each other's line of sight (obstructions cannot be between them). The curvature of the earth therefore requires that microwave stations be approximately 30 miles apart. The difference between the highest and lowest possible frequencies, also called the limiting frequencies, of a microwave channel is called the channel's **bandwidth**. Bandwidth is an indicator of a medium's speed. The bandwidth of a microwave channel can be subdivided into many subchannels similar to the multiple channels in broadband transmission. The subchannels may be used for voice-grade transmission, high-speed data links, or both. Bandwidth and other measures of carrying capacity are discussed later in this chapter.

bandwidth   The difference between the minimum and the maximum frequencies allowed. Bandwidth is a measure of the amount of data that can be transmitted per unit of time. The greater the bandwidth, the higher the possible data transmission rate.

Figure 1-8

A Microwave Relay Station

Advantages and Disadvantages   Microwave transmission offers speed, cost-effectiveness, and ease of implementation; however, it has the unfortunate potential for interference from other radio waves. It also is limited by line-of-sight considerations, and commercial transmissions are insecure because they can be intercepted by anyone with a receiver in the line of transmission. Microwaves can also be affected by environmental conditions. Transmissions at the same or nearly the same frequencies can interfere with each other, and some atmospheric conditions, such as high humidity, can affect the signal. Figure 1-8 shows a picture of a microwave relay station.

Satellite Radio

satellite radio transmission
Transmits data via very-high-frequency (VHF) radio waves and requires line-of-sight transmission between stations.

Satellite radio transmission, like microwave radio transmission, transmits data via very-high-frequency (VHF) radio waves; both media require line-of-sight transmission between stations. The primary difference between the two media is station location. Microwave makes use of land-based stations only,

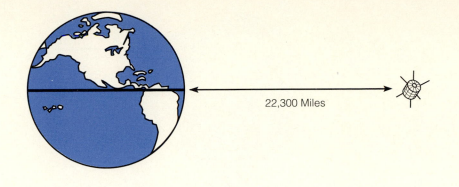

Figure 1-9

A Geosynchronous
Satellite Orbit

22,300 Miles

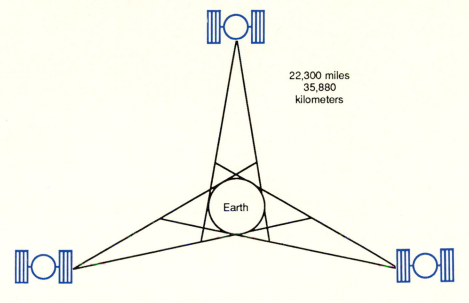

Figure 1-10

Satellite Positioning

22,300 miles
35,880
kilometers

Earth

whereas satellite uses both land-based stations and orbiting stations. Commercial communication satellites are placed in an equatorial, geosynchronous orbit at an altitude of 22,300 miles. A **geosynchronous orbit** means the satellite remains stationary relative to a given position on the earth, as illustrated in Figure 1-9. At this altitude, only three satellites are required to have all points on the earth within range, as shown in Figure 1-10. Because there is limited room for geosynchronous orbiting satellites, a variation called inclined orbit satellites is being used more frequently. Inclined orbit satellites also rotate at a distance of 22,300 miles above the equator; however, inclined orbit satellites move slightly north and south of the equator as illustrated in Figure 1-11. This movement requires that the earth stations track the movement of the satellites. Typically, tracking antennas are smaller (1.2 to 2.5 meters in diameter) than the more traditional earth stations (7 meter diameters or larger). These smaller antennas are called very small aperture terminals (VSATs). The added expense of having a tracking antenna is typically offset by lower transmission costs.

geosynchronous orbit   A satellite orbit in which the satellite is stationary with respect to the earth: The satellite is always positioned over the same location.

Figure 1-11

Inclined Orbit Satellite

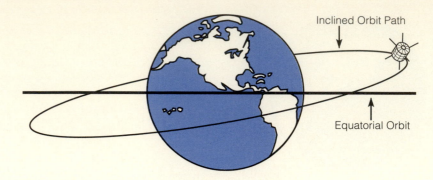

Figure 1-11

Inclined Orbit Satellite

Figure 1-12

Satellite Separation

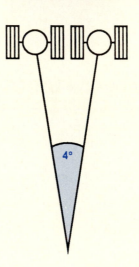

Technology   The basic components of satellite transmission are the earth stations, for sending and receiving, and the satellite component called a **transponder**. The transponder functions to receive the transmission from earth (uplink), amplify the signal, change the frequency, and transmit the data to a receiving earth station (downlink). The uplink frequency differs from the downlink frequency so the weaker incoming signals are not interfered with by the stronger outgoing signals. Satellite frequencies are spoken of in pairs, such as 12/14 gigahertz. The first number represents the downlink frequency and the second, the uplink frequency. *Giga* means 1 billion, and 1 hertz is 1 cycle per second. Thus, 12/14 gigahertz means a downlink transmission frequency of 12 billion cycles per second and an uplink transmission frequency of 14 billion cycles per second. To avoid interference, communication satellites in space must be separated by an arc of at least 4 degrees, as depicted in Figure 1-12. (This has led to concern, especially among countries presently incapable of launching satellites, that only a limited amount of space is available for these satellites and that the space will be allocated without them obtaining a slot.) Each transponder has a transmission rate of approximately 50 Mbps, which can be divided into 16 1.5-Mbps channels, 400 64-Kbps channels (Kbps means kilobits per second, or 1000 bits per second), or 600 40-Kbps channels. Although this transmission rate is high, there still is a

transponder   In satellite communications, a transponder receives the transmission from earth (uplink), amplifies the signal, changes frequency, and retransmits the data to a receiving earth station (downlink).

TABLE 1-2 Satellite Propagation Delay

Remote-satellite input uplink	22,300 miles
Satellite-host input downlink	22,300
Host-satellite response uplink	22,300
Satellite-remote response downlink	22,300
Total distance	89,200 miles

$$\text{Travel time} = \frac{89{,}200 \text{ miles}}{186{,}000 \text{ miles/second}} = 0.48 \text{ seconds}$$

significant delay because the signals must travel a long distance from source to destination.

Propagation Delay   The amount of time it takes for a signal to travel from its source to its destination is called **propagation delay**. Because most data communications signals travel at nearly the speed of light, propagation delay on earth is insignificant (about 16 milliseconds for a 3000-mile transcontinental journey). Across the extremely long distances of space, however, propagation delay can be noticeable. The delay includes travel time as well as the time required to accept, enhance, and retransmit the signal. Propagation delay becomes significant for applications that have sending times of less than a quarter-second or response times of a half-second or less. Propagation delay is ordinarily ignored for terrestrial links, but satellite transmission system designers must be aware of this factor. Table 1-2 gives an example of how propagation delay is computed for a transaction in which a remote terminal sends a message to a host computer and receives a reply from it.

propagation delay   The amount of time it takes for a signal to travel from its source to its destination.

Satellite Providers   The several providers of transponders for satellite communication include Hughes Network Systems, Comsat, AT&T Tridom, GTE Spacenet, and Scientific Atlanta, as well as broadcast agencies in Canada, Japan, Europe, and the Soviet Union. The number of transponders per satellite is typically between 12 and 24. Providers of satellite time usually lease a whole transponder, but it is also possible to sublease transponder subchannels from another user. Satellites make expansion of a data communications network relatively easy. All that is required is to add earth stations (except when the area being served is outside the area serviced by the satellite(s) being used). Satellite networks can present security problems, however, because transmission can be intercepted by anyone with proper receiving equipment.

Spread Spectrum Radio

The primary application of **Spread Spectrum Radio (SSR)** for data communications is wireless LANs. SSR has long been used by the military to provide reliable radio communications in battlefield environments where signal jam-

Spread Spectrum Radio (SSR)   The primary application for data communications is for use with wireless LANs. It has a characteristic reliability in environments where signal interference is likely.

ming can be expected. One characteristic of SSR is reliability in environments where signal interference is likely.

Two methods, frequency hopping and direct sequencing, are used to provide SSR signals. With **frequency hopping**, data is transmitted at one frequency, then the frequency is changed and data is transmitted at the new frequency, and so on. Each piece of data is transmitted over several frequencies to increase the probability that it will be successfully received. **Direct sequencing** sends data over several different frequencies simultaneously. When used in wireless LANs, SSR distances are limited to approximately 1000 feet, making it useful for small LANs or as the medium for small segments of larger LANs. Examples of SSR being used in a large LAN include the use of portable computers and providing LAN connections in an area in which it is difficult or expensive to install conducted media. SSR signals can penetrate normal office walls but signal strength is reduced considerably by concrete and metal walls. Like most radiated media, SSR has the disadvantage of being susceptible to signal interference and signal interception. The speed of data transmission (2 Mbps) also is lower than that of many of today's LANs using conducted media.

Infrared Transmission

Infrared transmission uses electromagnetic radiation of wavelengths between visible light and radio waves. Infrared transmission is another line-of-sight technology. It is used to provide local area connections between buildings and also is the medium used in some wireless local area networks. Data transmission rates are typically on the order of 4 Mbps or less.

Radiated Media Frequencies

The frequencies of various radiated media are given in Table 1-3.

MEDIA SELECTION CRITERIA

Several factors (Table 1-4) influence the choice of a medium for a data communications network. Because every configuration has its own set of constraints, not all factors apply in every situation; in some situations, there may even be only a single viable alternative. However, system designers must consider each criterion, either implicitly or explicitly. The factors also may influence one another. For example, a strong correlation often exists between a medium's application and its required speed, so much so that the application usually dictates a minimum acceptable transmission speed (although other factors such as cost and expandability can also pertain).

---

frequency hopping   Data is transmitted at one frequency, the frequency changes, and the data is transmitted at the new frequency. Each piece of data is transmitted over several frequencies to increase the probability that the data will be successfully received.

direct sequencing   Sends data out over several different frequencies simultaneously to increase the probability of success.

infrared transmission   Uses electromagnetic radiation of wavelengths between visible light and radio waves. It is a line-of-sight technology used to provide local area connections between buildings and is also the medium used in some wireless local area networks.

TABLE 1-3   Frequency Spectrum Classification

Frequency (Hz)	Wave Length
10^{16}	X-rays, Gamma rays
10^{15}	Ultraviolet light Visible light
10^{14}	Infrared light
10^{13}	Millimeter waves
10^{12}	
10^{11}	Microwaves
10^{10}	UHF television
10^{9}	VHF television VHF TV (high band)
10^{8}	FM radio
10^{7}	VHF TV (low band) Shortwave radio
10^{6}	AM radio
10^{5}	
10^{4}	
10^{3}	Very low frequency
10^{2}	
10^{1}	

TABLE 1-4   Media Selection Criteria

Cost	Security
Speed or Capacity	Distance
Availability	Environment
Expandability	Application
Error Rates	Maintenance

Cost

A dramatic expansion in the application of data communications began during the 1970s, influenced strongly by improvements in technology and lower costs. Cost reductions were the result of improved technology and competition among the common carriers providing transmission services. The technological advances included communications equipment capable of supporting higher data transmission rates at lower costs, as well as the commercial availability of fiber optics and satellite transmission.

The costs associated with a given transmission medium include not only the costs of the medium but also ancillary fees, such as the costs for additional hardware and software that might be required. A deferred ancillary cost that is important to consider when making an initial selection is the cost of expansion. An emerging marketing organization located in Houston, Texas, might initially select the specific market areas of New York City, Chicago, Houston, and Los Angeles. The logical choice for connecting the remote offices to the host computer in Houston is to lease a line from a common carrier. As the corporation expands into other cities, however, a satellite link could be more economical because the expense of adding new locations might be less than that of leasing more land lines.

Speed

aggregate data rate   The amount of information that can be transmitted per unit of time.

A tremendous range of transmission speeds is available. Low-speed circuits transmit at rates less than 100 bps; high-speed circuits, at more than 100 Mbps. Within a given medium, higher speeds mean higher costs, though this is not necessarily attributable to the medium itself. Higher data transmission rates require more sophisticated (expensive) communications equipment. Two factors dictate the required speed of a medium: response time and **aggregate data rate**. Design goals for an online application should include the expected response time for each type of transaction. Aggregate data rate refers to the amount of information that can be transmitted per unit of time. Media speeds are summarized in Table 1-5.

TABLE 1-5   Media and Their Common Transmission Speeds

Private line	300, 1200, 2400, 4800, 9600, 19,200, 38,400, 56,000 64,000 80,000
Switched line	300, 1200, 2400, 4800, 9600, 19,200, 38,400
Leased line	2400, 4800, 9600, 19,200, 56,000, 64,000
T1, T2, T3, T4	1.5M, 6.3M, 46M, 281M
Unshielded Twisted Pair	1M, 10M, 16M, 100M
Shielded Twisted Pair	1M, 10M, 16M, 100M
Coaxial cable	1M, 2M, 10M, 50M, 100M (over 400M potential)
Fiber optics	over 2 Gbps
Microwave	to 45M
Broadcast radio	9600
Spread Spectrum radio	2M
Infrared light	1M, 4M
Satellite	to 50M

Response Time   Response time has two components, transmission time and processing time, and each of these can be broken down into subcomponents. Suppose the design objective is a response time of 3 seconds for 95% of one type of transaction. If processing takes 1 second, transmission must take 2 seconds or less. If the transaction involves the exchange of 500 characters of information, then the speed of the medium must be at least 250 characters per second (500 characters divided by 2 seconds), which represents approximately 2400 bps. This assumes there is no sharing of the communications link. If the line is shared, allowances must be made for the amount of time that the line might be unavailable to a specific user. Chapter 8 discusses several ways that one communications line can be shared among several users.

Aggregate Data Rate   In applications such as bulk data transfers, aggregate data rate may be the factor dictating line speed. Suppose the application just discussed required that the line be available to office personnel during the day for inquiries and updates and that within an hour of closing time a file of 2 million characters had to be transmitted to a host computer. The business day requirements for response time could be satisfied with a 2400-bps channel, but the file transfer would require an aggregate data rate of about 555 characters per second (2 million characters per hour divided by 3600 seconds per hour), which is a 7200-bps channel. (Note: These examples do not allow for any overhead or retransmissions due to errors.)

Availability

Availability has two aspects: (1) Is the medium available when it is needed? (2) Is there sufficient carrying capacity to handle the volume of data? An operation that uses a switched telephone line would be at a disadvantage when phone lines are busy, as on certain holidays. Imagine a fast-food chain with stores throughout the United States that maintains a central file of sales and inventory data. Each store's terminals record the daily receipts and foods dispensed. At the end of the business day the central location dials the phone number of each store's computer, transfers and processes the data collected during the day, and then orders supplies for each restaurant. On Mother's Day the phone circuits are extremely busy, which interferes with the chain's ability to contact all of its locations. This lack of availability would not be catastrophic for this application, but for a process control or factory control application, lack of availability could produce disastrous results.

Shared Lines   Shared lines also can create problems of availability. One user may monopolize the line, thus making it unavailable to others. Suppose two terminals share a line, and one user is attempting interactive queries into a database while the other attempts to copy a lengthy file to an attached printer. The line's capacity may be taken up with the file transfer, making the line unavailable to the other user.

Control Messages   Some of a line's capacity must be reserved for control messages. For instance, error detection requires additional bits of information to be appended to the data. A long message that must be broken down into segments for transmission requires extra information to delimit the message's beginning, end, and segments. Acknowledging receipt of transmitted data creates additional line congestion. When erroneous messages are received, then the last message, and perhaps several previous messages, must be retransmitted. Using multiple devices per line requires that addresses be appended to messages; in many instances, control sequences need to be transmitted to establish when each device can use the medium and receive data. Idle time also may occur on the circuit because there is no data to send or because the state of the circuit is being changed, such as a control message to disconnect from a switched connection. These types of control functions can take up a considerable amount of the carrying capacity of a circuit—as much as 30%, excluding idle time. Figure 1-13 illustrates some of the extra fields appended to a message for transmission and for segmenting a long message.

Expandability

Frequently it becomes necessary to expand the scope of a data communications configuration, either by adding more devices at a given location or by adding new locations. Some media—such as coaxial cable and satellites—make expansion into new locations relatively easy, whereas others—such as leased telephone lines—make expansion more difficult or more costly. It is important that communications networks be designed for the future as well as for immediate needs. Suppose a rapidly growing computer company used private wires to attach terminals for some employees in the head office. The initial applications were extremely successful, and new applications and employees were quickly

Figure 1-13

Message Transmission

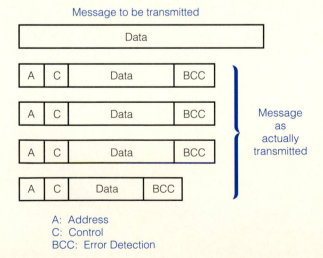

A: Address
C: Control
BCC: Error Detection

added. This created a need for more terminals, which required additional communications circuits. The company had to go through the time-consuming and expensive process of stringing additional wires throughout the facility. Had they anticipated their growth correctly, the additional wires could have been installed with the initial set.

Several alternatives are also available in such situations. Instead of supplying additional circuits, the company could have added new hardware, such as concentrators, multiplexers, or addressable terminals. Such solutions are the subject of Chapter 8. Expandability is a problem not just of media availability but also of hardware. When a system has reached its maximum capacity with respect to the available number of devices and communications circuits, a larger machine or additional machines must be added. The airline industry's reservations systems have faced this problem several times as more subscribers were added to the network.

Error Rates

All transmission media are subject to signal distortion, which can produce errors in the data. The propensity for error influences not only the quality of transmission but also its speed. Switched telephone lines are subject to noise from switching equipment and other sources, which typically limits the speed to 38,400 bps or less. Such errors pose no problem in voice communication because humans are adept at detecting errors and recovering from them; either a person does not understand what is being said or the context is incorrect, and recovery is simple because a person can usually ask that a message be repeated from a particular point. Computers, on the other hand, do not understand context, and therefore are unable to detect a corrupted data bit. The impact of even one undetected inverted bit can be significant. Suppose a bank must use data communications to transfer several million dollars to another bank. If just one of the high-order bits in the money field is changed, a difference of several million dollars can result. To detect transmission errors in data communications environments requires that redundant information be included with the transferred data. This technique reduces the efficiency of the link and still cannot ensure absolute accuracy of the data. The common methods for detecting errors are discussed in Chapter 2.

Security

The lack of security in data communications networks was made clear by several widely publicized incidents of hackers or espionage agents penetrating several major networks (Hafner, 1991; Mungo, 1992; Stoll, 1989). Personal computers equipped with a modem provide a low-cost capability for connecting to computer networks. With this equipment all an intruder needs is sufficient low-cost or free network connect time to find and exploit the network's security weaknesses. The above references show that costs for connect time can be avoided or minimized through the use of toll-free numbers, local calls to installations in the hacker's calling area, use of an established low-cost access network such as the Internet, use of stolen telephone credit cards, or illegally bypassing a common carrier's toll system.

Providing complete security, like providing an error-free medium, is impossible. However, some media, such as fiber optics, are more difficult to penetrate than others, such as microwave and satellite. Microwave and satellite transmissions are easy to intercept because they are broadcast and anyone with the proper receiver can pick up the signals. The conducted medium most vulnerable to the average hacker is switched telephone lines. Most companies providing data communications have switched telephone line access. In some instances computer vendors insist on such an access capability for emergency maintenance and diagnostic purposes. To avoid misuse of these lines, the lines should be deactivated when not needed and protected by security devices such as a call-back unit when operational. A call-back unit and other security devices are described in Chapter 8.

Distance

Distance includes not only transmission distance but also the number of locations served. If the distances are short (within one building or complex of buildings), private media such as wires, coaxial cable, or fiber optics may be feasible. With greater distance or number of locations, it usually becomes necessary to obtain media from a common carrier. As the number of locations to be reached becomes very great, or when it is necessary to communicate with remote locations, a broadcast medium such as a satellite may be the only viable solution.

Environment

The constraints of environment can eliminate certain types of media. Even when the distance between two buildings to be connected in a data communications network is small enough to make private lines feasible, local ordinances may prohibit the user from installing such lines. If a locale prohibits the stringing of wire over or under a public street, the user might have to pick a medium other than private wires. Direct satellite links in leased office facilities might be impossible because the lease prohibits installing earth stations on the premises. Private lines that must be strung through areas with considerable electrical or magnetic interference might be impractical because of the potential for inducing error in transmission. Environment clearly plays a critical role in the selection of a transmission medium.

Application

Certain applications (such as environmental monitoring) employ devices designed to connect to a system in a very specific way and at specific speeds. In such applications, the characteristics of the required equipment may dictate the type of medium and interfaces to be used. As noted above, the particulars of an application also help determine other required characteristics of the medium, such as speed, security, and availability. For instance, the most obvious media for a high-speed local area network are twisted-pair wires, coaxial cable, and fiber optics, whereas the private branch exchange (PBX) telephone system would be a lower speed alternative.

Maintenance

Just as all media are subject to error, all are subject to failure. In some cases repair or replacement is simple — a telephone cable severed in an excavation accident can be repaired within several days, and while repairs are being made an alternate path might be made available. Repair or replacement of a defective satellite, however, is a lengthy process, which is why communications companies frequently have a backup transponder available. Maintenance concerns do not have a high priority because such failures are infrequent. Nonetheless, system designers must consider the impact of medium failures and their probable duration and must prepare a backup or contingency plan so communications can continue while repairs are being made. Consider a major bank in Australia that depended heavily on its computer center. The bank established multiple computer centers, each serviced by different telecommunications trunk lines. It also made provisions for switching lines from one center to another should the communications links to one of the centers be severed. As a result, no failure at a single point was able to disrupt the bank's ability to process data.

A comparison of the principal data communications media is provided in Table 1-6. In some instances it is difficult to separate one criterion from another. Consider the expandability of a network that uses wires. An expansion can take place in several ways. One expansion option may be to add new hardware instead of new lines. Suppose a company needs to add two more terminals in a location that currently has only one. Instead of adding two new communication lines, a hardware device called a multiplexer can be installed at each end of the connection. A multiplexer will allow all three terminals to

TABLE 1-6 Media Comparison Table

	Wires	Coaxial Cable	Fiber Optics	Microwave	Broadcast Radio	Satellite
Availability	Good	Good	Good	Good	Possible contention	Fair to good
Expandability	Fair	Good in local area	Good	Good	Good	Good
Errors	Fair	Good	Good	Fair	Fair	Fair
Security	Fair	Fair	Good	Poor	Poor	Poor
Distance	Good	Poor	Good	Good	Good	Good
Environment	Fair	Good	Good	Fair	Fair	Fair

share the same line. Multiplexers are covered in Chapter 8. Another expansion option is to allow the three terminals to share the same line using a technique called polling. Polling is also discussed in Chapter 8. Another alternative is to add two new communication lines. If this last alternative is chosen, there is usually no problem in obtaining the circuit. Unfortunately, the cost may be high, which is why this cell in the table is assigned a rating of fair. This table should be used in conjunction with Table 1-5, on transmission speeds, because it is important that each device communicating on a medium have sufficient access and speed to perform its task. Configurations such as the line-sharing ones just mentioned will reduce the availability of the medium to individual attached devices. This means that with one type of multiplexer on a 9600-bps line with four devices, the available speed to an individual device will be only 2400 bps.

SIGNAL REPRESENTATION AND MODULATION

As noted above, each medium has individual characteristics that determine how and where it might be used. The medium serves as a conduit for data. It is also important to understand how data can be represented on the medium. The two basic classes of representing data are analog and digital. Let us now look at how data are transmitted.

Bit Rates, Baud Rates, and Bandwidth

bit rate   One method of measuring data transmission speed — bits per second.

Up to this point, data transmission speed has been discussed exclusively in bits per second, or **bit rate**. This bit rate is the most appropriate unit for systems analysis; however, two other terms also are commonly used: bandwidth and baud rate.

Bandwidth   The bandwidth of a channel is the difference between the minimum and maximum frequencies allowed. A voice-grade channel that can transmit frequencies between 300 and 3400 hertz (Hz) has a bandwidth of 3100 Hz. Bandwidth is a measure of the amount of data that can be transmitted per unit of time and is directly proportional to the maximum data transmission speed of a medium. The higher the bandwidth, the greater the data-carrying capacity.

baud rate   A measure of the number of discrete signals that can be observed per unit of time.

Baud Rate   The **baud rate** is a measure of the number of discrete signals that can be observed per unit of time. Only in the binary situation is the baud rate exactly the same as the bit rate. Unfortunately, the two terms are frequently used interchangeably. But the bit rate is higher than the baud rate when a baud represents more than one bit of information. In the binary amplitude modulation situation, two different signal levels can represent the bits 0 and 1 (as discussed earlier). If the signal changed 1200 times a second, the baud rate would be 1200 and the bit rate would be 1200 bps. Suppose, instead, that four different amplitudes were represented — 1, 2, 3, and 4 per

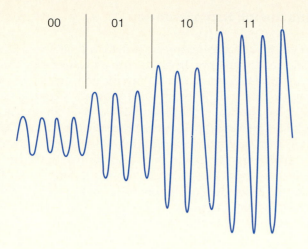

Figure 1-14

Dibits Using Amplitude
Modulation

00　01　10　11

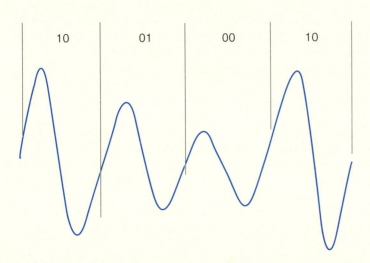

Figure 1-15

Example of Dibits Using
Amplitude Modulation

10　01　00　10

unit of time—as in Figure 1-14. Each level could then be used to represent two bits. This technique is referred to as **dibits**.

Now suppose a signaling rate of 1200 changes per second is maintained. The baud rate remains at 1200, but the bit rate doubles to 2400 bps because each signal represents two bits. Figure 1-15 shows the transmission of the bit pattern 1001001 using dibits (with one bit added to make the number of bits even). Similarly, eight signal levels could represent three bits with each signal, a technique referred to as **tribits**. If 16 different signaling levels were used, four bits per signal could be represented, a technique referred to as **quadbits**. Hence, with current technology the bit rate equals the baud rate or a multiple thereof (two, three, or four times the baud rate). **Phase Shift Keying (PSK)** or a derivative is the most common method of achieving dibit and tribit transfer; **Quadrature Amplitude Modulation (QAM)** is the most common method for quadbit transfer. Later in this chapter we explain how PSK and QAM are implemented.

dibits　A transmission mode in which each signal conveys two bits of data.

tribits　A method of modulation that allows three bits to be represented by each signal.

quadbits　A technique in which each signal carries four bits of data. Requires 16 different signals.

Phase Shift Keying (PSK)　A form of phase modulation.

Quadrature Amplitude Modulation (QAM)　A modulation technique using both phase and amplitude modulation.

Digital Versus Analog Representation

digital transmission   A transmission mode in which data is represented by binary digits rather than by an analog signal.

All the computers we are considering store data in digital form and transmit this data in analog or digital form. In **digital transmission**, data is represented by a series of distinct entities. In data communications equipment this series is almost always a binary digit, or bit—either 0 or 1. **Analog transmission** refers to measurable physical quantities, which in data communications take the form of voltages and variations in the properties of waves. Data is represented in analog form by varying the amplitude (height), frequency (period), and/or phase (relative starting point) of a wave. Translation from digital format to analog format and back to digital format is accomplished by a device known as a **data set** or **modem** (an acronym for modulator-demodulator). A modem functions to accept digital data (a string of bits), transform the data into an analog signal, and pass the signal along a medium to another modem. The receiving modem translates the analog signal back into digital data. Because the telephone companies' original communications systems transmit information in analog form, these systems must change the data to analog form to meet the requirements of data communications transmission facilities. In a subsequent section we discuss modem capabilities. First, we look at a method for representing data in an analog format.

analog transmission   Refers to measureable physical quantities, which in data communications take the form of voltage and variations in the properties of waves. Data is represented in analog form by varying the amplitude, frequency, and/or phase of a wave or by changing current on a line.

data set/modem   Short for *modulator-demodulator*. A device that changes digital signals to analog signals for transmitting data over telephone circuits. Also used for some fiber optic transmission (digital fiber optics do not require a modem) and any transmission mode requiring a change from one form of signal to another.

Carrier Signals

carrier signal   A wave that continues without change, carrying information that cannot be discerned but can be modulated by a modem so a receiver can interpret the information.

One of the trigonometric relationships between angles in a right triangle is called the sine of the angle. The values for the sine of an angle vary from 1 to −1 and a continuous curve of this function can be plotted. Figure 1-16 depicts a simple sine wave. A wave of this form has the potential for carrying information. If the wave continues without change, as depicted, no information can be discerned. Such an unmodulated signal is called a **carrier signal**. The purpose of a modem is to change, or modulate, the characteristics of the carrier wave so a receiver can interpret information. The simple sine wave has several properties that can be altered to represent data: amplitude (height), frequency (period), and phase (relative starting point). Modems alter one or more of these characteristics to represent data.

Amplitude Modulation

Amplitude Modulation (AM)   One method of changing the properties of a wave to represent data.

The simplest characteristic to visualize is **Amplitude Modulation (AM)**. Figure 1-17 represents two sine waves superimposed on one another. One curve represents sin x and the other represents 2 sin x. Note that the 2 sin x curve has twice the amplitude of the sin x curve. (Varying the amplitude of a curve is similar to changing the voltage on a line.) How is this variation used to convey information? Suppose the bit pattern 1001001 is to be transmitted. If a 1 bit is represented by the curve of 2 sin x, and a 0 bit by the curve traced by sin x, the bit pattern would be represented by the modulated sine curve depicted in Figure 1-18.

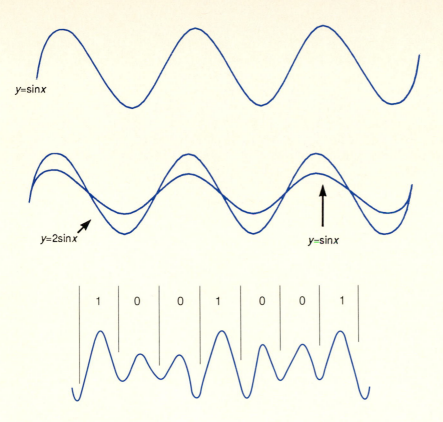

$y=\sin x$

$y=2\sin x$ $y=\sin x$

1   0   0   1   0   0   1

Frequency Modulation

The period, or frequency, of a sine curve is the interval required for the curve to complete one entire cycle. In the simple sine curve the period is 2 pi, where pi is approximately 3.14159. In data transmission such intervals are only seconds, so the period is the number of seconds required for the wave to complete one cycle. The mathematical function that alters the period is sin x. Figure 1-19 shows the curve of sin $2x$. When the horizontal axis represents time, the period is frequency (oscillations) per unit of time. **Hertz (Hz)** is the term used to denote frequency; one hertz is one cycle per second. The human ear can detect sound waves with frequencies between 20 and 20,000 Hz. Telephone systems use the much smaller frequency range between 300 and 3400 Hz, which is satisfactory for carrying voice transmission.

To convey information by **Frequency Modulation (FM)** is to vary the frequency of the transmission. To transmit the binary pattern 1001001 by frequency modulation on a voice-grade line, a frequency of 1300 Hz can represent the 1 bit and a frequency of 2100 Hz can represent the 0 bit (one of the actual values used by some modems). The signal received must be within 10 Hz of these values to be acceptable, which means the range for a 1 bit is 1290–1310 Hz. These frequency values must be different enough to minimize the possibility of signal distortion altering the values transmitted. Thus, if the 1 bit were represented by 1500 Hz and the 0 bit by 1510 Hz, a decrease of only

Hertz (Hz) The term used to denote frequency; one hertz is one cycle per second.

Frequency Modulation (FM)/Frequency Shift Keying (FSK) One method of changing the characteristics of a signal to represent data. The frequency of the carrier signal is changed. Often used by lower speed modems.

Figure 1-19

The Curve of Sin 2x

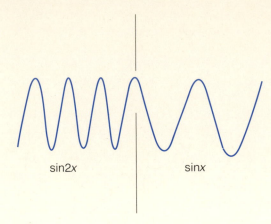

sin2x sin$x$

Figure 1-20

Frequency Modulation

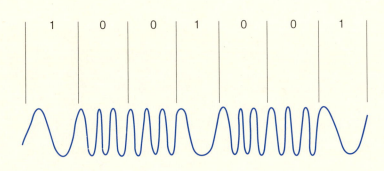

Figure 1-21

The Curve of Sin x

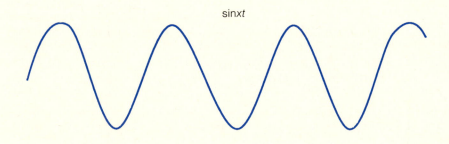

sinxt

10 Hz would change a 0 bit into a 1 bit. Figure 1-20 shows an example of frequency modulation for our selected bit pattern 1001001.

Phase Modulation

phase modulation   A change in the phase of a carrier signal. Commonly used alone or in conjunction with amplitude modulation to provide high-speed transmission (4800 bits per second and higher).

A third modulation technique is **phase modulation** (phase shifting). If the simple sine curve is represented by sin x, then a change of phase is represented by sin (x + n). Figure 1-21 shows the curve of sin x, Figure 1-22 shows the curve of sin (x + pi), and Figure 1-23 shows the two curves superimposed on one another. Transmitting the bit pattern of 1001001 using phase modula-

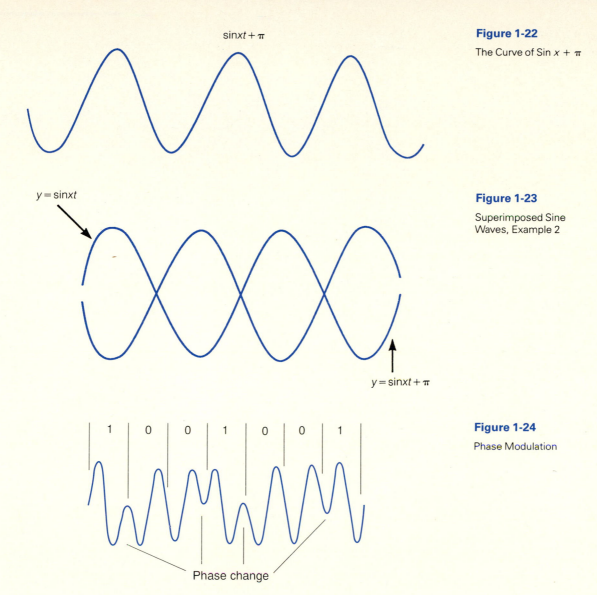

$\sin xt + \pi$

Figure 1-22

The Curve of Sin $x + \pi$

$y = \sin xt$

Figure 1-23

Superimposed Sine
Waves, Example 2

$y = \sin xt + \pi$

| 1 | 0 | 0 | 1 | 0 | 0 | 1 |

Figure 1-24

Phase Modulation

Phase change

tion — where a 1 bit is represented by no phase change and a 0 bit by a change in phase of pi radians — yields the curve in Figure 1-24.

Phase modulation is often used for high-speed modems because it lends itself well to the implementation of dibits, tribits, and quadbits. Figure 1-25(a) shows 8 different angles in a full circle. Suppose each angle is used as a phase shift in phase modulation. Thus, with 8 different signals we can represent 3 bits of information per signal, or tribits. In Figure 1-25(b) the 8 angles are combined with two levels (amplitudes) of signal, providing 16 different signals, each of which can represent 4 bits. This combination provides a quadbit capability known as quadrature amplitude modulation (QAM). QAM on a 1200-baud line can provide transmission of 9600 bps. The most common

Figure 1-25(a)

Phase Modulation Angles

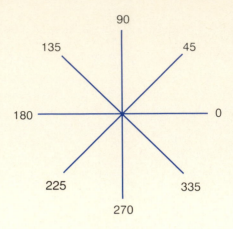

(a) Eight different phase changes,
suitable for tribits

Figure 1-25(b)

Phase Modulation Angles
and Amplitudes

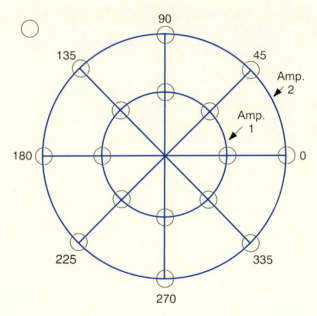

(b) Eight phase changes plus two amplitudes
yields 16 different signals, for quadbits

The 16 different signals are represented by circles

**Differential Phase Shift
Keying (DPSK)**   A modulation technique that uses
phase modulation. DPSK
changes phase each time a
1 bit is transmitted and does
not change phase for 0 bits.

modulation techniques in data communications are frequency modulation,
also known as **Frequency Shift Keying (FSK)**, and phase modulation, also
known as phase shift keying (PSK). Also available are a variation known as
Differential Phase Shift Keying (DPSK) and QAM.

The analog representation just described is used in many common carrier
communications networks. Be aware, however, that there are other ways of

Figure 1-26

A Codex 2680 High-Speed Modem

representing data in analog format. For example, changing the voltage on a wire can also be used to represent data. No voltage may represent a 0 bit and three volts may be used to represent a 1 bit.

Modems and Their Capabilities

Modems fall into two categories; copper-based and fiber optic. Copper-based modems are used to interface to twisted-pair wires, and fiber optic modems are used with fiber optic cable. The principle of both types of modems is essentially the same — changing signals from one format to another and then back again. Copper-based modems change a device's digital signals to analog electrical signals, whereas fiber optic modems change a device's digital signals to optical digital signals. When the supplier of fiber optic cable is a common carrier, the common carrier is responsible for signal generation. A company that installs its own fiber optic cables may need to purchase it's own fiber optic modems.

When modems are used to transmit data over communications links, they are always used in pairs. The modems in a pair must be configured alike. Most modems have a variety of available options. Figure 1-26 shows a modem. Some modem capabilities are presented in Table 1-7, and a terminal-computer connection using modems is illustrated in Figure 1-27. Most modems on the market do not offer all of these capabilities. Some options are explained here; the remainder are discussed in Chapters 2, 8, and 9.

Speed   All modems are designed to operate at a specific speed or range of discrete speeds. A variable-speed modem can be set via switches on the modem, via program control, or by automatic adjustment to the transmission speed.

TABLE 1-7   Some Modem Capabilities

Speed and variable speed

Auto-answer

Manual answer

Auto-dial

Manual dial

Auto-disconnect

Manual disconnect

Programmable control (e.g., computer-controlled dialing and setting of data rate)

Automatic redial

Keyboard dial

Speaker (to monitor dialing and connection)

Synchronous or asynchronous

Full or half duplex

Reverse channel

Secondary channel

Multiport

Line conditioning capabilities (equalization)

Self-testing mode

Voice-over data

Compatibility with:

  Bell modems

  Hayes modems

  Microcomputer Network Protocol (MNP)

    MNP 4 — error correction

    MNP 5 — data compression

  Consultative Committees on International Telegraph and Telephony (CCITT) standards

  Electronic Industries Association (EIA) standards

  U.S. government standards

Telephone Options   Auto-answer, manual answer, auto-dial, auto-disconnect, automatic redialing, and keyboard dialing all refer to use of switched telephone lines. Most newer modems can react to the ring indicator on the line and automatically answer a call. For a manual-answer modem, someone must help in making the connection. This "inconvenience" actually promotes security. Auto-dialing means the modem can dial a number itself. Many modems can remember frequently called numbers. Each memory location can usually be associated with a code name, making dialing even easier. For

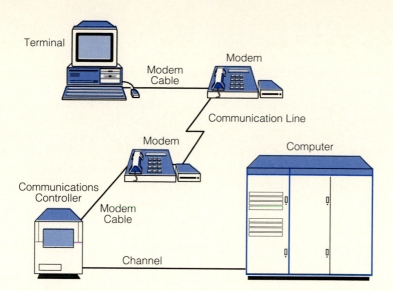

Figure 1-27

Terminal-Computer
Connection Using Modems

example, the code name "school" can be used to represent the telephone
number for the school's computer center. The user can then direct the modem
to dial school rather than selecting the specific number. With auto-disconnect
a modem terminates a call automatically when the other party hangs up or a
disconnect message is received. Automatic redialing modems automatically
redial a call that resulted in a busy signal or no connection. Finally, keyboard
or programmable dialing means the number can be dialed using the keyboard
of a terminal or via program control. For mobile computing, cellular radio,
broadcast radio, and pocket modems are available. Pocket modems are small
pocket-size modems used primarily for portable computers. Modems con-
forming to the Personal Computer Memory Card International Association
(PCMCIA) standards are available for notebook-class computers. Pocket,
PCMCIA, and radio frequency modems are relatively recent technologies and
show that mobile computing is becoming an important segment of the data
communications market.

Self-Testing   Most new modems, and many older models, have some
type of self-testing mode. These include a loop-back test, in which the modem's outgoing signal is looped back to itself; memory diagnostic checks; and
modem-to-modem test transmissions. These self-tests are quite valuable in
isolating problems in the communications equipment.

Voice-Over   Voice-over data capability allows voice communication over
the same circuit as the data, either as voice or data or as voice and data simultaneously. This arrangement is beneficial when the data transmission application
requires a dedicated circuit to a remote location. Suppose a company requires
voice telephone communication between offices already linked by leased lines.
Every such call can be dialed, incurring a toll for each, or voice-over data modems can be used, occupying a portion of the line capacity already leased. The

only additional costs of voice transmission, then, are the price of the modems and the reduced data capacity on the line.

Compatibility A variety of modem standards exist, and adherence to widely accepted standards helps establish modem compatibility. One of the references for compatibility is the modems supplied by AT&T; more recently, compatibility with modems manufactured by the Hayes Corporation is often cited. Two other entities involved in modem standards are the **Consultative Committee on International Telegraph and Telephony (CCITT)** and Microcom, Inc. Microcom has established or helped to establish a series of standards referred to as **Microcomputer Network Protocols (MNP)**. Some of the standards to which modems might adhere include:

- CCITT V.32, modulation specifications for high-speed modems commonly operating at 9600 with speeds of more than 38,400 bps possible with data compression.
- CCITT V.42, error correction.
- CCITT V.42bis, data compression. Data compression can significantly increase the apparent speed of a modem by reducing the number of bits transferred. Compression ratios of 4:1 or higher may be attained depending on the data being transmitted. A modem rated at 9600 bps may attain transmission speeds of 38,400 via compression.
- V.Fast, a 28,800-bps modem standard. If the V.42bis standard for data compression is added to a V.Fast modem, the effective speed can be 115 Kbps or higher.
- MNP 1, 2, 3, and 4, error correction.
- MNP 5, data compression.

Multiport modems are discussed in Chapter 8; reverse and secondary channels, full and half duplex operations, and conditioning are covered in Chapter 2; and synchronous and asynchronous transmission are addressed in Chapter 9.

Cost The price of modems is much like that of media — constantly changing and, in general, dropping as a result of new technology and competition. As summarized in Table 1-8, the price also varies according to the capabilities offered, with speed being the most influential factor.

Short-Haul Modems For short distances, short-haul modems can be used. These allow for transmission distances up to about 20 miles, at varying speeds. As distance increases, speed decreases. Table 1-9 presents the relationship between distance and speed with short-haul modems. Strictly speaking, distance is a function of the resistance of the conductor, and speed is a function of the capacitance and resistance of the conductor. For practical purposes, distance and speed are functions of the thickness or gauge of the conductor. Table 1-9 holds for 22-gauge wire; greater speeds or distances are possible with 19-gauge wire, and lower speeds or distances would result from the use

Consultative Committee on International Telegraph and Telephony (CCITT) An international standards organization.

Microcomputer Network Protocols (MNP) A set of modem protocols providing for data compression and error checking, such as MNP Level 4 and MNP Level 5.

TABLE 1-8   Representative Modem Costs

Speed in bps (Speed will typically be higher if compression is used)	Cost
2400	$60–70
9600	$185–200
14,400	$240–260
19,200	$635–650
24,000	$1350–1400

TABLE 1-9   Short-Haul Modems, Speed vs. Distance

Distance (miles)	Maximum Speed (bps)
17	2,400
15	4,800
12	9,600
7	19,200

Figure 1-28

A Modem Eliminator

of 26-gauge wire. The advantage of short-haul modems is a significant reduction in cost—tenfold savings or better are possible.

Modem Eliminators   For very short distances, **modem eliminators** provide additional savings and very high data transmission rates. Modem eliminators, also referred to as line drivers or null modems, can connect two devices that are in close proximity. A modem eliminator provides clocking and interface functions between two devices. One modem eliminator can replace two modems, as illustrated in Figure 1-28. The spannable distances are covered by interface specifications such as the RS-232-C standard, which recommends a distance of 50 feet for standard wires, or the RS-449 standard, which specifies 200 feet. Although manufacturers usually certify their modem eliminators at these standard distances, longer distances are possible.

modem eliminator   A device that allows data transmission over short distances without a modem. Provides for signal timing as well as data transmission.

acoustic coupler An acoustic coupler converts digital signals to analog and analog to digital. It is used mostly in switched communications and uses the telephone handset to pass data between a terminal or computer and the acoustic coupler.

current loop A transmission technique that uses changes in current flow to represent data. Does not require a modem and operates at speeds up to 19.2 K bits per second without modems.

neutral working A method of transmitting data in a current loop where current represents a 1 bit and the absence of current indicates a 0 bit.

polar working One method used to implement current loop transmission.

One use of modem eliminators is high-speed, computer-to-computer communications links. Data transmission rates up to 1 million bps can be supported by modem eliminators.

The previously described modems are connected directly to communications wires. An **acoustic coupler** allows for data transmission across telephone lines, using the telephone handset to pass the data. Acoustic couplers have a send-and-receive receptacle into which the handset is placed. Transmission rates for acoustic couplers are usually either 300 or 1200 bps. Acoustic couplers are frequently used with portable terminals, some of which even incorporate the acoustic coupler as an integral part of the terminal.

Current Loops   For distances up to 1500 feet, **current loop** technology allows data transmission speeds up to 19,200 bps without any type of modem. The common model is a 20-milliampere current loop. To transmit data by this technology, the current on the line is switched on and off or the direction of the current is changed. In the first method, the presence of current represents a 1 bit and the absence of current indicates a 0 bit. This technique is referred to as **neutral working**. When current direction is switched, current flowing in one direction represents a 1 bit and current in the opposite direction is a 0 bit. This technique is called **polar working**.

Fiber Optic Modems   Modems are also used for fiber optic transmission at speeds ranging from 1200 bps up to 50 Mbps, with popular intermediate speeds of 56 Kbps, 100 Kbps, 250 Kbps, 1.544 Mbps, 5 Mbps, and 10 Mbps.

CASE STUDY

Business at the Syncrasy Corporation has been progressing. President Ima Overseer and the other two founders report that business has been excellent and expansion is in order. The first phase of expansion will include a larger computer system and two new locations in New York City and Los Angeles. The remote offices will each have ten terminals connected to the host computer in the Kansas City office, where all inventory, pricing, and customer information is stored. It is expected that sales activity will occur throughout the day in both remote locations. The average order consists of 500 input characters and 100 response characters. The company's objective is to provide 5-second response time for each order; it has been determined that processing time per order averages 2.5 seconds. Thus far, each terminal operator enters 20 orders per hour on the average, with peak loads of 30 transactions per hour. Ms. Overseer wants to know which medium will best serve Syncrasy's immediate needs. Determining this requires some basic calculations, the first of which is to figure the necessary speed of the lines.

Line Speed

Usually a system is configured to meet the peak transaction load; if it can handle the peaks, it can definitely handle the valleys. Although configuring for peak loads is not absolutely necessary, it is undesirable to have the system bog down when it is needed the most. Configuring to the peak workload also provides latitude for expanding work during off-peak periods, including development activities such as program compiling and batch operations such as payroll and periodic reports.

Line speed is based on response time and throughput. Syncrasy has decided to use the conservative response time definition, which requires all response characters to be received. It is assumed that two or more terminals might share a communications path (Chapter 8 discusses how this is done). First the needs of a single terminal are considered. Five hundred input characters and 100 output characters total to 600 characters transmitted per average transaction. The expected response time is 5 seconds, of which 2.5 seconds is communication time (estimated processing time was 2.5 seconds). Thus, one terminal will require a path with a speed of $600/2.5 = 240$ characters per second. Assuming 10 bits per character, a line speed of 2400 bps is required. It is inconceivable that a line can operate at 100% capacity, so a 4800-bps line is preferable.

Number of Terminals per Line

To determine how many terminals could effectively share a line demands some intuition: A peak rate of 30 transactions per hour per terminal translates to 300 transactions per hour, or 5 transactions per minute. This rate is not excessive, and all 10 terminals could conceivably use the same 2400-bps line. The only problem would be if two users were to enter data at exactly the same time; one response time would be the expected 5 seconds, whereas the other would be approximately 7 seconds. The logic behind this is provided in Table 1-10, in which T represents transmission time, P represents processing time, and W represents wait time. Terminal 2 sees a slower response time because it must hold off transmitting until Terminal 1 has sent its data. If the line speed were twice as fast (4800 bps), two concurrent terminals could be handled within the 5-second response time.

If three users enter information at exactly the same time, one of them, of course, will have a lower response time. However, the chances of that happening with ten terminals on a line is slight. Assuming a random arrival rate, the probability of three transactions arriving in a 2-second interval is less than one in a thousand (0.00065) (see Exercise 4). A 4800-bps line should be satisfactory for all ten terminals.

TABLE 1-10   Transaction Activity

Terminal 1	TTTTTTTTTTPPPPPPPPPPPPPPTT
Terminal 2	WWWWWWWWWWTTTTTTTTTTPPPPPPPPPPPPPPTT
	----1----2----3----4----5----6----7----8
	Time in Seconds

Additional Criteria

There are no special environmental, security, expansion, maintenance, or error rate concerns to resolve in this system, and the application issues have already been addressed. The calculations show that a high-speed path is not necessary. Distance is a factor in the remote connections, and transmission facilities should therefore be acquired from a common carrier. Private wires are best for the local terminals in the Kansas City offices because the offices are free of environmental disturbances and there are no distance problems to overcome. Private wires also are far more cost-effective than other solutions, and their speed can be greater than that of leased lines. Fiber optics and coaxial cable are possibilities, but they would be more costly if privately implemented, and such high data transmission rates are not presently required.

SUMMARY

A wide variety of transmission media are available to the network designer, and many networks employ several of them. If the telephone companies' use of fiber optics, microwave, and satellite channels is considered, most long-distance networks are a combination of media. Numerous factors influence the selection of transmission media. Each medium has information-carrying capacity, which varies from a few characters per second to millions of characters per second. The terms *bit rate, baud rate*, and *bandwidth* are used to describe a medium's carrying capacity, and these measures are interrelated.

In transmitting information between devices in a computer network, it is frequently necessary to convert a device's digital signals to analog format. There are several ways to do this; frequency modulation, phase modulation, and phase modulation plus amplitude modulation are the most common. The device that translates digital signals to analog signals and then back again is known as a modem or data set. Modems differ greatly in the bit rate provided as well as in the options available.

KEY TERMS

acoustic coupler, *76*	baud rate, *64*
aggregate data rate, *58*	bit rate, *64*
Amplitude Modulation (AM), *66*	bits per second (bps), *44*
analog transmission, *66*	broadband transmission, *47*
attenuation, *48*	broadcast radio, *50*
bandwidth, *51*	carrier signal, *66*
baseband transmission, *47*	conditioning, *46*

REVIEW QUESTIONS

1. What are the advantages and disadvantages of private lines?

2. Distinguish between switched lines and leased lines.

3. Compare broadband and baseband transmission.

4. Rank wires, coaxial cable, and fiber optics with respect to speed, cost, and resistance to noise. Which is fastest? Which is least expensive? Which is least error prone?

5. Describe the effects of propagation delay on satellite transmission.

6. Describe:
   a. Amplitude Modulation
   b. Frequency Modulation
   c. Phase Modulation

7. Compare broadcast, microwave, and satellite radio.

8. How does spread spectrum radio work? What is its primary data communications application?

9. Why do some experts believe that television signals should be transmitted by conducted media rather than by radiated media? Do you agree or disagree with this premise?

10. Explain how the terms *baud rate*, *bit rate*, and *bandwidth* are used to describe the speed of a communications link.

11. Describe what a modem does.

12. What are the advantages of current loop transmission?

PROBLEMS AND EXERCISES

1. Given the different modes of communication — private lines, switched lines, leased lines, coaxial cable, fiber optic cable, microwave, satellite, or a wireless LAN media — which would be the most suitable for the following applications (a–g)? Why?

   a. A U.S. marketing organization must transmit large amounts of product information, sales data, facsimiles, and electronic mail to 40 cities. Each of the 40 locations has computers and sends volumes of sales data, facsimiles, and electronic mail. Response time is not critical.

   b. A manufacturing plant has multiple computers, data-processing workstations, and terminals, all spread throughout 6 buildings. All facilities are located within 1 kilometer of each other and all rights of way are controlled by the company. The data being transmitted includes small files, memos, electronic mail, and online transactions. Response time is critical for the online transactions.

   c. A hospital has automated its patient care system. Terminals have been placed in all administrative offices, laboratory facilities, doctors' and nurses' offices, and nursing stations. The online transactions include data entry, inquiries, and short reports. Rapid response time is important.

   d. A research corporation is evaluating solar energy systems. It has data collection devices attached to several experimental wind and solar collectors. A large, continuous volume of data is transmitted to the computer center, which is 10 miles from the test grounds. The computer center can be seen from the test grounds.

   e. A major fast-food chain has chosen to centralize its inventory and sales data. Each restaurant maintains its sales and inventory data on a small computer located in the store. This computer is attached to point-of-sale terminals that serve as data entry devices. Every time an item is sold, the inventory and sales data on the local computer are updated. Every evening the central office must retrieve the information from each store. The amount of information to be transmitted is approximately 10,000 characters per restaurant.

   f. A major car rental agency has decided to regionalize its inventory and reservations system. Approximately 75% of the reservation requests are resolved by the regional center, and the remaining 25% must be forwarded to another regional processing center. The peak amount of data to be transmitted to another center is approximately 10,000 characters per minute. This also means that each regional center will receive approximately 10,000 characters per minute.

   g. A research corporation must exchange data among three computers located in different departments within one building. The data is highly sensitive, so security is a major concern. The data consists of text, research results, graphics, and electronic mail. Response time is not critical. A communication speed of 9600 bps would be adequate. The optimum path for private wires would require the wires to pass through research areas with a considerable amount of electrical or magnetic activity.

2. A small insurance company wants to connect its ten microcomputers in a LAN. The company is situated in an old house that has been renovated. Speeds must be at least 2 Mbps but will not exceed 16 Mbps. There are no devices that have potential for disrupting signals on radiated or conducted media. What medium would you recommend? Justify your answer.

3. A corporate office needs to connect several departmental LANs. The interconnection will be made using a LAN to which the departmental LANs are connected. The interconnection LAN must operate at 100 Mbps. The medium will be run through elevator shafts and a machine room, so signal distortion is a concern. What medium would you recommend? Justify your answer.

4. The probability of k random arrivals in an interval of length T is given by the formula

$$P_k(T) = \frac{(LT)^k}{k!} \times e^{-LT} \text{ for } K = 0, 1, 2, 3, \ldots$$

where

$P_k(T)$ is the probability that k transactions will arrive in time interval T

k is the number of arrivals

T is the time interval being considered

e is the natural base for logarithms

L is the average number of transactions per unit of time

! is the factorial function

If the arrival rate of transactions per second is 0.25, the probability that two transactions will arrive in 5 seconds is given by

$$P_2(5) = (0.25 \times 5)^2/2! \times e^{-(0.25 \times 5)} = (1.25)^2/2 \times e^{-1.25} = 0.22$$

Using this formula, verify that the probability of three transactions arriving in a 2-second interval is approximately 0.00065 when the number of transactions arriving per hour is 300. In making your calculations, make sure that your time units match.

REFERENCES

Briere, Daniel. "Fast Modems Just Got Faster." *Network World*, April 19, 1993.

Coden, Michael H. "Why Fiber Will Fly." *LAN Technology*, Volume 8, Number 11, October 15, 1992.

Flanagan, Patrick. "VSAT: A Market and Technology Overview." *Telecommunications*, Volume 27, Number 3, March 1993.

Hafner, Katie. *CyberPunk*. New York: Simon and Schuster, 1991.

Head, Joe. "Fiber Optics in the '90s: Fact and Fiction." *Data Communications*, Volume 19, Number 12, September 21, 1990.

Johnson, Johna Till, and James K. Hurd. "High-Speed Modems: A Price Worth Paying." *Data Communications*, Volume 22, Number 10, July 1993.

Leeds, Frank, and Jim Chorey. "Cutting Cable Confusion: The Facts About Coax." *LAN Technology*, Volume 7, Number 3, March 1991.

————. "Round Up Your Cable Woes." *LAN Technology*, Volume 7, Number 10, October 1991.

Mell, John P., Jr., and Peter Wayner. "Wireless Mobile Communications." *Byte*, Volume 18, Number 2, February 1993.

Methvin, Dave. "V.32 Modems: Closer to the Mainstream." *PC Week*, January 29, 1990.

Mungo, Paul. *Approaching Zero*. New York: Random House, 1992.

Politi, Carol A., and John A. Stein. "VSATs Give Corporate Networks a Lift." *Data Communications*, Volume 20, Number 2, February 1991.

Sanders, Russel. "Mapping the Wiring Maze." *LAN Technology*, Volume 8, Number 11, October 15, 1992.

Saunders, Stephen. "Premises Wiring Gets the Standard Treatment." *Data Communications*, Volume 21, Number 16, November 1992.

Stoll, Clifford. *The Cuckoo's Egg*. New York: Doubleday, 1989.

Turner, Steven E. "Upgrading to V.Fast: Facts and Fictions." *Telecommunications*, Volume 27, Number 7, July 1993.

More Physical Aspects of Data Communications

....

CHAPTER OBJECTIVES

After studying this chapter you should be able to:

- Describe the three basic flow control protocols used in data communications
- Discuss the characteristics of major data codes
- Explain the types and sources of errors that can affect data transmissions
- Describe the ways errors are detected and corrected
- Compare and contrast digital and analog data transmission
- List the transmission services provided by common carriers

This chapter, an extension of Chapter 1, continues the discussion of physical transmission of data and data transmission utilities. Setting up and managing today's communications networks is more complex than ever. More vendors are providing communications services over a wider variety of speeds. Different forms of communication also are increasingly being integrated onto one transmission medium. As a result, the sphere of responsibility for the modern data communications manager is expanding. In addition to selecting communications facilities for data transmission, the communications manager may also be responsible for selecting hardware and software that can meet the corporate needs for data, voice, video, facsimile, and other forms of electronic communication. In this chapter you will learn about data transmission facilities and other common communication facilities.

DATA FLOW

Every data communications network must have some mechanism of control over the flow of data. This is accomplished at two levels. The first level provides for contention control, which determines which stations may transmit, the conditions under which transmission of data is allowed, and the pacing of data transmission. Contention control is discussed in subsequent chapters. The other, more basic level of data flow relates to the transmission equipment used — lines, modems, and devices. The three elementary types of data flow are simplex, half duplex, and full duplex.

Simplex Transmission

In simplex transmissions data may flow in only one direction, like traffic on a one-way street. Radio and television transmissions, illustrated in Figure 2-1(a), are examples. In simplex transmission one station assumes the role of transmitter and the other station is the receiver; these roles may not be reversed. Although this may appear rather limiting, simplex transmission has numerous applications. Receive-only devices such as keyboards, microcomputer monitors, and optical character recognition (OCR) scanners involve simplex communication. Communications with printers that are capable of transmitting status information back to the host are not classified as simplex,

Figure 2-1

Examples of Data Flow

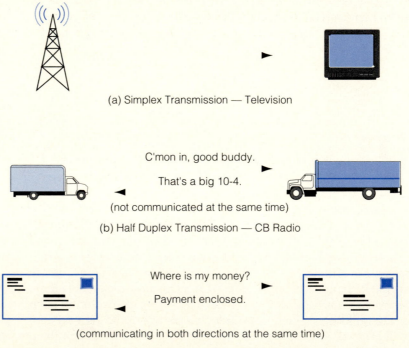

(a) Simplex Transmission — Television

C'mon in, good buddy.

That's a big 10-4.

(not communicated at the same time)

(b) Half Duplex Transmission — CB Radio

Where is my money?

Payment enclosed.

(communicating in both directions at the same time)

(c) Full Duplex Transmission — Mail System

but data collection devices that serve as input devices only do use simplex communication. In solar energy research installations, heat sensors, solar monitors, and flow meters have been used to monitor the environment and transmit samples of data via a simplex line. A building environmental monitoring system also operates in this mode, sending temperature and humidity readings to a computer that controls the heating and cooling of the building. Simplex lines are less common in business applications than half duplex or full duplex. Simplex lines are used for some printers, for monitoring devices in environment and process-control applications, for transmitting stock exchange data (stock tickers), and for most radio and cable television data transmissions.

Half Duplex Transmission

In half duplex transmission, data may travel in both directions, although only in one direction at a time, like traffic on a one-lane bridge. Figure 2-1(b) shows the example of citizens band (CB) radio, where radio operators on the same frequency may be either sender or receiver but not both at the same time.

Continuous Versus Noncontinuous Carriers   When data flow is controlled by a modem, two half duplex options are available: continuous carrier and noncontinuous carrier. A carrier signal, which involves a continuous frequency, is the signal that is modulated to represent data. In continuous carrier mode, even though data may only pass in one direction at a time, the carrier signal on which the data is imposed is passed in both directions, as shown in Figure 2-2(a). Noncontinuous carrier mode allows a carrier signal to be passed in either direction but only in one direction at a time, as shown in Figure 2-2(b). A transmitter "raises" the carrier signal that is propagated along the medium to the receiver.

Modem Turnaround Time   Noncontinuous carrier mode introduces an additional delay in transmitting the data. This delay is called **modem turnaround time**, which is the period required for the old sender to drop the carrier signal, for the new sender to recognize that the carrier signal has been dropped, and for the new sender to raise the carrier signal that must be detected by the new receiver. Most of today's modems do not incur this delay.

modem turnaround time   The time required for a modem to make the transition from sender to receiver on half duplex links. It includes the time for the old sender to drop the carrier signal, for the new sender to recognize that the carrier signal has been dropped, and for the new sender to raise the carrier signal that must be detected by the new receiver.

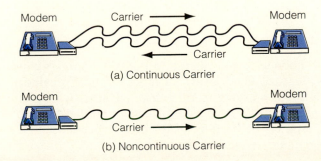

(a) Continuous Carrier

(b) Noncontinuous Carrier

Figure 2-2

Carriers

Figure 2-3

Reverse Channel Modem

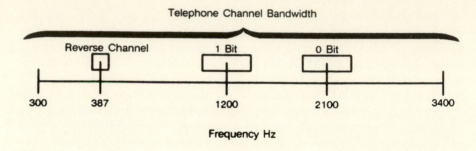

Reverse Channel Capability   To lessen the effect of modem turnaround time, some half duplex modems provide a **reverse channel**. For example, certain communications systems require the receiver to briefly (with a few characters) acknowledge receipt of each data transmission before another can be sent. Printers pass back brief status signals to indicate their readiness to receive more data. One set of conventions is known as XON and XOFF: When a terminal or printer wants the host to send more data it transmits an XON signal, and when it does not want more data transmitted it sends an XOFF signal. If modem turnaround were required for each of these short sequences, then overall turnaround time would be significant. A reverse channel provides a very slow circuit that allows the receiver to send these short messages without forcing a line turnaround. Reverse channel capability is a subcase of continuous carrier mode: There is a carrier in both directions, but the reverse channel has a lower transmission rate than the forward channel. A reverse channel is illustrated in Figure 2-3.

reverse channel   Allows transmission in both directions on a line that is essentially half duplex. The reverse channel generally has a lower transmission rate than the forward channel and is used to acknowledge receipt of data. Reverse channels help reduce the need for modem turnaround.

Full Duplex Transmission

In full duplex mode, data can be transmitted in both directions simultaneously, like traffic on a two-way street. An example of data transmission using full duplex capabilities is the postal service: Letters can be transmitted in both directions simultaneously, as illustrated in Figure 2-1(c). Figure 2-4 shows full duplex communication. Full duplex transmission does not involve modem turnaround time. Full duplex operations are effected in radio-wave transmissions by using two different frequencies, one for each direction. With coaxial cable, full duplex operations require broadband transmission.

DATA CODES

As already mentioned, data is stored in digital computers as sequences of binary digits (bits), each with a value of either 0 or 1. To provide meaning to a sequence of bits, you must set up the number of bits that are grouped to form a data character and create an encoding scheme, or translation table, by which the system translates each group of bits into a character. In the encoding scheme of telegraphy—Morse code—each character is represented as a combination of dots and dashes. Although these could be also interpreted as bits,

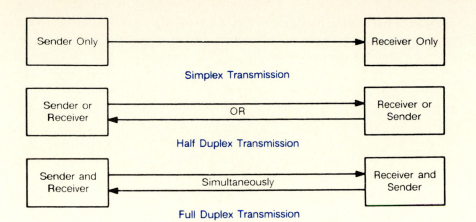

Figure 2-4

Data Flow Alternatives

Simplex Transmission

Half Duplex Transmission

Full Duplex Transmission

TABLE 2-1   Common Data Codes

Coding Scheme	Number of Bits	Characters Representable
BCD	4	16
Baudot	5	32 (62 using Shift key)
BCD	6	64
SBT	6	64
Standard ASCII	7	128
Extended ASCII	8	256
EBCDIC	8	256
Touch-tone telephone		12 frequencies

Morse code is not suitable for data communications because characters are represented by a different number of bits (the letter *A* is represented by dot-dash and the letter *S* by dot-dot-dot). Telegraphers distinguish one letter grouping from another by the time delay between characters. Such a scheme is not practical for computer-based systems. As a result, virtually all computer codes use a fixed number of bits per character. The number of bits that makes up the characters also determines the number of distinct characters that can be represented. Table 2-1 lists several data encoding schemes as well as the number of bits per character and the number of characters that can be represented by those codes.

BCD

Binary Coded Decimal (BCD) exists in both 4-bit and 6-bit versions. The 4-bit code is used for economy in transmission of numeric data. With 4 bits, at most 16 different entities can be represented, so 4-bit BCD is not suited to

Binary Coded Decimal (BCD)   A coding scheme for the storage of data in digital computers. The code may either be four-bit or six-bit.

TABLE 2-2   **The 4-Bit BCD Code**

Bit Pattern	Numeric Equivalent	Bit Pattern	Numeric Equivalent
0000	0	0101	5
0001	1	0110	6
0010	2	0111	7
0011	3	1000	8
0100	4	1001	9

the transmission of alphabetic or punctuation characters. However, for transmitting strings of numeric data, 4-bit BCD uses 3 bits fewer than ASCII and 4 bits fewer than EBCDIC or extended ASCII, thus increasing the effective line utilization. When used in this manner, 4-bit BCD is normally transmitted in mixed mode with another code, making it the responsibility of the application to determine the context of the data. The 4-bit BCD code is given in Table 2-2. The 6-bit BCD code is not used extensively because it can represent only 64 different symbols, a rather limited number. Using 6-bit BCD code, one could represent only 26 letters (uppercase or lowercase but not both), 10 numeric digits, and 28 other symbols for punctuation and control. A standard typewriter has 24 special punctuation or use symbols alone.

Baudot

Baudot   A code obtained from the telegraph industry that is used in data communications with telegraph lines or equipment originally designed for telegraphy. It is limited in its number of representable characters.

Baudot is a code derived from the telegraph industry, so its primary use in data communications is with telegraph lines or equipment originally designed for telegraphy. Its biggest limitation is in the number of representable characters: With only 5 bits per character, Baudot can represent at most 32 distinct characters, which is inadequate for all 26 letters of the Roman alphabet and the 10 numeric digits, let alone uppercase and lowercase letters and punctuation. Consequently, a technique is needed to extend the limited character set. One additional bit would allow a total of 64 characters to be represented. But because Baudot cannot physically be extended to 6 bits, obtaining this additional bit requires upshift and downshift modes, as on a typewriter (upshift produces capital letters and punctuation, downshift produces lowercase letters and numbers — in this way, 47 typewriter keys create 94 characters). In the Baudot code, the 5 bits transmitted must be interpreted according to whether they are upshifted (uppercase) or downshifted (lowercase). The bit pattern 11111 represents downshift characters and the bit pattern 11011 represents upshift characters. All characters transmitted after the sequence 11111 but before the shifted sequence 11011 are treated as downshift characters. Similarly, all characters transmitted after the sequence 11011 are treated as upshift (uppercase) characters until the pattern 11111 is recognized. Because two bit patterns are reserved to indicate the shift mode and therefore may not be used to represent transmitted characters, the total number of

TABLE 2-3   The USASCII 7-Bit Code

High Order Bits

		000	001	010	011	100	101	110	111
	0000	NUL	DLE	SPACE	0	@	P	`	p
	0001	SOH	DC1	!	1	A	Q	a	q
	0010	STX	DC2	"	2	B	R	b	r
	0011	ETX	DC3	#	3	C	S	c	s
	0100	EOT	DC4	$	4	D	T	d	t
	0101	ENQ	NAK	%	5	E	U	e	u
	0110	ACK	SYN	&	6	F	V	f	v
	0111	BEL	ETB	'	7	G	W	g	w
	1000	BS	CAN	(	8	H	X	h	x
	1001	HT	EM	)	9	I	Y	i	y
	1010	LF	SUB	*	:	J	Z	j	z
	1011	VT	ESC	+	;	K	[	k	{
	1100	FF	FS	,	<	L	\	l	|
	1101	CR	GS	-	=	M	]	m	}
	1110	SO	RS	.	>	N	^	n	~
	1111	SI	US	/	?	O	_	o	DEL

Low Order Bits

characters that can be represented is reduced to 30 bit patterns, each of which represents two characters.

SBT

Six-Bit Transcode (SBT) was created by IBM primarily for remote job entry communications. It is not used extensively.

Six-Bit Transcode (SBT)   A six-bit computer code developed by IBM primarily for RJE.

ASCII

American Standard Code for Information Interchange (ASCII) and EBCDIC (see next section) are the codes most commonly used. ASCII (also known as USASCII) is implemented primarily as a 7-bit code, although an extended 8-bit version also exists. With 7 bits, 128 characters can be represented; with 8 bits, 256 characters are available. As an alternative to the 8-bit code, the 7-bit form can be extended in the same manner as the Baudot code (using the special characters shift out and shift in, with bit patterns of 0001110 and 0001111, respectively). Extending the number of characters provides for additional character sets for graphics and for foreign languages such as Katakana. The 7-bit ASCII code is presented in Table 2-3.

American Standard Code for Information Interchange (ASCII)   A code that uses seven or eight bits to represent characters. One of the two common computer codes. *See also* EBCDIC.

TABLE 2-4a The EBCDIC 8-Bit Code

High Order Bits

<table>
<tr><th>Low Order Bits</th><th>0000</th><th>0001</th><th>0010</th><th>0011</th><th>0100</th><th>0101</th><th>0110</th><th>0111</th></tr>
<tr><td>0000</td><td>NUL</td><td>DLE</td><td>DS</td><td></td><td>SPACE</td><td>@</td><td>-</td><td></td></tr>
<tr><td>0001</td><td>SOH</td><td>DC1</td><td>SOS</td><td></td><td></td><td></td><td></td><td></td></tr>
<tr><td>0010</td><td>STX</td><td>DC2</td><td>FS</td><td>SYN</td><td></td><td></td><td></td><td></td></tr>
<tr><td>0011</td><td>ETX</td><td>DC3</td><td></td><td></td><td></td><td></td><td></td><td></td></tr>
<tr><td>0100</td><td>PF</td><td>RES</td><td>BYP</td><td>PN</td><td></td><td></td><td></td><td></td></tr>
<tr><td>0101</td><td>HT</td><td>NL</td><td>LF</td><td>RS</td><td></td><td></td><td></td><td></td></tr>
<tr><td>0110</td><td>LC</td><td>BS</td><td>ETB</td><td>UC</td><td></td><td></td><td></td><td></td></tr>
<tr><td>0111</td><td>DEL</td><td>IL</td><td>ESC</td><td>EOT</td><td></td><td></td><td></td><td></td></tr>
<tr><td>1000</td><td></td><td>CAN</td><td></td><td></td><td></td><td></td><td></td><td></td></tr>
<tr><td>1001</td><td>RLF</td><td>EM</td><td></td><td></td><td></td><td></td><td></td><td>\</td></tr>
<tr><td>1010</td><td>SMN</td><td>CC</td><td>SM</td><td></td><td>¢</td><td>!</td><td>|</td><td>:</td></tr>
<tr><td>1011</td><td></td><td></td><td></td><td></td><td>.</td><td>$</td><td>,</td><td>#</td></tr>
<tr><td>1100</td><td>FF</td><td>IFS</td><td></td><td>DC4</td><td><</td><td>*</td><td>%</td><td>@</td></tr>
<tr><td>1101</td><td>CR</td><td>IGS</td><td>ENQ</td><td>NAK</td><td>(</td><td>)</td><td>-</td><td>'</td></tr>
<tr><td>1110</td><td>SO</td><td>IRS</td><td>ACK</td><td></td><td>+</td><td>;</td><td>></td><td>=</td></tr>
<tr><td>1111</td><td>SI</td><td>IUS</td><td>BEL</td><td>SUB</td><td>|</td><td></td><td>?</td><td>"</td></tr>
</table>

EBCDIC

Extended Binary-Coded Decimal Interchange Code (EBCDIC) A code that uses eight bits to represent a character of information. One of the most common computer codes. *See also* ASCII.

Extended Binary-Coded Decimal Interchange Code (EBCDIC) utilizes 8 bits to form a character; 256 characters can be represented. The EBCDIC code is presented in Table 2-4a & b. As Tables 2-3 and 2-4 show, both ASCII and EBCDIC have some codes (such as ASCII 0000000 and 0000011) with mnemonic names such as NUL and ETX. These special characters, which are discussed in more detail in Chapter 10, are used to provide control information to nodes on the network as well as to represent binary data.

The EBCDIC tables show gaps following the letters *i, r, z, I, R,* and *Z*. The gaps represent unassigned bit values. This is a disadvantage relative to the ASCII tables, which have no such gaps, because the unassigned bit values fall within the letter sequence. If these values are ever assigned, it may interrupt the collating sequence of the letters. The gaps also make arithmetic operations on the characters more difficult. In ASCII, we can obtain the numeric value of an ASCII character and manipulate it arithmetically, such as by adding 15 to the numeric representation of the letter *A* to obtain the letter 15 characters down the alphabet from *A*. Another disadvantage of EBCDIC is that some characters—such as [and]—have not been defined. Omission of these characters raises problems in programming languages such as Pascal and C, which use these symbols.

TABLE 2-4b   The EBCDIC 8-Bit Code

High Order Bits

Low Order Bits

	1000	1001	1010	1011	1100	1101	1110	1111
0000					{	}	\	0
0001	a	j	~		A	J		1
0010	b	k	s		B	K	S	2
0011	c	l	t		C	L	T	3
0100	d	m	u		D	M	U	4
0101	e	n	v		E	N	V	5
0110	f	o	w		F	O	W	6
0111	g	p	x		G	P	X	7
1000	h	q	y		H	Q	Y	8
1001	i	r	z		I	R	Z	9
1010								
1011								
1100								
1101								
1110								
1111								

Touch-Tone Telephone

The touch-tone telephone code turns a touch-tone telephone into a data communications terminal. Some banks allow customers to pay bills and transfer money between accounts using their touch-tone telephone. Many colleges and universities allow students to register for classes using a touch-tone telephone. Telephone sets have 12 keys, so 12 different codes can be transmitted. Each key on the telephone keypad transmits a high frequency and a low frequency. The combination of the two frequencies uniquely defines which key has been pressed. Figure 2-5 shows the relationship between the telephone keypad and the frequencies each transmits. If a user presses the *9* key, the frequencies 852 Hz and 1446 Hz are transmitted. Because only 12 key codes are available, the telephone is limited in its use as a data communications input device.

Data Code Size

The transition from 5-bit and 6-bit codes to 7-bit and 8-bit codes became necessary to increase the number of unique code sequences that could be represented. The two most common data communications codes are 7-bit and

Figure 2-5

Touch-Tone Telephone Code

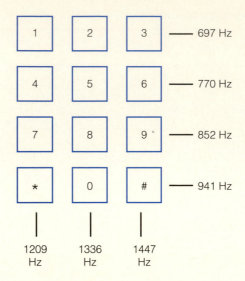

8-bit codes, which are able to represent 128 and 256 unique symbols, respectively. Is this a sufficient number of symbols? An 8-bit code can represent the 26-letter Roman alphabet (both uppercase and lowercase), the 10 Arabic numerals (0 through 9), and punctuation, totaling approximately 100 characters and symbols. Additional bit patterns may be required for line control, so perhaps up to 128 characters can be used. What are the rest used for?

For one thing, there may be a need to accommodate other alphabets, such as Greek and Cyrillic (Russian), and their accompanying diacritical marks, such as the tilde, umlaut, and accents. Still, 256 bits can accommodate the Roman alphabet and one other alphabet, with characters left over — until we look at Asian and Middle Eastern languages. The Kanji character set used for written communication in Japan and China contains more than 30,000 ideograms and symbols. Clearly, 256 unique symbols do not really go very far.

In addition to accommodating various alphabets, a data code may need to transmit, store, manipulate, and display graphics information, thus requiring additional characters. Line drawing characters can easily exceed 100 different symbols. Several microcomputers use an extended ASCII code to permit use of business graphics symbols. It is also likely that some of the newer technologies, such as videotex (in which text and images are transmitted together), will require a large number of characters. The data communications codes in current use have proved to be inadequate in meeting the communication demands among different cultures and languages, as well as the anticipated demands for extended services such as videotex. Now that the limitations of 8-bit codes are apparent, perhaps an international code using 16 bits will emerge. In Japan this has already been addressed by several standards.

To be effective a good communications code also must provide three other capabilities: It must be standardized, it must be nonsequential, and it must provide for error detection. Being standardized means the bit representations are sanctioned by a recognized standards group. Being nonsequential means the sequence in which characters are detected is immaterial. The Baudot code

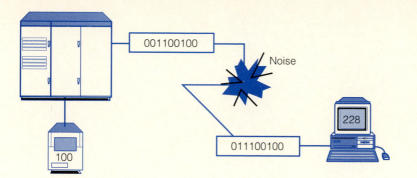

Figure 2-6

A Transmission Error

is sequential, as the upshift and downshift characters are critical to the meaning of characters received. If an upshift or downshift character is missed in the transmission, the message text following the missed shift character is incorrectly interpreted. An error detection capability inherent in the code allows detection of transmission errors. A parity bit is often appended to 7-bit ASCII to detect errors. Parity is less commonly used with 8-bit codes such as EBCDIC. In the next section we discuss how errors are caused and how they can be detected.

ERROR SOURCES

All data transmissions are subject to error, although some media are more susceptible than others. Contextual recognition of errors is usually impossible in data communications systems. If the data transmitter and receiver are computers, it is virtually impossible for editing routines to determine whether one or more bits have been changed; even if data is displayed on a terminal, the operator may be unable to discern all the errors. If a bank teller interrogates a customer's account balance as illustrated in Figure 2-6, it is unlikely that the teller would recognize that a 1-bit error had altered the balance from $100 to $228. Errors can be induced during data transmission in a number of ways. The most common are white noise, impulse noise, crosstalk, echo, phase jitter, attenuation, and envelope delay distortion.

White Noise

White noise, also referred to as **thermal noise** and **Gaussian noise**, results from the normal movements of electrons and is present in all transmission media at temperatures above absolute zero. The amount of white noise is directly proportional to the temperature of the medium (hence the term *thermal noise*). White noise also is distributed randomly throughout a medium (hence the term *Gaussian noise*). White noise in telephone circuits is sometimes heard as static or hissing on the line. The magnitude of white noise usually is

white noise   One source of data communication errors. It results from the normal movements of electrons and is present in all transmission media at temperatures above absolute zero. Also known as thermal noise and Gaussian noise.

Figure 2-7

The Impact of Noise on a
Data Signal

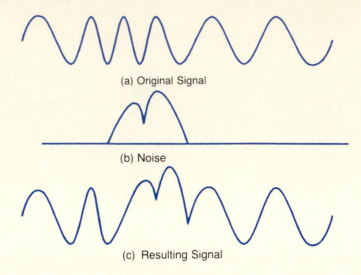

(a) Original Signal

(b) Noise

(c) Resulting Signal

not sufficient to create data loss in wire circuits, but it can become significant in radio frequency links such as microwave and satellite. Because white noise is proportional to bandwidth as well as temperature, improperly focused antennas (such as those directed toward the sun) can create enough disturbance to produce errors. Figure 2-7 illustrates the impact of noise on a data communications signal.

Impulse Noise

impulse noise A noise characterized by signal "spikes." In telephone circuits it can be caused by switching equipment or by lightning strikes and in other situations by transient electrical impulses such as those occurring on a shop floor. Impulse noise is a common cause of transmission errors.

Impulse noise is characterized by signal "spikes." In telephone circuits it can be caused by switching equipment or by lightning strikes, and in other situations, by transient electrical impulses such as those occurring on a shop floor. The various pieces of equipment on a shop floor require large amounts of electricity. This equipment also frequently cycles up and down, drawing more and less power. Setting an electrical charge in motion generates a magnetic field, and magnetic fields can, in turn, affect electrical transmissions. Unshielded data communications wires passing through a shop floor in close proximity to current-carrying wires can have their signals affected. Impulse noise, the primary cause of data errors in telephone circuits, is heard as a clicking or crackling sound. It usually is short (several milliseconds), with varying levels of magnitude.

Crosstalk

crosstalk When the signals from one channel distort or interfere with the signals of a different channel.

Crosstalk occurs when signals from one channel distort or interfere with the signals of a different channel. In telephone connections, crosstalk sometimes appears in the form of another party's conversation heard in the background. Crosstalk is also present in radio frequency and multiplexed transmissions (see Chapter 8) when the frequency ranges are too close together. Crosstalk in wire-pair transmission occurs when wire pairs interfere with each other as a result of strong signals, improper shielding, or both. Another common cause of crosstalk is interference between receivers and transmitters when a strong outgoing signal interferes with a weaker incoming signal. Crosstalk is directly proportional to distance, bandwidth, signal strength, and proximity to other transmission channels; it is inversely proportional to shielding or channel separation. Crosstalk is not usually a significant factor in data communications errors.

One special form of crosstalk is **intermodulation noise**, which is the result of two or more signals combining, or "adding together," to produce a signal outside the limits of the communications channel. Suppose one mode of FSK modulation represents a 1 bit as a frequency of 1300 Hz and a 0 bit as a frequency of 2100 Hz with a variation of 10 Hz. Intermodulation noise might result in two acceptable signals, such as 1305 Hz and 2105 Hz, combining to form a signal of 3410 Hz (1305 + 2105 = 3410). This signal is out of the accepted frequency range of voice communication over telephone lines (300 − 3400 Hz).

intermodulation noise A special form of crosstalk, which is the result of two or more signals combining to produce a distorted signal.

Echo

Echo is essentially the reflection or reversal of the signal being transmitted. This is most likely to occur at junctions where wires are interconnected or at the end of a line in a local area network. Telephone companies have installed **echo suppressors** on their networks to minimize this echo effect. The echo suppressor works by allowing the signal to pass in one direction only. In voice transmission, the suppressor continually reverses itself to match the direction of conversation. Obviously this would impede data transmission in full duplex mode, so echo suppressors are disengaged when full duplex transmission is required.

echo The reflection or reversal of the signal being transmitted. Also used to define a transmission convention in which the receiver of data sends the data back to the sender to assist in error detection.

echo suppressor A device that allows a transmitted signal to pass in one direction only, thus minimizing the echo effect.

Phase Jitter

Phase jitter is a variation in the phase of a continuous signal from cycle to cycle; it is especially significant when the modulation mode involves phase shifting.

phase jitter A variation in the phase of a continuous signal from cycle to cycle.

Attenuation

Attenuation, the weakening of a signal as a result of distance and characteristics of the medium, can produce a significant number of data errors. For a given gauge of wire and bit rate, a signal can be carried for a certain distance without enhancement. Beyond that distance a signal repeater or amplifier would have to be included to ensure that the receiving station can properly recognize the data.

Envelope Delay Distortion

Envelope delay distortion occurs when signals that have been weakened or subjected to outside interference by transmission over long distances are enhanced by being passed through filters. Passing the signals through a filter delays them a certain amount, depending on the frequency of the signal.

Impact of Data Errors

Table 2-5 shows the possible effects of impulse noise of various durations, for different line speeds. It is significant that fewer bits are subject to error when transmission is at lower rather than higher speeds. Although the figure applies to any type of noise for the same durations, impulse noise was chosen because it is one of the most common types of noise affecting telephone wires. The most significant thing shown by Table 2-5 is that the potential number of bit errors increases with both duration of the noise and line speed. Although the ideal is to eliminate all errors in data, a goal of fewer than 1 error per 100,000 bits is considered satisfactory. (Most line media and radio-wave transmission systems are designed for fewer than 1 error per 1 million bits transmitted.)

PREVENTION

The best method to guard against data errors is to correct their source. Eliminating all noise is impossible, but error prevention techniques can reduce the probability of error corruption in the data. Such techniques include telephone line conditioning, reducing transmission speed, shielding, line drivers, and using better quality equipment.

TABLE 2-5   **Potential Number of Corrupted Data Bits**

Line Speed (bps)	Impulse Noise Duration (milliseconds)				
	0.2	0.4	0.6	0.8	1.0
300	0.06	0.12	0.18	0.24	0.30
1200	0.24	0.48	0.72	0.96	1.20
2400	0.48	0.96	1.44	1.92	2.40
4800	0.96	1.92	2.88	3.84	4.80
9600	1.92	3.84	5.76	7.68	9.60
19,200	3.84	7.68	11.52	15.36	19.20

Telephone Line Conditioning

When a line is leased from a telephone company, conditioning—sometimes referred to as equalization—can be included for an additional charge. The two classes of conditioning are Class C and Class D, with four commercial levels of Class C conditioning—C1, C2, C4, and C5. Each level of Class C conditioning provides increasingly stringent constraints on the amplitude and phase distortion permitted on the line. A line with C5 conditioning should be more error-free than a line with C1 conditioning. One useful aspect of Class D conditioning—a relatively new service—is that the telephone company will inspect the circuits available between the desired communication points to select the one with the least amount of noise. Users can also obtain equipment, such as certain modems, that aids in the conditioning of lines.

Lower Transmission Speed

A bit error is much less likely to occur at lower transmission speeds. Some modems adjust their speed automatically or via program control to accommodate noisy lines. With a high-quality line, such a modem will operate at 9600 bps; if the quality of the line deteriorates, the modem has the capability of switching to a lower speed.

Shielding

Although additional shielding of leased telephone cables is not a user option, shielding can be provided for private lines to reduce the amount of crosstalk and impulse noise from the environment. Media shielding in the form of coaxial cable or shield twisted pair wires is frequently used for LAN media.

Line Drivers (Repeaters)

Line drivers, or repeaters, can be placed at intervals along a communications line to amplify and forward the signal. Digital signal noise can usually be eliminated, because the signal is being regenerated. For analog signals, however, it is difficult to separate most noise from the signal; noise that is picked up also will be amplified by the repeaters. The function of repeaters is to restore signals to their full strength and overcome signal loss due to attenuation.

Better Equipment

Because some older mechanical equipment and some older transformers and power supplies are more likely to produce noise than newer equipment (such as electronic switches), replacing older components with better equipment can reduce the amount of noise.

ERROR DETECTION

Unfortunately, the remedies just cited to minimize the number of errors may be impractical from either a cost or a feasibility standpoint. Because error elimination is impossible, it is also necessary to determine whether a transmission error has occurred and, if errors have occurred, to return the data to proper form. Error detection algorithms in data communications networks are based on the transmission of redundant information. In telegraphy, one way to ensure correctness of data is to transmit each character twice. This is not entirely error-proof, so it could be taken one or more steps further by sending each character three or more times. Although this might increase the reliability of the transmission, line utilization drops dramatically. As the error rate approaches zero, so does the effective utilization of the medium. Some middle-ground approach clearly is required that can detect almost all errors without significantly reducing the data-carrying capacity of the medium.

Parity Check

parity check/Vertical Redundancy Check (VRC)   The same as parity error checking. For each character transmitted, an additional bit, the parity bit, is attached to help detect errors. The bit is chosen so that the number of 1 bits is even (even parity) or odd (odd parity).

One of the simplest and most widely used forms of error detection is known as a **parity check** or **Vertical Redundancy Check (VRC)**. A parity check involves adding a bit — known as the parity bit — to each character during transmission. The parity bit is selected so the total number of 1 bits in the code representation of each character adds up to either an even number (even parity) or an odd number (odd parity). Each character is checked upon receipt to see whether the number of 1 bits is even or odd. Consider the string of characters *DATA COMM* as coded in 7-bit ASCII with odd parity. The representations of these characters plus the parity bit for odd parity are given in Table 2-6. It can be seen that the number of 1 bits in each 8-bit sequence (octet) is always odd (either one, three, five, or seven); it is the parity bit that ensures this. If even parity were chosen, the parity bit would be selected so the number of 1 bits would always be an even number.

Besides even and odd parity, you can have no parity, a parity bit with no parity checking, mark parity, or space parity. If there is no parity bit or if the parity bit is not checked (called no parity check), the ability to detect errors using this method is lost (although other methods, described later, could be utilized). Mark parity means that the parity bit is always transmitted as a 1 bit, and space parity means the parity bit is always transmitted as a 0 bit. Clearly, mark and space parity are ineffective as error detection schemes. If two stations attempting to communicate disagree on the parity scheme, all messages will be seen as being in error and will be rejected.

In the odd parity example in Table 2-6 each character transmitted consists of eight bits — seven for data and one for parity. Parity enables the user to detect whether one, three, five, or seven bits have been altered in transmission, but it will not catch whether an even number (two, four, six, or eight bits) has been altered. One common error situation involves burst errors, or a grouping of errors (recall the possible effect of impulse noise during high transmission rates). The likelihood of detecting errors of this nature with a

TABLE 2-6   Parity Bit Generation

Letter	ASCII	Parity Bit	Transmitted Bits
D	1000100	1	10001001
A	1000001	1	10000011
T	1010100	0	10101000
A	1000001	1	10000011
space	0100000	0	01000000
C	1000011	0	10000110
O	1001111	0	10011110
M	1001101	1	10011011
M	1001101	1	10011011

parity check is approximately 50%. At higher transmission speeds this limitation becomes significant. (A burst error for the duration of two bits does not necessarily result in two bit errors. None, one, or two bits could be affected.)

Longitudinal Redundancy Check (LRC)

We can increase the probability of error detection beyond that provided by parity by making, in addition, a **Longitudinal Redundancy Check (LRC)**. With LRC, which is similar to VRC, an additional, redundant character called the **Block Check Character (BCC)** is appended to a block of transmitted characters, typically at the end of the block. The first bit of the BCC serves as a parity check for all of the first bits of the characters in the block, the second bit of the BCC serves as parity for all of the second bits in the block, and so on. Table 2-7 is an example of LRC. An odd parity scheme has been chosen to perform the redundancy check, so each column has an odd number of 1 bits.

LRC combined with VRC is still not sufficient to detect all errors (no scheme is completely dependable). Table 2-8 presents the same *DATA COMM* message transmission, with errors introduced in rows and columns marked by an asterisk. Although both LRC and VRC appear correct, the data received is not the same as that transmitted. Adding LRC to VRC brings a greater probability of detecting errors in transmission.

Cyclic Redundancy Check (CRC)

A **Cyclic Redundancy Check (CRC)** can detect bit errors better than either VRC or LRC or both. A CRC is computed for a block of transmitted data. The transmitting station generates the CRC and transmits it with the data. The receiving station computes the CRC for the data received and compares it to

Longitudinal Redundancy Check (LRC)   An error-checking technique in which a block check character is appended to a block of transmitted characters, typically at the end of the block. The block check character checks parity on a row of bits.

Block Check Character (BCC)   In the error detection methods of longitudinal redundancy check (LRC) or cyclic redundancy check (CRC), an error detection character or characters, called the BCC, is appended to a block of transmitted characters, typically at the end of the block.

Cyclic Redundancy Check (CRC)   An error detection algorithm that uses a polynomial function to generate the block check characters. CRC is a very efficient error detection method.

TABLE 2-7 **Longitudinal Redundancy Check (LRC) Generation**

Letter	ASCII	Parity Bit	Transmitted Bits
D	1000100	1	10001001
A	1000001	1	10000011
T	1010100	0	10101000
A	1000001	1	10000011
space	0100000	0	01000000
C	1000011	0	10000110
O	1001111	0	10011110
M	1001101	1	10011011
M	1001101	1	10011011
BCC	1000011	0	10000110

TABLE 2-8 **LRC Transmission Errors**

Letter	ASCII	Parity Bit	Transmitted Bits
D	****** 1000100	1	10001001
A	1000001	1	10000011
T	*1100100	0	10101000
A	*1110001	1	10000011
space	0100000	0	01000000
C	1000011	0	10000110
O	1001111	0	10011110
M	1001101	1	10011011
M	1001101	1	10011011
BCC	1000011	0	10000110

the CRC transmitted by the sender. If the two are equal, then the block is assumed to be error-free. The mathematics behind CRC requires the use of a generating polynomial and is beyond the scope of this book.

If the CRC generator polynomial is chosen with care and is of sufficient degree, more than 99% of multiple-bit errors can be detected. Several standards—CRC-12, CRC-16, and CRC-CCITT—define both the degree of the generating polynomial and the generating polynomial itself. Because CRC-12 specifies a polynomial of degree 12 and the last two standards specify a polynomial of degree 16, the BCC will have 12 or 16 bits. CRC-16 and CRC-CCITT can detect:

- All single-bit and double-bit errors
- All errors in cases in which an odd number of bits are erroneous
- Two pairs of adjacent errors
- All burst errors of 16 bits or fewer
- More than 99.998% of all burst errors greater than 16 bits

Because of its reliability, CRC is becoming the standard method of error detection for block data transmission (as opposed to transmission of one character at a time). Chapters 5 and 9 discuss different data transmission protocols and their associated error detection schemes.

Sequence Checks

If sending and receiving nodes are connected directly, the receiving station receives all transmissions without the intercession of other nodes. However, large communications networks may have one or more intermediate nodes responsible for forwarding a message to its final destination, and one complete message may be divided into a number of transmission blocks. These blocks also may not all be routed along the same path and could be received out of order. In such a case, it is important to assign sequence numbers to each block so the ultimate receiver can determine that all blocks have indeed arrived and can put the blocks back into proper sequence.

Message Sequence Numbers   Suppose you send someone one letter per day for five days through the postal system. There is no guarantee that the letters will be received in the order sent. Several might arrive on the same day (and out of order), one might be lost, or all five might arrive at the same time. If the letters are intended to be read in order, you can number them sequentially, such as 1/5, 2/5, 3/5, and so on. This alerts the recipient to the order and allows him or her to detect missing messages. A similar scheme can be used for data communications messages.

One sequencing technique appends a message sequence number to each data block transmitted between two stations. If a processor is communicating with two different stations, each link would have its own sequence number. Every time a message is transmitted, the sequence number is sent along with the message. The receiving station compares the received sequence number with a number maintained in its memory. If the message numbers agree, no messages have been lost; if the received message number disagrees with the expected message number, an error condition is created and the receiver requests that the sender retransmit the missing messages.

Packet Sequence Numbers   In some networks, messages are segmented into smaller transmission groups, or packets. If there are multiple communication paths between sender and receiver, the packet routing strategy may use several of the paths simultaneously to speed delivery of the entire message; the packets could arrive out of order. To ensure that such a message can be reassembled in proper sequence, packet sequence numbers are appended to each packet. These sequence numbers also allow for error control.

In any of the situations just discussed, if a data block arrives and an error is detected, or if some of the blocks in a sequence have not been received, the recovery method is to ask the sending station to retransmit the erroneous or lost data. An acknowledgment usually is sent for all blocks received correctly; if a block is not positively acknowledged, the transmitter must resend it. This obligates the transmitting node to retain all transmitted blocks until they have been acknowledged. Being able to request that a message be retransmitted implies that the flow control is either half duplex or full duplex. If an error is detected on a simplex line, the recipient cannot send a request for retransmission. The only recourse in this case is to ignore the message or to use the message as received.

Error-Correction Codes

Some error detecting schemes allow the receiving station not only to detect errors but also to correct some of them. Such codes are called forward error-correcting codes, the most common being Hamming codes. As with straight error detection codes, additional, redundant information is transmitted with the data. Error-correcting codes are convenient for situations in which single-bit errors occur, but for multiple-bit errors the amount of redundant information that must be sent is cumbersome. The effectiveness of forward error-correcting codes is reduced by transmission noise that frequently creates bursts of errors, so these codes are not used as commonly as are error detection schemes. Error-correcting codes have good applications in other areas, such as memory error detection and correction, where the probability of single-bit errors is higher. Some semiconductor memories use a 6-bit Hamming code for each 16 bits of data to allow for single-bit error correction and double-bit error detection.

Miscellaneous Error Detection Techniques

Several other methods increase the probability of detecting data errors.

Check Digits   Check digits or check numbers are one or more characters (often simply the sum of fields being checked) that are appended to the data being transmitted. They are usually generated by the sending application or device and checked by the receiving application or device.

Hash Totals   One technique that validates operator input as well as augmenting an error detection scheme involves appending a hash total, which is the sum of a group of items. For a batch of credit card authorizations, the sum of all charges can be computed separately or by the input device. Computing separately prior to operator input provides an accuracy check of data entry as well as transmission. The receiving computer sums the number of fields transmitted and compares its total with the transmitted hash total. If the totals agree, it is assumed that there are no errors; if the hash totals do not agree, the data must be retransmitted.

Byte Counts   A byte count field can be added to a message. When an entire block of data is sent at one time (synchronous transmission), the loss of a character would ordinarily be detected either by LRC with VRC or by CRC. When every character is transmitted individually with its own error detection scheme (asynchronous transmission using parity checking), a lost character can go undetected. Transmitting one or more characters that indicate the total number of characters in the message helps detect transmission errors in which entire characters may be lost.

Character Echoing   In some systems, especially with asynchronous transmission, the characters transmitted are echoed to the user as a check. Because of the additional line time required, this technique is less frequently used in synchronous transmissions. Consider an operator at an asynchronous terminal: When a key is struck the character is transmitted to the host computer, which echoes (resends) the received character to the terminal. If the character displayed at the originating terminal is incorrect, the operator backs up the cursor to the character position and enters the correct character. With a high-speed communications line it appears to the operator as though the character is locally displayed as well as being transmitted to the host; with low-speed communications links, or when communicating with a busy processor, the echoing may become somewhat apparent. Echoing has the disadvantage of doubling the chances of obtaining an error, as the message must be transmitted twice. The original message may be received correctly, but if the echoed message has been corrupted, the original sender will detect an error.

Error Correction

Whenever an error is detected, it must be corrected. If an error-correcting code is used, the transmitted data can be corrected by the receiver. This is seldom the case in data communications. The most common error-correction mechanism is to retransmit the data. In asynchronous transmission, individual characters are retransmitted, whereas in synchronous transmissions, one or more blocks may need to be retransmitted. This type of correction is known as ARQ, which stands for automatic request for retransmission or automatic request for repetition.

Message Acknowledgment   The mechanism used to effect retransmission is the positive or negative acknowledgment, often referred to as ACK and NAK, respectively. When a station receives a message, it computes the number of error detection bit(s) or characters and compares the result with the check number received. If the two are equal, the message is assumed to be error-free and the receiver returns a positive acknowledgment to the sender; if the two are unequal, a negative acknowledgment is returned and the sending station retransmits the message. Of course, the sending station must retain all messages until they have been positively acknowledged.

Retry Limit   In some instances the second message will also be received in error, perhaps due to an error-prone communications link or to faulty hardware or software. To cut down on continual retransmission of messages, a retry limit—typically between 3 and 100—can be set. A retry limit of 5 means a message received in error will be retransmitted five times; if the message is not successfully received by the fifth try, the receiving station either disables the link or disables the sending station itself. The objective of a retry limit is to avoid the unproductive work of continually processing corrupted messages. Once the cause of the problem has been corrected, the communications path is reinstated.

DIGITAL DATA TRANSMISSION

All communications media are capable of transmitting information in either digital or analog form; despite the fact that computer data is represented in digital form, originally computer data was transmitted mostly in analog form. The primary reason for this is that the providers of communications transmission facilities had established analog facilities for voice transmission. However, advances in digital technology and lower prices for digital transmission electronics are bringing about a change to digital transmission. Within several decades most major metropolitan areas will have made the transition; were it not for the considerable existing investment in analog transmission facilities, the changeover might come even sooner. If telephone companies were to begin today, it is likely that their transmission facilities would be digital rather than analog. There are four primary reasons for this.

Advantages of Digital Transmission

The advantages of digital transmission for data communications are lower error rates, higher transmission rates, elimination of the need to convert from digital format to analog and back to digital, and better security.

Lower Error Rates   Current telephone networks transmit signals over wires or via radio broadcast, continually amplifying the signals to overcome weakening from attenuation. Long-distance transmission demands that the signals be amplified multiple times to overcome attenuation. Because any frequency within the bandwidth is acceptable, it is difficult to filter out introduced noise or distortion, so both are amplified and propagated along with the original signals.

Like analog signals, digital signals also lose strength due to attenuation. Figure 2-8(a) shows a digital signal as it is originated. Figure 2-8(b) illustrates a possible effect of attenuation on that signal. A digital signal represents only

Figure 2-8

Digital Signal Regeneration

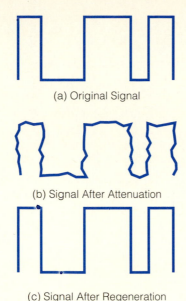

(a) Original Signal

(b) Signal After Attenuation

(c) Signal After Regeneration

two discrete values, so it is possible to completely regenerate the signal. Restored to its original state and strength, the data can be forwarded to the next regeneration point or to the final destination without any associated noise. This is accomplished by a digital regenerator. Figure 2-8(c) shows a regenerated signal.

Higher Transmission Rates   Another benefit of digital transmission is increased transmission speed. With digital transmission, switched connections can operate at speeds up to 56 Kbps. The current limit is 38,400 bps for switched circuits and leased lines.

No Digital-Analog Conversion   Digital transmission theoretically avoids the need for conversion between formats. Unfortunately, not all locations are serviced by digital networks, whose implementation has been restricted thus far to highly populated urban centers. In addition, the connection from a given location to the digital transmission and switching equipment is still an analog link in many cases. This makes it necessary to convert a signal from digital to analog and back to digital for transmission to the message's destination. The device that converts the analog signal to digital is known as a codec, an acronym for coder-decoder.

Security   Companies are becoming increasingly concerned about security of data and voice transmissions. One method for protecting these transmissions is encryption. You may be familiar with this concept as voice scramblers used on secure telephone lines. Although encryption algorithms exist for both analog and digital formats, digital encryption algorithms are more advanced and hence more secure and difficult to crack. Therefore, digital transmissions have the *potential* of greater security.

Figure 2-9

Codec Converting Analog
and Digital Signals

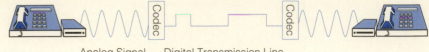

Analog Signal   Digital Transmission Line

Figure 2-10

Pulse Code Modulation

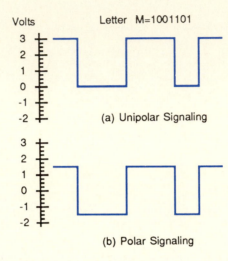

Digital Voice Using Pulse Code Modulation

In converting from analog to digital transmission lines, telephone companies are faced with the opposite problem faced by the data communications industry: On a digital line it becomes necessary to transform analog voice patterns into digital representation and then convert the digital patterns back to analog format. This is illustrated in Figure 2-9. A variety of conversion techniques exist, but the most commonly used is known as **Pulse Code Modulation (PCM)**. On a communications wire, PCM is represented as pulses of current. A pulse of 3 volts could represent a 1 bit, and 0 voltage could represent a 0 bit. In some schemes a 1 bit would be represented by a voltage of $+1.5$, and the 0 bit, by a voltage of -1.5. The first technique is referred to as unipolar signaling; the latter is polar signaling. These techniques are illustrated in Figures 2-10(a) and 2-10(b), respectively.

INTERFACE

Once a medium has been selected, it is necessary to connect it to the computer equipment. The two classes of equipment in data communications are **Data Communications Equipment (DCE)** (modems, media, and media-support facilities such as telephone switching equipment, microwave relay stations, and transponders) and **Data Terminal (or terminating) Equipment (DTE)** (including terminals, computers, concentrators, and multiplexers, all

Pulse Code Modulation (PCM)   A method for transmitting data in digital format.

Data Communications Equipment (DCE)   One class of equipment in data communications, including modems, media, and media support facilities.

Data Terminal Equipment (DTE)   The second class of equipment in data communications, including terminals, computers, concentrators, and multiplexers.

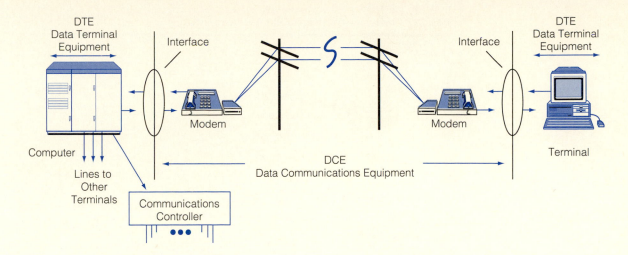

Figure 2-11

DTE and DCE Components

of which are covered in Chapter 8). The physical interface is the manner in which these two classes of equipment are joined together. Figure 2-11 depicts a data communications linkage with the DCE and DTE components identified.

The interface between DCE and DTE can be divided into four aspects: mechanical, electrical, functional, and procedural. The mechanical portion includes the type of connectors to be used, the number of pin connections in the connectors, and the maximum allowable cable lengths. The electrical characteristics include the allowable line voltages and the representations for the various voltage levels. The functional interface specifies which signals — timing, control, data, or ground leads — are to be carried by each pin in the connector. Table 2-9 lists the signals assigned to each of the 25 pins in an RS-232-C interface.

Procedural characteristics define how signals are exchanged and delineate the environment necessary to transmit and receive data. One pin or conducting wire in the connector might represent the ability of a terminal to accept a transmission; when the terminal is ready to receive data, a signal will be raised on that lead. When no signal is raised on that circuit, transmission to the terminal is not valid. Table 2-10 shows a procedural interface to transmit from a processor to a terminal.

Interface Standards

Numerous standards are adhered to in establishing an interface between DCE and DTE. The following brief descriptions familiarize you with these standards and what they generally cover.

RS-232-C   Currently in the United States the predominant interface standard is the Electronic Industries Association (EIA) **RS-232-C standard**, established in October 1969 and reaffirmed in June 1981. RS-232-C encompasses

RS-232-C standard   An Electronic Industries Association (EIA) standard for asynchronous transmission.

TABLE 2-9   Interface Connector Pin Assignments

Pin Number	Circuit	Description
1	AA	Protective Ground
2	BA	Transmitted Data
3	BB	Received Data
4	CA	Request to Send
5	CB	Clear to Send
6	CC	Data Set Ready
7	AB	Signal Ground (Common Return)
8	CF	Received Line Signal Detector
9	—	(Reserved for Modem Testing)
10	—	(Reserved for Modem Testing)
11		Unassigned
12	SCF	Secondary for Pin 8
13	SCB	Secondary Clear to Send
14	SBA	Secondary Transmitted Data
15	DB	Transmission Signal Timing
16	SBB	Secondary Received Data
17	DD	Receiver Signal Timing
18		Unassigned
19	SCA	Secondary Request to Send
20	CD	Data Terminal Ready
21	CG	Signal Quality Detector
22	CE	Ring Indicator
23	CH/CI	Data Signal Rate Selector
24	DA	Transmit Signal Element Timing
25		Unassigned

serial binary data interchange at rates up to 20,000 bps and a recommended distance of up to 50 feet; longer distances are possible for shielded wires. (Shielded wire is certified by the manufacturer as capable of spanning 500 feet at 9600 bps.) Because of the speed limitations, RS-232-C has its greatest application in interfacing to wire media, where this bit transmission rate is most common. It covers private, switched, and leased connections, with pro-

TABLE 2-10   Procedural Interface Between Processor and Terminal

1. Processor and terminal raise DTR (data terminal ready) signal to modem.
2. Modems raise DSR (data set ready) signal.
3. Processor raises RTS (request to send) signal.
4. Processor's modem sends a carrier signal.
5. Terminal's modem detects carrier and raises CD (carrier detect) signal to processor's modem.
6. Processor sends data on TD (transmit data).
7. Processor's modem modulates data onto the carrier wave.
8. Terminal's modem demodulates data onto RD (received data).
9. Processor lowers RTS signal.
10. Processor's modem drops CTS and carrier wave.
11. Terminal's modem drops CD.
12. Transmission is complete.

Message to Be Transmitted: LINE
Representation: ASCII

L	1001100
I	1001001
N	1001110
E	1000101

1001100   1001001   1001110   1000101
L   I   N   E

(a) Bit Serial Transmission

```
1 1 1 1
0 0 0 0
0 0 0 0
1 1 1 0
1 0 1 1
0 0 1 0
0 1 0 1
L I N E
```

(b) Bit Parallel Transmission

Figure 2-12

Serial vs. Parallel Transmission

visions for auto-answer switched connections. In **serial binary transmission** (or bit serial transmission), bits are transmitted in single file. This is contrasted with **bit parallel transmission**, wherein bits are transmitted in parallel. Figure 2-12 illustrates the difference between these two techniques.

The RS-232-C standard does not specify size or type of connectors to be used in the interface. It does define 25 signal leads, 3 of them unassigned, 2 reserved for testing, and the remaining 20 used for grounding, data, control,

serial binary transmission
The successive transmission of bits over a wire medium.

bit parallel transmission
The simultaneous transmission of bits over a wire medium.

Figure 2-13

Cable Connectors

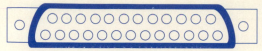

(a) 25-pin connector for RS-232-C or CCITT V.24 interface

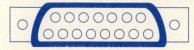

(b) 15-pin connector for RS-232-C or CCITT V.24 interface

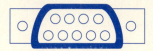

(c) 9-pin connector for RS-232-C, RS-449 or CCITT V.24 interface

and timing. In the absence of a standard, one connector—a 25-pin connector—has become common in implementing RS-232-C connections. Figure 2-13(a) depicts this type of connector. Actual transmissions typically use fewer than 25 signal leads. A simple modem interface can require that only 7 pins be active; yet on occasion, connectors supporting 15, 9, and 7 pins are used to interface with these devices. A 15-pin connector and a 9-pin connector are illustrated in Figures 2-13(b) and 2-13(c). The RS-232-C standard covers all four aspects of the interface: mechanical, electrical, functional, and procedural. This is significant because other interface specifications treat them separately, which means two or three standards may be cited that together form the equivalent of what is specified by RS-232-C.

RS-449 standard   An Electronic Industries Association (EIA) standard that improves on the capabilities of RS-232-C.

RS-449   Because of the speed and distance constraints of the RS-232-C standard, the EIA **RS-449 standard** was adopted. It provides for a 37-pin connection, cable lengths up to 200 feet, and data transmission rates up to 2 million bps. RS-449 equates with the functional and procedural portions of RS-232-C (the electrical and mechanical specifications are covered by RS-422 and RS-423). Because of RS-449's enhanced capabilities over RS-232-C, it should eventually replace RS-232-C as the predominant interface within the United States.

RS-366 standard   An Electronic Industries Association (EIA) standard for automatic-call unit interface.

RS-366   EIA has also adopted an **RS-366 standard**, a 25-pin connection with enhanced capabilities for automatic calling equipment. RS-366 covers interface details such as what signals need to be present when the dial tone is detected, when dialing, and so on. (The electrical portion of the interface is covered by the RS-423 standard.)

ISO and CCITT Standards   The International Standards Organization (ISO) and the Consultative Committee on International Telegraph and Telephony (CCITT) also have adopted standards that are widely adhered to. The most significant of these international standards for interfaces are briefly described below.

- **ISO-2110:** A functional interface standard similar to the functional portion of RS-232-C. It describes which signals will be carried on specific pins.
- **CCITT V.10 and V.11:** Electrical interfaces similar to those specified by RS-422 and RS-423.
- **CCITT V.24:** Covers both the functional and the procedural aspects of a 25-pin interface similar to that specified by RS-232-C.
- **CCITT V.25:** Covers the procedural aspects of establishing and terminating automatic calling unit connections over switched lines.
- **CCITT V.28:** Covers the electrical interface in a manner similar to that of RS-232-C.
- **CCITT V.35:** Defines a 34-pin connection for interfaces with speeds of 48,000 bps.
- **CCITT X.20 and X.21:** Cover the interface between DCE and DTE for packet distribution networks (PDNs). (PDNs are discussed in detail in Chapter 11.)
- **CCITT X.24:** Covers the functional aspects of interface for PDNs.

Other Standards   The U.S. government and U.S. military have their own interface standards. Specifically, MIL-STD-188-114 and U.S. government standards 1020 and 1030 provide for electrical interfaces similar to those of RS-422 and RS-423.

COMMON CARRIER SERVICES

In the past, a marked distinction existed between communications facilities used for voice and video and those used for transmitting data. In today's networks that distinction is less apparent. Today's high-speed transmission facilities are available at low cost. We are able to combine data, voice, and graphic images on one of these high-speed communications links. Thus, the modern data communications manager may be responsible for the entire spectrum of corporate electronic communications; knowledge of the basic services and operations of the common carriers is important. Major offerings are briefly summarized below.

Common Carrier Network Organization

First we look at the organization of the common carrier communications network. We consider how the network was organized in the United States prior to the **AT&T divestiture**. Some telephone networks outside the United States still are organized along these lines. Next, we examine how the U.S. network is organized after the divestiture.

ISO–2110   A functional interface standard that describes which signals will be carried on specific pins.

CCITT V.10 and V.11   Electrical interfaces for data transmission.

CCITT V.24   A functional interface similar to RS-232-C.

CCITT V.25   A specification for establishing and terminating sessions with an auto-call unit.

CCITT V.28   A specification for electrical interface similar to that of RS-232-C.

CCITT V.35   A standard for data transmission at speeds up to 48,000 bits per second using a 34-pin connection.

CCITT X.20 and X.21   Standards that cover the interface between DCE and DTE for packet distribution networks.

CCITT X.24   A functional interface for packet distribution networks.

AT&T divestiture   In 1984, AT&T was broken up into independent RBOCs and a separate AT&T company. The divestiture ended the regulated monopoly of AT&T as well as freeing AT&T and the RBOCs to enter into business areas previously denied to them.

end office A telephone company office to which a subscriber is connected. Also called a class 5 office.

toll center In the telephone network, a toll center is a class 4 switching office. Also called a class 4 station.

primary center A telephone company class 3 station. A primary center is one station higher than a toll center.

sectional center In the telephone network, a class 2 station.

regional center A class 1 telephone station.

Regional Bell Operating Company (RBOC) The AT&T divestiture resulted in the formation of RBOCs and a separate AT&T company. An RBOC is responsible for local telephone services within a region of the United States.

Local Access and Transport Area (LATA) The region served by a regional Bell operating company (RBOC) following the divestiture of AT&T is divided into local access and transport areas. LATAs are not rigidly defined, but calls within a LATA are handled exclusively by the RBOC (the call is not handled by a long-distance carrier but still may be a toll call).

Pre-Divestiture Organization Prior to the divestiture, one company, AT&T, dominated the telephone service industry. Other general service providers included GTE, and competition for long-distance service had begun to appear. The AT&T network is described here. Figure 2-14 illustrates the organization of the AT&T network. Note that there is a hierarchy of switching stations through which a call can be forwarded. A telephone subscriber is connected to a local switching office called a **class 5 office**. Class 5 offices are also called **end offices** because they are at the extremities of the telephone switching network. If the subscriber calls another subscriber who is also attached to the same local office, the call is switched through that single end office. This is illustrated in Figure 2-14 by Subscriber A's connection to Subscriber B. It is also possible for Subscriber C to call Subscriber D, whose telephone is connected to another class 5 office in the same general area. C's call goes directly from C's end office to D's end office and then to D's local line. Both calls are local calls and will incur no long-distance fee.

If the call is not local, as in Subscriber E's connection to Subscriber F, the call is routed from the class 5 station to a **class 4 station** called a **toll center**. This initiates the billing process for the call. From the class 4 station, the call goes to a **class 3 station** called a **primary center**. At this point, if the call is destined for a regional high-use area, the class 3 station might route the call directly to the recipient's class 5 local switch. Alternatively, the call is routed up through the **class 2 station**, termed a **sectional center**, to a **class 1 station**, called a **regional center**. The class 1 station then passes the call to another class 1 station. A class 1 station might then send the call to another class 1 center. Class 1 centers form a backbone transmission network. When the call reaches the class 1 station "closest" to the call's recipient, the connection is switched down through the hierarchy until it reaches the recipient's class 5 end office. At the end office, the call is switched to the recipient's local line.

Post-Divestiture Network The divestiture in 1984 broke up AT&T into independent **Regional Bell Operating Companies (RBOCs)** and a separate AT&T company. The divestiture not only ended the regulated monopoly AT&T had enjoyed but also freed AT&T and the RBOCs to enter into business areas formerly denied them, such as the computer industry. RBOCs are responsible for handling subscriber services within their area; one of the functions of AT&T is to provide long-distance services. The divestiture resulted in a revamping of how long-distance calls are handled.

Local calls are handled in much the same way as in the pre-divestiture era. However, the regions served by RBOCs were divided into **Local Access and Transport Areas (LATAs)**. A LATA is roughly equivalent to the area serviced by an area code. More generally, a LATA corresponds to a common calling area. In areas of high population density, such as the San Francisco Bay area, several area codes may fall within the same LATA. All calls originating and terminating within a LATA are handled exclusively by the RBOC. Any call that crosses a LATA boundary becomes the responsibility of a long-distance carrier, such as AT&T, MCI, or Sprint.

Each telephone subscriber is free to choose a long-distance carrier, and long-distance carriers are required to have equal access to subscribers. To

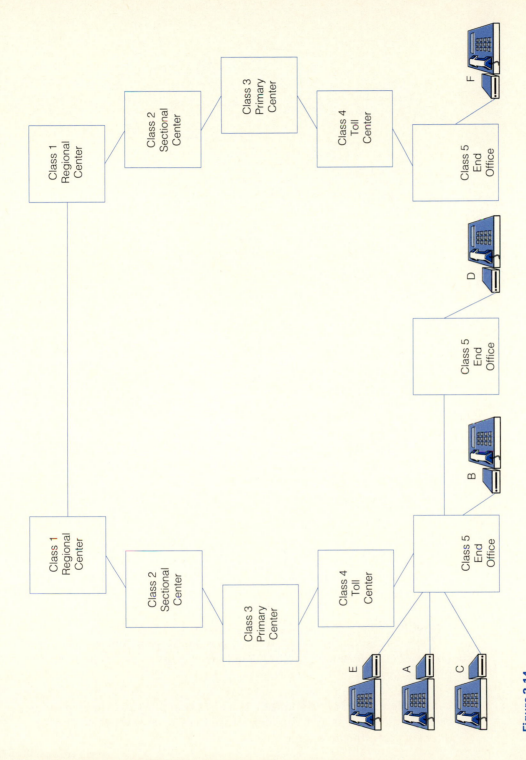

Figure 2-14

Pre-Divestiture Telephone
Switching Network

Figure 2-15

Post-Divestiture Long-
Distance Switching

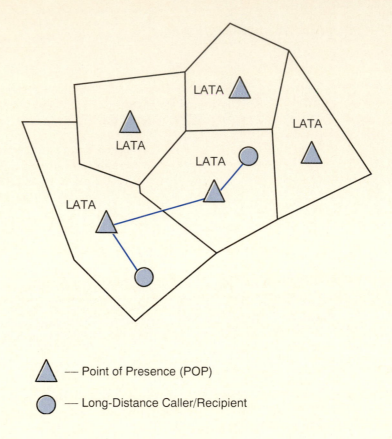

⏥ — Point of Presence (POP)

⏺ — Long-Distance Caller/Recipient

Point of Presence (POP) In
the U.S. public telephone
network, a point of presence
is a point at which a transfer
is made from a local telephone company to the long-
distance carrier.

provide equal access, each LATA has a designated interexchange **Point of Presence (POP)**. An inter-LATA call is routed to the POP, where it is accepted by the designated long-distance carrier. The long-distance carrier routes the call to the POP in the recipient's LATA and the call is switched to the recipient's end office and telephone. This is illustrated in Figure 2-15.

Available Services

A common carrier typically provides a broad range of services. The primary services are discussed in the following sections.

Switched Lines Switched lines, as defined in Chapter 1, simply make use of the existing telephone circuits and switching equipment to establish a connection between sender and receiver. This facility is available wherever telephone wires exist.

Leased Telegraph-Grade Lines Leased telegraph-grade lines provide lower transmission rates than the voice-grade lines described below. They are used for very low transmission rates.

Leased Voice-Grade Lines   Leased lines also were discussed in Chapter 1. Leased lines may be conditioned to reduce error rates, which allows higher transmission speeds.

Wide Band Transmission   Wide band transmission allows very high data transmission rates. Transmission rates in this category are in the range of 48 Kbps to 80 Kbps. Most wide band services available today are digital rather than analog.

T-1 Service   **T-1 service**, also referred to as **DS-1 signaling**, provides digital transmission rates of 1.544 Mbps. A T-1 communications link is created by multiplexing (combining) a number of lower speed lines. Although the implementation may vary, generally a T-1 circuit is created by multiplexing 24 64-Kbps lines. The product of 24 and 64,000 is 1.536 million. The additional 8000 bits per second are control bits. The 8000 bps derives from the PCM algorithm discussed earlier.

Higher speeds are available with **T-3** and **T-4 services**, also referred to as **DS-3** and **DS-4 signaling**, respectively. T-3 service provides a data rate of 45 Mbps and is derived from multiplexing 672 64-Kbps lines. T-4 service provides transmission at 274 Mbps and is derived from multiplexing 4032 64-Kbps lines. T-1 is the most common option; however, as the need for speed increases and the rates for T-3 and T-4 services decline, higher speed services such as T-3 are likely to become more common. One of the needs for higher data rates may be full motion video. With current technology, T-1 and T-2 speeds are insufficient for full motion video transmission.

Fractional T-*n*   A T-1 service that began to appear in the late 1980s is known as **fractional T-1** service. Before fractional T-1, high-speed transmission options were 56 or 64 Kbps or 1.544 Mbps with few options in between. Fractional T-1 is intended to fill this void by providing a portion of a T-1 line to customers. Organizations needing data rates higher than 64 Kbps but less than the 1.5 Mbps of a T-1 line can subscribe to fractional T-1 service. For speeds between T-1 and T-3, fractional T-3 services are available. Fractional T-*n* service allows a user to share a T-*n* line with another subscriber by using only a portion of the 64 Kbps lines that are multiplexed together to form the T-*n* circuit. A fractional T-1 subscriber could subscribe to 64, 128, 192, 256, and so on Kbps. Some common carriers limit the available increments by allowing multiples of 1, 2, 4, 6, 8, and 12 channels for speeds of 64, 128, 256, 384, 512, and 768 Kbps. Fractional T-*n* services allow the subscriber to optimize the line speed and the cost of the service.

Switched Multimegabit Data Service   Switched Multimegabit Data Service **(SMDS)** is a high-speed connectionless digital transmission service. *Connectionless* means the sender and receiver do not need to be connected via a dedicated line. In SMDS, the common carrier provides the user with access points for both sender and receiver. With SMDS, data is broken down into 53-byte cells for transmission. The common carrier provides high-speed

T1/DS1 through T4/ DS4 High-speed data transmission circuits from a common carrier.

fractional T-1 A T-1 service that fills the void of high-speed transmission options between 64 Kbps and 1.5 Mbps by providing a portion of T-1 line to customers.

Switched Multimegabit Data Service (SMDS) A high-speed connectionless digital transmission service.

switching equipment that routes these cells to their destination address. SMDS speeds are 44 Mbps but 155 Mbps services are soon likely. SMDS can be used for high-speed data transmissions such as the long-distance interconnection of LANs.

Asynchronous Transfer Mode (ATM) A high-speed transmission protocol in which data blocks are broken into small cells that are transmitted individually and possibly via different routs in a manner similar to packet-switching technology.

Asynchronous Transfer Mode and Frame Relay   **Asynchronous Transfer Mode (ATM)** and frame relay are similar services that provide high-speed switching of data packets. Both provide high-speed data transfers ranging into the hundreds of megabits per second. Although differences exist between the two, we use ATM as an example of both. In ATM a user starts the transmission process by sending a block of data addressed to the recipient. The data is broken into 48-byte data packets for transmission. Five bytes of control data are appended to the 48-byte data packets, forming a 53-byte transmission frame. These frames are then transmitted to the recipient, where the 5-byte control data is stripped and the message is reassembled.

Wide Area Telecommunications or Telephone Service (WATS) An inbound or outbound telephone service that allows long-distance telephone service. In the United States the inbound service is associated with the 800 area code toll-free numbers.

WATS   WATS is an acronym for **Wide Area Telecommunications** or **Telephone Service**. Both inbound and outbound services are available. The inbound WATS service is the familiar toll-free 800-prefix numbers. A customer may subscribe to an inbound service, an outbound service, or both. The common carrier charges a flat monthly fee for the service, which provides for a specific number of hours of connect time to designated regions. The cost of the service is based on both the number of hours of connect time and the distance to be covered by the service. When WATS service is used for data transmission, the effect is the same as using switched lines, but the cost of the call differs.

Packet-Switching Network Service   This service allows users to establish connections between many locations for a fixed monthly fee plus a cost per packet of data sent. This facility is discussed in more detail in Chapter 11.

Satellite Service   Users may rent satellite transponder time from a number of common carriers. Satellite transmission was described in Chapter 1.

Integrated Services Digital Network (ISDN) The integration of voice and data transmission (and other formats such as video and graphics images) over a digital transmission network. This network configuration is proposed by numerous common carriers.

Integrated Services Digital Networks (ISDNs)   Increased use of common carrier facilities for data communications has prompted providers of such services to evaluate their networks. One conclusion that has been drawn is the need for one network capable of transmitting data in various forms. These forms could include digital data, voice, facsimile, graphics, and video. The benefits to the user community of this type of network are higher transmission speed and potential cost reductions for communications services resulting from the ability to combine multiple data forms onto one network.

One objective of **Integrated Services Digital Networks (ISDNs)** is to allow international data exchange. This requires interfaces between a number of national and regional providers of such services. The first mission of the ISDN program has been to define the functions and characteristics of the network and to establish implementation standards. In 1984, the CCITT produced the

TABLE 2-11   ISDN Channel Types and Options

ISDN Channel Types

B — 64 Kbps

H0 — 384 Kbps (= 6B)

H11 — 1.544 Mbps (= 23B + $1D_{64}$) — North America and Japan

H12 — 2.048 Mbps (= 30B + $1D_{64}$) — Europe

Control Data

D — Both 16 and 64 Kbps

Basic Service Options

$2B_{64} + D_{16}$ = 144 Kbps

Primary Service

$23B_{64} + D_{64}$ = 1.544 Mbps — North America and Japan

$30B_{64} + D_{64}$ = 2.048 Mbps — Europe

first of what is likely to become several standards for ISDN implementations. This standard provides for several different types of service.

The ISDN system specifies three basic types of channels designated as B, D, and H types. Within the type H channel several options are available. These options are shown in Table 2-11. ISDNs will initially provide two interface structures designated as basic service and primary service. The basic service is designated as $2B_{64} + D_{16}$, which indicates that it consists of two type B channels and one 16-Kbps type D channel, for an aggregate speed of 144 Kbps. The primary service has a different configuration for North America and Japan than for Europe. The North American and Japanese specification is designated as $23B_{64} + D_{64}$, for an aggregate speed of 1.544 Mbps. This is the same speed as the T-1 service. In Europe, the primary service is designated as $30B_{64} + D_{64}$, for an aggregate speed of 2.048 Mbps, equivalent to the European version of T-1 transmission.

As an emerging technology, ISDNs have great potential for data transfer and the integration of different forms of data. All the uses for ISDNs have not yet been identified, but applications that have been identified include:

- Digital voice transmission
- Local area networks (see Chapter 7 for additional information about this use of ISDNs)
- Office automation (routing and access to documents)
- Security via transmission of graphic images, such as signatures for check cashing verification or freeze-frame images to security guards
- High-speed switched data lines
- Video telephone service

• Concurrent transfer of voice and data (for example, two users can be engaged in a telephone conversation while simultaneously transmitting data between their workstations)

Cellular Radio Telephone Cellular radio telephone provides mobile telephone connections. The telephones often are installed in vehicles, but that is not required. A mobile telephone can be carried by a pedestrian or cyclist. Currently cellular telephones are only available in major metropolitan areas because it is not economical to establish the facilities in areas of low population density. It is likely that satellite transmission will be added to existing systems and thereby overcome this limitation.

Figure 2-16 shows a diagram of a cellular system. Transmission is via FM radio broadcast. Before cellular technology, signals for a major metropolitan area were broadcast from a central site like ordinary radio station signals. Because of the limited available channels (dictated by the assigned frequencies), only a limited number of calls could be in progress at one time. With cellular technology, the calling area is divided into cells, each of which is serviced by a transmitting station. The transmissions are low power and thus serve only that cell, allowing the same frequency to be used concurrently by nonadjacent cells. As a mobile user moves from one cell to another, the responsibility for transmission is passed from the cell being exited to the cell being entered. Because cellular technology provides connection to line-based telephone networks, the full range of data transmission capabilities that exists for regular telephone service is available. Some cars are now equipped with

Figure 2-16

A Cellular Radio Telephone System

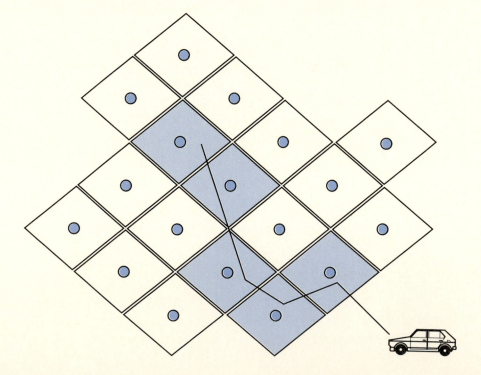

facsimile machines for mobile fax transfers, and it is possible to connect portable computers in mobile stations to computer networks.

PBX and Centrex Services PBX is an abbreviation for **Private Branch Exchange**. PBXs are discussed in more detail in Chapter 7 as a delivery mechanism for a local area network. **Centrex service** is essentially a PBX service provided by a common carrier. Instead of the switching equipment being located on the customer's premises, the common carrier provides the switching equipment on the common carrier's site. This allows several locations in a city to share the same switch and use the same calling prefix and allows extension dialing as though the telephones were located in one building and serviced by an onsite PBX. As with a PBX, Centrex service can be used to transmit data as well as voice.

Service Providers In the United States the following companies provide some or all of the above capabilities.

AT&T

MCI

U.S. Sprint

Western Union

Allnet

Contel/American

CompuServe

ITT

IBM Information Services

GTE

Computer Sciences Corporation

McDonnell Douglas

Comsat

> **Private Branch Exchange (PBX)** Telephone switching equipment located on corporate premises and owned by the corporation. A PBX allows telephone calls within an office to be connected locally without using the telephone company's end office or transmission circuits.
>
> **Centrex Service** A telephone company service that provides PBX capabilities to a company. With the Centrex service, the PBX equipment is located on the telephone company's premises.

SUMMARY

The three basic types of data flow are simplex, half duplex, and full duplex. Most business data communications systems use either full or half duplex. In half duplex mode, modem turnaround time may adversely affect terminal response time. Several different communications codes are used in data communications, the most common being ASCII and EBCDIC.

All media are subject to error. Detecting errors requires that redundant information be transmitted with the data. The three most common error detection schemes in data communications are vertical redundancy check (VRC), longitudinal redundancy check (LRC), and cyclic redundancy check (CRC). The most effective is CRC. In some protocols, sequence checking is also used to improve the reliability of transmission.

Digital data transmission provides both higher transmission speeds and fewer errors. The common carriers are gradually making the conversion from analog transmission equipment to digital equipment. Digital transmission has led to new transmission capabilities, specifically the integration of different services over one medium. It is now common for both data and voice to be transmitted over the same circuits. One of the technologies rapidly being implemented to provide this capability is the integrated services digital network, or ISDN.

Interface standards exist regarding connections between data terminal equipment (DTE) and data communications equipment (DCE). Both domestic and international standards address mechanical, functional, procedural, and electrical interfaces; unfortunately, these standards do not always agree.

KEY TERMS

REVIEW QUESTIONS

1. Define:

    a. simplex transmission

    b. half duplex transmission

    c. full duplex transmission

2. What effect does modem turnaround time have on data transmission? Does it have a more significant effect on short messages or long messages? Why?

3. How is a reverse channel used?

4. What are the limitations of a 6-bit data code?

5. What are the limitations of an 8-bit data code?

6. Describe:

    a. white noise

    b. impulse noise

    c. echo

    d. attenuation

    Which of the four is most likely to cause an error in data transmission?

7. Describe four ways to *prevent* transmission errors.

8. Describe how parity checking works. If even parity is used, what will the parity bit be for the ASCII characters *P, A, R, I, T,* and *Y*?

9. Explain why CRC is a better error detection scheme than parity or longitudinal redundancy checks.

10. Explain how sequence checks can increase the integrity of data transmission.

11. What are the advantages of digital data transmission?

12. Explain how digital data transmission can obtain higher speeds than analog and at the same time have fewer errors.

13. Why are interface standards important?

14. What are ISDNs? Give two examples where ISDNs might be used for data transmission.

15. How does a cellular radio telephone system work?

16. Briefly describe:

   a. Switched Multimegabit Data Service

   b. Asynchronous Transfer Mode

   c. fractional T-*n*

PROBLEMS AND EXERCISES

1. Label each of the following items as simplex, half duplex, or full duplex.

   a. commercial radio

   b. CB radio

   c. television

   d. smoke signals

   e. classroom discussion

   f. family arguments

   g. ocean tides

   h. shortwave radio communications

2. Calculate the line time and modem turnaround time required for the following transaction. Assume a modem turnaround time of 20 milliseconds, a line speed of 2400 bps, and 10 bits per character.

   a. Operator enters 10-character employee ID.

   b. System returns 500-character employee record.

   c. Operator changes zip code and retransmits only the 5-character zip code back to the system.

   d. System acknowledges receipt and positive action by sending operator 20-character message.

3. Identify instances other than those mentioned in the chapter in which a code with 256 different characters may be insufficient.

4. Obtain and examine the Japanese Industrial Standard (JIS) for data codes that contain a portion of the Kanji character set. What other characters are allowed? How many bits are required to support this standard? What, if any, special features are included?

5. Why is Morse code not a viable alternative for computers?

6. If the speed of transmission on a line is 7200 bps and that line is hit by lightning that causes an impulse distortion of 3.5 milliseconds, what is the maximum number of bits that could be in error?

7. Assuming the worst case in Exercise 6, what percentage of the errors incurred would be caught by VRC?

8. ISDN services are widely written about in data communications magazines and journals. Research the literature and describe four different applications that use this technology.

9. Interfaces are being defined for attaching microcomputers to ISDNs. Research the literature and find the cost and capabilities of one such interface.

10. Determine whether cellular radio telephone service is available in your area. What are the distance limitations of the service? What is the cost?

REFERENCES

Abrahams, John R. "Centrex Versus PBX: The Battle for Features and Functionality." *Telecommunications*, March 1989.

Briere, Daniel, and Mark Langner. "Sizing Up Switched Digital Services." *Network World*, Volume 9, Number 45, November 9, 1992.

———. "Users Wonder if ISDN Can Endure." *Network World*, Volume 9, Number 51, December 21, 1992.

Budwey, James N. "ISDN Progress in the USA." *Telecommunications*, Volume 24, Number 3, March 1990.

Electronic Industries Association. *Interface Between Data Terminal Equipment and Data Communications Equipment Employing Serial Binary Data Interchange.* RS-232-C Standards Document. Washington, DC: Electronics Industries Association, 1969, 1981.

Herman, James, and Christopher Serjak. "ATM Switches and Hubs Lead the Way to a New Era of Switched Internetworks." *Data Communications*, Volume 22, Number 4, March 1993.

Johnson, Johna Till. "Rebuilding the World's Public Networks." *Data Communications*, Volume 21, Number 18, December 1992.

———. "U.S. Carriers: Variations on a Rebuilding Theme." *Data Communications*, Volume 21, Number 18, December 1992.

Layland, Robin. "Unfinished Business: A Theory of Evolution for ATM Technology." *Data Communications*, Volume 22, Number 4, March 1993.

Noel, Joe. "Why Is Frame Relay Moving So Slowly?" *Telecommunications*, Volume 27, Number 2, February 1993.

Wallage, Bob. "AT&T Unveils Fractional T-1 Speeds, DDS Objectives." *Network World*, Volume 9, Number 49, December 7, 1992.

Williams, Jay. "ISDN in the Small Business World." *Telecommunications*, Volume 26, Number 12, December 1992.

Many companies operate one or more LANs, and today's workers access the applications and data they need via a LAN workstation. The role of a LAN as a provider of access to computing resources formed the basis on which LAN technology emerged. However, software technology has turned the LAN into a tool for improving the productivity of people who work together as a project team, also known as a workgroup. One outgrowth of LANs on microcomputers is a new class of software called groupware, which is designed to make workgroups more effective.

Collins, Komiski, Materi, and Schultz (CKMS) is a law firm with 50 attorneys and 45 support personnel. A major data-processing effort at CKMS is preparing, modifying, and distributing legal documents. Many of these documents consist of hundreds of pages and represent the collaborative efforts of several people. CKMS uses a LAN and one type of groupware called a document management system to assist its employees in managing document processing. The document management system provides storage, retrieval, and version control of documents. CKMS's document management system also allows several workers to make concurrent changes to different portions of the same document. Other workgroup members may be designated as editors who can read the document and make "margin" notations but are unable to change the document text itself. Using this system, CKMS has been able to produce more accurate documents in less time.

Because of their high data transmission speeds, LANs are beginning to provide another new service: multimedia capabilities. Multimedia combines text, video and graphical images, and audio data to deliver information in a more understandable and usable format. Video, graphics, and audio require the transmission of large amounts of data as well as proper timing of signal transmission to avoid distortion of the recipient's image. With today's networking technology, a LAN is the most effective method of transmitting this time sensitive volume of data to multiple users.

LAN applications have changed and will continue to change the way in which individuals and workgroups interact. In this part we look at some of today's LAN applications, the way a LAN is organized and how data is transmitted over the LAN medium, the hardware and software components of a LAN, and considerations in selecting a LAN system. ■

Part II

LOCAL AREA NETWORKS

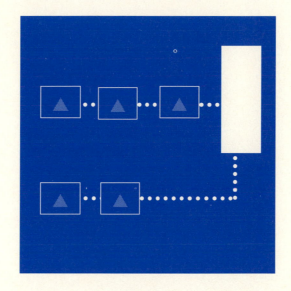

Introduction to Networks

CHAPTER OBJECTIVES

After studying this chapter you should be able to:

- Define the characteristics of a local area network (LAN) and a wide area network (WAN)
- Compare and contrast a LAN and a WAN
- Discuss the rationale behind LANs and WANs
- Describe major LAN and WAN applications
- Compare and contrast LAN administration and stand-alone microcomputer administration

*A*s noted in the discussion of data communications history in the Introduction, the decade of the 1970s brought a significant growth in wide area network (WAN) technology, and one of the biggest growth segments of the communications industry during the 1980s was local area network (LAN) technology. The LAN boom has resulted from lower hardware costs, availability of network and application software, and the integration of microcomputers into the workplace. This is not to say that all LANs use microcomputers as workstations. LANs were in operation before microcomputers became commonplace, and high-speed LANs are still used to connect large computing systems. The 1990s are likely to be characterized by the continued growth of LANs; the widespread interconnection of networks of all types; mobile networking; expansion of the use of multimedia over networks; integration of telecommunications networks such as telephone, computer, radio, and television networks; and a significant increase in network speeds. In a few years the differences between WANs and LANs may be slight and we will be able to once again just talk about networks. Until that time, we need to recognize the existence of the two basic network types and where each fits in the world of data communications.

In this chapter we first define LANs and WANs, including the reasons for having them and applications that lend themselves to these types of network. We also introduce common network terms. Some of these terms are generic to all network types and some are specific to either a LAN or a WAN. This chapter also introduces the concept of network management and specifically addresses the differences between LAN administration and the management of stand-alone microcomputers. An understanding of this material will aid in your understanding of the details of network hardware, topologies, media access control, system software, and network implementations, which are covered in Chapters 4 through 7 for LANs and Chapters 8 through 11 for WANs. We start by comparing WANs and LANs.

THE RATIONALE BEHIND NETWORKS

The first type of network to be developed was the WAN. The major motivations for WANs were to overcome distance, to overcome the computational limitations of a single computer, and to provide for departmental computing. Companies that are national or international frequently have multiple computing sites. Networks are used to connect these geographically dispersed sites, and provide for the exchange of data and software. In some instances, the computing needs at one location exceeded the capacity of a single computer. In these instances multiple computers were installed at one location and then networked to provide resource sharing as well as greater computing capacity. Resources that were shared included hardware and data. As computers became smaller and less expensive with the introduction of minicomputers, some departments purchased computers to better control their computing environment. The department-level computers usually were networked with corporate computers and other department-level computers.

The last two motivations for WAN networking resulted in several computers being located in a small geographical area. The mode of interconnection, however, was basically the same as that being used to connect computers over long distances. LAN technology developed to overcome the speed limitations of this type of network. Originally LANs were installed to connect mainframe and minicomputers, and most LANs were implemented for two reasons: high-speed data transfer and resource sharing in a local area. Today there are several additional reasons including group-oriented software, communication among workers, management control, cost-effectiveness, and downsizing in which large computer systems are replaced by LANs. We consider each motivation.

Large Data Transfers

In a large data-processing installation with a variety of processors, moving data from one system to another once was accomplished by magnetic tape or low-speed communications links (less than 100 Kbps). Magnetic tapes provide high data transfer rates but have two disadvantages. First, manual intervention is required to effect data transfers. Operators are required to mount and dismount tapes. This not only tends to slow down the transfer but also often means the transfer must be scheduled, reducing the potential for as-needed transfers. Second, incompatibilities between tape formats on different systems must be accommodated when tapes are used as a transfer medium.

When using communications links slower than 100 Kbps, large file transfers are very time-consuming. If we consider a speed of 56 Kbps in transferring 1 million records of 100 bytes each, the transfer requires

$$(1,000,000 \text{ records})(100 \text{ bytes per record})(8 \text{ bits per byte})/56,000 \text{ bits per second} = 14,286 \text{ seconds} = 238 \text{ minutes} = 3.97 \text{ hours}$$

The above figures assume that the line is operating at 100% capacity and there is no protocol overhead, both ridiculous assumptions. The actual transfer time would likely be more than 6 hours. The corresponding time for a 100-Mbps LAN is 8 seconds.

A LAN can provide the best attributes of each of the above solutions: high speed coupled with operator-free implementation. LANs operating at speeds of 10–100 Mbps are approximately 200–2,000 times faster than the 56-Kbps link. A caveat is required at this point: Although the medium can transmit data at a rate of 100 Mbps, actual transfer between two systems is often considerably slower because of the CPU time necessary to send and receive the message. Still, the transfers both are time efficient and can be initiated under program or terminal control without operator intervention.

Resource Sharing

Resource sharing is best exemplified by microcomputer LANs. Early microcomputer LAN systems were primarily oriented toward printer and file sharing—**print server** and file server technology. Printer sharing allows several users to direct their printed output to the same printer. In Chapter 6 we explain how this is done. With file sharing, two or more users can share a single file. The file can be an application program, a database file, or a work file such as a spreadsheet or word processing document. In the next chapter we consider server technology and ways in which files can be shared. LANs now are used to share more than printers, disks, and data. Other hardware shared on a LAN includes facsimile (fax) machines, modems, and terminals.

print server   A computer that allows several users to direct their printed output to the same printer.

Groupware

LANs have expanded the potential of the microcomputer from individual productivity to work-group productivity; however, work-group software is not exclusively a microcomputer technology. Work-group productivity tools, collectively referred to as **groupware**, have their roots in WANs. Groupware allows a group of users to communicate and coordinate activities. Basic groupware capabilities such as electronic mail and project management systems

groupware   A collective of work-group productivity tools that allows a group of users to communicate and to coordinate activities.

were common WAN applications before the introduction of microcomputers. Some work-group productivity tools are described below.

Electronic mail   One of the earliest workgroup applications was **electronic** or **E-mail**. An E-mail system has many of the capabilities of a conventional postal system, such as collecting and distributing correspondence of various sizes and types and routing the correspondence to recipients in a timely manner. We have, however, come to expect many more capabilities from an E-mail system than from a conventional postal system. Today's E-mail systems allow correspondents to exchange communications containing text, graphics, and voice images in batch or real-time mode. For many companies, E-mail has become a primary mode of communications, and because of its importance, we discuss its characteristics in some detail in Chapter 15.

Electronic Appointment Calendars   Electronic appointment calendars are stored on the network. One user can consult other users' appointment calendars to find a time at which each user is available for a meeting. The electronic calendar system can then schedule the meeting for each participant.

Electronic Filing Cabinets   E-mail and other machine-readable documents can be stored in disk folders that are equivalent to file folders in conventional filing cabinets. Messages and documents in the folder can later be retrieved, modified, or deleted. Most filing systems maintain an index of the folders and their contents.

File Exchange Utilities   File exchange utilities allow files to be easily copied from one network node to another.

Project Management Systems   Project management systems assist in planning projects and allocating resources. The introduction of LAN implementations has allowed these systems to be integrated more completely into the work group. A manager and team member can agree on the parameters of a task, the team member can update his or her progress, and the manager can monitor the progress. Projects can therefore be managed more effectively.

Group Decision Support Systems   Group Decision Support Systems (**GDSSs**) assist individuals and groups in the decision-making process and help them set objectives. There are two levels of GDSSs. A lower level GDSS does not have an underlying decision support system, but simply serves as a bulletin board for the exchange and development of ideas. A higher level GDSS includes a decision support system that provides more tools for group users than a lower level GDSS.

Electronic Meeting Systems   Electronic meeting systems go beyond simple teleconferencing. The inclusion of networks allows participants to exchange machine-readable information in the form of graphics, text, audio, and full-motion video. If electronic meeting systems are combined with decision support system software, meeting participants can work in parallel to reach solutions.

E-mail   Electronic mail.

electronic appointment calendar   A work-group productivity tool that is stored on the network, so that users can consult each other's appointment calendars.

file exchange utilities   Work-group productivity tools that allow files to be easily copied from one network node to another.

project management system   A management tool that assists in planning projects and allocating resources.

Group Decision Support System (GDSS)   System that assists individuals and groups in the decision-making process and helps them set objectives.

electronic meeting system   Network that allows participants to exchange machine-readable information in the form of graphics, text, audio, and full-motion video.

Document Management Systems   Document management systems help an organization manage and control its documents. Capabilities include indexing documents, finding documents based on keywords contained in the document, controlling document changes, and allowing several users to collaborate on document editing.

The motivation for using microcomputer LANs has evolved from that of simple hardware resource sharing to data and application sharing to idea sharing and personnel coordination. Although LANs are still used to share hardware, software, and data, the biggest benefit of LANs may lie in groupware applications. We discuss groupware in more detail in Chapter 15.

document management system   System that helps an organization manage and control its documents.

Communication

Most of us view telephone networks as a way to allow people to communicate. We use data communications networks for the same reason. However, in a data communications network, the entities that communicate with each other are not necessarily people. The network depicted in Figure 3-1 represents a variety of users and applications communicating—a person-to-person communication, a person-to-application communication, and an application-to-application communication.

The "messages" being exchanged can also differ. The person-to-person communication may be an electronic conversation with the two parties exchanging messages in real time as illustrated in Figure 3-1. User A types a message on the terminal and presses the Enter key, and the message is immediately displayed on User B's workstation. The person-to-application communication may be a user making an inquiry into the corporate database. In

Figure 3-1

Objects Communicating in a Network

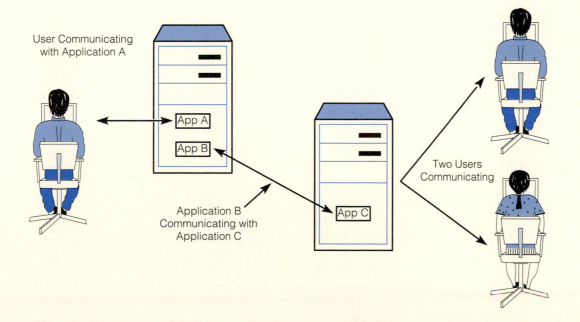

User Communicating with Application A

App A

App B

Application B Communicating with Application C

App C

Two Users Communicating

Figure 3-1, the user communicating with the application might be checking on a shipment for a customer. The application-to-application communication may be the transfer of a file from one node to another. Examples of other network applications are given in Chapter 15.

Management Control

Another reason for using a LAN is management control. A LAN can help a company standardize the microcomputer environment.

Application standards can be set up more easily in a network because most application programs can be installed on one or more network nodes called **servers**. In general, a server provides a service commonly needed by applications. Some common server classes are file, database, print, terminal, and modem. Servers in these classes allow applications to share the hardware and capabilities that the servers provide. Users access these services over the network. In a small network, all users may run the same word processing program that is located on a specific network node. All users will use the same version of the same word processor, making document interchange a simple matter. Contrast this with two or more users having different versions of the same word processor or, worse yet, completely different word processing software. In this case, documents created under one system would likely need to be converted and possibly reformatted before being used by the other word processing system.

LANs can also help control one of the most unsettling problems facing computer users today, computer viruses. A computer virus is a segment of code that attaches itself to a file (usually a program), to memory, or to system portions of a disk. A computer virus is intended, first, to replicate itself and, second, to disrupt the normal functioning of the computer. With **diskless workstations** and **virus detection software**, management can reduce the risk of viral infections. Virus detection software analyzes a system and attempts to discover any viruses that have infected the system. Once a virus is detected, the virus detection software or a complement software utility can be used to remove the virus. A diskless workstation has no local disk drives, which reduces the ways in which a virus can be introduced. An added security benefit of diskless workstations is that a company's workers are unable to copy software or corporate data for personal gain. The disadvantage of diskless workstations is the complete dependence on the network. They cannot be used in a stand-alone mode or in a location that does not have access to the network.

Cost-Effectiveness

Communicating, sharing, and management control are three benefits of using networks. However, the primary reason for using a network is cost-effectiveness. The ability to share resources has a direct impact on an organization's expenses. If users can share hardware, less hardware is needed. If a network were used only for resource sharing, it would be cost-effective when

server The routine, process, or node that provides a common service for one or more other entities. In one configuration for online transaction processing, application programs act as servers for users' requests. This is called a requester server environment.

diskless workstation A workstation that has no local disk drives, reducing the ways in which a virus can be introduced.

virus detection software Software that analyzes a system and attempts to discover and remove any viruses that have infected the system.

installing and operating the network is less expensive than or equal to the hardware, software, data preparation, and other costs in a non-networked environment. Less obviously, cost-effectiveness may derive from the ability of users to communicate and thus improve their productivity. One direct benefit is the reduction of paperwork. Electronic data exchange is converting paper offices to electronic offices.

Downsizing

In some companies, LANs have been used to downsize the data processing hardware, software, and personnel requirements. Downsizing, also sometimes referred to as rightsizing, refers to using smaller computer platforms in place of large computers or to choosing the correct size of computer for the job. Some companies have replaced their mainframe computers by one or more microcomputer LANs. These companies found they could provide better data processing services for their users. The better services were obtained at lower hardware, software, and personnel costs; however, reduced costs are not always the result of downsizing. Other companies that have downsized have not realized reduced costs as a result. "Downsizing: The Business Decision" in *LAN Times* reports that, "While the size of FGIC's [Financial Guaranty Insurance Company's] portfolio grew by 40 percent, downsizing cut the company's annual systems budget from $10 million to $2 million and reduced its information services staff from 70 programmers to 20." This represented an 80% cost savings. Diagrams of that company's computer configuration before and after downsizing are shown in Figure 3-2(a) and Figure 3-2(b) respectively. For more detail on companies' experiences with downsizing, refer to Chivvis, 1991.

NETWORK APPLICATIONS

In the Introduction we generally characterized network applications. In this section we concentrate on applications common to both WANs and LANs. Many applications fall into this category. The more common include office automation, multimedia applications, factory automation, computer-aided design (CAD), computer-aided manufacturing (CAM), and computer-aided instruction (CAI). Some of the functions performed in these application areas are described below.

Office Automation

Over time, a few technologies have significantly affected office procedures. Among these are telephones, calculators, copy machines, and computers. Two of the most recent influences are microcomputers and LANs. Microcomputers have provided office workers with some autonomy regarding their processing needs. The vast array of microcomputer software with user-friendly

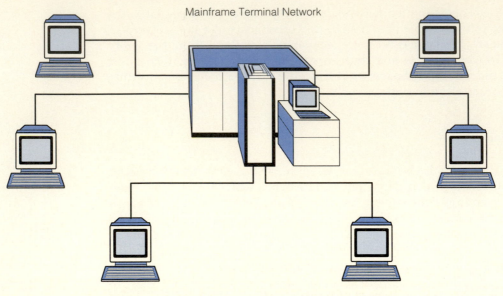

Mainframe Terminal Network

(a) Computer System Before Downsizing

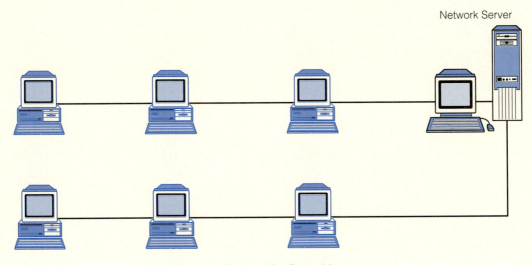

Network Server

(b) Computer System After Downsizing

Figure 3-2

Computer Configuration

interfaces has given end users significant local processing capability. This ability, coupled with shared access to centralized databases and documentation, has added a new dimension to data access and manipulation. Together with electronic mail and document exchange systems, these capabilities have significantly changed the way many offices conduct business. Some office activities an office worker can perform include:

- Distributing memos to a list of recipients using the electronic mail system.

- Scheduling a meeting by accessing electronic appointment calendars. The scheduler software chooses a time at which all participants are available. The calendars of the attendees can be accessed over the network, a common convenient time determined, and appointments made in affected calendars without contacting each participant personally.

- Running an application stored on a file server's disk. The speed at which the application is transferred to the workstation is relatively equal to that of executing the software from a locally attached disk drive.

- Accessing a shared plotter or color printer to output a graph.

- Accessing a document for editing and returning the changes to a central repository, the shared disk drive.

- Extracting data from a centralized database and manipulating the data locally with spreadsheet, database management system, word processor, or other software.

- Composing a portion of a document and submitting it to a centralized system for integration with work accomplished elsewhere.

- Inputting transactions for processing on another node in the network.

- Transmitting data from the LAN to other corporate users on a WAN or another LAN.

- Accessing public or quasi-public networks such as CompuServe, Prodigy, Internet, or Bitnet. Networks such as these provide a wide range of services including electronic mail, information databases, and services such as banking, stock trading, and catalog shopping.

Multimedia on LANs

Multimedia technology extends a computer's capabilities by adding audio and video to data. Multimedia is much more than just being able to produce sound, pictures, and animation on a computer. The promise of this technology is the full integration of audio and video into existing software. Additional hardware is needed to bring these capabilities to a computer. Typically, the components of a multimedia personal computer (MPC) are a compact disk–read-only memory (CD-ROM) drive, an audio board, a computer with a fast processor, a high-resolution color monitor, and ample memory and disk capacity. Multimedia technology is rapidly expanding on both stand-alone microcomputers and LANs. In this section we do not address the technology of multimedia; instead, we examine its impact on LANs.

Multimedia on LANs is already being used. A multimedia server on a LAN delivers digitized audio and video signals to client workstations capable of supporting the technology. The issue is not whether multimedia can be done on LANs but how to do it successfully. The current problem with this technology is the speed of the common LAN. Today's LANs operate at approximately 4–16 Mbps. These speeds are inadequate for extensive use of multimedia. Full-motion video to a monitor with a resolution of 640 by 480 picture elements (pixels) with 24-bit true color at a frame rate of 30 frames per

multimedia technology
Technology that extends a computer's capabilities by adding audio and video to data.

second requires a data rate of 240 Mbps (Lippis, 1993). This is far in excess of common LAN speeds. Still-frame video and audio signals do not require such high bit rates, but sustained transfers of between 16 and 384 Kbps are needed for the duration of many multimedia video and audio sessions (Davidson, 1992). At the higher rate, 30 users would require more than the entire capacity of a 10-Mbps LAN. It also is not possible to sustain a 10-Mbps data rate over a 10-Mbps network because of overheads in the data link protocol, transmission errors, and delays in media access. LANs operating at 10 Mbps are not designed to sustain such constant high data rates.

A combination of several techniques will likely be necessary to realize the full potential of multimedia for large numbers of users. Among these are data compression, higher speed networks, LAN segmentation, and the asynchronous transfer mode switches described earlier.

Data Compression   Data compression reduces the number of bits that need to be transferred. You may be familiar with this technology through disk compression programs that approximately double the storage capacity of disk drives. Thus, an 80-MB disk might be able to store 160 MB of data via compression. If data are compressed prior to transmission and then decompressed at the receiving end, the demand on the transmission media can be significantly lowered. Compression/decompression chips are available that perform these two operations faster than software. Equipping multimedia clients and servers with compression/decompression capability will help by reducing the number of bits being transferred.

Higher Speed Networks   Even with compression, the capacity of LANs running slower than 20 Mbps will be strained by several concurrent users. LANs with a large number of users and without multimedia are already candidates for higher speed transmissions. Several options are available to accommodate these users as well as those moving to heavy multimedia use. High-speed LAN technologies are described in Chapter 5.

LAN Segmentation   Even 100-Mbps LANs will be unable to meet the needs of large numbers of concurrent multimedia users. To allow for greater numbers of concurrent multimedia users, LANs may need to be broken down into small segments as illustrated in Figure 3-3. Each multimedia segment can be serviced by a dedicated multimedia server or by a multimedia server on a high-speed backbone network, as shown in Figure 3-4. With few users on each segment, the data-carrying capacity of each segment will not be exceeded. It is even conceivable that an individual intensive multimedia user will need to be placed on a LAN segment by him- or herself.

Computer-Aided Design (CAD)   An application of computers in the design process. One component is computer drafting.

Computer-Aided Manufacturing (CAM)   The use of computers to solve manufacturing problems. CAM includes robotic control, machine control, and process control components.

CAD/CAM

In addition to the office automation functions above, networks can serve as the communications medium for **Computer-Aided Design/Computer-Aided Manufacturing (CAD/CAM)** applications. In a CAD/CAM application a user

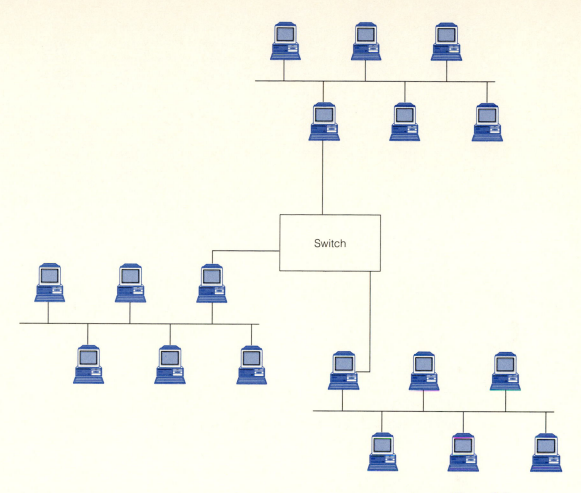

Figure 3-3

Segmenting a LAN for
Multimedia Applications

can check out a drawing and continue work on it, compose a new drawing, and exchange information with other users of the system. The draftsperson can access a designer's notes, change or create a drawing from those notes, and print the drawing on a shared device such as a plotter. Engineering drawings are usually represented by very large data files; LAN transmission speeds are essential to effectively transfer these drawings from one node to another. CAD is used extensively by automobile, aerospace, computer, and engineering corporations. With a CAD system, an engineer can go directly from drawings to constructing a model of the system to sending the plans to manufacturing in a seamless operation. *Seamless* means the flow of work and control is highly integrated and the system user is not aware of the interfaces in going from one operation, such as an engineering drawing, to another, such as model construction.

CAM systems control assembly line operations, robots, manufacturing processes, and machinery. CAM systems are designed to make the manufacturing process more efficient through automation. In the aerospace industry, computer control of machinery effects precision fabrication of parts. Computer-

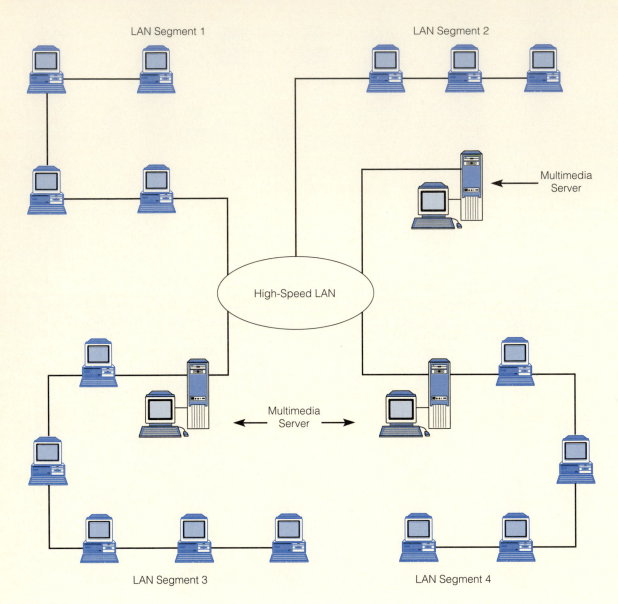

LAN Segment 1

LAN Segment 2

Multimedia
Server

High-Speed LAN

Multimedia
Server

LAN Segment 3

LAN Segment 4

Figure 3-4

A High-Speed Backbone
Network for Multimedia
Applications

controlled robots are used to weld bodies on automobile assembly lines. As
in CAD applications, transmission speed is critical in many CAM applications
because events must be triggered at precisely the right time.

Computer-Aided Instruction

Computer-Aided Instruc-
tion (CAI)   The use of
networks to facilitate the
education process.

Educational institutions have found that networks in general and LANs in particular can facilitate the education process with what is known as **Computer-**
Aided Instruction (CAI). Most education capabilities of stand-alone micro-

computer systems are also available on LANs. These capabilities include computer-based instruction and testing. In educational institutions the LAN may be used for many reasons, including device sharing, access to application software, and electronic mail. Other possible uses include assignment, collection, and return of exercises. An English professor could assign a term paper, require that it be "typed" on a word processor, have the papers submitted electronically, grade the papers, insert grading comments, print a copy of each paper for archival purposes, and return the graded papers to the students. Clubs and committees can use the LAN to post information for other students on electronic bulletin boards. Electronic bulletin boards are the computer equivalent of the physical bulletin board. Users of the LAN typically access the electronic bulletin board through a switched telephone connection. Once attached, the user can "post" notices on the board, such as asking how to connect a specific printer to a LAN printer server. A user also could post answers to existing questions or make software or hardware available. In general, the electronic bulletin is a clearinghouse for public (group) dialogue and equipment exchange.

LAN AND WAN CHARACTERISTICS

The applications described above have several things in common:

- Communication between a variety of devices in a limited geographical area
- Utilization of several different applications
- High-speed data transfer
- High reliability
- Device and data sharing
- Transparent interface to shared resources
- Adaptability to meet changing hardware and software requirements
- Potential access to other networks such as a wide area network, a PDN, or another LAN
- Potential access to a multiuser host system such as a minicomputer or a mainframe
- Security from interference from other users, either accidental or intentional
- Ease of management
- Private ownership

This, then, is the basis for a local area network: multiple devices of different types and capabilities providing transparent access to diverse applications in a limited geographical area, all requiring reliability and rapid response for common services needed by the devices. The network must be manageable,

able to accommodate changing requirements and devices, and able to interface to other communication networks. Most important, the LAN must contribute to the solution of business problems.

High speeds over limited distance make LANs very suitable for joining computers in a building or building complex. Typically, LAN speeds are 1 million (M) bits per second (bps) or faster, and speeds of more than 2 billion (G) bps have been attained. The distance spanned depends on the specific implementation. Usually workstations are not dispersed over a distance of more than a few miles; a few LAN implementations support distances of 100 miles or more.

The LAN itself consists of communications software, a communications medium, nodes, connectors that attach the nodes to the medium, and network software. In contrast, a WAN usually consists of data terminal equipment owned or controlled by the user and data communications equipment provided by a common carrier; however, some WANs are implemented as totally private networks without using the services of a common carrier. It also is common for LANs and WANs to be connected into a larger enterprise network, and the distinction between the two regarding speed and distance is decreasing. Perhaps in several years we will just talk about networks without making distinctions between the two.

ADDED RESPONSIBILITIES OF NETWORKS

Thus far, we have mentioned several problems that networks can help solve and benefits that can result from implementing a LAN or a WAN. Networks also mean additional responsibilities. With stand-alone computer systems, whether it is a microcomputer, minicomputer, or mainframe, each individual microcomputer user or individual data processing organization is responsible for computer operations. These single entities are principally responsible for their own management tasks such as making backups, keeping the system running, reporting problems, replacing paper in the printer, and so on. A network provides sharing of many resources, but the responsibility for network management should not be shared. When management is everyone's responsibility it is also no one's responsibility. Thus, a network must be managed and someone must be given that responsibility and authority. Computer system management for large systems is the rule; although some new technical skills may have been required, management of networks was a natural extension of computer system management. Formal management of stand-alone microcomputers is the exception. A significant change must take place when a company converts from stand-alone microcomputers to a LAN. Effectively managing a LAN requires additional skills to those usually required for individual microcomputer users. Depending on the number of users and applications, LAN management will range in scope from a part-time responsibility to a full-time job for one or more employees.

Now it is time to get into some details of how networks work. We start the discussion of implementation details by introducing some networking terms.

Figure 3-5

Links and Paths in a Network

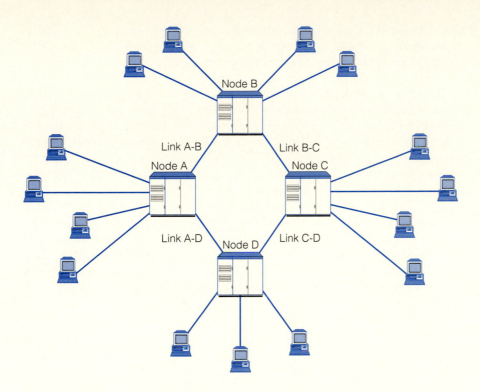

NETWORK TERMINOLOGY

Network and Node   The term **network** as used in Chapters 3 through 11 means a group or set of computer systems and their attached communications devices, such as terminals and multiplexers. Each computer system is called a network **node**. *Computer system* is the term used rather than *processor* or *computer* because of the existence of multiple processor systems. Thus, a node is one or more processors that collectively serve as a termination point for a communications link with another node.

Link, Path, and Circuit   In the Introduction you read about the data link layer and how it helps move data from one node to another. We can also talk about the path a message takes to get from the sender to the receiver. There is often a difference between a link and a path: A **path** represents end-to-end message routing, whereas a **link** connects one node to an adjacent node or one node to a terminal. A link is also known as a circuit, because a **circuit** is a conduit for data and in some instances multiple, lower speed, individual connections are combined to form a single higher speed connection through a technique called multiplexing. In Figure 3-5, the lines represent communications links connecting nodes. Figure 3-5 shows two paths available for communication between Node A and Node C (the path A -> B, B -> C and the path A -> D, D -> C), with two links on each path. We sometimes also refer

network   Two or more computers connected by a communications medium, together with all communications, hardware, and software components. Alternatively, a host processor together with its attached terminals, workstations, and communications equipment, such as transmission media, modems, and so on.

node   Processor in a network, either a LAN or a WAN.

path   A group of links that allows a message to move from its point of origin to its destination.

link   The circuit established between two adjacent nodes, with no intervening nodes.

circuit   Either the medium connecting two communicating devices or a path between a sender and a receiver where there may be one or more intermediary nodes. The exact meaning depends on the context.

virtual circuit   A connection, established when setting up a communications session, between a sender and a receiver in which all messages are sent over the same path.

routing   An algorithm used to determine how to move a message from its source to its destination. Several algorithms are used.

packet switching   The transmission of a message by dividing the message into fixed length packets and then routing the packets to the recipient. Packets may be sent over different paths and arrive out of order. At the receiving end, the packets are reordered. Routing is determined during transmission of the packet. AKA packet distribution network (PDN), public data network, X.25 network, or value-added network. *See also* circuit switching.

store-and-forward system   When transmitting data between two nodes, the messages are logged at intermediate nodes, which then forward them to the next node.

to a **virtual circuit**, which is a connection established between a sender and a receiver upon setting up a communications session. In a virtual circuit, all messages are sent over the same path.

Routing   Routing is a function of the OSI network layer and refers to how the path from sending node to receiving node is determined. In general, routing in a LAN is simple: The message is broadcast to all nodes. This can be done efficiently because of the speed of data transmission. In WANs routing is usually more selective in that a single optimum path is selected for sending data or several paths may be used concurrently. It is seldom the case, however, that a message is sent to all nodes as in a LAN.

Session and User   Session refers to a communications dialogue between two users of a network and is a function of the OSI session layer. A user can be a terminal operator, an application, or any other originator of messages. In some systems, sessions are quite formal, with well-defined conventions for establishing, continuing, and terminating the dialogue.

Packet Switching, Packet Distribution Network (PDN), and Circuit Switching   Packet switching refers to the technology of transmitting a message in one or more fixed-length data packets. A packet-switching network is also sometimes referred to as a **packet distribution network (PDN)**, **public data network (also PDN)**, **X.25 network** (X.25 is a standard designation), or **value-added network (VAN)**. Henceforth, the abbreviation PDN is used. A PDN generally connects a user and the nearest node in the PDN. The PDN routes the data packets to their final destination by finding the best route for each packet (packet switching).

Store-and-Forward   In a **store-and-forward system**, messages may be stored at nodes along the transmission path before these nodes deliver the messages to the next node. There are several reasons for using store-and-forward. First, there is the responsibility for being able to resend the message. If Node A is transmitting a message to Node Z, the path between the two may pass through several intermediate nodes. To ensure delivery, either A must keep the message until it is delivered or an intermediate node that has received the message must assume this responsibility. In a store-and-forward system, a node that receives the message will write it to disk or store it in memory and then acknowledge to the sender that the message has been received. This relieves the sender of accountability for the message. Store-and-forward is attractive for financial transactions as it provides a trace of the progress of the transaction.

Second, store-and-forward algorithms are used for time-staged delivery systems. These systems allow users not only to send messages but also to specify a required delivery time, providing several benefits. Corporations with offices in various time zones can assign a delivery time for their mail messages. If the delivery time is not immediate, the system can process the message during a period of low activity. Suppose that a mail message is posted at 2:00 P.M. for delivery to a time zone that is four hours later, where it is 6:00 P.M. If the delivery time is set as 9:00 A.M. the next day, the message can be stored locally and sent at midnight when both the sending and receiving systems are less busy. Time-staged delivery of large files can also allow their transmission to be paced over time, making the communications links more available for other transmissions.

Third, store-and-forward systems may be used if no path to the destination is available. If a link fails during the process of sending the message and the message cannot be delivered, the node at the point of failure can store the message. When the link is restored, the message is forwarded to the next node in the path. This practice relieves the message originator from the responsibility of saving the message until it reaches its destination.

Finally, store-and-forward techniques can be used in systems where messages have different priorities. Low priority messages may be stored for later delivery to give higher priority messages better access to a link during periods of congestion.

Network Architecture and Topology　　The physical layout of a network, which is the way that nodes are attached to the medium, is referred to as the **network topology**. The **network architecture** is the way that the media, hardware, and software are integrated to form the network.

> **network topology**　A model for the way in which network nodes are connected. Network topologies include bus, ring, and star.

> **network architecture**　The way in which media, hardware, and software are integrated to form a network.

SUMMARY

A LAN is a high-speed network serving a limited geographic area. Originally, LANs were used primarily for sharing hardware and software and high-speed data transfers. Recent reasons for using a LAN include the ability to use work-group software or groupware, serving as a communications vehicle among workers, downsizing applications, and management control of computing resources. Four classes of LAN applications are office automation, computer-aided manufacturing, computer-aided drafting and design, and computer-aided instruction.

LANs extend the capabilities of stand-alone computers. LANs also mean additional responsibilities. Stand-alone microcomputers are managed by those who use them. A LAN requires more centralized management and control. This is a part-time responsibility for small LANs but is a full-time responsibility for one or more employees for medium to large-scale LANs. Poor management can ruin the effectiveness of even the best configured LANs.

KEY TERMS

circuit, *141*
Computer-Aided Design (CAD), *136*
Computer-Aided Instruction (CAI), *138*

Computer-Aided Manufacturing (CAM), *136*
diskless workstation, *132*

REVIEW QUESTIONS

1. What is the difference between a link and a path?

2. What is a store-and-forward system?

3. What were the motivating factors for the development of LANs?

4. What are the distinguishing features of a LAN? What are those of a WAN?

5. What is a computer virus?

6. Describe three LAN applications.

7. Describe four LAN hardware components.

8. Describe three LAN software functions.

9. Explain the differences between managing a LAN and managing stand-alone computers.

PROBLEMS AND EXERCISES

1. Your company has decided to implement multimedia applications on a LAN with 100 users. The speed of the LAN is 10 Mbps and it is estimated that as many as 30 users will be using multimedia applications at the same time. Suggest a configuration that will support the additional load on the network.

2. Investigate the literature and describe the behavior of four different computer viruses.

3. Choose a specific LAN installation. Describe the hardware, software, and vendor details. Cover such items as maintenance policies, support fees, cost of adding a station, number of stations that can be supported by the system, system management procedures and costs, and the type of work accomplished by workstations.

REFERENCES

Chivvis, Andrei M. "Downsizing: The Business Decision." *LAN Times*, Volume 8, Issue 10, May 20, 1991.

Davidson, Peter. "Multimedia Finally Appears Within Networks' Reach." *Network World*, Volume 9, Number 14, April 6, 1992.

Frank, Howard. "The Downside of Downsizing." *Network Management*, Volume 10, Number 13, December 1992.

Lippis, Nick. "Multimedia Networking." *Data Communications*, Volume 22, Number 3, February 1993.

Nunamaker, Jay F., Jr. "Teamwork Tools Lead the Way to Creative Collaboration." *Corporate Computing*, Volume 1, Number 2, August 1992.

Powell, Dave. "Safeguarding the Enterprise Network." *Networking Management*, Volume 10, Number 12, November 1992.

White, David. "SQL Database Servers: Networking Meets Data Management." *Data Communications*, Volume 19, Number 12, September 21, 1990.

4

LAN Hardware

CHAPTER OBJECTIVES

After studying this chapter you should be able to:

- Identify the major classes of LAN servers
- Compare and contrast file and database servers
- Identify the principal hardware components of a LAN
- Discuss LAN hardware needs
- Design the hardware components of a LAN for a specific application
- Recognize the tradeoffs made in designing LAN hardware

When selecting and installing a LAN you have several important decisions to make. You must choose the medium, media access control protocol, topology, hardware, and software. We discussed media in Chapters 1 and 2. Chapter 5 discusses the topology and media access control, and Chapter 6 covers LAN software. In this chapter we look at the principal hardware components of a LAN. A wide variety of components are available — servers, workstations, adapters, and so on — but the key to success is choosing components that can be integrated to form an effective system. In this chapter you will read about servers, backup devices, workstation hardware, LAN adapters, printers, and miscellaneous hardware devices.

SERVER PLATFORMS

To make an informed decision regarding server hardware, you must understand what the server does. Services provided by a server include disk, file, database, printer, terminal, modem, facsimile (fax), and remote access. Disk servers allow a disk to be logically segmented into individual user disks; this older technology has been replaced by file servers that manage disk storage more efficiently. A terminal server allows terminals to be attached to a LAN; the terminal server provides the necessary computation capabilities. Modem and facsimile servers allow users to share modems and fax machines. A remote access server provides LAN services to users who access the LAN remotely via telephone lines. File, database, and printer servers are the most common server types and are the focus of our attention in this chapter. We begin by comparing file and database servers.

File Services

File services is one of the primary jobs of a server. The objective of file services is to provide users access to data, programs, and other files stored on the server's disk drives. It should be transparent to the user that the data or files he or she is using are located on the server's disk drives rather than on a local disk drive. Over time several technologies have been developed to provide file services. File and database servers are the most commonly used today.

File Servers   A file server allows users to share files. If several LAN users need access to an application such as word processing, only one copy of the application software needs to reside on a file server. Individual users can share this application provided the users' company has observed the product's license agreement. In this case, one copy of the program files can satisfy the needs of all application users. When a user enters a command to start an application, that application is downloaded into the user's workstation. Consider the savings in disk space in a company having 100 users for a product that requires 5 MB of disk storage. Storage on a file server requires only 5 MB of disk space for all users. Storing the same application on 100 users' local disk drives will require 500 MB of disk space. File server technology is illustrated in Figure 4-1.

When a user needs data from the file server, that data is transferred to the user's workstation. This is suitable for small files, but consider the impact of such technology when accessing a large database. If a user enters a request that requires looking at thousands of records, each record must be transferred over the LAN to the user's workstation.

Suppose you want to determine the average grade point average (GPA) for all students in your school and that there are 40,000 records in the student file. With file server technology the database application runs on your workstation; it is downloaded to your workstation when you start the application. When you make your request to find the average GPA, each student record is transferred over the network to your workstation, where the grade-point-average data is extracted and computations are made. Transferring all 40,000

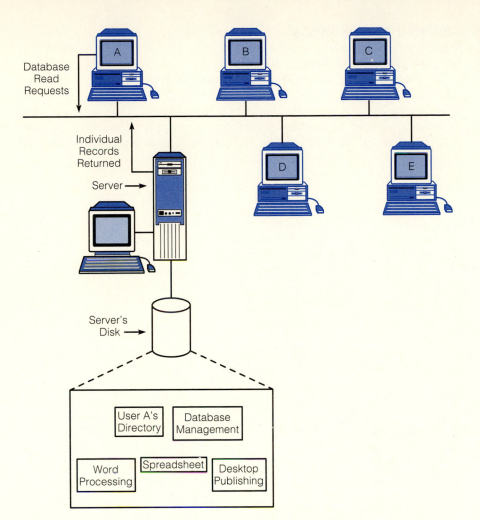

Figure 4-1

File Server Technology

database records over the network can place a heavy load on the medium and reduce its performance. In a case like this it is more efficient to have the server do the calculations and pass only the response over the network. A database server performs this function.

Database Servers   The database server was developed to solve the problem of passing an entire file over the medium. The most common example of a database server is the SQL server. **Structured Query Language (SQL)** is a standard database definition, access, and update language for relational databases. An SQL server accepts a database request, accesses all necessary records locally, and then sends only the results back to the requester. In the GPA example, all 40,000 student records still must be read, but the computation is done by the SQL server. Only one record containing the average GPA is sent back over the network to the requester. This reduces the load on the network medium, but it does place an extra load on the server. The server not only must access the records, but also must perform some database processing.

Structured Query Language (SQL)   A relational database language developed by IBM and later standardized by the American National Standards Institute (ANSI).

This can affect other users who are also requesting SQL services. The SQL server must be powerful enough to provide effective services for all users and avoid becoming a performance bottleneck.

An interface also must exist between the application software making the database request and the SQL server. The interface must be capable of translating an application's data needs into an SQL statement. This means an SQL server cannot work unless the application or an application interface exists that can generate the SQL syntax. SQL server technology is illustrated in Figure 4-2.

Server Disk Drives

File and database servers share a common need to efficiently access data. When choosing a file or database server, you should carefully select the server's disk subsystem, which consists of the disk drives and the disk controllers.

Figure 4-2

SQL Server Technology

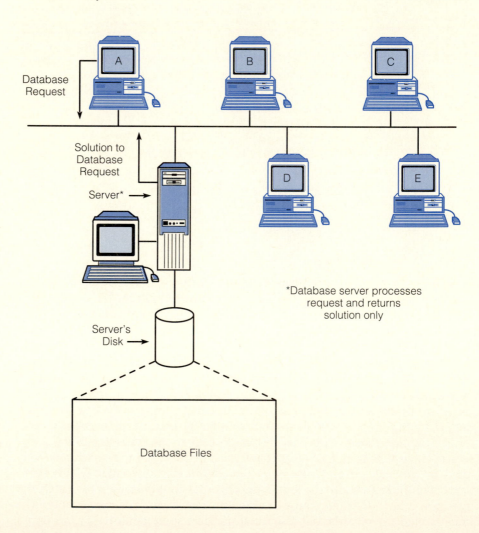

Two factors are critical when choosing a disk drive: storage capacity and average access time.

Server disk drives are typically high-capacity units, which means they can store large amounts of data and have fast access times. The capacity to store large amounts of data is important because the server must store many data and program files. A file server is essentially each user's hard disk. Individual data storage, together with shared storage needed for application software, databases, several versions of operating system software, utility programs, and electronic mail messages, can easily require several hundred megabytes of storage. Some operating systems require more than 5 MB of disk storage. An SQL server holds database files as well as the SQL server software. Organizations adopting SQL server technology will likely have large databases and high-volume storage needs.

The need for large amounts of data storage might be satisfied with one high-capacity drive or with several lower-capacity ones; both alternatives offer benefits. Having fewer disk drives provides a configuration that is easier to manage. Having several smaller-capacity drives is beneficial because several disks can be working simultaneously to satisfy user requests, and the impact of a disk failure can be lessened. Suppose you need 300 MB of storage. You could select one 300-MB drive or three 100-MB drives. With one drive it is simple to determine file allocation: All files are placed on that drive. With three drives your objective should to be to spread the files over the three drives to provide equal access and to ensure equal activity.

If an application requires 45 disk accesses per second, a single fast disk drive may have difficulty keeping up with this load. With three drives and a good distribution of files, you would have only 15 requests per drive per second. This configuration may be more expensive but it provides better performance. Remember, for file or SQL server disk drives, you should select those with sufficient storage capacity and speed to meet your performance objectives. A powerful processor with a slow disk subsystem can cripple your network. This point cannot be emphasized enough.

A second factor to consider when choosing a disk drive is the **access time** of the disk itself. The three components of disk access are seek time, latency, and transfer time. The **seek time** is the time required to move the read/write heads to the proper cylinder. Once the heads are positioned, you must wait until the data revolves under the read/write heads; this is called **latency**. The average latency is one-half the time required for the disk to make a complete revolution. **Transfer time** is the time required to move the data from the disk to the computer's memory. Fast disks will have average access times of approximately 15 milliseconds. In contrast, many floppy disk drives have access times of approximately 200 milliseconds. In general, your file server should have disks with fast average access times.

Finally, you also need to consider the **disk drive interface**, or the **controller**. The disk drive interface sets the standards for connecting the disk drive to the microprocessor and the software commands used to access the drive. There are a variety of disk drive interfaces. Some are well suited for server operations and some are too slow for most LANs. You must choose an interface supported by your LAN operating system. The three interfaces most

access time The total time required in accessing a disk, including seek time, latency, and transfer time.

seek time In disk accessing, the time it takes to move the read/write heads to the proper cylinder.

latency On disk drives, the average time required for the data being read to revolve under the read/write heads.

transfer time In disk accessing, the amount of time required for the data to be moved from the disk to the processor's memory. In data communications, the amount of time required for a message to move from the sender to the receiver.

disk drive interface/ controller Sets the standards for connecting the disk drive to the microprocessor and the software commands used to access the drive.

commonly used for microcomputer-based servers are the small computer system interface (SCSI, pronounced "scuzzy"), the enhanced small device interface (ESDI, pronounced "es-dee"), and the integrated drive electronics (IDE) interface. All interfaces provide high-speed data transfers and large-capacity disk drives. SCSI generally provides more efficiency and is currently the interface of choice. ESDI drives, once the best choice, are becoming less common.

Server Memory

A server is a combination of hardware and software. The software should be designed to take full advantage of the hardware, and in the next chapter you will learn techniques for ensuring this compatibility. Memory is often a good hardware investment, because many software systems can take advantage of available memory to provide better performance. High-speed **cache memory** can significantly improve a computer's performance. Today, microcomputer memories operate at speeds of 70–80 nanoseconds. High-speed cache memory operates at speeds of approximately 15 nanoseconds, and is thus 4–5 times faster than RAM. Obviously, it is faster to fetch instructions from cache memory than from RAM. The processor first looks for the instruction in cache memory. If it is found in cache, the fetch is very efficient. If the instruction is not in cache, it and a block of the following instructions are transferred from RAM into cache. This increases the chances that the next instruction will be efficiently found in cache memory. Another form of caching is called disk caching. **Disk caching** is similar in function to cache memory except that main memory serves as a high-speed buffer for slower disk drives. In both types of cache, memory is used as a buffer for lower speed hardware.

When choosing a LAN operating system that provides disk caching, you need to configure the server with sufficient memory to make caching effective. The fundamental premise of disk caching is that a memory access is faster than a disk access. A disk cache therefore attempts to keep highly accessed data in memory. Essentially caching works as follows: If a user's request for data is received, cache memory is searched prior to the data being physically read from the disk. If the data is found in cache memory — a process known as a logical read — then the data is made available almost instantly. If the data is not found in cache memory, then it is read from disk, which is called a physical access. As data is read from disk, it is also placed into cache memory so any subsequent read for that data might be a logical read.

Disk caching taken to the fullest extent results in all data residing in memory and all reads being logical reads. This is rarely the case. However, it should be clear that effective use of cache memory can improve performance. Because disk caching requires memory, sufficient memory must be available to provide a large percentage of cache hits. A cache hit means that the data being read is found in cache memory. (This process is also called a logical read.) Consider the following example, which illustrates the effects of having too little memory.

Suppose that LAN data requests cycle through four records, A, B, C, and D, and that you only have enough cache memory for three records. When

cache memory   High-speed memory that improves a computer's performance.

disk caching   Similar in function to cache memory except that main memory serves as a high-speed buffer for slower disk drives.

additional space is needed, the cache-management scheme typically replaces the record that has been dormant the longest with a new record. Records A, B, and C have been read in that order and are in cache memory as illustrated in Figure 4-3(a). A request is issued for Record D, but it is not in cache memory, so a physical read is required. Record D is read and must be inserted into cache memory. Because Record A is the least recently used, Record D replaces Record A, as illustrated in Figure 4-3(b). Next a request is received for Record A. Because it is not in cache memory, a physical read is issued and Record A replaces the least recently used record, Record B. Cache memory now looks like Figure 4-3(c). Next a request is made for Record B, which is also not in cache memory, as illustrated in Figure 4-3(d). Record B is read and replaces Record C. Unfortunately, Record C is the next record to be read and again requires a physical read. It is read into cache memory, replacing Record D. Then the cycle repeats again. In this simple example, the cache is one record too small and is totally ineffective. In fact, it is counterproductive, as it only incurs extra overhead by searching cache memory for records that are not cache resident.

The problem of insufficient cache memory can be corrected by expanding the cache memory. In the example, just one more record slot results in 100 percent cache hits after the four initial reads. Of course, this example is contrived, and 100 percent cache-hit rates are rarely attainable. The example demonstrates that there is a critical threshold for cache memory. If the available memory is under this threshold, cache can be ineffective. When the available cache memory is over this threshold, cache can be very effective. Some users

Figure 4-3

Example of Disk Cache Memory

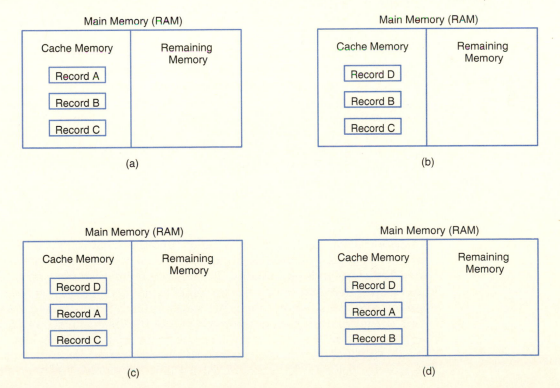

have experienced cache hits as high as 80 to 90 percent. The hit rate depends on the access patterns, so do not expect this figure to hold true for all systems.

An ample amount of memory is important for reasons other than disk caching. You also should have sufficient memory to avoid disk swapping. Most of today's memory-management schemes are based on **virtual memory management**, which uses the disk as an extension of memory so each program has virtually all the memory it needs. Virtual memory management allows the real memory of a system to be less than the aggregate memory required by all the applications. To do this, application code and data are swapped back and forth between the disk and memory. The swap rate goes up if the available memory is too small. When the swap rate increases, the operating system is spending extra time managing memory and less time is available for doing application work. The amount of application work done per unit of time decreases as the swap rate increases.

virtual memory management A memory management scheme that uses the disk as an extension of memory so each program has virtually all the memory it needs.

Processor Speed

The processing power of the server is also a critical factor. It seldom makes sense to select a server that has fast disks and sufficient memory but a slow CPU. In general, the server ought to be one of the fastest (if not the fastest) computers on the network. One exception to this generalization is a server providing small amounts of data to graphics workstations. Most graphics applications require high-speed processors to create and print graphic images. In these networks the workstation computing power may equal or exceed that of the server.

Expansion and Power

A server should have sufficient expansion capability and the power to effectively use the expansion slots. Network server capacity can be expanded by adding hardware to the existing server or by adding servers. Expanding the capabilities of an existing server is less expensive than adding a new server, so the server you choose should support expansion. This allows you to add more memory, disks, printers, or other hardware devices that users can share, such as modems, facsimile machines, tape drives, and optical disk drives.

System Bus

A computer's bus provides the connection among system components such as the CPU, memory, and device controllers. The size, speed, and type of bus affect the computer's performance. The bus size determines how many data bits can be transferred among system components at one time. A server with a 16-bit bus will take twice as many transfers for 1000 bytes of data as a system with a 32-bit bus, and the operation will take approximately twice as long to perform. A 64-bit bus will provide better performance than a 32-bit bus. The speed of the bus determines how fast data is transferred along the bus. A faster bus will provide better performance than a slower one. The type of the bus refers to the interface standard the bus supports. Microcomputers use three main bus architectures: industry standard architecture (ISA), extended industry standard architecture (EISA), and microchannel architecture (MCA). The ISA bus is the one on which the original IBM PC was based and is still widely used. The EISA and MCA buses represent improvements over the original ISA bus and are better suited for high-capacity servers. Some systems have more than one bus, such as a separate bus for the monitor and for disk drives. Having two or more buses allows multiple data paths between devices and can further improve performance.

WORKSTATIONS

Some LANs are homogeneous, which means all the workstations are of the same basic type, all are running the same level of the same operating system, and all use essentially the same applications. It is easier to configure this type of network than one that is heterogenous, but homogeneous networks are less common. Often a network is assembled from workstations acquired over time. These workstations usually represent different levels of technology and perhaps use different versions of operating systems. Consider a network with the following workstations:

- IBM or compatible with an industry standard architecture (ISA) bus
- IBM or compatible with an extended industry standard architecture (EISA) bus
- IBM or compatible with a microchannel architecture (MCA) bus
- Apple Macintosh or compatible
- Sun workstation

If you are selecting components for a heterogenous network, your hardware and software options are more limited than for a homogeneous network. You may be limited in your choice of network operating systems (see Chapter 5) or LAN adapters. The limitations arise from the inability of some LAN software to support different workstations or from the limited availability of required hardware, such as a LAN adapter. You will find many options for a LAN with only IBM-compatible workstations and several for LANs with only Apple workstations, but some of these options will not support both types of microcomputers. Fortunately, interoperability of different hardware platforms on a single LAN is becoming more common.

Diskless Workstations

You may want to consider diskless workstations when configuring your LAN. A diskless workstation does not have any local disk drives. Instead a diskless workstation has its operating system boot logic in a read-only memory (ROM) chip. This chip contains the logic to connect to the network and download the operating system from the server. A diskless workstation cannot be used in a stand-alone mode; it is fully dependent on the server for all of its software, and it cannot function if the network or server is not operating. This is the disadvantage of a diskless system. Its advantages are lower cost, better security, and tighter control.

Because diskless workstations have no disk drives, they are inherently less expensive than those with disk drives. The maintenance costs for diskless systems also are less than for systems with disk drives. Diskless systems provide extra security because users are unable to copy the organization's data onto local hard or floppy disk drives. This is important because an organization's primary security risk is its employees. Diskless systems also provide a greater measure of control because employees cannot introduce their own software into the system. This not only ensures that standard software and data are used but also reduces the chances of computer viruses being introduced into the network.

Workstation Memory and Speed

Like servers, workstation memory configurations are important. If you have stand-alone microcomputer systems, each with the minimum application memory configuration, you may need to add more memory to those systems to run the same applications on a network because LAN software must also run in the workstations. In addition, LAN software stays memory resident. Suppose you have a microcomputer with 512 KB of memory and that this is just enough to load the operating system and your database management system. Placing that same microcomputer on a network requires that some of the memory be allocated to the LAN interface software; you may be unable to run your database management system because of insufficient memory. The solution is to expand the computer's memory. The amount of memory required for LAN software varies from one LAN to another. Some require fewer than 20 KB, and some require more than 70 KB of resident memory.

The speed of the workstation's processor needs to be compatible with the type of work for which the workstation is being used. If you use the workstation for word processing, a low-speed processor probably is satisfactory. A workstation used for graphics work requires a high-speed processor. Basically it is the application and not the LAN that determines the required power of the workstations.

BACKUP DEVICES

No LAN is complete without a backup device. One of the LAN administrator's most important duties is to make periodic file backups. A backup is a copy of files at a specific time and is used to restore the system to a workable state following a system failure or an event that damages the data, or to restore data that needs to be available only on a periodic basis. Research data needed only once or twice a month and year-end payroll data needed temporarily to file workers' tax notices can be backed up and then replaced on disk on an as-needed basis.

TABLE 4-1   Primary Hardware Backup Technologies

Diskette Backup

    360 KB

    720 KB

    1.2 MB

    1.44 MB

    2.88 MB

    20 MB

Hard Drive, Fixed

    Multiple capacities

Hard Drive, Removable Cartridge

    40 MB to more than 250 MB

Tape Backup

    4mm or ¼-inch
        to 5 GB
        60 MB, 150 MB, 160 MB, 500 MB, 1.2 GB, 2.2 GB are common

    8mm or VCR
        to 2.2 GB

    9-track
        to 100 MB

(Some backup systems provide autoloading multitape systems with capacities to 100 GB.)

Optical Drives

    WORM (write once, read many)
        to 4 GB

    Rewritable
        to 4 GB

    The principal backup device is a magnetic tape drive. Removable disk drives and optical disk drives are alternatives. The primary backup technologies are described below and are listed in Table 4-1.

Magnetic Tape Drives

Magnetic tape drives are inexpensive relative to the other backup options. Magnetic tapes can hold large volumes of data, are easy to use and store, and generally provide good performance. A variety of tape backup devices are available. The drives themselves are less expensive than disk or optical drives with comparable storage characteristics, and a wide range of data capacities are available. Tape drives vary in the size of the tape and the recording method. If more than one tape drive is to be used in one organization, it is best to establish a standard tape configuration so the tapes can be exchanged among the different drives.

Like other hardware, the tape drive must be compatible with the server or workstation on which it is installed. A drive usually has a controller that must be installed in the computer, so you must select a drive that has a controller compatible with your equipment. You also need backup software and procedures to make your backups. Backup software is covered in the next chapter.

Floppy Disk Drives

You may use floppy disks as the backup medium. The disk drives may be server or workstation drives. The major disadvantage of this backup method is the low capacity and speed of the backup medium. Typical floppy disk capacities for IBM-compatible systems are 360 KB, 720 KB, 1.2 MB, 1.44 MB, and 2.88 MB. Disks with capacities up to 20 MB are also available. Often the capacity of server drives is 100 MB or more. A large LAN may have several hundred million or even several billion bytes of disk storage. Backing up this amount of data to 1 MB (or even 20 MB) disks is cumbersome. The advantages of floppy disk backup are high availability on workstations and servers and low cost. Disk backup for LANs with small disk requirements or for backing up a few small files can be practical, but for large-disk systems, the number of diskettes needed to store all the data is too high to be time effective. Backing up to floppy disks is slow, subject to errors, and requires handling many disks.

Hard Disk Drives

A hard disk drive on either a server or a workstation may also be used for backup. The arguments for and against this alternative are much the same as those for floppy disks. The major difference is that the capacity of hard disks is greater than that of floppy disks. If the hard disk is not removable, however, it is difficult to keep multiple generations of backups, a procedure that is important for a comprehensive backup plan. You should have at least three generations or more of backups, which means that if you take a backup weekly, three weeks' worth of backups are always available. Some hard disk drives have removable disk cartridges, which are an excellent backup alternative because they provide high capacity (90 MB or more per cartridge) and rapid access. Some newer computers also allow for easy removal of hard disk drives, making them better suited as a backup medium.

Optical Disk Drives

Optical disk drives are gaining popularity as backup devices. The reasons for this are their decreasing costs and large storage capacity, and the recently introduced ability to erase and write to optical disks. The two classes of writeable optical disk drives are WORM (write once, read many) and erasable drives. WORM technology allows you to write to the medium only once. You cannot erase data on a WORM disk and reuse the medium. This can make the cost of backups expensive because the cost of cartridges for many such drives on microcomputers is more than $150. An advantage of WORM technology is that the data cannot be changed, so the backup cannot be accidentally destroyed. The newest optical disk technology allows data to be rewritten. Rewritable optical drives are more expensive than WORM drives, but you can expect these prices to come down. The capacities of optical drives range from 300 MB to 1 GB or more.

LAN ADAPTERS

LAN adapters provide the connection between the medium and the bus of the workstation or server. LAN adapters are designed to support a specific protocol using a specific medium, although a few can support two different medium types. One type of Ethernet card supports twisted-pair wires and another type supports coaxial cable. After you match medium and protocol, there are additional alternatives regarding vendor and architecture. We discuss protocols in the next chapter.

The choice of a LAN adapter vendor determines the support, quality, and price of the LAN adapter. Just as you should be careful when selecting a LAN vendor, you should also be careful regarding the vendor of individual components such as a LAN adapter. The LAN adapter that is initially the least expensive may prove to be more costly in the long term if it is of inferior quality, if it does not have a good vendor-support policy, or if replacement LAN adapters are difficult to obtain should the vendor go out of business.

LAN adapters are installed in each workstation and server. Naturally the LAN adapter must be compatible with the hardware architecture of the computer into which it is installed. You also need to ensure that a LAN adapter is available for each type of network node you anticipate having. Certain combinations of equipment may not be supported. You may have difficulty finding ARCnet cards for each node in a network consisting of a Digital Equipment Corporation VAX server and Apple Macintosh, Sun, and IBM workstations. LAN adapters also must be compatible with the bus of the host computer. For IBM and Apple microcomputer-based LANs, you may need ISA-, EISA-, MCA-, Personal Computer Memory Card International Association-(PCMCIA), and NuBus-compatible cards.

LAN adapters also have their own architecture. LAN adapters for IBM or compatible systems often come in 8-bit, 16-bit, and 32-bit architectures. The 32-bit adapters are almost always more expensive and faster than the corresponding 16-bit and 8-bit adapters. By faster we mean that a 32-bit adapter can transfer data between the computer and the medium faster than a 16-bit adapter, which is faster than an 8-bit adapter; the architecture does not affect the speed at which data is transferred over the network medium. A 32-bit adapter is faster than a 16-bit adapter because it transfers data between the adapter and memory 32 bits at a time, whereas the 16-bit adapter transfers data in 16-bit groups.

PRINTERS

One major factor that affects the success of a LAN is printer support. Some LANs have restrictions regarding the distribution of printers and the number of printers that can be supported by 1 server. Suppose that network printers must be attached to a server and that each server can support a maximum of 5 printers. An organization that needs 20 printers therefore must have at least 4 servers.

You must be concerned not only with the number of printers but also with the type of printers supported and the way in which they are supported. A **printer driver** is a software module that determines how to format data for proper printing on a specific type of printer. The printers you intend to use must be supported by the software drivers provided by the vendor. You may find that a laser printer you attach to the LAN can operate in text mode but is restricted in its graphic mode operation or in its ability to download fonts. Be sure to consider interoperability of hardware and software components to ensure that your needs are realized. Some LAN systems provide a utility program that allows you to tailor a generic printer driver to meet the needs of a specific printer you want to use. This utility allows you to define printer functions and the command sequences essential to invoking those functions. Because new printer technologies are constantly appearing, this utility is quite useful.

> **printer driver**   A software module that determines how to format data for proper printing on a specific type of printer.

ADDITIONAL LAN HARDWARE

Other hardware components you may find in a LAN are:

- Terminal servers, which allow terminals to access the network. However, a terminal attached to a LAN will not have the same functionality as a microcomputer attached to a LAN.
- Modem servers, which allow users to share one or more modems.
- Facsimile (fax) machines, which may be attached to a server and shared by network users.
- Remote access servers, which allow remote users dial-in access to the network.

These services are important but are less common than either file, database, or printer services. As such, we do not devote more coverage to them.

Earlier we discussed the principle of disk caching. Most efficient network operating systems use this to enhance performance. A disadvantage to using disk caching is that several disk updates can be lost if the server experiences a power failure. To reduce the risk of this happening, many companies protect their servers with an **Uninterruptible Power Supply (UPS)**. A UPS uses batteries to provide power to a connected computer in the event of blackout or reduced power conditions. Some UPSs also provide protection against power spikes and momentary power loss. For many business applications a UPS that costs several hundred dollars is a good investment.

UPSs come in different sizes. The size of a UPS is given in watts, which is a measure of power. It is important to select a UPS that matches or exceeds the power demands of the computer it is protecting. Each computer has a power supply rated in the number of watts it delivers to the system. The easiest way to select the proper UPS size is to meet or exceed the wattage of the power supplies for all computers protected by the UPS. A more precise but time-consuming method is to sum the power requirements of all components serviced by the UPS.

Uninterruptible Power Supply (UPS)   A backup power unit that continues to provide power to a computer system during the failure of the normal power supply. A UPS is frequently used to protect LAN servers from power failures.

MAKING CONNECTIONS

Thus far we have discussed the medium, the network nodes, and the LAN adapter. All that remains is to connect the nodes to the medium. Connections can be made in a variety of ways. You have already learned that you must pick a LAN adapter that is compatible with the medium you choose. Therefore it is the medium that primarily influences the way in which physical connections are made. Let us look at the problem from a generic perspective.

The objective of network connection — connecting a computer to the LAN medium — is to provide a data path between the medium and the computer's memory. To accomplish this there must be a connection to the medium and a connection to the computer's bus or channel. The interface or connection to the medium is referred to as the **Communications Interface Unit (CIU)**, and the interface or connection to the computer's bus is referred to as the **Bus Interface Unit (BIU)**. These functions, illustrated in Figure 4-4, are provided by the LAN adapter.

A key component of the network connection is a **transceiver**, which establishes the connection to the medium and implements the transmit and receive portion of the protocol. In a few Ethernet LANs, the transceiver is connected directly to the medium. Most of today's Ethernet implementations have a transceiver that is located on the LAN adapter, as illustrated in Figure 4-5.

The physical connection between the computer and the medium is established through **connectors**. Many different types of connectors are used, but the principal ones are:

- BNC-, TNC-, or N-type connectors for coaxial cable
- RJ-11, RJ-45, or DB-*nn* (DB-25 or DB-15) connectors for wires
- SMA connectors for fiber optic cable

The type of connector you need is determined by your LAN adapter. A wide variety of connector adapters allow you to change connector types. One

Communications Interface Unit (CIU)   In a local area network, the communications interface unit provides the physical connection to the transmission medium.

Bus Interface Unit (BIU)   In a local area network, the bus interface unit provides the physical connection to the computer's I/O bus.

transceiver   A device that receives and sends signals. A transceiver helps form the interface between a network node and the medium.

connector   Establishes the physical connection between the computer and the medium.

Figure 4-4

Bus/Communications Interface Units and Transceiver

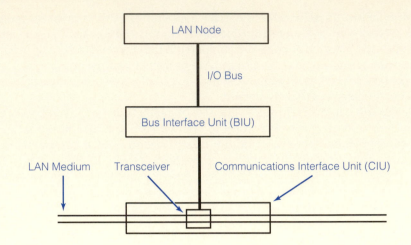

Figure 4-5

A Transceiver on a LAN Adapter

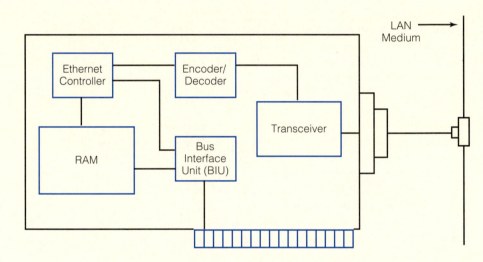

baluns adapters that change coaxial cable connectors into twisted-pair wire connectors, allowing transfer from one medium to another or from a connector for one medium to a different medium.

wiring hubs Used by some LAN implementations to provide node-to-node connection.

Multistation Access Unit (MAU) In an IBM token ring LAN, an MAU is used to interconnect workstations.

active hub A node connection hub used in an ARCnet LAN that provides signal regeneration and allows nodes to be located up to 2000 feet from the hub.

adapter can change a bayonet nut connector (BNC) to a TNC-type connector. **Baluns** are adapters that change coaxial cable connectors to twisted-pair wire connectors. These adapters allow you to transfer from one medium to another or from a connector for one medium to a different medium. Several connectors are illustrated in Figure 4-6.

In some networks, connecting a computer to the medium is sufficient for making that computer active on the network. Some LAN implementations use **wiring hubs** to provide node-to-node connection. Several kinds of connection hubs are commonly used. In an IBM token ring LAN, individual stations are connected to a wiring hub called a **Multistation Access Unit (MAU)**. The ring is established via internal connections within the MAU as illustrated in Figure 4-7. An ARCnet LAN may use active and passive hubs for node connections, as illustrated in Figure 4-8. An **active hub** provides signal regeneration and allows nodes to be located at distances up to 2000 feet

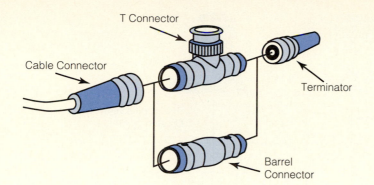

Figure 4-6

Use of Connectors and a Terminator

T Connector

Cable Connector

Terminator

Barrel Connector

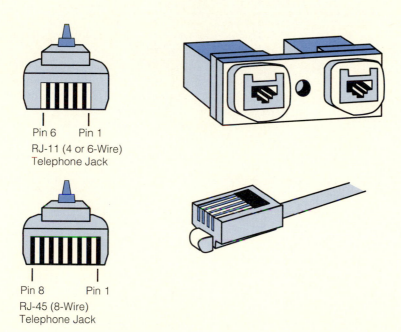

Pin 6   Pin 1

RJ-11 (4 or 6-Wire)
Telephone Jack

Pin 8   Pin 1

RJ-45 (8-Wire)
Telephone Jack

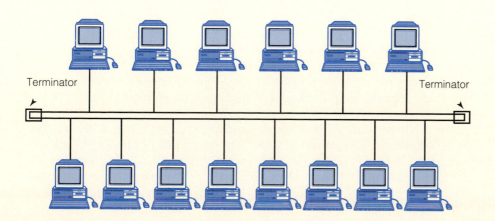

Terminator   Terminator

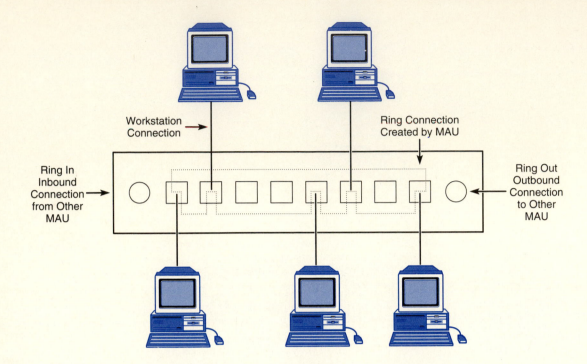

Workstation Connection →

Ring Connection Created by MAU

Ring In Inbound Connection from Other MAU →

Ring Out Outbound Connection to Other MAU

Figure 4-7

A Multistation Access Unit (MAU)

passive hub   A node connection hub used in an ARCnet LAN that does not provide signal regeneration, so nodes can be located no farther than 100 feet from the hub.

terminator   A resistor at a cable end that absorbs the signal and prevents echo or other signal noise.

from the hub. A **passive hub** does not provide signal regeneration, so nodes can be located no more than 100 feet from the hub.

A variety of other hardware components are sometimes needed to make the network function. On bus networks or networks using wiring hubs, terminators are often needed to prevent signal loss. **Terminators** are used at the ends of a bus to prevent echo and are required on unused passive hub ports in an ARCnet network for the same reason. The location of terminators in a LAN configuration is shown in Figure 4-6.

Sometimes LAN connections go further than simply connecting a node to the medium. You may also need to connect one LAN to another or connect a LAN to a WAN. We discuss this subject in detail in Chapter 12.

SUMMARY

LAN hardware mainly consists of server platforms, workstations, LAN adapters, printers, a medium, and connectors. The hardware combines with software to provide the LAN services. LAN adapters are protocol- and medium-oriented. One LAN adapter supports Carrier Sense with Multiple Access/Collision Detection (CSMA/CD) on twisted-pair wires, another supports CSMA/CD on coaxial cable, and a different LAN adapter is necessary for token passing using fiber optic cable. Servers must be properly configured to provide the performance and backup services required by an

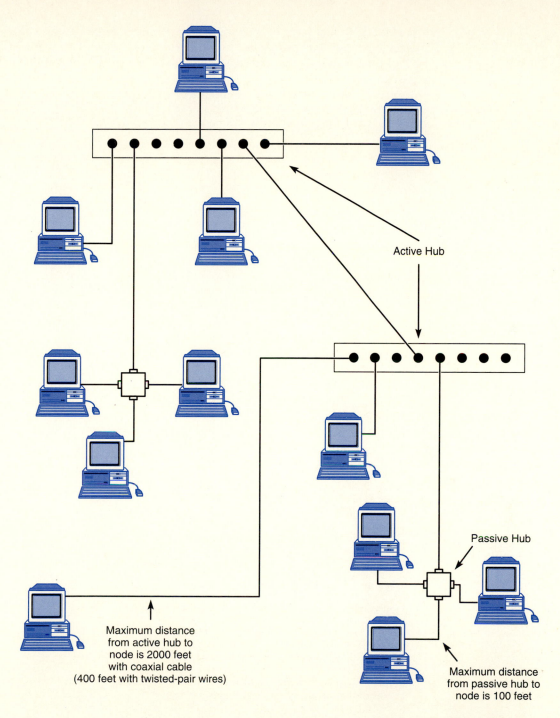

Active Hub

Maximum distance
from active hub to
node is 2000 feet
with coaxial cable
(400 feet with twisted-pair wires)

Passive Hub

Maximum distance
from passive hub to
node is 100 feet

Figure 4-8

ARCnet with Active
and Passive Hubs

efficient LAN. The keys to meeting this requirement are having sufficient memory, a powerful processor, high-performance disk drives, and a file backup unit. Naturally the software also must be available to exploit the hardware configuration.

You can choose from many combinations of hardware and software when you are building a LAN. The key to success is combining the alternatives so that the hardware and the software form an effective team.

KEY TERMS

access time, *151*

active hub, *162*

baluns, *162*

Bus Interface Unit (BIU), *161*

cache memory, *152*

Communications Interface Unit
   (CIU), *161*

connectors, *161*

controller, *151*

disk caching, *152*

disk drive interface, *151*

latency, *151*

Multistation Access Unit (MAU), *162*

passive hub, *164*

printer driver, *160*

seek time, *151*

Structured Query Language (SQL), *149*

terminator, *164*

transceiver, *161*

transfer time, *151*

Uninterruptible Power Supply
   (UPS), *161*

virtual memory management, *154*

wiring hubs, *162*

REVIEW QUESTIONS

1. What are the generic functions of a server?

2. Distinguish between file and SQL server technology.

3. What must you take into consideration when you select a server disk drive?

4. How do servers use memory to improve performance?

5. Explain how disk caching works. What is its benefit?

6. Why should servers have high processor speeds?

7. How do diskless systems work? What advantages do they have over disk systems? What are the disadvantages of a diskless system?

8. What is data backup? What devices are used to effect backup?

9. Why are floppy disks usually ineffective as a backup device?

10. What options need to be considered when selecting a LAN adapter?

11. What are wiring hubs, baluns, and terminators? What function does each provide?

12. What does an Uninterruptible Power Supply (UPS) do?

PROBLEMS AND EXERCISES

1. You need to establish a small network having 1 server and 15 workstations. Describe a hardware configuration for the server and for the workstations. Make all workstation configurations the same. Consult one or more recent magazines to help you determine the hardware costs for your LAN. Include the server, workstations, LAN adapters, a backup tape device, three laser printers, and three dot-matrix printers in your cost estimates. Configure the server with at least 1.2 GB of disk storage and 16 MB of memory.

2. You have a file server with 600 MB of data. If you use 1.4-MB disks to back up this data, how many disks are necessary? Your backup utility provides data compression and you get 1.8:1 compression for your files. A 1.8:1 compression ratio means that on the average, 1.8 bytes can be compressed into 1 byte. Using this compression ratio, how many disks are required? List the advantages and cost of a more suitable backup medium.

3. Examine the references listed and give an example of how each of the following are used:

   a. a terminal server

   b. a modem server

   c. a fax server

   d. an Uninterruptible Power Supply

4. A company has an IBM or IBM-compatible microcomputer with an 80386 processor, 2 MB of memory, and an 8-MB disk drive. The company wants to know whether this computer will work as a file server for a 25-node network. The primary applications are word processing, spreadsheets, and desktop publishing. What would your response be to this inquiry? Justify your response.

5. Assuming that you decided the microcomputer in Problem 4 could handle the job if it is upgraded, what upgrades would you recommend?

REFERENCES

Axner, David H. "Wiring Hubs: Keys to the Network Infrastructure." *Networking Management*, Volume 10, Number 12, November 1992.

Barrett, Ed. "The Critical Steps to Hub Selection." *LAN Technology*, Volume 8, Number 11, October 15, 1992.

Cummings, Syndi. "Prepare for the CD-ROM Invasion." *LAN Times*, Volume 10, Number 1, January 11, 1993.

Ga Cote, Raymond, Steve Apiki, and Stan Wszola. "Network FAX on Tap." *Byte*, Volume 18, Number 2, February 1993.

Harbison, Robert. "LAN Linchpin." *LAN*, Volume 9, Number 2, February 1994.

Kent, Les. "Backup to the Rescue." *InfoWorld*, Volume 14, Number 45, November 9, 1992.

Krivda, Cheryl. "Enterprising Hubs." *LAN Interoperability*, Volume 3, Number 2, Fall 1992.

Salamone, Salvatore. "Terminal Servers: No End in Sight." *Data Communications*, Volume 21, Number 13, September 21, 1992.

St. Clair, Melanie. "Beyond Batteries." *LAN Magazine*, Volume 7, Number 11, November 1992.

5

LAN Topologies and Media Access Control

CHAPTER OBJECTIVES

After studying this chapter you should be able to:

- Describe several important LAN standards
- Identify the three major LAN topologies
- Compare and contrast the three major LAN topologies
- Describe the LAN media access control protocols
- Recognize the advantages and disadvantages of each media access control protocol
- Discuss the ways in which topologies and media access control protocols are combined
- Compare and contrast the major LAN architectures

When you build a LAN, you will probably investigate the capabilities provided by a variety of vendors. You will discover several ways in which you can build a LAN, and you also might hear conflicting statements about the relative merits of each. In this chapter you will learn about the network layouts that vendors most commonly propose. You will also read about LAN topologies, media access control protocols, common ways in which topologies and media access control protocols are combined, and the strengths and weaknesses of several LAN configurations.

The LAN components covered in this chapter exist at the OSI physical and data link layers.

THE LAN SYSTEM

If you evaluate vendor responses to a LAN selection process, you may first read statements intended to give you a general idea of the type of solution proposed. Here are some examples:

"We are happy to propose a Novell IEEE 802.3 network for your consideration."

"We believe a Banyan Vines token ring network will best suit your purposes."

"Our solution uses Microsoft's Windows NT software and Ethernet."

network topology   A model for the way in which network nodes are connected.

Media Access Control (MAC) protocol   A sublayer of the OSI reference model's data link layer. The media access control protocol defines station access to the media and data transmission. Common MAC protocols are carrier sense with multiple access and collision detection (CSMA/CD) and token passing.

These statements encapsulate three major LAN components: the LAN software, the topology, and the media access control protocol. A **network topology** is the model used to lay out the LAN medium and connect computers to the medium. A **Media Access Control (MAC) protocol** operates at the OSI data link layer and describes the way in which a network node gains access to the medium and transmits data. The combination of these three components is what we call the LAN architecture and provides much of the uniqueness of a LAN. In general, you will be considering three basic topologies—ring, bus, and star—and two basic media access control protocols—contention and token passing. The major distinctions between one token ring, contention bus, or token bus and another are in the network operating system, the hardware, and the medium. A number of vendors, such as Apple, Artisoft, Banyan, IBM, Microsoft, and Novell, provide networking software.

When selecting a LAN you must keep one idea paramount: You are selecting a *system*. The system has many components, and the overall success of the LAN is how well these components can be integrated to form a system. Interoperability is the key, not the efficiency of a single component. For example, you must be able to attach workstations to the LAN and support each workstation's operating systems. The LAN might have IBM or IBM-compatible workstations together with Apple Macintosh or compatible systems, all with a variety of operating systems and printers. In this case the system you choose must support all of these components; some networks cannot do this.

LAN TOPOLOGIES AND STANDARDS

What do we mean when we talk about a LAN topology? First, the term *topology* derives from a mathematics field that deals with points and surfaces in space—that is, with the layout of objects in space. Thus, LAN topology is the physical layout of the network. Another way you can look at a topology is as a model for the way in which you configure the medium and attach the nodes to that medium. In general, LAN topologies correspond to the OSI physical layer described in the Introduction.

LANS have three basic topologies: ring, bus, and star. Each configuration is illustrated in Figure 5-1. Let's take a closer look at each topology.

Figure 5-1

Basic LAN Topologies

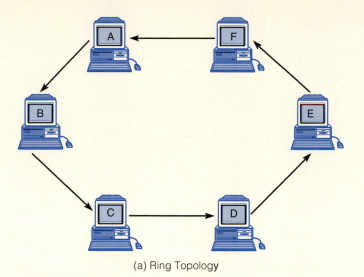

(a) Ring Topology

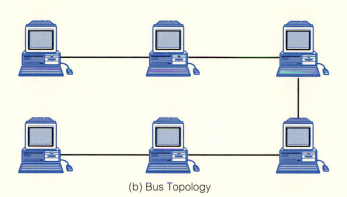

(b) Bus Topology

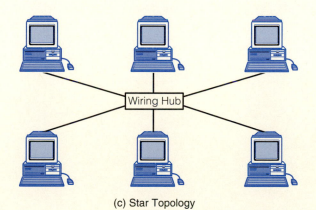

(c) Star Topology

Ring Topology

ring topology   A network
configuration commonly
used to implement local area
networks. The medium
forms a loop to which workstations are attached. Data is
transmitted from one station
to the next around the ring.
Generally the access protocol
is token passing.

active node   A node capable of sending or receiving
network messages.

inactive node   A node that
may be powered down and
is incapable of sending or receiving messages.

In a **ring topology** the medium forms a closed loop, and all stations are
connected to the loop or ring. We first look at the basics of a ring and then at
some specifics of two implementations.

On a ring, data is transmitted from node to node in one direction. Thus if
Node A in Figure 5-2 wants to send a message to Node F, the message is sent
from A to B, from B to C, from C to D, and so on, until it reaches Node F.
Usually Node F then sends an acknowledgment that the message was successfully received back to Node A, the originator of the message. The acknowledgment is sent from Node F to G, and then from G back to A, completing one journey around the loop.

Nodes attached to the ring may be active or inactive. An **active node** is
capable of sending or receiving network messages. An **inactive node** is incapable of sending or receiving network messages; for example, an inactive node
may be powered down. Naturally, nodes may go both from inactive to active
and from active to inactive. For example, when a worker leaves at night, she
might turn her workstation off, placing the workstation in an inactive state.
In the morning she powers up her system and brings it into the active state.
A failed or inactive network node must not cause the network to fail; an
overview of how such a network failure can be prevented is included later in
this chapter.

The most frequently used microcomputer ring network is a token-passing
ring. IBM's LAN approach has been widely adopted and conforms to the

Figure 5-2

A Token-Passing Ring
Configuration

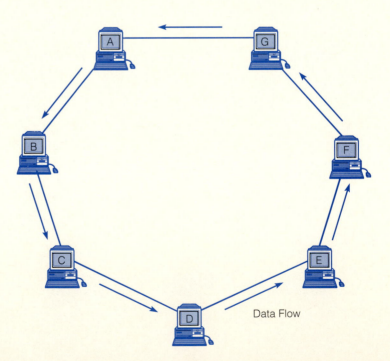

Data Flow

Institute of Electrical and Electronics Engineers (IEEE) 802.5 standard, so we describe it here. Realize, however, that we are only discussing the topology and media access control. The token-passing ring we are describing can be implemented using a variety of different network operating systems to include Novell Netware, Banyan Vines, and IBM's LAN Server.

As pointed out in Chapter 4 (Figure 4-7), in IBM's token-passing ring network, stations (nodes) are connected to a multistation access unit (MAU or MSAU). You can see that this configuration looks somewhat like the star configuration of Figure 5-1(c): The MAU forms the ring internally. Figure 5-3 shows the connection of two MAUs. IBM token-passing ring speeds are 4 and 16 Mbps using twisted-pair wires or fiber optic cable as the medium. Speeds of 100 Mbps are also now available. For best results at 16- and 100-Mbps speeds, you should use fiber optic cable or shielded twisted-pair wires. Unshielded twisted-pair wires have been used at 16 Mbps, but this medium is subject to signal disruption at high speeds. With technology improvements, unshielded twisted-pair wires may become better suited to high data transfer rates. IEEE 802.5 speeds are 1 and 4 Mbps, but you can expect these speeds to increase.

Another network that uses a ring topology is a high-speed metropolitan area LAN, which is designed to cover a wider geographical area than a typical LAN. The ANSI standard for this type of network is called the **Fiber Distributed Data Interface (FDDI)** standard. It uses fiber optics for the medium and spans distances of up to 200 kilometers at a speed of 100 Mbps. An alternative to FDDI is **Copper Distributed Data Interface (CDDI)**, which uses shielded or unshielded twisted-pair wires as the medium. As LAN workstations become more powerful and the volume of data transmission increases (perhaps due to the transmission of graphic and video images), high-speed LANs may be used to connect microcomputers in one department within a company. Currently one use for an FDDI LAN is as a backbone network connecting microcomputer LANs within a company complex or within a metropolitan area. A **backbone network**, illustrated in Figure 5-4, is used to interconnect other networks or to connect a cluster of network nodes.

Bus Topology

In a **bus topology**, illustrated in Figure 5-5(a), the medium consists of a single wire or cable to which nodes are attached. Unlike a ring, the ends of the bus are not connected. Instead the ends are terminated by a hardware device called a terminator, as we discussed in Chapter 4. A variation of a bus topology, illustrated in Figure 5-5(b), has spurs to the primary bus formed by interconnected minibuses. This variation of the bus topology is quite common.

As with ring topologies, several standards describe a bus implementation. The most common of these is an implementation originally known as Ethernet. **Ethernet** LAN specifications were originally proposed by Xerox Corporation in 1972. Soon thereafter Xerox was joined in establishing the Ethernet standard by Digital Equipment Corporation (DEC) and Intel Corporation. The

---

Institute of Electrical and Electronics Engineers (IEEE) A professional society that establishes and publishes documents and standards for data communications. IEEE has established several standards for local area networks, including the IEEE 802.3 and IEEE 802.5 standards for LAN technology.

Fiber Distributed Data Interface (FDDI) An ANSI LAN standard for fiber optic LANs spanning a distance of approximately 200 kilometers and providing speeds of 100 Mbps.

Copper Distributed Data Interface (CDDI) An ANSI LAN standard for twisted-pair-wire LANs providing speeds of 100 Mbps. An extension of the fiber distributed data interface LAN.

backbone network A network used to interconnect other networks or to connect a cluster of network nodes.

bus topology A communications medium for transmitting data or power. A local area network topology.

Ethernet A local area network implementation using the CSMA/CD protocol on a bus. The IEEE 802.3 standard is based on Ethernet. One of the popular local area network implementations.

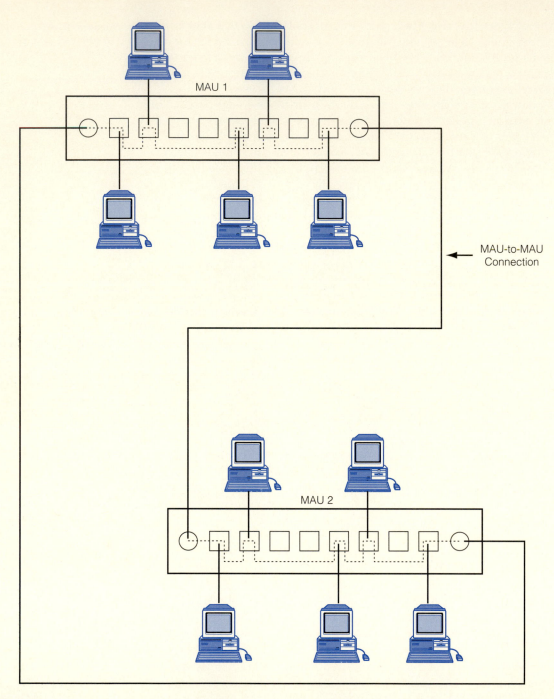

Figure 5-3

MAU Connection

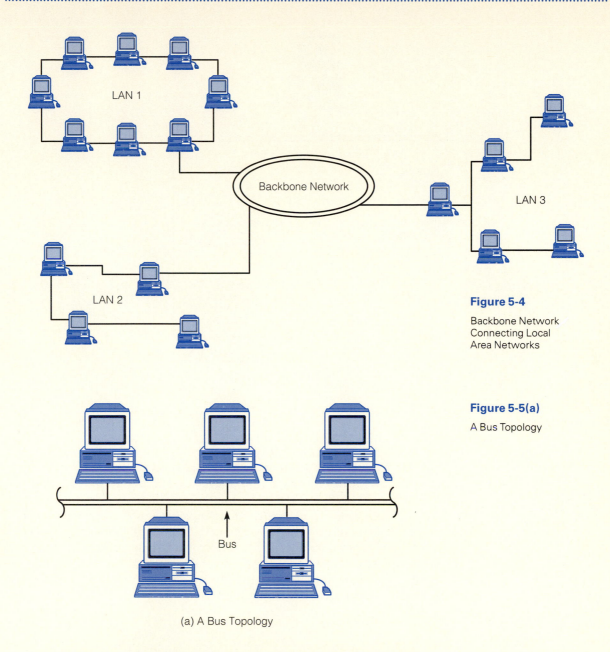

Figure 5-4

Backbone Network
Connecting Local
Area Networks

Figure 5-5(a)

A Bus Topology

(a) A Bus Topology

IEEE 802 Committee then developed the IEEE 802.3 standard, which encompasses most of the premises of the original Ethernet specification. Thus, the IEEE 802.3 standard is sometimes referred to as an Ethernet implementation. The IEEE 802.4 standard also proposes a bus technology. The primary difference between the two is the media access control protocol. The IEEE 802.3 standard specifies a contention protocol, and the 802.4 standard uses a token-passing protocol. Again, these protocols are covered later in this chapter.

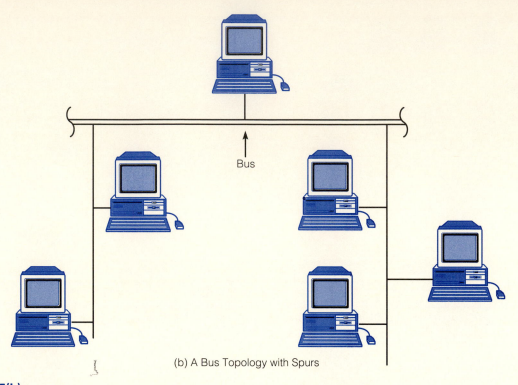

(b) A Bus Topology with Spurs

Figure 5-5(b)

A Bus Topology with Spurs

The common speeds of bus LANs are 1, 2.5, 5, and 10 Mbps. Versions of the IEEE 802.3 and 802.4 standards specify each of these speeds. Currently, 100-Mbps LANs are in fairly common use and standards for this speed are forthcoming. IEEE 802.3 and 802.4 media are either twisted-pair wires or coaxial cables. Very high speed bus architectures use twisted-pair wires, coaxial cables, or fiber optic cables as media. Fiber optic cables are also used for 802.3 LANs. However, the IEEE 802.3 and 802.4 standards have not included specifications for a fiber optic interface as of this writing. You can expect these standards to eventually encompass fiber optic cables. Ethernet technology has also been implemented using microwave radio as the medium.

star topology   A network topology using a central system to which all other nodes are connected. All data are transmitted to or through the central system.

star-wired LAN   A variation of star topology in which a wiring hub is used to form the connection between network nodes.

Star Topology

Figure 5-6 shows true **star topology**, which consists of a central computing node to which all other nodes are directly connected. This type of topology, however, is rare in microcomputer networks. A variation called a **star-wired LAN** has gained wide acceptance. In a star-wired LAN, a wiring hub is used to form the connection between network nodes. Two common star-wired LANs are known as ARCnet and StarLAN.

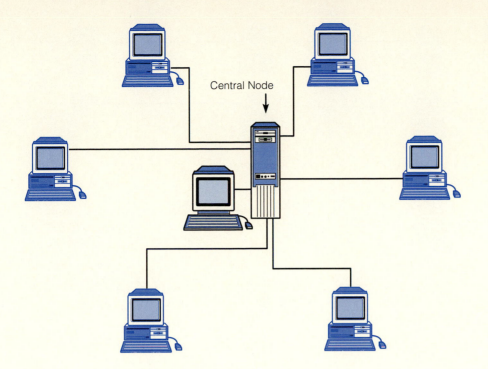

Figure 5-6

A Star Topology

Central Node

ARCnet technology was developed in the 1970s by Datapoint Corporation to form networks of their minicomputers. The technology was well developed when microcomputer LANs were evolving, and the technology was readily adopted. Because it has been so widely used, ARCnet has become a de facto microcomputer LAN standard and also has been submitted to the American National Standards Institute (ANSI) for formal standardization. An ARCnet configuration, illustrated in Figure 5-7, is a token-passing bus but does not conform to the IEEE 802.4 standard. As discussed in Chapter 4, ARCnet uses both active and passive hubs to connect network nodes. ARCnet speeds are 2.5 Mbps and 20 Mbps, and both speeds can be used in the same network. ARCnet media are usually either twisted-pair wires or coaxial cables. Fiber optic cables are also used for ARCnet LANs, primarily in higher-speed implementations.

StarLAN technology was developed by American Telephone and Telegraph (AT&T) Corporation. The topology was also adopted and marketed by several other companies and has been included as a low-cost, low-speed option in the IEEE 802.3 standard. Originally the StarLAN speed was 1 Mbps but today 10 Mbps implementations are also available. A StarLAN configuration is similar to the basic star topology (Figure 5-1(c)) in that each workstation is connected to a wiring hub. Note that the configuration is also similar to that of the ARCnet configuration (Figure 5-7). The primary medium used for StarLAN implementations is twisted-pair wires.

ARCnet   Local area network implementation based on Datapoint's attached resource computer network.

American National Standards Institute (ANSI) A U.S. standards-making agency.

StarLAN   A configuration similar to the basic star topology in that each workstation is connected to a wiring hub. The primary medium used for implementations is twisted-pair wires.

Figure 5-7(a)

ARCnet Bus Configuration

Maximum distance is
1000 feet

Figure 5-7(b)

ARCnet with Active
and Passive Hubs

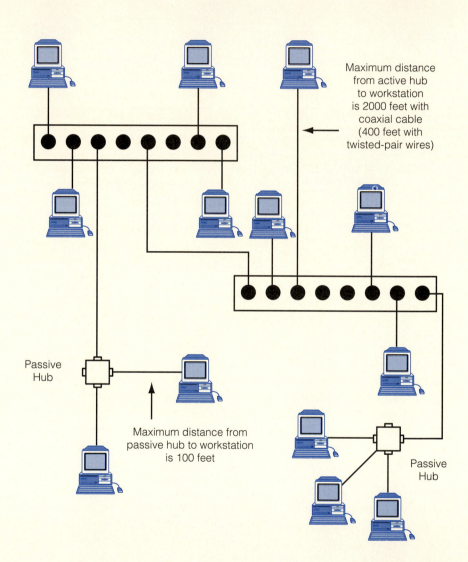

Maximum distance
from active hub
to workstation
is 2000 feet with
coaxial cable
(400 feet with
twisted-pair wires)

Passive
Hub

Maximum distance from
passive hub to workstation
is 100 feet

Passive
Hub

IEEE Project 802 Subcommittees

In addition to the IEEE 802.*n* standards described above, other IEEE 802 subcommittees are formulating standards. The subcommittees and their objectives are described below.

802.1 — High-Level Interface The high-level interface subcommittee addresses matters relating to network architecture, network management, network interconnection, and all other issues related to the OSI layers above the data link layer, which are the network, transport, session, presentation, and application layers.

802.2 — Logical Link Control IEEE has divided the OSI data link layer into two sublayers: **Logical Link Control (LLC)** and media access control (MAC). The MAC sublayer implements protocols such as token passing or CSMA/CD. Figure 5-8 illustrates the relationship between the LLC and the MAC sublayers. The objective of the LLC is to provide a consistent, transparent interface to the MAC layer, so the network layers above the data link layer are able to function correctly regardless of the MAC protocol.

Logical Link Control (LLC) A sublayer of the OSI reference model data link layer. The logical link control forms the interface between the network layer and the media access control protocols.

802.3 — CSMA/CD The **IEEE 802.3 standard** covers a variety of CSMA/CD architectures that are generally based on Ethernet. Several alternatives are available under this standard. Some of these are:

IEEE 802.3 standard A standard that covers a variety of CSMA/CD architectures that are generally based on Ethernet.

1. 1Base5 is a 1-Mbps baseband medium with a maximum segment length of 500 meters. The segment length is the length of cable that can be used without repeaters to amplify the signal. This standard encompasses implementations commonly known as StarLAN.

2. 10Base5 is a 10-Mbps baseband medium with a maximum segment length of 500 meters.

3. 10Base2 is a 10-Mbps baseband medium with a maximum segment length of 200 meters. The cable used in this implementation is commonly called Thinnet or Cheapernet.

4. 10BaseT is a 10-Mbps baseband medium with twisted-pair wires as the medium.

5. 10Broad36 is a 10-Mbps broadband medium with a 3600-meter segment length.

You may infer from this nomenclature that, in general:

- The initial number represents the speed of the medium in millions of bits per second.

- The "base" or "broad" designator represents baseband or broadband, respectively.

- With one exception, the last number represents the segment length of the medium in hundreds of meters.

Figure 5-8

LLC and MAC Sublayers of
the OSI Data Link Layer

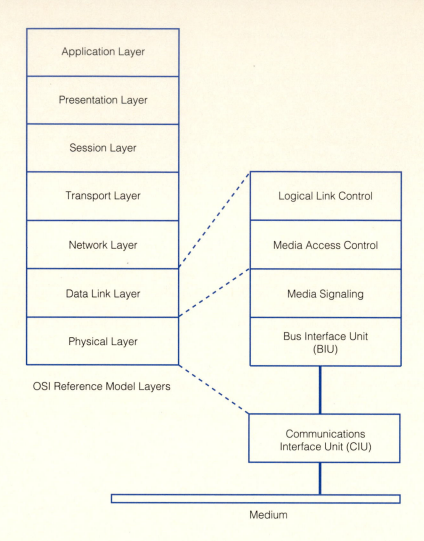

OSI Reference Model Layers

IEEE 802.4 standard A
subcommittee that sets
standards for token bus
networks.

802.4 — Token Bus   The **IEEE 802.4 standard** subcommittee sets standards for token bus networks. The standard describes how the network is initialized, how new stations can insert themselves into the set of nodes receiving the token, how to recover if the token is lost, and how node priority can be established. The standard also describes the format of the message frames.

IEEE 802.5 standard A
subcommittee that sets
standards for token-ring
networks.

802.5 — Token Ring   The **IEEE 802.5 standard** subcommittee sets standards for token-ring networks. The standard describes essentially the same functions as those described by the token bus network.

802.6 — Metropolitan Area Networks (MANs)   The FDDI family of technologies is not the only MAN proposal. The IEEE 802 LAN standards committee has also developed specifications, IEEE 802.6, for a MAN. The IEEE 802.6 standard has also been adopted by ANSI. The standard is also referred to as the distributed queue dual bus (DQDB) standard.

Bus A, Unidirectional

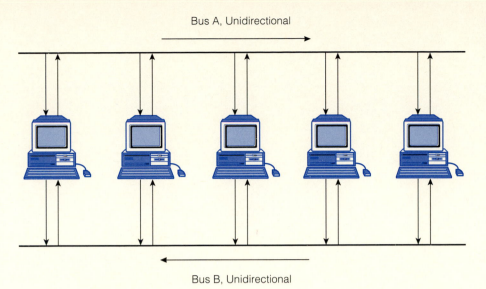

Bus B, Unidirectional

Figure 5-9

ANSI Distributed Queue
Dual Bus LAN

As the name DQDB indicates, the architecture uses two buses. Each bus is unidirectional, meaning that data is transmitted in one direction on one bus and in the other direction on the second bus, as illustrated in Figure 5-9. Each node must therefore be attached to both buses. The specification also allows for a variation called a looped bus. The looped bus still uses two one-direction buses; however, each bus forms a closed loop as illustrated in Figure 5-10. Several speeds are defined in the standard. Speeds are dependent on the medium used. With coaxial cable the speed is 45 Mbps; the speed is 156 Mbps over fiber optic cable. Distances up to 200 miles are supported. This subcommittee sets standards for networks that can cover a wide area and operate at high speed. Distances of up to 200 miles and speeds on the order of 100 Mbps are being considered for metropolitan area networks. A metropolitan area network could transmit voice and video in addition to data.

802.7 — Broadband Technical Advisory Group   This group provides guidance and technical expertise to other groups that are establishing broadband LAN standards, such as the 802.3 subcommittee for 10Broad36.

802.8 — Fiber Optic Technical Advisory Group   This group provides guidance and technical expertise to other groups that are establishing standards for LANs using fiber optic cable.

802.9 — Integrated Data and Voice Networks   This committee sets standards for networks that carry both voice and data. Specifically, it is setting standards for interfaces to the **Integrated Services Digital Networks (ISDNs)**.

802.11 — Wireless LANs   This committee is expected to issue its findings in mid-1994. It is expected that the standards will cover multiple transmission methods to include infrared light, as well as a variety of broadcast

Integrated Services Digital Network (ISDN)   The integration of voice and data transmission (and other formats such as video and graphics images) over a digital transmission network. A network proposed by numerous common carriers.

Direction of
Data Flow

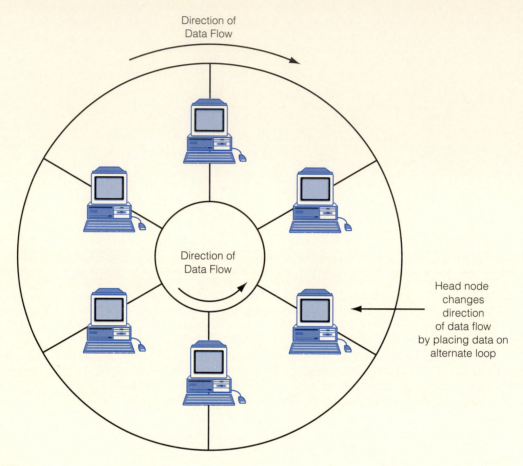

Direction of
Data Flow

Head node
changes
direction
of data flow
by placing data on
alternate loop

Figure 5-10

ANSI Looped Bus LAN

frequencies to include spread spectrum radiowaves and microwaves. Thus, it is expected that many of the existing wireless implementations will be covered under the standards proposed.

The ANSI Fiber Distributed Data Interface (FDDI) Standard

Two major uses have been suggested for high-speed LANs. The obvious one is the high-speed exchange of data among computers located within a large urban area. Frequently, companies have several offices distributed throughout a large metropolitan area, and a MAN will allow computers in these locations to exchange large amounts of data almost instantly. The second purpose is as a backbone network to interconnect distributed LANs. This is illustrated in Figure 5-4.

ANSI originally established the fiber distributed data interface (FDDI) for a high-speed LAN using fiber optic cable. The CDDI extension uses twisted-pair wires as the medium. The FDDI is similar to the metropolitan area network (MAN) being proposed by the IEEE.

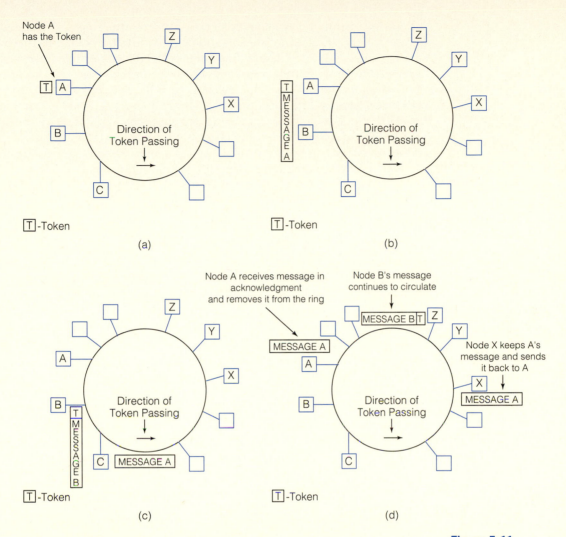

Figure 5-11

Message Passing in an FDDI LAN

The FDDI specifications call for a token ring LAN operating at a speed of 100 Mbps over distances up to 200 kilometers. As the name implies, the medium is fiber optic cable. The maximum cable segment allowed without repeaters is 2 kilometers. The 200-kilometer distance can be attained by connecting 100 such segments. Up to 1000 nodes can be connected to the ring. With a LAN spanning this distance, it is not efficient to have only one message on the ring at one time. Multiple messages may be circulating at a given time. The protocol for doing this is as follows: Only one token circulates around the line. When a station receives the token, such as Node A in Figure 5-11(a), it removes the token from the ring and transmits its message. At the end of its message, A appends the token, as illustrated in Figure 5-11(b). The next node, Node B, sees the token and can piggy-back a message onto the existing message. Node B then appends the token onto the message as illustrated in Figure 5-11(c). A's message continues to circulate around the ring until it gets to the recipient, Node X. X returns the message to A as an acknowledgment, and A removes its message from the ring as illustrated in Figure 5-11(d). The specification also allows a node to transmit multiple messages in succession. A transmit time limit is established during which a node is allowed to send multiple messages while it holds the token.

Two addressing modes are allowed in an FDDI network. One mode uses a 15-bit address and the other uses a 46-bit address. The standard does not, however, stipulate the exact format of addresses. The FDDI LAN can be used as a backbone network to connect multiple LANs, as a high-speed LAN connecting large computing systems, and as a high-speed document delivery system for office automation and graphics applications.

DATA LINK AND MEDIA ACCESS CONTROL PROTOCOLS

The physical layer of the OSI reference model describes the medium, the connectors required to attach workstations and servers to the medium, and the representation of signals using the medium, such as voltage levels for baseband transmission or frequencies for broadband transmission.

Once connected to the medium, a network node must have the ability to send and receive network messages. This function is described by the data link layer of the OSI reference mode. A convention, or protocol, must exist to define how this function is accomplished. The method by which a LAN workstation is able to gain control of the medium and transmit a message is called a media access control (MAC) protocol. The MAC protocol is implemented in LANs as one of two sublayers of the OSI reference model's data link layer. The other sublayer is called the logical link control (LLC) sublayer. We first look more closely at the functions provided by a data link protocol.

Data Link Protocols

In general, a data link protocol establishes the rules for gaining access to the medium and for exchanging messages. To do this the protocol describes several aspects of the message-exchange process. Five of the most important aspects are:

  delineation of data
  error control
  addressing
  transparency
  code independence

Delineation of Data   A data link protocol must define or delineate where the data portion of the transmitted message begins and ends. You may recall from the discussion of the OSI reference model in the Introduction that each layer may add data to the message it receives from the layers above it. The data link layer is no exception to this. Some of the characters or bits it adds to the message may include line control information, error detection data, and so on. When these fields are added, a data link protocol must provide a way to distinguish among the various pieces of data. This can be accomplished in two basic ways: by framing the data with certain control characters or by using a standard message format wherein a data segment is identified by its position within the message.

The framing technique is used in two types of data link protocols: asynchronous transmission and binary synchronous transmission. These protocols are common to WANs and are discussed in Chapter 10.

Many of today's LANs use a standard message format for sending data. For example, an Ethernet message has several distinct parts, as illustrated in Figure 5-12. The message frame begins with a 64-bit synchronization pattern. The synchronization bits give the receiving node an opportunity to sense the incoming message and establish time or synchronization with the sending node. The message is a stream of continuous bits, so it is important that the receiving node is able to clock the bits in as they arrive. The IEEE 802.3 standard uses a 64-bit synchronization pattern; however, the standard divides this into a 56-bit group and an 8-bit group. The first 56 bits are for synchronization, and the 8 bits that follow signal the start of the frame and thus indicate where the first bit of the remaining frame can be found. The next two fields are the addresses of the destination node and the sending node. Each address is 48 bits long.

The 16-bit field type is a control field. In the IEEE 802.3 standard, this represents the length of the data field that follows. The length is expressed as the number of octets of data. An **octet** is a group of 8 bits. If the message is short, extra bits may be added to make the entire message long enough to allow the message to clear the length of the network before the sending node stops transmitting. This is essential to ensure correct transmission. The frame check sequence, a 32-bit cyclic redundancy check (CRC) field as illustrated in Figure 5-12, provides for error detection.

octet A group of eight bits used in bit synchronous protocols. Data, regardless of its code, is treated as octets.

Error Control Error control is used to detect transmission errors. Common error-detection techniques are parity and cyclic redundancy checks. These techniques are discussed in Chapter 2.

Addressing Communication between two network nodes is accomplished through an addressing scheme. Network addressing is similar to addressing we use for postal mail. A postal address is a hierarchical addressing scheme, with the hierarchy being individual recipient, street address, city,

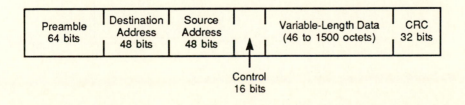

Figure 5-12

The Ethernet Message Format

state, country, and zip code. Networks also use a hierarchical addressing scheme, with the hierarchy being application, network node, and network. Like postal addresses, network addresses must be unique; otherwise, ambiguity arises as to which node is the recipient. At this point, we are concerned only with network node addressing, not network or application addressing.

Each network has a specific way in which it forms station addresses. In Ethernet and the IBM token ring, each address is 48 bits long. Each Ethernet or IBM token-ring LAN adapter card has its address set by the manufacturer. This ensures that all nodes, regardless of location, have a unique address. In ARCnet a node address is an 8-bit entity, and the LAN administrator typically sets the node address through switches on the LAN adapter. On a LAN, node source and destination addresses typically are included in the headers of messages being transmitted.

transparency　The ability to send any bit string as data in a message. The data bits are not interpreted as control characters.

Transparency　When concerned with data link protocols, **transparency** refers to the ability of the data link to transmit any bit combination. In the binary synchronous data link protocol (shown in Figure 5-13) the start-of-text and end-of-text framing characters have special meaning. These characters can be sent as part of the data only when special considerations are made. Without these special considerations, the protocol is not transparent. We want protocols to be transparent because they can be used to transfer binary data such as object programs as well as text data. The Ethernet message illustrated in Figure 5-12 does provide transparency: No bit patterns in the data field can cause confusion in the message.

code independence　The ability to successfully transmit data regardless of the data code, such as ASCII or EBCDIC.

Code Independence　**Code independence** means that any data code, such as ASCII or EBCDIC, can be transmitted. These codes use different bit patterns to represent many of the characters. Code independence is important because often you must communicate with or through computers having a data code different from that of your computer. In the Ethernet protocol this is accomplished by sending data in groups of 8 bits called octets. The 8 bits are not tied to any particular code, and thus any code can be used. If your computer uses a 7-bit code, such as one of the two ASCII codes, the only requirement is that the total number of bits transmitted be divisible by 8. Thus, if you are sending 100 7-bit characters, the total number of bits in the

Figure 5-13

Framing in the Binary Synchronous Data Link Protocol

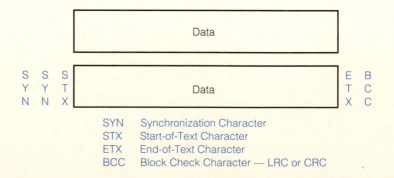

SYN　Synchronization Character
STX　Start-of-Text Character
ETX　End-of-Text Character
BCC　Block Check Character — LRC or CRC

data portion must be 704. The last 4 bits are added to pad out to an integral number of octets (700/8 = 87.5, and an integral number of octets must be transmitted; thus 704 bits are necessary because 704 is a multiple of 8).

MAC Protocols

LAN technology adheres to two primary data link protocols: token passing and contention. In the IEEE 802 standards, the data link layer is divided into the two sublayers of logical link control (LLC) and MAC. The LLC provides the functions of flow control, message sequencing, message acknowledgment, and error checking. The MAC layer describes token passing and contention.

Contention   In a true **contention** MAC protocol, each network node has equal access to the medium. Although variations of this protocol exist, essentially it works like this:

1. Each node monitors the medium to see whether a message is being transmitted.
2. If no message is detected, any node can begin a transmission.

The act of listening to the medium for a message is called carrier sensing, because when a message is being transmitted, a carrier signal is present. Several nodes can have messages to send. Each of them may detect a quiet medium, and each may begin to transmit at one time. The ability for several nodes to access a medium that is not carrying a message is called **multiple access**.

If two or more nodes begin to transmit at the same time, a **collision** is said to occur. Multiple simultaneous transmissions cause the messages to interfere with each other and become garbled. It is imperative that collisions be detected and that recovery be effected. When a collision occurs, the messages will not be transmitted successfully. On detecting a collision, the sending nodes need to resend their messages. If both nodes immediately attempt to retransmit their messages, another collision might occur. Therefore, each node waits a small, randomly selected interval before attempting to retransmit. This reduces the probability of another collision.

There is only a small time interval during which a collision can occur. For example, suppose that two nodes at the extremities of a 1000-meter bus network have a message to send and that the medium is not being used. The collision interval is the time it takes for a signal to travel the length of the cable. Because the signal travels at the speed of light, the collision window is the time it takes for the signal to travel 1000 meters, the signal's propagation delay. The propagation delay is approximately 5 nanoseconds per meter. For a 1000-meter segment, the maximum propagation delay is therefore approximately 5 microseconds (5 millionths of a second). Although this interval is small, collisions can still occur.

The media access control technique just described is known as **Carrier Sense with Multiple Access and Collision Detection (CSMA/CD)**. It is the most common of the access strategies for bus architectures. The CSMA/CD

contention   A convention whereby devices obtain control of a communications link. In contention mode, devices compete for control of the line either by transmitting directly on an idle line or by issuing a request for line control.

multiple access   The ability for several nodes to access a medium that is not carrying a message.

collision   In a CSMA/CD media access control protocol, a collision occurs when two stations attempt to send a message at the same time. The messages interfere with each other, so correct communication is not possible.

Carrier Sense with Multiple Access and Collision Detection (CSMA/CD)   A media access control technique that attempts to detect collisions and is the most common of the access strategies for bus architectures.

TABLE 5-1   CSMA/CD Media Access Control Protocol

1. Listen to the medium to see whether a message is being transmitted.

2. If the medium is quiet, transmit message. If the medium is busy, wait for the signal to clear and then transmit.

3. If a collision occurs, wait for the signal to clear, wait a random interval, and then retransmit.

media access control protocol, sometimes referred to as listen-before-talk, is summarized in Table 5-1. You should note that the CSMA/CD protocol is a broadcast protocol. All workstations on the network listen to the medium and accept the message. Each message has a destination address. Only a workstation having an address equal to the destination address can use the message. Using a broadcast technique makes it easy for new workstations to be added to and removed from the network.

CSMA/CD is known as a **fair protocol**, meaning that each node has equal access to the medium. In a pure CSMA/CD scheme, no one node has priority over another. Variations of this protocol exist that give one workstation priority over another and minimize the likelihood of collisions. One of these protocol variations divides time into transmission slots. The length of a slot is the time it takes a message to travel the length of the medium. Nodes on the network are synchronized, and each node can begin a transmission only at the beginning of its allocated time slot. This protocol has proven to be more efficient for networks with lots of message traffic.

A variation of CSMA/CD is **Carrier Sense with Multiple Access and Collision Avoidance (CSMA/CA)**. This protocol attempts to avoid collisions that are possible with the CSMA/CD protocol. Collisions are avoided because each node is given a wait time before it can begin transmitting. For example, suppose there are 100 nodes on the network and the propagation delay time for the network is 1 millisecond. Node 1 can transmit after the medium has been idle for 1 millisecond. Node 2 must wait 2 milliseconds before attempting to transmit, Node 3 must wait 3 milliseconds, and so on. Each node, therefore, has a specific time slot during which it can transmit, and no collisions will occur. However, the node with the lowest priority time slot may experience long delays in getting access to the medium.

Token Passing   The second major medium access control protocol is **token passing**. It is used on both bus and ring topologies. Token passing is a round-robin protocol in which each node gets an equal opportunity to transmit. An overview of the token-passing protocol is given in Table 5-2. With token passing, the right to transmit is granted by a token that is passed from one node to another. Remember that a token is a predefined bit pattern that is recognized by each node. In a ring topology, the token is passed from one node to the adjacent node. On a token-passing bus, the order of token passing is determined by the address of each node. The token is passed in either ascending or descending address order. If it is passed in descending order,

fair protocol   A protocol in which each node has equal access to the medium.

Carrier Sense with Multiple Access and Collision Avoidance (CSMA/CA)   A media access control technique that attempts to avoid collisions.

token passing   A media access control protocol in which a string of bits called the token is distributed among the network nodes. A computer that receives the token is allowed to transmit data onto the network. Only the stations receiving a token can transmit. Token passing is implemented on ring and bus LANs.

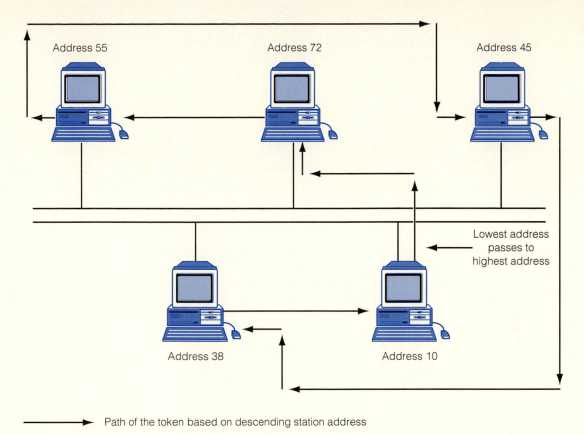

Address 55   Address 72   Address 45

Lowest address
passes to
highest address

Address 38   Address 10

Path of the token based on descending station address

Figure 5-14

Token-Passing Bus

TABLE 5-2   Token-Passing Media Access Control Protocol

1. Wait for transmit token.

2. If transmit token is received and there is no message to send, send the token to
   the next node.

3. If transmit token is received and there is a message to send, then:
   a) transmit message
   b) wait for acknowledgment
   c) when acknowledgment is received, pass token to the next node

the lowest address station passes the token to the node with the highest
address. The routing of a token from high to low addresses in a token-passing
bus is illustrated in Figure 5-14.

When a node obtains the token, it has two options: It can transmit a
message or, if it has no message to send, it can pass the token to its neighbor
node. If the node has a message to transmit, it keeps the token by changing
the format of the message header from "token" to "transmit" and sends the
message. The message recipient keeps the message and then transmits it back
onto the network. The message eventually arrives back at the sending node.

When a node receives the message it sent, it accepts the message as an acknowledgment that the message was successfully received. The transmitting node then activates the token by sending it to the next node. The token-passing protocol does not allow a node to monopolize the token and the network. Note that, unlike the CSMA/CD protocol, the token-passing protocol does not allow collisions to occur.

token-passing ring   A configuration that allows recovery from a failed node or a transmission error. It does this by designating one node as the active monitor and the others as standby monitors.

Token-Passing Ring   In a **token-passing ring**, the token can become lost if a node holding the token fails or if transmission errors occur. To allow recovery from this, one node is designated as the active monitor. Other nodes are designated as standby monitors. The active monitor periodically issues a message indicating that it is active. The standby monitors accept this status and remain in standby mode. If the active monitor message fails to appear on time, a standby monitor assumes the active monitor role. A major function of the active monitor is to ensure that the token is circulating. If the token does not arrive within a certain amount of time, the active monitor generates a new token. This technique is guaranteed to work because the token transmit time is very predictable.

token-passing bus   A protocol where a token is passed from one workstation to another based on station addresses.

Token-Passing Bus   Token passing is slightly different on a **token-passing bus**. On a bus, the token is passed from one workstation to another based on station addresses. As mentioned earlier, the token can be passed in ascending or descending address order. Let us assume that the token is passed in descending address order so the station with the lowest address forwards the token to the station with the highest address. This token passing scheme is illustrated in Figure 5-14. Such a protocol must allow for new workstations to be inserted and active ones deactivated.

Suppose a station attempts to send the token to the next station, and the next station has been shut down. Recovery must be possible when a station goes from active to inactive status. For example, when a sending station does not receive the token back in a prescribed interval, the sending station transmits the token to its neighbor again. If a second failure occurs, the sending station assumes that the neighboring station is inactive and issues a message, asking for the address of the next station. The "who is next" message contains the address of the unresponsive station. The successor of the failed station recognizes the address in the "who is next" message as its predecessor station and responds. If the successor node has also failed, another "who is next" message is then sent out with the entire address range of the LAN. If any other stations are active, they respond.

Allowance also is made in the token-passing bus protocol for new stations to enter the LAN. Periodically stations issue a "solicit successor" message. This message contains the sending station's address and the address of that station's current successor node. Stations receiving this message inspect the addresses of the sender and the successor. If a station has an address that falls between these two addresses, it responds to the message. Two stations can respond at the same time, in which case a collision occurs as in CSMA/CD, and collision resolution is effected. This allows an orderly process for insertion of new stations.

MAKING THE DECISIONS

Without even considering the network operating system software alternatives, the number of alternatives available in choosing a LAN can be overwhelming. You have three basic conducted media choices or three choices in the new wireless medium technology, three major topology choices, two primary media access control choices, and a wide variety of vendor choices. The issue then becomes which is the best configuration for your company and applications. If one clear option were superior for all applications and for all users, the choice would be easy. However, applications vary significantly with respect to the number of nodes, number of concurrent users, data access needs, distance spanned, and budget. Next, we explore tradeoffs you can consider when making LAN choices.

Token Passing and CSMA/CD Compared

The pros and cons of the token-passing and CSMA/CD protocols are summarized in Table 5-3. Note that each protocol has advantages and disadvantages. In practice both have been noted to have good performance.

TABLE 5-3   MAC Protocol Comparison

Token Passing	CSMA/CD
Equal access for all nodes	Equal access for all nodes
Predictable access window	Access window can be unpredictable
Maximum wait time to transmit is token circulation time	Maximum wait time to transmit is unpredictable and depends on collisions
Average wait time to transmit is predictable — half the maximum circulation time	Average wait time to transmit is unpredictable
Network congestion does not adversely affect network efficiency	Network congestion may result in collisions and reduce network efficiency
A node needs to wait for the token before being able to transmit	A node may be able to transmit immediately
One node cannot monopolize the network	One node may be able to monopolize the network
Large rings can result in long delays before a node obtains a ring	A node can transmit when the network is quiet
Consistent performance for large, busy networks	Unpredictable performance for large, busy networks due to possibility of collisions

Topology and Protocol Tradeoffs

We consider the three primary combinations of topology and protocol: CSMA/CD bus, token bus, and token ring. The StarLAN model LAN is covered under the IEEE 802.3 standard, and its characteristics are similar to that of the CSMA/CD bus. As of this writing, wireless LANs are so new that tradeoff data regarding their use is not readily available. When specifics are required, we will use popular implementations as examples: Ethernet or an IEEE 802.3 implementation for CSMA/CD buses, ARCnet for token buses, and IBM's token ring. Table 5-4 summarizes the topologies and protocols, which are described in the following sections.

CSMA/CD Buses   Most CSMA/CD bus implementations use either twisted-pair wires or coaxial cable. Less frequently, fiber optic cable and microwave radio are used. As previously stated, the IEEE 802.3 standard has not yet set the standard for using fiber optic cable. Common speeds for these LANs are 1, 10, and 100 Mbps, with 10 Mbps being the most common. The distances spanned by these networks vary, but the IEEE 802.3 standard, which covers several implementations, specifies 925, 2500, and 3600 meters. The number of supported nodes also varies. In the IEEE standard, one implementation allows 150 nodes and another allows 500. The number of nodes allowed is a hardware-based limit and addresses the issue of connectivity. The network operating system and performance needs also may limit the number of network nodes. Some network operating systems restrict the number of network nodes. We discuss network operating systems in Chapter 6.

A network's performance is a critical factor in its productivity. Performance depends on both the hardware and the software. There are many different combinations of hardware and software, so we consider the general outlook for CSMA/CD bus systems. The major concern people have voiced regarding CSMA/CD bus performance is its capacity under load. As the number of users and the number of messages being sent increase, so does the probability of collisions. If the collision rate is high, the effectiveness of the LAN decreases. When the LAN is busy, the efficiency may drop, and you might lose effectiveness just when you need it most. LAN vendors and researchers have run numerous tests to gauge the effect of high collision rates. Under these tests the performance characteristics did not drop appreciably. However, the true test of performance comes from actual use. Under light load conditions, access to the medium and the ability to transmit are good; there is little waiting time to transmit. Performance under heavy loads can be unpredictable.

Token Buses and Token Rings   We discuss these two implementations together because their media access control characteristics are similar. ARCnet can be implemented in a bus or a star-wired topology. ARCnet operates at speeds of 2.5 Mbps on twisted-pair wires, coaxial cable, or fiber optic cable. At this writing, a 20-Mbps capability has been introduced, but availability is limited. Both speeds can be used in the same LAN, because the 20-Mbps cards can work at either speed. The maximum distance that can be spanned

TABLE 5-4   **LAN Topology and Protocol Summary**

	IEEE 802.3 or Ethernet	IBM's Token Ring	ARCnet	StarLAN
Speed	10 or 100 Mbps	4, 16, or 100 Mbps	2.5 or 20 Mbps	1 Mbps
Medium	Twisted-pair wires, coaxial cable, or fiber optic cable	Twisted-pair wires	Twisted-pair wires or coaxial cable	Twisted-pair wires
Distance	500 meters for thick cable, 185 meters for thinnet cable segments; 5 segments can be connected with repeaters to give maximum lengths of 2500 and 925 meters	366 meters for the main ring; can be extended to 750 meters with repeaters and to 4000 meters with fiber optic cable	6110 meters; maximum distance between active hubs is 62 meters and between passive hubs is 31 meters	500 meters
Number of Stations	802.3-100 per thick cable segment, 30 per thinnet segment Ethernet-1024	260	255	Not stated by 1Base5 standard (early StarLANs set limit at 50)
Standards	IEEE 802.3	IEEE 802.5	De facto (submitted for approval as an ANSI standard)	IEEE 802.3 1Base5
Cost for NIC and Connectors Only	Low (approx. $100 per station)	High (approx. $250 per station)	Low (approx. $75 per station)	Low (approx. $100 per station)

by ARCnet is 20,000 feet (6110 meters). An example of an ARCnet configuration is shown in Figure 5-7.

IBM's token ring operates at 4, 16, or 100 Mbps. Stations on the LAN connect to a multistation access unit (MAU). A typical MAU contains ports for eight workstations plus an input and output connector to another MAU. Like all LANs, a token-passing ring has limitations on distance and number of stations. The maximum distance spanned by a ring is 770 meters and the maximum number of nodes allowed is 260. These limitations can be extended by setting up two or more token-ring LANs and connecting them with a device called a bridge. When LANs are connected in this way, a user on one ring can communicate with users or devices on another connected ring; from the user's perspective the interconnected rings appear as a single LAN.

Predictability is the key of token LAN performance. Because the medium is accessed through the possession of a token, and because each station is assured of receiving the token, you can predict the maximum and average times needed for a station to transmit its message. The problem of collision, inherent in contention LANs, does not exist in a token-passing LAN. When network traffic is light, a station may need to wait longer than a station on a contention bus; however, when network traffic is heavy, the token-passing station may wait less time. Regardless of the wait time, a station is assured that it can transmit in a predictable amount of time. The maximum time a station must wait is given by

$$T_{Max} = (\text{number of stations} - 1) *$$
$$(\text{message transmit time} + \text{token-passing time})$$

Thus, a station that has just passed the token to its neighbor may become ready to send a message. That station must wait until the token comes back around. The worst-case scenario would be that every other station has a message to transmit. Thus, the station must wait on all other stations in the ring to transmit their messages and pass the token. On average, a station ready to transmit must wait for half the other stations.

Of the common microcomputer LAN implementations, token-passing solutions provide both the lowest and the highest cost solutions. In general, ARCnet LANs have a lower per station cost than Ethernet LANs, and Ethernet LANs have a lower per station cost than token rings. This statement is based on the cost of the hardware—LAN adapters, MAUs, wiring hubs, cables, connectors, and wiring. Because prices fluctuate over time and from one vendor to another, you should verify these costs.

SUMMARY

A LAN topology is the pattern used to lay out the LAN. The main LAN topologies are a bus, a ring, and a star. The medium access control protocol is the way in which a station interfaces with the medium. The main media access control protocols for LANs are carrier sense with multiple access and collision detection (CSMA/CD) and token passing. CSMA/CD is used on bus topologies and star topologies. Token passing is used on bus and ring topologies.

A variety of standards covering medium access control, LAN topology, medium distances, and the maximum number of LAN nodes have been developed. The two principal standards organizations for LANs are IEEE and ANSI. Standards have resulted in open architectures. With open architectures, a variety of manufacturers can develop products that will interoperate on a LAN. As a consequence LAN administrators usually have several product choices, and competition among product developers leads to product innovation and lower prices.

KEY TERMS

active node, *172*

American National Standards Institute (ANSI), *177*

ARCnet, *177*

backbone network, *173*

bus topology, *173*

Carrier Sense with Multiple Access and Collision Avoidance (CSMA/CA), *188*

Carrier Sense with Multiple Access and Collision Detection (CSMA/CD), *187*

code independence, *186*

collision, *187*

contention, *187*

Copper Distributed Data Interface (CDDI), *173*

Ethernet, *173*

fair protocol, *188*

Fiber Distributed Data Interface (FDDI), *173*

IEEE 802.3 standard, *179*

IEEE 802.4 standard, *180*

IEEE 802.5 standard, *180*

inactive node, *172*

Institute of Electrical and Electronics Engineers (IEEE), *173*

Integrated Services Digital Network (ISDN), *181*

Logical Link Control (LLC), *179*

Media Access Control (MAC) protocol, *170*

multiple access, *187*

network topology, *170*

octet, *185*

ring topology, *172*

star topology, *176*

StarLAN, *177*

star-wired LAN, *176*

token passing, *188*

token-passing bus, *190*

token-passing ring, *190*

transparency, *186*

REVIEW QUESTIONS

1. What is a topology?

2. What are the primary LAN topologies?

3. What is a media access control protocol?

4. What are the primary LAN media access control protocols?

5. What are the IEEE 802.3, 802.4, and 802.5 standards?

6. What is the ANSI fiber distributed data interface (FDDI)? How does it differ from the CDDI?

7. What function is performed by a multistation access unit (MAU)?

8. List four items that are specified in the IEEE LAN standards.

9. Compare ARCnet and Ethernet.

10. Compare Ethernet and token-passing ring LANs.

PROBLEMS AND EXERCISES

1. The ALOHAnet, an early example of a local area network, was developed by the University of Hawaii. Research the literature to find the details of this network's architecture.

2. What are some of the uses of a metropolitan area network such as the fiber distributed data interface?

3. What are the advantages and disadvantages of LAN standards?

4. Suppose you had a LAN application in which guaranteed access to the medium within a specified time was essential. Which media access control protocol would you choose? Justify your choice.

REFERENCES

Hurwicz, Mike. "The Fastest Gun in the LAN World." *Network World*, Volume 9, Number 50, December 14, 1992.

Keiffer, Tom, Leslie Richey, and Tim Christian. "Charting Network Topologies." *LAN Technology*, Volume 5, Number 3, March 1989.

Ough, Steven T., Carol G. Rosaire III, and Harvey J. Roth. "Analyzing FDDI as a Backbone." *LAN Technology*, Volume 8, Number 6, June 1992.

Stallings, William. *Handbook of Computer-Communications Standards: Local Network Standards*. New York: Macmillan, 1987.

6

LAN System Software

CHAPTER OBJECTIVES

After studying this chapter you should be able to:

- Describe the functions of LAN system software
- Discuss the functions performed by LAN workstation software
- Explain important characteristics of LAN server software
- Describe how a spooler works
- Explain the importance of making backups
- List backup options and elements of backup procedures
- Discuss the software requirements for shared data and application usage
- Describe several types of software licenses

*I*n Chapter 4 you examined the details of the LAN hardware system. In this chapter you will learn about the software system that drives the hardware. We separate LAN software into two classes: workstation system software and server system software. The success of the LAN depends on how these two software classes and the application software interact in setting up the communications capability.

GENERIC FUNCTIONS OF LAN SYSTEM SOFTWARE

Application software is designed to solve business problems. It is assisted in this goal by supporting system software such as the operating system (OS), database management systems (DBMSs), and data communications systems. Like all system software, LAN system software is essentially an extension of the operating system. It carries out hardware-oriented LAN tasks, such as interfacing to the medium, and input/output (I/O) oriented tasks, such as directing print jobs and disk read and write requests to a server. A few operating systems are designed specifically to carry out LAN server tasks and have these functions integrated with other OS tasks such as the user interface and job, file, and memory management. Other LAN system software implementations operate in partnership with a general-purpose OS such as UNIX or OS/2. The general-purpose OS is responsible for providing much of the user interface and job, file, and memory management. The LAN extensions are responsible for implementing the LAN-oriented tasks such as the LAN interface and file and printer server functions.

System software is designed to insulate applications from hardware details such as I/O and memory management. System software provides an interface through which the applications can request hardware services. The applications make requests for services, and system software contains the logic to carry out those requests for a specific type of hardware. For example, an application makes disk access requests independent of the type of disk drive being used. A disk driver is a component of the operating system that fulfills the request for a specific type of disk drive.

LAN system software resides both in the application's workstation and in the server(s), as illustrated in Figure 6-1. The workstation's LAN system software includes the redirector and the medium interface software. We use the example of a workstation environment to examine the interaction between workstation and server software components.

A Workstation Environment

Consider a workstation in which the server provides file and printer services. The workstation has local disk drives A, B, and C. The file server's disk drives are known to the workstation as drives F and G. The workstation's local printer ports are LPT1 and LPT2. A local dot-matrix printer is attached to LPT1; output to LPT2 is directed to a network laser printer. The key to making this environment work is transparent access to all devices. From the user's perspective, printing to a network printer and accessing a network disk drive are transparent. Thus, the workstation user accesses remote drives F and G in exactly the same way as he or she accesses local drives A, B, and C. The user also prints to the laser printer as though it were locally attached. This transparency is accomplished by the LAN system software. To see how, we consider an application that issues a read for a record located on the file server.

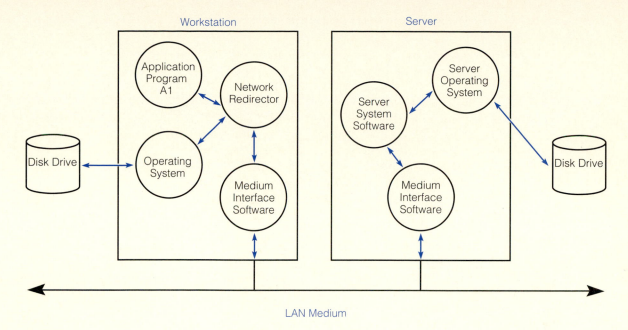

Figure 6-1

LAN Systems Software in
Server and Workstation

System Software Functions

You learned in Chapters 3 and 4 that the hardware provides the physical
connection between a workstation and a server. The software forms the logical connection by using the hardware to carry on sessions between applications on a workstation and the server. The first function of the LAN software
is to set up these logical connections. For now, we assume that this is done by
the user issuing a server logon request. If the logon is successful, the user can
use the server in accordance with his or her security controls.

The operating system (OS) running in the workstation is aware only of the
devices physically attached to that workstation. In our example, the OS is
capable of handling requests to drives A, B, and C and to LPT1 on its own.
However, it cannot handle I/O requests to drives F and G or direct output to
the network printer at LPT2. Ordinarily, when an application issues a file or
print request, the request is accepted and carried out by the OS. If a request
is made to access a device not attached to the workstation, the OS returns the
error message "device not found." To prevent this error message from being
returned in a LAN situation, the requests for drives F and G must be intercepted before they get to the OS. The software that reroutes I/O requests is
generically called a **redirector**.

The redirector is a software module that intercepts all application I/O
requests before they get to the workstation's OS. If the request is for a local
device, the redirector passes the request to the computer's OS. Thus, local
device access requests are carried out as usual. If the redirector gets a request
for a remote access to a LAN server, it sends the request over the network to
the server. This is illustrated in Figure 6-2.

redirector   A software
module that intercepts and
reroutes network application
I/O requests before they get
to the workstation's OS.

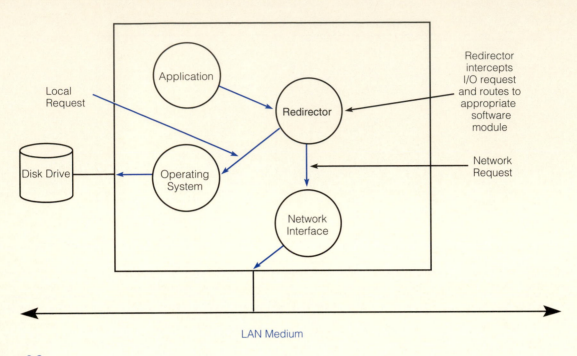

LAN Medium

Figure 6-2

Redirector Software

multithreading The capacity a server has to work on multiple requests at once.

The server receives a request for file or print service, in this case, a request for a database record. Many workstations are attached to the network, and any of them can make server requests at any time. The server may receive several requests simultaneously, and efficiency requires that the server be able to work on multiple requests at once. This capability is known as **multithreading**, because the server can have multiple transactions in progress at the same time. The server software must keep track of the progress of each transaction.

Suppose the server simultaneously receives two requests for a database record, three requests to write to a network printer, and one request to download an application program. These requests arrive in single file as illustrated in Figure 6-3. The server accepts the first request, a database record read, and searches disk cache memory. If the record is not in cache memory, the server issues a disk read to satisfy the request. It also remembers the address of the workstation that requested the read. While the disk is working to find the requested record, the server takes the next request, a printer write request, and issues a write to the print file. The server then accepts the next request, one for downloading an application program, and issues a read request for the first segment of the program.

At this point the server is notified that its read for the first database record has been completed. The server recalls the address of the workstation making the request and sends the record back to that workstation. Then the server takes the next request, a database read, and issues the read that satisfies the request. Thus the server software spends most of its time changing between accepting requests, issuing reads or writes to satisfy them, reacting to completions of those reads and writes, and sending the results back to the requester.

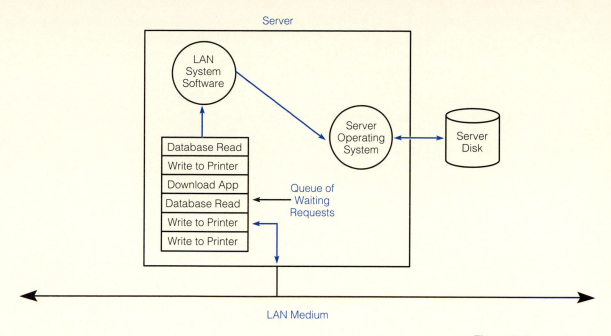

Figure 6-3

Server Request Queue

The application/server protocol just described is called a **client/server protocol** or requester/server protocol. To understand the importance of the multithreading capability of the server, consider the following example of single threading versus multithreading. Suppose you went to a restaurant and your waitperson could only wait on you when all tables ahead of you were done. You would end up waiting a long time before getting service, but the service would be great when you finally got it. However, the waitperson would have large amounts of idle time waiting for the food to be cooked. In a fast-food restaurant, you may be willing to wait for the person ahead of you in line to be served before placing your order. Likewise, in a small LAN such a service protocol might work well; however, a larger LAN may have multiple concurrent requests, so the use of multithreading becomes essential.

We now look at the LAN system software in more detail. We discuss the software components and explore how each component becomes involved in handling a server request.

client/server protocol An application framework in which the processing load is divided among several processes called clients and servers. Clients issue requests to servers, which provide specialized services such as database processing and mail distribution. Within this framework, clients are able to concentrate on business logic while servers can use specialized hardware and software that allows them to provide their services more efficiently. When clients and servers are located in different computers, application processing is distributed over multiple computers and, in effect, the network becomes the computer.

LAN WORKSTATION SOFTWARE

LAN workstation software can also be divided into three classes: application software, workstation system software, and LAN system software. LAN workstation software is simple when compared to server software, but do not expect this to continue. The simplicity of today's environment results from workstations being primarily single-application, single-user systems in which the workstation is doing only one thing at a time. This means the LAN workstation software can be single threaded. As workstations become more powerful, you can expect the associated software to also become more powerful to fully exploit the hardware. We limit our discussion to the current workstation environment.

Workstation Software Interface

We use computers as tools to solve problems. Application software has the logic necessary for solving specific problems, but it does not do all the work essential to the problem solution; instead it relies on system software to perform hardware-oriented tasks such as interfacing with disk drives and printers. Applications make requests to system software, which then assists the applications in carrying out their work. System software support may come from workstation system software or from LAN system software, depending on the application's needs. Workstation system software assists with local requests and LAN system software assists with requests needing LAN services.

If you have experience with a programming language, you may be familiar with procedures that contain the logic to perform a certain kind of processing. You pass input to a procedure, and it carries out the necessary processing on the input and returns output. For example, a procedure called FIND_MAXI-MUM accepts a list of numbers as input and returns the largest value in the list. When you invoke the procedure, you are making a request. The procedure acts on your request and returns the results. It is not important that you know how the procedure arrived at its conclusion, only that the conclusion is correct. Similarly, when you make a read or write request to a disk drive, you do not write directly to the disk. Instead you actually pass data to the operating system, which carries out this activity on your behalf.

When an application requests a service from the operating system, it does so by issuing a signal called an **interrupt**. A computer's operating system recognizes many interrupts, some generated by application software and some generated by the hardware. Each interrupt reflects a different class of service. The LAN system software reacts to the interrupt and decides whether it is a LAN request or a local request. Thus, the interrupt generated by the application must match those that are expected by the LAN software.

Today, most widely used software packages can run on a LAN; however, some applications operate correctly on one LAN implementation but not on a different one. This can happen because some application software is written specifically for one type of LAN and generates the proper interrupts only for that LAN's software. When selecting software that is compatible with your hardware and LAN software, you also must determine whether the software will run on the specific LAN you will be using and whether it will support concurrent users.

An application communicates with the network through an **Application Program Interface (API)**. Some APIs are listed in Table 6-1. The basic function of an API is to accept a request from an application, format the request in an API standard format, and send the request over the network to the server.

interrupt   A signal issued by hardware or an application requesting a service from the operating system.

Application Program Interface (API)   In LANs, the interface between application programs and the network software.

TABLE 6-1   Some Application Program Interfaces (APIs)

NETBIOS

Named Pipes

Xerox Network System (XNS)

Advanced Program-to-Program Communications (APPC)

Novell's Internetwork Packet Exchange and Sequenced Packet Exchange (IPX/SPX)

When an API protocol is set up, both the server and the workstation use that protocol to transfer data. If the protocol is not followed, communication is disrupted. When selecting your LAN software, you must be careful to ensure that the server and workstations have a common API through which they can communicate. Some LANs support several different APIs. The more APIs supported, the greater the likelihood that an application can run on the LAN.

Workstation System Software

An application uses an API to communicate with the LAN and the operating system. The LAN system software basically consists of two parts: One part interfaces with the applications and the operating system, and one part interfaces with the network hardware.

The portion of the software that interfaces with the applications, the redirector, is responsible for handling the application's interrupts. The application generally is not aware that the device it is reading from or writing to is a LAN device. This means each potential LAN service interrupt must be acted on. The LAN redirector therefore accepts all such interrupts, whether they are for local or remote requests. Local requests are sent to the operating system, and network requests are passed to the medium-oriented portion of the LAN system software.

Workstations connected to the LAN may use different versions of operating systems. In one LAN system, some workstations may use DOS versions 2, 3, 4, 5, or 6; some may use OS/2; some may use Apple DOS; and some may use a version of UNIX. The API for a heterogeneous system must be able to accommodate each of these versions and the interrupts they expect. Inability to do so limits the operating systems that can be used and, as an extension, limits which workstations can be used.

The medium-interface portion of the LAN workstation software has two basic functions: placing data onto the network and receiving data from the network. This portion of the software is responsible for formatting a message block for transmission over the network. It is closely tied to the LAN server software because it must format message blocks so they are compatible with what is expected by the server, and the workstation software must be able to recognize the format of messages received from the server. The data communications software also interfaces directly to the LAN adapter card.

SPECIFICS OF SERVER SOFTWARE

As previously stated, server software is more complex than workstation software, because server software is usually multithreaded and because the software must work well with the hardware to provide efficient service. We have already discussed the benefits and general strategy of multithreading. Now we consider several other functions that might be found in LAN server system software.

Server Operating Systems

Two basic approaches are taken in creating server software. One approach is to integrate the server and operating system functions into one complete software package. The other approach is to write LAN functions that run under an existing operating system, such as UNIX or OS/2. Each approach has advantages and disadvantages. Table 6-2 lists several leading LAN operating systems.

TABLE 6-2   **Leading LAN Operating Systems**

LAN	Vendor	Topology	Protocol
Novell	Novell, Inc.	Ring, bus (supporting Ethernet, IBM token ring, ARCnet)	CSMA/CD or token passing
LAN Server	IBM Corporation	Ring	Token passing
Windows NT	Microsoft, Inc.	Bus, ring	CSMA/CD or token passing
Apple Talk	Apple Computers, Inc.	Bus	CSMA/CA
PC Network	IBM Corporation	Bus	CSMA/CD
LANtastic	Artisoft, Inc.	Bus	CSMA/CD
TOPS	Sun Microsystems, Inc.	Bus, star	CSMA/CD
ViaNet	Western Digital Corporation	Bus, star	CSMA/CD
StarLAN	AT&T Corporation	Star	CSMA/CD
Nexos	DSC Communications Corporation	Bus, ring	CSMA/CD or token passing
VMS	Digital Equipment Corp.	Bus	CSMA/CD
PC/NOS	Corvus Systems, Inc.	Bus (supporting Ethernet, IBM token ring, and ARCnet)	CSMA/CD
Vines	Banyan Systems, Inc.	LAN OS (supporting Ethernet, IBM token ring, and ARCnet)	

Novell's **NetWare** and Microsoft's **Windows NT** are leading examples of the integrated software approach. The primary advantage of this approach is that the designers can optimize the software for LAN operation. The system is designed specifically to provide server functions and can be custom-tailored for that purpose. The disadvantage is that this approach requires writing complex software that may already be provided by an existing operating system. This makes the development effort longer and the maintenance more complex.

Creating LAN software that runs under an existing operating system overcomes the disadvantages cited for the integrated approach. Examples of LAN software that run under an existing OS are Banyan **Vines**, which runs under UNIX, and IBM's **LAN Server**, which runs under OS/2. The disadvantages are that a general-purpose operating system may be less efficient than one designed to carry out only the special functions required for LAN services.

Some operating systems, such as MS-DOS, are not well suited for hosting a LAN, primarily because of their inherent memory limitations, single-user orientation, and lack of security provisions. Despite these limitations, some LAN software runs under DOS and is successful in supporting LANs with few workstations or with limited server requirements. The operating systems that most frequently host LAN software are UNIX and OS/2.

First, let us look at some functions you might find in a LAN OS. Then we look briefly at specific LAN operating systems by Novell, IBM, and Banyan. The other OS options listed in Table 6-2 are competitive with those systems, although we do not discuss them in detail here.

NetWare   A leading example of the integrated LAN operating system software approach by Novell.

Windows NT   A leading example of the integrated LAN operating system software approach by Microsoft.

Vines (Banyan)   An example of LAN software that runs under an existing OS, UNIX.

LAN Server (IBM)   An example of LAN software that runs under an existing OS, OS/2.

LAN Operating System Functions

A LAN OS provides a variety of special capabilities. Among these are I/O optimization and fault tolerance.

Optimized I/O   A primary service provided by a server is file access. Optimizing this task, or **I/O optimization**, increases the performance of the server. Some optimization methods are hardware oriented and some are software oriented. One frequently used technique is called disk caching, which we discussed in Chapter 4.

Another I/O optimization technique is **disk seek enhancement**. A disk read requires that the read/write heads be positioned to the proper disk location. The act of moving the read/write heads is called a seek. The place to which the heads are moved is called a cylinder or track. Disk requests typically arrive in random order. Disk seek enhancement arranges the requests in order so the read/write heads move methodically over the disk, reading data from the nearest location. This is illustrated in Table 6-3. In Table 6-3(a) you can see the order in which several disk requests are received. Table 6-3(b) shows the optimum way to access those records and the savings in number of cylinders when processing the requests in the optimum order. Reducing the number of seeks improves performance.

I/O optimization   A variety of ways to optimize the task of file access, which increases the performance of the server.

disk seek enhancement An I/O optimization technique that reduces the head movement during seeks and improves performance.

TABLE 6-3   **Disk Seek Enhancement**

(a)

Disk Read Requests (cylinder or track) in order of arrival	Number of Cylinders Moved (assume a starting position of cylinder 0)
50, 250, 25, 300, 250, 50, 300	50 + 200 + 225 + 275 + 50 + 200 + 250 = 1250

(b)

Disk Read Requests (cylinder or track) in optimal order		
25, 50, 50, 250, 250, 300, 300	25 + 25 + 0 + 200 + 0 + 50 + 0 = 300	Savings = 950 Cylinders

---

read-after-write   A fault tolerance technique in which the system reads the data again after it has been written to a disk to ensure that no disk write errors occurred.

mirrored disks   A fault tolerance technique in which two disks containing the same data are provided so that if one fails, the other is available, allowing processing to continue.

Redundant Arrays of Independent Disks (RAID)   A fault-tolerant disk storage technique that spreads one file plus the file's checksum information over several disk drives. If any single disk drive fails, the data stored thereon can be reconstructed from data stored on the remaining drives.

parity data   In RAID technology, additional data that provides the ability to reconstruct data that has been corrupted.

Fault Tolerance   Some network operating systems provide increased reliability through a feature called fault tolerance. If you have only one server and it fails, the network is down. A LAN with fault tolerance allows the server to survive some failures that ordinarily would be disabling. Fault tolerance is usually provided by a combination of backup hardware components and software capable of using the backup hardware.

The lowest level of fault tolerance is the ability to recover quickly from a failure. This means that a failure that shuts the server down may occur, but the system can quickly be recovered to an operational state. One technique that makes this possible involves writing backup copies of critical disk information — disk directories, file allocation tables, and so on — to an alternate disk drive. Another helpful technique is called **read-after-write**. After writing data to a disk, the system reads the data again to ensure that no disk write errors occurred. If the data cannot be read again, the area of the disk containing that data is removed from future use and the data is written to a good area of the disk.

Fault tolerance can also be provided by **mirrored disks**, which are two disks that contain the same data. Whenever a disk write occurs, the data is written to both disk drives. If one disk fails, the other is available and processing continues. Mirrored disks have an additional benefit: Two disk drives are available so both disks can work simultaneously on behalf of two different requests. For added support some LAN servers also allow duplexed disk controllers. In this configuration, if a controller fails, another is available to continue working. Thus you can survive a controller failure and a disk failure.

Mirrored disk reliability can be extended using **Redundant Arrays of Independent Disks (RAID)**. RAID technology spreads data over three or more disk drives. The stored data consists of the actual data plus **parity data** — additional data that provides the ability to reconstruct data that has been corrupted. If one drive fails, the data stored on that drive can be reconstructed from data stored on the remaining drives. Parity data can be reconstructed because the remaining parts of the file are still available. If a section of the file

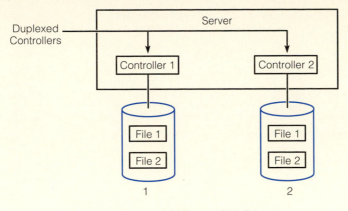

(a) Mirrored Disk Drives

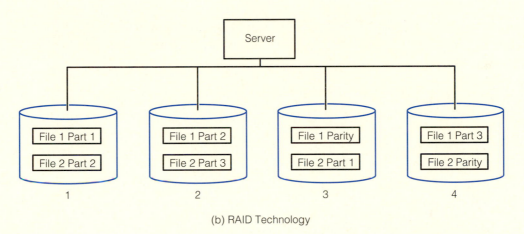

(b) RAID Technology

Figure 6-4

Mirrored Disk RAID Technology

is lost, it can be reconstructed from the parity data and the remaining parts of the file. The advantage of RAID over mirroring is that fewer disk drives are required for redundancy. With mirroring, two drives of data require four disk drives; with RAID, the same information can be stored on three drives with the same level of reliability. Disk mirroring and RAID technology, illustrated in Figure 6-4, can provide more efficient data access because multiple disk drives are available for reading and writing.

The best fault tolerance is provided by **duplexed servers**. With this configuration one server can fail and another is available to continue working. Even though it appears that this fault tolerance capability is primarily hardware oriented, software must exist that takes advantage of the duplexed hardware. A duplexed server is illustrated in Figure 6-5. Fault tolerance has been provided commercially by large systems since 1977. Fault tolerance features are currently available in most of the leading network operating systems.

duplexed servers The fault-tolerance technique in which one server can fail and another is available to continue working.

Figure 6-5

Duplexed Servers

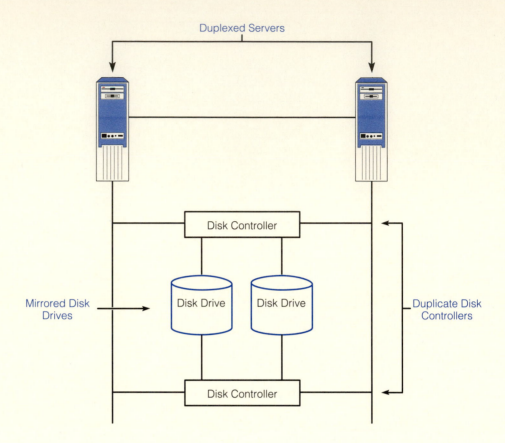

Duplexed Servers

Disk Controller

Mirrored Disk Drives

Disk Drive　　Disk Drive

Duplicate Disk Controllers

Disk Controller

Novell Operating Systems

Over time Novell has offered several versions of network operating systems. Novell now offers three basic systems with a variety of configuration options for two of the versions. For very small networks using peer-to-peer workstations, Novell offers Personal Netware. A peer-to-peer network is one that has no dedicated servers, and the network administrator can make the resources of each network node accessible to other network nodes. This technique is most suitable for networks with few nodes.

For high-end networks, Novell offers NetWare 2.x, NetWare 3.x, and NetWare 4.x. Fault tolerance capabilities are available with each version. NetWare 4.0 is Novell's newest network operating system. Its market is companies with very large networks and companies having several networks. NetWare 4.x supports up to 1000 nodes per LAN; simultaneous connection to multiple servers; and a network naming directory, which helps users locate local and remote network resources. NetWare 3.x and 4.x run on server hardware based on the 80386, 80486, Pentium, and later model processors only. Netware 2.x runs on 80286 server platforms as well as on the more advanced processors. These network operating systems are available for networks with a wide range of users and can be operated in either dedicated or nondedicated server mode. Netware 3.x can be purchased for networks ranging from five users to several hundred users, and Netware 4.x fills the need for larger networks. The cost of the system is scaled according to the maximum number of supported users. Thus small networks can realize the same operating system technology as that used on very large LANs but at a much lower cost (the cost per user for the LAN software remains somewhat constant). Netware 4.x also is available in a variety of languages including French, Italian, German, Spanish, Chinese, and Japanese.

One significant feature available from Novell is System Fault Tolerance (SFT), which provides an environment in which certain hardware failures do not cause network failures. For example, SFT supports mirrored disk drives, so that if one of the mirrored disk drives fails, the other is available to provide continuous service.

All Novell OS versions are designed to optimize LAN performance. An efficient file server must be able to quickly retrieve data from its disks. Novell provides optimized disk directory support and disk caching to maximize performance.

Microsoft's Windows NT

For several years Microsoft has provided LAN server OS support via its LAN Manager product that runs under the OS/2 operating system. LAN Manager is due to be replaced by a new, more powerful product, Windows NT (which stands for new technology). At this writing, Windows NT has not been officially released and has not experienced extensive production use. Despite this, public and press reaction to Windows NT has been generally favorable and it is expected to become a network OS that will compete with Novell's NetWare and other leading LAN OSs.

Windows NT is one of a family of Microsoft products that span a wide range of user needs and hardware platforms. The low-end product is Windows 3.x, and Windows NT provides the high-end operating environment. Between these two products are Windows for Workgroups (WFWG) and announced upgrades to Windows 3.x. Windows NT has two versions: NT for client workstations and NT Advanced Server (NTAS) for LAN servers. When NTAS matures, a typical NTAS-based LAN might have client workstations using a variety of operating environments including DOS, Windows 3.x, WFWG, UNIX, and Novell NetWare.

NT is a 32-bit operating system that provides multitasking and multithreading, both of which are essential to efficient server operation. On client workstations these services are needed primarily by power users who need to run multiple tasks on powerful desktop systems. NT's effective memory requirements of 16 MB and an anticipated software cost of several hundred dollars will likely result in lower-end users choosing a less costly operating environment such as DOS or a low-end Windows product.

On server platforms, NTAS should have hardware and software costs comparable to those of its competitive network OSs. NTAS's ability to support systems with multiple processors also makes it well suited for use with the most powerful servers. NTAS will support the two most common LAN architectures, Ethernet and token-passing rings. It also will support interfaces to WANs and has the ability to make WAN resources appear as local LAN resources. These interfaces are available because NTAS supports a wide variety of internetworking protocols, such as the TCP/IP protocols discussed in Chapter 12.

IBM's LAN Server and OS/2 Operating System

OS/2 is the second generation of operating systems for IBM and IBM-compatible microcomputers. It incorporates several data communications capabilities, including both LAN interfaces and terminal emulation features. The OS/2 operating system provides multitasking, presentation services, and data communications capabilities similar to those of the original IBM PC operating system, DOS. Communications products that run under OS/2 provide several enhanced data communications capabilities via their LAN Server and a communications manager and a database manager, as illustrated in Table 6-4.

The communications manager provides terminal and gateway support. Terminal support includes asynchronous terminal emulation, IBM 3270 terminal emulation, X.25 services, and a program-to-program gateway to an IBM host system. Other capabilities include a variety of interfaces to IBM's Systems Network Architecture (SNA), which is discussed in Chapter 11. Some of these communications manager functions also exist under DOS; however, OS/2 provides these functions in one comprehensive package rather than as a variety of individual packages from various vendors. OS/2's multitasking capabilities also allow more terminal sessions to be active than in the DOS environment. Connections to multiple hosts as well as to a LAN can be supported concurrently. The LAN Server software provides file and printer sharing services; provides an interface to IBM's network management system, NetView, and its wide area network architecture, Systems Network Architecture (SNA); and provides support for Apple Macintosh computers. Because of these interfaces, LAN Server is well suited for companies with SNA networks that need to interface to the LAN.

TABLE 6-4   **LAN Manager/LAN Server Configuration**

Services Software		
Printer	Communications	SQL Server
	LAN Manager/LAN Server	
	OS/2 Operating System	

Banyan Vines

Banyan Vines is recognized for its support for large networks and network interconnections. Banyan Vines runs on UNIX-based servers — a distinct advantage because many WANs contain nodes running the UNIX operating system. This makes it easier for Vines systems to connect to those nodes. A server based on UNIX also can be used effectively as an application system in addition to providing LAN services, which means the server platform can function not only as a server but also as a platform for running application programs. OS/2 operating systems allow multitasking but not multiuser capabilities and thus cannot match UNIX-based machines, which allow several users to run applications.

One major strength of Vines is a global naming strategy called **StreetTalk**. StreetTalk is a database that provides **network directory services** such as identifying network resources such as users, files, hardware, and so on. This database is replicated on each server in the network, providing a measure of fault tolerance as well as making resource lookup more efficient. Applications use StreetTalk to locate needed resources; A mail application can use it to find the location of mail recipients. LAN managers use StreetTalk to assist in controlling the network and network users: The access rights of each user can be placed in the StreetTalk database. A unique feature of StreetTalk, particularly for international networks, is the ability to store information such as status and error messages in several languages.

Interoperability of Server Software

A large LAN may need more than one file server (the point at which a second server is needed varies according to the number of active, concurrent users and their server access profiles). If two or more servers are required, you must ensure that they operate correctly. If all servers are using the same hardware and software platforms, they often can operate correctly in concert. It is not always true, however, that two different server software packages can interoperate correctly.

Interoperability basically means the ability of all network components to connect to the network and to communicate with shared network resources. With a global view, this means the ability to interconnect different networks so that nodes on one network are able to communicate with nodes on the same network or on another network. On a single network, it means any node can access resources to which it has appropriate security. Interoperability is usually easy in a homogeneous network, in which only one network operating system version is used and the workstations are all the same type and use the same operating system. Networks using a mixture of network operating systems and workstation platforms make interoperability more complex.

We now look at interoperability in a single network. Consider a network that has two servers with different network operating systems, such as Novell

StreetTalk (Banyan) A database that provides network directory services.

network directory services A database that contains the names, types, and network addresses of network resources. Examples of resource types include users, printers, and servers. The directory database may be replicated on several network nodes, thus allowing users and processes to locate resources they need to complete their work.

interoperability The ability of all network components to connect to the network and to communicate with shared network resources.

TABLE 6-5   Possible Complications of Having Two Network Operating Systems in One LAN

Compatibility of user identifiers and passwords

Synchronization of user identifiers and passwords across servers

Ability to simultaneously access data on two servers

Ability to access data on one server and print to spooler on another

Applications that can run from both servers

Support for common application program interfaces (APIs)

Support for common protocols at the OSI network and transport layers

Ability to use/have two redirector processes

NetWare and Banyan Vines. If users were to use only one or the other server, it would probably be easier to divide the network into a Novell network and a Banyan Vines network. If both servers are available on one network, we may assume that some users must have access to both servers. Table 6-5 lists complications that may exist as a result. How well the server operating systems handle these issues affects the interoperability of the network.

PRINT SPOOLER

LAN users share LAN printers. It may be obvious that only one user can be physically printing to a printer at one time, and yet several users will need to logically write to one printer at the same time. Logically writing to a printer means the user has opened a printer and has written to that printer; however, the printed output may not be physically written to the printer at that time. The output is first written to a disk file and is printed after the complete output has been collected. The software subsystem that allows several users to logically write to one printer at the same time is called a **spooler**. The operation of a spooler is shown in Figure 6-6. Let us trace the activity of a print job through the spooler.

spooler   A software system that collects printer output (typically on disk) and schedules the data for printing. *Spool* is an acronym for simultaneous peripheral operation on-line.

A user at one workstation is using a word processing program to create a report, and a user at another workstation is using a spreadsheet program to prepare a budget. At nearly the same time, each user prints the document he or she is working on. The output is directed to LPT2 on each system. On each system, LPT2 is mapped by the network software to a laser printer attached to the server. Before writing to the printer, each application first opens the printer. The redirector at each system directs the "open" request to the server. When the server receives the printer open request, it is passed to the spooler software. The spooler software prepares to receive each workstation's printed output into a disk file. When each application receives an acknowledgment that the "printer" has been successfully opened, it begins to send output to the printer.

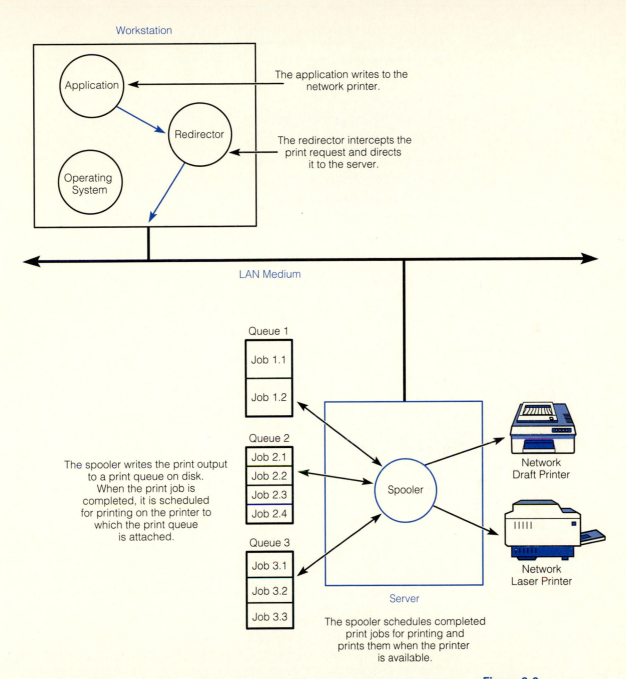

The application writes to the network printer.

The redirector intercepts the print request and directs it to the server.

The spooler writes the print output to a print queue on disk. When the print job is completed, it is scheduled for printing on the printer to which the print queue is attached.

The spooler schedules completed print jobs for printing and prints them when the printer is available.

Figure 6-6

Spooler Operation

The spooler receives the output from each workstation and stores the output in that workstation's print file on disk. This process continues until each workstation is finished. When the application closes the printer file, the print job is ready to be physically written to the printer.

Be aware that some applications, such as some versions of Lotus 1-2-3, do not close the print file until the user explicitly chooses a close printer option

TABLE 6-6   Spooler Options

Collect printed output

Direct print jobs to designated printers

Hold jobs in disk queue after printing

Hold jobs in disk queue before printing

View jobs on hold in print queue

Set number of print copies

Setting print job priorities

Delete jobs from print queue

Attach/detach printers from print queue

Set/change job priorities

Add/delete printers

Start/stop printers

Start/stop spooler process

Print banners

Close print jobs based on time-out interval

Print statistical reports

or until the application terminates. If this occurs, a user may not get a printout when expected. Suppose Maria is working on a spreadsheet and prints a portion of it. If the printing had been sent to a locally attached printer, it would print immediately. With a spooler, however, the spreadsheet program does not close the printer, and the job is left open. This allows for another portion of the spreadsheet to be printed directly after the first print range. The spreadsheet program continues to hold the file open until Maria exits from the spreadsheet. Her job then is scheduled for printing. In this case, printing on a LAN differs from printing to a local printer and may not be what Maria needs. She may want the range to be printed immediately so she can use that information for further work. For such instances, some spoolers also allow the print job to be closed if a certain time elapses before receiving additional print data. This feature allows the user to obtain the printed results without exiting from the application.

When a print job has been closed, the spooler schedules the job for printing. Spoolers have a priority scheme by which they decide which job prints next. Some spoolers print the jobs in the order in which they became ready to print (first in, first out); some print the smallest available job; others print jobs according to user-assigned priorities. When the job has been printed, it may be removed from the disk to make room for other print jobs. Alternatively, the job may be held on disk for printing at a later time, for printing to a different device, or for perusal from a workstation. Spooler systems provide a variety of options regarding the association of logical print devices with physical printers and the treatment of jobs captured in the spooler files. Some of these options are listed in Table 6-6.

TABLE 6-7   Backup Software Capabilities

Back up all files

Back up all files modified since a particular date

Back up by directory

Back up by list of files

Back up all but a list of files to be excluded

Back up by index

Back up by interface to a database

Back up using wildcard characters in filenames

Create new index on tape and disk

Maintain cross-reference of tape serial numbers and backup

Manual backup

Automatic backup by time or calendar

Start backup from workstation or server

Data compression

Multivolume backup

Generate reports

BACKUP SOFTWARE

In Chapter 4 we discussed backup hardware. The software used to perform the backups is as important as the hardware. **Backup software** is responsible for reading the files being backed up and writing them to the backup device. During recovery, a restoration module reads the backup medium and writes the data back to disk. Several backup software options are available. They all provide the basic functions of backing up and restoring data. However, they differ with respect to backup and restoration procedure including the options they provide, the devices they support, and their ease of use. Backup devices frequently come with a backup/restore program (both capabilities are contained on one program), and most LAN system software includes a backup/restore module. Novell's backup/restore program for one version of their network software is NBACKUP. Some LAN administrators choose to purchase a separate, more functional backup system than the LAN or backup device version. Table 6-7 lists some features supported by backup software.

backup software Software that is responsible for reading the files being backed up and writing them to the backup device.

SOFTWARE REQUIREMENTS FOR SHARED USAGE

Most early microcomputer applications were written for single-user systems, which means the software developers could make certain simplifying design decisions. To use these applications in a shared LAN system, accommodations must be made by the LAN administrators, by the LAN system software, or by the application itself. Let us now consider the required changes.

TABLE 6-8   User Configuration Options

Default disk drive

Default disk directory

Disk drive mappings

Disk drive/directory search paths

Printer mappings

Initial program/menu

Hardware Configuration

Software written for a single user need not be concerned with problems of computer configuration. You are probably aware that microcomputers may be configured with a variety of options. The primary variations are in memory, disk configurations, printer configuration, and monitor support. In a stand-alone system the application software is set up to match the configuration of that system. However, a LAN might have many different workstation configurations, and application software should support each configuration as much as possible.

Some applications support only one configuration. The hardware settings of such applications are stored in a single file. One way to use this type of application is to configure the application for the lowest common denominator of hardware and have each user get essentially the same configuration. Users with high-resolution color graphics monitors might have images displayed in monochrome at low resolution, or a user with a hard disk drive might have to use a floppy disk drive rather than the hard disk for some files. Usually LAN administrators can avoid this type of configuration by storing multiple versions of the application in different disk directories. Users can then use the configuration that most closely matches their computer's profile.

Some applications allow several configuration files and decide which to use by a run-time parameter or by making a default choice if the startup parameter is not specified. LAN administrators can provide each user with a tailored environment by virtue of a batch startup file.

Applications designed for LAN use usually have a user-oriented configuration file. Each LAN user has his or her personal configuration that is custom-tailored for the specific user and the specific hardware. This provides users with the most flexibility and requires little or no customization by the LAN administrator. These options are listed in Table 6-8.

Application Settings

The software equivalent to hardware configurations are application settings. Ideally, users tailor application settings to meet personal preferences. One user may prefer his or her word processor application to display green characters on a black background with tabs at every five character positions. Another user might prefer white characters on a blue background with tabs at every four character positions. Each user should receive these settings as the default. Application settings can be defined in a way similar to setting hardware options.

Contention

You learned a little about contention in the Introduction and in Chapter 2. Remember that whenever two users are capable of accessing the same resource at the same time, contention for that resource can occur. Similar problems occur when accessing files.

A classic contention problem is illustrated by two users working on one document at the same time. The same type of problem can occur when two users access and update the same database record. A primitive way to handle contention is simply to avoid it by scheduling user activities so they do not interfere with each other. On small LANs this may be possible, but as the number of concurrent users increases, this method becomes clumsy. Rather than avoiding contention, an application or LAN software should *prevent* contention problems by exerting controls over files or records.

One prevention mechanism is activated when an application opens a file. The three basic file open modes are exclusive, protected, and shared. In **exclusive open mode**, an open request is granted only if no other user already has the file open. File open requests from other users also are denied until the application having an exclusive open closes the file.

Exclusive opens may be too restrictive for some applications. Suppose two users, Alice and Tom, are both working on the same word processing document. Alice needs to update the document, and Tom only needs to read it. In this case Tom will not interfere with Alice's work. A **protected open mode** can satisfy both users' needs. Protected open mode is granted only if no other user has already been granted exclusive or protected mode. Once a file is open in protected mode, only the application with protected open can update the document. **Shared open mode** allows several users to have the file open concurrently. In shared update mode, all users can update the file. In shared read-only mode, all users can read the file but cannot write to it. If Alice opens the document in protected mode and Tom opens the document in shared read-only mode, Alice can read and update the document but Tom can only read it. Furthermore, Tom cannot open the document in exclusive, protected, or shared update mode while a protected open exists.

Sometimes a read-only application must be protected against file updates. An application that is doing a trial balance of an accounting file must prohibit updates during the reading and calculations. If another application makes changes while the file is being read, the figures may not balance. The trial-balance application can protect against this by opening the accounts file in protected read-only mode. This prevents other processes from opening the file in update mode while allowing processes to open the file in shared read-only mode. Table 6-9 shows the combinations of exclusive, protected, and shared open modes.

exclusive open mode   A mode in which an open request is granted only if no other user has the file opened already.

protected open mode   A mode that is granted only if no other user has already been granted exclusive or protected mode.

shared open mode   A mode that allows several users to have a file open concurrently.

TABLE 6-9   **Comparison of Open Modes**

Open Mode Requested	Currently Opened As			
	Exclusive	*Protected*	*Shared Update*	*Shared Read-Only*
Exclusive	Denied	Denied	Denied	Denied
Protected	Denied	Denied	Denied	Granted
Shared, update	Denied	Denied	Granted	Granted
Shared, read-only	Denied	Granted	Granted	Granted

Exclusive and protected open modes are sufficient for meeting some contention problems, such as our word processing example. However, they are overly restrictive for other applications, such as database processing. One objective of database applications is to help several users share data. Exclusive opens allow only one user at a time to use the data. The problem with file-open contention resolution is overcome by exerting controls at a lower level, the record level. Record level controls are called **locks**.

Suppose Alice and Tom want to update a database. So long as they are using different records, they will not interfere with each other. However, suppose that at some time both Alice and Tom need to access and update the same record, leading to contention problems. If Alice locks the record when accessing it, Tom's read request will be denied until Alice unlocks the record. This process is illustrated in Figure 6-7. Note that Tom must wait until the record has been unlocked before being allowed to proceed.

Record locking can, however, cause another problem: **deadlock**, or deadly embrace. Suppose that Alice and Tom are accessing the database. Alice's application reads and locks Record A and, at nearly the same time, Tom's application reads and locks Record B. After reading Record A, Alice attempts to read Record B and, of course, waits because the record is locked. If Tom then attempts to read Record A, deadlock occurs: Alice and Tom are waiting for each other, and neither can continue until the record they are waiting for is unlocked, which can never happen because there is a circular chain of users waiting on each other. Three or more users can also be involved in this circular chain of events. The deadlock problem is illustrated in Figure 6-8. Deadlock avoidance or resolution methods exist but are beyond the scope of this text. You can read about these methods in many database texts.

Some database systems take care of contention for users. These systems recognize when contention is occurring and prevent the problems associated with it. One convention used to do this is outlined as follows:

1. User A reads Record X.
2. User B reads Record X (and the read is allowed).
3. User A updates Record X (and the update is allowed).
4. User B attempts to update Record X.
5. The database management system recognizes that the record has been changed since User B read it.

lock   Record- or file- level control that overcomes the problem with file open contention.

deadlock   A state that exists when two or more processes are unable to proceed. It occurs when two or more transactions have locked a resource and request resources that other involved processes already have locked.

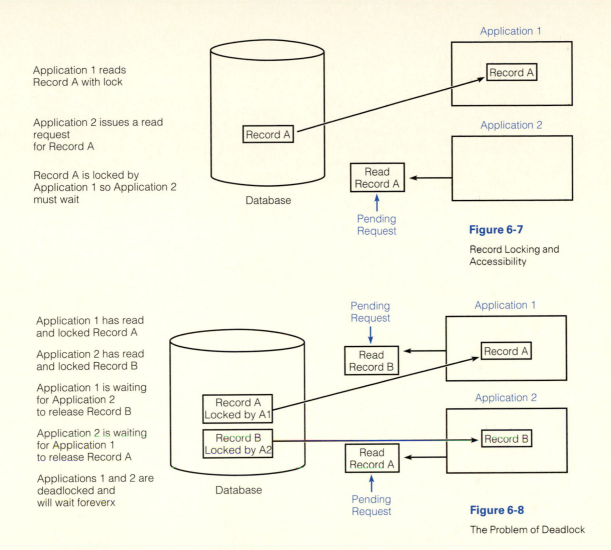

Application 1 reads
Record A with lock

Application 2 issues a read
request
for Record A

Record A is locked by
Application 1 so Application 2
must wait

Figure 6-7

Record Locking and
Accessibility

Application 1 has read
and locked Record A

Application 2 has read
and locked Record B

Application 1 is waiting
for Application 2
to release Record B

Application 2 is waiting
for Application 1
to release Record A

Applications 1 and 2 are
deadlocked and
will wait foreverx

Figure 6-8

The Problem of Deadlock

6. The database management system sends the revised copy of Record X to User B and notifies the user that the update was rejected because the record was changed by another user.

7. User B reissues the update or takes another course of action.

In selecting LAN software, it is critical that you understand the problems of configuration and contention. If these issues are not resolved the effectiveness of the system is reduced or, worse yet, the data becomes corrupted. Sharing data has another side effect that must be addressed — security.

Access Security

Early operating systems, and many current ones for stand-alone microcomputers, do not provide file security. Even though only one user can use a microcomputer at one time, several users might use one system. Without

access security Security that controls a user's access to data. The controls may regulate a user's ability to read and update data, to delete files, and to run programs.

access security these users not only have access to another user's sensitive data, but also might accidentally (or intentionally) remove another user's files. Access to the computer essentially provides access to all data stored on that computer. Users might store sensitive data on a stand-alone microcomputer's disks, but those users are limited with respect to their ability to protect that data from unauthorized reading, changes, or destruction. Instead, a user could store data on a removable disk and store it in a secure place when not being used. Another alternative is buying an application that provides password security or allows hiding or encrypting data to protect it from misuse.

When you install a LAN, data that must be shared and was once stored as "private" data on one or more stand-alone systems is likely to be placed in a database on a server. Without security, all data on the servers can be accessed, updated, and deleted by any LAN user. For most applications this is not acceptable. Therefore, the LAN system software must provide protection through security. Other security concerns include protecting against software piracy and preventing the introduction of computer viruses. We discuss security in more detail in Chapter 15.

SOFTWARE LICENSE AGREEMENTS

license agreement An agreement that covers the rules under which you are allowed to use a product.

One of the most important things to know about your software is its licensing agreement. Virtually all software you buy is covered by a **license agreement**. This is true for both systems and applications software. The license agreement covers the rules under which you are allowed to use the product. It is a way of protecting both the manufacturer and the user of the product. To better understand the need for license agreements, we first look at an analogy.

Consider the books you purchased for school, which probably were rather expensive. Of course, the publisher does not pay nearly that much to print the book. Part of your book price goes to profit, but the publisher also incurs other expenses. One or more authors worked many hours to write the material; editors worked many hours with the authors to develop the format and content; designers laid out the style (graphics and page formats); marketing analysts determined a marketing strategy and created advertising brochures; and the salesforce were told about the book, its target markets, and key selling points. All of this activity required a considerable investment. Some books never become popular and the publishing company loses money on them. Others become very popular and the publishing company makes a profit. Some of that profit is used to offset losses on other projects. Now, suppose someone decides to illegally reprint a text and sell the successful books. With today's technology, it does not cost much just to print these copies. This person can sell the copies for much less than the publisher because he or she has not had to make the investment of developing the work, paying the salaries of editors and production workers, the royalties to the developers, and so on.

Patent and copyright laws are intended to protect the investment of designers, artists, filmmakers, authors, publishing companies, and so on. Software companies also make a sizable investment in creating application or system software. Systems analysts design the product, programmers write and debug the code, marketing analysts create a marketing plan, advertising campaigns are developed and implemented, manuals are created, a support organization is staffed and trained, and the product is brought to market.

Several years probably elapsed from the time the product was conceived to the point at which it was ready to sell and make a profit. Thousands of dollars were probably expended before there was any opportunity to sell the software. In addition, once a software product is released, expenses continue. Support staff must be paid and new enhancements designed. As with illegal book printing, the gain from all this effort can be eroded by illegal copying. To give you an idea of the magnitude of this problem, at the end of the 1980s several software piracy shops in Hong Kong were raided. Some estimated the annual loss of revenues to software companies resulting from software piracy in one building alone to be hundreds of millions of dollars.

Software vendors must therefore take steps to protect their investment. Like books, pictures, films, and fashion designs, software can be illegally copied and sold. Software is protected in six basic ways:

1. The code is kept secret so other software houses cannot use special algorithms developed by the company to write a competing system.

2. The code is copyrighted to prevent another company from copying the code and writing a competing system.

3. The software is copy protected to deter the making of illegal copies.

4. The software requires a special hardware device to run.

5. License agreements are used to establish the terms of ownership and use.

6. Legislation penalizing those who do not adhere to the copyright and license restrictions are applied.

The first two of these measures protect the source code from being used by someone else. During development, it is common to keep the source code of software secret. However, after the product has been released, it is always possible to derive the source code, even if the software is released only in object code format. Deriving the source code from object code is done through reverse engineering. To protect themselves from reverse engineering, software manufacturers usually copyright their software. Copyright laws, originally intended to cover writing, films, and works of art, have been extended to include software. New legislation also has been enacted to further define the restrictions and penalties for unauthorized software copying.

Each of these measures is rather clear; most people understand and observe the rules. However, the remaining two issues—copy protection and license agreements—are less standard and directly involve how the software is used. Software piracy has always been a problem, even before the introduction of microcomputers. With minicomputers and mainframe systems, software piracy is easier to detect and hence its incidence is negligible relative to its occurrence on microcomputers. There are two good reasons for easier detection of large system software piracy. First, large computers are used by large organizations with professional data processing departments. Software piracy is difficult to hide in such organizations, and ordinarily anyone found using pirated software is subject to dismissal and the company is subject to lawsuits. Second, large computer sites typically work closely with the software vendor's personnel. The vendor's employees are aware of the software its customers are authorized to use, and it is easy to detect the presence of unauthorized software. Easy piracy detection is not the case with microcomputer software.

A few software companies protect their software by requiring the use of a special hardware device that attaches to a serial or parallel port. The device and an application work together to provide application security. When started, the application attempts to read data encoded in the device. If the device is not attached, the application terminates. One disadvantage to this approach is having several applications each of which need a different device. Because the number of serial or parallel ports is limited, changing from one application to another may require changing the device. Other companies have accomplished somewhat the same effect by requiring a **key disk**. The key disk is usually a flexible disk that must be in a disk drive when the application is run. The application uses the key disk only to verify the disk's presence. This technique is seldom used today and, of course, cannot be used with diskless systems.

key disk   A security system in which a flexible disk must be in the disk drive when the application is run.

Originally many microcomputer software vendors used copy protection to deter software piracy. The software diskette was encoded to prevent copying using standard operating system copy facilities such as DOS's COPY or DISKCOPY commands. In general, copy protection only gave rise to a new software industry; software to allow copying of copy-protected software. Of course, vendors of such software were careful to point out that the sole purpose of their software was to make a backup copy and not to make illegal duplicate copies. Many companies that once copy protected their software have abandoned that means because it proved relatively ineffective. Instead of or in addition to copy protection, software vendors now rely on copyright protection together with software license agreements.

When you buy software, both application software and LAN system software, often the diskettes that hold the software are sealed in an envelope. Written on or attached to the envelope is text regarding the license agreement and a message that opening and using the software is a commitment to adhere to the stipulations of that license agreement. The license agreement states the conditions under which you are allowed to use the product.

In essence, when you buy software, you do not get ownership of that product; you are simply given the right to use the product. An attorney might quibble with this statement, but the basic premise is correct. Some license agreements explicitly state that you own the diskette but not the contents of the diskette. This means you cannot make copies of the software to give to your friends, you may not be able to run it on several workstations at the same time, you may not reverse engineer it to produce source code for modification or resale, and so on. Your rights to the software are limited to using the software in the intended manner. You can, if you like, destroy the software, cease to use it, sell it, or give it as a gift. In the last two cases you also transfer the license agreement to the recipient. Some software vendors go so far as to state that transferring the software must be approved by the software vendor. In some cases the software license covers the use of the accompanying documentation as well.

One of the problems with license agreements is that there are no standards. If you buy two different applications, you are liable to find two different license agreements. To protect yourself and your organization from civil and criminal suits, you must understand the provisions of each agreement. Several companies including a major state university have been investigated for illegally copying software, have been found guilty of the offense, and have been heavily fined. It is important that a company and individuals respect license agreements. We look at some general licensing provisions, namely:

- Single user, single workstation
- Restricted number of concurrent users
- Site license
- Single user, multiple workstation
- Server license
- Corporate license

Single User, Single Workstation   Single-user, single-workstation license agreements are the most restrictive. They specify that the software is to be used on one workstation only and by only one person at a time. If you have a multiuser microcomputer, only one user can be running the software at any time. In most instances, restricting the software to only one machine also implies a single user.

This license agreement also means that if an office has two or more computers, a separate copy of the software must be purchased for each machine on which the software is to be used. If you have two employees, one on a day shift and one on a night shift, using the same software but on different workstations, each needs an individual copy of the software. In this situation, the software is never used concurrently, yet two copies are required. One of the ways in which software vendors enforce this policy is through the software installation procedure. The install process counts the number of installations. When you install the product the counter is decremented to zero and you are not able to install the programs on another system. To move the software to another system you must uninstall the software. The uninstall process removes the application from the computer's disks and increments the installation count. Another method used to enforce a single-user, single-workstation license is the requirement for a key disk described earlier.

Single User, Multiple Workstation   This type of license agreement relaxes the constraints of the single-user, single-workstation agreement. It usually also relies on the honor system for enforcement. Software vendors that use this agreement recognize that different people may want to use the software and at different workstations, such as in the office and on a portable computer. The purchase of a single copy of the software allows the owner to install it on several systems. However, the license restricts *use* of the software to one user at a time per software copy. Suppose an office with ten worksta-tions must do word processing. Each of ten employees can use the word processor, but only five employees can use the product concurrently. With this license agreement, the company can buy five copies of the software and install them on ten different systems. So long as five or fewer employees use the word processing application at any one time, the company has lived up to the license provisions. Note that it is possible for six users to inadvertently use the application at the same time, in violation of the license agreement.

Restricted Number of Concurrent Users   On a LAN it is common for several users to run an application concurrently. Three employees may be doing word processing, 10 may be using the spreadsheet software, and 25 may be using the database software. With file or database server technology, only 1 copy of each application is on the server's disks. Most LAN-compatible software is inherently designed for multiple users; however, some software vendors place restrictions on the number of concurrent users. The main idea behind this strategy is to charge by the number of users.

Consider the database needs of the company just mentioned, where the maximum number of concurrent database users is 25. The database vendor has a license agreement that allows 10 concurrent users for a certain fee. The company also has an expansion policy that allows additional concurrent users to be added in groups of 10 with an additional fee for each such group. The company must purchase three modules, to satisfy its need of 25 concurrent users. This type of license is typically enforced by a meter program that controls the concurrent use of the application. When a user starts the appli-cation, the meter program increments a counter by 1. When a user exits the application, the counter is decremented by 1. If the license agreement is for 30 users, a user can run the application so long as the counter is 29 or fewer. If the counter is 30, a user requesting the application receives an error mes-sage indicating that the file is not available.

server license   A license that allows an application to be installed on one server.

Server License   A **server license** allows an application to be installed on one server. All users attached to that server may use the application. If a company has three servers and wants to use the application on each of them, the company must purchase three licenses or three copies of the software.

site license   A license that gives the user unlimited rights to use the software at a given site.

Site License   A **site license** gives the user unlimited rights to use the software at a given site. The site may be a single LAN or multiple LANs at one location.

corporate license   A license that gives a corporation un-limited use of software at all locations.

Corporate License   A **corporate license** gives a corporation unlimited use of the software at all locations. Some companies restrict a corporate license to all locations within one country. Sometimes the right to reproduce docu-mentation is also granted.

The license agreement is intended primarily to protect the rights of the manufacturer. However, the holder of a license agreement also has certain rights. Among these rights may be:

1. The owner can transfer or assign the license to another user.

2. The owner can get a refund if the product is defective or does not work as stated.

3. Legal rights may be granted by certain states or countries regarding the exclusion of liability for losses or damage resulting from the use of the software.

4. The user can terminate the license by destroying the software and documentation.

When selecting your application and system software, you must take care to understand fully all the conditions of the license agreements. You want each user to have the necessary software services available. Different license and pricing policies among competing products can result in substantial differences in availability to you or cost to your company.

CASE STUDY

The Syncrasy Corporation has installed two separate LANs in the home office. Two LANs were decided upon for several reasons, two of which are separation of department functions and the number of users. The two LANs are connected but the connection is used primarily to allow users to exchange electronic mail messages. The intention is for all users to access applications located on a server attached to their LAN, so that a user on LAN A does not access applications located on a LAN B server. To meet most users' application needs, Syncrasy has chosen five core microcomputer products — word processing, spreadsheet, database management, presentation graphics, and desktop publishing — that are to be available to all LAN users in the home office. It was decided to use individual software packages for these core products rather than purchasing one of the combined office program packages. A consequence of using multiple software vendors is having to understand and adhere to several different license agreements. The license agreement provisions of each of the core products are as follows:

Word processing	Basic network licenses on one server for 25 and 50 users are $2500 and $4500, respectively. A 25-user license includes 5 sets of manuals and a 50-user license has 10 sets. Additional sets of documentation are available for $20. Additional user licenses come in 25-user increments and cost $2000. The 25- and 50-user licenses for an additional server are $2000 and $4000, respectively.
Spreadsheet	A basic network license for 25 users is $2000. This includes 2 sets of documentation. Additional licenses are available in 10-user increments for $750. Additional copies of manuals are available for $20. No additional costs are charged per server at the same location.

Database management	A site license is available for $6000. This allows an unlimited number of users and installation on multiple servers. The cost includes 2 sets of documentation. Additional manual sets are available for $25.
Presentation graphics	A single server license covering 25 users costs $2500 and allows installation on 1 server only. Additional server licenses for 25 users cost $2500. Additional users on a single server can be added in increments of 25 at a cost of $2000. Each server license includes 5 sets of documents, and additional sets of documents can be purchased for $30.
Desktop publishing	License fees are independent of the number of servers. A network license for 25 users costs $10,000, for 50 users the cost is $17,500, and for 100 users the cost is $30,000. Beyond 100 users, additional users can be added in increments of 10 for $250. A 25-user package comes with 2 sets of manuals, the 50-user has 5 sets, and the 100-user has 10 sets. Additional manual sets can be purchased for $25.

Once the software selection was made, it was necessary to order the proper number of licenses to ensure that Syncrasy was compliant with each vendor's license provisions. Determining the cost for each product required an understanding of the license provisions for the product and the parameters under which the product would be used at Syncrasy. Table 6-10 shows the factors that were gathered to complete the cost analysis. Some of the data in Table 6-10 may not need to be applied in the license analysis for a specific product. We consider the analysis that was conducted to determine the product costs for the word processing and spreadsheet applications. Analysis for the three remaining products is left as an exercise.

Word Processing License and Manual Costs   For the LAN A server (Server A), Syncrasy needs a 50-user license and a 25-user extension to cover 60 concurrent users. This will cost $4500 + $2000 for a total of $6500. For LAN B's server (Server B) an additional server license for 25 users must be purchased for a price of $2000. The total license cost is therefore $6500 + $2000, or $8500. A 50-user license includes 10 manual sets and a 25-user license includes 5 sets. From the license costs, 20 manual sets are available, 15 on Server A and 5 on Server B. Syncrasy must purchase an additional 30 manual sets to have 50 sets of manuals available. Each manual set costs $20, so the manual cost will be $600. The total software license and manual costs for word processing are therefore $8500 + $600, or $9100.

Spreadsheet License and Manual Costs   The cost of the spreadsheet software must be calculated differently than the cost for word processing because the license provisions are different. Syncrasy must be able to accom-

TABLE 6-10   Software License Cost Analysis

Product	LAN A Server Maximum Concurrent Users	LAN B Server Maximum Concurrent Users	Maximum Concurrent Users on Both Servers	Document Sets Required
Word Processing	60	25	75	50
Spreadsheet	60	20	70	50
Database Management	40	30	60	50
Presentation Graphics	25	20	40	50
Desktop Publishing	25	25	45	50

modate 70 concurrent users on both LANs. This is accomplished by purchasing the basic 25-user license and adding 5 extensions of 10 users each. The costs for this is $2000 + (5)($750), or $5750. The license fees include 2 manual sets, so 48 additional sets at a cost of $20 each are needed; the additional manuals will cost $960. The total software and manual costs for the spreadsheet are $5750 + $960, or $6710. ❖

SUMMARY

LAN software can be separated into systems software and application software. LAN system software in the servers and workstations is responsible for carrying out the LAN functions. Application software solves business problems. LAN system software is found on servers and workstations.

Workstation system software is responsible for intercepting application I/O requests and deciding whether the request is local or network. If the request is local, the workstation LAN software passes it along to the workstation operating system. If the request is for a network resource, the workstation LAN software formats a network message and sends the request over the network for processing. The workstation LAN software is also responsible for accepting LAN messages and passing them along to the proper application. Because LAN workstation software must remain resident in the workstation memory, a stand-alone workstation may need a memory upgrade to run some LAN applications.

LAN server software is more complex than workstation software. Some functions it may provide are

- I/O optimization
- Fault tolerance

- Printer services
- Utility and administrative support
- Access security
- File backup and restore
- Contention resolution

These functions help to make performance better, to improve reliability, or to protect data from accidental or intentional damage.

When choosing LAN software, you need to consider how that software will interoperate with other software, other networks, and your hardware. Poor interoperability increases the complexity of using a LAN and decreases its usability.

A major difference between stand-alone microcomputers and microcomputers attached to a LAN is resource sharing. Sharing hardware and data may lead to contention problems, and mechanisms must be available to arbitrate resource contention. Spoolers manage contention for network printers. Open modes and file or record locks are commonly used to resolve data contention. These forms of data contention resolution may lead to another problem called deadlock. If two or more processes are involved in a deadlock, none of the processes is able to proceed until one of them releases the resources it has locked. Resolving contention and deadlock problems is essential to preserving the integrity of data and ensuring the progress of applications.

Purchased software is covered by a license agreement that describes the manner in which the software may be used. In using the software, an organization agrees to abide by the licensing provisions, which typically limit the number of concurrent users and the hardware platforms on which the software may be installed. License agreements protect the software vendor's investment in manufacturing and distributing the software and give the user rights to use and upgrade a product. System administrators must ensure that the licensing provisions are adhered to. Numerous organizations that have ignored licensing provisions have been assessed large fines and were required to pay for additional licenses to cover the way in which the software was being used.

KEY TERMS

access security, *220*

Application Program Interface (API), *202*

backup software, *215*

client/server protocol, *201*

corporate license, *224*

deadlock, *218*

disk seek enhancement, *205*

duplexed servers, *207*

exclusive open mode, *217*

I/O optimization, *205*

interoperability, *211*

interrupt, *202*

key disk, *222*

LAN Server (IBM), *205*

license agreement, *220*

REVIEW QUESTIONS

1. Explain the functions of the workstation redirector software.

2. Explain how an application's network request is processed by both the workstation and the server.

3. Why may a stand-alone workstation need a memory upgrade when added to a LAN?

4. Explain why multithreaded server operation is important.

5. What is a client server or requester server protocol? Give an example.

6. What is an application program interface (API)?

7. What is the purpose of I/O optimization? Give two examples.

8. What is the benefit of fault-tolerant servers?

9. Describe three fault tolerance capabilities.

10. Explain how a print spooler works.

11. Explain two ways application software can be tailored to individual users.

12. Describe two ways data contention can be avoided.

13. What is deadlock? Give an example.

14. What is a software license? Why are software licenses necessary?

PROBLEMS AND EXERCISES

1. Use the literature to identify and briefly describe five capabilities of fault tolerance systems, such as Novell's SFT or Tandem's NonStop systems. The following magazine sources may prove helpful: *Network Management, LAN Times, LAN Technology, LAN,* and *Network Computing.* You also may use CD-ROM sources, such as *Computer Select.*

2. Evaluate a LAN-compatible database management system to determine how it resolves contention. Is contention resolution the responsibility of the user or the

database management system? Systems you may want to examine include Paradox and dBASE IV from Borland and FoxBase from Microsoft.

3. Research the literature for references to a LAN server that runs under the DOS operating system. How many users does the system support? Attempt to determine the expected level of performance.

4. Investigate one of the backup/restore software packages available. What functions does it provide?

5. You have been asked to configure the hardware for a local area network to provide office automation capabilities for a small office. The office manager wants you to provide a LAN that will make use of four IBM ATs with 1 MB of memory, two IBM XTs with 640 KB of memory, two IBM XTs with 512 KB of memory, one laser printer, and two dot-matrix printers that the office currently owns. Draw a network diagram of your proposed LAN using a bus topology. Label all hardware components in your diagram. Prepare a report to accompany your diagram that gives the following details:

   a. the equipment, software, and cabling that will be needed to connect each device to the LAN

   b. necessary upgrades to any of the existing hardware to make it LAN usable

6. Consider the office LAN described in problem 5. Some employees want to access the LAN from their homes to transfer files and do remote printing. Configure the hardware, software, and communications capabilities required at the LAN and user ends of the connection.

7. The office described in problem 5 wants to add fax capabilities to the network. The capabilities needed include the ability to send and receive fax transmissions and to store fax images on disk. Images sent and received may be in either hard copy or disk image format. Describe the hardware, software, and communications equipment necessary to create this capability.

8. Investigate several LAN software systems and describe the type of license agreement each uses.

9. The Software Publishers Association is an organization funded by many software firms. The charter of the association includes protecting against software piracy and the violation of software license agreements. Research the literature and find three instances of actions taken against companies or universities for violation of software license agreements.

10. Complete the case study in this chapter by calculating the remaining license and manual costs for database management, presentation graphics, and desktop publishing. What are the total software and manual costs for all five products?

REFERENCES

Allinger, Doug. "Fault Tolerance Comes to LAN Servers." *LAN Technology*, Volume 7, Number 1, January 1991.

Bolt, Robert C. "Battle of the Database Servers." *LAN Technology*, Volume 7, Number 1, January 1991.

Cavanagh, James P. "Anatomy of a Network OS Selection." *LAN Technology*, Volume 6, Number 8, August 1990.

Cavanagh, James P., Robert L. Guaraldi, Kathleen McKinney, and Mary Anne Cleary. "Anatomy of a Network OS Selection." *LAN Technology*, Volume 6, Number 6, June 1990.

————. "Anatomy of a Network OS Selection." *LAN Technology*, Volume 6, Number 7, July 1990.

Cavanaugh, Jim. "Decision '92: The Network Choice." *LAN Technology*, Volume 8, Number 12, November 1992.

Chacon, Michael, and Claude King. "Far and Wide with NT." *LAN*, Volume 9, Number 3, March 1994.

Day, Mike. "Network Printing: The Second Generation." *LAN Times*, Volume 9, Issue 15, August 10, 1992.

Derfler, Frank J., Jr. "Network Operating Systems Go Corporate." *PC Magazine*, Volume 11, Number 11, June 16, 1992.

Gilliland, Jim. "Surveying OS/2 2.0 Networking Options." *LAN Technology*, Volume 8, Number 10, October 1992.

Gillooly, Caryn. "Prepping Peer NOSes for the Enterprise." *Network World*, Volume 9, Number 33, August 17, 1992.

Janusaitis, Robert. "Meeting the NOS Selection Challenge." *Network World*, Volume 9, Number 41, October 12, 1992.

Korzeniowski, Paul. "Windows NT Advanced Server." *InfoWorld*, November 15, 1993.

Mendelson, Edward. "Premium Insurance: Backup Software Gets Better." *PC Magazine*, Volume 10, Number 11, June 11, 1991.

Nance, Barry. "Interoperability Today." *Byte*, Volume 16, Number 12, November 1991.

7

LAN Considerations

CHAPTER OBJECTIVES

After studying this chapter you should be able to:

- Describe several LAN alternatives
- List several LAN selection criteria
- Discuss how a specific selection criterion influences the selection process
- Evaluate a company's needs and develop a basic LAN strategy that meets those needs

*A*lthough originally designed to connect minicomputers, mainframes, and supercomputers, most LANs being installed today are used to link microcomputers. In this chapter, you will learn about the selection, implementation, and use of microcomputer-oriented LANs and alternatives to microcomputer LANs.

LAN ALTERNATIVES

We can look at LAN alternatives from two perspectives: different types of LAN implementations or hardware and software alternatives to LANs. In this section we discuss both. We start by looking at the ways LANs can be implemented.

LAN Implementation Alternatives

A LAN can be implemented using dedicated servers, using nondedicated servers, and peer to peer.

dedicated server   One or more computers that operate only as designated file, database, or other types of servers.

Dedicated Servers
In a **dedicated server** LAN, one or more computers are designated as file or database servers and these computers serve only in that capacity. They do not double as user computers. Many current LANs use client/server technology with dedicated server nodes. This is certainly true of most large LANs. However, the average number of nodes per microcomputer LAN is 6.3. This implies that many LANs have six or fewer nodes. For these small LANs, dedicating an expensive server machine (which will probably be underutilized) reduces the cost-effectiveness of the network. Two other technologies, nondedicated servers and peer-to-peer LANs, provide users an alternative to dedicated servers.

nondedicated server   A computer that can operate as both a server and a workstation.

Nondedicated Server
A few LAN operating systems allow **nondedicated servers**. A nondedicated server works as both a server and a workstation. A nondedicated server usually is the workstation with the most resources. For example, it is hard to imagine four users in a typical office keeping a dedicated server busy most of the time. If the server is allowed to also function as a workstation, it can be used more effectively.

The advantage of nondedicated servers is more effective use of resources. There are also some disadvantages. A nondedicated server must divide its workload between its application work and its server work. Sometimes it might be very busy in both roles. In these instances, both those using the server as a server and the person(s) using the server as a workstation will experience service degradation. If these conflicts occur too often, the LAN administrator should think of making the server dedicated. Another disadvantage of nondedicated servers is the increased likelihood of server failures. Simply running both applications and server software increases the possibility of failures because the server is doing more and the environment is more complicated. However, the most probable source of a nondedicated server failure is the user's application or the user him- or herself. If the application gets locked, the server may be unable to attend to its server duties. If the user powers the server down or unintentionally formats the server disk, the server function will also be disrupted.

Peer-to-Peer LANs
Taking nondedicated servers one step further leads to peer-to-peer LANs. In a peer-to-peer LAN, any or all nodes can operate as servers. If five microcomputers are networked in a peer-to-peer LAN, the network administrator can designate which computer resources are shareable and which are not. On one computer, a laser printer may be shared but a dot-matrix printer may be private to the user of that system. The computer's hard disk drive and one floppy disk drive may be shared but a second floppy disk drive may be private. All of the computers in this network are primary workstations for a user. Thus, the activities of a user can directly affect other users. If a user powers down the computer, its resources are not available to other

users, and if a user's program gets caught in a loop, that computer's resources will not be available to other users. Some peer-to-peer network operating systems allow you to designate each node as client only, server only, or both.

A peer-to-peer LAN is primarily used when there are few LAN workstations. The main benefit of peer-to-peer networks is the low cost per node, usually less than $200 for both hardware and software. Two disadvantages of peer-to-peer LANs are (1) centralized network management is more difficult and (2) fewer capabilities are provided for linking to other networks than are typically found in server-based LANs.

Other Implementations

Alternative implementations to a LAN include large, centralized computer systems; service bureaus; multi-user microcomputer systems; sub-LANs; and zero-slot LANs.

Large, Central Computer Systems For years the traditional approach to computing was to have a central host computer as shown in Figure 7-1. These large, central computers are still the mainstay of many data-processing operations. They are the primary means for processing large volumes of data, producing big reports, supporting special-purpose hardware devices such as

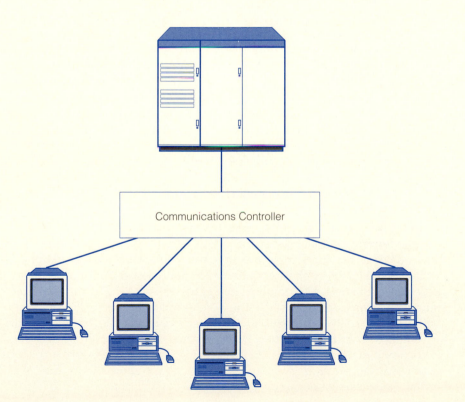

Figure 7-1

Central Host Computer

Communications Controller

check reader/sorters, and so on. It is unlikely that a large bank would be able to process its daily closing work with a microcomputer or a network of microcomputers. However, most companies augment their processing capabilities with microcomputers for personal productivity applications, and as noted earlier, downsizing from large computer systems to LANs is more common than replacing LANs with large systems.

Service Bureaus   Another alternative that a potential LAN user might consider is contracting with a computer **service bureau**. This alternative basically provides the same computing and connectivity capabilities as the large, central host alternative but without the high initial costs. The subscriber pays for the amount of computing resources — disk storage, processing time, and printed output — actually used. Subscribers also pay for custom software modifications and possibly a monthly subscription fee. This pricing structure is similar to that offered by the telephone systems, with a monthly connection charge regardless of usage and a second charge based on the amount of use. If usage is high, costs can be significant.

Multiuser Microcomputer Systems   A multiuser computer system allows two or more users to share a computer's resources. Several years ago, a multiuser computer system required a large computer. Today's microcomputers are as powerful as some low-end mainframes and minicomputers; a high-end microcomputer equipped with the right operating system can provide multiuser capabilities for a small number of users. As microcomputer technology expands, the number of users that can be supported will grow. This solution can provide complete compatibility with microcomputer software at a cost lower than that of most LANs.

The key to a multiuser system is the operating system. The hardware can be an off-the-shelf microcomputer as long as it has sufficient memory, disk space, and speed to support multiple users. However, the operating system must be able to support multiple concurrent users, display devices, and peripherals — features not available in common microcomputer operating systems such as MS-DOS and OS/2. Several multiuser operating systems are currently available, and more are likely to be added. In addition to the operating system, a multiuser system needs a printed circuit board that provides the interface to user terminals or microcomputers.

Sub–Local Area Networks   **Sub-LANs** provide a subset of LAN capabilities, primarily peripheral sharing and file transfer. They differ from a LAN in two ways: A sub-LAN's data transfer rates and costs are lower than those of a LAN, and file transfer capabilities are typically less transparent than on a LAN. On most sub-LANs, if a user needs to transfer a file to another workstation, the sender must first call the person operating the receiving workstation to manually establish the setting for data transfer. Sub-LANs are implemented with **data switches**. Data switches provide connection between microcomputers in much the same way a telephone company provides connections between callers. A switch configuration is shown in Figure 7-2. If Device A needs to connect with Device B, the switch establishes the connec-

---

service bureau   A subscription service in which the customer commissions disk storage, processing time, and printed output services of a large central host system based on usage.

sub-LAN   A network that provides a subset of LAN capabilities, primarily peripheral sharing and file transfer, but has lower data transfer rates and diminished transparency than a LAN.

data switch   A device implemented on sub-LANs to provide connection between microcomputers.

Figure 7-2

A Switch Configuration

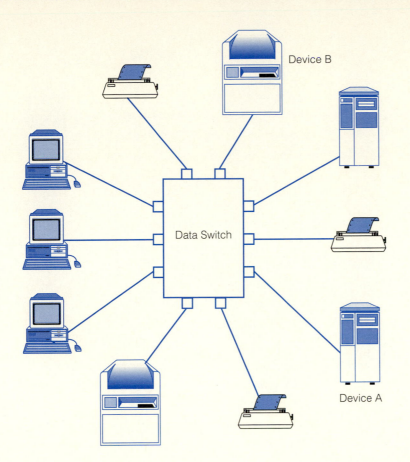

tion as illustrated in Figure 7-3. Many data switches are designed specifically for sharing peripheral devices, such as printers and plotters, and use manual switching. This means a user must turn a switch selector knob on the switch box to make the proper connection. With keyboard command switching, a user can enter the address of a desired device. If the device is not already in use, the connection is made; otherwise, the user must wait until the device is available. The connection remains active until one of the two stations requests a disconnect; alternatively, a disconnect may occur after a specified time of inactivity. Keyboard command switching does not solve the file transfer problem described above. Operators at the sending and receiving computers still must coordinate file transfer by starting the file transfer software at each end of the connection.

Sub-LANs are relatively inexpensive. A serial or parallel interface is used between the microcomputers and the switch. Because serial and parallel ports are either standard or low-cost options, the cost for the microcomputer components is limited to those ports and a cable. A switch that can support eight devices together with the essential operating software can be purchased for less than $2500, making the cost per connection about $325.

The disadvantages of a data switch are the low speed of the communications link; lack of user transparency, expandability, and ability to interface to other

Figure 7-3

Connecting Hardware with a
Switch

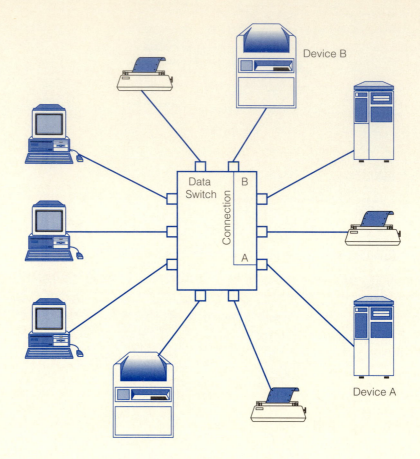

networks; and contention. The line speeds supported are typically 19.2 Kbps or slower. This speed is adequate for small file transfers and individual database records but not for large data transfers such as downloading program files, large documents, or large portions of a database. The ability to connect to other networks is generally poor. Although one of the switch ports might be connected to a terminal port on a large system, making the connection is not simple. The number of such connection ports is also limited.

Contention can also occur when using a data switch. If two users want to connect to a device such as a printer, only one of the connections can be made. The first request received is granted, and the second user must wait until the first connection is severed. Some data switches have on-board random access memory (RAM) to alleviate this contention problem. If multiple outputs for the same printer are received, one can be held in the switch's RAM until the printer becomes available. In the above situation, both users would perceive that their connection request was honored. Data switches are an effective, low-cost way to share peripherals and accomplish infrequent transfers of small files. They are not well suited for downloading software programs or large data files or for frequent file exchanges.

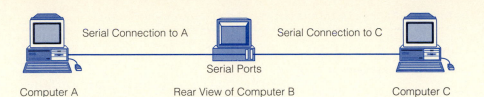

Figure 7-4

A Zero-Slot LAN

Serial Connection to A   Serial Connection to C

Serial Ports

Computer A   Rear View of Computer B   Computer C

Low-Cost LAN Alternatives

Just as there is a broad range of microcomputer workstations capable of meeting a variety of user needs, there is a broad range of microcomputer connection technologies collectively referred to as LANs. One major variant among these technologies is transmission speed, with speeds ranging from a low of 9600 bps to more than 2 billion (G) bps. In this text, the major emphasis is on technologies supporting speeds of 1 Mbps or faster. In this section, you will learn about several low-speed LAN alternatives. The advantage of these alternatives is low cost. The disadvantages are low transmission speeds and, in general, the inability to add many workstations. Low-speed LANs function well for small file transfers, database record access, and printer output; they perform poorly in an environment with many users or where large files and programs are downloaded.

The least expensive LAN alternatives use existing microcomputer hardware for connection. High-speed LANs use a LAN adapter or network interface card (NIC) as the interface between the communications medium and the workstation. Low-speed LANs use "standard" microcomputer components such as a serial or a parallel port. These LAN implementations are sometimes referred to as **zero-slot LANs** because they do not require an additional slot on the motherboard for a LAN adapter. When a LAN adapter is used, each station is assigned a unique address, which is set on the LAN adapter at the factory or through dual inline package (DIP) switch settings. Sometimes two serial or parallel ports are required by zero-slot LANs, as illustrated in Figure 7-4. Thus, the costs of implementing this type of LAN are cables, LAN software, and perhaps server hardware.

Low-cost alternatives other than zero-slot LANs exist. These systems use LAN adapters that run at speeds of 1 Mbps or slower and that cost less than the higher speed LAN adapters. The number of supported workstations usually is fewer than that supported on more expensive LANs, and the network software is not as developed as that used with most higher speed LANs. The software limitations are in support for file sharing, microcomputer applications, security, and network management. With zero-slot LANs based on DOS, the ability to perform multitasking operations is limited, resulting in less responsiveness to concurrent users. Some low-cost LANs do not support user passwords for security; of those that do, some provide only limited file protection schemes, such as the ability to provide certain file attributes — read, write, create, erase, and execute — to users and user groups.

zero-slot LAN   A low-speed LAN using "standard" microcomputer components that do not require an additional slot on the motherboard for a LAN adapter.

TABLE 7-1   **Rating of LAN Alternatives and a "Conventional" LAN**

	A	B	C	D	E	F
Number of workstations	1	2	3	3	3	1
Initial cost	5	4	2	1	1	3
Personnel costs	5	1	1	1	1	2
Operations/maintenance costs	5	4	1	1	3	3
Expandability	1	2	3	3	3	1
Microcomputer workstation support	4	3	2	2	1	1
User transparency	3	3	2	4	1	1
Accommodation for multiple users	1	1	4	4	3	2
Ease of user	3	4	2	4	2	1
Ease of management	3	1	2	2	4	3
Interface to other networks	1	5	5	5	4	1

     A = large, centralized computer systems

     B = use of a service bureau

     C = multi-user microcomputer systems

     D = sub-LANs

     E = zero-slot and low-cost LANs

     F = conventional LAN, for example, Ethernet or Token

Comparison of Alternatives

Table 7-1 compares the LAN alternatives just discussed. The evaluation rates several criteria on a scale of 1 to 5, with 1 being best. As an example of how to interpret Table 7-1, consider the first line that rates the number of workstations. A large, conventional LAN and a mainframe or minicomputer will allow hundreds or thousands of workstations or terminals; therefore, these two alternatives receive the highest rating. A service bureau will also provide access to a large number of terminals but generally at a higher cost, so this alternative is rated below the mainframe and large, conventional LAN alternatives. Multi-user microcomputers, sub-LANs, and zero-slot or low cost LANs are usually quite restrictive regarding the number of workstations allowed and thus tie for the lowest rating in this category.

LAN SELECTION CRITERIA

In preceding chapters we discussed LAN hardware, software, topologies, media, and media access control protocols. This material provides the foundation for evaluating a company's LAN needs and for selecting the components neces-

TABLE 7-2   Major Factors Influencing LAN Selection

Cost	Device Connectivity
Number of Concurrent Users	Vendor
Medium and Distance	Manageability
Expandability	Type of Workstations
LAN Software and Hardware	Number of Printers
Vendor Support	Applications
Number of Workstations	Connectivity with Other Networks
Type of Use	Adherence to Established Standards
Speed	Security

sary to build an effective LAN system. We now look at the major factors influencing LAN selection. These criteria are summarized in Table 7-2.

Cost

If cost were not a consideration, LAN selection would be easier. You could buy the fastest, biggest workstations and servers available and use the most comprehensive LAN software available. Deciding which hardware and software modules fit this description would not be simple, but lack of price constraints would make selection much easier. However, cost often is an overriding constraint, and you must choose the best solution within your budget. In the final analysis the LAN must be a cost-effective solution for your situation.

Hardware and software are not the only costs you will incur. Other costs you must plan for include the immediate and recurring costs shown in Table 7-3. Immediate costs are those you incur when installing a LAN. Recurring costs are the costs of operating and updating the LAN and training LAN users and administrators.

Number of Workstations

The effect the number of workstations has on the immediate costs of attaching a LAN has already been discussed. The number of workstations is also a key factor in network configuration. Each LAN is physically capable of supporting a specific maximum number of workstations. If you exceed that maximum, you must make some provision for extending the maximum number. A variety of techniques exist for doing this, and each increases the cost of the LAN. Other workstation costs can be incurred as well. If you intend to use existing microcomputers on the LAN, they may need to be upgraded. For example, because LAN software will be resident in each workstation, the amount of

TABLE 7-3   Immediate and Recurring LAN Costs

Immediate Costs

Equipment upgrades	Training — users, operators, administrators
Documentation	
Installation of cabling	Site preparation
System software installation	Hardware installation
Creating user environments	Installing applications
Space required for new equipment	Testing
	Supplies and spares

Recurring Costs

LAN management — personnel costs	Hardware and software maintenance
	Training — new users, administrators
Consumable supplies	

memory available to applications will be reduced. You therefore may need to add memory to some workstations.

Type of Workstations

The type of workstations you use will be a significant influence in your LAN alternatives. If your LAN will consist of Apple Macintoshes, a number of DOS-oriented LAN systems will be eliminated. If your workstations are IBM-compatible systems, Apple LANs will be eliminated. The same logic applies if your LAN consists of any of the other possible workstation platforms, such as those of Sun Microsystems. The LAN hardware and software must be compatible with the workstations used. If you need to mix the types of workstations on the LAN to allow both Apple and IBM-compatible workstations, you will again eliminate a number of LAN options and, perhaps, increase the cost.

Number of Concurrent Users

The number of concurrent users may differ from the number of workstations. Some networks have restrictions regarding the number of active users. One network operating system allows four concurrent users, but more than four workstations can be attached. An increase in the number of concurrent users also increases the LAN workload. As the LAN workload increases, you have two basic choices: You can allow system responsiveness to decrease, or you can increase the work potential of the system to maintain or improve the responsiveness. Naturally the second option involves higher costs. Some ways to improve LAN responsiveness are to select a faster LAN (one with higher transmission speeds), to use additional or more powerful servers (which means more expensive computers), or to use more efficient (and typically more costly) LAN software. The number of concurrent users of an application also has an impact on the cost of the application. Software vendors vary in their user license provisions; in general, application costs are directly proportional to the number of concurrent users. As the number of concurrent users goes up, so do software costs.

Type of Use

The impression you may have gained from the preceding paragraph is that having more concurrent users increases the LAN workload. However, you need to understand more about the effect of concurrent users on LAN performance. To do so, we look at two very different ways of using a LAN.

Suppose the primary LAN application is word processing, and the operating mode is as follows: LAN users access the word processing software on the file server at the beginning of their work shift, they save their documents on a local disk drive, and they periodically print documents. What demands are there on the LAN? The demand is heavy when a user starts the word processing program. The program must be downloaded, or transferred from the server to the workstation. The user does not need LAN services again until he or she prints a document or, in some cases, requires an **overlay module** for the word processor. An example of an overlay module is a spelling checker. Current microcomputer software is so rich in capabilities that all the functions cannot always be included in one memory-resident module. An overlay module overcomes this constraint by sharing memory with other overlay modules. LAN requests are therefore infrequent, but the amount of data transferred is large. Adding users may not significantly increase the LAN workload if there is a considerable amount of idle time. If you have used a LAN in a classroom situation, you probably have experienced this type of usage. At the beginning of the class, LAN response is slow because many students are starting an application at nearly the same time, and the demand for LAN resources is high. After that, however, LAN responsiveness improves because the LAN usage becomes intermittent.

Suppose instead that the primary LAN activity is database access, with users continually accessing and updating a database. In this case the LAN is constantly busy transferring large and small amounts of data. Adding new users in this instance can have a noticeable impact on LAN performance.

overlay module Overlaying is a memory management technique that divides a program into one resident segment and multiple overlay segments or modules. The resident module resides permanently in memory. The overlay segments occupy a common memory area. When code or data in an overlay module is referenced, it is either in the overlay memory area or on disk. If on disk, the overlay module is read into the overlay memory area and replaces the current overlay module.

Number and Type of Printers

The number and distribution of printers can affect your LAN decision as well. Some LAN operating systems require that network printers be attached to file servers, and each file server can support only so many printers. With such systems, if you have a need for a large number of printers, you may need to add server hardware and software simply to provide printing services. You also must be sure that the LAN you select is capable of supporting the types of printers you will be using. Each printer requires printer driver software to direct its operation. The driver software knows how to activate the special printer features needed to print special typefaces, underlining, graphics, and so on. Spooler software is responsible for writing printed output to shared printers. It follows that there must be an interface between the spooler and the printer drivers. Drivers are often included as part of the server software. When selecting a LAN you must ensure both that the printers you plan to use are supported and that they are supported in the manner in which you plan to use them. For example, a certain printer may be supported for printing text but not for printing graphics.

Distance and Medium

LANs serve a limited geographical area at high speeds. Distance and speed are related. Attaining high speed over long distances can be very expensive, and each LAN has a maximum distance it can cover. Different types of LANs also have different distance limitations. The distance is measured in wiring length. If you snake a cable back and forth through an office complex, you may not cover a wide geographical area, but the cable distance can be quite long. In general, as the distance your LAN needs to cover increases, your LAN options decrease. Distances for popular microcomputer LANs range from a few hundred meters to several thousand meters.

The type of medium also influences the selection process. If your facility already has wiring installed, you may select a LAN that can use that type of wiring. Each medium has speed and error characteristics. Earlier you read that twisted-pair wires support lower speeds and are more susceptible to errors than either coaxial cable or fiber optic cable. If your LAN wiring needs to pass through areas that can induce transmission errors (such as areas that produce electrical or magnetic interference), you may need to select a LAN that can use a more noise-resistant medium such as coaxial cable or fiber optic cable. One company came to this realization the hard way. In wiring the building with unshielded twisted-pair wires, the company ran the wiring through the shaft of a freight elevator. The freight elevator was seldom used; however, every time it was operated, the motor interfered with the data being transmitted on the LAN, causing numerous transmission errors. Replacing the cabling in the elevator shaft with more error-resistant wiring eliminated the periodic failures.

Speed

LAN speeds can be somewhat deceptive. A LAN speed quoted by the vendor is the speed at which data are transmitted over the medium. You cannot expect the LAN to sustain this speed at all times. Time is required to place data onto the medium and to clear data from the medium. This is done in a variety of ways, which you learned about in Chapter 5. It is important that you select a LAN capable of meeting your performance goals. If you expect access to data on your LAN's file server to have a transfer rate comparable to that of a hard disk, such as 5 Mbps, this requirement eliminates a number of low-speed LANs. Common LAN speeds available for microcomputers are 1, 2.5, 4, 10, 16, 20, and 100 Mbps. The trend is toward higher speeds because of greater LAN use and because of the types of data now being used in LAN applications. Applications using graphics, audio, and full-motion video are becoming more common. These applications require the transfer of large amounts of data and place a heavy load on the media and servers.

Applications

Most major application software packages are now available in LAN-compatible versions. This does not mean that all applications can run on all LANs. Applications communicate with the network through interfaces called application program interfaces (APIs), and a variety of APIs are in use. If the application uses an interface not supported by a particular LAN, then the application probably will not work on that network. Some software simply is not LAN compatible. It either cannot run on a LAN at all or it does not support sharing on a LAN but can be used by one user at a time. Custom-written applications also may not be LAN compatible. It is important to determine whether software you need to use will work on the LAN you are considering.

Expandability

After installing a LAN you probably will need to add workstations to it or move workstations from one location to another. The ease of doing this varies among implementations. The ease may depend on the medium used and on the way in which the medium was installed. Adding new nodes to some systems using twisted-pair wires or coaxial cable is relatively easy. Adding a new node to a fiber optic cable may require cable splicing, which means you must cut the cable, add the connectors, and rejoin the cable so the light pulses can continue along the cable. Fiber optic cable splicing technology has improved and is not difficult; however, adding a new node is still more difficult than for twisted-pair wires or coaxial cable.

Device Connectivity

Some organizations need to attach special devices to the LAN, such as an optical disk. LAN interfaces for such devices may not be available on some LANs or LAN file servers. This, of course, reduces your options to the LANs and servers that support the interface.

Connectivity to Other Networks

A LAN is often only one part of an organization's computing resources. Other facets may be a WAN, a large stand-alone computer, or other LANs. If there are other LANs, they may be of different types. When a variety of computing resources are available, it is frequently desirable to connect these resources. This allows a node on the LAN to communicate with a node on a WAN or to access data on a central mainframe system. A variety of connection capabilities exist, but a given LAN may not support all of them. If you have immediate connectivity needs or anticipate them in the future, you need to select a LAN that will support the connection protocols you expect to use.

LAN Software and Hardware

If you already have microcomputers and associated software and hardware, you probably want to preserve your investment in them. That means you need to select LAN software and hardware that will be compatible with your existing equipment. Notable differences between capabilities of LAN software and hardware also may be important in making your LAN selection.

Adherence to Established Standards

Some LANs conform to the standards for LAN implementation, whereas others do not. Several nonstandard LANs have been adopted by many users and have thus become de facto standards. Other LANs are neither covered by standards nor very widely adopted. A LAN's adherence to a standard does not necessarily mean it is superior to nonstandard LANs. However, there are benefits to choosing a LAN that conforms to a standard. Because standards are published, any company is able to design components that work on the LAN. This creates competition, gives users alternative sources of equipment, and usually drives down the cost of components. Adopting a standardized LAN also is often regarded as a "safe" decision because the community of users is frequently large. This generates a body of expertise that new users can tap for either information or personnel. On the other hand, a nonstandard LAN may provide innovative features that are not yet covered by standards. Adopting such a LAN can place an organization ahead of competition that is using a more conventional system. You can read about more LAN standards in Chapter 5.

Vendor and Support

When you select a LAN, you are selecting much more than hardware and software. You also are selecting a vendor or vendors with whom you expect to have a long-term relationship. Your vendors ought to be available to help you in times of problems; provide you with maintenance and support; and supply you with spare parts, hardware and software upgrades, and new equipment. You can be more successful with a good vendor and a less capable LAN than with a poor vendor and a superior LAN, especially if your vendor can quickly resolve problems, obtain needed equipment, and so on. Evaluate prospective vendors and their support policies as carefully as you evaluate the equipment itself.

Manageability

Do not underestimate the time and effort required to operate and manage a LAN. Even a small, static LAN requires some management once it has been installed and set up. Occasionally a user might be added or deleted, applications may be added or updated, and so on. The major ongoing activities will be backing up of files, taking care of printer problems, and solving occasional user problems. In a large LAN, management can be a full-time job — perhaps for more than one person. In Part IV you will learn about network management. During the selection process you must ensure that your LAN will have the necessary management tools or that third-party tools are available. Third-party tools are those written by someone other than the LAN vendor. The tools you need depend on the size of the LAN and complexity of the users and applications involved. As a minimum you should be able to easily accomplish the tasks listed in Table 7-4.

TABLE 7-4   LAN Management Tasks

User/Group Oriented

Add, delete users and groups	Set user/group security
Set user environment	Solve user problems

Printer Oriented

Install/remove printers	Set up user/printer environment
Maintain printers	

Hardware/Software Oriented

Add/change/delete software	Add/change/delete hardware
Diagnose problems	Establish connections with other networks
Plan and implement changes	

General

Make backups	Maintain operating procedures
Carry out recovery as necessary	Educate users
Plan capacity needs	Monitor the network
Serve as liaison with other network administrators	

Security

With stand-alone microcomputers, security generally is not an issue because stand-alone microcomputer systems are usually single-user systems, and thus, no security provisions were built into the operating systems or application software. As a result, access to the system is tantamount to access to all data stored on that system. By contrast, data in a LAN is shared. This does not imply that all users have unlimited access to all data. The LAN software must have the ability to control access to data. For each user you should at least be able to establish read, write, create, and purge rights for each file. Chapter 15 gives more comprehensive coverage of LAN security.

CASE STUDY

With these selection criteria in mind, we look in on the Syncrasy Corporation. Recall from Chapter 6 that Syncrasy has two interconnected LANs in the home office. The multiple LAN configuration evolved from an original single LAN. As Syncrasy's business grew and as LAN software evolved, Syncrasy decided that splitting the original LAN into two department-oriented LANs would better meet the company's computing needs. In this case study we describe Syncrasy's original LAN acquisition analysis. As this analysis began, Syncrasy soon found that choosing a microcomputer LAN is no easy task. Of the four primary architectures—CSMA/CD bus, StarLAN, token bus, and token ring—each has several variations, which may include speed and baseband or broadband as well as hardware and software. It became apparent to Syncrasy that the most important aspect of choosing a LAN implementation was to understand and define the problem they were attempting to solve.

LAN Requirements

The following points were formulated as some of Syncrasy Corporation's LAN requirements.

Data Sharing   Data maintained on the host system must be available to be used on microcomputer workstations. This data includes data in the database, text files, and graphics images.

Security   User access to the network must be controlled. Users will have to login to the network to use it and the login procedure must support passwords. User access to files must also be controlled so that on a user-by-user basis a user can be

- prevented from detecting the existence of a file
- able to detect a file's presence but not be able to read from or write to it
- able to read a file but not write to it

- able to read and write to a file
- able to erase a file or not

These important issues, common to LANs and WANs, are covered as an aspect of network management in Chapter 15.

Software Downloading   Most of the software that is to be run on the microcomputers must reside on one or more file servers. A user needing access to a particular program will run it from one of the file servers. This requirement is subject to software licensing agreements.

Printers   Approximately 20 printers will be distributed throughout the work areas. These laser printers, high-speed dot matrix printers, and plotters must be accessible to all users, which means they must be attached to printer servers.

User Access   Users must be able to easily access the resources of both file and printer servers.

Remote Access   Remote access to the network must be available. Users on the wide area network already installed must be able to attach to the LAN and utilize its resources.

Compatibility   The LAN should support all the IBM-compatible microcomputers currently owned by Syncrasy. New workstation technology should also be able to attach to the LAN and coexist with the current technology.

Other Hardware   Other hardware should be able to be attached to the LAN as well, such as minicomputers and mainframe systems.

Fault Tolerance   Some level of fault tolerance is required either through hardware and software features or through multiple components such as file and print servers.

Support of User Base   The LAN must have the ability to support the current user base of 150 workstations.

Expansion   The LAN must have the ability to expand in a modular fashion. Support of up to 250 workstations within 2 years is considered essential.

Vendor Requirements   Vendors are requested to provide system configuration and costs for hardware, software, cabling, education, manuals, maintenance, and installation for the system capable of supporting 150 workstations. They also are required to explain how the system could be expanded to accommodate 250 workstations and to estimate the cost required to effect this expansion.

To obtain the best information on obtaining and implementing a LAN, Syncrasy launched a three-pronged effort. A request for information (RFI) was drafted asking LAN vendors to indicate how their systems would meet the above requirements. Application software vendors were contacted to determine whether their software was LAN compatible, which LAN implementations were certified, and their licensing agreements. Finally, the selection committee made arrangements to visit a variety of comparable LAN implementations.

Hardware Evaluations

When the LAN vendors returned their responses, Syncrasy was amazed at the variations in suggested approaches. Twenty responses were received. LAN speeds of 1, 2, 4, 10, 16, and 100 Mbps were proposed. Implementations included token rings, token buses, CSMA/CD buses, and StarLANs. The number of file servers recommended to provide service for 150 workstations varied from 1 to 6. In addition, for the configuration proposing 1 file server, the apparent processing capacity of the file server was equivalent to that of one of the file servers in the configuration proposing 6 servers! The supporting operating systems included MS-DOS, OS/2, UNIX, and custom server-oriented ones. Equating capabilities among the alternatives was not an easy task. After reviewing all responses, Syncrasy decided to attempt to reduce the systems being considered to a more manageable size of five. The company established a set of criteria to provide a fair elimination process. A summary of the process used to do this follows.

Resolve Areas of Uncertainty   Some RFI responses were not clear on certain points. These vendors were contacted for clarification.

Cost   At the outset Syncrasy had anticipated the cost for workstation LAN adapters, cabling, servers, server software, installation, education, and manuals at $150,000. This estimate did not include the costs of workstations or application software. This cost was based on the following rough calculations:

- LAN adapters, 150 at $200 each: $30,000
- Cable, 2000 feet at $2 per foot: $4000
- Cable installation: $15,000
- Education: $20,000
- Three servers: $30,000
- LAN operating system, 3 copies, 100 users each: $18,000
- Manuals: $5000
- First-year maintenance: $5000
- Miscellaneous, including network management and so on: $23,000

The only figure in the entire original estimate in which there was a high degree of confidence was the LAN controller cards. Syncrasy knew how many they needed and documentation was available indicating that the per unit cost was a reasonable approximation. The other figures were mostly speculation.

The variation among vendor responses was considerable. Some vendors did not propose a configuration or price. The lowest cost was approximately $100,000, and the highest was more than $500,000! Because several attractive proposals were less than $200,000, it was decided to table all proposals over that figure.

Speed   Syncrasy wanted to run file server software at close to floppy disk speed. Some of the literature they had read indicated that they would be fortunate to realize 50% of the rated LAN speed. In fact, some literature indicates that only 20% effective use may be attained (Cashin, 1987). Floppy disks have a transfer rate of about 250 Kbps. Factoring in seek and latency time, Syncrasy estimated an effective transfer rate of 100 Kbps for a program located on adjacent tracks. Running a 100-Kbyte program would thus require transferring 1 million bits. This would take 10 seconds on a floppy disk drive using the 100 Kbytes per second speed. Empirical timings on some software packages indicated that this figure was reasonable.

Using the 50% LAN utilization factor (which some thought optimistic), a 1-Mbps LAN would be required for a 2-second download time for a 100-Kbyte program. Because 150 users would be on the LAN, multiple requests for downloading could be received simultaneously — particularly at common start times such as the first thing in the morning and after lunch. The selection committee decided the minimum speed for their network should be 4 Mbps. Had there been fewer users, lower speeds would have been sufficient.

Manageability   Network management consists of establishing user IDs, setting security on files, making backups, managing disk usage, monitoring performance, tuning, and so on. Without working with a system it is difficult to determine the management involvement. Syncrasy believed, however, that the greater the number of components involved, the more difficult the management tasks. Several viable solutions that used three or fewer file servers were proposed. Therefore, Syncrasy decided that all solutions calling for more than three file servers would be tabled. It also turned out that some of the solutions that had the most file servers also were among the most costly.

Connectivity   One requirement Syncrasy had placed on the system was to be able to connect existing computers to the LAN. Although they did not have plans for this at the outset, it was an option they wanted to hold open for the future. Some of the LANs proposed were limited in this capability. Interfaces must exist on two sides to make connections, the LAN side and the equipment side. Almost all proposals supported connections such as asynchronous interfaces, but Syncrasy desired a direct LAN attachment that could operate at LAN speeds. Connectivity also pertains to the number of workstations that can be added, the configuration for workstations, and how many printer servers can be supported. All LANs have limits; however, these limits are encountered in different areas. Examples of limitations include a maximum of 5 shared printers and a maximum of 64 workstations per file server.

Adherence to Established Standards   Syncrasy decided to implement a LAN for which a standard existed. This meant adherence to one of the IEEE 802 standards or to the ANSI FDDI standard. It was Syncrasy's belief that a standardized implementation would protect them from future isolation regarding attaching equipment to the LAN and the ability to take advantage of new technology.

Vendor Reliability   One or two vendors were rejected because Syncrasy was skeptical of their reliability, ability to support the product, and/or the reliability of the manufacturer of the equipment they proposed.

Viability of Proposal   As mentioned above, there were considerable differences among the proposed solutions. A small number of proposals were rejected because they did not seem plausible.

Syncrasy drew two key conclusions from this research: First, do not assume anything and, second, ask questions even if the answers seem obvious. We do not divulge Syncrasy's final selection; it is left as a reader exercise. There is another reason for not indicating the final selection. There are many LAN alternatives and all fulfill certain user needs. Picking one over another here could be erroneously construed as an endorsement of that technology. There are many good solutions to a given LAN problem, and different constraints and emphases will lead to different implementations.

Software Evaluations

Just as there were considerable differences in the hardware proposals, Syncrasy found considerable differences regarding how application software vendors approached site licensing. For an organization to use software, it must comply with the software vendor's licensing agreements. Most software for microcomputers is licensed to operate on one system only, or at least on only one system at a time. Networks have added a new dimension to software use. The software resides on a file server and is available for any LAN user to access. For leading software packages, Syncrasy encountered all the following variations.

- There was no such thing as a site license.
- Running the software on the LAN was a violation of the licensing agreement, even if the site purchased one package for each potential user.
- The site license required that an individual package be purchased for every workstation.
- The site license required that an individual package be purchased for each simultaneous user. A counter was used to control simultaneous access to the program.

- The site license was a one-time fee for the software, which allowed as many multiple users as the site needed.

- The site license was based on a per server charge. There were no restrictions regarding concurrent use.

- There was a license fee for each server and for each workstation that would have access to the software.

Some leading software packages also would not run on a LAN because of copy protection or because they were not capable of supporting multiple users. Some software would work on one LAN implementation and not another. Syncrasy decided to adopt a standardized set of software for common functions such as word processing, database management, graphics, spreadsheets, desktop publishing, and statistics. Before Syncrasy made the final selection, the vendor was required to demonstrate each of these programs running on the proposed network in a multiuser environment. ❖

SUMMARY

Microcomputer LANs are increasing in number. You can expect to encounter them or a LAN alternative whenever two or more microcomputers are located near each other. The variety of LAN alternatives include large mainframe systems and service bureaus on the high end and multiuser microcomputers, sub-LANs, and zero-slot LANs on the low end. These alternatives ought to be considered before you implement a LAN.

A variety of factors must be considered when selecting a LAN. First, you should decide whether a LAN is required or whether a LAN alternative will suffice. If a LAN is required, factors to consider include cost-effectiveness, available system and application software, security, compatibility with existing hardware and software, LAN organization (dedicated server, nondedicated server, or peer-to-peer), adherence to established standards, number of concurrent users supported, ability to interconnect with other networks and computers, and vendor support and expertise. The weight associated with each selection criterion may differ among organizations. In making the right selections, you need to evaluate the alternatives from the perspective of your organization's immediate and future communications objectives.

KEY TERMS

data switch, *236*

dedicated server, *234*

nondedicated server, *234*

overlay module, *243*

service bureau, *236*

sub-LAN, *236*

zero-slot LAN, *239*

REVIEW QUESTIONS

1. Compare and contrast a dedicated and nondedicated server.

2. Describe a peer-to-peer LAN. How does it differ from a dedicated server LAN?

3. What are the advantages and disadvantages of a large, central computer system vis-à-vis a LAN?

4. Compare and contrast a multiuser microcomputer with a multiuser mainframe computer.

5. Describe how a data switch works. What are its weaknesses as a LAN alternative?

6. What is a zero-slot LAN? What are the advantages and disadvantages of zero-slot LANs?

PROBLEMS AND EXERCISES

1. You have decided that a LAN alternative is the correct solution for your application. You want to connect 5 microcomputers in one 20-by-30-foot room of your office complex. You want to share printers extensively and do a limited amount of file sharing. Cost is a critical consideration in your implementation. What LAN alternative should you use? Explain why you reached your decision.

2. If user transparency were a critical issue in exercise 1, which LAN alternative would be best? Which alternative would likely be unsuitable? Explain your decisions.

3. Consider the case study at the end of this chapter. Using the material in the preceding chapters and current hardware and software references, configure a LAN for Syncrasy showing the hardware and software costs involved. Recall that Syncrasy already has the 150 workstations. Assume that no upgrades to any workstation will be necessary except for inclusion of the LAN adapter. You must include servers, server and workstation software, and LAN adapters in your configuration.

REFERENCES

Allinger, Doug. "A Look at Low-End LANs." *LAN Technology,* December 1989.

Cashin, Jerry. "Local Area Networks Play the 20% Game." *Software News*, April 1987.

Derfler, Frank J., Jr. "Building Network Solutions: Is ISDN Tomorrow's Interoffice Network?" *PC Magazine*, February 13, 1990.

————. "Building Workgroup Solutions—Low-Cost LANs." *PC Magazine,* March 28, 1989.

————."Building Workgroup Solutions—The X.25 Alternative." *PC Magazine,* May 15, 1990.

————. "Connectivity Simplified." *PC Magazine*, Volume 11, Number 6, March 31, 1992.

————. "Making Do with DOS." *PC Magazine*, Volume 9, Number 10, May 29, 1990.

Nance, Barry. "Peer LANs Offer a Low-Cost Network Alternative." *Byte*, Volume 16, Number 12, November 1991.

Nash, Jim. "Peer Pressure." *LAN*, Volume 7, Number 10, October 1992.

Today you may be sitting in your classroom or at home reading this material from a printed book. If you want to see a movie you go to a theater, or rent a video from a video store. A printed newspaper is delivered to your home by a delivery person. Within a few years, each of these communications delivery methods will seem decidedly old-fashioned. With the information superhighway, a wide area network (WAN), all these conveniences and many more will be available to you electronically, on demand, and within seconds — and all in your own home. The information superhighway will dramatically change the ways Americans work and play. Many postal letters will be replaced by electronic mail; newspapers and books will be transmitted and stored electronically; and you will shop, attend classes, and telecommute — all using the services of a WAN.

Some of these services are currently available via one or more information networks, such as the Internet. The Internet is a network of networks connecting hundreds of subnetworks and millions of computers and users representing academia, governments, military units, and private corporations.

Although they are not as widely publicized as LANs, many businesses use WANs to connect geographically distributed offices. One such company is the Associated Banks Corporation (ABC). ABC is a national bank with four regional data-processing centers located in Atlanta, Boston, San Francisco, and Chicago. ABC maintains a network of automatic teller machines (ATMs) in its service areas and LANs in each bank and at the home office. ABC's WAN was placed in service long before ABC had ATMs and LANs. In its early days the WAN provided computational services via a network of terminals. Although the WAN has undergone many changes since its initial implementation, it remains the foundation of ABC's data-processing activities. In addition to providing high-volume computing services such as check clearing, loan approval and upkeep, interest computations, and account maintenance, ABC's WAN provides connectivity among the WAN nodes, ATMs, and LANs.

In this part we see how companies such as ABC implement their WANs. We start by discussing the key components of a WAN — hardware, topologies, transmission services, and software. These topics are followed by descriptions of several specific WAN implementations. ∎

Part III

WIDE AREA NETWORKS

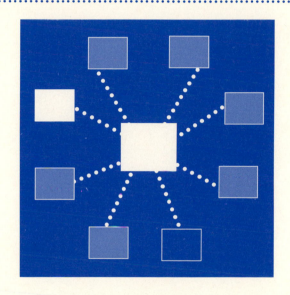

8

WAN Hardware

CHAPTER OBJECTIVES

After studying this chapter you should be able to:

- Define the differences between dumb, smart, and intelligent terminals
- Discuss a variety of terminal attributes
- Explain what ergonomics means and the importance of ergonomically designed terminals
- Describe ways that two or more terminals can share the same communications line
- Apply considerations for choosing the best terminal for a given task
- Describe how multiplexers work
- Compare and contrast front-end processors and concentrators
- Define the use of several types of WAN hardware and diagnostic devices

*I*n this chapter we discuss WAN hardware, starting with terminals attached to the end of a communications line. After describing the terminal equipment we move toward the primary processors of a system, host computers. Along the way, we examine devices that make the use of a medium more efficient, more cost-effective, or both. One configuration of some of the hardware we discuss is illustrated in Figure 8-1.

259

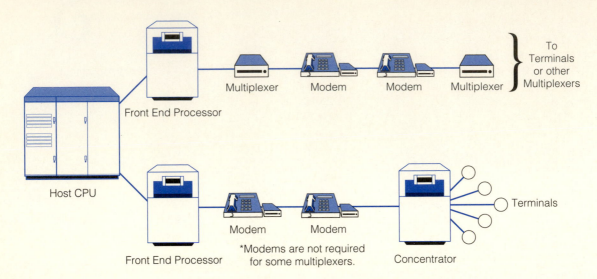

Figure 8-1

A Hardware Configuration

TERMINALS

terminal   An input/output device that can be connected to a local or remote computer called a host computer.

We define a **terminal** as an input and/or output device that may be connected to a local or remote computer, called a host computer. The terminal is at certain times dependent on the host for either computation or data access or both. The phrase *may be connected* allows for switched connections and devices that have some degree of processing power and are connected to a host on a periodic basis, such as a microcomputer.

Terminal Types

Microcomputers   Microcomputers are an integral component of computer networks because they can augment the host by doing a portion of the processing. They may be grouped together in a local area network or as terminal devices connected to a host computer or both. Some ways microcomputers are being used in networks include uploading processed data to the host, downloading host data for processing, and terminal emulation. **Uploading** happens when the terminal transfers files or programs to the host. Downloading is the act of transferring programs or data from a host to a terminal. With **terminal emulation**, a software program and a hardware interface allows one microcomputer to function as a variety of terminals in support of changing requirements.

uploading   The transfer of files or programs from the terminal to the host.

terminal emulation   A software program and a hardware interface that allow one microcomputer to function as a variety of terminals in support of changing requirements.

Remote Job Entry (RJE) Stations   A terminal can be used to forward record images to a host system and possibly to receive updated reports back from the host. Historically, input from such terminals has been card images and the resulting output has been printed reports or punched cards. Tape has also served as an input or output medium. This type of operation is sometimes referred to as remote batch processing.

Figure 8-2
A VDU Terminal

Data Entry and Display A **video display unit (VDU)** or a hard-copy device such as a teletypewriter (TTY) can serve for data entry, data display, or both. Such devices can carry on a dialogue with the host(s) and get data from and provide data to the business's applications. A VDU is also sometimes referred to as a Video Display Terminal (VDT) or a Cathode Ray Tube (CRT). A VDU terminal is shown in Figure 8-2.

Sensor Devices Sensor devices are used in laboratory, hospital, or data collection applications, frequently for input only. For example, many newer, large office buildings have a computer-controlled environmental monitoring system. Sensors located throughout the building alert the system to areas in which temperature is outside the comfort zone. The host responds by sending a message to an output-only terminal device that switches on either heating or cooling.

Display-Only Devices A display-only device frequently serves as a receiver of data. The display monitors in stock-market applications are display-only devices. Remote printers also fit in this class, although some also have the ability to transmit control information such as "out of paper" or "not ready to receive."

Video Display Unit (VDU) A terminal that uses a technique such as a cathode ray tube or a liquid crystal display to represent data. Also referred to as a Video Display Terminal (VDT) or Cathode Ray Tube (CRT).

Point-of-Sale Terminals   Point-of-sale (POS) terminals are used to help maintain inventory, record gross receipts, and — in some instances — participate in money transfers from a buyer's account to a merchant's account. The capabilities of POS terminals vary significantly.

Portable Terminals   One application for portable terminals or microcomputers is in direct sales. Some marketing agencies provide their salesforce with portable terminals capable of storing information in memory. The salesperson records customer orders during the day and can use a telephone link to transmit the orders to the home office for processing. Figure 8-3 features a portable microcomputer.

Touch-Tone Telephones   Touch-tone telephones can be used in bill paying, account inquiry or transfer applications, and student registration. Although not employed extensively because of their limited input and output capabilities, they work well for certain applications.

Automatic Teller Machines (ATMs)   Most banks now have networks of teller machines that enable the customer to personally handle simple banking

Figure 8-3

A Portable Microcomputer

transactions such as deposits, withdrawals, and account balance inquiries. ATMs have had a significant impact on the way people use banking services. Through the ATM, bank customers can get cash or make deposits 24 hours a day and without the assistance of a teller. The ATM provides convenience to the bank customer and reduces the number of personnel a bank needs to provide services, because the customer and the computer combine to accomplish services that formerly required the assistance of a bank teller.

Terminal Capabilities

Rather than discussing the wide variety of terminal types in depth, we focus our discussion on terminal capabilities and then present a list of attributes to be considered when selecting the proper terminal for a given application. Terminals can be classified as dumb, smart, or intelligent, although no distinct lines separate these classes.

A **dumb terminal** passively serves for input and/or output and does no additional processing. Because dumb terminals usually have no memory to store data, each character entered must be transmitted immediately to the host, unsolicited, and the host must always be ready to accept data from the terminal. A dumb terminal generally operates in **conversational mode**, in which the terminal user and the host exchange messages in response to each other.

Smart terminals can do anything a dumb terminal can; however, smart terminals have memory. Data entered by the operator can be saved in the terminal's memory until an entire record or several screens of data have been entered. The terminal can then transmit all the entered data in one or more blocks, a capability referred to as **block mode**. Often the screen can be divided into multiple windows, with each window representing a different object set. One window might represent text being written, one might contain notes about the text, another might contain a graphic image of an item being described in the text, and a fourth might contain a menu of tasks or commands that are valid in the current window. Most smart terminals are also addressable, which means they can be given a name that both they and the host recognize. Thus, the host can transmit data addressed to that terminal, and the terminal will recognize that the data is intended for it and store the data in its memory. Smart terminals are subject to host control, which means the host can specify when the terminal is allowed to:

- send or receive data
- position the cursor on the display
- designate that certain fields — such as an employee's salary — be protected from alteration
- control the keyboard and disallow any data entry
- specify the display attributes of fields such as blink and half intensity
- read from or write to selected portions of the display

dumb terminal   A terminal that passively serves for input and/or output but performs no local processing.

conversational mode   A mode in which the terminal and the host exchange messages.

smart terminal   A terminal that can save data entered by the operator into memory.

block mode   A mode in which data is entered and transmitted in one or more sets or blocks.

Addressing, memory, and host-control capabilities enable several terminals to share the same medium and thereby reduce transmission costs.

Smart terminals may also support auxiliary data entry devices such as lightpens, mice, and touch-screens. Many can have a printer attached, for printing a displayed page and for automatic logging of data received by the terminal. Many smart terminals have additional keys known as function keys, or program attention keys, that transmit specific character sequences to the host. Function keys allow the operator to indicate to the application what function is to be performed on the data provided. The number of function keys per terminal typically ranges from 4 to 32; some special-purpose terminals have 50 or more function keys.

intelligent terminal   A
terminal that has both memory and data processing
capabilities.

An **intelligent terminal**, such as a microcomputer, has all or most of the capabilities of a smart terminal, but it can also participate in the data-processing requirements of the system. In some situations the intelligent terminal is completely independent of the host; however, to satisfy our definition of terminal, at some point the intelligent terminal must be connected to a host processor for processing or data access. Because this terminal is programmable, it is also possible for an intelligent terminal to act as host for another terminal. Intelligent terminals may have secondary storage in the form of disk or tape, and an attached printer is a common option. If no auxiliary storage is available, programs can be downloaded to the terminal from the host computer. Like smart terminals, intelligent terminals can be controlled from the host and can operate in both conversational and block modes. Processing functions available on intelligent terminals include storage and display of screen formats, data editing, data formatting, compression/decompression, and possibly some local database access and validation.

Relative Advantages of Dumb, Smart, and Intelligent Terminals

The advantage of smart terminals over dumb terminals is a certain amount of independence between the terminal operator and host. Once a data entry screen is displayed, the operator is free to enter data at his or her own pace, unrestricted by the transmission speed of the line. Any errors made by the operator can be corrected without the host's involvement. The operator can move the cursor to any field in the record and can correct any data before transmission to the host. The host then controls the terminal and solicits inputs and outputs according to its priorities rather than being periodically interrupted by unsolicited inputs, as is the case with dumb terminals. The advantages of intelligent terminals over smart terminals stem from the fact that control and processing are local. Some data, such as customer data, can be maintained locally where it is frequently used, and line time is not required for obtaining customer information, transmitting screen templates, or correcting edit errors.

Several terminal attributes are listed in Table 8-1. These attributes are among the criteria to consider when selecting a terminal for a given application.

TABLE 8-1 Some Terminal Attributes

Cost	Synchronous	Auxiliary storage	EBCDIC
Conversational	Batch	Protected fields	Protocol support
Block mode	Point-to-point	Graphics	Attached devices
TTY-compatible	Multipoint	Formatting	Duplex
Dumb	Function keys	Character sets	Screen size
Smart	Editing	Keyboard	Character size
Intelligent	Cursor control	Blink	Modified data
Printer	Host control	Half intensity	tags
Speed	Color	Reverse video	CPU
Asynchronous	Programmable	ASCII	Interface
			Portability

Input and Output

Terminal output can be hard copy and soft copy. Hard-copy output leaves a permanent record of the data sent to the terminals, whereas soft-copy output leaves no record of the inputs or outputs. Hard copy uses some type of printed output, and soft-copy format uses a display monitor such as a CRT. The most common input mechanism is the keyboard, which can be configured in a variety of ways. Some configurations support foreign languages whereas others have preprogrammed keys that support specific applications, such as specimen description keys for medical laboratories. Other input devices include various types of readers—badge readers and OCR readers—and light-pens, mice, trackballs, joysticks, touch-screens, sensors, voice recognition and generation equipment, and digital image processing devices that scan graphic images and create digital images of them.

Cost

The cost of terminals varies dramatically, from several hundred dollars for a dumb terminal to tens of thousands of dollars for special terminals such as RJE or very high resolution graphics terminals with imaging devices. Cost analysis is difficult, as cost factors such as line utilization, operator acceptance, efficiency, and local processing ability are not always easy to quantify.

Speed

The speed at which a terminal accepts and transmits data is dependent on the terminal hardware, the type of line to which it is attached, and the types of modems used (if any). Any given terminal can receive and transmit information at a discrete set of rates. An unbuffered hard-copy terminal may have a maximum receive speed of 1200 bps because its print capacity is 120 characters per second. A CRT device, on the other hand, may be capable of receiving data at 19.2 Kbps or more. In addition to the maximum available speed, the intermediate speeds available should be considered. Some terminals have one or two speed settings, whereas others support several common speeds, such as 75, 300, 600, 1200, 2400, 4800, 9600, 19,200, and 38,400 bps.

Maintenance and Support

Some computer manufacturers sell terminals that are manufactured by other companies. These computer manufacturers usually provide the support for these terminals. Other computer vendors build their own terminals and design them to complement their computer systems. These terminals usually receive support consistent with the support for the rest of the system. An advantage of such vendor support is having only one organization to contact regardless of the problem. For instance, what appears to be a terminal problem may actually be an error in the software or hardware communicating with that terminal. Single-vendor support tends to eliminate the question of who is responsible for errors. Determining which vendor is responsible for a problem can become a difficult issue in multiple-vendor installations. Single-vendor support has one disadvantage for both terminals and computer equipment: Computer manufacturers sometimes charge more for their terminals than manufacturers who specialize in terminal equipment.

Display Attributes

Hard-copy devices have very few display attributes to select, with the possible exception of colored pens for plotters, graphics, italics, underline, type fonts, or overprint. Video display units have several display attributes to consider, including multiple colors, shading or intensity, reverse video, and highlighting such as blinking fields. Screen size and character size also should be taken into consideration, because the number of characters per line and the number of lines per screen can vary significantly.

Ergonomics

ergonomics The science of designing equipment to maximize worker productivity by reducing operator fatigue and discomfort while improving safety.

Ergonomics, also called human engineering, is the science of designing equipment to maximize worker productivity by reducing operator fatigue and discomfort while improving safety. Currently, a very important consideration in terminal and microcomputer design and selection is the unit's human engineering. Several physical problems have been attributed to poor terminal design, including radiation side effects, headaches, eye strain, muscle and tendon problems, and arthritic conditions. Perhaps the major side effect of VDU terminals is their emission of radiation. Terminal and microcomputer monitors emit low-level radiation, and users working near the monitors are exposed to those emissions. Some companies have noted a higher incidence of birth defects among women working at VDUs, and several lawsuits have been filed in this regard. According to U.S. law, radiation emitted from a terminal must be less than 0.0005 rems per hour at a distance of 2 inches from the screen. Radiation reduction is usually achieved by filtering the radiation with a glass screen. Radiation emission is one factor to consider when selecting a monitor.

Three other ergonomic factors to consider include monitor position, monitor display, and keyboard position. Among the most common user complaints are head, neck, and eye strain. Head and neck strain can be caused by the user having to adjust to the relatively fixed position of a monitor. An ergonomically designed monitor can be tilted and swiveled to a position that is comfortable for the user. Finger, hand, and wrist strains result from improper positioning of the keyboard. The keyboard should be detached from the monitor so it can be moved to a position comfortable for the user. Computer furniture is also an ergonomic factor to consider. With a chair that can be raised and lowered and a movable keyboard platform, the computer system can be adjusted comfortably to the user. Again, the key is to have a unit capable of adjusting to a user rather than requiring a user to adjust to the equipment.

Eye strain can be caused by poorly formed characters, flickering screens, and poor foreground/background colors. A good monitor has crisp, well-formed characters and images, and the contrast between foreground and background colors should be visually pleasing. Ergonomic studies have shown that green or amber foreground characters on a black background is easier on the eyes than other combinations, such as white letters on a black background. Another factor affecting eye strain is screen flickering. CRT screen images are constantly refreshed by "repainting" the screen image. Low refresh rates cause screen images to fade before being refreshed, creating a flickering effect that can cause headaches and eye strain.

Ideal Terminal Characteristics   The ideal display should be easy on the eyes, with a non-glare surface. Green phosphor or amber characters on a black background are preferred to white characters on a black background. The display should tilt and swivel for ease of reading. The screen image should be refreshed at a sufficient rate to avoid flicker, and contrast should be adjustable to ease eye strain. Display characters should be well formed and easy to read. The keyboard should be detachable and at a convenient height. Keys should be sculpted and arranged for easy access. The keyboard should emit a click to reinforce each keystroke, and the loudness of the click should be controllable, from inaudible to somewhat loud.

Data Link Protocol

Terminals communicate by a convention that transmits either a character at a time or a block at a time. In Chapter 5 we discussed LAN data link protocols. WANs also use data link protocols, but typically WAN data link protocols differ from LAN protocols. WAN data link protocols (discussed in more detail in Chapter 9) are a primary concern when purchasing a terminal. Many terminals communicate via only one of these conventions, such as an asynchronous protocol or one of several synchronous protocols.

Terminal Configurations

point-to-point connection A connection using a communication line to connect one terminal to a host computer.

On any communications channel, the two options for attaching terminals are point to point and multipoint. **Point-to-point connections** use a communications line to connect one terminal to the host computer. Point-to-point connections are common in computer-to-computer communications, local connections between a host and a terminal where the cost of the line is negligible, and remote connections with only one remote terminal. The methodology for controlling which station is allowed to use the communications link is sometimes referred to as a line discipline. Data flow in a point-to-point configuration is usually determined by contention.

contention mode A mode in which the host and the terminal contend for control of the medium by issuing a bid for the channel.

In the **contention mode**, the host and the terminal contend for control of the medium much like nodes on a CSMA/CD LAN. The terminal and the host are considered to have an equal right to transmit to the other. To transmit, one station issues a bid for the channel, asking the other party for control. If the other is ready to receive data, control is granted to the requester. Upon completion of the transfer, control is relinquished and the link goes into an idle state, awaiting the next bid for control. A collision can occur when both stations simultaneously bid for the line. If this occurs, either one station is granted the request based on some predetermined priority scheme or each station waits awhile and then reattempts the bid. With the latter approach, the time-out intervals must not be the same, or another collision would occur. Conflicts for the use of the channel in a point-to-point configuration typically are few, because only the host and the terminal are candidates for transmission.

For communication among several terminals over a long distance, true point-to-point connections would be quite expensive, as each terminal would require a separate line with a pair of modems. Several techniques have been developed to allow several terminals to share one communications link. One such technology is called a **multipoint connection**. The number of terminals allowed to share the medium depends on the speed of the medium and the aggregate transmission rate of the terminals. As the number of terminals on the line increases, the average time each terminal has access to the link decreases. With terminals, the most common approaches to multipoint connections are polling and multiplexing.

multipoint connection A connection in which several terminals share one communications link.

polling The process of asking terminals whether they have data to transmit. One terminal, usually the host, is designated as the primary station and the rest are referred to as secondary stations.

Polling   The process of asking terminals whether they have data to transmit is referred to as **polling**. In polling, one station is designated as the supervisor or primary station. This role is almost always assumed by the host computer, although other pieces of equipment such as controllers or concentrators may be used instead. There is only one primary station per multipoint link; all other stations are referred to as secondary stations. In the discussion that follows we assume that the host computer is the primary.

The primary station is in complete control of the link. Secondary stations may transmit data only when given permission by the primary station. Each secondary station is given a unique address, and each terminal must be able to recognize its own address. Although there are several distinct methods of polling, essentially the process works as follows. The primary is provided a list of addresses for terminals on a particular link. Several multipoint lines may be controlled by one primary, although addresses on a given line are unique. The primary picks an address from the list and sends a poll message across the link using that address. The poll message is very short, consisting of the poll address and a string of characters that has been designated as a poll message. All secondary stations receive the poll message, but only the addressee responds. The poll message is an inquiry to the secondary station as to whether it has any data to transmit to the primary. If it has data to transmit, the secondary responds either with the data or with a positive acknowledgment and then the data. If the secondary station has no data to send, it responds with a negative acknowledgment. Upon receipt of either the data or the negative acknowledgment, the primary selects another station's polling address and repeats the process.

Selection   When the primary has data to send to one or more secondary stations, it selects the station in much the same manner as with polling. Some terminals have two addresses, one for polling and one for selecting. In the selection process, the primary sends a selection message to the terminal. A selection message consists of the terminal's selection address and an inquiry to determine whether the terminal is ready to accept data. The terminal may respond positively or negatively. If the terminal's buffer is full, it cannot accept additional data and responds negatively. After a positive acknowledgment to the selection message, the primary transmits the data to the terminal. In some multipoint networks the primary can send a message to all stations simultaneously via a broadcast address, which is one address that all terminals recognize as their own.

Types of Polling   The two basic types of polling are roll call and hub polling. In roll-call polling the primary obtains a list of addresses for terminals on the line and then proceeds sequentially down the list, polling each terminal in turn. If one or more stations on the link are of higher priority or are more likely to have data to send, their address could be included in the list multiple times so they can be polled more frequently. Roll-call polling is illustrated in Figure 8-4.

Hub polling requires the terminals to become involved in the polling process. The primary sends a poll message to one station on the link. If that station has data to transmit, it does so. After transmitting its data or if it has no data to transmit, the secondary terminal passes the poll to an adjacent terminal. This process is repeated until all terminals have had the opportunity to transmit. The primary then starts the process again. Hub polling is illustrated in Figure 8-5. In the diagram, if T2 were not operational, T3 would pass the poll to T1.

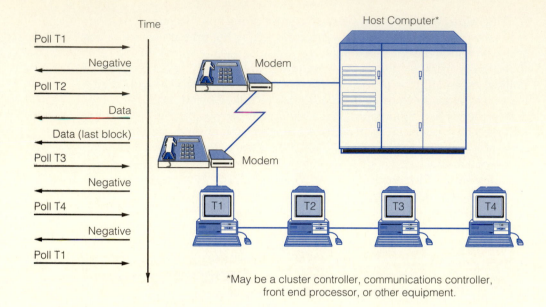

Figure 8-4

Roll-Call Polling

*May be a cluster controller, communications controller, front end processor, or other equipment.

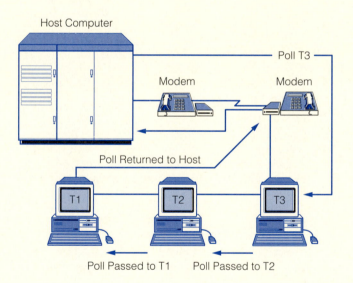

Figure 8-5

Hub Polling

Advantage of Multipoint Connections   The advantage of multipoint lines is economic. First, only one communications link is required for a host to communicate with several terminals; second, if modems are required on the link, fewer modems are necessary. In a true point-to-point link, a pair of modems is often required for each terminal, one at the host end and one at the terminal end. For multipoint links, at most one modem per terminal and one at the host are required. In some instances a terminal cluster controller may be used at the terminal end, and if the terminals are sufficiently close to the controller, individual terminal modems are not necessary: Only a host and cluster controller modem are required. If 10 terminals are to be located

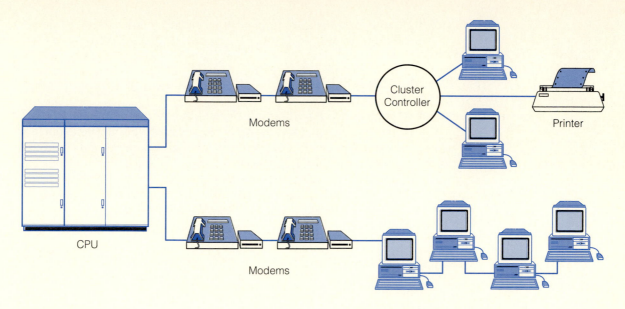

Figure 8-6

Multipoint Configurations

remotely, 10 point-to-point lines would require 20 modems. For a multipoint line, at most 11 modems would be required, and possibly 2 would be sufficient. Figure 8-6 presents several multipoint configurations, together with their required modems.

Disadvantages of Multipoint Connections   There are also disadvantages to the multipoint configuration. First, terminals used in this environment must have some intelligence, making them more expensive than terminals in the point-to-point connection. This higher cost is usually negligible, however, when compared with the savings in medium and modems. Because the medium is shared among several terminals, a terminal may have to wait to transmit its information. If messages are short, the wait time should not be long; on the other hand, if messages are lengthy, such as when a microcomputer transfers a file, the other terminals may be required to wait an inordinate amount of time. Delays also have an impact on response times, and this delay should be factored into the response time calculations for a multipoint line.

MULTIPLEXERS

Polling requires the use of smart terminals that are addressable and have memory. Another line-sharing technique, **multiplexing**, does not generally require the use of smart terminals. Multiplexing technology allows multiple signals to be transmitted over a single link. Multiplexing has been used by telephone companies for many years to combine multiple voice-grade circuits into a single high-speed circuit for long-distance communication. In data

multiplexing   A line-sharing technology that allows multiple signals to be transmitted over a single link.

communications networks, multiplexers, or muxes, allow several devices to share a common circuit.

How Multiplexers Work

Remote locations often have multiple devices that must communicate with a host. Multiplexing provides an alternative to a point-to-point connection and polling. Figure 8-7 presents a general mux configuration. Several communication lines enter the mux from the host side. The mux combines the data from all incoming lines and transmits it via one line to a mux at the receiving end. This receiving mux separates the data and distributes it among the outgoing terminal lines. The number of lines going into the mux on the host side is the same as the number going out to terminals (or other muxes) on the remote side.

To the user, the multiplexer appears to function as though there were several physical lines as opposed to just one. The configuration of one high-speed link and a pair of multiplexers, however, costs less than that of several lower speed links with a pair of modems for each. Applications written for a point-to-point terminal connection also can be used without change. The multiplexer makes the line sharing transparent to the user, because the application essentially sees a point-to-point line.

Figure 8-7

General Multiplexer
Configuration

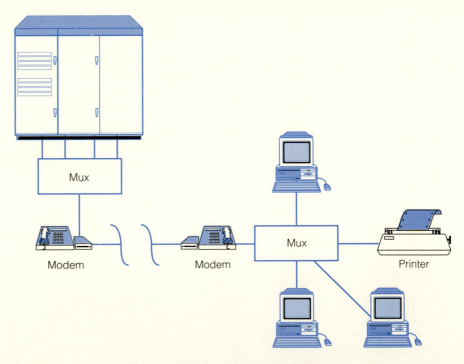

Four host lines combined with one long distance line.
A modem is not required by all types of multiplexers.

Types of Multiplexers

A communications link is divided among several users in two basic ways. The first technique, known as frequency division multiplexing (FDM), separates the link by frequencies. The second technique, known as time division multiplexing (TDM), separates the link into time slots.

Frequency Division Multiplexing (FDM)   In **Frequency Division Multiplexing (FDM)** the available bandwidth of the circuit is broken into subchannels, each of which has smaller bandwidths. Consider a telephone circuit with a bandwidth of 3100 Hz, a frequency range of 300 to 3400 Hz, and a line-carrying capacity of 1200 bps. On this line we could have one terminal operating at 1200 bps; however, instead of one terminal running at 1200 bps we want to have three terminals operating at 300 bps. Although arithmetically it appears possible to have four 300-bps terminals on the line, this is impossible because frequency separation of the subchannels must be maintained to avoid crosstalk. The recommended separation for a 300-bps circuit is 480 Hz. The subchannel separators are referred to as **guardbands**. This situation requires two guardbands of 480 Hz each. Each of the three 300-bps subchannels therefore has a bandwidth of 713 Hz, derived as follows:

3100 Hz (total bandwidth of circuit) − 960 Hz (two guardbands at 480 Hz each)
= 2140 Hz ÷ 3 channels = 713 Hz per channel

Similarly, a 9600-bps channel can be divided into four 1200-bps channels. The higher the speed of individual channels, the larger the guardbands must be. Figure 8-8 illustrates an FDM configuration and the division of the channel into several subchannels. There is no need for modems in this configuration because the FDM functions as a modem by accepting the signal from the data terminal equipment (DTE) and transforming it into a signal within a given frequency range. Thus, the modem is integrated into the FDM. Each line in the FDM is mapped onto one of the subchannels. The first line's signal is passed along the first subchannel; the second line's, along the second subchannel; and so on. If terminals on that line are not busy, that portion of the carrying capacity goes unused.

Frequency Division Multiplexing (FDM)   A technique that divides the available bandwidth of the circuit into subchannels of different frequency ranges, each of which is assigned to one device.

guardbands   Subchannel separators that are implemented in frequency division multiplexing to avoid crosstalk.

Figure 8-8

A Frequency Division Multiplexer Configuration

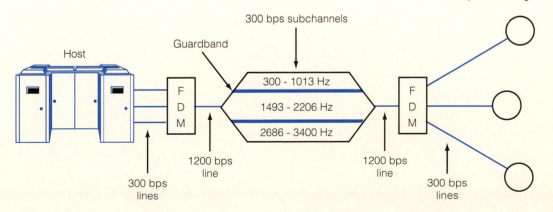

Time Division Multiplexing (TDM)   Time Division Multiplexing (TDM) is roughly equivalent to time-sharing systems. As with FDM, TDM has a group of lines entering the mux, one circuit shared by all, and the same number of lines leaving the mux at the other end. Instead of splitting the frequency, however, TDM shares time: Each line is given a time slot for transmitting, which is accomplished by interleaving either bits or characters. Bit interleaving is more common for synchronous (block at a time) transmissions and character interleaving is more common with asynchronous (character at a time) transmissions.

To understand how TDM operates, look at the four-port TDM in Figure 8-9. This mux combines signals from the four lines onto a single communications circuit. Data entering the TDM from the devices on the input line are placed in a buffer or register. With character interleaving, first a character from Line 1 is transmitted, then a character from Line 2, one from Line 3, one from Line 4, and back again to Line 1 to repeat the process. Bit interleaving works in the same manner except that a bit instead of a character is taken from each line in turn to form a transmission block. The mux at the other end breaks the data back out and places it on the appropriate line.

As with FDM, each line gets a portion of the available transfer time. However, TDM requires no guardbands, so there is no loss of carrying capacity. Each line is given a portion of the circuit's carrying capacity even though there are no data to be transmitted. Still, the improvement is significant:

Figure 8-9

A Time Division Multiplexer

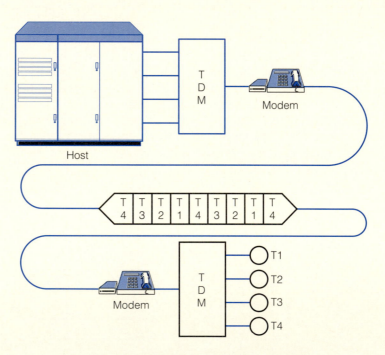

*A modem is not required for all TDMs; for example, an in-house digital TDM may not require modems.

Instead of only three 300-bps sublines on a 1200-bps line, there can be four lines, each capable of 300-bps transmission. A 9600-bps line can be multiplexed into eight 1200-bps lines or four 2400-bps lines, as illustrated in Figure 8-10.

Statistical Time Division Multiplexing (STDM)   Statistical Time Division Multiplexing (STDM) (also known as a **stat mux**) improves on the efficiency of TDM by transmitting data only for those lines with data to send, so idle lines take up none of the carrying capacity of the communications circuit. Figure 8-11 illustrates STDM. Because neither time slot nor frequency is allocated to a specific terminal, an STDM must also transmit a terminal identification along with the data block. When all lines have data to transmit, an STDM looks just like a TDM; when only one line has data to send, the entire line capacity is devoted to that line.

Under good conditions, an STDM on a 9600-bps line can support five or six 2400-bps sublines, as illustrated in Figure 8-11, or three to four 4800-bps sublines. The reason for this apparent increase in carrying capacity stems from the probability that none of the incoming lines will be 100% busy. If each line is only 50% utilized, then four 4800-bps lines could be placed on one 9600-bps link. STDMs also have internal buffers for holding data from a line

Statistical Time Division Multiplexing (STDM)   A technique that provides improved time-sharing efficiency by transmitting data only for those lines with data to send, rather than allowing idle lines to occupy carrying capacity of the communications circuit. Also known as a stat mux.

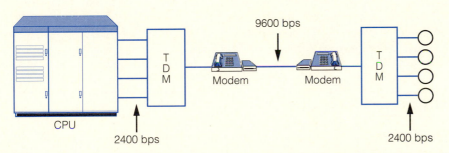

Figure 8-10

Time Division Multiplexing

One 9600 bps line supporting four 2400 bps devices.

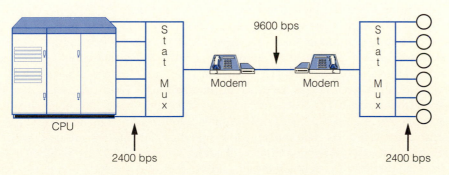

Figure 8-11

Statistical Time Division Multiplexing

One 9600 bps line supporting six 2400 bps devices.

in case all lines try to transmit at once. Newer stat muxes provide additional capabilities including:

- data compression
- digital data support
- line priorities
- mixed-speed lines
- integrated modems
- network control ports for monitoring the multiplexed line
- host port sharing where two or more lines at the terminal end are mapped onto one line at the host end
- port switching wherein a terminal can be switched from one port to another
- accumulation and reporting of performance statistics
- automatic speed detection
- memory expansion
- internal diagnostics

All of these features are not likely to be found in one mux. Different makes offer one or more of these capabilities as standard or optional functions. A few of these features can also be found in TDMs. Most of the development and enhancements in the past several years have been devoted to stat muxes because of their higher performance capabilities.

Multiplexer Configurations

daisy chain   A connection arrangement in which each device is connected directly to the next device. For example, a daisy chain of devices A, B, C, and D might have A connected to B, B connected to C, and C connected to D. Also known as cascading.

inverse multiplexer   A mux that provides a high-speed data path between two devices by separating an incoming line into multiple lower-speed communications circuits.

In addition to attaching terminals to muxes, other muxes can be added in **daisy-chain** fashion, a configuration illustrated in Figure 8-12. Daisy chaining, also referred to as **cascading**, allows some circuits to be extended to another remote point, which is useful in a situation with two areas for data entry. With eight terminals in each area, a 16-port stat mux could provide linkage between the host and Area A, and eight lines from Area A could travel via an eight-port mux to Area B. The number of ports on a mux can vary, though commonly there are 4, 8, 16, 32, 48, or 64 ports. Multiplexer prices vary according to the number of ports and features provided. For a relatively plain four-port or eight-port stat mux, prices start at about $1000.

A less common mux known as an **inverse multiplexer** provides a high-speed data path between two devices, usually computers. An inverse mux accepts one line from a host and separates it into multiple lower speed communications circuits. The multiple low-speed circuits are recombined at the other end into a high-speed link, as illustrated in Figure 8-13. A 56-Kbps link from a computer to an inverse mux can be split into six 9600-bps lines and then back to a 56-Kbps line at the remote end. Telephone companies use this type of multiplexing to provide high-speed communications lines.

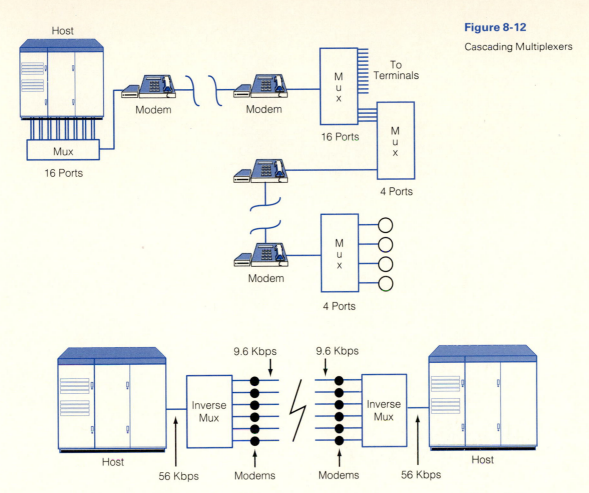

Figure 8-12

Cascading Multiplexers

Figure 8-13

An Inverse Multiplexer

CONCENTRATORS

A **concentrator** is also a line-sharing device. It functions similar to a mux, allowing multiple devices to share communications circuits. Because a concentrator is a computer, however, it can participate more actively than a mux in any application. In the early 1970s there was a marked distinction between a concentrator and a multiplexer. As multiplexers took on the additional functions just described, the difference between the two devices narrowed. Currently the principal differences between a mux and a concentrator are:

1. Concentrators are used one at a time; multiplexers are used in pairs.

2. A concentrator may have multiple incoming and outgoing lines, with a different number of incoming lines than outgoing lines; a multiplexer takes a certain number of incoming lines onto one line and converts back to the same number of outgoing lines.

3. A concentrator is a computer and may have auxiliary storage for use in support of an application.

concentrator A computer that provides line-sharing capabilities, data editing, polling, error handling, code conversion, compression, and encryption.

Figure 8-14

A Concentrator
Configuration

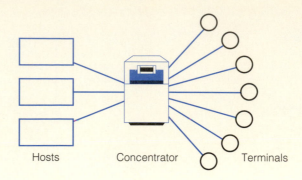

Hosts   Concentrator   Terminals

4. A concentrator may perform some data-processing functions, such as
   device polling and data validation.

One possible concentrator configuration is illustrated in Figure 8-14.

Concentrators can further aid an application by providing data editing,
polling, error handling, code conversion, compression, and encryption.
Concentrators can also switch messages between terminals and hosts. In a
banking ATM environment where three regional processing centers are
responsible for authorizing transactions, each city with multiple ATMs could
use a concentrator to handle ATM traffic. The concentrator would have three
lines, one each for the three hosts in the three regional processing centers.
There would also be one line for each ATM or cluster of ATMs. Based on the
customer's ATM card number, the concentrator would switch each transaction
to the processing center closest to the customer's home branch.

FRONT-END PROCESSORS

Front-End Processor (FEP)
A communications compo-
nent placed at the host end
of a circuit to take over a portion of the line management
work from the host. Also referred to as a communica-
tions controller or a message
switch.

A **Front-End Processor (FEP)**, sometimes referred to as a communications
controller or message switch, is employed at the host end of the communications circuit much like a concentrator is used at the remote end. The FEP takes
over much of the line management work from the host; in many respects,
FEPs and concentrators serve the same function. An FEP configuration is
shown in Figure 8-15.

An FEP interface with a host system uses one or more high-speed links.
The FEP is responsible for controlling the more numerous low-speed circuits.
All functions of a concentrator can also be performed by an FEP, except, of
course, concentrating message traffic for multiple remote terminals onto one
communications line. FEPs may be either special purpose or general purpose.
Special-purpose FEPs, such as the IBM 3745 communications controller, are
designed specifically for data communications. Their operating system and
software are solely communications oriented. General-purpose computers,
such as minicomputers, are also used as FEPs. When general-purpose com-

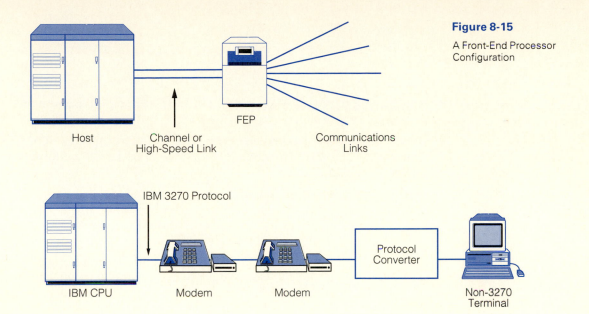

Figure 8-15

A Front-End Processor
Configuration

Host

Channel or
High-Speed Link

FEP

Communications
Links

IBM 3270 Protocol

IBM CPU

Modem

Modem

Protocol
Converter

Non-3270
Terminal

Figure 8-16

Protocol Conversion

puters are used in this way, their role is generally restricted to providing data communications functions.

PROTOCOL CONVERTERS

In Chapter 5 we discussed protocols, which are conventions for communication between devices. Protocols determine the sequences in which data exchanges may take place and the bit or character sequences required to provide device and line control. Each maker of terminals typically has its own proprietary protocols, which means that a Digital Equipment Corporation (DEC) VT420 terminal will not be able to directly communicate with an IBM system over a line configured for IBM 3270 terminals. To bridge these differences, companies have developed **protocol converters**, which are special-purpose devices that allow a terminal to look like a different type of terminal. A protocol converter also enables different computer systems to transmit to and receive from a given terminal model. Protocol conversion is accomplished by hardware and/or software. Figure 8-16 shows an example of protocol converters connecting several different devices. Many different types of protocol converters are available. Some of the more common types are:

- asynchronous to synchronous
- teletypewriter (TTY) to IBM 3270
- asynchronous to IBM SDLC
- IBM 3270 to IBM 2260 poll/select

protocol converter   A special-purpose device that allows a terminal to look like a different type of terminal in order to facilitate interconnection between different computer systems.

- IBM 2780/3780 to IBM 3270
- PARS (airline reservations system protocol) to binary synchronous

DIAGNOSTIC AND MISCELLANEOUS EQUIPMENT

The hardware discussed thus far is involved in the transportation or receipt of data. Another set of hardware is frequently necessary to perform the following functions:

- provide security of transmission and facilities
- monitor data
- control the sequences being transmitted
- provide connection for switched communications lines
- provide other functions necessary to control and manage the communications network

Some of these devices are described below.

Security Hardware

Security of data transmission and storage is becoming increasingly important. Several types of hardware are available to assist in the protection of data.

call-back unit   A security device for switched connections. It operates by receiving a call, verifying the user, severing the call, and calling the user back.

Call-Back Units   One simple but effective device is a **call-back unit**, which participates in making switched connections. A person trying to access a system using a switched connection must identify himself or herself with an ID and a password. The opening connection is severed after the ID and password are entered, and the call-back unit scans its tables for that user's number and calls the number to make the connection.

A call-back system has at least two problems. First, the host computer becomes responsible for the costs of the connection. Second, the call-back system prohibits portable terminal connections, such as that needed by a traveling salesperson or executive with a portable computer. However, some call-back units allow users with certain passwords to bypass the call-back. The bypass may be allowed at all times for certain users or may be programmed to allow bypass only during specific hours. This feature has the disadvantage of lowering security.

Encryption Equipment   Encryption equipment allows transmitted data to be scrambled at the sending location and reconstructed at the receiving end. The U.S. National Bureau of Standards (NBS) has approved a standard called the data encryption standard (DES), which uses a 64-bit pattern as the encryption key. The DES algorithm is available on a chip contained in commercially available encryption boxes. Figure 8-17 shows an encryption device installed on a communications link. Encryption is discussed in more detail in Chapter 15.

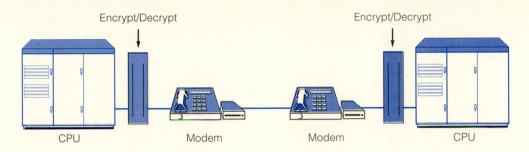

Figure 8-17

Data Encryption Box

Line Monitors

Line monitors, also known as protocol analyzers, are used to diagnose problems on a communications link. Their basic function is to attach to a communications circuit so the bit patterns being transmitted over the link can be displayed for analysis and problem solving by a data communications expert. The two types of line monitors are digital and analog. Analog monitors are used primarily by common carrier personnel to analyze their lines. Digital monitors are used by data-processing technicians to check for adherence to protocols. In this discussion we refer to digital monitors such as the one shown in Figure 8-18. Features commonly available on line monitors are:

line monitor   A device used to diagnose problems on a communications link. Also known as a protocol analyzer.

video display	memory
recording tape or disk	programmability
trap setting for selected bit patterns	multiple protocol support
variable character-length support	multiple interfaces
multiple speeds	function keys
graphics display	integrated breakout box
importing/exporting data	

Figure 8-18

A Digital Line Monitor

If a corporation requires multiple line monitors to cover multiple locations, it is best to use models from one manufacturer. Each manufacturer usually has several models with varying capabilities, which allows the user to buy the minimum required capability for a specific location. There are two reasons for using equipment from only one manufacturer. First, personnel education is easier when there is only one manufacturer. Even though different models may be used, the operations are usually quite similar, especially for simple functions. Second, and more important, recordings made at one site may be shipped to another and analyzed; because there is no industry-standard recording mode, tape or disk recorded on Manufacturer A's machine is probably not readable on Manufacturer B's equipment.

Some microcomputers can be enhanced to provide line-monitoring capabilities. A microcomputer may be enhanced with an adapter board, connector, and software that will provide network and protocol analyzer capabilities. The price for this capability is usually less than that for a dedicated analyzer because some of the components of an analyzer—monitor, disk drives, and cabinetry—are already part of the microcomputer. Some of the necessary hardware and software to equip a microcomputer with this ability is priced under $1500.

Breakout Boxes

breakout box A passive, multipurpose diagnostic device that is patched or temporarily inserted into a circuit at an interface.

A **breakout box** is a passive, multipurpose device that is patched or temporarily inserted into a circuit at an interface. Figure 8-19 shows a programmable breakout box. Once the breakout box is installed, it is possible to monitor activity on each of the circuits, change circuit connections, isolate a circuit to prevent its signal from passing through to the receiver, and measure circuit voltage levels. Some breakout boxes are equipped with bit pattern generators and receivers, which allow for both transmitting and receiving a small number of selected bit patterns. This beneficial feature allows the individual doing the testing to determine what effect a known data pattern has on the circuit.

Auto-Call Units

Auto-Call Unit (ACU) A device used to place a telephone call automatically without manual intervention.

An **Auto-Call Unit (ACU)** is used to place a telephone call without manual intervention. The ACU is able to open the line (equivalent to lifting the handset from its cradle), detect the dial tone, dial the number (through either pulse dialing or touch-tone dialing), detect the ring indicator or busy signal, and determine whether the call is complete or incomplete. Incomplete calls are usually the result of a busy signal, failure to answer, a busy circuit, or a number out of order. In the United States, ACUs could originally be sold only by the telephone companies. This policy changed with the Carterphone decision. The ACU and auto-answer functions are now common in modem equipment. The interface to ACU equipment in the United States is via either the RS-232-C interface or the RS-366 interface. The latter specifically addresses the electrical and functional interface for automatic calling equipment.

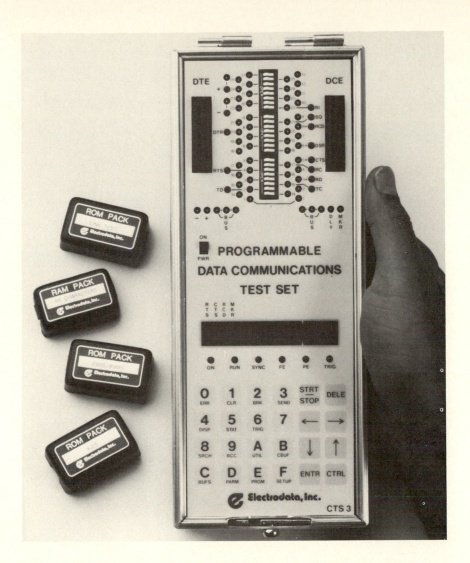

Figure 8-19

A Programmable Breakout Box

Port Concentrator

Multiplexers allow multiple terminals to share one communications link. However, for each terminal attached to a multiplexer there must be one communications port at the host end to receive the signal, which makes the multiplexer appear to be a point-to-point connection for both terminal and host. All systems have an upper limit to the number of communication ports that may be configured, and, of course, there is a cost to providing ports. A **port concentrator**, illustrated in Figure 8-20, allows multiple input streams from a multiplexer to be passed to the host through a single communications port. This is beneficial not only in reducing the hardware cost of the host but also in allowing for expansion beyond the port limitations of a particular processor. Port concentration requires that a software module be available in the host to receive the multiple terminal messages and then route them to the appropriate applications.

port concentrator A device that allows multiple input streams from a multiplexer to be passed to the host through a single communications port.

Figure 8-20

A Port Concentrator

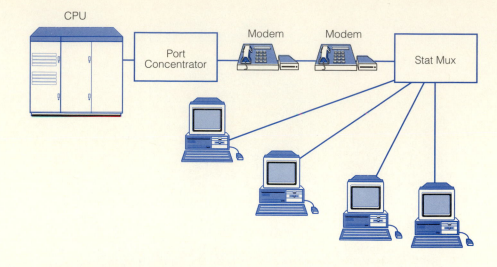

Figure 8-21

A Port Selector Schematic

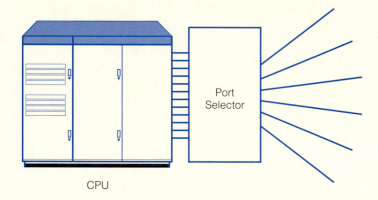

Port Selector or Data Switch

port selector   A device that
helps determine which users
· are granted access to applications where the number of
potential terminal users far
exceeds the number of available lines. Also known as a
data switch.

A **port selector** helps determine which users are granted access to applications where the number of potential terminal users far exceeds the number of available lines, as in reservations systems and library systems. If a particular system allows a total of 1000 terminals to communicate with a host at one time and there are 8000 potential users, obviously not all of these users can have access to the system at once. A port selector helps to determine which users are granted access. For switched lines the port selector can act as a rotary, allowing users to dial one number and connecting the incoming calls to any available switched port. It can also enable switched users to connect to an unused dedicated port. Port selectors can also sometimes make connections to several hosts. Some port selectors give the user considerable control over how many ports will be used for switched calls, how many can be shared between dedicated and switched users, and how many can be routed to another host. Thus, the ports and the class of users who may select them can be configured to meet specific needs. Figure 8-21 shows how a port selector is used.

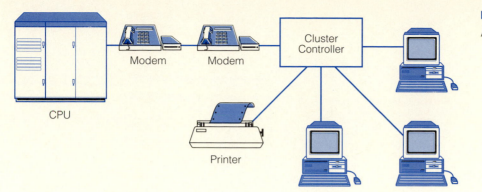

Figure 8-22

A Cluster Controller

Cluster Controllers

A **cluster controller**, depicted in Figure 8-22, is designed to support several terminals. It manages the terminals, buffers data being transmitted to or from the terminals, performs error detection and correction, and polls. The controller may be attached to the host either locally or remotely. Although every terminal attached to a cluster controller usually uses the same communications protocol, the devices themselves may differ. The remote cluster controller in Figure 8-22 has VDUs and a printer attached.

cluster controller A device that manages multiple terminals by buffering data transmitted to and from the terminals and performing error detection and correction.

Private Branch Exchanges

A private branch exchange (PBX) is a private telephone switch. Within a company, some of the telephone calls are between employees in the same building complex. Rather than routing these calls through the telephone company's switch, a PBX switches the calls internally while routing external calls through the telephone company's system. In the past, private branch exchange (PBX) telephone switches have been separate from data communications networks. More recently, PBXs have been integrated into networks, primarily to provide LAN capabilities. Using the PBX system as a LAN medium can be efficient because the wiring is already in place. The disadvantage of using PBX systems for LANs is lower speed transmission and competition between data and voice for available transmission capacity.

Matrix Switches

Some installations have multiple host processors, and terminal users may attach to a specific host in a variety of ways. One way is through a **matrix switch**, such as that shown in Figure 8-23. The switch allows terminal connections to be switched among the available processors. This is effected manually through a patch panel or automatically through program control. Matrix switches prevent the need to physically move communication lines between terminals and processors. Three ways a matrix switch may be used include:

matrix switch A device that allows terminal connections to be switched among the available processors.

Figure 8-23

Matrix Switch Hardware

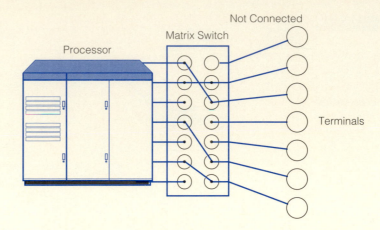

Figure 8-23

Matrix Switch Hardware

1. Users can be evenly distributed over several processors. If one processor in the system becomes saturated, some users can be quickly and efficiently transferred to another processor.

2. If a failure occurs in one line, the terminal(s) attached to that line are switched to a functional line.

3. More terminals can be distributed than direct physical line attachment would permit. For example, it may be necessary to have terminals in conference rooms, demonstration areas, and unoccupied offices, where they are seldom used. For a system that supports 256 directly connected terminals, there may actually be 275 installed terminals. Using a matrix switch, terminals in low-use areas can easily be connected or disconnected from the system as needed.

CASE STUDY

The Syncrasy Corporation is considering expanding operations into several major marketing areas. A preliminary analysis has been initiated to determine the costs of expansion and a portion of the analysis has already been completed. System design objectives and system goals have been formulated. A feasibility study is under way to determine whether the design objectives can be met within the budget. One goal of this study is to determine the number of terminals required in each location, which necessitates first estimating transaction time.

Transaction Time

Syncrasy's preliminary analysis has indicated that expansion needs will be met by a single host processor with multiple terminals at remote locations. For one location it has been determined that five types of transactions—order entry, credit check, customer maintenance, and send and receive mail—constitute the major transaction load. These transaction types are described in Table 8-2.

TABLE 8-2   Projected Transactions for Syncrasy Corporation

	Order Entry	Transaction Credit Check	Type Customer Maintenance	Send Mail	Receive Mail
Think/wait time (secs)	10	5	120	60	180
No. of input characters	600	50	150	2000	50
No. of output characters	20	500	500	50	2000
Disk/CPU/ queuing time (secs)	1	0.5	0.5	1.5	1.5
Hourly peak	40	10	4	5	5

Think/Wait Time   **Think/wait time** is the amount of time the operator will wait or think while entering data for each transaction. A long think/wait time for a customer maintenance transaction (120 seconds) reflects the time the operator is obtaining the information from the telephone. Other possible sources of think/wait time are drinking coffee or tea, reading documents, rearranging papers, and so on.

Data Entry (Input/Output) Time   The number of input characters represents the number of keystrokes the operator enters to complete a transaction. Depending on the type of data being entered, operators are capable of entering 5 characters per second or more. The following analysis assumes a more conservative keystroke rate of 1.5 characters per second. Number of output characters is the number of characters received in response to the transaction. We account for protocol overhead by assuming that each character transmitted requires 10 bits.

Disk/CPU/Queuing Time   Disk/CPU/queuing time is the amount of time the transaction is held by the processor and the time spent waiting in queues at different places in the system. For this analysis the cumulative times for these activities have been given. In reality, some of these times are difficult to determine. Disk access time is important because each transaction type requires records to be read from or written into the database. For order entry transactions, the inventory levels of each item ordered are adjusted by reading and writing the inventory record for each item, which might require that one or more index tables be accessed and searched. Database access times depend on the type of disk drive used and the organization of the database. There are usually three major components of disk access time: seek time, rotational delay or latency, and transfer time.

CPU time is the amount of time required for the CPU to execute the processing instructions, including those executed by the database management system, the operating system, the data communications software, and

think/wait time   The amount of time an operator will wait or think while entering data for each transaction.

CPU time   The amount of time required for the CPU to execute the processing instructions, including those executed by the database management system, operating system, data communications software, and applications programs.

the application programs. CPU time is a function of the speed of the processor and memory, as well as of the number and type of instructions to be executed, and it is small relative to disk access time and data transmission time. Because most business transactions tend to be input/output (I/O) intensive, and because I/O time is usually much greater than CPU time, CPU time usually has little impact on the final calculations.

queuing time   The amount of time the transaction must wait in queues for service.

Queuing time is the amount of time the transaction must wait in queues for service. Queuing time, like CPU time, is difficult to determine accurately; unlike CPU time, it can represent a significant portion of overall transaction time. A transaction can wait in queues in various places within a system: at the terminal waiting to be polled, at an application or data communications activity waiting to be processed, and at the disk drive awaiting the completion of other disk requests. Transaction queues can be compared to lines at a grocery store, where a customer might wait in one line for a parking space, another line for check approval, and a third line for checkout. In the store situation, wait time is a function of line length or customer arrival rate; mean service time for customers in line; number of servers available; and the service convention, such as first-in-first-out (FIFO) or last-in-first-out (LIFO). The same is true of computer systems. The specifics of how to calculate the disk, CPU, and queuing times are quite complex. These times have been provided without derivation for this exercise.

Number of Terminals

The amount of time required to completely process a single transaction is the total of operator think/wait time, data entry time, transmission time, and disk/CPU/queuing time, as seen in Table 8-2. The minimum number of terminals required can be found by determining the total time required to process all transactions in a given period, such as 1 hour. If 1200 transactions per hour were to be processed, each requiring 30 seconds (0.5 minutes) to complete, the number of terminals required would be:

$$\frac{1200 \text{ trans.}}{\text{hour}} \times \frac{0.5 \text{ terminal minutes}}{\text{trans.}} \times \frac{1 \text{ hour}}{60 \text{ minutes}} = 10 \text{ terminals}$$

This is the minimum number of terminals required based on utilization.

For several reasons, a user might decide to install additional terminals. There may be more potential operators than there are required terminals, such as in an office in which every employee is given a terminal even though each employee uses it only part of the day. To place ATMs more conveniently for customers, a bank might install more ATMs than actually required to meet transaction demand. Additional terminals might also be installed to accommodate expansion, to provide spares, and to provide a margin for calculation error.

It is assumed that all wait-time components are included in the transaction times. If this were not the case, the calculated number of terminals would be less than the minimum number required. Consider a polled communications line. Two types of messages are sent over the line, data and polling requests. If only the data transmission time were considered and the average wait time for polling were ignored, the results would not reflect the actual time of a given transaction. To determine the number of terminals required for Syncrasy Corporation, we calculate the transaction time for each type of transaction, multiply each transaction time by the number of transactions of that type per hour, and then total the results for each type of transaction. Shorter approaches could be taken, but they would be less instructive. Only the order entry transaction is computed in detail; the calculations for the remainder are left as an exercise.

Transaction time for the order entry transaction is given by

$$\text{transaction time} = \text{think/wait time} + \text{data entry time}$$
$$+ \text{transmission time} + \text{disk/CPU/queuing time}$$

To determine transmission time, a transmission speed must be selected; for this exercise a speed of 4800 bps is assumed. Order entry transaction time is

$$10 + \frac{600}{1.5} + \frac{(620)\,(10)}{4800} + 1 = 412.3 \text{ seconds}$$

The transaction times required for credit check, customer maintenance, sending electronic mail, and receiving electronic mail are, respectively, 39.9, 221.9, 1399.1, and 219.1 seconds (perform the necessary calculations yourself to test your understanding). The total amount of time for all transactions in an hour is

$$(421.3)\,(40) + (39.9)\,(10) + (221.9)\,(4) + (1399.1)\,(5) + (219.1)(5)$$
$$= 26{,}229.6 \text{ seconds}$$

In one hour's time, 26,229.6 seconds of terminal, communications link, and CPU/disk/wait time will be required, and the number of terminals needed is

$$\frac{26{,}229.6}{3600} = 7.29 \text{ terminals}$$

To provide for the total number of transactions from one location, eight terminals will be needed. ❖

SUMMARY

There is a wide variety of terminals, terminal capabilities, and terminal prices. The industry has been moving toward terminals with more intelligence, which provide functions that are simple to use and may also reduce overall communications cost and host processor work. Intelligent terminals in the form of microcomputers have replaced standard terminals in many networks. Their flexibility and local processing ability make them very effective in the modern communications network. Ergonomic features are important to consider when selecting a terminal.

If several terminals are placed near each other in a remote location, it is impractical to have one line for each terminal, so the terminals must share one communications line. One way in which this is done is polling, which requires addressable terminals. In polling, a supervisor station asks each terminal in turn whether it has data to send. A terminal that is polled returns either data or a negative acknowledgment that indicates it has no data to send. *Selection* is the name given to the procedure by which the supervisor sends data to a terminal. Line sharing is also accomplished with multiplexers and concentrators.

Many alternatives are available when configuring a data communications system. The hardware components—multiplexers, concentrators, and front-end processors—overlap in the functions they can provide. These components can reduce circuit costs significantly as well as make more efficient use of the circuits and reduce some of the processing load of the hosts. Configuration modeling tools, which have been designed for telephone company or similar common-carrier lines, are available to help system designers select the lowest cost or most efficient communications lines. A wide variety of protocol conversion equipment is available to enable different manufacturers' terminals to interface with host equipment. Such conversion equipment can protect a user's investment in terminals. Diagnostic tools are necessary because errors can be encountered in connecting data terminal equipment to data communications networks. If properly used, these tools can reduce the time and effort in tracking down such problems.

KEY TERMS

Auto-Call Unit (ACU), *282*

block mode, *263*

breakout box, *282*

call-back unit, *280*

cascading, *276*

cluster controller, *285*

concentrator, *277*

contention mode, *268*

conversational mode, *263*

CPU time, *287*

daisy chain, *276*

dumb terminal, *263*

ergonomics, *266*

Frequency Division Multiplexing (FDM), *273*

Front-End Processor (FEP), *278*

guardbands, *273*

intelligent terminal, *264*

inverse multiplexer, *276*

line monitor, *281*

matrix switch, *285*

multiplexing, *271*

multipoint connection, *268*

point-to-point connection, *268*

polling, *268*

port concentrator, *283*

port selector, *284*

protocol converter, *279*

queuing time, *288*

smart terminal, *263*

Statistical Time Division Multiplexing (STDM or stat mux), *275*

terminal, *260*

terminal emulation, *260*

think/wait time, *287*

Time Division Multiplexing (TDM), *274*

uploading, *260*

Video Display Unit (VDU), *261*

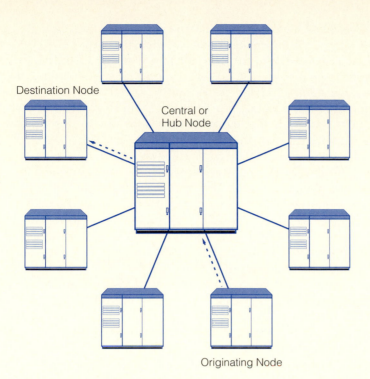

Destination Node

Central or
Hub Node

Originating Node

Figure 9-1

A Star Configuration

Star systems have a relatively low reliability. The loss of the central node is equivalent to loss of the network. Failure of a peripheral node has little impact on the network as a whole, however, as only messages bound for that node are undeliverable. The best candidate for the central node is a fault-tolerant system that is almost immune to failure.

Star systems have the additional disadvantage in a long-distance network of possibly higher circuit costs. This is exemplified in the case study at the end of this chapter, in which the point-to-point configuration has a monthly circuit cost almost $1500 higher than that of the minimum media distance configuration. This is particularly true when the centralized node is not geographically in the center of the network. Other topologies are better able to configure the links between nodes so the distance spanned by the media is minimized.

Hierarchical Network

Hierarchical topology, shown in Figure 9-2, is also referred to as a tree structure. Directly connected to the single root node (Node A) are several nodes at the second level. Each of these can have several cascaded nodes attached. This type of network, often found in corporate computer networks, closely resembles corporate organization charts. With the corporate computer center as root node, division systems are attached directly to the root, regional systems to divisional systems, districts to regions, and so on. Corporate reports from

hierarchical topology A network topology in which the nodes are arranged hierarchically. Also known as a tree structure.

a lower level are easily consolidated at the next higher level, and the network generally mirrors the information flow pattern in the corporation. Information flowing from a district in one division to a district in a different division would need to go through the root or corporate node. As with a star system, this allows for a great deal of network control.

Media costs for the hierarchical topology are likely to be lower than for the star topology, assuming that the lower level nodes are in closer proximity to the next higher level than they are to the root. It is possible, of course, to devise configurations in which media costs are higher than for a centralized system. A hierarchical network can require quite a few hops for a message to reach its destination. If Node F in Figure 9-2 needed to send a message to Node Z, the message would have to pass through five intermediate nodes (F -> D -> C -> A -> S -> Y -> Z). In the hierarchical topology, nodes tend to communicate with neighboring nodes, so the instance of long paths where a leaf node on one side of the hierarchy communicates with a leaf node on the other side of the hierarchy is presumably small.

Expansion and reconfiguration of a hierarchical network can pose problems. In the configuration of Figure 9-2, splitting Node C into Nodes C and K, with D and F under C and E under K, would require more work than in the star configuration. Node K would have to be linked to Node A, and Node E would have to be unlinked from C and relinked to K. Although this may not sound difficult, it costs time and money to change circuits from one location to another, especially with circuits provided by a common carrier. As with most configuration changes, network routing tables must be updated,

Figure 9-2

A Hierarchical Configuration

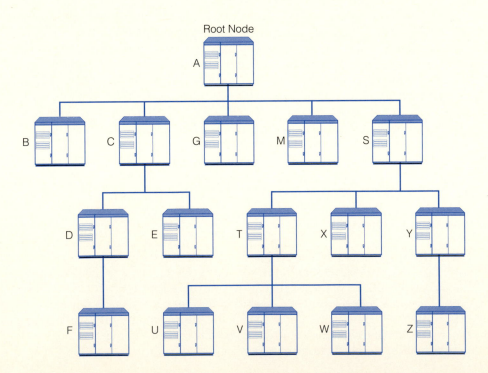

and a system or network regeneration may be needed. Failure of the root node in a hierarchical configuration is less costly than in a star configuration, but it does present a serious reliability problem. In fact, the failure of any node other than those at the extremities will make it impossible to reach that node or any of its subordinate nodes. Congestion at the root and higher level nodes is also a potential problem.

Interconnected (Plex) Network

Two forms of an **interconnected (plex** or **mesh) network** are shown in Figure 9-3. In the fully interconnected network, Figure 9-3(a), every node is connected to every other node with which it must communicate. In the past, fully interconnected topology was required because the available network software was not sophisticated enough to perform the routing and forwarding functions. Current network software allows for but does not require fully interconnected nodes. Message traffic patterns are used to determine where links should be installed. As might be expected, the links in a fully interconnected network are quite costly. The number of links required for a fully interconnected network of n nodes is $n(n-1)/2$. The performance of an interconnected system is generally good, as direct links can be established between nodes with high amounts of data to exchange. Costs can also be controlled because interconnected topology is capable of the shortest or least expensive configuration. Any of the other topology types can be mimicked by an interconnected topology, although routing and control mechanisms would probably be different.

The expandability of interconnected configurations depends upon the type of network and how the new node is to be connected. In the fully interconnected network, expansion is costly and time-consuming because a link must be established to every node with which the new node must communicate. In networks that do not require full interconnection, insertion of a new node can be simple. Adding Node H in Figure 9-3(b) would be very simple, requiring only adding a link from Node G to the new Node H. Adding a node such as Node C in Figure 9-3(b) would be more involved and costly.

The impact of node failure depends on the specific configuration. Alternate paths around a failed node are sometimes available. If Node C in Figure

interconnected (plex or mesh) network A network topology in which any node can be directly connected to any other node.

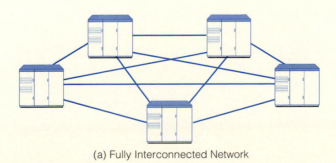

(a) Fully Interconnected Network

Figure 9-3a

Interconnected Configuration

Figure 9-3b

Interconnected
Configuration

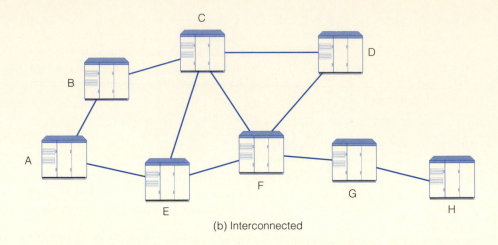

(b) Interconnected

9-3(b) fails, all other nodes are still able to communicate. The loss of Node F, however, would isolate Nodes G and H. Because all nodes in an interconnected topology are equal, control is distributed rather than centralized.

Hybrid Networks

Combinations of the above topologies are sometimes integrated into one network. One such combination is a backbone network—such as a ring—with spurs attached. The backbone nodes can be dedicated to message transfer and data communications while the other nodes are used for both data processing and data communications. In widely distributed systems with many nodes, this helps reduce the number of hops, the length of the links, and congestion problems. If the backbone is implemented as a ring or with multiple paths available, reliability is also high. The cost of hybrid networks can be quite low because different topologies can be used for network segments. Table 9-1 summarizes the different types of topology with respect to cost, control, number of hops (speed), reliability, and expandability.

TABLE 9-1   **Network Topology Characteristics**

Topology Type	Cost	Control	Number of Hops	Reliability	Expandability
Star	Can be high	Very good	Maximum of two	Poor	Good
Hierarchical	Can be high	Good	Can be many	Fair	Fair to good
Interconnected					
Full	Highest	Distributed	One only	Good	Very poor
Other	Can be lowest	Distributed	Can be many	Good	Good
Ring	Good	Distributed	Can be many	Good	Good
Bus	Good	Distributed	N/A	Good	Good

WAN DATA LINK PROTOCOLS

Most LANs use contention and token passing for data link control. WAN data link protocols are typically either asynchronous or a form of synchronous protocols. Asynchronous is most often used to connect hosts with terminals. Synchronous protocols are used between computers and between computers and terminals. We begin the discussion with asynchronous, the first WAN data link protocol.

Asynchronous Transmission

Asynchronous transmission (async) is the oldest and one of the most common data link protocols. Like many of the techniques used in data communications, it is derived from the telegraph and telephone industries. In asynchronous transmission, data is transmitted one character at a time, and sender and receiver are not synchronized with each other. The sender is thus able to transmit a character at any time. The receiver must be prepared to recognize that information is arriving; accept the data; possibly check for errors; and print, display, or store the data in memory. Individual characters also can be separated over different time intervals, meaning no synchronization exists between individual transmitted characters.

Most dumb terminals are async devices, and many smart and intelligent terminals can also communicate asynchronously. Personal computers often use async transmission via their serial port to communicate with each other and with host systems. Async transmission is also referred to as a start-stop protocol. This term and the terms *mark* (1 bit) and *space* (0 bit) are holdovers from telegraphy. It is called start-stop because each character is framed by a start bit and a stop bit, as illustrated in Figure 9-4.

Compatibility of Sending and Receiving Stations   A communications link is either idling or transmitting data. In the idle state, an async line is held in the mark condition, which is continuous 1 bits. The sending and receiving stations must agree on the number of bits per character before establishing the communications link. If parity is to be transmitted for error detection, both stations must agree on either even or odd parity and on whether the parity bit is to be checked (the parity bit could be transmitted but not checked

asynchronous transmission (async)   The oldest and one of the most common data link protocols. Each character is transmitted individually with its own error detection scheme, usually a parity bit. The sender and receiver are not synchronized with each other. Also known as the start-stop protocol.

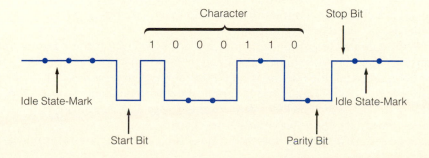

Figure 9-4

Asynchronous Transmission of the Letter F

by the data link software or hardware). The stations also must agree on a transmission speed, because this determines the interval at which the line is sampled. Finally, there must be agreement as to what will terminate the message. A message terminator usually is a defined set of characters called **interrupt characters**, a count of a specific number of characters, or a time-out interval. For the following discussion we will assume that sending and receiving stations are the same with respect to the number of bits sent per character, parity, message termination, and maximum speed of the link (as detected by the receiving modem). The line is in the idle state, meaning that a continuous stream of 1 bits is being transmitted. There are seven data bits and one parity bit, and odd parity will be checked.

Transmitting a Character   A character's arrival is signaled by a start bit, which is a change in the state of the line from a mark to a space, or a 0 bit. The start bit is followed by seven data bits, one parity bit, and a stop bit, which is a return to a 1 bit or mark condition. If parity does not check or if the tenth bit is not a 1, it is assumed that an error has occurred. Appendix A describes how checking for start, stop, data, and parity bits is physically accomplished. The ASCII representation for the character *F* is 1000110; the async representation for transmitting this character is given in Figure 9-4. After a character is transmitted, the line goes back to the idle state until the next start bit is encountered.

Interrupt Characters   If interrupt characters are being used to end transmission, each character received must be examined to determine whether it matches one of the interrupt characters. If they match, the message is considered complete and is delivered to the intended application. This is the usual way async communications are completed. On terminals, the character that is transmitted when the operator presses the Return key—usually a carriage-return character—is frequently one of these termination characters. Other interrupt characters can also be specified.

Character Count   **Character-count termination** is used when the number of characters transmitted is large or when data are received from a device that transmits continuously without sending termination characters. Some news wire services send large amounts of text for a story without including message termination characters. The receiving computer must be capable of accepting the entire story regardless of its length. Because the message is received by the computer into a buffer that may be smaller than the entire message, a character-count termination allows the computer to save the data in blocks and avoid buffer overflow.

With character-count termination, a read is posted on the communications line for a specific number of characters. When that number of characters has been received, the transmission is considered completed, and the data is delivered to the application. It is the application's responsibility to make sense of the message, which includes determining the end of the transmission. On staffed terminals, character-count termination is usually used only for entering fixed-length data fields. Interactive questions with one-character answers

---

interrupt characters   A set of characters that terminate a message or cause an interruption in transmission to perform a special action, such as a backspace.

character-count termination   A transmission termination technique wherein a transmission is complete when a specified number of characters have been received. Allows the computer to save the data in blocks and avoid buffer overflow.

often use this technique. Character-count termination may be used with the other termination methods. A continuous stream of data on the line as described above can cause another problem, buffer overflow.

Double Buffering   **Buffer overflow**, or **overrun**, can arise when the data block being transmitted is larger than the receiving buffer area or when data from a subsequent block are received before the previous block's data has been emptied from the buffer. In such cases, there is no place to store the arriving characters, and they are lost. Frequently in such instances the data link protocol uses a technique known as **double buffering** to avoid losing characters.

Double buffering means there are two (or more) input buffers capable of receiving data. The buffers are alternated: When one buffer is filled, new incoming characters are stored in the alternate buffer. While an alternate buffer is being used, data in the full buffer can be passed to the application, which makes that buffer available for receiving new data. Double buffering might be used when transmitting data from a microcomputer's disk to the host. Such data may form a continuous character stream that can arrive at any time at nearly maximum data link speed and in variable-length blocks. A receiving computer with single buffering may not be fast enough to empty its buffer and be ready to accept the next arriving characters.

Time-Out Interval   Another termination mechanism is the **time-out interval**. This method is effective with a character count or when data is received from sensor-based or laboratory equipment. In conjunction with character count, the time-out interval is beneficial when the size of a message can vary. Suppose the termination character count is 100 and the message is 350 characters. If only character-count termination is used, the first 300 characters would be received routinely in three data groups, but the last 50 characters would be held in the buffer until it was filled, which would only occur when the next message is sent. A time-out termination prevents unnecessary delays in completing such a message. In the laboratory situation, a long interval between data arrival means the entire data stream has arrived or the equipment is out of order. The time-out interval is not a good terminator for data being input by an operator, because if the operator should take a break in the midst of input, a time-out interval would prematurely terminate the message.

buffer overflow/overrun   A situation that arises when the buffer is either too small or too full to receive the transmitted data. In either case there is no place to store the arriving characters, and the data is lost.

double buffering   Used when buffer overflow/overrun occurs to avoid losing characters.

time-out interval   A period of time allowed for an event to occur. If the event does not happen, the time-out expires and the process initiating the event is notified.

Effectiveness of Asynchronous Transmission

The following rating of asynchronous transmission, with respect to the data link objectives described earlier, uses a three-level grading system: poor, adequate, and good. The data delineation and contention control objectives are not rated, as they are both essential functions; exactly how they are implemented, however, can influence the effectiveness rating. The ratings are based on the data link layer functions discussed in Chapter 5. The effectiveness of asynchronous protocols is summarized in Table 9-2.

TABLE 9-2   **Effectiveness of Asynchronous Protocols**

Capability	Comments	Rating
Error detection	Usually parity	Poor
Transparency	Not possible when interrupt characters are used	Poor
	Possible under other message termination options	Adequate
Addressing	No limitations	Good
Code independence	Number of bits per character established before communicating, and hence there is no code independence	Poor
Configurations	No inherent restrictions	Adequate
Efficiency	Protocol overhead is 30%; character-at-a-time transmission is slower than block-at-a-time transmission	Poor
Growth	Limited	Poor

Why Asynchronous Transmission Is so Popular

Despite the poor rating given to asynchronous transmission, it remains one of the most common data link protocols for several reasons. Async was the first protocol, and for several years it was the only way to transmit data. Many terminals and controller boards were designed for async operation. Thus, async technology is well developed, and a wide variety of hardware options are available at a relatively low price. Async also is very well suited to many types of applications. People performing data entry in a conversational mode or even in block mode operate at speeds compatible with async protocol. The primary penalty paid with async is its inefficient use of the circuit.

SYNCHRONOUS TRANSMISSION

synchronous   A transmission protocol where the sender and receiver are synchronized. Data is generally transmitted in blocks, rather than a character at a time as in asynchronous transmission.

Synchronous data link protocols can be divided into three groups: character oriented, byte count oriented, and bit oriented. The last is the newest technology and the basis for many current data communications systems. Synchronous transmission allows sender and receiver to be synchronized with each other. Synchronous modems have internal clocks that are set in time with each other by a bit pattern, or sync pattern, transmitted at the beginning of a message. For long messages these sync patterns are periodically inserted within the text to ensure that the modem clocks remain synchronized. Synchronized clocks are one feature that separates asynchronous modems from synchronous ones; although there is a clocking function in async transmission, the clocks are not synchronized. The clocks on asynchronous modems are used to pace the bits on the line on the sending side and to sample the line when awaiting data on the receiving side. Once data start arriving, the

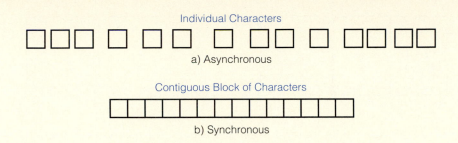

Figure 9-5

Asynchronous vs.
Synchronous Transmission

sampling rate is adjusted to the pace of the arriving characters so the characters can be recognized (see Appendix A).

Another difference between asynchronous and synchronous transmission is that instead of transmitting character by character, synchronous transmission involves sending a block of characters at a time. Failure to remain synchronized results in lost data. Figure 9-5 illustrates the differences between asynchronous and synchronous transmission.

CHARACTER SYNCHRONOUS PROTOCOLS

Types of Synchronous Protocols

Some synchronous protocols are positional, some use a framing technique, and others use a byte count to delineate data. **Positional protocols** delineate fields by the use of fixed-length fields on the message (except perhaps on the data field), by indicating the size of the message with a character count embedded in the message, or both. **Framing protocols** use reserved characters or bit patterns to delineate data and control fields within the message. **Byte count protocols** delineate data by including the number of characters being transmitted within the message.

Positional Protocols   A fixed-message format used in the CSMA/CD local area network is illustrated in Figure 9-6. All fields except the data field are a specific length and at a specific location within the message. The end of the message is indicated by dropping the carrier signal on the medium. Neither framing characters nor character counts are used to define where address fields and data begin. The first 64 bits are always the preamble field;

positional protocol   A type of synchronous protocol that delineates fields by the use of fixed-length fields on the message, by indicating the size of the message with a character count embedded in the message, or both.

framing protocol   A type of synchronous protocol that uses reserved characters or bit patterns to delineate data and control fields within the message.

byte count protocol   A type of synchronous protocol that delineates data by including the number of characters being transmitted within the message.

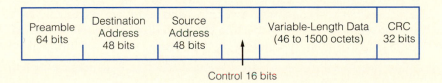

Figure 9-6

The CSMA/CD Message Format

Figure 9-7

Framing for a Character
Synchronous Message

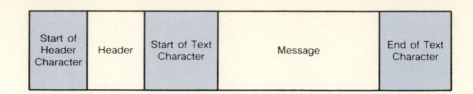

| Start of Header Character | Header | Start of Text Character | Message | End of Text Character |

the next 48, the destination address; and so on. All messages in Ethernet adhere to this fixed format.

Framing Protocols   A message may have several parts, a header, an address, data, and a block-check character. If a message contains both a header and data fields, a framing protocol would use a special control character to indicate the start of the header, another control character to indicate the start of the data field, and a third control character to designate the end of the data field. This is illustrated in Figure 9-7. Other framed messages between the same sender and receiver could have different parts; for example, the header field could be omitted.

character synchronous protocol   A type of synchronous protocol oriented toward specific data codes and specific characters within those codes.

Character synchronous protocols differ from byte count synchronous in that character synchronous message control is oriented toward specific transmission codes and specific characters within those codes. In a character synchronous protocol, a specific character, an STX character in ASCII and EBCDIC, is used as a control character to indicate the start of text. Other types of data may be transmitted before the text, such as a message header, in which case the header would be preceded by a start of header character (SOH).

Standards for Character Synchronous Protocols

Both corporate and national standards specify how character synchronous protocols are to be implemented. National standards include American National Standards Institute (ANSI) standards X3.1, X3.24, X3.28, and X3.36, all of which pertain to various aspects of character synchronous transmission. The IBM **Binary Synchronous Communications** (**BISYNC** or **BSC**) **protocol** has become a de facto industry standard communications protocol supported by many manufacturers. Because it is so common, BISYNC is used as a model of character synchronous protocols in the following discussion. Further details of binary synchronous transmission are discussed in Appendix B.

Binary Synchronous Communications (BISYNC or BSC) protocol   A transmission protocol introduced by IBM as the data link protocol for remote job entry. It later became a de facto standard for many types of data transmission, particularly between two computers. Data is transmitted a block at a time, and the sender and receiver need to be in time with each other. Specific control characters are used to indicate beginning of text, end of text, start of header, and so on.

BISYNC was introduced by IBM in 1967 as the data link protocol for remote job entry, using the 2780 workstation. Since that time its use has expanded to many other applications and with several other devices. Only three data codes are supported by BISYNC: 6-bit transcode (SBT), ASCII, and EBCDIC. One or more synchronization characters are transmitted at the beginning of each transmission block to synchronize sending and receiving modems. The receiving modem uses this bit pattern to establish timing and get in step with the sender. To maintain timing for long transmission blocks, additional sync characters are inserted at regular intervals. The number of sync characters required depends on the equipment being used, although two or three is the

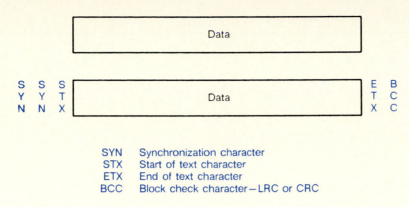

Figure 9-8

BISYNC Control Characters

SYN Synchronization character
STX Start of text character
ETX End of text character
BCC Block check character—LRC or CRC

usual number. Figure 9-8 shows a message with BISYNC control characters for synchronization (SYN), the start of text (STX), and the end of text (ETX). BISYNC supports both point-to-point and multipoint configurations.

Message Control   Each transmitted block can have an optional header field for message control that designates such items as routing information, priority, and message type. The beginning and end of text are identified by framing the data with control characters. An STX character signals that the data portion of the text is starting. One of several characters—such as ETX, ETB, or EOT—can be used to identify the end of a block of data, depending on whether an intermediate or final block is being transmitted. The ETB control character designates the end of the transmission block, ETX signals the end of the text, and EOT means end of transmission. Lengthy messages are ordinarily broken down into segments or blocks. If a message were broken into four different transmission blocks, the first three blocks would terminate with the ETB control character and the last would terminate with the EOT character.

Transparency   Transparent transmission is a BISYNC configuration option involving the insertion of extra characters in the message, which can be rather cumbersome. Appendix B includes a detailed discussion of the implementation.

Error Control   Error control is either parity or parity with LRC. Cyclic redundancy checks are used with EBCDIC and with ASCII when ASCII is configured for transparency. LRC and parity are used with nontransparent ASCII.

BISYNC's Half Duplex Nature   One limitation of BISYNC is that it is essentially a half duplex protocol, so each message transmitted must be acknowledged by the receiver before the next message can be sent. This is not a major concern for many applications, especially those involving terminal data entry, for which the amount of time required to acknowledge is short compared with the speed of data submission. For host-to-host communica-

TABLE 9-3   **Effectiveness of Binary Synchronous Protocol**

Capability	Comments	Rating
Error detection	With CRC	Good
	Without CRC	Adequate
Transparency	Possible, but design is clumsy	Adequate
Addressing	Wide range possible	Good
Code independence	None — only three codes supported	Poor
Configurations	Multipoint and point-to-point	Adequate
Efficiency	Fixed overhead per message. Good for large messages, high for very short messages. Inherent half-duplex nature is restrictive.	Good overall
Growth	Limited in supported configurations and lack of code independence	Adequate

tions, on the other hand, half duplex can be quite restrictive. Consider a file transmitted between two processors: It would be efficient for the sender to transmit several blocks before requiring an acknowledgment transmitted in parallel with the data, as would occur in full duplex mode.

Effectiveness of the BISYNC Protocol

The effectiveness of BISYNC is summarized in Table 9-3.

Byte Count Synchronous Protocols

The difference between byte count synchronous protocols and BISYNC lies in how they signal the beginning and end of messages. They are called *byte count protocols* because the number of characters in the message is given in a required message header, as illustrated in Figure 9-9. The header is a fixed length, and the data field is of variable length. One advantage of byte count protocols is their transparency. With the byte count provided, it is clear where the message begins and ends: The header is always x characters long. Therefore, the beginning of the data is x characters from the beginning of the message, the data span the byte-count number of characters, and following that may be a block-check character or CRC characters. Because there is no need to scan the input stream for termination characters, any bit pattern can be represented within the data stream.

Message Sequence Numbers   Some implementations of byte count protocols also include **message sequence numbers**. Each transmitted mes-

message sequence numbers
A system in which each transmitted message is given a sequential number, allowing multiple messages to be transmitted without acknowledgment.

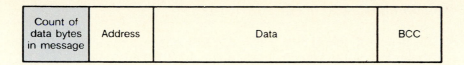

Count of data bytes in message	Address	Data	BCC

Figure 9-9

A Byte Count Message Format

sage is given a sequential number, allowing multiple messages to be transmitted without any acknowledgment. If three bits are used for sequencing messages, eight different sequence numbers (0 through 7) can be generated. When the count reaches 7, the next number assigned is 0. This allows up to eight messages to be transmitted before being acknowledged. The ability to send multiple messages without an acknowledgment can save a significant amount of time, especially on slower links or links with a high modem turnaround time.

Effectiveness of Byte Count Synchronous Protocols The performance of byte count synchronous protocols is much the same as for BISYNC, the differences being in transparency and efficiency. Transparency is inherent in byte count protocols. Byte count protocols also have greater efficiency if message sequencing or true full duplex operations are allowed. An example of a byte count synchronous protocol is Digital Equipment Corporation's DDCMP protocol. Its message sequencing allows 256 message numbers.

Bit Synchronous Protocols

Bit-oriented synchronous data link protocols use bits rather than bytes to delineate data and provide message control. The first bit-oriented synchronous data link protocol, **Synchronous Data Link Control (SDLC)**, was introduced by IBM in 1972. Since then, numerous other bit-oriented data link controls have surfaced. The major bit synchronous protocols are:

- **SDLC, Synchronous Data Link Control**, from IBM
- **ADCCP, Advanced Data Communications Control Procedure**, an ANSI standard data link protocol (ADCCP is frequently pronounced "addcap")
- **HDLC, High-level Data Link Control**, a standard of the International Standards Organization (ISO)
- **LAPB, Link Access Procedure, Balanced**, designated as the data link protocol for the X.25 packet distribution networks (LAPB is an adaptation of HDLC)

All of these bit synchronous protocols operate similarly. Although there are both national and international standards, SDLC is used in the following discussion as the model for bit-oriented data link protocols because it is used in many IBM installations and represents many of the bit synchronous implementations. Many vendors also support SDLC as a connection to IBM networks and devices. More detailed information regarding SDLC may be found in Appendix C.

bit-oriented synchronous data link protocol A data link protocol in which one or more bits are used to control the communications link. Bit synchronous protocols are commonly used on both LANs and WANs.

Synchronous Data Link Control (SDLC) An IBM positional synchronous protocol that operates in full duplex or half duplex mode in both point-to-point and multipoint configurations. Data is transmitted in fixed-format frames consisting of start flag, address, control information, block check character (BCC), and end-of-frame flag.

Advanced Data Communications Control Procedure (ADCCP) An ANSI standard bit-oriented data link control. Pronounced "addcap."

High-level Data Link Control (HDLC) A positional synchronous protocol that operates in full duplex or half duplex mode in both point-to-point and multipoint configurations. Data is transmitted in fixed-format frames consisting of start flag, address, control information, block check character (CRC), an end-of-frame flag. HDLC is an International Standards Organization standard similar to IBM's SDLC.

Link Access Procedure, Balanced (LAPB) A bit synchronous protocol similar to high-level data link control. LAPB is the protocol specified for X.25 networks.

Synchronous Data Link Control (SDLC)

SDLC operates in full duplex or half duplex mode on nonswitched lines in both point-to-point and multipoint configurations. In half duplex mode it also allows switched, point-to-point configurations. Under SDLC it is possible to configure stations in a loop, as depicted in Figure 9-10. Data are transmitted in one direction around the loop, as with hub polling. In all configurations, including point to point, one station is designated as the primary station and the others are secondary stations. The primary controls the link and determines which station is allowed to transmit.

The Frame   At the application level a given application will transmit a message. At the transport layer the message may be broken down into packets. At the data link layer a packet may be broken down into frames. Thus, the basic unit of transmission in SDLC is the **frame**, presented in Figure 9-11. The flag field is used to indicate the beginning and end of the frame. The bit pattern for the flag—01111110—is the only bit pattern in the protocol that is specifically reserved; all other bit patterns are acceptable. (This is discussed further in the SDLC section on transparency.) The second field within the frame—the address field—is eight bits. A maximum of 256 unique addresses is possible. Other data link protocols, such as ADCCP and HDLC, allow the address field to be expanded in multiples of eight bits, significantly increasing the number of addressable stations per link. The control field, also eight bits, identifies the frame type as either unnumbered, informational, or supervisory. Only the first two of these three types are used to transmit data, with the primary data transport frame being the information frame.

frame A term used to describe a transmission packet in bit-oriented protocols.

Figure 9-10

An SDLC Loop Configuration

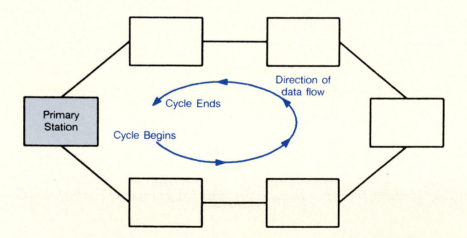

Figure 9-11

An SDLC Frame Format

8 bits	8 bits	8 bits	Variable	16 bits	8 bits
Flag 01111110	Address	Control	Data (Optional Octets)	Frame Check Sequence	Flag 01111110

The data field, always omitted for supervisory frames, is optional on unnumbered frames and is usually present on information frames. The only restriction on the data field is that the number of bits must be a multiple of eight, or an octet. This restriction does not mean an 8-bit code must be used; in fact, any code is acceptable. But if necessary, the data being transmitted must be padded with additional bits to maintain an integral number of octets (no partial octets). If the data being transmitted consist of 5 Baudot characters, at 5 bits each, only 25 bits would be required for the data and an additional 7 bits would be required to complete the last octet. Following the optional data field is a frame check sequence for error detection, which is 16 bits. The final field of the frame is the flag that signals the end of the message. The bit pattern for the ending flag is the same as that for the beginning flag. Thus, the ending flag for one frame may serve as the beginning flag for the next.

SDLC is a positional protocol, which means each field except the data field has a specific length and location relative to adjacent fields. No special control characters (except for the flag characters) are used to delimit the data or headings in the message. For control frames, which are either unnumbered or supervisory, the control function is encoded in the control field. Unnumbered frames have 5 bits available to identify the control function, so 32 different function types are possible. The supervisory frame has only 2 bits available, so a maximum of four functions can be defined.

Number Sent (Ns) and Number Received (Nr) Subfields   In information frames, the control field contains two three-bit fields known as the **number sent** (**Ns**) and **number received** (**Nr**) **subfields**. The Ns and Nr counts are used to sequence messages. Three bits allow for eight numbers, 0 through 7. When transmitting an information frame the sender increments the Ns field value. The Ns or Nr number following 7 is 0; thus, the number sequence cycles through those eight values. The Nr field is used to acknowledge receipt of messages. Every time a message is received, the receiver increments the Nr count, which represents the number of the frame expected next. An Nr count of 5 means message number 5 should arrive next. The Ns and Nr counts are compared every time a frame is received to make sure no messages have been lost. This scheme allows seven messages to be sent before an acknowledgment is required. The ability to receive up to seven frames without acknowledgment improves performance; however, it also places a burden on the sender, which must be ready to retransmit any unacknowledged frames. This requires that messages be saved in the sender's buffers until acknowledged, which can create problems for systems with small buffers or memory. Examples of how the Ns and Nr fields are used are found in Appendix C.

Both ADCCP and HDLC allow the control field to be expanded to provide for larger Ns and Nr counts, as illustrated in Figure 9-12. When expanded to 16 bits, the Ns and Nr fields can each be 7 bits, which allows 128 sequence numbers, and up to 127 messages can be transmitted before being acknowledged. This arrangement is especially beneficial with satellite links because of the propagation delay for response, which can cause a small number of unacknowledged frames to create undesirable delays. Recall from Chapter 1 that satellite signals incur a one-way propagation delay of approximately a quarter of a second. If 10,000-bit blocks are being transmitted on a 1-Mbps

number sent (Ns) subfield In bit synchronous transmission such as HDLC, a field on the transmission frame and on the sender's system used to represent the frame sequence number being transmitted.

number received (Nr) subfield In bit synchronous transmission such as HDLC, a field on the transmission frame and on the receiver's system used to represent the frame sequence number the receiving station expects to receive next.

Figure 9-12

Control Fields for
Information Frames

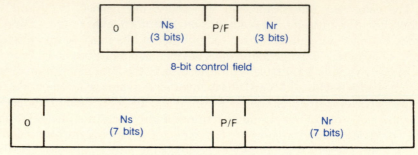

8-bit control field

Expanded 16-bit control field

Figure 9-13

SDLC Transparency

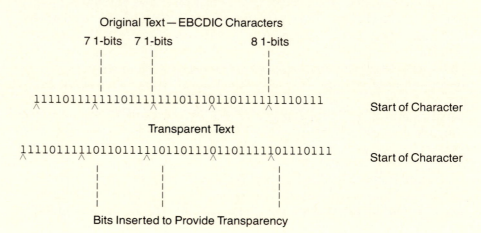

Original Text — EBCDIC Characters

7 1-bits   7 1-bits   8 1-bits

111101111111011111110110110111111110111   Start of Character

Transparent Text

111101111101101111101101110110101111101110111   Start of Character

Bits Inserted to Provide Transparency

satellite link, then 25 blocks theoretically could be transmitted every quarter of a second. With 3-bit Ns and Nr fields, only 7 blocks could be sent before waiting for an acknowledgment. In this case, transmission time for 18 blocks would be lost, limiting the available capacity.

Transparency   Transparency is implemented in SDLC by bit insertion, also known as **bit stuffing**. Because the beginning and ending flags use the only reserved bit sequence, their bit pattern — 01111110 — must never appear in the data portion of the record. This is accomplished by inserting a 0 bit after five consecutive 1 bits are encountered in the data. After the control field, the receiver looks for two specific bit patterns: the ending flag and five consecutive 1 bits. If the ending flag is encountered the receiver knows that the preceding 16 bits are frame check characters and that all bits between the end of the control field and the start of the frame check are data. If, on the other hand, five consecutive 1 bits arrive followed by a 0 bit, the receiver also knows that the 0 bit has been inserted for transparency. The inserted 0 bit is then stripped out and the receiver continues evaluating the input stream. An example of SDLC transparency is illustrated in Figure 9-13.

bit stuffing   The implementation of transparency in SDLC through bit insertion.

Effectiveness of the SDLC Protocol   The effectiveness of SDLC is summarized in Table 9-4.

TABLE 9-4   Effectiveness of SDLC Bit Synchronous Protocol

Capability	Comments	Rating
Error detection	CRC	Good
Transparency	Designed in	Good
Addressing	8-bit address field	Fair
	Expandable address field	Good
Code independence	Inherent — only limit is that data must be in octets	Good
Configurations	Wide variety allowed	Good
Efficiency	Fixed overhead is better for long messages. Full duplex exchanges can enhance performance.	Good
Growth	Designed for changing circumstances	Good

TABLE 9-5   Comparison of Asynchronous and Synchronous Protocols

Asynchronous	Synchronous
Character-at-a-time transmission	Block transmission
Modems are not synchronized	Modems are synchronized
Error detection commonly is parity	Error detection commonly is CRC or parity plus LRC
Fixed overhead per character	Fixed overhead per block (may be less efficient for small messages but more efficient for large ones)
Less efficient use of communications link	More efficient use of communications link
Lower cost devices	Higher cost devices

CHOOSING A DATA LINK PROTOCOL

Although several other data link protocols exist, those described in this chapter are the most common. The question is, which one is appropriate for which application? Table 9-5 compares synchronous and asynchronous protocols. When selecting the proper protocol, the network designer must first choose a protocol supported by the hardware vendor. Most vendors support some version of asynchronous, character synchronous, and bit synchronous protocols. CSMA/CD and token passing are found primarily in local area networks. Second, the type of hardware used in an application partly dictates the data link protocol. Most terminals support one or possibly two protocols; the exception is intelligent terminals, which can support a wide variety of protocols. Third, the network support provided by the vendor affects the choice of data link protocol. Many newer network systems have been designed around a bit-oriented synchronous protocol. Because not all users have compatible terminals, accommodations are frequently made to support other protocols, such as BISYNC.

In practice, do not select a protocol and then gather the equipment to support it. Instead select a network design, a hardware vendor, and associated hardware, each of which dictates a particular protocol. Most current data link technology and development for wide area networks are based on bit-oriented synchronous protocols. There are several bit-oriented implementations and several standards exist. The industry trend is toward higher speed transmission and efficient use of the data link, which definitely favor synchronous transmission protocols.

THE OSI NETWORK LAYER

The OSI network layer performs four major functions: routing, network control, congestion control, and collection of accounting data. Whereas the data link layer is concerned with moving data between two adjacent nodes, the network layer is concerned with end-to-end routing, or getting data from the originating node to its ultimate destination. Data may take a variety of paths from the originating node to the destination node. The network layer must be aware of alternative paths in the network and choose the best one. Selection of the best path depends on several factors, including congestion, number of intervening nodes, speed of links, and so on.

network control Involves the sending and receiving of node status information to other nodes to determine the best routing for messages.

Network control involves sending node status information to other nodes and receiving status information from other nodes to determine the best routing for messages. The network layer must enforce the priority scheme when priorities are associated with messages. **Congestion control** means reducing transmission delays that might result from overuse of some circuits or because a particular node in the network is busy and unable to process messages in a timely fashion. The network layer should adapt to these transient conditions and attempt to route messages around such points of congestion. Not all systems can adapt to the changing characteristics of the communications links. In broadcast-type systems, very little can be done to overcome this problem.

congestion control The reduction of transmission delays.

Message Routing

routing An algorithm used to determine how to move a message from its source to its destination. Several algorithms are used.

One function of the network layer, **routing**, is achievable through several algorithms used to direct messages from the point of origination to final destination. Determination of message routing can be either centralized or distributed. Routing itself can be either static, adaptive, or broadcast and is governed by a network routing table resident at each node. The network routing table is a matrix of other nodes with the link or path to that node. If a message destined for Node X arrives at Node K, the network routing table is consulted for the next node on the path from K to X. Network routing tables can also contain more information than just the next link, such as congestion statistics. The following discussion covers a sample of routing techniques.

Centralized Routing Determination: The Network Routing Manager

In centralized determination of routing tables, one node is designated as the **network routing manager** to whom all nodes periodically forward such status information as queue lengths on outgoing and incoming lines and the number of messages processed within the most recent interval. The routing manager is thereby provided with an overview of network functioning, location of any bottlenecks, and location of underutilized facilities. The routing manager periodically recalculates the optimal paths between nodes and constructs and distributes new routing tables to all nodes.

The disadvantages of this form of network routing are manifold. The routing manager's ability to receive many messages from the other nodes increases the probability of congestion, a problem that can be exacerbated if the routing manager is itself a node used to accept and forward messages. Networks are sometimes subject to transient conditions, such as when the internode transfer of a file saturates a link for a short period of time. By the time this information is relayed to the routing manager and a new routing is calculated, the activity may have already ceased, making the newly calculated paths less than optimal. Some nodes also will receive the newly calculated routing tables before others, leading to inconsistencies in how messages are to be routed. Figure 9-14 shows a change in the message path. Under the old routing mechanism the route was A -> B -> D -> X, whereas the new path is A -> C -> D -> X, as indicated in Figure 9-14. Also, the new path from Node B to Node X is B -> A -> C -> D -> X. If Node B receives its new routing chart while Node A is still using the old chart, then for a message destined from A to X, A will route it to B and B will route it back to A, continuing until A receives the new routing table. Transmission of the routing tables themselves also may bias the statistics being gathered to compute the next routing algorithm.

network routing manager
A designated node that has an overview of network functioning, location of any bottlenecks, and location of utilized facilities.

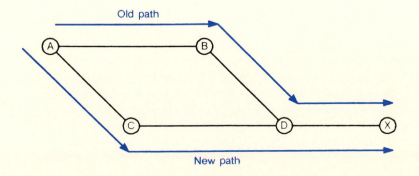

Figure 9-14

A Change in the Message Path

An additional problem with centralized route calculations is the amount of CPU processing power needed. Reliability of the routing manager is another important factor. If this node fails, either the routing remains unchanged until the system is recovered or an alternate routing manager must be selected. The best situation is to have alternate routing managers available in case the primary routing node fails. This is implemented most efficiently by having the routing manager send the alternates "I'm alive" messages at predefined intervals; if the backup manager fails to receive this message within the prescribed interval, it assumes the manager has failed and takes over. The backup manager's first responsibility is to broadcast that network status messages should now be routed to it.

Distributed Routing Determination

distributed routing determination   A routing algorithm in which each node calculates its own routing table based on status information periodically received from other nodes.

Distributed routing determination relies on each node to calculate its own best routing table, which requires each node to periodically transmit its status to its neighbors. As this information ripples through the network, each node updates its tables accordingly. This technique avoids the potential bottleneck at a centralized route manager, although the time required for changes to flow through all the nodes may be quite long.

Static Routing

static routing   A form of routing in which one particular path between two nodes is always used.

The purest form of **static routing** involves always using one particular path between two nodes; if a link in that path is down, communication between those nodes is impossible. Fully interconnected networks were sometimes used for this approach. The only path between any two nodes was the link between them. If that link was down, the available network software was incapable of using any alternate paths. This type of system has largely disappeared. Static routing generally now refers to the situation in which a selected path is used until some drastic condition makes that path unavailable. An alternate path is then selected and used, until the route is switched manually, a failure occurs on the alternate path, or the original path is restored.

weighted routing   When multiple paths exist, each is given a weight according to perceived utilization. A random number is generated to determine which of the available paths to use based upon their weights.

When multiple paths exist, some implementations weight each path according to perceived utilization, which is referred to as **weighted routing**. The path is then randomly selected from the weighted alternatives. Figure 9-15 shows three paths from Node A to Node X, via Nodes B, C, and D. Suppose the network designers had determined that the path through Node B would be best 50% of the time, the path through Node C would be best 30% of the time, and the path through Node D would be best 20% of the time. When a message is to be sent from Node A to Node X, a random number between 0 and 1 is generated. If the random number is 0.50 or less, the path through Node B is traversed; if the random number is greater than 0.50 and less than or equal to 0.80, the path through Node C is selected; otherwise, the path through Node

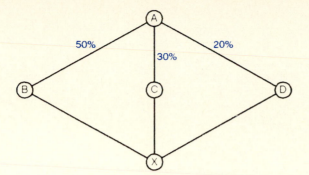

Figure 9-15

Weighted Routing

D is selected. The path may alternate, but each path is used with the same frequency as in the routing tables. This type of routing can only be changed by altering the route weighting in the routing tables.

Adaptive Routing

Adaptive routing, occasionally referred to as dynamic routing, attempts to select the best current route for the message or session. The best route may be determined by several different parameters, such as link congestion, link speed, and so on.

adaptive routing A routing algorithm that evaluates the existing paths and chooses the one that will provide the best path for a message. Routes may change due to congestion and path failures.

Quickest Link   The simplest adaptive routing algorithm is to have a node pass along the message as quickly as possible, with the only restriction being not to pass it back to the sending node. The receiving node looks at all potential outbound links, selects the one with the least amount of activity, and sends the message out on that line. There is no attempt to determine whether that path will bring the message closer to its destination. This type of algorithm is not very efficient and causes messages to be shuffled to more nodes than necessary, which adds to network congestion. The message could conceivably be shifted around the network for hours before arriving at its destination.

Best Route   The more intelligent adaptive routing techniques attempt to select the best route, as determined by one or more of the following parameters: the number of required hops, the speed of the links, the type of link, and congestion. Link congestion occurs when message traffic on a link is heavy, similar to freeway congestion during rush hours. Routing of this type requires current information on the status of the network. If a node is added to the network or if one is taken off the network, that information must be relayed to the nodes doing route calculation. Knowing the speed of the links as well as the number of hops is important. Traversing two links at 4800 bps is more costly than traversing one link at 2400 bps. The line time for both will

Figure 9-16

Routing Based on
Congestions

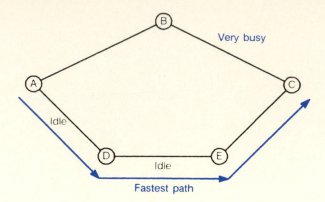

be the same, but some time is lost in receiving and forwarding the message. Avoiding congested areas will prevent messages from being stuck on inbound and outbound queues. In Figure 9-16, if Node A is transmitting a file to Node C, the route from Node A to Node C through B is the shortest but probably not the quickest at that time. The route through Nodes E and D would be more efficient, because the link from B to C is congested.

Broadcast Routing

broadcast routing   Routing in which the message is broadcast to all stations. Only the stations to which the message is addressed accept it.

Broadcast routing is exemplified by the CSMA/CD link protocol discussed in Chapter 5. Routing is quite easy, the message is broadcast to all stations, and only the station to whom the message is addressed accepts it. The network layer of the OSI recommendation has fewer functions with broadcast routing.

THE OSI TRANSPORT LAYER

transport layer   One layer of the International Standards Organization's open systems interconnection reference model. The transport layer is responsible for generating the end user's address and for the integrity of the receipt of message blocks.

The OSI **transport layer** is involved in end-to-end transmission services and assists the session layer in establishing the connections for a session. The transport layer may accept messages of any length; however, the communications link may have limitations regarding message size. The transport layer must segment these large messages into smaller transmission blocks and establish sequence numbers for each. The transport layer is responsible for end-to-end sequence number control and error detection and recovery. If a segment of a long message is lost, the transport layer effects recovery to ensure correct, complete message transfer.

Transport Service Access Point (TSAP)   An address used by the transport layer to uniquely identify session entities.

Another service that may be provided by the transport layer is addressing. Each user of the system is identified by an address called a **Transport Service Access Point (TSAP)** to identify entities unique to that session. The transport layer is responsible for translating user identifiers into TSAPs. TSAPs of the source and destination session entity, together with a checksum to detect errors, are appended to the message received from the session layer.

Seymour Opportunity, vice-president of marketing for the Syncrasy Corporation, has convinced the other corporate executives that the future lies not only in mail-order operations but also in discount computer stores. Wanting to expand into several areas at once, Syncrasy is opening discount computer stores in Chicago, New York City, Atlanta, Houston, Los Angeles, San Francisco, and Kansas City. Penny Pincher, the comptroller, has exerted her influence by obtaining commitments that the cost of expansion will be held to a minimum.

The computer stores in Chicago, New York, and Los Angeles will have five terminals each, and the other stores will have three each. Mail-order operations will continue, although on a diminished scale. The catalog stores in Kansas City, New York, and Los Angeles will be located 15, 20, and 40 miles from the discount stores, respectively.

Computer Store Transaction Types

The two basic transactions at each computer store will be (1) inventory and receipt transactions and (2) parts and customer inquiries.

Inventory and Receipts   The first type of transaction deals with inventory control and receipts. Every time a sale is made, the part number, quantity sold, unit price, discount rate, and total amount of the sale are transmitted to the central computer. The line item for each part sold consists of 22 characters, and the total amount of the sale is a 10-character field. The usual response to the transaction is 10 characters. Orders that total more than $1000 are an exception and require a credit check. These transactions, which comprise an estimated 30% of all inventory transactions, have 10 additional characters in the response portion of the message. Average processing time for normal orders is 0.5 seconds; for orders of more than $1000, it is 0.8 seconds. There is an average of 6 items per order and an average of 20 orders per terminal per hour, with peaks of 40 orders per terminal per hour. Peak transaction periods are from noon to 1:00 P.M. and from 5:00 P.M. to 6:00 P.M. It is required that 95% of all transactions of this type have a 3-second response time.

Parts and Customer Inquiries   The second type of store transaction is a parts or customer inquiry. Average input is 10 characters and average response is 500 characters. Average and peak rates for this transaction are both 10 per hour per terminal. A response time of 4 seconds is required. Processing time for these transactions is 1.5 seconds per order.

Catalog Store Activity

The third type of transaction will be in the catalog stores. Activity in the catalog store operations will decline as a result of having discount stores in the area. Catalog stores will have eight terminals each. The typical catalog store transaction has 500 characters of input data and a 100-character response. Each terminal averages 20 orders per hour, with a peak of 30 orders per hour. Five-second response time is required for these transactions. Processing time is 2.5 seconds per order.

Prices, Equipment, and Mileage

Only leased transmission lines from a common carrier are considered. Satellite transmission was considered by Syncrasy at the outset, but it was dismissed because of the relatively light amount of traffic from the stores and the effect of propagation delay on response times. The following rates are used in this case study (and in the exercises at the end of this chapter).

Modems   The cost of modems has declined in recent years, so it is unlikely that modems will be leased. The following calculations are for monthly fees only, excluding modem costs. Syncrasy also has opted to buy statistical multiplexers with integrated modems.

Interstate Communication Lines   The line can handle speeds up to 38,400 bps. Line speed is governed by the modem.

First 100 miles	$2.52 per mile (including monthly fee)
101–1000 miles	$0.94 per mile
Each mile over 1000	$0.58 per mile

Local Communication Lines   The line can handle speeds up to 38,400 bps. Line speed is governed by the modem.

Each mile	$4.70

Statistical Multiplexer   Syncrasy chose stat muxes with additional memory and built-in modems. These muxes are more expensive than the entry-level muxes with the price of $1000 quoted earlier in the chapter. Because the unit costs of these muxes are relatively high, Syncrasy decided to lease them. The costs of the multiplexers Syncrasy has chosen are:

Number of Channels	Purchase Price	Monthly Lease Price
4	$1700	$150
8	$2600	$225
16	$4300	$358
32	$6500	$540

Concentrators   The price of concentrators can vary enormously. This case uses two configurations. The first configuration will handle up to 32 output lines, which could be point-to-point terminals, multipoint communication lines, or lines to another concentrator or multiplexer. It sells for $30,000, with a monthly lease price of $1500. The second configuration must be large enough to handle all transactions. It sells for $40,000 and leases for $2000 per month. Each of these

TABLE 9-6   Mileage Chart

	Chicago	Houston	Kansas City	L.A.	N.Y.C.	S.F.
Atlanta	708	791	822	2191	854	2483
Chicago		1091	542	2048	809	2173
Houston			743	1555	1610	1911
Kansas City				1547	1233	1861
Los Angeles					2794	387
New York City						2930

concentrators will be able to accommodate up to eight incoming lines from the host processor.

Front-End Processors   The price of the FEP, $40,000, is the same as that of the more expensive concentrator.

Terminals   Dumb terminals sell for $500, with a monthly lease price of $50. Smart terminals sell for $1200, with a monthly lease price of $95. Intelligent terminals sell for $1500, with a monthly lease price of $105.

Mileage   Airline miles are used for determining communication rates between cities. Table 9-6 lists the mileage between cities.

Preliminary Considerations   A simple case study has been constructed, with few locations and a centrally located computer center. Even so, the variation between media costs of the best and worst cases alone can be significant. Because of their extended capabilities, intelligent terminals have been selected.

Mileage Costs

In actual practice, several common carriers would be consulted and their bids solicited for the best configuration. If there were many more locations, one of the network modeling systems would also be utilized to analyze all possible routes and provide a listing of the best alternatives. Instead, this exercise uses the brute force method of hand calculations.

Long-Distance Line Costs   Although it is unusual to do so, point-to-point costs are calculated first. This allows comparison of the best- and worst-case line costs. The cost of the Kansas City–Los Angeles link is computed in detail; mileage and line costs for the remaining cities are simply listed. Because mileage rates are different for miles 0–100, 101–1000, and over 1000, the 1547 miles between Kansas City and Los Angeles must be broken down into these increments, yielding $100 + 900 + 547$ miles. The cost for the Kansas City–Los Angeles link, then, is:

$$(100)(2.52) + (900)(0.94) + (547)(0.58) = 1415.26$$

Figure 9-17

A Network Configuration of
the Shortest Route

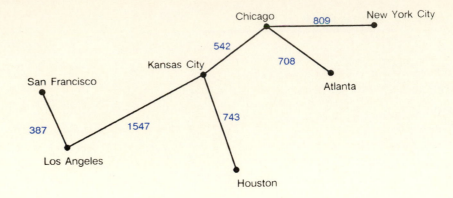

Monthly point-to-point link charges between the home city and all remote
locations are:

Kansas City to:

Atlanta	$ 930.68
Chicago	667.48
Houston	856.42
Los Angeles	1415.26
New York City	1233.14
San Francisco	1597.38
Total	$6700.36

Minimum-Distance Configuration Costs   Many combinations are
available to find the lowest rate based on a minimum-distance configuration.
The easiest way is to start with the shortest link—Kansas City to Chicago—
and work outward until all locations are accounted for. A simple program
could also be written to evaluate all combinations and pick the shortest route.
A network configuration of the shortest routes is given in Figure 9-17. The
costs of this network are:

From	To	Distance (miles)	Cost
Kansas City	Houston	743	$ 856.42
Kansas City	Chicago	542	667.48
Chicago	New York City	809	918.46
Chicago	Atlanta	708	823.52
Kansas City	Los Angeles	1547	1415.26
Los Angeles	San Francisco	387	521.78
Total			$5202.92

Local Line Costs   The costs of local links between the mail-order and
discount stores in Kansas City, New York City, and Los Angeles must be
calculated in addition to the costs of long-distance lines. These charges are
easier to compute because there is a flat rate per mile. The costs are:

Location	Distance (miles)	Cost
Kansas City	15	$ 70.50
New York City	20	94.00
Los Angeles	40	188.00
Total		$352.50

The difference between the low-cost and high-cost configurations is $1497.44 per month ($6700.36 − $5202.92). This does not mean the configuration is finalized. Whether the capacity of the lines can support the application is yet to be determined. For instance, the link from Kansas City to Chicago must be capable of supporting all message traffic from Chicago, New York City, and Atlanta. If one 9600-bps line is not capable of this, another alternative will be required, such as linking Houston and Atlanta.

Calculation of Line Utilization Costs

Five items must be considered in calculating the costs of line utilization: overhead, response time, aggregate data rate, line contention, and configuration. The first line-speed calculation is for response time. Following that, the aggregate data rate for a given link is considered to make sure there is sufficient capacity to meet all terminals' demands. Contention issues are then addressed, followed by an analysis of configuration.

Overhead   Overhead includes costs for several components: control messages, polling, and terminal access. Overhead involves how efficiently the lines are utilized. As we discuss in the next chapter, some of the purposes of data link protocols are to delimit data, provide error detection and line control, and allow for addressing. Each function requires that additional data be appended to the data message. In this case, control message overhead is approximated by using 10 bits per character rather than the actual 7 or 8 bits. Although not entirely accurate, this measure is adequate and certainly simplifies calculation.

A second overhead factor is polling costs, if a multipoint configuration is used. Determining polling overhead involves figuring the amount of time a terminal must wait to be polled. This averages out to be:

$$\text{wait time} = \text{polling interval} \times (\text{number of terminals} - 1) / 2$$

On average, a terminal will wait for half of the *other* terminals. Sometimes a terminal will wait for all of the other terminals, and at other times there will be no wait at all. Total wait time is the number of terminals that are waited for times the polling interval, or the amount of time required to send the poll message and wait for a reply. The amount of time required for a terminal to send data is not factored in because that is included in the contention calculations. Polling is ignored in this example because of the added complexity it requires.

The final component of overhead is the additional characters required for terminal access. Smart terminals using screen templates, protected fields, and video attributes require several characters to provide these capabilities. These include not only the characters needed for prompts, but also the control characters that position the cursor, allow for video attributes and protected fields, and so on. The number of additional characters required to support these capabilities varies from terminal to terminal. Although these additional characters are ignored in this case, the number of characters required for terminal access can be significant. Polling wait time can also be significant, especially with many terminals and half duplex lines with slow modem turnaround times. These factors must not be ignored in a real-life situation.

Response Time: Inventory and Receipts   First, the inventory and receipts transaction is considered. The average number of line items per transaction is 6. Each line item consists of the part number, quantity, discount rate, and line item price, with a total of 22 characters per line item. For 6 line items, $6 \times 22 = 132$ characters are required, plus a 10-character total field, giving a total input record length of 142 characters. The response consists of 10 characters. The expected response time is 3 seconds. With 0.5 seconds required for processing, this leaves 2.5 seconds to transmit 152 characters, or $152/2.5 = 61$ characters per second. At 10 bits per character for overhead of the data link protocol, a 610-bps line will be required. Thus, a 1200-bps line will be sufficient for this transaction's response time, hereafter referred to as transaction Type 1.

Transactions of this type that are more than $1000 in total sales require the same response time but have an additional 10 characters in the response and 0.3 seconds of processing time. The system must be able to transmit 162 characters in 2.2 seconds, which is 74 characters per second, or a 740-bps capacity. A 1200-bps line will also satisfy the response time for this transaction, hereafter called transaction Type 2.

Response Time: Parts and Customer Inquiries   The customer or inventory inquiry transaction requires 10 characters of input and generates a 500-character response, with 4-second response time and a 1.5-second processing time needed. The line time allowed is 2.5 seconds. The system must then transmit 510 characters in 2.5 seconds, or 204 characters per second. This equates to 2040 bps, which necessitates a 2400-bps line. This is hereafter referred to as transaction Type 3.

Response Time: Catalog Store Transactions   The catalog store transaction calculation was done in Chapter 1, where it was determined that 600 characters had to be transmitted in 2.5 seconds, for 240 characters per second or 2400 bps. This is hereafter called transaction Type 4. Overall, considering individual terminal response time only, a 2400-bps line will be adequate.

Aggregate Data Transmission Rate   In determining the aggregate data rate for Syncrasy's lines, we can start with the line from Kansas City to Chicago, which must support five terminals in Chicago, eight catalog store terminals in New York City, five store terminals in New York City, and three store terminals in Atlanta. Computation of the aggregate data rate must also consider the peak transaction load. Table 9-7 contains all of the pertinent information for this analysis.

TABLE 9-7   Transaction Analysis

Transaction Type (Location)	Number of Transactions per Hour	Number of Characters per Transaction	Number of Terminals	Total Number of Characters per Hour
1 (East Coast)	28	152	8	34,048
1 (Chicago)	21	152	5	15,960
2 (East Coast)	12	162	8	15,552
2 (Chicago)	9	162	5	7,290
3 (both)	10	510	13	66,300
4 (mail order)	30	600	8	144,000
			Total	283,150

In Table 9-7, the Chicago Type 1 transactions have been separated from the East Coast Type 1 transactions. Because peak transaction rates occur during specific hours and the East Coast cities of New York City and Atlanta are in a different time zone from Chicago, the worst condition of peak traffic on the East Coast has been assumed, for 40 transactions per hour; average load has been assumed for Chicago. Also, of the 40 transactions, 30% are transaction Type 2. Thus, there are 28 Type 1 transactions and 12 Type 2 transactions per hour on the East Coast and 21 Type 1 transactions and 9 Type 2 transactions in Chicago. The total 283,150 characters transmitted per hour is the product of the number of terminals, the number of transactions per terminal, and the number of characters per transaction, as indicated in the last column of Table 9-7.

An aggregate data rate of 283,150 characters per hour equates to approximately 78 characters per second, which is derived by dividing the number of characters per hour by 3600 seconds per hour. These calculations indicate that a 1200-bps line is sufficient to support the aggregate data rate. Thus far, response time is the dominant factor with respect to line speed.

Line Contention   As discussed in Chapter 1, a 2400-bps line is adequate in a point-to-point environment, although not if two terminals attempt to start a transaction at the same time. If a random transaction arrival rate is assumed, the following formula (from queuing theory) may be used to determine the probability of several transactions arriving within the same interval.

$$P_k(T) = (LT)^k \, (k!) \, (e^{-LT}) \qquad \text{for } K = 0, 1, 2, 3, \ldots$$

where

$P_k(T)$ is the probability that k transactions will arrive in interval T

L is the average number of transactions per unit of time

T is the interval being considered

e is the natural base for logarithms

k is the number of arrivals

$!$ is the factorial function

TABLE 9-8   Transaction Arrival Probabilities

Number of Arrivals	Probability
2	0.21
3	0.08
4	0.02
5	0.005

In this transaction environment there is a total of 840 transactions per hour, which is derived by summing the products of the number of transactions per hour and the number of terminals performing that transaction rate, as shown in Table 9-7. This results in an average of 0.23 transactions per second (840 divided by 3600). Thus, L in the formula is 0.23. Assuming an interval T of 5 seconds, which is the time for the longest transaction, the probability of two transactions arriving within a given 5-second interval is:

$$P_2(5) = (0.23 \times 5)^2 (2!) (e^{-(0.23 \times 5)}) = (1.15^2) (2) (e^{-1.15}) = 0.21$$

The complete probability table is given in Table 9-8, from which it can be determined that the probability of two or more transactions arriving in any 5-second interval is:

$$0.21 + 0.08 + 0.02 + 0.005 = 0.325$$

Thus, 33% of the time two or more transactions will be active in a 5-second time span. Doubling the line speed will allow two transactions within 5 seconds to meet the expected response time. The probability then becomes only 0.10, or 10%, that transactions will contend with each other (the probability that three or more transactions will arrive within 5 seconds). A 5-second interval is actually quite conservative, since it is not entirely devoted to line time — the element of interest. During the 5-second interval, for a given transaction, the line will be idle approximately 50% of the time at a speed of 2400 bps. Increasing the line speed to 4800 bps should adequately eliminate slow response time due to contention.

Configuring the System: East Coast   It would be most economical to use a short route-line configuration with cascading statistical multiplexers. If the configuration follows a path from Kansas City to Chicago, then from Chicago to New York City and Atlanta, and finally from New York City catalog store to New York City discount store, as shown in Figure 9-18, by the time the extremities have been reached, a stat mux is likely to have run out of capacity. Each time a line is dropped off, the speed generally steps down. In addition, cascading multiplexers down by five levels will likely result in performance problems. Another problem is the number of terminals in New York City that must be accounted for. A concentrator in Chicago will provide the following significant network capabilities:

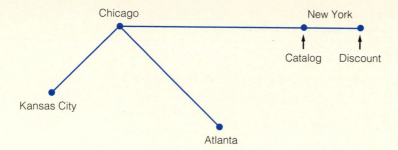

Figure 9-18

Syncrasy East Coast Network

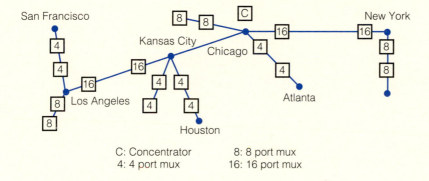

Figure 9-19

Syncrasy Configuration

C: Concentrator   8: 8 port mux
4: 4 port mux   16: 16 port mux

- allows terminals to be polled from Chicago rather than Kansas City
- provides for later expansion
- allows for more local terminal and error handling
- can provide some local support if the path to Kansas City is malfunctioning
- makes for a more workable configuration than extensive cascading of muxes
- can support higher speed circuits to the East Coast

Configuring the System: West Coast   A different configuration can be used for the West Coast link to Los Angeles and San Francisco: a direct link to Los Angeles and two separate drops — five terminals to the discount stores in Los Angeles and three to San Francisco. This contrasts with the link from Chicago to New York City, which involves 18 terminals. Cascading muxes are feasible for the West Coast. For the Houston link, a simple four-port statistical multiplexer on a 4800-bps line can be used. The final configuration is given in Figure 9-19.

Final Costs

The final monthly costs, broken down by branches of the network, are summarized on the following pages.

Monthly Equipment Cost for the Kansas City, Chicago, New York City, and Atlanta Branches of the Network

Multiplexers	2	16-port muxes at $358 each: $716
	4	8-port muxes at $225 each: $900
	2	4-port muxes at $150 each: $300
Modems	purchased or integrated with muxes	
Terminals	11	intelligent terminals at $105 each: $1155
	(Note: Two were available from the mail-order store.)	
Concentrator	1 at $1500 each: $1500	
Subtotal	$4571	

Monthly Equipment Cost for the Kansas City to Kansas City Branch of the Network

Multiplexers	2	4-port muxes at $150 each: $300
Modems	purchased or integrated with muxes	
Terminals	1	intelligent terminal at $105 each: $105
	(Note: Two terminals were available from the mail-order store.)	
Subtotal	$405	

Monthly Equipment Cost for the Kansas City to Houston Branch of the Network

Multiplexers	2	4-port muxes at $150 each: $300
Terminals	3	intelligent terminals at $105 each: $315
Subtotal	$615	

Monthly Equipment Cost for the Kansas City to Los Angeles to San Francisco Branches of the Network

Multiplexers	2	16-port muxes at $358 each: $716
	2	8-port muxes at $225 each: $450
	2	4-port muxes at $150 each: $300
Modems	purchased or integrated with muxes	
Terminals	6	intelligent terminals at $105 each: $630
	(Note: Two were available from the mail-order store.)	
Subtotal	$2096	

Total Monthly Costs for the Network

Total equipment: $7687

Total long-distance line costs: $5203

Total local line costs: $352

Total network costs: $13,242

Syncrasy will have to sell a lot of equipment to support this $13,242 per month configuration. However, there is the existing alternative of attaching to a Packet Distribution Network (PDN). PDNs are discussed in Chapter 11. Because the amount of data being transmitted is relatively small and PDNs charge by the number of packets and not by connect time, the overall cost could be lower. ❖

SUMMARY

This chapter covered WAN topologies and the transmission services of the OSI data link, network, and transport layers. The principal WAN topologies are the star, hierarchical, and interconnected topologies. Rings or loops and busses are also used in WANs, but are most common in LANs.

The primary WAN data link protocols are asynchronous and synchronous. Asynchronous protocols were adapted from pre-computer technologies such as telegraphy. Asynchronous transmission is widely used, particularly for connections between terminals and host computers and between microcomputers and other computers. There are several varieties of synchronous protocols. The preferred protocol today is a bit synchronous protocol such as SDLC, HDLC, LAPB, or ADCCP. Additional details of asynchronous and synchronous protocols can be found in Appendices A, B, and C.

The OSI network and transport layers also provide transmission services. The OSI network layer performs four major functions: routing, network control, congestion control, and collection of accounting data. Several routing algorithms exist, and can be classified into two broad categories: static and adaptive. Static routing algorithms choose a path and continue using that path so long as it is available. Adaptive routing algorithms may vary the path used in an attempt to always use the best path. Thus, adaptive routing may be able to avoid congestion and more effectively use all available paths between a sender and receiver.

The OSI transport layer is involved in end-to-end transmission services and assists the session layer in establishing the connections for a session. One of the services performed by the transport layer is message accountability. Message sequence numbers are generated by the transport layer in the sending computer and checked by the transport layer in the recipient's computer thus ensuring that the entire message was received. The transport layer also assists in finding the network address of the recipient.

KEY TERMS

REVIEW QUESTIONS

In answering some of the questions below, it may be helpful to refer to the material in Appendices A–C.

1. Explain why asynchronous protocols do not support code independence.

2. In asynchronous protocols, what function is provided by interrupt characters?

3. Why is double buffering necessary?

4. Explain the popularity of asynchronous protocols.

5. Distinguish between positional and framing synchronous protocols.

6. How does a byte count synchronous protocol work?

7. Name three implementations of bit-oriented synchronous data link controls. List those features indicated in the text that distinguish some of these from SDLC.

8. How do asynchronous and synchronous protocols differ? In what respects are they the same?

9. What advantages does SDLC have over BISYNC?

10. Which network topology provides the greatest amount of control? Which provides the lowest link costs? Which will have the highest link costs?

11. What are the advantages and disadvantages of centralized routing calculations?

12. What are the advantages and disadvantages of local route determination?

13. Distinguish between static and adaptive routing.

14. What are the advantages and disadvantages of the quickest link routing algorithm?

15. Describe the weighted routing algorithm.

PROBLEMS AND EXERCISES

1. Make a chart that compares the overhead of asynchronous, BISYNC, and SDLC protocols. Make the chart for message sizes of 25, 50, 100, 500, and 1000 characters. The chart should look like Table 9-9. In filling out the chart, assume a start, stop, and parity bit for async. For BISYNC, assume six control characters (SYN SYN STX ETX plus two for BCC). For BISYNC you should also include a point-to-point line bid (SYN SYN ENQ) and two acknowledgments (SYN SYN ACK0 and SYN SYN ACK1) of four characters each. One acknowledgment is for the line bid and one for the data. For SDLC, assume a frame overhead of 48 bits. Count the acknowledgment as 16 bits, because ordinarily several frames will be acknowledged at once. Which is the most efficient protocol and under what conditions? Assume seven-bit characters for each case.

2. Diagram a sequence of message exchanges between two stations using SDLC that shows the changing of the Ns and Nr subfields.

3. Is transparency a requirement of code independence? Justify your answer.

4. Can there be a start-stop flag in the address or control field of an SDLC message? If not, why not? If so, why does it not terminate the message?

5. You need a wide area network and want a topology that provides a low cost with good reliability and expandability. You also need good response times, which implies a limited number of hops. Which topology would you choose? Why?

TABLE 9-9 **Protocol Comparison Chart**

Number of Text Characters	Number of Bits Transferred		
	ASYNC	BISYNC	SDLC
25			
50			
100			
500			
1000			

TABLE 9-10   Mileage Chart

	Cleveland	Houston	Las Vegas	Phoenix	Portland	San Diego	Washington, D.C.
Boston	657	1830	2752	2670	3144	2984	448
Cleveland		1306	2093	2032	2432	2385	360
Houston			1467	1164	2243	1490	1365
Las Vegas				285	996	336	2420
Phoenix					1268	353	2300
Portland						1086	2784
San Diego							2602

6. Investigate three network implementations and answer the following questions.

    a. What topology does each use?

    b. What type of routing does each use?

    c. Are alternate paths available? If so, under what conditions are they used?

7. What is the lowest cost communications configuration that will link each of the cities in the mileage chart in Table 9-10? Use the line costs presented in the case study.

8. If Houston is the central location, what is the cost of a network connecting Houston to each of the cities in Exercise 7 via point-to-point links?

REFERENCES

IBM. *IBM Synchronous Data Link Control General Information*. Manual no. GA27-3093-2. Research Triangle Park, NC: IBM, 1979.

Stallings, William. *Handbook of Computer-Communications Standards: Local Network Standards*, Volume 2. New York: Macmillan, 1987.

10

WAN System Software

CHAPTER OBJECTIVES

After studying this chapter you should be able to:

- Describe the functions of the OSI session layer
- Discuss the functions provided by an operating system and device drivers
- Compare and contrast database and telecommunications access methods
- Explain the capabilities of a teleprocessing monitor
- Trace the flow of a transaction through a system

*I*n this chapter we discuss several major software components of a data communications network. In the OSI reference model, software exists at every layer from the data link level up. We have already looked at functions of the physical, data link, network, and transport layers. This chapter primarily addresses functions found in the OSI session layer. Consistent with prior approaches, the discussion moves from the level closest to the terminals and proceeds toward the host processor. In this chapter you will learn about systems software functions. By systems software, we mean software such as an operating system or data communications software that supports applications in carrying out their tasks.

THE OSI SESSION LAYER

Whenever two entities in a network communicate, a session is established between them. The major objectives of the session layer are to establish the dialogue rules between two entities, to manage the exchange of data between the entities, and to dissolve the session. The dialogue rules include the method of flow control, which can be either full duplex or half duplex. Simplex transmission is not supported in the OSI reference model.

Another aspect of the dialogue rules is establishing synchronization points. If a session is interrupted for any reason, the synchronization points help reestablish and recover the session. Other parameters that the session layer might stipulate for a session are message lengths and quality of service. Quality of service parameters include the ability to set priorities, security, and speed and quality of the communications link. When the entities involved in a session need to terminate the dialogue, the session must be dissolved. Dissolution may occur at the request of either session member. Prior to a session being dissolved, all data in transit must first be received and acknowledged. We now consider a generic software environment and then two WAN software systems that provide session-level services.

SOFTWARE OVERVIEW

Applications Software

applications software
Software that solves a business or scientific problem as opposed to system software that make the system easier to use.

A generic software configuration is depicted in Figure 10-1. At the heart of the system is the **applications software**. The goal of applications software is to solve a business or scientific problem, not to solve computer system problems. An example of a system problem is the details of how to display data on a terminal. In the early days of computer programming, an applications program needed to contain logic to communicate with specific hardware devices. If a new terminal was introduced into the system, applications programs had to be changed to support the differences between the new terminal and terminals the program already supported. If all currently supported terminals had monochrome screens and the new terminal had a color screen, the applications program had to be modified to be able to display colors. When applications software is responsible for device handling, the applications programs take longer to create, test, and modify. The applications programmer also must be knowledgeable of device interface skills as well as applications design skills.

Systems Software

Most current systems provide systems-level software that eliminates the need for hardware-dependent logic in applications software. This allows programmers to focus their attention on business problems. To support this objective,

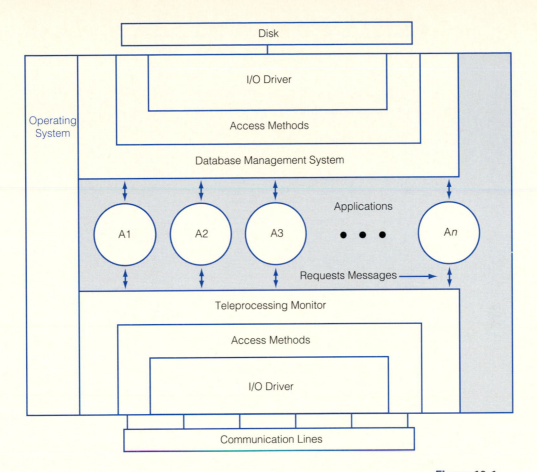

Figure 10-1

A Generic Software
Configuration

software such as database management systems and teleprocessing monitors were developed to control and manage data and terminal devices, and access methods were added to provide easier access to data and terminals. These software capabilities provide functions common to most applications programs and remove the details of file and device access from applications software. This follows a trend of systems-level software: making the system easier to program and use. Programmers interface to devices via well-defined user interfaces. Just as the adjacent levels of the OSI reference model have interfaces that allow data to flow between layers, messages and data flowing between applications programs and the database or data communications system pass through interfaces to reach their destination. Perhaps the most important piece of software in effecting this is the operating system.

Operating System

The **Operating System (OS)** helps applications by performing interface, process management, and file management functions as listed in Table 10-1. The OS performs all of these functions in a manner largely transparent to the

Operating System (OS)
The overall manager of the computing system that performs all of its functions transparent to the applications program and the programmer.

TABLE 10-1   Operating System Functions

Interface Functions — Provide Interface to:

    Users

    I/O system

    File system

Process Functions

    Schedule processes for execution

    Start/stop processes

    Establish process environment

    Enforce process priorities

    Prevent processes from interfering with each other

    Allow multiprocessing/multitasking

Management Functions

    Manage memory

    Manage I/O system and devices

    Manage access to CPU

    Manage user access through security provisions

File Management Functions

    Allocate disk space

    Maintain disk directories

Manage file attributes — owner, date, and time updated, and so on

Provide file security

applications program and the programmer. The OS also performs many functions for an executing program, but these functions are carried out without the programmer explicitly requesting them. The OS, the overall manager of the computing system, is loaded when the system is started and portions of the OS remain memory resident so it is always available to provide management and interface functions. One of the functions provided by the OS is managing the input/output (I/O) subsystem. The parts of the operating system that perform this task are called I/O drivers.

I/O Drivers   The **I/O drivers** in Figure 10-1 provide the low-level access to devices. On the database side the devices are tapes and disks, and on the data communications side they are communications lines. In data communications, low-level access involves implementing the data link protocol, such as asynchronous or HDLC; error detection; buffer management; and so on. For disk drives the I/O driver issues seek, read, and write commands. The specifics of I/O drivers are system and device dependent.

I/O driver   The part of the operating system that manages the input/output subsystem by providing low-level access to devices.

Access Methods   **Access methods** exist for both database and data communications systems. Access methods generally separate the application from physical characteristics of the data or devices the application is accessing. An access method essentially functions as a black box to translate user read and write requests into lower-level requests tailored to the file or device being accessed. Database access methods allow users to retrieve data. Applications often need several data retrieval methods. With personnel files, for instance, an employee record might need to be accessed via employee name, employee number, and Social Security number. Access methods provide the ability to select a specific record from the database with a small number of disk accesses. Some access methods also allow records to be retrieved in order on a key, which provides a logical ordering to the records. Thus, one access method might be used to retrieve personnel records in employee name order and another access method might be used to retrieve personnel records in department order.

Data communications access methods allow users to display data on a terminal and to retrieve data that has been entered on the terminal. How data is displayed on terminals may vary from one terminal to another. In Chapter 8, several terminal attributes were presented, including color, reverse video, and protected fields. Data communications access methods allow the user access to these attributes without knowing their implementation details. Access methods are covered in more detail later in this chapter.

Database and File Management Systems

A **Database Management System (DBMS)** organizes data into records, organizes records into files, and provides access to the data based on one or more access keys. A DBMS also provides a mechanism for relating one file to another. In a university database, records are maintained on students, classes, and teachers. File relationships allow users to answer questions such as, "What students are enrolled in section 4 of tapeworm taxonomy?" and "List the advisors for all students majoring in mathematics." Both requests require that data be extracted from at least two files via relationships that exist between the files (such as a teacher-advises-student relationship). A **File Management System (FMS)** provides a subset of the capabilities found in a DBMS. An FMS is basically oriented toward one file and hence does not provide file relationships. Database and file management systems provide data services to application processes. Applications issue database requests to store, modify, retrieve, or delete data, and the database management system carries out these requests.

Transaction Control Process

Whereas the database management system provides an application with access to data, application access to terminals or other nodes is provided by a transaction control process (TCP), also referred to as a teleprocessing monitor

access method   A software subsystem that provides input and output services as interface between an application and its associated devices. It eliminates device dependencies for an application programmer.

Database Management System (DBMS)   A system that organizes data into records, organizes records into files, provides access to the data based on one or more access keys, and provides the mechanism for relating one file to another.

File Management System (FMS)   A system that provides a subset of a database management system's capabilities. An FMS provides functions such as storage allocation and file access methods for a single file.

or message control system (MCS). A data communications access method can partially fulfill this function. Similar to the way in which a DBMS allows applications to share data, insulates the applications from the physical details of data storage, and provides data independence, the TCP enables different terminals to interface with multiple applications and removes an application from details such as the physical differences among terminals and among network nodes. Whereas the DBMS uses different data access methods to provide multiple paths to data, the TCP uses different terminal access methods to give access to multiple terminal types. A more detailed description of the transaction control process and its associated access methods can be found later in this chapter.

Example of Transaction Flow

With this brief overview of the applications software environment, we now see how the software components cooperate in processing a transaction. The following example assumes that our system is configured to allow recovery from most system failures and that the transaction will be entered by a user at a terminal.

Preparation for a transaction begins before the user enters the information. The first step in a system startup, of course, is loading the operating system. Following that, the systems and application software such as DBMS, TCP, spooler, and electronic mail systems are started.

The applications programs in Figure 10-1 receive their inputs from the TCP. Once the applications start, they must establish a session with the TCP. In some systems, such as IBM's **Customer Information Control System (CICS)**, applications run under the control of the TCP. In other systems, applications are relatively independent of the TCP. In the first case the applications are tightly coupled to a single TCP, whereas in the second case applications can receive messages from one or more TCPs as well as from other sources.

Customer Information Control System (CICS)   A TCP provided by IBM. Its primary function is as an interface between terminal users on one side and application programs or the database on the other.

Regardless of the implementation, a data path always exists or can be established between applications and a TCP. Once this path exists, the application issues a read request on its message file or otherwise indicates its readiness to accept a message for processing. The TCP displays an opening screen on each terminal under its control and then initiates a read for each terminal. Typical opening displays are a menu of available transactions or a user login screen.

Multiple TCPs may be in operation concurrently, and each TCP will exclusively control several terminals. Terminals may be moved from one TCP to another, but may only be attached to a single TCP at any one time. However, not all terminals in the system need to connect to a TCP. Some terminals may be used outside the TCP for applications such as program development. Terminals may also alternate between use for transaction processing under TCP control and use for other applications outside TCP control.

At this point in the transaction environment, each application is awaiting a transaction from the TCP, and the TCPs are awaiting data from their terminals. We assume that a user has successfully logged on to the system, a menu of transactions has been displayed on the user's terminal by the TCP, and the user is ready to enter a transaction. When a terminal transmits a transaction (such as admitting a patient to a hospital), the following actions are taken.

1. The user selects the "admit patient" transaction from the menu. This selection is transmitted to the TCP.

2. The TCP responds to the user's selection by displaying a patient identification form on the terminal and issues a read request for that terminal. The user fills in the form and transmits it to the TCP.

3. The TCP receives the transaction from the terminal, completing the read the TCP has issued for that device. For each of the other terminals, the TCP also has an outstanding read. Thus, at any time, a terminal operator may complete a task and transmit data to the TCP. The TCP must be able to accept these messages when they arrive.

4. The TCP sends the patient's ID to an application with a request to find a patient record that matches the requested ID. The objective is to determine whether this patient already has a hospital record.

5. The application issues a database read request to obtain a patient record with the ID sent to it by the TCP. If the record exists, it is returned to the application; otherwise, the application receives a message from the DBMS stating that the record does not exist.

6. The application returns the result to the TCP. In this case we assume the patient does not have a record on file.

7. The TCP displays a patient registration form and posts a read on the terminal. The user enters data into the form and sends it back to the TCP. At this point the TCP has all the data necessary for admitting the patient.

8. Data edits are performed on all fields for which they have been specified. For example, the TCP determines whether the patient's name has been entered, whether the data entered for the patient's gender is either M or F, whether the birth date entered is valid, and so on. If any of the fields are found to be in error, the TCP displays an error message on the terminal and highlights the field to be corrected. The user then corrects the mistake and the TCP rereads the data.

9. When all data edits have been successfully completed, the TCP writes the data received to a **transaction log**. The transaction log is used for recovering from failures and sometimes for system auditing.

transaction log Records all of the data received and is used in recovering from failures and in system auditing.

10. Because this transaction will modify the database, the TCP starts a transaction for recovery purposes. A transaction that changes data in the database must leave the database in a consistent state, which means the transaction must be completed in its entirety or leave the database as it was before the transaction started. Thus, a transaction

is a unit of work as well as a unit of database recovery. Starting a transaction is typically not necessary for read-only transactions because they do not change the database and do not need to be recovered. If the admissions clerk checks the database to see whether the patient already has a record on file, this activity does not require that a transaction be started.

11. The TCP examines the transaction and determines which application(s) should process it. Some transactions require the services of more than one application process. In this example, one application will create a patient record, another will locate a room and calculate room charges, and still another will generate a standard patient supplies issue and build supply charge records. The TCP may send each participating application its work at the same time, or the TCP may wait until one application finishes before sending the second application its portion of the work.

12. An application receives its portion of the transaction and begins processing. We consider here only the activity performed by the application that creates the patient record. The application uses the data received from the TCP to create a database record for the patient. The application sends the record to the database management system with a request to insert the new record.

13. The DBMS receives the request from the application and acts on it. Each time a record is updated or a new record inserted, images of the records being changed are inserted into the DBMS recovery log. Images of the record before and after the changes are written to the log. This allows the transaction to be reversed if it cannot be completed and also allows it to be re-created at a later time if necessary.

14. After logging the before- and after-images, the DBMS inserts the patient record and returns a successful result status to the application.

15. When the application has performed all of its work, including the database requests, it formats a reply message and returns it to the TCP. In this case, the reply is a status code indicating the success of the transaction. If the database operation is unsuccessful, the response will be an unsuccessful result code and a message or data to be returned to the terminal. This insert might have failed because the patient file was full.

16. The TCP determines whether another application process must become involved in the transaction. The other applications are given their work to accomplish, and they respond to the TCP with the results. When all applications have successfully completed their work, the TCP posts a transaction completion message on the transaction log, formats a response, and sends the response back to the terminal.

17. The application process(es), having finished the transaction, posts another read request on the message file, which indicates its ability to accept another transaction (another transaction may already be

queued on the application's input file). The TCP posts another read on the terminal, thus enabling additional transaction input.

While the above activity is being accomplished for this transaction, other transactions may also be in various states of completion. Examples of other transactions that may be in progress include:

- Another admission clerk may be admitting a different patient.
- A nurse may be reading a patient's record to find the patient's work telephone number.
- An accounting clerk may be consolidating the fees for a patient being dismissed.
- A clerk in the radiation laboratory may be entering a charge for a patient who has just been X-rayed.

We now consider the data communications software components in more detail, beginning with the access methods.

ACCESS METHODS

Data communications access methods give system users easier access to terminal devices. They relieve users from the device-specific attributes of terminals and provide connection, disconnection, and data transfer services to the applications. As with TCPs, the scope of access methods differs with the vendor and even within different access methods from a single vendor.

Application-Terminal Connection

Several approaches have been used to provide access methods, but we discuss only the most practical implementation. One function of an access method is to provide terminal-application connections. This may be accomplished by having a pool of applications and a pool of terminals available, as illustrated in Figure 10-2. The access method serves as a switch to connect terminal requests with the proper application(s).

Accessing a Terminal

Because an access method separates the application program from the terminal access logic, access methods can be used with or without a TCP, depending on the environment. Figure 10-3 illustrates two situations: TCP present and TCP absent. The access method performs fewer functions when the TCP is present because some functions, such as message routing and data editing, are performed by the TCP.

The first requirement of accessing a terminal from a program is to connect the two. The access method serves as an intermediary in this case. Either the

Figure 10-2

Access Method and Pooled
Application-Terminal
Connections

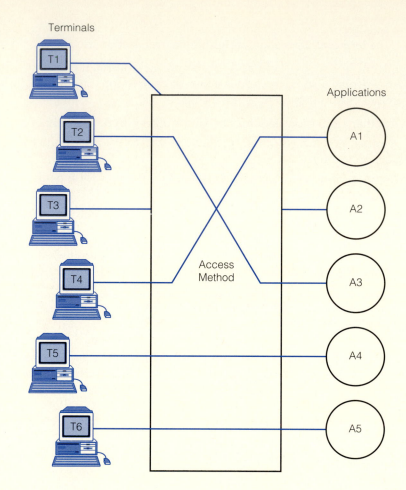

application initiates a connection by issuing an open or connect request to the access method or the terminal initiates the action by issuing an application logon request through the access method. Once the connection has been honored, a communication path exists, and the terminal and application can exchange data. Connection requests can be denied for security reasons or because the application or device is already occupied.

Without a TCP, the access method makes the connection between an application program and a terminal. In some implementations the connection is static: The application and terminal are attached to each other and the terminal can run only those transactions provided by that particular application. For the terminal user to access another application process, the terminal must first be disconnected from its current access application and then reconnected to the new one. Other systems provide more flexibility in making the connection between a terminal and an application. For example, IBM's **Virtual Telecommunications Access Method (VTAM)** provides several methods for terminal-application connections.

**Virtual Telecommunications
Access Method (VTAM)**
One of IBM's telecommunications access methods.

Figure 10-3

An Access Method with and
Without a TCP

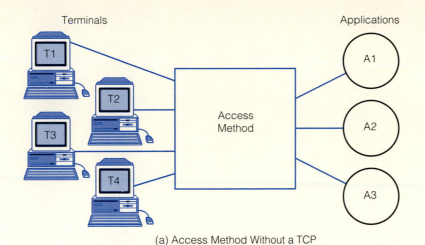

Terminals   Applications

(a) Access Method Without a TCP

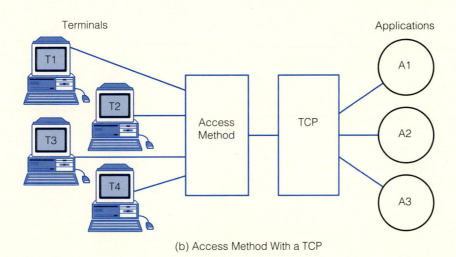

Terminals   Applications

(b) Access Method With a TCP

TRANSACTION CONTROL PROCESS

TCP Configuration

The configuration of the TCP is depicted in Figure 10-4. Because the TCP serves as a switch between applications and terminals, it must be aware of the terminals attached to it, the transactions that can be submitted, and the applications responsible for processing those transactions. In this environment, any terminal can access any application known to the TCP. Implementation can be as a monolithic process, as in Figure 10-5(a), or as multiple processes, as in Figure 10-5(b).

Figure 10-4

A Generic TCP Configuration

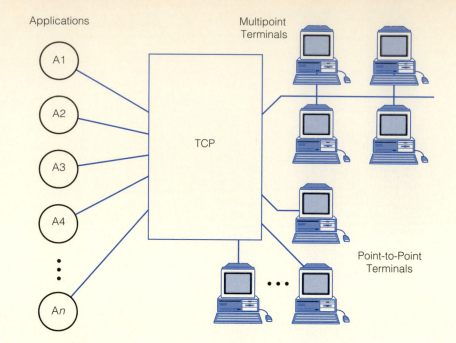

Figure 10-5

TCPs

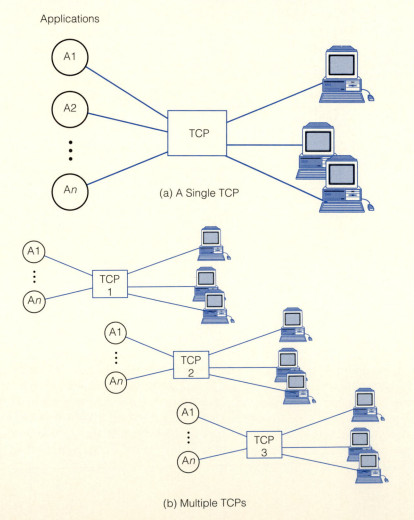

(a) A Single TCP

(b) Multiple TCPs

Single Threading Versus Multithreading

The efficiency of the application environment depends upon how quickly transactions can be processed. If multiple transactions can arrive at once, good performance requires that parallelism in transaction processing be provided. This means the TCP may need to process several transactions concurrently, a concept known as **multithreading**. With **single threading**, a process accepts an input, processes the input to completion, produces an output, and then is ready to accept another input for processing. A TCP operating in this manner would accept an input from one terminal, send the transaction to an application process, wait for the response, and send the result back to the terminal. Then, the TCP would accept another transaction and process it. Meanwhile, other terminals may be waiting for service. This processing method will result in long delays for terminals with queued requests.

    The difference between single threading and multithreading can be likened to what happens in a grocery store when people queue up at the checkout counter. The checkout clerk represents the TCP process, and the customers represent the terminals. The clerk ordinarily operates in a single-threaded manner, processing one customer and one customer only until the total order has been tabulated and the money collected before turning to the next customer. If an object does not scan correctly, everyone waits while an assistant checks the price. Looking up the price is analogous to accessing a disk, with the assistant as the DBMS. Everyone waits while the clerk scans each item, missing prices are checked, coupons are deducted, and the check is written and verified. To improve efficiency, the clerks could be multi-threaded: Everyone in the line would get attention as time allows. The clerks would maintain separate totals for each customer. While a missing price was being checked, the clerk could move on to the next customer's order. While a check is being written, another customer could be served. The multithreaded clerk must, of course, be much more flexible than the single-threaded clerk. Multiple totals are accumulated, items are taken from the correct basket and placed in the proper bag, and the totals are delivered to and collected from the proper customers. Multiple application threads are active within a multi-threaded process simultaneously. A comparison of single-threaded and multi-threaded processes is presented in Figure 10-6.

multithreading A technique that allows multiple operations to be processed concurrently.

single threading A technique in which only one operation is processed at a time.

Maintaining Context

An additional requirement of multithreaded processes is maintaining **context data**. Each single-threaded transaction is completely self-contained. In a multithreaded process, a transaction might be separated into several parts, and each part might be acted on by a different program. To unify this work, one program must (1) keep track of the completed parts and the parts yet to be worked on and (2) ensure that an interrupted transaction is restarted at the correct point. The action to be performed also may be contingent on a previous activity. For instance, in searching a database for an employee named Smith, an application might select and display the first ten Smiths plus additional identifying information. If none of the ten names is correct, the next

context data A requirement of multithreaded processes that entails unifying the work by keeping track of the completed parts as well as the parts yet to be worked on, and ensuring that an interrupted transaction is restarted at the correct point.

Figure 10-6

Single Threading vs.
Multithreading

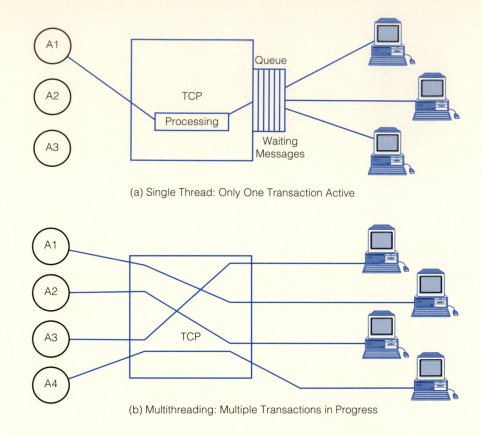

(a) Single Thread: Only One Transaction Active

(b) Multithreading: Multiple Transactions in Progress

ten are displayed, and so on until the proper Smith is found. The search for the next ten names is contingent on where the previous search stopped.

Like the multithreaded grocery clerk, the TCP must handle multiple customers at once. Suppose a TCP controls four terminals — T1, T2, T3, and T4 — and three applications — A1, A2, and A3. At the start of the system, all three applications request to open, or connect to the TCP. The TCP records this information and issues a command to open and display the first screen, and posts a read on each of the four terminals. At this point, the TCP is awaiting input from the terminals or a process. A chronological record of the TCP's activities is outlined in Table 10-2. This type of interleaved processing continues throughout the workday.

For the activities in Table 10-2, context was maintained in the TCP. It could also have been maintained within the application or the terminal. However, the application is not as logical a place as the TCP for maintaining context; multiple copies of one application may be used to increase efficiency, in which case the TCP would have to send the second part of a transaction to the same process that worked on the first part. Saving context in applications programs also makes those applications programs more complex. Some designers prefer to remove this type of complexity from the application. Because many TCP processes are supplied by software houses or computer vendors rather than being written by the end user, it benefits the user to have the multiuser complexity in the TCPs and not in the applications.

TABLE 10-2   Multiple TCP Transaction Threads

Accept update transaction from T2

Write T2's transaction on audit log

Accept inquiry transaction from T4

Route T4's request to application A1

Receive *write complete* on T2's audit log write

Begin transaction for T2

Route T2's transaction to A2

Receive inquiry transaction from T3

Route T3's transaction to A1

Receive A1's return message for T4

Write response to T4

Receive A2's return message for T2

End T2's transaction

Receive inquiry transaction from T1

Receive request for next ten records from T4

Send T1's request to A3

Receive notice that T2's transaction has ended

Send response to T2

Send T4's request together with stored context to A1

Memory Management

To manage context information and accept data from both terminals and applications, the TCP must provide **memory management** functions. At any time the TCP can receive a message from either terminals or applications, and multiple messages may be queued up simultaneously. The way in which TCPs manage memory varies. Essentially, the TCP must have sufficient memory available to provide storage for terminal and application messages as well as for context data. Sometimes this requires virtual memory algorithms similar to those employed by some operating systems: The disk is treated as an extension of memory and data is swapped back and forth between real memory and disk.

memory management Functions provided by the TCP that manage context information and accept data from both terminals and applications.

Transaction Routing

The TCP also must provide **transaction routing**, which means routing the transaction received from a terminal to one or more application programs. Several techniques are used to determine how to route a transaction. One method uses a transaction code embedded within the data message itself. The terminal operator enters the transaction code in the text of the message,

transaction routing The routing of a transaction received from a terminal to one or more application programs.

Figure 10-7

Transaction Routing in a TCP

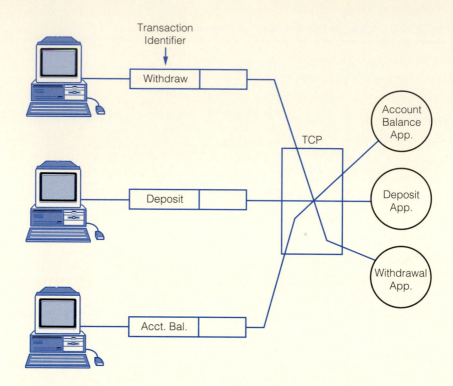

as illustrated in Figure 10-7. The TCP must recognize this code and route the transaction accordingly. Another method is based on context and a signal from the terminal. The signal is usually either a transaction code or the operator pressing a designated function key. Other signals may be indicated by using a lightpen, mouse, or touch-screen.

Transaction routing requires that the TCP know both which application handles a given transaction and the path or connection that leads to that application. Transaction routing could be table driven, in which case the TCP would look up the transaction ID in a table that provides directions to the proper application process. Alternatively, a procedural interface with a case statement or similar construct would result in a program call or a message being sent to that process.

Transaction Log

The TCP is a logical place to implement transaction logging. A transaction log captures the transaction inputs, usually on tape or disk. Once inputs are captured, the system can assure the user that the transaction will be processed. This does not necessarily mean the transaction will be successfully completed (errors could prevent that); it does mean the transaction will not be lost should a system failure occur. In addition to its use in recovery, transaction logging is sometimes required by auditors, especially in financial transactions. Electronic data processing (EDP) auditors will periodically check transaction sources and trace them through the system to determine whether they were correctly processed. If transaction logging is implemented, as soon as a transaction is received by the TCP, the transaction is written on the log file. Usually the TCP appends additional information to the message, such as a date-time stamp, transaction ID, or similar identifying information. Sometimes the completion of a transaction is also logged. In recovery situations this prevents a transaction from being processed twice.

In some systems the transaction log is synchronized with the database logging function to ensure that a message received by the system will be processed and that no duplicate transactions will be processed if a failure occurs. One system even guarantees that transactions requiring reprocessing in the event of a failure will be processed in the original order. This last is an important feature in banking applications. For instance, an account with an initial $100 balance receives a $500 deposit and then a $200 withdrawal. In the time-compressed recovery situation, the transaction could possibly be processed in reverse order, meaning that the withdrawal would be rejected for insufficient funds and the account would be overdrawn.

Security and Statistics

A TCP can be a focal point for online transactions entering the system, so it is a logical place to collect statistics and provide for security. Several statistics that are necessary to effectively manage a network system can be collected in the TCP, including the total number of transactions from all terminals, types of transactions, number of characters transmitted to and from a terminal, application processing time per transaction, and number of transactions per terminal. Security at the terminal and transaction levels could be enforced at the TCP. All online transactions for terminals managed by a TCP must be routed through the TCP, making the TCP is a logical place to implement security.

Message Priorities

The TCP is in an ideal position to assist with implementing message priorities within the online system. Every message received could be examined for priority, or priorities could be assigned by the TCP. Priorities could be established according to the source and type of message. Priority messages could then be given service first and routed to special server applications to expedite message processing.

Application Development

It is necessary to establish test environments consisting of terminals, access methods, TCPs, applications, and a database when designing an online system. This environment is also used to develop and test enhancements and problem fixes after a system has been placed in operation. The TCP can provide features to make testing and debugging easier, including the ability to trace or examine transactions received by the TCP, the ability to store transactions in a transaction file and pass them through the TCP as though they were entered at a terminal, and the ability to vary the rate of transaction submission. The TCP should also allow concurrent running of production applications and test applications.

Operations Interface

operations interface An interface that gives a network administrator the ability to monitor and control the TCP environment. Monitoring the TCP environment includes looking at statistics such as buffer utilization; number of transactions waiting in various queues for service; and busy rates for lines, devices, and the TCP. Controlling the TCP includes activities such as adding terminals and applications, starting or stopping devices, and reconfiguring the system.

An **operations interface** gives a network administrator the ability to monitor and control the TCP environment. Monitoring the TCP environment includes looking at statistics such as buffer utilization; number of transactions waiting in various queues for service; and busy rates for lines, devices, and the TCP. Controlling the TCP includes activities such as adding terminals and applications, starting or stopping devices, and reconfiguring the system. This may be accomplished through an operations interface program, illustrated in Figure 10-8. The operations interface provides some or all of the following capabilities:

TCP startup	TCP shutdown
Defining lines, terminals, or applications	Starting lines, terminals, or applications
Stopping lines, terminals, or applications	Adding lines, terminals, or applications
Deleting lines, terminals, or applications	Displaying statistics
Enabling/disabling statistics gathering	Moving lines, terminals, or applications from one TCP to another

Figure 10-8

TCP-Operations Interface

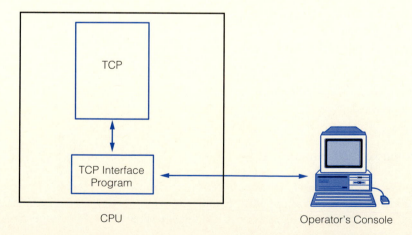

TCP

TCP Interface Program

CPU

Operator's Console

TABLE 10-3   TCP Activities

Provides a user interface with the TCP subsystem

Manages memory

Provides an interface between applications and terminals

Manages applications

Logs messages

Participates in recovery

Provides transaction definition

Edits data fields

Formats data for terminals and applications

Routes messages to server processes

Gathers statistics

Provides testing and debugging facilities

Assists in providing security

Assists in implementing a priority system

Other TCP Functions

Additional functions that a TCP might carry out include:

- If an application fails, the TCP should be able to automatically restart it. If a transaction arrives for a process that is not currently running, the TCP should be able to activate the process.
- If one application receives so many requests that response times become degraded, the TCP should be able to initiate additional copies of that process to enhance performance.
- If a process has been inactive for a long time, the TCP should be able to optionally delete that process to free the resources the process is holding.

Table 10-3 summarizes the activities of a TCP.

SUMMARY

Data communications software works closely with the applications, database, and operating system software to provide the functions required of today's systems. Two major components of networking software are access methods and transaction control processes (TCP). In some cases, access method software provides the linkage between application programs and terminal devices. Access methods always provide an interface with different terminal devices, providing terminal and application independence. TCPs also provide a link between applications software and terminal equipment. A TCP will also use the access method software to interface with terminal devices. The functions provided by TCPs in interfacing applications and devices go beyond those provided by the typical access method. These added capabilities include data edits, message switching, data formatting, and transaction definition and recovery.

KEY TERMS

access method, *335*

applications software, *332*

context data, *343*

Customer Information Control System (CICS), *336*

Database Management System (DBMS), *335*

File Management System (FMS), *335*

I/O driver, *334*

memory management, *345*

multithreading, *343*

operating system (OS), *333*

operations interface, *348*

single threading, *343*

transaction log, *337*

transaction routing, *345*

Virtual Telecommunications Access Method (VTAM), *340*

REVIEW QUESTIONS

1. What functions are performed by the operating system? Explain how two of these functions support applications.

2. Describe how a database access method is used to access a record.

3. Describe the functions of a data communications access method.

4. Describe how a transaction flows through an online system.

5. Describe the functions of a TCP.

6. Compare and contrast the functions of a TCP and a data communications access method.

7. Compare and contrast the operations of a TCP and an operating system.

8. Why are audit (log) trails important?

9. Compare multithreading and single threading.

10. Why is multithreading of a TCP an attractive feature?

PROBLEMS AND EXERCISES

1. Other than the banking example given in the chapter, describe another transaction that could create inconsistencies in a database if not recovered in the same order in which it was originally processed.

2. Is the saving of context necessary for multithreading? Why or why not?

3. Is it necessary for all user transactions to be recoverable units? If so, why? If not, give an example of a transaction that would not have to be recovered if the system failed.

4. Some data-processing professionals claim that a TCP uses a considerable amount of system resources and thus has a high overhead. This statement has some validity. How would you respond to such a statement in supporting the use of a TCP?

5. Research the literature to find an example of a TCP other than IBM's CICS. What features does this TCP provide?

6. Compare and contrast the functions of a local area network file server and a TCP.

REFERENCES

IBM. *Advanced Communications Function for VTAM General Information: Concepts*. Manual no. GC27-0463-3. Kingston, NY: IBM, 1982a.

————. *Customer Information Control System/Virtual Storage (CICS/VS) General Information*. Manual no. GC33-0155-1. Kingston, NY: IBM, 1982b.

11

WAN Implementations

CHAPTER OBJECTIVES

After studying this chapter you should be able to:

- Describe the workings and advantages of a packet distribution network (PDN)
- Explain the organization and workings of the Internet network
- Discuss the components and workings of IBM's systems network architecture (SNA)
- Describe the problems inherent in international networks

*I*n this chapter you will learn about wide area network (WAN) implementations. Specific networks covered in this chapter are packet distribution networks, the Internet, and IBM's systems network architecture. The chapter concludes with a case study that illustrates some considerations for implementing a WAN.

PACKET DISTRIBUTION NETWORKS

The concept of a packet distribution network (PDN) was first introduced in 1964 by Paul Baran of the Rand Corporation as a process of segmenting a message into specific-size packets, routing the packets to their destination, and reassembling the packets to re-create the message. In 1966, Donald Davies of the National Physics Laboratory in Great Britain published details of a store-and-forward packet distribution network. In 1967, plans were formulated for what is believed to be the first packet distribution network, ARPANET, which became operational in 1969 with four nodes. The ARPANET has since expanded to more than 125 nodes and generally evolved into the NSFNet. NSFNet and several other regional networks are integrated into one supernetwork called the Internet. The Internet is discussed later in this chapter.

A packet distribution network (PDN) is sometimes referred to as an X.25 network, a packet-switching network, a value-added network (VAN), or a public data network. Packet distribution and packet switching both refer to how data is transmitted: as one or more packets with a fixed length. The X.25 designation stems from CCITT's recommendation X.25, which defines the interface between data terminal equipment (DTE) and data circuit-terminating equipment (DCE) for terminals operating in the packet mode on public data networks. The term *public data network*, which derives from the X.25 recommendation, is somewhat of a misnomer because packet-switching networks also have been implemented in the private sector. When the network is public, users subscribe to the network services much like they subscribe to telephone services. The term *value-added network* is used because the network proprietor adds not only a communications link but also message routing, packet control, store-and-forward capability, network management, compatibility among devices, and error recovery. These are the services associated with the OSI physical, data link, and network layers.

Packet distribution networks specify a selection of different packet sizes, with sizes of 128, 256, 512, and 1024 bytes being most common. All packets transmitted must conform to one of the available packet lengths; individual users subscribe to a service providing one of the available packet sizes. Limiting the number of variations in packet size makes managing message buffers easier and evens out message traffic patterns.

PDNs and the OSI Layers

Only three OSI layers have been described for PDNs, because a PDN is only responsible for message delivery. The three layers of the OSI reference model responsible for message delivery are the physical, data link, and network layers. From the PDN user's perspective all seven OSI layers exist; the application, presentation, session, and transport layer functions are implemented in the user's segment of the network.

Current PDN Implementations

The use of PDNs has increased significantly since the first PDN was established, and most computerized countries currently have access to at least one. In addition to the privately implemented NSFNet, public networks in the United States include those offered by AT&T, CompuServe, GE Information Services, Infonet Services, MCI Communications, and the Sprint Corporation, to name a few. Implementations outside the United States include Datapac in Canada, Transpac in France, EuroNet in Europe (essentially an extension of Transpac), Britain's Packet Switching Service (PSS), Germany's DATEX-P, and Japan's Nippon Telephone and Telegraph (NTT) DDX-2 system. Interconnections exist among these networks, providing international networking capabilities at a reasonable cost. Several CCITT recommendations, covering different aspects of PDN access and use, are listed in Figure 11-1 where applicable.

Figure 11-1

A PDN General Configuration

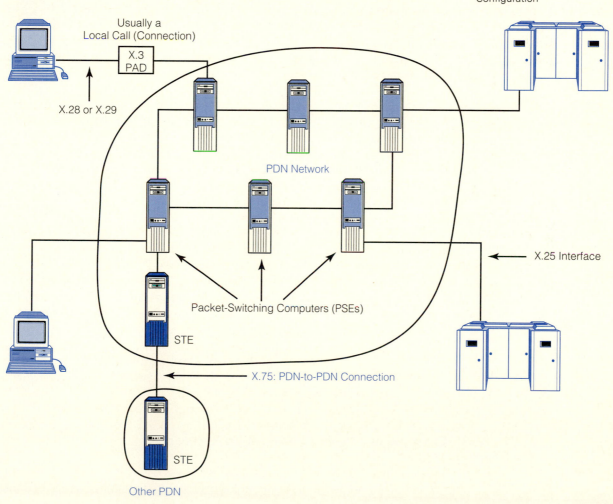

Connection Options

A PDN provides up to three types of connection options: switched virtual circuit, permanent virtual circuit, and datagram service. A virtual circuit is a communications path that is established between the sending and receiving nodes.

Switched Virtual Circuit (SVC) One of three types of circuits in a packet distribution network. When a session is required between two users, an end-to-end circuit is determined and allocated for the duration of the session. Similar to a switched connection.

call clearing The process that dissolves a switched virtual circuit.

Permanent Virtual Circuit (PVC) One of three types of connection for a packet distribution network. A PVC provides a permanent link (like a leased line) between two nodes. It is usually selected when two nodes require continual transmission.

datagram One type of connection option for a PDN. The message fits into the data field of one packet. There is less accountability for packet delivery than for other connection types.

Switched Virtual Circuit A **Switched Virtual Circuit (SVC)** is similar to a switched communications link in that both are established when needed by a session and dissolved when the session ends. When an SVC session is established between two users, an end-to-end circuit is allocated for the duration of the session. This is accomplished via a call-setup request that is initiated by the user. On receiving a call-setup request, the X.25 network establishes a transmission link for the session. The switched virtual circuit is dissolved at the end of the session, a process referred to as **call clearing**.

Permanent Virtual Circuit A **Permanent Virtual Circuit (PVC)** is usually selected when two nodes require almost continuous connection. A PVC is similar to a leased communications link, as described in Chapter 1. With a PVC a circuit is permanently allocated between two nodes and hence no call-setup is required.

Datagram Service The third type of connection option is a **datagram**, which is a message that fits completely into the data field of one packet. Because a temporary path is established for each datagram, two datagrams from the same source can have two different circuits established. This type of circuit allocation is called connectionless because a dedicated connection is not established. Datagram service has the potential of fast service for short, unrelated messages. Although they have lower overhead because they do not require a virtual circuit, certain features of datagrams make them undesirable for many applications. First, the arrival order of datagrams is not guaranteed, as each datagram sent by a particular node may take a different route. Second, and more important, arrival itself is not guaranteed, because the PDN establishes datagram arrival queue depths, and a datagram is discarded if the queue is full when the datagram arrives. This problem is compounded by the fact that recovery of lost datagrams is the responsibility of the user, not the PDN, making datagrams best suited to messages of relatively low importance and messages where speed is more critical than the possibility of lost data (such as in process control environments and certain military situations). Datagram service, though included in the X.25 standard, has seldom been implemented in existing systems.

Example of a Packet Distribution Network

To see how a PDN functions, we follow a message as it proceeds from the starting terminal to its destination address, using a switched virtual circuit connection.

Establishing the Virtual Circuit   The user connects to the PDN by dialing the nearest PDN access port (a local telephone call in most large cities). After a login procedure, the address of the other node is supplied. The PDN then goes through the process of establishing the virtual circuit. The call sequence is as follows:

1. A call-request packet is sent from the sending node to the receiver. The call request is delivered to the receiver as an incoming-call packet. The receiver may accept or reject the call.

2. If the receiver wishes to accept the connection, it transmits a call-accepted packet that is presented to the sender as a call-connected message. This establishes the connection, and data exchange may begin.

3. To terminate the connection, either node can transmit a clear request to the other. The recipient of the clear request acknowledges the disconnect with a clear-confirmation control packet.

Data Exchange   Data exchange can begin once the virtual circuit has been established. The recommended data link protocol is link access procedure balanced (LAPB), an HDLC-type protocol (see Chapter 9). Other data link protocols also have been specified for use on an interim basis, because many pieces of data terminal equipment do not support LAPB. The data portion of the frame is restricted to a specific maximum length, recommended at 128 octets, with 16, 32, 64, 256, 512, and 1024 specified as options. The Ns and Nr subfields (see Chapter 9) are defaulted to 3 bits each, but they also may be expanded to 7 bits. In the defaulted situation, up to seven frames can go unacknowledged, although the X.25 specification recommends that no more than three frames be sent before acknowledgment. This acknowledgment limit can be altered at the discretion of the implementer and would almost always be increased when the Ns and Nr subfields are expanded to 7 bits. The PDN uses a portion of the data field for control information: circuit addressing, packet sequence numbers, and packet confirmation. Three or four octets are used in information packets for this purpose, four when the sequence numbers are 7-bit entities. Figure 11-2 illustrates the format of a PDN packet.

Packet Assembly/Disassembly (PAD)   The first step in sending the data is to assemble the packets, a function performed by a **Packet Assembly/Disassembly (PAD)** module. The PAD function is not considered a part of the PDN; rather, it is the responsibility of the data terminal equipment. However, because many terminals used in PDNs lack the intelligence to perform this function, most PDNs still provide this capability. PAD functions are specified in the CCITT X.3 standard. The PAD acts on one end to transform a message into one or more packets of the required length and then reassembles the message at the other end. The PAD is also responsible for generating and monitoring control signals such as call setup and clearing.

Once the message has been transformed into packets, the packets are passed to the PDN in accordance with the X.25 interface. The PDN then

Packet Assembly/Disassembly (PAD)   A function in a packet-switching network that breaks messages into packets for transmission and reassembles packets into messages at the message's destination.

Figure 11-2

Call-Request and Incoming-Call Packet Format

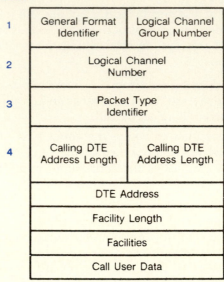

Octet

1	General Format Identifier	Logical Channel Group Number
2	Logical Channel Number	
3	Packet Type Identifier	
4	Calling DTE Address Length	Calling DTE Address Length
	DTE Address	
	Facility Length	
	Facilities	
	Call User Data	

moves the data through the network for delivery to the destination. The standards do not discuss the internal workings within the PDN, such as routing and congestion control. The receiving PAD takes the information from the data portion of the packet and reassembles the message.

PDN Equipment Two types of machines have been defined for use within a PDN: **Packet-Switching Equipment (PSE)**, which accepts and forwards messages, and **Signaling Terminal Equipment (STE)**, which is used to interface two different PDNs according to CCITT standard X.75. The standards for a packet-switching network specify interfaces and functions of the PSEs and STEs, but not the nature of the equipment itself. Figure 11-3 illustrates the connections between users' equipment and the PSE.

Packet-Switching Equipment (PSE) Equipment that accepts and forwards messages in a packet distribution network.

Signaling Terminal Equipment (STE) Node used to provide an interface between two different packet-switching networks.

Advantages and Disadvantages of a PDN PDNs have several advantages. First, the user is charged for the amount of data transmitted rather than for connect time. Applications that send low volumes of data over a relatively long period will find the charges for a PDN lower than those for either leased lines or switched lines. The PDN also gives access to many different locations without the cost of switched connections, which usually involve a charge for the initial connection plus a per minute use fee. Access to the PDN is most often via a local telephone call, which also reduces costs. Maintenance of the network and error recovery are the responsibilities of the PDN.

There are also disadvantages to using a PDN. Because the PDN is usually shared, users must compete with each other for circuits. Thus, it is possible for message traffic from other users to impede the delivery of a message. In the extreme case, a switched virtual circuit to the intended destination may even be unobtainable. This is also true for a switched connection from a

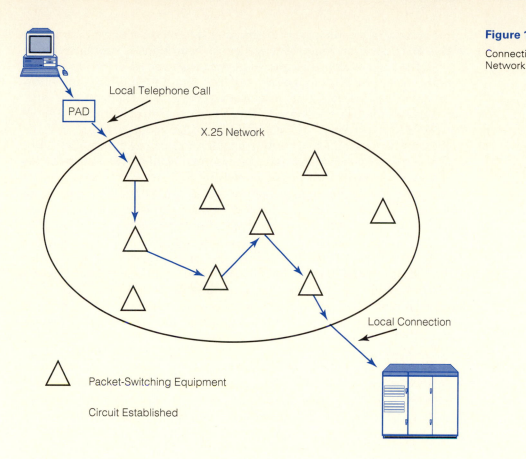

Figure 11-3

Connections in an X.25 Network

Local Telephone Call

PAD

X.25 Network

△ Packet-Switching Equipment

Circuit Established

Local Connection

common carrier. If the number of data packets to be transferred is great, the cost of using a PDN can exceed that of using leased facilities. Because the PDN is controlled by its proprietor, the individual user is unable to make changes that might benefit an individual application, such as longer messages or larger packets, longer message acknowledgment intervals, and higher transmission speeds, all of which are set by the PDN administrators.

THE INTERNET

What Is the Internet?

The term *internet* is used in two contexts. In one context, an internet refers to the interconnection of two or more networks. The **Internet** is a specific collection of interconnected networks spanning more than 40 countries throughout the world.

The NSFNet, which replaced the ARPANET, serves as the backbone network that provides the interconnection of the other networks. More than 2000

Internet A specific collection of interconnected networks spanning more than 40 countries throughout the world.

different networks participate in the Internet. The member networks are both WANs and LANs and represent academic institutions, research facilities, companies, and government agencies. As you will soon read, private individuals are also subscribers to Internet services, and, in the future, household Internet-like service subscriptions will be as common as telephone, newspaper, and cable television services. It is even likely that all of these services will be integrated into a single information and entertainment service.

Computers in the member networks fall into two basic categories. Host nodes are used to attach a network to the Internet. Nonhost nodes have access to the Internet through a host node but are not directly connected to the Internet. Access to the Internet is provided at three basic levels: national, regional, and local. National providers are commercial entities that sell access to the Internet in various cities. For example, Advanced Network and Services, Incorporated, provides ANS CO + RE Services and the Sprint Corporation provides SprintLink, both of which operate nationally in the United States and sell access to the Internet. You may also be able to access some Internet services through providers such as CompuServe, Uunet, and AppleLink. Regional providers sell access in a region. In the United States, a region might consist of several contiguous states and would probably provide toll-free access numbers within the region. Examples of regional providers in the United States are Midwestern States Network (MIDnet), New England Academic and Research Network (NEARNET), Southwestern States Network (WestNet), Colorado SuperNet, and California Education and Research Federation Network (CERFNet). Local providers are proprietors of networks attached to the Internet and provide individual access to the network. Examples are individual colleges, universities, businesses, and government facilities.

Internet Addressing and Access

To gain access to the Internet you need an access connection and a user ID. Access connections are issued by national, regional, and local providers. Many Internet users gain access through their place of employment or education. Private individuals can subscribe to services through a commercial provider such as Uunet, CompuServe, or AppleLink.

Every node on the Internet has a unique address called its internet number or its IP address. Addresses are 32 bits long and are usually written as four separate numbers delineated by a period, or as an address name. Using the first convention, a node address might be written as 101.209.33.17. Each number in the group represents an octet, or a range of numbers from 0 to 255. The address itself does not divide conveniently into 8-bit groups, but in general the first set of numbers represents the network identification of a node's network, called the **subnet**, and the last numbers identify a specific node on the subnet. The subnet address may consist of 1, 2, or 3 octets depending on the class of the node or subnet.

Currently there are four address classes, A through D; Class E is defined but reserved for future use. With the exception of Class D, classes are based on the number of nodes on the subnet. As the number of nodes on the subnet

subnet The first set of numbers in an address representing the network identification of a node's network.

increases, more bits of the address are needed to distinguish each node. Class A addresses are used for networks with more than 2^{16} nodes. The first bit of the 32-bit address is 0, to distinguish this class from the others, which start with a 1 bit; the next 7 bits represent the network ID. There can be no more than 128 sub networks in this class. The remaining 24 bits are used to distinguish among the subnet nodes.

Class B addresses are used for subnets with 2^8 through 2^{16} nodes. The first two bits in this class start with a 1 followed by a 0, and 14 bits are used to represent the subnet address, leaving 16 bits available for node addresses on the subnet. Class C addresses are used for subnets with fewer than 2^8 nodes; this class is distinguished by starting bits of 110. Class C addresses use 21 bits for the subnet address and 8 bits for subnet node addresses. Class D nodes begin with bits of 1110 and designate host nodes that want to receive broadcast messages.

In conclusion, Class A nodes use one octet to represent the subnet address, Class B nodes use two octets, and Class C nodes have three octets representing the subnet address (including the class designator with the subnet address). All network addresses are assigned by the Network Information Center to avoid address duplication.

Internet Naming Conventions

For most Internet users, the four-octet address representation, called a **dotted quad**, is too cumbersome. Therefore, most users substitute a naming convention that consists of a user name followed by what is essentially a node name. The node name includes a computer's name followed by a domain name. Common domain names are EDU, GOV, MIL, and COM, which stand for education, government, military, and company organizations, respectively. Domain names may also be qualified by country names. For example, AU, CA, and FR represent Australia, Canada, and France, respectively. Intercountry communications will use the country domain designator whereas intracountry communications would not need the country qualification because it defaults to the host's country. Generic network addresses using the naming convention are:

> user@computer.domain
> dstamper@frodo.edu
> jdoe@nasa.gov
> comgen@usahq.mil
> sysmgr@xyzcorp.com

The @ symbol is used to denote the node name and the period is used to specify domain names. The computer.domain notation is called a **Fully Qualified Domain Name (FQDN)**. Naturally, there is a correspondence between the dotted quad and the user @ FQDN addresses. Translation between the two is automatically provided by the host node through a mapping dictionary. Thus, users are able to use names as addresses rather than a series of numbers.

dotted quad The four-octet address representation on the Internet.

Fully Qualified Domain Name (FQDN) The computer.domain notation used to specify user addresses.

Figure 11-4

Internet Backbone Network

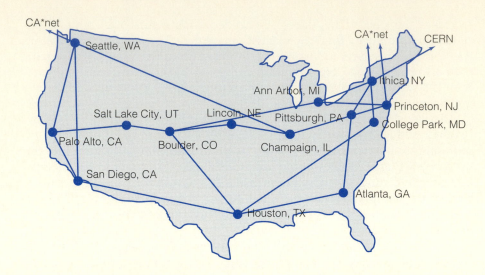

Internet Connections

The Internet uses a variety of communications lines. The backbone nodes use T1 or T3 links to provide speedy transmission from one area to another. Regional links may use T1, 56-Kbps or slower lines. The Internet backbone network configuration is shown in Figure 11-4. The connection services are accomplished using the Transmission Control Protocol/Internet Protocol (TCP/IP) protocol suite that is covered in Chapter 12.

Internet Services

The Internet provides a variety of services, including:

- electronic mail between Internet users
- file transfer
- remote login
- access to software archives
- news reports
- news groups and the distribution of news for special-interest groups
- bulletin boards
- library services
- electronic journals

The goal of the Internet is to promote research and scholarly activity. Over time, some usage has taken on a more commercial overtone; however, the spirit of the Internet remains that of research and scholarly activity and commercial usage is discouraged.

News groups are a feature of Usenet, a service of the Internet. Usenet is essentially a group of computers that provide news services. A site may or may not decide to have one of its nodes support this service depending on the needs and capacity of the site. News groups exist for a variety of special interests, including computer and scientific topics as well as social topics such as environmental or political action forums.

THE INFORMATION SUPERHIGHWAY

When the United States was primarily an industrial society, the federal government funded the building of a national highway system. This system, augmented by state and local roads, provided transportation for people, raw materials, and finished goods to needed locations. The national highway system helped establish the strength of the U.S. economy. Today the United States is primarily an information society, with more than half the workforce engaged in the business of information. We now envision a new national highway system geared to moving the raw materials (data) and finished goods (information and ideas) of information to their needed locations. This new highway system is formally called the National Information Infrastructure (NII), but is commonly and most often referred to as the **information superhighway**. We use the less formal term of information superhighway for our discussion. If built and used correctly, the information superhighway will help maintain and extend the economic strength of the United States.

information superhighway A national information system geared toward moving the raw materials (data) and finished goods (information and ideas) of information to their needed locations.

Building the Information Superhighway

The federal government was instrumental in funding and building the interstate highway system. In contrast, the information superhighway will be built largely by the private business sector. The role of the federal government will be to provide guidance, legislation, procedures, and prototype systems, and to fund research and development efforts for new technologies. After the information superhighway has been established, the federal government also may subsidize use of the system by public entities such as libraries, schools, and hospitals. In the areas of procedures and legislation, it has already been recognized that privacy and security issues need to be addressed. Federal regulations will undoubtedly be required to help control access and set penalties for abuses, much like the Interstate Commerce Commission regulates commercial use of the interstate highways and roads. To provide this guidance the federal government has established an Information Infrastructure Task Force (IITF) to oversee information superhighway development.

Like the interstate highway system, the information superhighway will evolve over time. Many technologies needed for building the information superhighway are currently in place; still needed is the investment to integrate and install the technologies so they can be made available throughout the country. Different companies or consortiums may form regional segments of the information superhighway, and then the regional infrastructures will be integrated into a national or perhaps a global supernetwork. This evolution will probably be similar to that of the Internet. The information superhighway also is likely to extend across country borders and become a global information superhighway. At this writing, no clear directions have been established and leadership roles have not materialized. However, activity is proceeding at a rapid pace, and the two key events thus far are:

The information superhighway is envisioned as an integration of communications networks, information and service providers, and computer hardware and software. To provide these components, mergers and alliances are being formed among common carriers, computer hardware and software companies, cable TV companies, and the entertainment industry.

A cross-industry working team of 28 companies has been formed to design the information superhighway. The original members represent communications, computer, banking, publishing, and cable TV companies. The cross-industry working team has formed four subgroups: applications, services, architecture, and portability. The role of the first three is apparent from their names. The portability subgroup will address the needs of mobile communications.

The architecture of the information superhighway will likely resemble that of the Internet in that a high-speed backbone network of fiber optic and satellite links will speed data from one region to another. Local delivery will be established by regional providers over fiber optic cable, coaxial cable, and copper media. Businesses that make heavy use of the information superhighway will likely have the data delivered to their premises by fiber optic cable. Local distribution within the company will be over fiber optic cable, coaxial cable, or twisted-pair wires.

For personal use, it is unlikely that fiber optic cable will be brought into homes. Instead, fiber optic cable will bring the data to a local distribution point from which coaxial cable or twisted-pair wires will distribute the data to individual homes. There are several reasons for copper-based delivery to individual subscribers. In many locations cable TV companies have already installed this type of delivery mechanism and it can be used for the last-mile delivery system. The data speeds required for home use also will be much lower than that of many businesses, so the higher speed of fiber optic cable will not be necessary. Finally, the current cost of fiber optic cable and the difficulty of splicing and making new connections favor the use of copper-based end delivery. Figure 11-5 illustrates a potential information superhighway implementation.

Information Superhighway Uses

Several potential information superhighway uses are:

- A business might use the information superhighway to conduct a conference among employees in different locations.
- A software company might use the information superhighway to distribute software directly to customers.

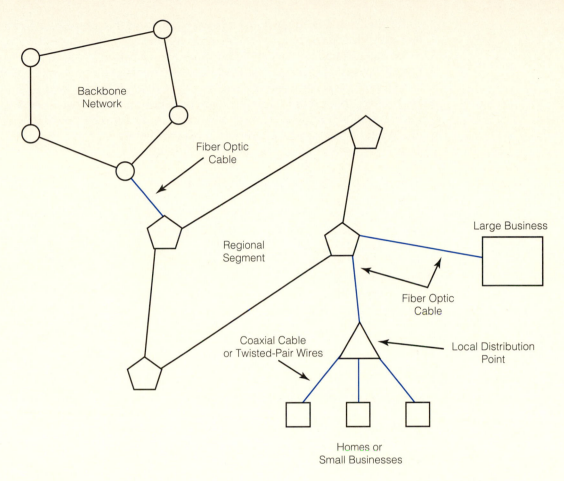

Backbone Network

Fiber Optic Cable

Regional Segment

Large Business

Fiber Optic Cable

Coaxial Cable or Twisted-Pair Wires

Local Distribution Point

Homes or Small Businesses

Figure 11-5

A Potential Information Superhighway Implementation

- A publishing company might distribute books or magazines directly to readers or perhaps to a local outlet for on-demand printing.

- Companies and individuals could subscribe to information utilities such as stock market and financial news, congressional records, and so on.

- Companies and individuals will be able to shop for merchandise via online catalogs and make airline, car, hotel, and entertainment reservations.

- Movies and games may be available on demand.

- Education classes at all levels may be available and allow people to learn new skills at their home or office.

- Health care may be delivered by patients getting advice remotely. A physician may be able to view patients at remote locations, coach paramedical personnel on procedures, and recommend cures.

- Electronic mail and video images may be exchanged. Interactive use of such technologies may give rise to online discussion groups and conferencing.

From these few suggestions it may be apparent that possible information superhighway uses are varied. The information superhighway will deliver far more that just data; it can deliver information in a variety of formats including data, voice, and video. At issue is how individuals and companies will gain access to these resources and how much it will cost to use them. For some services, costs of more than $200 per connect hour are likely. Access to the information superhighway also will require the media connections and equipment necessary to send and receive the signals.

Social Implications

The information superhighway is likely to bring a profound change in the way businesses operate and in individuals' private lives. The costs required for information superhighway connection and services may also lead to new social issues. People who cannot afford these services will have fewer opportunities than those who have the services. Consequently, publicly funded access through schools, libraries, and civic centers may be needed to ensure that all members of society have access to the opportunities the information superhighway will provide.

VENDOR WIDE AREA NETWORKS

Systems Network Architecture (SNA)   IBM's architecture for building a computer network. Encompasses hardware and software components, establishing sessions between users, and capabilities such as office and message/file distribution services.

Vendor offerings play a major role in network implementation and configuration, with almost every major computer vendor offering networking capabilities. Vendor networks compete with each other, with packet-switching or X.25 networks, and with common carrier networks. The following section is devoted to IBM's **Systems Network Architecture (SNA)**, which has become a de facto industry standard. Most networks currently being designed on IBM mainframe systems use SNA. If another vendor's equipment interfaces with an IBM network, it will likely do so via an SNA interface. Many computer manufacturers have implemented or are implementing the ability to attach to an SNA network as a type of SNA node.

IBM'S SYSTEMS NETWORK ARCHITECTURE

SNA, announced by IBM in 1974, provides the framework for implementing data communications networks using IBM or IBM-compatible equipment. SNA is not a product per se but a blueprint for how hardware, software, and users interact in exchanging data on IBM systems. A network based on SNA consists of a variety of hardware and software components in a well-defined configuration.

Why SNA?

Since the 1960s IBM has been the leader in computer sales and installations. The move to SNA was prompted not so much by competition from the outside but by competition from within IBM itself. Before 1974, the implementation of communications systems had been somewhat random: If a new terminal was developed, a new or modified access method and data link protocol were likely to accompany it. By 1974, IBM was offering more than 200 different models of communications hardware, 35 different device access methods, and more than a dozen data link protocols. Continuing this product proliferation would have created an enormous burden for IBM's support and maintenance. SNA was the result of integrating all these functions into one cohesive network architecture.

The objective of any network is to enable users to communicate with one another. Users in SNA either are people working at a terminal or operator's console or they are applications that provide services for other programs or terminal users. Thus, a user is an entity with some degree of intelligence. A terminal is not a user, though the terms *terminal operator* and *terminal* are frequently used synonymously. SNA has been developed to provide communications paths and dialogue rules between users. This is accomplished via a layered network architecture similar to the OSI reference model.

SNA Layers

The early releases of SNA referenced either six or four functional layers. The discrepancy between a six-layer and a four-layer definition is explained by the fact that layers three through five are sometimes referred to as a single layer, known as the **half-session layer**. The lowest OSI reference model layer, the physical layer, is not usually specified in SNA, nor is the application layer included. However, both layers obviously must exist. The four-layer definition is given in Table 11-1. The six layers are identified in parentheses, where applicable. In the current version of SNA, the layering has been somewhat redefined. The presentation service layer is omitted from the earlier definition and the services manager is now referred to as the function management

half-session layer
Represents a single layer (transmission control, flow control, and presentation service) in the four-layer definition of SNA functional layers.

TABLE 11-1   SNA Layers

Layer 1	Data link control
Layer 2	Path control
Layer 3	Half-session layer, consisting of:
	Transmission control (layer 3)
	Flow control (layer 4)
	Presentation service (layer 5)
Layer 4	Services manager (layer 6)

TABLE 11-2   SNA Physical Units

Physical Unit	Hardware Component
Type 1	A terminal device, e.g., 3278
Type 2	A cluster controller, e.g., 3274
Type 4	A communications controller, e.g., 3725
Type 5	A host processor, e.g., 4381 or 3094

Physical Unit (PU)   In SNA, a hardware unit. Four physical units have been defined: Type 5, host processor; Type 4, communications controller; Type 2, cluster or programmable controller; and Type 1, a terminal or controller that is not programmable.

layer. Although the layering carries different names, the functions each performs are similar to those for the OSI reference model.

SNA also defines four distinct hardware groupings called **Physical Units (PUs)**. The four physical units are numbered 1, 2, 4, and 5, with no PU currently assigned to number 3. These device types are listed in Table 11-2. The hardware configuration consists of IBM or IBM-compatible CPUs; communications controllers; terminal cluster controllers; and terminals, printers, or workstations. These are all connected by any of the media discussed in Chapter 1. Other vendors' equipment may also be included in the network if that equipment conforms to the SNA protocols. The preferred data link protocol is SDLC, but accommodations have been made for other protocols such as BSC and asynchronous.

Logical Units and Sessions

Logical Unit (LU)   In IBM's SNA, a unit that represents a system user. Sessions exist between LUs or between an LU and the SSCP. Several types of LUs have been defined.

session   The dialogue between two system users.

Users of SNA are represented in the system by entities known as **Logical Units (LUs)**. An LU is usually implemented as a software function in a device with some intelligence, such as a CPU or controller. The dialogue between two system users is known as a **session**. Because a logical unit is the agent of a user, when one user wants to establish a session with another user, the LUs are involved in establishing the communications path between the two. A session involves two different LUs; the activities and resources used by one LU in a session are called a half-session. In the SNA layering in Table 11-1, the half-session layers represent the functions that would be performed by an LU for its user.

Session Types   Many different types of sessions can be requested, such as program to terminal, program to program, or terminal to terminal. Each category can be further stratified as to terminal type (interactive, batch, or printer) and application type (batch, interactive, word processing, or the like). One logical unit also can represent several different users, and a user can have multiple sessions in progress concurrently. If a terminal (operator) desires to retrieve a record from a database, the terminal will need to use the services of an application program to obtain the record. Each user—the terminal and the database application—is represented by a logical unit. The terminal LU issues a request to enter into a session with the database appli-

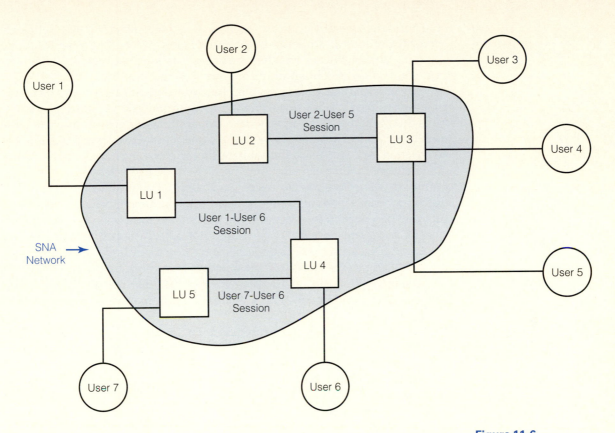

Figure 11-6

SNA Sessions and Logical Units

cation LU. The application LU can either accept or reject the session request. Rejection is typically either due to security reasons, because the requesting LU lacks authority to establish a session with the application LU, or due to congestion, because the application LU has already entered into the maximum number of sessions it can support. If the session request is granted, a communications path is established between the terminal and the application. The two users continue to communicate until one of them terminates the session. Figure 11-6 shows several sessions between users communicating through their respective logical units.

LU Types   Seven LU types have thus far been defined within SNA. These are numbered from 0 to 7, with the definition for LU Type 5 omitted. It is important to note that the LU types refer to session types and not to a specific LU. Thus, a specific LU can participate in a Type 1 LU session with one LU and a Type 4 LU session with another. For two LUs to communicate they must both support and use the same LU session type. Of the seven LU types all but Types 0 and 6 address sessions with hardware devices such as printers and terminals. LU Type 6 is defined for program-to-program communication. It has evolved through two definitions, LU 6.0 and LU 6.1, to its current definition, LU 6.2. LU 6.2 is a key SNA capability.

LU 6.2   An SNA logical unit type representing a program-to-program session.

There are several significant aspects of LU 6.2. First, **LU 6.2** defines a protocol for program-to-program communication. Most of the other LU types are somewhat hardware-oriented, involving sessions between 3270 devices, printers, and so on. A program-to-program communications interface is more general and can have wider uses than hardware-oriented interfaces. Second, program-to-program sessions provide a communications path for applications distributed over multiple nodes. Two applications communicating with each other are not required to be in the same node. This capability supports transaction processing systems with multiple processing nodes. For example, an inventory inquiry can start on a network node in a sales office and communicate with a warehouse node application to determine whether stock exists to cover a pending order. Finally, and perhaps most significantly, a program-to-program interface is more generic than a session type involving specific hardware devices. This means that other vendors' equipment can enter into SNA sessions with an application process running in an IBM processor so long as the communicating program in the vendor's processor adheres to the session rules. This allows an application on Vendor A's hardware to enter into a transaction with a database application running on an IBM node.

Many vendors have implemented an LU 6.2 capability for their SNA interface because such an interface can be made device-independent. Given a configuration as illustrated in Figure 11-7, a program in Vendor X's system can interface to its terminal device on one side and to an IBM application on the other. This logically provides the ability for a non-IBM terminal to interface to an IBM application system. Without LU 6.2, Vendor X would need to appear to the IBM application as one of the supported hardware types, such as a 3270 terminal or cluster controller. The International Standards Organization (ISO) also has agreed on a transaction interface that is compatible with IBM's LU 6.2 session. Computer manufacturers that have committed to an LU 6.2 interface include Tandem Computers, Inc.; Hewlett-Packard Co.; Sun Microsystems, Inc.; Banyan Systems, Inc.; and AT&T.

Figure 11-7

Non-IBM Vendor in an LU 6.2 Session

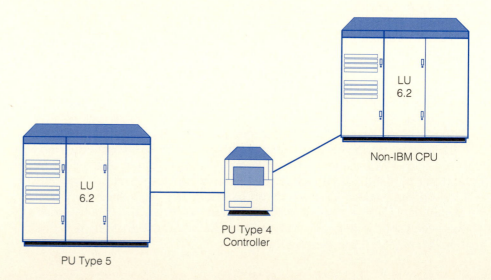

LU 6.2

Non-IBM CPU

LU 6.2

PU Type 4 Controller

PU Type 5

Systems Services Control Point

As mentioned above, a dialogue between two users within the SNA environment is called a session. A supervisor or intermediary is involved in establishing a session. In SNA this extremely important entity is known as the **Systems Services Control Point (SSCP)**; it resides in a host processor, which is a physical unit Type 5. Not all PU Type 5 devices house an SSCP. The SSCP is the software controlling its host's portion of the network. The devices controlled by the host and its SSCP represent a **domain**.

Networks implemented under early versions of SNA had only one SSCP and thus only one host computer. All of the network was controlled by this host. In 1979, SNA was enhanced to allow multiple-host systems, and hence multiple domains. This became necessary because large SNA networks were being implemented. Multiple SSCPs were better able to manage many devices and sessions. A two-domain SNA configuration is shown in Figure 11-8.

Within a given domain the SSCP is the controlling entity. It is responsible for the physical and logical units within its domain. In fulfilling this obligation, the SSCP manages its units, including unit initialization, maintaining the status of individual units, placing units on- and offline as necessary, and serving as mediator in the establishment of sessions. Physical units subordinate to an SSCP must be able to carry on a dialogue with the SSCP. To accomplish this, a subset of the SSCP functionality, called a **Physical Unit Control Point (PUCP)**, resides in SNA nodes that do not contain an SSCP. A PUCP is responsible for connecting the node to and disconnecting the node from the SNA network.

Systems Services Control Point (SSCP) In IBM's SNA, the process that controls a domain. It is responsible for initiating network components, establishing sessions, and maintaining unit status.

domain In IBM's SNA, the network components managed by a systems services control point.

Physical Unit Control Point (PUCP) In IBM's systems network architecture (SNA), a physical unit control point resides in nodes that do not contain a systems services control point (SSCP). The PUCP is responsible for connecting the node to and disconnecting the node from the network.

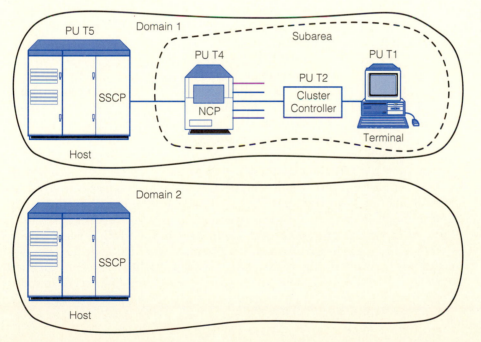

Figure 11-8

The IBM SNA Network

Addressing

For one user to communicate with another, an address is required because messages are sent to a specific unit by using its address. Addressable components in SNA are called **Network Addressable Units (NAUs)**. An NAU can be an SSCP, an LU, or a PU. Network addresses are hierarchical in nature. You have already learned that an SNA network consists of domains. Domains consist of subareas. A **subarea** consists of a communications controller (such as a 3745) and all its NAUs or of a host/SSCP together with all of the locally attached NAUs. Figure 11-9 shows two subareas. Each subarea has a unique address. NAUs within one subarea are known by a local address. An SNA address consists of two parts, a subarea address and a unit address. The combination of subarea address and unit address uniquely identifies an NAU in the network. In SNA, addresses may be either 16 or 23 bits. The longer address is known as **extended addressing**, which allows for a larger number of NAUs in a network.

In extended addressing mode, the first 8 bits represent the subarea, and the last 15 bits represent the device within the subarea. The 16-bit address can be decomposed into a subarea and device address on a network-by-network basis, which allows two networks to decompose the address in different manners. One network could have an 8-bit address for both subareas and devices, whereas another could adopt a split of 7 bits for subarea and 9 bits for devices.

Communication Between Users

If Users A and B are in the same domain, communication between them is established as follows. The logical unit representing User A sends a message to the SSCP requesting a session with User B. On behalf of User A, the SSCP contacts the User B LU to request a session and also to provide information about User A, including User A's access profile and type. User B either accepts or rejects the session request. If the session is rejected, User A is so notified. If User B accepts the invitation to enter into a session with A, a communications path must be established. Communication between users in different domains is established in a way similar to that for a single domain, except that the SSCPs in both domains are involved: The request goes from an LU to its SSCP to the SSCP in the other domain and then to its LU.

Path establishment was easy in early SNA implementations because only one path existed between LUs. Presently, two routing methods are supported: end-to-end routing and virtual routing. In **end-to-end routing**, for which at least one of the nodes must be a Type 5 physical unit or terminal, the path is determined and maintained through the entire session (unless the path is broken). In **virtual routing**, no permanently established path exists; instead, each node consults its routing table to determine to which node the message should be forwarded. The path control half-session layer is responsible for path allocation. Each available path is given a weighting that assists in route determination. A route might be selected based on best use according to such factors as security, speed, and propagation delay (as for satellite links). Up to five different paths between any two LUs can be described.

Network Addressable Unit (NAU)   In IBM's SNA, any device that has a network address, such as logical units and physical units.

subarea   The parts of a domain, consisting of a communications controller and all its NAUs or of a host/SSCP together with all of the locally attached NAUs.

extended addressing   The 23-bit address representing the combination of subarea address and unit address that uniquely identifies an NAU and allows for a larger number of NAUs in a network.

end-to-end routing   Routing for which at least one of the nodes must be a Type 5 physical unit or terminal and the path is determined and maintained through the entire session.

virtual routing   No permanently established path exists; instead, each node consults its routing table to determine which node should next receive the message.

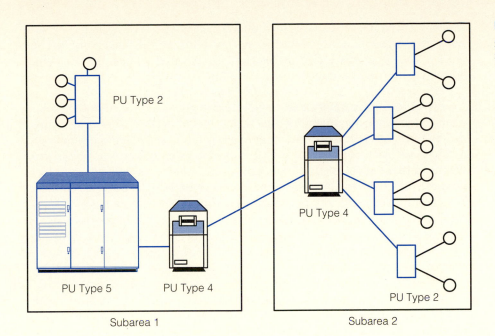

Figure 11-9

SNA Network with Two Subareas

PU Type 2

PU Type 4

PU Type 4

PU Type 5

PU Type 2

Subarea 1

Subarea 2

Additional SNA Elements and Capabilities

Network Control Program The **Network Control Program (NCP)**, which resides in a communication controller such as the 3745, controls communications lines and the devices attached to them. It works with the Virtual Terminal Access Method (VTAM) that resides in the host. VTAM serves as the interface between application programs and the network.

Advanced Communications Facility The **Advanced Communications Facility (ACF)** was introduced in 1979. It provides such features as interdomain communication, improved error and testing capabilities, and dynamic device configuration.

Network Performance Analyzer The **Network Performance Analyzer (NPA)** provides performance information for the system, including information on lines, buffers, errors, queue lengths, and data transmission rates.

Network Problem Determination Aid The **Network Problem Determination Aid (NPDA)** collects, maintains, and reports information on error conditions within the network. It also allows for testing of the system concurrent with production operations.

Netview, Netview/PC, and Netview/6000 In 1986 IBM announced two network management packages for use in SNA systems. Netview runs on IBM hosts, and Netview/PC, on microcomputers. With Netview, IBM has consolidated several previous network management facilities (including NPDA) and enhanced them to provide more comprehensive management

Network Control Program (NCP) A data communications program that helps manage a communications network. Specifically, a program that runs in IBM's 37xx line of communications controllers.

capabilities. Netview/6000 was introduced in 1992 and is designed to provide network management functions for open systems, specifically, non-SNA networks. The functions found in Netview are covered in Chapter 15, which addresses network management.

SNA Distribution Services (SNADS) An SNA facility that provides asynchronous distribution of documents throughout a network.

SNA Distribution Services   SNA Distribution Services (SNADS) allow users to exchange documents using the SNA network. Document interchange differs from the typical SNA session. In a typical SNA session the sender and receiver are synchronized regarding information exchange. By *synchronized* we mean that the users communicate (through their LUs) and agree to carry on a conversation. In contrast, with document exchanges the users may not be synchronized. A sender may dispatch a document without first coordinating the transmission with the recipient. The recipient can then request access to the document at its convenience. SNADS provides the ability to distribute documents in such a manner. This is particularly helpful for office automation applications such as network mail and document distribution.

Advanced Peer-to-Peer Networking (APPN)   APPN allows independent LUs to enter into sessions without the cooperation of the SSCP. APPN reduces the dependence on a host node and allows applications to specify session characteristics such as the type of path and security required. Non-IBM vendors have implemented APPN interfaces on their systems. This capability together with LU 6.2 provides an easy way for programs to independently enter into a session and provides a way for applications that run on non-IBM computers to communicate via the services of SNA.

Other SNA Capabilities   SNA is being continually upgraded to meet the changing demands of communications. It has evolved from an IBM-only network architecture to include internetworking with other networks. Accommodations made in this regard include:

- support for the TCP/IP protocol suite
- accommodations for LAN interfaces
- alterations that reduce the hierarchical nature of the network and provides support for peer-to-peer communications via APPN
- support for distributed databases
- internetworking

INTERNATIONAL NETWORKS

Data communications networks are not confined to national boundaries, and today many companies are international in scope. International computer networks help many of these companies manage their data and provide communication among employees. International networks are used by banks for money transfer and financial planning applications. With international networks, manufacturing companies can schedule production of parts in multiple locations for assembly at a central location. All international companies can use international networks and electronic mail for immediate, timely communications. Electronic mail also helps eliminate the problems of time-zone differences. For example, working hours may not overlap between offices in England and Australia, but electronic mail provides quick communication during an employee's normal working hours.

Designing and implementing international networks is more difficult than building a national network. The problems that may be encountered include politics, regulations, hardware, and language.

Politics

On occasion the problems to be resolved with international networks are political rather than technical. One company reported that it was given permission to install a microwave link in a particular country. That country's government, however, suggested that the company double the capacity of the network. Upon completion, the microwave system was nationalized by the government, and the company that built it was "given" half of the carrying capacity of the network (Jenkins, 1987).

Regulations

Networks require communication links. In many countries the communications networks are controlled by an agency we shall call the postal, telephone, and telegraph (PTT) authority. The PTT often is a government agency or government-regulated agency with exclusive rights to provide communication facilities. The regulations under which the PTTs operate generally were designed for their original mission of postal, telephone, and telegraph communications. These regulations sometimes impede the establishment of international data communications.

Sometimes regulations are established to protect or subsidize certain interests. In some countries, restrictions exist regarding which equipment can be connected to a network. A few countries require that hardware used in a network be manufactured in whole or in part within the country. Pricing regulations in some countries are structured so data communications services help subsidize individual telephone services. Regulations frequently prohibit competition in providing communication facilities. Thus, it is often difficult to set up a network using services provided by a single communications carrier. Many PTTs recognize that regulations need to be changed to meet the needs of international networks; therefore, some countries have begun to deregulate their communications industry. Deregulation typically means opening competition regarding equipment that can be attached to the network and the cost and provision of communications facilities.

International networks sometimes also conflict with other national interests. Some countries impose an import duty on software. Sometimes the duty is on the value of the carrying medium, such as a magnetic tape; other countries tax the value of the imported software. International networks provide the ability to import software over the network, making the collection of tariffs more difficult. Some countries view international networks as potential threats to national security. Data regarding national resources, the economy, and people can be more easily collected and transmitted to another country through international networks. Several nations are attempting to legislate solutions to these concerns.

Hardware

When discussing regulations we mentioned that in some countries restrictions exist regarding the source or type of equipment that can be attached to the communications facilities of a PTT. Several countries require that all or part of the equipment used within the country be locally manufactured. Some do not require the equipment to be manufactured in-country but still restrict the equipment that can be used to that manufactured by a select group of companies. Most countries require that equipment attached to communications networks meet minimum technical specifications. Specifications also differ among countries. A communications controller that is certified for operation in the United States may not meet the tighter specifications for grounding that exist in Australia.

Another technical difference that must be accommodated is variations in power supplies among countries. When ordering equipment for a specific node, we must be sure that the equipment's power supply needs are consistent with the power available in that location. Many times new hardware also must be certified by a host country before it can be attached to the communications network. For example, a company that introduces a facsimile controller that connects to the common carrier's network must first undergo testing and evaluation by the host country. It is not unusual for certification to take several months and require that equipment and circuit schematics be provided for the evaluation process. Thus, introduction of new equipment into a network can incur substantial delays.

Language

Another problem needing resolution in international networks is language related. Network managers at different locations must be able to communicate to resolve differences. Several different countries and hence several different languages may be involved in solving one problem. This makes it necessary to have not only technical expertise but also linguistic expertise in the network management organization. Data generated in one location in the in-country language also may need to be translated when used in another country. Such translation may be manual or through language translation programs. Accompanying the need to translate from one language to another is the need to have hardware and software capable of displaying local character sets, such as Kanji in China and Japan, Hongul in Korea, and Farsi in Arab countries. Accommodations also must be made when the number of characters in a national character set exceeds the capacity of a particular code. For example, 7-bit ASCII codes can accommodate 128 distinct characters, but the number of Kanji characters exceeds 30,000.

Other Issues

An international network typically involves the coordination of several communications providers. One of the easier methods of creating an international network is to use the services of existing X.25 networks. The ease derives from the fact that most public X.25 network providers have established interconnections and the network implementer need not be concerned about PTT interfaces. If a company decides to procure exclusive links such as leased lines, creating the network may be more difficult. Determining the correct interfaces and problem resolution must be assumed by the company. Problem resolution can be somewhat difficult in an international network. Consider a link from Australia to France. The end-to-end connection may use links from Australia to the United States, to England, and then to France. Thus, four PTTs, several protocols, a variety of vendor equipment, and several time zones may be involved. If a problem arises in transmitting data between the French and Australian nodes, the multiplicity of involved vendors can cause delays in resolution. On more than one occasion a problem has been allowed to continue while two PTTs debated which was responsible for the problem.

Costing an international network can present several difficulties. First, collecting tariff information can be time-consuming. When multiple nodes exist within a country, we typically must deal with local tariffs and international tariffs. In some cases, there may be multiple circuit providers, a variety of available rates, and variations between local and long-distance rates. In addition to tariffs for the use of lines, in some countries we also must determine the costs of taxes applied to the movement of data over a country's borders and taxes on imported software.

The International Telecommunications Union (ITU), the Consultative Committee on International Telegraph and Telephony (CCITT), and other international communications organizations realize the existing limitations and problems in implementing international connections and are addressing the issues. Standards such as OSI, X.25, and X.400 electronic-mail interface ease the burden of establishing international networks. Deregulation of the communications industries in some countries has allowed the introduction of new equipment and competition among providers of communications links. Issues such as the rights of communication facilities provided from a foreign country, such as a Canadian PTT operating circuits in the United States, are being discussed. All these efforts should make establishing international networks easier; however, the problems inherent in international networks will always be greater than those for domestic networks. Another international body, the **General Agreement on Trade and Tariffs (GATT)**, an organization of 97 nations, has proposed a treaty that will ease the problems of international networks. Among the treaty provisions are stipulations regarding the use and cost of private lines.

CASE STUDY

The Syncrasy Corporation, once again expanding, intends to open retail outlets in several additional cities. A tentative list of these new cities is given in Table 11-3.

Network Requirements

Each city on the network will have at least one processor, and the existing network, discussed in Chapter 9, might be abandoned if a better configuration exists.

Reliability   The requirements of the new network include high reliability among the major centers in New York City, Chicago, Kansas City, and Los Angeles and among the European cities. For the Pacific area, however, it has been decided that distance and the related communications costs prohibit the redundant links required for reliability. Reliability for Syncrasy means that all nodes can continue to communicate should a link fail and that all remaining nodes can still communicate should a node fail.

Low Cost   The second design criterion is cost. Syncrasy wants the lowest cost network that can provide the necessary functions.

U.S. Network Configuration

The long-distance network in the United States must, of course, interface with the local area network, designed in Chapter 7. The gateway function should be performed by a processor attached to both networks.

TABLE 11-3   **Expansion Cities**

Seattle	Detroit	Rome
Phoenix	Denver	Oslo
Boston	Montreal	Hong Kong
Miami	Toronto	Sydney
Dallas	London	Tokyo
Washington, D.C.	Paris	Mexico City
Philadelphia	Frankfurt	

Backbone Network   The need for reliability in the four major U.S. cities demands a loop configuration, as depicted in Figure 11-10. As a minimum, the network routing algorithm must be able to alter paths if a node or link fails. This type of configuration is sometimes called a backbone network, and the nodes are referred to as backbone nodes. From the mileage chart given in Table 11-4, it can be determined that the backbone network in Figure 11-10 is the minimum-distance configuration.

One possible U.S. configuration is depicted in Figure 11-11. The backbone network serves as the delivery system for many of the nodes, such as from Seattle to Boston. However, a message sent from Seattle to San Francisco will not make use of the backbone system. Syncrasy has decided that the backbone nodes should be dedicated to the network task, so they will not be used for application processing. This decision was made because the amount of anticipated message traffic is high enough to allow dedicated backbone nodes. To increase the reliability of the backbone network, fault-tolerant computers were chosen.

Remaining U.S. Network   Three primary options were considered in configuring the remainder of the network: leased media, switched media, and public data network (PDN). Which of these is most cost-effective is a function of distance and message traffic. Distance becomes a factor when determining the rates charged for leased and switched connections; it usually

TABLE 11-4   **Mileage Chart**

	Chicago	Houston	Kansas City	L.A.	N.Y.C.	S.F.
Atlanta	708	791	822	2191	854	2483
Chicago		1091	542	2048	809	2173
Houston			743	1555	1610	1911
Kansas City				1547	1233	1861
Los Angeles					2794	387
New York City						2930

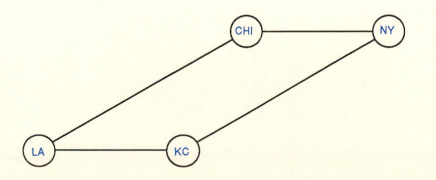

Figure 11-10

A Backbone Network

Figure 11-11

A Possible U.S. Network

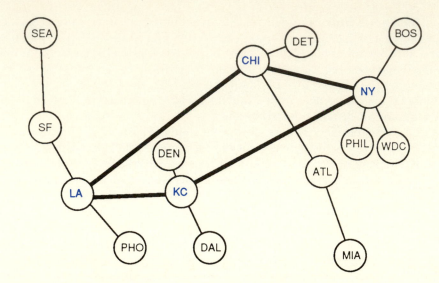

is not a factor with respect to PDN rates. Message traffic affects the connect time for switched connections and the packet charges for a PDN. For all U.S. nodes not in the backbone network, an analysis was performed to determine which of the three options would be most cost effective. The analysis for the Seattle node follows.

Seattle–San Francisco Line Costs   The following rate information on the three options for connecting the Seattle node to the San Francisco node (the closest) are approximate and are intended for use only in this case study. Actual rates may vary. Leased line rates are given in Table 11-5, switched telephone rates, in Table 11-6; and PDN rates, in Table 11-7. Additional comparison information must be derived. To evaluate the switched connections, the number of connections per day and the total amount of connect time must be approximated. Seattle, being a relatively low volume node at a network extremity, will not be involved in store and forward operations. In contrast, the San Francisco node will originate and receive its own messages and will forward messages to and from Seattle and other nodes. It is estimated there will be three connections per day, requiring 250 minutes total connect time. A message traffic of 30,000 characters per day also is anticipated. A 23-day work month is assumed. The total distance between Seattle and San Francisco is 810 miles. Leased line charges are:

$$\text{(first 100 miles @ \$2.52 per mile)} + \text{(710 miles @ \$0.94 per mile)}$$
$$= 252 + 667.40 = \$919.40$$

Daily switched line costs are:

$$\text{(3 connections @ \$0.60 per first minute)} + \text{(247 remaining minutes @ \$0.40}$$
$$\text{per minute)} = 1.80 + 98.80 = \$100.60$$

TABLE 11-5   Leased Line Rates, Seattle to San Francisco

First 100 miles	$2.52 per mile (includes monthly service charge fee)
Next 900 miles (101–1000)	$0.94 per mile
Each mile over 1000	$0.58 per mile

TABLE 11-6   Switched Line Rates, Seattle to San Francisco

First minute of connect time	$0.60
Each additional minute	$0.40

TABLE 11-7   PDN Charges, Seattle to San Francisco

Connection charge per node	$400 per month
Packet charge	$1.50 per 1000 packets
Packet size	128 characters

Monthly switched line costs are therefore:

$$23 \text{ days @ } \$100.60 \text{ per day} = \$2313.80$$

No additional telephone service charges are included in the analysis because telephones are already installed on the premises. If one or more telephones were dedicated to data communications, then their cost would have to be included.

PDN charges are derived as follows: Two stations must be connected at a fee of $400 each. There are 30,000 characters transmitted per day, which, at 128 characters per packet, is 235 packets. This assumes that all packets are full, which will not be the case. A message of 140 characters requires that two packets be sent. The 30,000 characters transmitted per day was approximated to include this variance. There is a charge of $1.50 per 1000 packets, and there are 23 workdays per month. Thus, the monthly PDN charges are:

$$(2 \times 400) + (30,000 \div 128 \times 1.50 \div 1000 \times 23)$$
$$= 800 + (235 \times 0.0015 \times 23) = 800 + 8.11 = \$808.11$$

This analysis shows that PDN will be the most economical link between Seattle and San Francisco. This configuration has the added benefit of allowing the Seattle node to transmit directly to any node with a PDN port, meaning that such messages would not always need to be routed through San Francisco.

Breakeven Point   One more computation will complete the analysis of the link between Seattle and San Francisco. A break-even figure will show the amount of message traffic necessary to make the cost of a leased link the same as that for a PDN. (From the above analysis, it seems unlikely that a switched connection will ever be practical.) The break-even number of characters per day, x, is given by:

$$(2 \times 400) + (x \div 128 \times 0.0015 \times 23) = \$919.40$$
$$x = 442{,}991 \text{ characters per day}$$

This is not a significant amount of message traffic; a 120-page typed document, at 80 characters per line and 55 lines per page, with no compression, exceeds this amount.

The above calculations assumed that neither node had a PDN port and that there was one connection charge per node. If one of the nodes already had a PDN connection, the cost for that port either should not be included or should be distributed throughout the network. Thus, if San Francisco already had been configured with a PDN port, the PDN cost would decrease by $400, or the cost of that port should be apportioned among the nodes that must be connected to San Francisco.

San Francisco–Los Angeles Line   A similar analysis was performed for the San Francisco–Los Angeles connection. A switched line was not considered in this instance; a leased line was the most economical. The leased line rates between San Francisco and Los Angeles are different from those given in Table 11-5 because the link is intrastate. A leased line is available for $425. Because approximately 200,000 characters per day are transferred between the two cities, PDN charges are:

$$400 + (200{,}000 \div 128 \times 0.0015 \times 23) = 400 + 53.90 = \$453.90$$

International Lines   All the European cities will be connected by a backbone network. The connections between Europe, the United States, Canada, Mexico, Japan, Australia, and Hong Kong will be made via X.25 networks. The amount of message traffic between these entities does not warrant the use of leased facilities. Configuring the other parts of the network is left as an exercise. ❖

SUMMARY

Packet distribution networks have evolved into an efficient, effective networking alternative to private networks. PDNs offer circuit acquisition, message routing, error detection and correction, and maintenance. Interconnection of PDNs provides users with an instant international network. The cost of a PDN is reasonable so long as the number of data packets being transferred is low. However, this advantage comes at the price of contending with other users for the facility and a lack of control over network operations. The success of packet switching networks has made them a potential standard for future network implementations as well as for gateways between different network systems.

Wide area networks are usually built around a particular vendor's network software. Although most major computer vendors offer network capabilities, the leader in proprietary network software is IBM's SNA. SNA provides an architecture for building networks, and many vendors support some type of connection to SNA networks. One of the ways that vendors can communicate with an SNA network is via the LU 6.2 protocol. Microcomputers are increasingly found as wide area network components. Their versatility makes them a cost-effective network tool.

SNA continues to evolve and mature as a network product. Internally, new network functions such as those provided by LU 6.2 and SNADS are being included in the architecture. Gateways to other networking products continue to be implemented, together with SNA interfaces between IBM SNA components and other manufacturers' equipment. Some vendors have gone so far as to implement PU Type 4 and PU Type 5 capabilities within their systems. SNA may be the most significant influence in WAN implementations today.

KEY TERMS

call clearing, 356
datagram, 356
domain, 371
dotted quad, 361
end-to-end routing, 372
extended addressing, 372
Fully Qualified Domain Name (FQDN), 361
half-session layer, 367
information superhighway, 363
Internet, 359
Logical Unit (LU), 368
LU 6.2, 370
Network Addressable Unit (NAU), 372
Network Control Program (NCP), 373
Packet Assembly/Disassembly (PAD), 357

Packet-Switching Equipment (PSE), 358
Permanent Virtual Circuit (PVC), 356
Physical Unit (PU), 368
Physical Unit Control Point (PUCP), 371
session, 368
Signaling Terminal Equipment (STE), 358
SNA Distribution Services (SNADS), 374
subarea, 372
subnet, 360
Switched Virtual Circuit (SVC), 356
Systems Network Architecture (SNA), 366
Systems Services Control Point (SSCP), 371
virtual routing, 372

REVIEW QUESTIONS

1. Why are only three layers defined for PDNs? Do the other OSI layers exist? Explain your answer.

2. Why is datagram service generally unsuited to business applications?

3. Are there any business applications for which datagram service is useful? If so, list them.

4. Describe the configuration of the Internet.

5. Explain the two Internet address formats.

6. What services are provided by the Internet?

7. What are the four types of physical units in SNA? What is the role of each in the network?

8. What is a half-session layer in SNA? What is its purpose?

9. Explain how a session is established in SNA.

10. Compare and contrast a WAN and a PDN.

11. Discuss the influence of SNA on other computer vendors.

12. How does SNA relate to the OSI reference model?

13. Describe three potential problem areas when setting up an international network.

PROBLEMS AND EXERCISES

1. Suppose message traffic between New York City and Boston is 600,000 characters per day. If the cost of a leased line is $650 per month, which will be more economical, a leased line or a PDN? Assume that New York City already has a PDN port. How many characters must be exchanged for a leased line to cost the same as a PDN? Use the costs included in the case study in your analysis.

2. Would a PDN be a suitable network for the Syncrasy Corporation's network of catalog and discount stores (see Chapter 9)? What would be the advantages and disadvantages of using a PDN for that application?

3. Obtain the costs for subscribing to a PDN. What are the monthly charges and what are the packet charges?

REFERENCES

Barrett, John J., and Eberhard F. Wunderlich. "LAN Interconnect Using X.25 Network Services." *IEEE Network*, Volume 5, September 1991.

Bernt, Phyllis, and Martin Weiss. *International Telecommunications*. Carmel, IN: Sams Publishing, 1993.

Briere, Daniel, and Christopher Finn. "Not Just X.25 Anymore." *Network World*, Volume 10, March 22, 1993.

Byrnes, Philippe. "Using SNA to Link LAN to Host." *LAN Technology*, Volume 6, December 1990.

Crockett, Barton. "Treaty Could Reform Int'l. Network Rules." *Network World*, Volume 7, May 21, 1990.

Guruge, Anura. "AnyNet Anyone?" *Network World*, Volume 10, June 14, 1993.

————. "The New SNA: Router Backbones Unite Terminals and LANs." *Data Communications*, Volume 20, June 21, 1991.

Jenkins, Avery. "Networks in a Strange Land." *Computerworld Focus—Critical Connections*, Volume 15, March 1986.

Kapoor, Atul. "The New SNA." *Network World*, Volume 8, Number 22, May 27, 1991.

Kehoe, Brendan P. *Zen and the Art of the Internet*. Englewood Cliffs, NJ: PTR Prentice Hall, 1993.

Miller, Mark. "Get a Grip on Internet Access." *Network World*, Volume 10, Number 29, July 19, 1993.

Salamone, Salvatore. "SNA Update: Users Mixed on IBM Net Vision." *Network World*, Volume 9, Number 18, May 4, 1992.

St. Clair, Melanie. "Europe's Borders Open to Networking." *LAN Times*, March 9, 1992.

Sweet, Walter. "Overseas Laws Throw Kink in Bank's Net." *Network World*, Volume 7, Number 27, July 2, 1990.

Tolly, Kevin. "Opening the Gateways to SNA Connectivity." *Data Communications*, Volume 19, Number 3, March 1990.

*I*n the previous two parts you read about two classes of networks, LANs and WANs. Numerous companies that have a WAN also have one or more LANs, and some LAN-only companies have several LANs. Often companies that have several networks need to connect those networks together to form a corporate internetwork or an enterprise network.

Worldwide Labs (WL) is a specialized chemical company. WL develops, manufactures, and distributes chemical compounds that are used in perfumes, cosmetics, food, and other products requiring distinctive aromas. WL also develops flavoring compounds that are added to food products to provide tastes tailored to cultural palates. At its world headquarters in Paris, WL has ten LANs organized around departments. WL also has manufacturing and marketing offices on all continents, and these offices are connected via a corporate WAN. Manufacturing offices also have one or more LANs.

For WL's business style, it is imperative that all employees be able to communicate. A LAN user in Tokyo should be able to communicate with a WAN user in San Francisco or another LAN user in Paris. Providing this capability means that all networks must be interconnected, the WANs to LANs and, in some cases, LANs to LANs. With this enterprise network, WL essentially has a single large network.

With a large internetwork like that used by WL, managing network resources and diagnosing and correcting problems are significant issues. They involve dealing with differences in languages, standards, common carriers, network types and protocols, hardware, software, and time zones. WL's network is complex, so one could expect complexity in its management; however, even relatively simple networks such as a small, fairly homogenous LAN can provide management challenges.

In this part we discuss the various ways in which two networks can be connected and the conditions under which each connection type can be used. Subsequently, we cover the essentials of network management — management objectives, the organization of the network management team, network management tools and protocols, network management software, setting up security, systems analysis, capacity planning, tuning, and system configurations. ∎

Part IV

....

NETWORK INTERCONNECTIONS AND MANAGEMENT

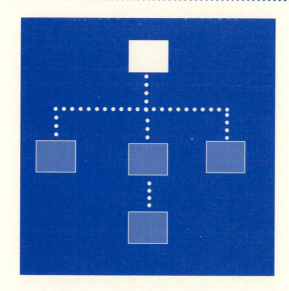

12

Network Interconnections

CHAPTER OBJECTIVES

After studying this chapter you should be able to:

- List the ways networks can be interconnected
- Describe the principal methods for making network connections: repeaters, bridges, routers, and gateways
- List the capabilities of Transmission Control Protocol/Internet Protocol (TCP/IP)
- Describe the network interconnection capabilities of TCP/IP
- List capabilities of network interconnection utilities

The computing resources of organizations are diverse. They range from a single microcomputer to multiple local and wide area networks that connect hundreds of different types of computers—microcomputers, minicomputers, mainframes, and supercomputers. Today, a large organization may have several microcomputer LANs, a WAN, and perhaps connections to public computer networks. When one organization has a variety of computers and networks, those computers ordinarily must be interconnected to provide better use of hardware and software and to allow users to communicate easier. A LAN may need to be connected to another LAN, to a single, large host computer, to a WAN, to remote workstations or terminals, or to public networks, and it may be necessary to connect two or more different WANs. In this chapter we cover the principal ways these connections are made.

THE OSI REFERENCE MODEL REVISITED

Throughout this text, we have discussed the OSI reference model. Because network interconnections are established at the physical, data link, and network layers of the OSI reference model, at this time you may wish to review the sections covering the functions of these three layers.

What do we mean when we say the connection interface is made at the physical, data link, or network layer? An interface that operates at the physical layer must be sensitive to signals on the medium, and one that operates at the data link layer must be aware of data link protocol formats, and one that operates at the network layer must use a common network layer protocol and be able to route messages to the next node along the path to its destination. The interconnection at a specific layer must be knowledgeable of the implementation details of that layer. We begin by looking at physical layer interconnections.

As signals are transmitted through a medium, the signals weaken. A signal eventually will become unintelligible unless it can be amplified or regenerated. To guard against this in the telephone system, repeaters are placed at regular intervals to amplify or regenerate the signal. If the transmission is analog, any frequency is allowed and, therefore, signals must be amplified. Amplification simply strengthens the signal and will also amplify any errors that have crept into the transmission. This is illustrated in Figure 12-1(a). A digital signal can be regenerated and restored to its original strength and values. Because a digital signal has only two states, a 0 or a 1, a regenerator can examine an incoming signal, decide which of the two states the signal represents, and restore the signal to its original value and strength as illustrated in Figure 12-1(b).

Figure 12-1

Signal Amplification and
Regeneration

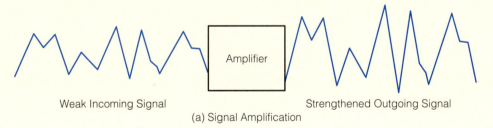

Weak Incoming Signal   Strengthened Outgoing Signal

(a) Signal Amplification

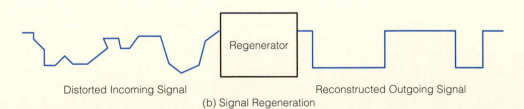

Distorted Incoming Signal   Reconstructed Outgoing Signal

(b) Signal Regeneration

A hardware device that amplifies or regenerates a signal at the physical layer is called a **repeater**. The function of a repeater is similar to that of some nonelectronic data transmission techniques. You may be familiar with communications techniques such as semaphore flags. Semaphores are line-of-sight transmissions. If the message must be transmitted over relatively long distances, relay stations are necessary. If Station A in Figure 12-2 needs to transmit a message to Station D, the signaler at Station B will read the signal sent from Station A and resend the message to Station C, where the message will be repeated and sent to Station D. At each relay station the signal is essentially amplified. If an error in transcribing or transmitting the message is made at any point, the error will be propagated to subsequent stations.

In a similar manner, the length of the medium on a LAN can be extended by repeaters. A repeater is a physical layer device and hence must know and

repeater A device used to amplify signals on a network. Repeaters allow the medium distance to be extended.

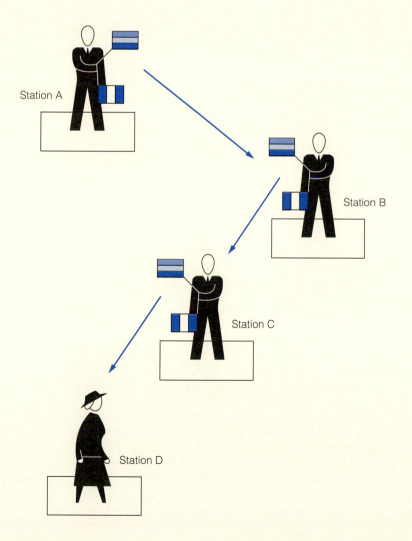

Figure 12-2

Signal Relay Stations

Station A

Station B

Station C

Station D

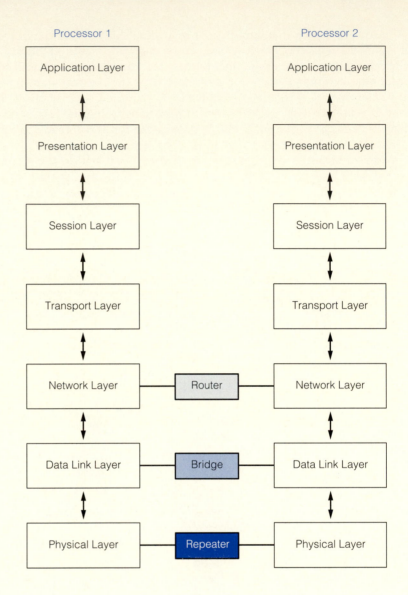

Figure 12-3

A Repeater, Bridge, and
Router and the OSI
Reference Model

obey all the physical layer conventions regarding signaling and connections. Repeaters are commonly used in LANs to extend the distance the signal can travel over the medium and still maintain signal strength. Unlike the repeaters used in the telephone system, LAN standards limit the number of repeaters that can be used for a single LAN and hence limit the maximum length of the LAN medium. Figure 12-3 illustrates the relationship between a repeater and the OSI model.

Three functions of the data link layer of the OSI reference model are delineation of data, error detection, and address formatting. A data link protocol is concerned with getting data from the current node to the next node. A message may pass through several data link protocols on its path from the source node

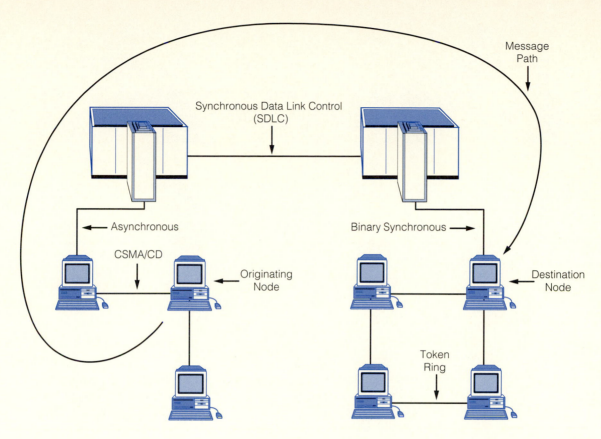

Figure 12-4

Message Passing Through Several Different Data Link Protocols

to the destination node as illustrated in Figure 12-4. In this example, a message passes from a LAN data link protocol to a WAN data link protocol and back to another (possibly different) LAN data link protocol. The data link protocol at each node is concerned only with moving the data to the next node.

An interface that operates at the data link or media access control (MAC) layer is called a **bridge**. Bridges are most commonly used in LANs to overcome limitations in distance or in number of workstations per LAN. A bridge is seldom necessary in WANs because they do not have distance limitations. WANs that limit the number of nodes per network usually use routers (see below) to interconnect two or more WANs.

Bridges originally connected LANs of the same type, such as two token ring LANs or two IEEE 802.3 LANs. These early bridges indiscriminately forwarded all message traffic from one LAN onto the other LAN. Today's bridge technology is more sophisticated and can connect LANs using different data link protocols, such as bridging a token ring LAN to a CSMA/CD bus LAN. Now, a bridge selectively forwards packets of data. Packets sent between two nodes on the same LAN are not acted on by the bridge; only internetwork packets are forwarded by a bridge, as illustrated in Figure 12-5. The relationship between a bridge and the OSI model is illustrated in Figure 12-3. Note that although the

bridge The interface used to connect networks using similar data link protocols.

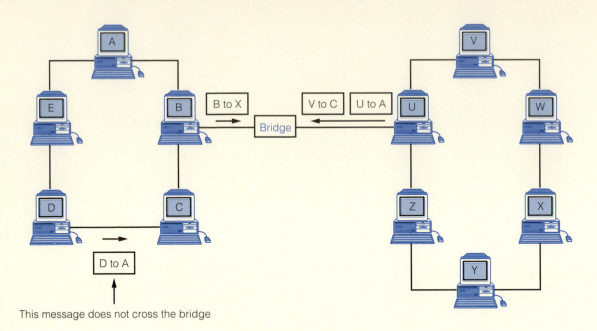

This message does not cross the bridge

Figure 12-5

Bridge Packet Forwarding

bridge is shown at the data link layer, the data is transmitted from the data link layer down to the physical layer, over the medium to a physical layer, and back up to the data link layer. When a bridge that has a physical connection to two LANs receives a message, the message passes from the bridge's physical layer to its data link layer. The bridge examines the destination address in the header attached as part of the data link protocol and determines the destination address of the packet. This address tells the bridge which of the two LANs has the message's recipient, and the bridge passes the message to the proper LAN using the services of the physical layer connection.

The network layer of the OSI reference model is responsible for packet routing and the collection of accounting information. Networks use a variety of routing algorithms. CSMA/CD and token-passing LANs send messages to each node using broadcast routing. WANs are more selective in their routing because broadcast routing in a WAN causes too much overhead and delay. You may want to refer back to Chapter 9 for a review of WAN routing algorithms. Several routing paths may be available in some networks, as illustrated in Figure 12-6. The network layer is responsible for routing an incoming message for another node onto an appropriate outbound path. Thus, a message for Node X that arrives at Node B in Figure 12-6 will arrive at the physical layer and be moved up through the data link layer to the network layer. If the packet is not intended for an application on Node B, the network layer determines the outbound path for the message and sends it down to the data link layer, which formats the packet with the proper data link control data (perhaps a data link protocol different from that of the arriving message). The data link layer then passes the packet down to the physical layer for transmission to the next node along the path to the final destination.

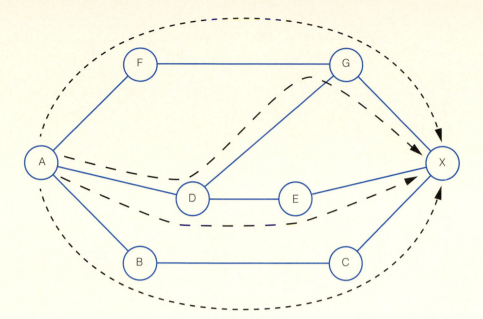

Figure 12-6

Several Routing Paths in a
Network

An interconnection interface that operates at the network layer is called a **router**. A router is not sensitive to the details of the data link and physical layers. Thus, a router can be used to connect different types of networks, such as a token ring LAN to an IEEE 802.3 LAN or a LAN to a WAN. A router looks at the destination address of a message, determines a route the message should follow to reach that address, and provides the addressing required by the network and data link layers for delivery. This function is provided by **Transmission Control Protocol/Internet Protocol (TCP/IP)** in the Internet, whereas Novell networks typically use a protocol called Sequenced Packet Exchange/Internetwork Packet Exchange (SPX/IPX) to transfer packets between nodes. The TCP and SPX protocols operate at the transport layer, and IP and IPX protocols operate at the network layer. Some networks use a different type of protocol, such as the Xerox Network System (XNS). An SPX/IPX router will not be able to forward TCP/IP packets, and a router that knows only the XNS protocol cannot forward SPX/IPX packets. For two nodes to exchange data using a router, they must share a common network layer protocol. Figure 12-3 shows the relationship between a router and the OSI layers.

Network connections that operate at the network layer or above are generically called **gateways**. A gateway is used to connect dissimilar networks or systems by providing conversion from one network protocol to another. A gateway might be used to connect a LAN to a WAN as illustrated in Figure 12-7. In making this interconnection, the gateway must accept packets from the LAN, extract the data from the packets, and format the data in a packet according to the WAN protocol, or vice versa.

Now that we have introduced the basic types of network interconnections, we examine some of their details.

router A network interconnection device and associated software that links two networks. The networks being linked can be different, but they must use a common routing protocol.

Transmission Control Protocol/Internet Protocol (TCP/IP) A suite of internetwork protocols developed by the U.S. Department of Defense for internetwork file transfers, electronic mail transfer, remote logons, and terminal services.

gateway The interface used to connect two dissimilar networks or systems by providing conversion from one network to another.

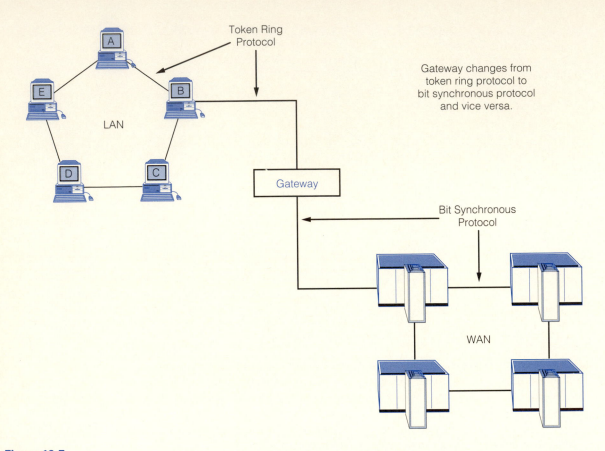

Token Ring
Protocol

Gateway changes from
token ring protocol to
bit synchronous protocol
and vice versa.

LAN

Gateway

Bit Synchronous
Protocol

WAN

Figure 12-7

A Gateway Connecting a
LAN and a WAN

LAN-TO-LAN AND WAN-TO-WAN CONNECTIONS

By definition, a LAN serves a limited geographic area, and most LAN specifications place a limit on the length of the medium used. Companies that have
LANs in geographically separated locations, or LANs that cover distances
longer than the maximum allowed, frequently have a need for interLAN
exchanges. Users on one LAN may want to exchange electronic mail messages with users on the other LAN, or a user on one LAN may want to use
resources located on another LAN.

Distance or geographic separation is not the only reason for having several
LANs. Departmental computing is another rationale for having a multiple
LAN environment. A company that is interested in department-level computing might implement a LAN for each department or for groups of departments. For example, a computer software manufacturer may go to great
lengths to protect the integrity of their new products. Often details of new
developments are not shared with those employees who are not directly involved with a new product. Having separate LANs allows the company to
separate functions and provides additional security of information. Among
the software company's departments, there might be a LAN shared by soft-

ware development and documentation, one for software support, one for accounting, one for personnel, and one for marketing. This separation will reduce the likelihood that software being developed will inadvertently or intentionally be made available to customers through the support or marketing LAN. Likewise, personnel information can be more easily protected if it is on a separate LAN.

A third reason for LAN connections is to consolidate independent LANs that were formed in an ad hoc manner. Superficially this reason is similar to connecting departmental LANs. The difference is that department-oriented LANs are a planned separation whereas workgroup-oriented LANs were implemented as needed by individual departments or workgroups. This situation is common in many colleges and universities, where the departments or colleges of computer science, business, engineering, and nursing may have implemented LANs independently. Another reason for forming several small LANs rather than one large one is limitations on medium capacity. LANs supporting graphics and multimedia applications need to send high volumes of full-motion video and sound data in short amounts of time. Only a small number of multimedia workstations can be supported on media operating at 10 or 16 Mbps. Regardless of the original reasons for setting up several LANs, often a need arises for inter-LAN message exchanges and LAN interconnections to support them.

A fourth reason for having multiple LANs is the number of users per LAN. A LAN with hundreds of users might provide poorer performance than the same LAN with tens of users. A LAN administrator attempts to maintain the responsiveness of a LAN even when more users are added. Responsiveness can be maintained by adding more resources to an existing LAN — more memory, more disks, or another server — or by splitting the LAN into two or more smaller LANs. When splitting a LAN, the administrator strives for a proper balance of users and resources; however, a perfect balance is not always attainable due to distance, physical location, or differences in workgroup sizes. Because inter-LAN communications involves more overhead than intra-LAN communications, an administrator must consider grouping of users and resources so the number of inter-LAN messages is reduced. Members of a department or workgroup often communicate with each other more than with members of other departments or workgroups. Thus, splitting a LAN because many users are being serviced frequently results in a configuration split along departmental or workgroup lines.

Companies may also have several WANs. One reason for having multiple WANs arises from corporate mergers and acquisitions. When two companies combine, each may have a WAN already in place. These WANs sometimes use different vendors' network architectures. After the merger, it is usually desirable to interconnect those networks; however, preexisting incompatibilities may make it necessary to retain separate WANs. Sometimes independent networks are started in regional areas and later need to be connected to form national and international networks. Finally, a company may want to connect its network to external networks such as the Internet. Different WANs also can arise from the need to support different work tasks. A bank might use one vendor's hardware and network architecture to set up a network of automatic teller machines and a different network to support its back office, platform, and administrative applications. Similarly, a manufacturing company may use one type of hardware and network to support research and development operations and another for sales and administrative purposes.

There are many good reasons for having several different networks in an organization. At some point, there is often a need to have these separate networks connected into one enterprise network. As a generic model for connecting separate networks, we use LANs as an example of both LAN-to-LAN and WAN-to-WAN connections. This is appropriate because the first two types of connections, repeaters and bridges, are most common in LANs. Routers are common to both network types.

Repeaters

Every LAN has a distance restriction. One of the IEEE 802.3 standards, 10Base5, specifies a maximum medium segment length of 500 meters. To span longer distances, a repeater can be used to connect two segments. The standard allows for a maximum of four repeaters, for a total distance of 2500 meters per LAN. Two repeaters connecting three segments in an IEEE 802.3 network is illustrated in Figure 12-8.

As signals travel along the medium, they lose strength due to attenuation. Weak signals can result in transmission errors. A repeater is a simple hardware device that accepts a signal, regenerates or amplifies it, and passes it along at full strength. This is illustrated in Figure 12-9. A repeater does not

Figure 12-8

Repeaters Connecting Three
LAN Segments

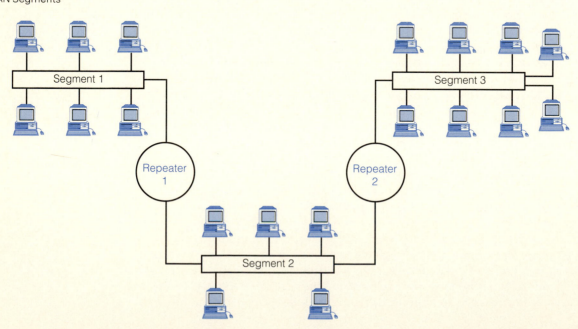

buffer messages and does not know about MAC protocols or data packets. A repeater also does not separate one segment of the network from another. If a station in segment 1 and a station in segment 3 of the network in Figure 12-8 try to transmit at the same time, a collision will occur.

Table 12-1 is a list of repeater capabilities and characteristics. Note that one capability of some repeaters is media transfer. Although it is not commonly needed, this capability allows an administrator to change media from twisted-pair wires on one LAN segment to coaxial cable on another segment at a repeater junction; the MAC protocol remains the same even though the medium changes. The LAN administrator must also keep in mind that a change in the medium can result in a change in the overall maximum length of the LAN.

Bridges

Early bridges were used to connect two networks that both used the same MAC protocol. Today, we have products called bridges that connect LANs having different MAC protocols. These newer bridges must be able to reformat packets from one data link protocol to another. Be aware that the use of the term *bridge* can vary. Sometimes a bridge is defined in the original sense — a device connecting two identical networks. Others use the broader definition of a device used to connect two networks at the data link layer. For example, you may encounter bridges that connect a token ring to an Ethernet LAN. Sometimes a device providing this capability will also be referred to as a **brouter**. Figure 12-10 illustrates two LANs, LAN A and LAN B, using a token ring protocol. These two rings may be configured around departments, with one ring per department, or around distance if the distance spanned by the workstations is greater than what can be supported by a single LAN. Regard-

brouter A term used to describe new bridges that are able to connect two different LANs using the data link layer.

TABLE 12-1   Repeater Characteristics and Capabilities

Media transfer, such as coaxial cable to twisted-pair wires

Multiple ports allowing one repeater to connect three or more segments

Diagnostic and status indicators

Automatic partitioning and reconnection in the event of a segment failure

Manual partitioning

Backup power supply

Figure 12-9

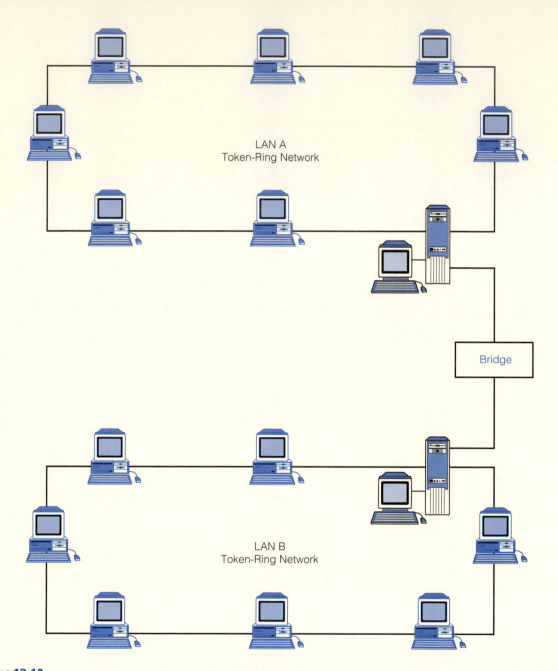

LAN A
Token-Ring Network

Bridge

LAN B
Token-Ring Network

Figure 12-10

Token Rings Connected by a
Bridge

less of the reason for having two rings, it is likely that an application on Ring
A will want to communicate with a server on Ring B or that a user on Ring A
will want to send E-mail to a user on Ring B. A bridge can provide this ability.

In Figure 12-10 the bridge's function is to move data packets between the
two LANs. Unlike a repeater, a bridge is selective in what it does. It accepts
packets from both LANs and transfers LAN A packets addressed to nodes
on LAN B and transfers LAN B packets addressed to nodes on LAN A. Some
bridge functions are listed in Table 12-2.

TABLE 12-2 Basic Bridge Functions

Packet Routing Function

1. Accept packet from LAN A.

2. Examine address of packet.

3. If packet address is a LAN A address, allow the packet to continue on LAN A.

4. If packet address is a LAN B address, transmit the packet onto the LAN B medium.

5. Do the equivalent for LAN B packets.

Additional Functions

Media conversion	Learning
Remote connection	Signal conversion
Speed conversion	Packet statistics
Token ring to Ethernet conversion	

TABLE 12-3 Bridge B1's Network Routing Table

Node	Port	Comments
N1	P1	
N2	P1	
N3	P2	
N4	P1	Bridge B2 routes
N5	P1	Bridge B2 routes

A bridge must know about addresses on each network. Because the bridge knows the MAC protocol being used, the bridge can find the source and destination addresses in the packet and use those addresses for routing. (We use the term *routing* here to describe the process of the bridge deciding to which LAN the message must be transferred. In using this term we do not imply that the bridge is performing the functions of a router.) The only additional information the bridge must know is the LAN to which the destination node is connected. This is determined in several ways. Older bridges indiscriminately transferred each message onto both LANs or required network managers to provide a network routing table. A **routing table** contains node addresses and the LAN identifier for the LAN to which the node is connected. These older bridges are static regarding their ability to forward messages. If a new node is added to one of the networks, the routing tables in all bridges must be manually updated, and until that happens the new node will not receive inter-LAN messages. As shown in Figure 12-11, network interconnections using bridges can also be more complex than a single bridge connecting two networks. A network routing table for Bridge B1 in Figure 12-11 is shown in Table 12-3.

routing table An information source containing the node address and the identification of the LAN to which the receiving node is connected.

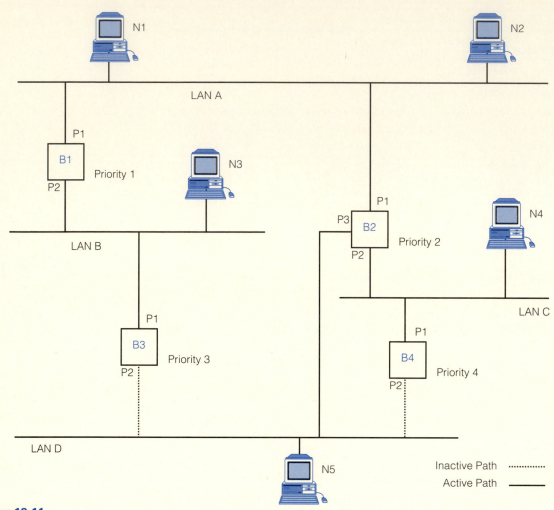

Figure 12-11

Network Interconnections
Using Bridges

learning bridge Bridge
that builds its own routing
table from the messages it
receives, rather than having
a predefined routing table.
Also known as a transparent
bridge.

Most bridges being sold today are referred to as **learning bridges** or **transparent bridges**. Learning bridges build their routing table from messages they receive. They do not need to be loaded with a predefined routing table. Essentially the network administrator need only connect the bridge to both LANs and the bridge is immediately operational. Two methods are commonly used for bridges to learn and build their routing table: spanning tree and source routing (both are described later). To understand how bridges of this type work, we start with a sample bridge configuration, as illustrated in Figure 12-11. Figure 12-11 shows four LANs (A, B, C, and D), four bridges (B1, B2, B3, and B4), and five nodes (N1, N2, N3, N4, and N5). In this figure, each bridge has two ports labeled P1 and P2. Bridge B2 has a third port, P3.

Note that in this configuration, at least two paths exist between each pair of LANs. LAN A can get to LAN D via bridges B1 and B3 or directly via Bridge B2; LAN D can get to LAN C directly through either Bridge B4 or

Bridge B2 or indirectly through bridges B3, B1, and B2. We start by explaining how a bridge works. In this example we assume each bridge has a fully developed routing table like the one shown for Bridge B1 in Table 12-3. Note also that there is only one route for each node. If a route changes for some reason, the bridge will update its routing table to show the new route. Some networks use routing algorithms that allow multiple active paths between two nodes, but this is atypical of bridges. Following this example, we examine the two ways in which a bridge learns its routing information.

In Figure 12-11, suppose Bridge B1 receives a packet from N1 destined for N2. Recall that each LAN packet contains the address of the sender, or source, and the recipient, or destination. The bridge examines its routing table for the destination address. In this case, the address is local because both the source and the destination addresses are on LAN A. Because the destination address is local, no further action is required; the bridge essentially does nothing. In a token-passing LAN, the bridge may need to forward the packet to the next node on the LAN. In a CSMA/CD LAN, the bridge will do nothing because packets are broadcast to all nodes.

Suppose Bridge B1 receives a packet on Port P2 from LAN B, with a source address of N3 and a destination address of N2 (LAN A). The bridge again consults its routing table for the destination address and finds the address to be a nonlocal node. The routing table shows the outbound port on which to send the packet, P1 in this instance. The bridge takes the packet as received and transmits through Port P1 onto LAN A (if the LANs have a different MAC protocol, the bridge will format the packet to make the packet compatible with the receiving MAC protocol). Similarly, if Bridge B3 receives a packet from Node N5 with a destination of N2, B3 will consult its routing table, find that the path to N2 is Port P1, and transmit the packet on LAN B. Bridge B1 on LAN B will receive this packet, consult its routing table, and forward the packet to LAN A through Port P1. You may be wondering why Bridge B4 did not also transmit the packet onto LAN C, or why Bridge B2 did not also transmit the packet, causing a duplicate packet. The answer lies in how bridges operate and learn.

The Spanning Tree Algorithm

Spanning tree algorithms, in which bridges exchange routing information with each other, can be used on any type of LAN. The spanning tree algorithm has been evaluated by the IEEE 802.1 Media Access Control Bridge Standards Committee. The committee selected the spanning tree algorithm as the standard for all IEEE 802 LAN standards.

In developing the algorithm for spanning trees let us first look at a simple case. You may wish to refer back to Figure 12-11 during this discussion. Recall that each LAN packet contains the source address and the destination address. If Bridge B1 receives a packet on Port P1, the bridge assumes that the source address is a node local to LAN A. Because a bridge receives all network traffic on a LAN to which the bridge is connected (Bridge B1 gets all message traffic on LANs A and B), a bridge soon learns all of the "local" node addresses

spanning tree algorithm A learning bridge algorithm in which bridges exchange routing information with one another. Based on the routing information thus received, each bridge maintains a routing table that shows how to route messages to other LANs.

from the source addresses in these messages. If a source address is not found in the bridge's routing table, the address is added to the table.

Suppose Node N3 in Figure 12-11 sends a message to Node N2. If the destination address N2 is already in B1's routing table, the bridge forwards the packet accordingly. If the destination address is not already in the bridge's routing table, the bridge needs to locate the address. The bridge does this by sending the packet out on all ports other than the one on which it was received, which is called **flooding** (the packet will also be sent to all nodes on the LAN on which it was received). In this instance, the packet will be transmitted on Port P1.

Flooding assures that a packet will arrive at its destination by sending it along all possible paths. The bridge will eventually receive either an acknowledgment that the packet was received or a message from the receiving station. The acknowledgment contains the address of the original recipient, N2 in this case. From this acknowledgment, the bridge will be able to determine the direction in which the node lies, and it adds this information to its routing table.

Sometimes a path may become unavailable, or new bridges or paths may become operational, which may cause routing information to change. To keep routing as efficient as possible, each bridge sends status messages periodically to let other bridges know of its current state. Also, status messages are sent immediately if the topology changes.

Now we consider a more complex situation, in which multiple bridges are connected to the same network and there may be multiple paths between LANs and perhaps multiple ports per bridge, as illustrated in Figure 12-11. If Node N5 sends a message to Node N2, does the packet get sent via Bridge B2 or via Bridges B3 and B1 or even via Bridge B4 and then Bridge B2? To reconcile such decisions, each bridge is given a priority. If two or more bridges are available, the bridge with the highest priority is chosen. If the path along that route becomes disrupted, the path can change and the highest priority alternate path will be activated. We consider in more detail how this occurs.

A bridge has at least two ports. An **active port** will accept packets from the LAN end of the port, and an **inactive port** will block or not accept packets from the LAN end of the port. An inactive port still can be used to transmit packets. These packets, however, must originate from the bridge end of the port. Each bridge is assigned a priority by the administrator.

The bridge with the highest priority is designated as the **root bridge**. Each bridge has an active port in the direction of the root bridge. Other ports are active or inactive depending on the priority of the bridge and the configuration. Figure 12-11 also shows the priority of each bridge (with 1 representing the highest priority) and the active and inactive paths. A port is active if its path is active; otherwise it is inactive. All bridges have their port in the direction of the root bridge active. Therefore, packets from the root direction can be forwarded and received. For all other cases, the active port from a LAN is toward the bridge with the highest priority. Ports on the root bridge are always active. Thus, in Figure 12-11, LAN A and B will choose Bridge B1's ports as the active ports. LAN C is connected to two bridges, B2 and B4. B2 will be chosen because it has the higher priority, and B2's Port P2 will be

flooding   A technique used by a bridge to locate a destination address not present in the bridge's routing table by sending a packet out on all possible paths. An acknowledgment from the receiving station will contain the destination address of the packet, which can then be added to the bridge's routing table.

active port   The status of a port that will accept packets from the LAN end of the port.

inactive port   The status of a port that will not accept packets from the LAN end of the port.

root bridge   The bridge assigned the highest priority.

active. B4's Port P1 is also active because P1 is in the direction of the root bridge. LAN D is connected to three bridges, B2, B3, and B4. Because B2 has the highest priority, it will be chosen as the active bridge. Ports P2 on bridges B3 and B4 will be inactive and will not accept packets from LAN D.

The advantages of the spanning tree algorithm are (1) it is MAC layer independent, (2) bridges can learn the topology of the network without manual intervention, and (3) paths can change if an existing path becomes inoperable or if a better path is introduced. The algorithm overhead is the size of the routing table for networks with many communicating nodes, and the extra network traffic resulting from status messages and flooding.

Source Routing

In practice, spanning tree algorithms have been more commonly used for CSMA/CD LANs, and **source routing** is more common for token-passing LANs. Source routing is also being considered by an IEEE standards committee as a routing algorithm for token-passing networks.

Source routing relies on the sending station to designate the path for a packet. In Figure 12-11, suppose Node N5 wants to send a packet to Node N2. If N2 is in N5's routing table, the packet is sent along that route; otherwise, N5 must "discover" the best route to N2. N5 does this by sending a **discovery packet** on all routes available. In this case, the discovery packet will be sent on Port P2 of Bridge B4, Port P3 of Bridge B2, and Port P2 of Bridge B3. Each bridge will, in turn, transmit the packet on each port except the one on which the packet was received. Moreover, each bridge appends its information to the packet. Thus, Node N2 will receive several packets, each containing the identity of each bridge through which the packet traveled. All of these packets are returned to Node N5. N5 selects the path from all the alternatives returned. In our example, Node N5 will likely receive four discovery packets with paths B4-B2, B2, B3-B1, and B4-B2-B3-B1. Upon receiving the four responses from its discovery packets, Node N5 will choose one. B2 would probably be the best route as there is only one bridge through which the message must pass. Realize, however, that path B3-B1 might be faster if B2's connections on ports P1 or P3 are slower than the connections for bridges B3 and B1.

After N5 discovers the path to Node N2, whenever Node N5 needs to transmit to Node N2, it appends the selected routing information to its packet. Each bridge along the way investigates this information to determine by which route to send the packet.

You might have already noticed that the algorithm as just explained has one possible fault. The discovery packet sent from Bridge B4 will reach Bridge B2, and B2 will send the packet out on all ports except the one on which it was received (ports P3 and P1). The packet on Port P3 will be directed back to LAN D and will again reach bridges B4 and B3. A mechanism must be in place to prevent discovery packets from looping through the network. This is accomplished in one of two ways. First, a maximum number of hops is specified. If the maximum is set to ten, then a packet that has not reached its

source routing   A learning bridge algorithm in which the sending node is responsible for determining the route to the destination node. The routing information is appended to the message and the bridges along the route use the routing information to move the message from source to destination.

discovery packet   A packet sent by the sending station on all available routes to evaluate and determine the best route from the information collected by the packet.

destination after traversing ten bridges will be discarded. The second way to prevent a loop is to discard a packet that recirculates through the same bridge. For example, one of N5's discovery packets will go from B4 to B2 and then back to B4. When B4 finds that it has already handled that packet, it will discard the packet.

The advantage of the source routing algorithm is that bridges are not responsible for maintaining large routing tables for extensive networks. Each node is responsible for maintaining routing information only for those nodes with which it communicates. The disadvantages are the overhead of sending numerous packets during discovery and the extra routing data that must be appended to each message.

Other Bridge Capabilities

In the preceding discussion, we did not consider the interconnected LANs' location and media. Bridges are available that will accommodate media differences. Suppose LAN A in Figure 12-11 uses coaxial cable and LAN B uses twisted-pair wires as the medium. You could therefore select a bridge that has BNC connectors for coaxial cable on one port and RJ-45 connectors for twisted-pair wires on the other port.

There are also several interconnection options for connecting geographically distributed LANs. The most common of these are listed in Table 12-4. The speed of the connection between remote LANs usually is much slower than the speed within either LAN. This speed difference can cause the bridge to become saturated with messages if there are many internet packets. Bridges have memory that allows some messages to be buffered, which helps reconcile the differences in transmission speed. If too many messages arrive in a short period, the buffer will become full, and newly arriving packets will be lost. Note that this condition can occur when two local LANs are connected. A bridge also must do some processing to determine where a packet must be routed. Except for very slow LANs, the processing time may exceed the arrival rate. Thus, bridges connecting LANs with high packet arrival rates can also become saturated.

TABLE 12-4   Remote Bridge Connection Alternatives

RS-232 serial lines

RS-422 serial lines to 19.2 Kbps to 2 Mbps

Synchronous transmission at 56 Kbps or 64 Kbps

T-1 Line, 1.5 Mbps

Fractional T-1, 64Kbps

X.25 packet-switching network

Integrated Services Digital Network (ISDN)

Routers

Networks sometimes are connected at the network layer. This type of connection, called a router, is used to connect LANs to LANs, WANs to WANs, and LANs to WANs. As in any form of communication, a common language or protocol is needed. In a bridge the common protocol is the data link protocol. Because the data link protocol may not be common for all links on networks connected with a router, the common internetwork protocol is formed at the network layer. Although the network interconnection is established at the network layer, data link and physical layer services are also involved.

A variety of network protocols are used for network interconnection. Novell's native network protocol is SPX/IPX. SPX/IPX can therefore be used to establish the common basis of communication between a Novell token-ring LAN and a Novell CSMA/CD LAN. However, SPX/IPX may not be implemented in WANs and in LANs provided by other network vendors, and SPX/IPX cannot be used as a routing protocol for these networks. Thus network administrators must find one network layer protocol supported by at least one node on each network. Several internetwork protocols have been developed, but the most common of these is TCP/IP. As a result, we use TCP/IP as our router example.

TCP/IP

TCP/IP was developed by the Advanced Research Projects Agency (ARPA) of the U.S. Department of Defense (DOD). Originated as an internetwork protocol, it has evolved over time into a suite of protocols addressing a variety of network communications needs, one of which is that of a router. Note that TCP/IP is not just a microcomputer protocol. On the contrary, it was developed on large systems and was later transported to microcomputers. Because TCP/IP runs on a wide variety of platforms, it is an ideal choice for a routing protocol. Other functions provided by the TCP/IP protocol suite include file transfer, electronic mail, and logins to remote nodes.

Using TCP/IP's routing capabilities, users may be on (1) either the same or different networks, (2) networks that are directly connected by a bridge or router, or (3) networks with one or more intermediate networks as illustrated in Figure 12-12. In addition to providing network interconnection, TCP/IP also provides services for file transfers, electronic mail, and provisions for a user on one network to log onto another network. Although these capabilities are important, we consider only the router functions of the protocol.

Figure 12-12 illustrates how networks might be connected using TCP/IP. Routing nodes are denoted by R and nonrouting nodes by WS. Note that internetwork connections are made through specific network nodes. Thus, Node R1 on Network A has a physical connection to Node R2 on Network B, and Node R3 on Network A has a physical connection to Node R4 on Network C. You should also realize that the networks we are discussing can be either a LAN or a WAN, and routing nodes that communicate with each other must

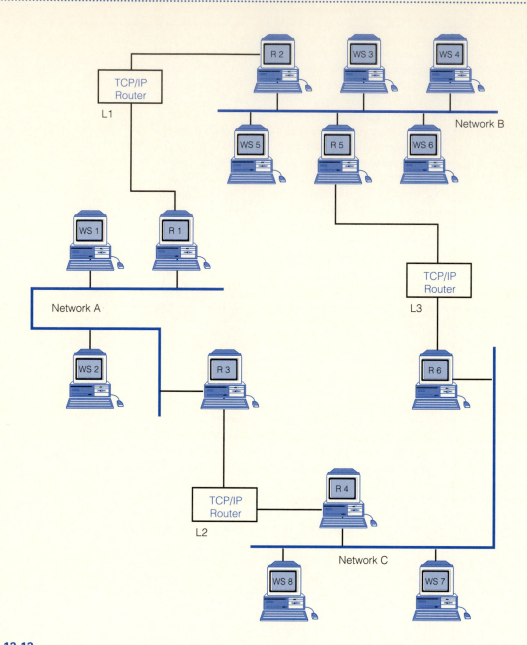

Figure 12-12

TCP/IP Routing in a Network

share a common data link protocol and a physical link. Although we speak of routers operating at the network level, for messages to transmit from one node to another they must pass through the data link and physical layers of each computer. The key is that the information needed to determine how to forward the message is understood by the network layer's logic. In Figure 12-12, assume that Network A is a CSMA/CD LAN, Network B is a token-ring LAN, and Network C is a WAN. Nodes R1 and R2 must share a common data link protocol over Link L1, and nodes R3 and R4 must share a common data link protocol and medium over Link L2. The data link protocols at L1 and L2 may be different. A key concept for a router is that any data link protocol can be used.

As the abbreviation implies, TCP/IP consists of two distinct protocols, the Transmission Control Protocol (TCP) and the Internet Protocol (IP). The TCP operates at the transport layer and the IP operates at the network layer. Before tracing the flow of a message transfer using TCP/IP, let us first look at the functions of each protocol.

The IP provides two basic services: breaking the message up into transmission packets and addressing. Figure 12-12 shows several network interconnections, and each connection may use a different data link protocol. Many data link protocols have a maximum size for transmission packets. For example, an Ethernet LAN packet contains at most 1500 characters. Some networks have a maximum packet size of 128 characters. An IP must be aware of these data link differences. The IP is also responsible for packet routing. On occasion this requires that the IP break a message into smaller packets of the appropriate size. To do this, the IP must determine the address of the next node on the path to the message's destination.

There are several functions an IP does not perform. The IP is not responsible for guaranteeing end-to-end message delivery. The TCP protocol is held accountable for message delivery. If a packet is lost during transmission, the TCP, not the IP, is responsible for resending the message. Also, the IP does not guarantee that individual packets will arrive in the correct order, a function that is also provided by the TCP. Thus, the primary functions of the TCP are to provide message integrity, to provide acknowledgment that a complete message has been received by a destination node, and to regulate the flow of messages between source and destination nodes. The TCP also may divide the message into smaller transmission segments. These segments usually will correspond to an IP transmission packet.

We now consider how the TCP and IP cooperate in sending a message from one node to another. This example also serves as a model for the functions of a router. For this example we assume that Node WS1 on Network A needs to send a message to Node WS5 on Network B in Figure 12-12. TCP/IP uses the following procedure to carry out this transmission.

1. To start the process, the TCP in Node WS1 receives a message from an application. The TCP attaches a header to the message and passes it down to the IP in Node WS1. The message header contains the destination address and error detection fields such as a Cyclic Redundancy Check (CRC) and a message sequence number. These are used to ensure that the message is received without errors and to ensure that messages are received in the proper sequence or can be reordered into the proper sequence.

2. Node WS1's IP determines whether the destination is an internetwork address. If the address is on the local network, such as Node WS2, then the IP passes the message to the local network routing facility, which transports the message to the proper node. If the destination is a node on another network, the IP finds the best path to the destination and

forwards the message to the next IP node along that path. In this case, the IP in Node WS1 will send the message to Node R1.

3. The IP at Node R1 receives the message, examines the address, and determines the address of the next node, R2 in this example. The IP may break the message up into packets of the appropriate size. The IP adds a header to each packet and passes it down to the data link layer. The data link layer appends its transmission information and transmits the packets over the link between R1 and R2.

4. The data link layer at R2 receives a packet, strips off the data link layer control data, and passes the message to R2's IP. If the destination is local to that IP's network, as it is in this instance, the IP delivers the message to the local network routing facility for delivery. If the destination is on another network, the IP determines the next node along the path and sends the message to it. If the node address were WS7, the packet would be routed to Node R5 and then to Node R6. Ultimately the message arrives at the destination node.

5. When the message arrives at the final destination node, it is passed up to the TCP, which then decodes the header attached by the sender's TCP. The receiving TCP checks for errors, such as message sequence errors or CRC errors. If no errors are detected, the TCP determines the destination program and sends the message to it.

On the path from source to destination, the message may pass through several IP nodes and traverse links with several different data link protocols. The router, TCP/IP in this example, is responsible for generating the destination address and intermediate addresses along the way, and for ensuring the correct delivery of the message.

Xpress Transfer Protocol (XTP)   An extension of TCP/IP that enhances performance by reducing the amount of processing and allowing some functions to be worked on simultaneously.

TCP/IP is continually being extended to meet new communications needs. One extension, **Xpress Transfer Protocol** (**XTP**) enhances TCP/IP performance by reducing the amount of processing and allowing some functions to be worked on in parallel. One example of parallelism is the ability to transmit data while the CRC is being computed.

From the preceding discussion you should realize that a LAN node that must communicate with a node on another network must run both the TCP and the IP software. Most of today's LAN operating system vendors have TCP/IP software available in DOS, OS/2, and UNIX versions. You will also find this software and associated utilities available from independent software vendors. A variety of TCP/IP utilities can be found in the public domain and are thus available at no cost or at a minimal cost.

ISO Routing Standards

Connectionless Network Protocol (CLNP)   The counterpart to the Internet Protocol (IP), this protocol provides message services such as message priorities, route selection parameters, and security parameters.

The International Standards Organization (ISO) has also developed standards for functions similar to those provided by TCP/IP. The counterpart to IP is the **Connectionless Network Protocol** (**CLNP**). In addition to forwarding messages, CLNP can provide message services such as message priorities, route selection parameters, and security parameters. The ISO has defined five classes of transport protocols that are abbreviated as TP0, TP1, TP2, TP3, and TP4. The classes are based on the error characteristics of the network. The lower classes assume better network error performance and hence provide less end-to-end support. TP4 makes no assumptions about the error characteristics of the network and provides the highest level of error detection and recovery. Combining the transport protocols with CLNP yields a service similar to that of TCP/IP. The ISO services are abbreviated TP*n*/CLNP, where *n* represents a number between 0 and 4.

Gateways

The interface between two dissimilar networks is called a gateway, which is basically a protocol converter. A gateway reconciles the differences between the networks it connects. With a repeater, a bridge, or a router, the communicating nodes share a common protocol at the physical, the data link, or the network layer, respectively. If it is necessary to connect two nodes that do not share a common protocol, a gateway or protocol converter can be used to make the connection. Naturally, the gateway must be able to understand the protocol of the two nodes being connected and also must be able to translate from one protocol to the other. The components of a gateway are the network interfaces and the logic that carries out the conversion necessary when moving messages between networks. The conversion must change the header and trailer of the packet to make it consistent with the protocol of the network or data link to which the message is being transferred. This may include accommodating differences in speed, packet sizes, and packet formats. If both a LAN and a WAN interface to an X.25 network, the X.25 network can serve as a gateway that allows stations on the LAN and the WAN to communicate; in this case, there are two gateways, one from the LAN to the X.25 network and one from the X.25 network to the WAN. This is illustrated in Figure 12-13.

Which Interface Is Right for You?

We have defined three network interconnection capabilities: repeaters, bridges, and routers. How do you choose the right one? In general, you should choose the connection at the lowest OSI level possible. Thus, a repeater is usually preferable to a bridge, and a bridge is usually preferable to a router. As you move up the OSI layers, your connection must be more intelligent, do more work, and have a lower packet exchange rate. These are not the only deciding factors, however.

A bridge can replace a repeater, and a router can replace a repeater or a bridge; however, the opposite is not always true. A repeater cannot always substitute for a bridge and a bridge cannot always substitute for a router. If you have the option of using a repeater, you might instead choose to use a bridge. This decision makes sense if the bridge can handle the message traffic and if you already have the bridge components. A bridge also allows some

Figure 12-13

LAN-WAN Interconnection
Using an X.25 Network

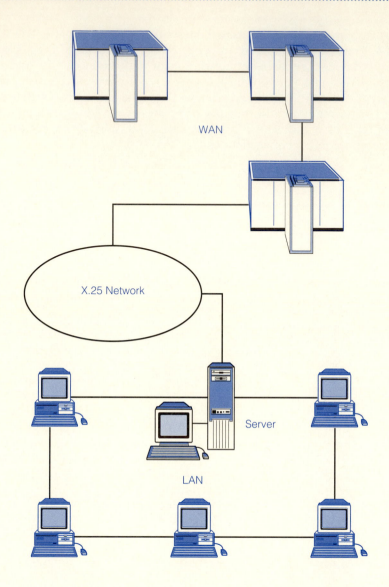

LAN isolation capability that a repeater does not provide. Thus, you might choose a bridge over a repeater to provide an extra level of network security.

LAN-TO-HOST CONNECTIONS

The preceding discussion explored ways of connecting networks, specifically, ways in which a LAN can be connected to another LAN or to a WAN. For many companies another LAN connection need is that of connecting a LAN to a stand-alone computer.

Many companies entered the microcomputer age with a large computer already installed. As these companies increased their use of microcomputers

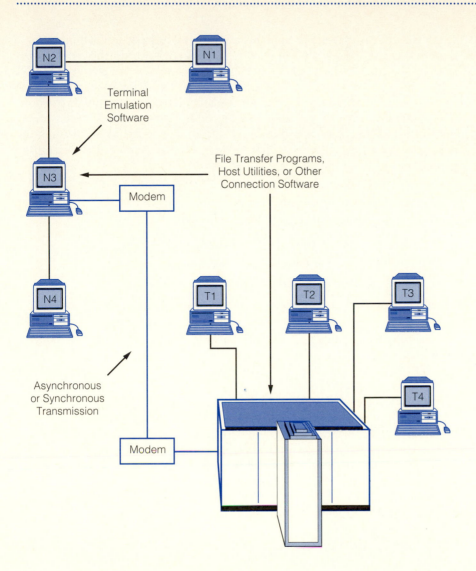

Figure 12-14

LAN-to-Host Connection

Terminal
Emulation
Software

File Transfer Programs,
Host Utilities, or Other
Connection Software

Modem

Asynchronous
or Synchronous
Transmission

Modem

and then installed one or more LANs, the large computer continued to play
an important role in those companies' computing needs. For example, the
large computer, often called a host, might be used for payroll or large database
applications. Even companies that replaced or are replacing the host with
LAN technology go through a period when both computing environments
exist. Companies that use hosts and LANs usually need to exchange data
between the two environments. This can be done via media exchange: Data
on the host can be copied onto a disk or tape and transferred to the LAN and
vice versa. Often, a LAN-host direct connection is a more efficient way to
accomplish data exchange. Figure 12-14 illustrates a host computer connected
to a LAN. Before discussing the ways in which the LAN-host connection can
be made, we look at several ways in which a LAN user can interact with a
host.

In Figure 12-14, a user at Node N1 might need to view, update, or evaluate data that is stored in the host's database. This user can do the work on the host or she can do the work on her LAN workstation. A user at Node N2 might need to send an electronic mail message to a user at Terminal T1. A user at Node N3 might need to run an application that exists only on the host. The application may be available only on the host for a variety of reasons: It has not yet been implemented on the LAN, it needs special hardware available only on the host (such as a typesetting machine), or it requires computing power beyond that available on the LAN.

The three preceding examples cover most of the general connection needs of LAN users. These needs can be summarized as follows:

- using host data and applications
- transferring data from host to LAN or LAN to host
- using host hardware or software resources
- communicating with host users

A host user will likely have the same basic needs for LAN resources. You have already read about two ways in which a LAN-host connection can be made, routers and gateways. We now consider some other ways these connections can be made.

The Host as a LAN Node

Some hosts have the ability to connect to the LAN as a node. This is the most effective way of establishing the connection. The host can thus operate as a server, providing all of the above needs.

Asynchronous Connections

In Chapter 9 we discussed the asynchronous data link protocol. Virtually every computer has the ability to send and receive asynchronously. You are probably familiar with the term *serial port* on a microcomputer. The serial port is an asynchronous communications port. Because most computers support this protocol, it is sometimes used to link a microcomputer to a host. Usually a microcomputer attached to a host asynchronously operates in one of two modes, file transfer or terminal emulation. Terminal emulation software capabilities are listed in Table 12-5.

Dedicated Connection per Microcomputer   Host computers can usually accommodate many asynchronous connections. Small minicomputers will usually support 32 or more, and large mainframes may accommodate hundreds. One way to connect a LAN node to a host is to provide a direct connection between a port on the host and each microcomputer needing a host connection. This is illustrated in Figure 12-15. In the figure, nodes N1, N2, N4, and N5 each have a dedicated connection to the host. Nodes N3 and N6 are not connected to the host.

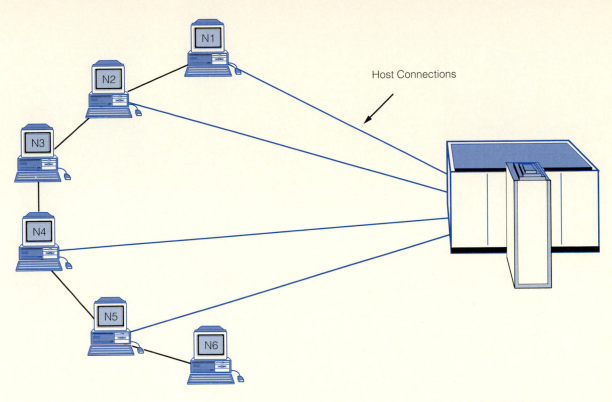

Host Connections

Figure 12-15

Multiple Direct LAN-to-Host
Connections

TABLE 12-5   Terminal Emulation Software Capabilities

Scripts

Mouse support

File transfer: CompuServe, XModem, YModem, Kermit

Terminal emulation: ANSI, DEC VT 220, IBM 3101, TTY

Electronic mail

Phone directory

Capture of data to a disk

Text editor

Password security

A **dedicated connection** provides direct host access and the microcomputer does not use LAN resources for communicating with the host. The typical connection has the microcomputer appear to the host as though the microcomputer were a host terminal. In addition to the serial port, the microcomputer needs terminal emulation software to establish the connection and carry on a host session. Terminal emulation software is available from many sources and has the ability to emulate a wide variety of terminals. With dedicated connections, the LAN administrator and data processing depart-

dedicated connection   A connection providing direct access to the host using non-LAN resources for communication between the host and the microcomputer.

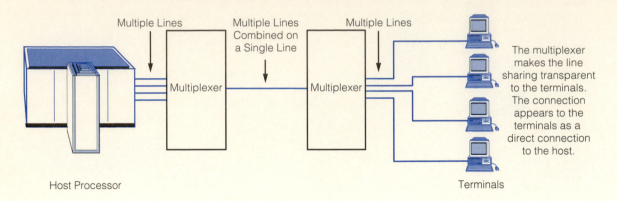

Multiple Lines   Multiple Lines   Multiple Lines
                        Combined on
                        a Single Line

Multiplexer   Multiplexer

The multiplexer
makes the line
sharing transparent
to the terminals.
The connection
appears to the
terminals as a
direct connection
to the host.

Host Processor   Terminals

Figure 12-16

A Multiplexer Connection

ment can easily control which LAN nodes have access to the host. Nodes without a direct connection will be unable to make a host connection.

A dedicated connection has several disadvantages. First, as with all asynchronous connections, the speed of the link is slow. Asynchronous speeds can be faster than 100,000 bits per second (bps), but typically for microcomputer connections the speed is 19,200 bps or less. If many LAN nodes must communicate with the host, many host ports will be required. This not only reduces the number of ports available to the host's terminal users but also is somewhat costly. The cost for host ports can be significant and is burdensome for microcomputers that need only occasional access. Finally, when operating in terminal emulation mode, the microcomputer loses some of its processing capabilities. It can essentially do only what a terminal can do. Specifically, the microcomputer can send and receive data but (usually) cannot use this interface to have a local application, such as a database management system, directly access data on the host.

multiplexer A hardware device that allows several devices to share one communications channel.

Multiplexing   A **multiplexer** is a hardware device that allows several devices to share one communications channel. Multiplexing typically is used to consolidate the message traffic between a computer and several remotely located terminals, as illustrated in Figure 12-16. This technique can also be used to allow several microcomputers to share a communications link to a host processor.

communications server A server that monitors connections to the host by determining whether there is a free port to make the connection and granting or denying the request accordingly.

Shared Asynchronous Connections   In some applications, each LAN node needs occasional access to the host but the number of concurrent connections is far fewer than the number of LAN nodes. A dedicated line per node is excessive in such situations. A better solution is to share asynchronous connections. The most common way to share connections is via a **communications server** or Front-End Processor (FEP) as illustrated in Figure 12-17.

In the figure, the communications server has four connections to the host. A microcomputer needing host services will request a connection through the communications server. If all four ports are in use, the request will be denied. If a host port is free, the request will be honored and the microcomputer will be connected to a vacant host port. You might note that the communications server functions much like a telephone switch.

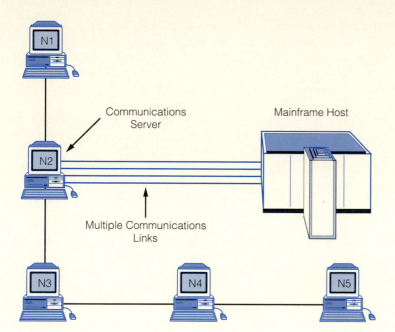

Figure 12-17

LAN-to-Host Connections
Using a Communications
Server

Communications servers also may provide connections for remote hosts. The usual way a connection is made to a remote host is via a modem connection. The line to the remote host may be dedicated or switched. A dedicated line is continuously available; a switched line connection is established on an as-needed basis. The typical example of a switched line is a dial-up telephone line. The link between two devices is made via a telephone call, remains active during the length of the session, and is broken when the session is completed. Rather than providing each LAN node with a dedicated modem, the communications server can provide modem sharing. The technique for doing this is much like the sharing technique described in the previous paragraph.

Other Types of Host Connections

Asynchronous connections are common because they are easily implemented and are supported by most host systems. On the microcomputer side, all that is necessary is a serial port and terminal emulation or file transfer software. The only host-specific characteristic is the type of terminal being emulated or the file transfer software. Other types of vendor-specific connections exist.

IBM System Connections

Because of the dominant role played by IBM systems, many of these connections are based on IBM software and hardware technologies. These connections might also work on non-IBM equipment because many large-computer companies support one or more IBM communications protocols. Two of the most common IBM interfaces are described here.

IBM-3270 Emulation   A mainstay of IBM's communications networks is the family of 3270 terminals. The family consists of a variety of terminals, printers, and cluster controllers. The communication protocol used for 3270 devices is a synchronous protocol, either binary synchronous (BISYNC) or synchronous data link control (SDLC), both of which were discussed in Chapter 9.

IBM-3270 emulation can be effected through a communications server or through individual LAN nodes. When emulation is implemented at individual LAN nodes, a synchronous communications controller must be installed in the microcomputer. The controller provides the necessary line interface. If a communications server is used, the server must have a synchronous communications port. Aside from the protocol interface, the connection works much like the asynchronous connection described earlier.

LU 6.2 Connection   For many years IBM networks have been designed around IBM's Systems Network Architecture (SNA), which is discussed in Chapter 11. In SNA users communicate through sessions and a variety of session types are defined. Logical Units (LUs) represent users in establishing, using, and ending a session. One type of session allows programs to communicate with other programs. This type of session is called an LU 6.2 session. Support for LU 6.2 sessions is available for microcomputers and is being increasingly used to establish host connections. The advantage of an LU 6.2 interface is that a microcomputer application can communicate directly with a host application or with an application on another network node (as opposed to the microcomputer simply acting as though it were a terminal).

INTERCONNECTION UTILITIES

Having the ability to establish network connections is one part of communicating among networks. Another part is having utilities that help you exploit those connections. Many such utilities are available. Some are commercial products whereas others are available in the public domain for no or little cost. Some utilities you may find useful are briefly described below.

file transfer utility   An intrinsic part of many routers, this utility allows files to be moved between network nodes.

File Transfer Utilities   File transfer utilities allow you to move files between network nodes. File transfer capabilities are an intrinsic part of many routers. Part of the TCP/IP protocol suite is a file transfer capability. Kermit is another file transfer utility that runs on a wide variety of computer platforms. It uses asynchronous communications links to transfer ASCII format files. Two common microcomputer file transfer utilities are XMODEM and YMODEM. Kermit, XMODEM, and YMODEM are often included in terminal emulation programs.

remote login facility   A network utility that allows users to log onto a remote system by establishing the remote user as a local user on the remote node.

Remote Login   Remote login facilities allow users to logon to a remote system. A remote login essentially establishes a remote user as a local user on the remote node. Once a user has successfully logged on to the remote node, commands issued by that user are processed and acted on by the remote node rather than by the local node. When the user logs off from the remote node, his session is reestablished on the local node.

Access Servers   **Access servers** allow remote microcomputers to access LAN resources remotely. Suppose you are working at your home microcomputer and must do some work at your office. Specifically, you may have remembered that you had a report due in the morning. If the software, files, and electronic mail essential to creating and distributing the report are available only on the LAN in your office, you have two options: You can drive to the office to complete the work or you can use the facilities of an access server. To access your LAN remotely, you need a serial port and a modem and a modem on the LAN end plus the communications software. This type of connection was described earlier.

Access servers provide more than just modem connections. If you tried to run a LAN application such as word processing remotely, the word processing program would have to be downloaded into your computer. If your line speed is 2400 bits per second (bps) and the size of the application is 360 Kb, it will take at least 25 minutes to download the program (2400 bps is about 240 characters per second). This level of performance is hardly acceptable. An access server is one solution to this problem. The access server runs applications at the LAN end of the connection and passes only the monitor display and keyboard data over the communications link. The remote processing can be accomplished by connections to remote access CPU boards (the user essentially has a dedicated remote CPU at the LAN) or by multiprocessing on a high-capacity microcomputer. The two approaches to access server technology are illustrated in Figure 12-18.

access server   An interconnection utility that allows remote microcomputers to access LAN resources from remote locations.

Figure 12-18

Two Remote Access Server Technologies

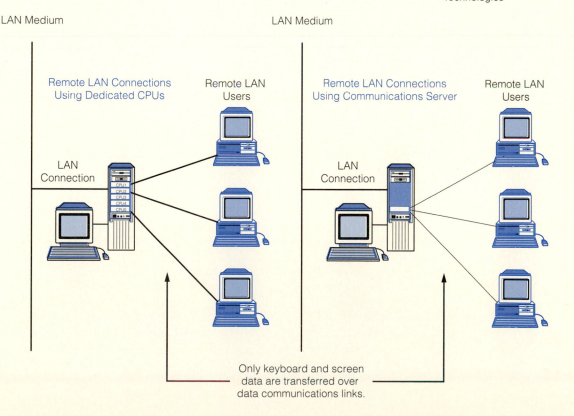

LAN Medium

LAN Medium

Remote LAN Connections Using Dedicated CPUs

Remote LAN Users

LAN Connection

Remote LAN Connections Using Communications Server

Remote LAN Users

LAN Connection

Only keyboard and screen data are transferred over data communications links.

SUMMARY

Networks are not necessarily isolated islands of computing. Often there is a need to connect several LAN segments, connect homogeneous but separate LANs, connect heterogeneous LANs, connect LANs to WANs, connect one WAN to another WAN, or connect LANs to a single host. These connections can be made in many ways.

Repeaters are used to connect segments of a homogeneous LAN and thereby extend the length of the LAN medium. Repeaters operate at the physical level. They simply accept a signal from one segment, amplify or regenerate the signal, and forward the signal the next segment.

Bridges connect homogeneous but distinct LANs. A bridge operates at the data link (MAC) level. A bridge receives a packet, looks at its destination address, and, if the address is a node on a LAN other than the one on which the packet was received, the bridge transmits the packet onto another LAN. Most of today's bridges are learning bridges. Learning bridges use spanning tree or source routing algorithms to learn the location of network nodes. Learning bridges can adapt to changes in network paths.

Routers operate at the network layer and can connect homogeneous or heterogeneous networks. A router receives a message, determines the address of the destination, and chooses a route for the message to take. The message may travel through several intermediate networks to reach the destination. Different data link protocols may be used in moving the message from the source to its recipient. Because they operate at the network layer, routers are independent of data link protocols.

A gateway is a name applied to network connections between heterogeneous networks. A gateway must perform translation functions such as packet formatting, speed conversion, error checking, and so on.

Sometimes LAN nodes must be connected to a host machine. A variety of connection types exist. Some hosts can connect directly to the LAN and operate as a LAN node. Asynchronous connections are common and easy to implement but are quite slow. Synchronous connections offer greater speed but usually require additional microcomputer hardware. Because of the wide variety of connection services available, you should be able to find ready-made solutions to most of your LAN connection needs.

KEY TERMS

access server, *419*

active port, *404*

bridge, *393*

brouter, *399*

communications server, *416*

Connectionless Network Protocol (CLNP), *410*

dedicated connection, *415*

discovery packet, *405*

file transfer utility, *418*

flooding, *404*

gateway, *395*

inactive port, *404*

learning bridge (transparent bridge), *402*

multiplexer, *416*

REVIEW QUESTIONS

1. Give two reasons that a company might have two LANs in the same general location.

2. Identify the OSI level at which each of the following operates.

   a. bridge

   b. repeater

   c. router

3. Under what conditions can a repeater be used? What does a repeater do?

4. What does a bridge do? Under what conditions can a bridge be used?

5. What does a router do? Under what conditions can a router be used?

6. Compare the capabilities of repeaters, bridges, and routers.

7. Describe how TCP/IP sends a message from a node on one network to a node on another network.

8. Besides providing network interconnections, list three other functions you might find in TCP/IP.

9. What is a gateway?

10. Describe three distinct LAN-to-host interfaces.

11. What are the advantages and disadvantages of asynchronous LAN-to-host interfaces?

12. Describe two common types of microcomputer interfaces to IBM systems.

PROBLEMS AND EXERCISES

1. Evaluate the following LAN situations. State whether the LANs can be consolidated with a repeater, bridge, or router. Give all possible types of connection. State which connection alternative you would choose and state why you chose it.

   a. A token ring and a token bus.

   b. Two IEEE 802.3 LANs. One LAN has a total cable span of 1000 meters and the other has a total cable span of 2500 meters.

   c. Two IEEE 802.3 LANs. Each has a total cable span of 1000 meters. Assume that the cable being used meets the IEEE 802.3 standard for maximum segment lengths of 500 meters and a maximum distance of 2500 meters per LAN.

   d. Three Novell LANS. One LAN is ARCnet, one is a token ring, and one is a CSMA/CD bus.

2. Your company has two IEEE 802.3 LANs, one in your eastern office and one in your western office (the distance between them is several hundred miles). The company wants to connect these LANs so users can more easily exchange data. The data being exchanged is primarily small messages, such as electronic mail messages and small data files. Occasionally a file several megabytes in size must be exchanged but in these situations, the exchange is not time critical (for example, it could occur overnight). Devise a way to connect these LANs. Describe the type and speed of communications channel you would use to make the connection. Explain your decision.

3. Suppose the two LANs described in problem 2 were different, such as a token ring and a CSMA/CD bus. Would your decision be different? Explain any differences and the reason for your decision.

4. Suppose the situation in problem 2 were different in that the large files (2 MB or less) had to be exchanged within two minutes or less. Would your solution to the connection be different? Explain any differences and the reason for your decision.

5. A company has two large computers connected by a synchronous communications line having a speed of 56Kbps. These computers are geographically separated, one in the eastern office and one in the western office. Each location also has a LAN. The company wants to allow all computer users, those connected to the LANs as well as those connected to the large computers, to be able to communicate. Can the connection be made using the existing communications link? Explain your answer.

6. Assuming the existing communications link described in Problem 5 were used for the long-distance connection, answer each of the following:

    a. How can the LANs be connected to the large systems?

    b. Describe the changes a LAN packet will undergo as it moves from a LAN, to a large system, to the other large system, and then to the other LAN. Assume the LANs are homogeneous.

REFERENCES

Byrnes, Philippe. "Using SNA to Link LAN to Host." *LAN Technology*, Volume 6, Number 12, December 1990.

Comer, Douglas E. *Internetworking with TCP/IP*. Englewood Cliffs, NJ: Prentice Hall, 1991.

Derfler, Frank J., Jr., and Rigney, Steve. "Bringing Your Networks Together." *PC Magazine*, Volume 10, Number 15, September 10, 1991.

Dryden, Patrick. "LAN Bridges Get Cheaper, More Powerful." *LAN Times*, Volume 8, Issue 19, October 7, 1991.

Duncan, Thom. "Comparing TCP/IP Gateways." *LAN Times*, Volume 7, Issue 8, August 1990.

Nolle, Thomas. "Making the LAN-to-WAN Connection." *LAN Technology*, Volume 5, Number 9, September 1989.

Sheltzer, Alan, and Blotter, Ned. "Making the LAN-to-Mini Connection." *LAN Technology*, Volume 7, Number 5, May 1991.

Stephenson, Peter. "Mixing and Matching LANs." *Byte*, Volume 16, Number 3, March 1991.

13

Network Management Objectives

CHAPTER OBJECTIVES

After studying this chapter you should be able to:

- Present a brief history of network management
- List the objectives of network management
- Describe ways of meeting network management objectives
- Describe the network management organization
- Distinguish between managing a WAN and managing a LAN

*O*nce a network is installed and operational, it must be managed. Proper management keeps the network components functioning in an optimal way. In this chapter we look at some techniques and tools for network management. This chapter begins with a discussion of the objectives and functions of network management, and how those objectives can be met. You then learn about both generic and specific network management systems and some of the issues surrounding managing a WAN and managing a LAN.

HISTORY OF NETWORK MANAGEMENT

The network management team has historically been responsible for the selection, implementation, testing, expansion, operation, and maintenance of the data communications portion of the data-processing environment because early networks were concerned with the transmission of character-oriented data. Currently, data being transmitted by high-speed networks also includes graphics, voice clips, and video. Some companies are also combining telephone services with computer data on the same medium. With the integration of voice, data, and video transmissions on a common medium, the role of network management is expanding to include management of the entire telecommunications needs of an organization. In the past, voice, video, and data communications were usually separate and were managed by different groups. In today's communications environment, integrating and sharing media and hardware components can produce significant savings for a company. Despite these changes, covering all facets of telecommunications management is beyond the scope of this text. In this chapter we confine the discussion to management of a data communications network.

The role of network manager, like that of database administrator, is a relatively new position within the data-processing industry. Both positions were created by the technological expansion of the 1970s and the recognition of the increasing importance of these technologies to the storage, retrieval, and maintenance of business data. These positions are similar in several respects. Both have high visibility among system users. The database administrator is called when required data is unavailable. If terminals do not work or response time is unsatisfactory, the network manager is notified. Both roles are responsible for configurations, planning, tuning, and establishing standards and procedures in their respective areas. Both positions require personnel with a strong technical background, good leadership qualities, and an ability to work well with people who have wide ranges of technical expertise. In the remainder of this chapter, the terms **network manager**, **network administrator**, and **LAN administrator** refer to the function of network management, and therefore to a team of people rather than to a single individual.

network manager   An individual or management team responsible for configuring, planning, tuning, and establishing standards and procedures for a network. Also known as a network administrator or LAN administrator.

NETWORK MANAGEMENT OBJECTIVES

The three primary objectives of network management are to:

- support system users
- keep the network operating efficiently
- provide cost-effective solutions to an organization's telecommunications requirements

If these three objectives are met, the network management team will be successful.

Supporting System Users

Supporting system users means empowering them with the hardware and software tools to do their jobs effectively. Essentially it means keeping the network users satisfied. User satisfaction can also be enhanced by:

- providing proper user training
- forewarning users of periods when the network will be taken out of operation
- fixing problems that limit user access to required network resources
- keeping users informed of system changes and their consequences

Keeping the user community informed is one of the easiest and most overlooked ways to achieve user satisfaction. Users should be informed of scheduled down time, imminent down time, periods when other processing requirements are likely to adversely affect response times, certain changes in hardware or software, and changes in personnel with whom users will be interfacing. This information can be disseminated in several ways, the most direct being to reserve a portion of the terminal output area for system or network news bulletins. Users are generally understanding when down time is unanticipated and no prior warning is possible. On the other hand, users may be less understanding if they arrive on Saturday afternoon to catch up on some work and find the system down for a scheduled but unannounced reason. Many systems can send notices to users when they logon to the system and can send notice of system status for short-term, emergency network interruptions.

Another useful communication medium is newsletters, which can alert users to down times scheduled for preventive maintenance and reconfigurations, announce new capabilities, serve as a training aid, answer frequently asked questions, solicit comments and suggestions, and generally help people feel they are an integral part of the network team. Newsletters are able to reach all users of a system and so are a valuable communication resource.

Meetings between users and the network management team should be held at least quarterly. Mature systems not undergoing change may require meetings less frequently than those that are new, changing, or experiencing problems. Such forums can serve to air grievances, disseminate information, propose new ideas, educate both users and network managers, resolve problems, plan for future changes, and establish new goals. For more hands-on communication, formal and informal training can be helpful. Some companies find informal seminars at lunchtime or after hours a very effective way to exchange information. Formal training classes serve not only to educate users but also to establish contacts within the organization. New users, in particular, will find it easier to call on an expert should a problem arise if they have been given an opportunity to work with that individual during a non-crisis situation.

Measures of System Effectiveness

A system is effective if it provides good performance, is available when needed, and is reliable when being used. If all three factors are present, the system will be effective.

Good Performance   Good performance means a predictable transaction response time. Response time depends on the nature of the transaction. Transactions differ in the amount of work to be accomplished and the number of characters to be transmitted. For every transaction in the system, a realistic response time objective should be established. Predictable response times require that most transactions be completed within a small range around the established response time goal. For example, for an expected transaction response time of 10 seconds, it is realistic to expect 95% of all transactions of that type to be completed within 9–11 seconds and 100% of such transactions to be completed within 20 seconds. Erratic response times are generally perceived by users to be worse than slow but predictable responses. Of the two response time components—processing time and communications time—the network manager ordinarily has little or no control over the application processing and database access components, but does have control over configuration and line speed. The configuration aspects include the number of terminals on a given line, hardware employed (such as multiplexers, front-end processors, and concentrators), types of terminals used, number of intermediate nodes through which the message must travel (hops), networking software, and error characteristics. Each of these affects the performance of the system.

availability   All necessary components of a network are operable and accessible when a user requires them.

Availability   Availability means that all necessary components are operable and accessible when a user requires them; for a terminal operator, these include the terminal, cables, connectors, modems, medium or media, controllers, processors, and software. Accessibility means the user can make use of the component when needed. In a network that has 10 available modems and 100 users, all modems may be operable, but if all are in use when a user requests a modem connection, a modem is not available. Three factors influence availability: operational considerations, Mean Time Between Failures (MTBF), and Mean Time to Repair (MTTR).

Operational considerations may require that portions of the system be taken out of service. Some areas of the online system may be available only during standard working hours. Thus, the payroll system may be unavailable at night, when payroll transactions are not anticipated. In some installations the online system is given priority during the day, whereas batch operations have priority on night shifts, when all or portions of the online system are shut down. Other operational requirements such as preventive maintenance and installation of new hardware or software can remove all or parts of the system from use. Generally, operational considerations can be planned so online users are able to work without being disrupted.

Mean time between failures (MTBF) is the average period that a component will operate before failing. A CRT terminal with MTBF of 2000 hours that operates an average of 8 hours a day, 23 days a month, would be expected to fail once every $2000/(8 \times 23) = 10.86$ months. MTBF figures are provided by manufacturers to indicate the reliability of their products. The figures provided are sometimes unreliable and should not be assumed to be exact. Also, an MTBF figure does not predict the reliability of a single component. Mean time to repair (MTTR) is the average amount of time required to place a failed component back into service. For certain components, repair time is relatively constant, such as replacing a failed modem with a spare. For a CPU, however, there may be considerable variations in repair time. CPU repairs often require the repair person to travel to the site and run a varying number of diagnostic routines and testing procedures. Availability can be defined by the following probability function (Nickel, 1978):

$$A(t) = \frac{a}{a + b} + \frac{b}{a + b}e^{-(a + b)t}$$

where $a = 1/\text{MTTR}$, $b = 1/\text{MTBF}$, e is the natural logarithm, and t is a time interval. The equation gives the probability that a component will be available when required by a user. For a terminal with an MTBF of 2000 hours and an MTTR of 0.5 hours (typical of replacement with an onsite spare),

$$a = 1/0.5 = 2 \text{ and } b = 1/2000 = 0.0005$$

Availability for an 8-hour period, then, is

$$A(8) = \frac{2}{2 + 0.0005} + \frac{0.0005e^{-(2 + 0.0005)8}}{2 + 0.0005}$$

$$= \frac{2}{2.0005} + \frac{(0.0005)(0.0000001121)}{2.005}$$

$$= 0.99975 + 2.8 \times 10^{-11} = 0.9997$$

On average, an operator can expect the terminal to be unavailable three times in every 10,000 tries. Because the exponential term approaches zero and becomes insignificant as the time interval increases, availability in such cases becomes

$$A = \frac{MTBF}{MTBF + MTTR}$$

Table 13-1 shows availability given different values for MTBF and MTTR.

Availability with Multiple Components   If several components — such as terminal, modem, medium, and CPU — must be linked together to make the system available to the user, then system availability is given by the product of the availabilities of the component parts (Nickel, 1978):

$$A_s = A_t \times A_m \times A_l \times A_m \times A_c$$

TABLE 13-1   Availability for Several MTBF and MTTR Values

MTTR	MTBF				
	10	*100*	*1000*	*10,000*	*100,000*
1	0.90909091	0.99009901	0.99900100	0.99990001	0.99999000
2	0.83333333	0.98039216	0.99800399	0.99980004	0.99998000
5	0.66666667	0.95238095	0.99502488	0.99950025	0.99995000
10	0.50000000	0.90909091	0.99009901	0.99900100	0.99990001
20	0.33333333	0.83333333	0.98039216	0.99800399	0.99980004

where A represents availability and the subscripts s, t, m, l, m, and c represent the system, terminal, modem, link, modem, and CPU, respectively. If each component has an availability of 0.999, the user will see a system availability of

$$A_s = 0.999^5 = 0.995$$

In this situation, statistically the user would find the system unavailable 5 times every 1000 attempts, or once every 200 attempts. The availability factor is important in determining how many spare components to stock and how much productive time might be lost when the system is unavailable. Figure 13-1 illustrates system availability as a function of MTBF and MTTR.

reliability   The probability that the system will continue to function over a given operating period.

Reliability   Reliability is the probability that the system will continue to function over a given operating period. If a transaction requires 3 seconds for a response to be received, then the reliability of the system is the probability that the system will not fail during that 3 seconds. Reliability of the network includes error characteristics of the medium and stability of the hardware and software components. More specifically, network reliability is a function of the MTBF. In some cases the user will see circuit errors in the form of slow response times. Data received in error will cause retransmissions, slower response times, and congestion of the medium. If the errors are persistent, the retry threshold for the link might be exceeded and the link consequently removed from service. For some modems, a large number of errors will cause the modem to change to a lower speed to minimize the impact of the errors. Failure of hardware and software components is usually seen by the user as down time on the system. With fault-tolerant systems the effect is either negligible or somewhat slower response times, depending on the system load. Even though the processor and all components of the system except one are functioning properly, the user, who is unable to continue working because of that one failed component, views the system as being down.

The reliability function, which is the probability that the system will not fail during a given period, is given by (Nickel, 1978):

$$R(t) = e^{-bt}$$

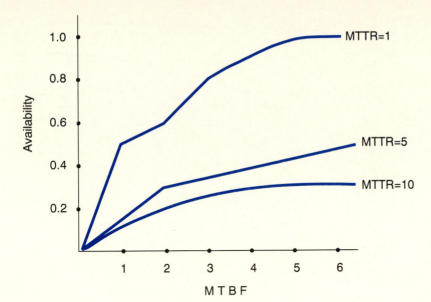

Figure 13-1

Availability, MTBF, and MTTR

where b is the inverse of the MTBF, as described earlier. The time units used for MTBF and t must be the same. If the MTBF for a terminal is 2000 hours, and a transaction requires 1 minute to complete, then the reliability is

$$R(160) = e^{-(1/2000)(1/60)}$$

$$= e^{-(1/120,000)} = 0.999992$$

All times are expressed in hours. This equation shows that if the terminal is available at the beginning of the transaction, the probability is high that it will remain available throughout a 1-minute transaction.

Reliability with Multiple Components   Like availability, system reliability is the product of the reliability of its components. If a system consists of a terminal, a medium, two modems, and a CPU, the reliability of the system from the user's perspective is

$$R_s = R_t \times R_m \times R_l \times R_m \times R_c$$

where s, t, m, l, m, and c represent the reliability of the system, terminal, modem, medium link, modem, and CPU, respectively. Figure 13-2 shows reliability as a function of the MTBF.

Overall Effectiveness   The overall **effectiveness** of a system is a measure of how well it serves users' needs. Mathematically, effectiveness is given by the following formula:

$$E = A \times R$$

where E is the effectiveness, A is the availability, and R is the reliability of the system. The formula shows that, for a given system effectiveness, when R is

effectiveness   A measure of how well a system serves users' needs.

Figure 13-2

Reliability and MTBF

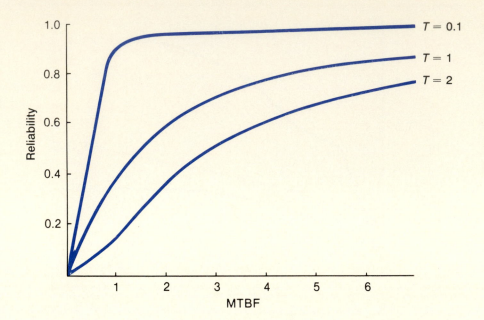

greater than A the amount of time available for repairing a fault increases, whereas if A is greater than R the repair time is reduced (Nickel, 1978). Because R is entirely a function of the MTBF, an increase in R means that more time can be devoted to repairing the system to attain the same overall effectiveness. This is illustrated in Figure 13-3.

Reliability of Backup Components   In many networks, alternate components are available should one component fail. Communication paths frequently have alternate links available, and fault-tolerant systems have available a backup CPU, disk drive, or other components. These backup components increase the MTBF of the system, which increases reliability, availability, and effectiveness. With backup components available, the reliability of the components operating in parallel is given by (Nickel, 1978):

$$R_p = 1 - (1 - R_s)^2$$

where R represents reliability, p represents the components operating in parallel, and s represents a single component. If the reliability of a communications link is 0.995, the reliability of the link with a backup is

$$R = 1 - (1 - 0.995)^2 = 0.999975$$

Cost-Effectiveness

The third objective of network management is to provide cost-effective solutions to the data communications needs of an organization. As shown in previous chapters, there are many solutions to communications problems. Network management is responsible for selecting solutions that are feasible

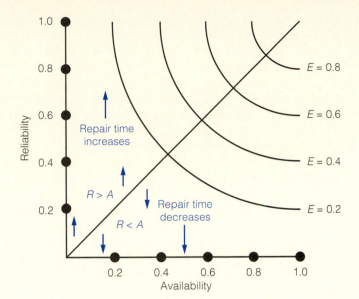

Figure 13-3

Reliability, Availability, and Effectiveness

and cost-efficient. If the network is unable to contribute positively to the financial position of a company, it probably should not be implemented.

Prior Planning   Prior planning is one way to save money. In configuring a network two basic alternatives exist: installing equipment to meet immediate needs and paying the price of upgrading when the time comes — which sometimes leads to lower immediate costs but a higher cost of expansion — or immediately buying equipment in anticipation of future needs — which creates higher immediate costs, with relatively low-cost, easy expansion. Buying immediately for future needs is sometimes risky because technology changes so quickly. Usually the best alternative is to purchase modular equipment, which can be upgraded in small increments so overpurchasing is seldom necessary and expansion is relatively easy. A variation of this approach is the planned movement of equipment, whereby lower-capacity equipment is gradually pushed outward and absorbed elsewhere in the network as newer, higher-capacity equipment is acquired.

Modular Expansion   Modular growth is available for several network components, the most fundamental being the computer itself. Many computer vendors offer a broad line of systems that allow growth within the product line. Most vendors have several different models spanning the distance between small systems and very large systems, and within each model there is also a certain amount of growth potential. The transition from one model to another is not always easy, often requiring a recompilation of programs and frequently causing significant rewrites. When an organization has finally reached the top of one model line and is ready to upgrade to the next model, the processors, operating systems, and network software often are not the same as those in current use, even if they are produced by the same vendor.

modular expansion   A
single-vendor system that
allows the user to upgrade
from a small system to a
more powerful system by
adding more of the same
type of processor to the
existing system.

This approach can be contrasted with those vendors' systems that allow **modular expansion** from a relatively small system to an extremely powerful one by adding more of the same type of processor. There is no need to remove, sell, or return the existing equipment; it is simply augmented to provide the additional processing power. Computer vendors that offer this capability, such as Tandem Computers, Inc., and Stratus Computers, Inc., often have systems designed for the transaction processing market, where expansion is very common. Modular expansion is also possible with front-end processors (FEPs) and multiplexers. Some vendors offer multiplexers that can be expanded from 4 to 32 or more lines, in increments of 4, 8, or 16 lines, so the user company pays for the cost of expansion only when necessary.

Planned Equipment Moves   Planned equipment moves are an alternative when modular expansion is not possible. For example, the central site could begin with a four-port multiplexer, with remote sites also having four-port multiplexers. As the number of applications in a remote site grows, the central-site four-port mux could be moved there, a new eight-port mux added to the central site, and the old four-port mux used in a new location or cascaded off the eight-port mux. This is illustrated in Figure 13-4. Similarly, low-speed modems can be moved to lower traffic locations as they are replaced by high-speed modems. If the older equipment is not needed, it could be kept in inventory to be used as replacements for failed equipment. This type of activity requires longer range planning than the other options; however, the financial rewards may make it preferable to the disposal of old equipment—possibly at a significant loss—every time a new piece is acquired.

Figure 13-4

Relocation of Components

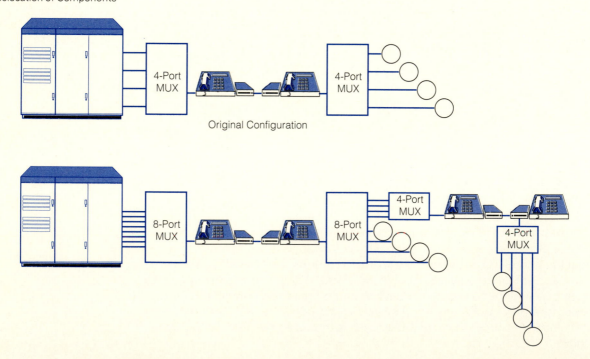

MEETING THE OBJECTIVES

The objectives of network management are met by a combination of competent staff, hard work, careful planning, good documentation, implementing standards and procedures, communicating with users, and being able to work with other people to resolve problems. Although every one of these elements may not be present in a successful network, the probability of success is directly proportional to how well these elements are realized.

Competent Staff

The most important element is creating a competent staff, who can even overcome deficiencies in other areas. Specific staff qualifications depend on the hardware and software employed, but some generalizations can be made. The functions of network management can be grouped into the areas of design and configuration, testing, diagnosis, documentation, repair, and, on rare occasions, coding. The team must have detailed knowledge of both hardware and software; ideally, every member of the team would know both areas, but often one person is an expert on hardware, whereas another's specialty is software. The staff should be versatile and creative in resolving problems, because many solutions are ad hoc, temporary ones that require ingenuity. Finally, and perhaps most important, staff should be able to work well with both technical and nontechnical personnel. Being able to describe the technology to those not "in the know" and to elicit the necessary technical information from nontechnical users is critical to the team's success.

Design and Configuration

The staff should be skilled in use of the diagnostic and planning tools described later in this chapter. In design and configuration, they should be knowledgeable of configuration alternatives and their strengths and weaknesses. They must be willing and able to keep up with changes in hardware and software of the existing system as well as capabilities continually offered by other vendors, including a multitude of different tariff structures from a growing number of common carriers.

Diagnosis

Skill in diagnosing the cause of problems, often under considerable pressure, is essential. Whenever a problem in a production system is encountered that disables all or a portion of an online application, immediate resolution is needed. A failed system prevents employees from fully performing their job functions and decreases productivity. In some situations, direct revenue is also lost, such as in an airline reservation system.

Planning

Planning is another key to success. Because of the dynamic nature of networks, constant planning and replanning are necessary to ensure that objectives are met. Too often, network managers are so caught up in day-to-day activities that they ignore longer range planning. This type of behavior is both common and self-perpetuating. Without good planning, problems occur more frequently and require a greater amount of time to be solved. There is often truth to the adage, "If you fail to plan, you plan to fail." Corporate goals are set by upper-level management. Planning that defines the actions essential to accomplishing these goals should include short-term and long-term objectives. Short-term planning includes scheduling of personnel, hiring, training, budgeting, and network maintenance and enhancement activities. Long-term planning involves predicting and resolving expansion issues, integrating new technologies, and budgeting.

Documentation, Standards, and Procedures

Documentation, standards, and procedures are an outgrowth of good planning. Good documentation includes listings of the software, logic diagrams, internal and external specifications for the system, wiring and connection diagrams, hardware specifications, and users' manuals. Documentation is used in all phases of the management of the network. Standards and procedures together provide consistency in system management. Standards set minimal acceptable levels of performance and implementation. Procedural guidelines aid in operating and maintaining the system and are especially necessary in resolving problem situations.

In summary, meeting network management objectives requires a group of talented individuals who:

- have the right tools in place
- have a well-defined but flexible direction for the short term and the long term
- are willing to work unusual hours in sometimes difficult or stressful environments
- can work effectively with people at all levels of capability

The growth in network management has placed large demands on the supply of qualified people. As a result, network management personnel are currently among the most difficult to find and highest paid in the computer industry.

NETWORK MANAGEMENT ORGANIZATION

Once a system has been successfully installed, tested, and made operational, the day-to-day management of the network begins. Operations tasks include monitoring, control, diagnostics, and repair. Just as application developers design a system to solve business problems, network managers should design a system — part manual, part automated — that solves the problems of operations. The manual portion of the system is necessary for restoring a down system, a task that cannot be accomplished with software when the hardware is not running.

Control

Control functions to be performed include putting failed lines or terminals back in operation, adding new lines or terminals, and taking failed components out of the system. Control of a geographically separated, multiple-computer network is somewhat more difficult, because parts of the control function must also be distributed. The distributed case is discussed here, because a subset of it applies to single-node or colocated-node networks.

Control Center   The **control center** is responsible for monitoring the network and taking corrective action where necessary. In a distributed network, it is not uncommon to have more than one control center. In a network of cooperating, independent users, such as a network of universities, each node can participate in the management and control functions, with each installation being responsible for control of its part of the network. However, the central control site is usually able to resolve any problem.

> **control center**   A network component responsible for monitoring the network and taking corrective action when necessary.

A processor may be dedicated to the control function in very large networks. Several companies provide computers and software designed specifically for network control. A network control system typically consists of special microprocessor-based modems that collect **network statistics** that are periodically transmitted to the network monitor node for storage and analysis. The monitoring systems gather information such as error rates, data rates, and the number of retransmission attempts resulting from errors. Trend analysis of this data can help determine gradual degradation so faults are immediately reported and corrective measures taken.

> **network statistics**   Information, such as error rates, data rates, and the number of retransmission attempts resulting from errors, that is collected to analyze network performance trends.

Network Monitors   The control facility must have a minimum of one or more hardware/software monitors so the management team can probe every node for problems and gather network parameters and statistics. The monitors also enable managers to make any necessary changes to the system. These include:

- bring lines and terminals into and out of service
- bring network applications to an orderly halt and start network applications
- alter network parameters, such as the process controlling a terminal
- check for line errors and implement corrections
- initiate and evaluate line traces
- run diagnostic routines
- add and delete users from the system
- control passwords for local and remote nodes
- maintain the control center database

A network database contains data about the network configuration, the release level of all software and hardware components, the names of contact individuals at remote sites, histories of problems and solutions, outside contact points for vendors, and documentation.

problem-reporting system
A system for recording and managing error reports.

Problem-Reporting System   Ideally an online **problem-reporting system** should also be available for retrieving trouble reports via keywords. This capability is especially helpful in managing a distributed network in which problems can be encountered and resolved in multiple locations simultaneously. An online problem-reporting system can help avoid having to repeatedly solve the same problem.

Problem-Reporting Procedure

Another important function of a control center is the acceptance and resolution of problems. Some solutions may lie outside the control center itself; however, the center should remain active as an intermediary in resolving the problem. This section describes a prototype control center's operation with respect to problem reporting and resolution. Although a computerized problem-reporting system is assumed, a manual system with the same functionality could exist.

Network managers should publish a problem-reporting procedure that describes the information users must gather to report a problem, and to whom the report should be made. It is assumed that users have been directed to contact their control center about network problems by telephone rather than by any automated problem-reporting system. An end user, such as a terminal operator, ordinarily should not be expected to interface with an automated problem-reporting system. When the problem report call is received, the network manager obtains all relevant information, including:

- date and time of the call
- date and time the problem was first observed
- name of the caller and how the caller might be reached
- names and contact information for any other personnel involved in the problem
- a brief but detailed description of the problem
- whether the problem is reproducible or intermittent
- possible contributing external influences such as installation of a new software release, reconfiguration, power glitches, or the equipment being used

A problem report containing the relevant information is generated and a copy returned to the reporting person. As soon as the problem is resolved, the solution is noted in the trouble report, a final copy is sent to the reporting installation, and the trouble report is marked closed. If the solution is not immediately known, the control center begins its evaluation, first searching the problem database to determine whether such a problem was resolved before. If not, then problem investigation begins. The first objective of such an investigation is to isolate the problem and pinpoint the source of the difficulty, which can involve looking at statistics and system console or log messages, initiating line traces, using line monitors, taking program dumps or traces, debugging, or running hardware diagnostics. If the problem is isolated to an area of vendor responsibility, such as network control programs, the vendor is contacted and the supporting documentation is passed to the vendor for analysis. The degree of vendor involvement varies among vendors, and even within one vendor company the support level can vary among individual customers, depending on the expertise available. Some users provide a vendor with a complete analysis and suggested solution, whereas others simply report the existence of a problem and leave the diagnostics to the vendor.

Additional Control Center Responsibilities

The additional responsibilities of the control center are creating and maintaining documentation, security, establishing procedures, release control, and training of personnel. Documentation, which should be kept current, includes operations manuals, procedures for emergency and routine activities, notification lists, contingency plans, inventory, program listings, and statistics. Security measures include creating and assigning passwords, setting user access levels, monitoring and reacting to unsuccessful logon attempts, ensuring that passwords are changed periodically, and checking physical security where applicable. Procedures should cover normal operating guidelines as well as those for handling abnormal situations such as network failures. Escalation policies that bring problems to the attention of higher management levels if the problem persists and contact names and numbers are also included. **Release control** includes the installation, testing, and implementation of new versions of hardware and software to ensure compatibility of new features with existing software and hardware, and to uncover any new problems, which are frequently introduced with new releases. Finally, training involves all levels of personnel who use or maintain the network.

release control Procedure including the installation, testing, and implementation of new versions of hardware and software to ensure compatibility of new features with existing software and hardware.

LAN VERSUS WAN MANAGEMENT

In theory, you might expect LAN management to be essentially the same as WAN management. In practice that is not usually the case. WAN management typically involves:

- geographically distributed nodes
- some local autonomy in node management and control
- diverse hardware platforms and network protocols
- a variety of media types and speeds
- third-party media vendors

Figure 13-5

Network Management in an
Enterprise Network

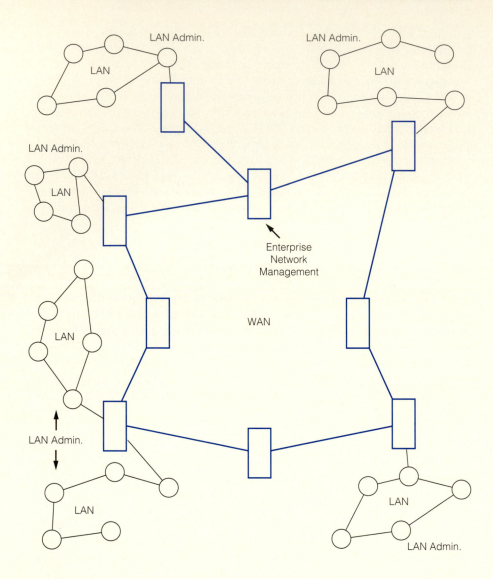

WANs typically grew out of data-processing departments and the management concerns are more technically oriented than those for LANs, which grew out of stand-alone microcomputer environments. If a site has interconnected LANs and WANs, responsibility for management of the interconnection interfaces often falls on the WAN management team. This means the WAN management team must be aware of large and small system concepts whereas the LAN administrator is not usually required to have knowledge of large systems and WANs.

Consider the enterprise network portrayed in Figure 13-5. Each LAN will likely have an administrator who is responsible for keeping the LAN functioning. The WAN managers are responsible for:

- keeping all WAN nodes operating properly

- working with common carriers to obtain and maintain links between nodes
- maintaining connections between subnetworks
- coordinating efforts of subnet managers
- managing LANs co-located with the WAN

Having evolved from mainframe management environments, WAN management personnel are typically highly experienced data-processing personnel who know the intricacies of data communications subsystems and large system operating systems. In contrast, a LAN administrator may be chosen from the ranks of skilled microcomputer users. Sometimes personnel chosen for this position have limited technical backgrounds as compared to their counterparts in WAN management. We have already described the profile of a network management team and the skills they need. Let us now look more closely at one of the entry levels of network management, LAN administration.

In a six-person office in which each person has a microcomputer workstation, how do you imagine the management and operations of the workstations are conducted? In most offices:

- Each person is responsible for backing up his or her data (if it is done at all).
- Each person is responsible for operating a micro.
- There is no office data-processing manager (although there may be a local "expert" upon whom others rely for help).
- No provisions are made for security.
- If resource sharing exists, it is done via disk exchange or printer switches.
- If someone makes a mistake or if one system fails, it has little impact on the others.
- A certain amount of "trading" of software occurs because the office does not have one copy for each user.
- Everyone wants the best printer attached to their computer.

Now, suppose the office manager informs everyone that a LAN is about to be installed and that, after the dust settles, a more effective computing system will be available. The manager probably is correct with respect to the LAN providing a more effective computing platform. However, let us look at another implication of a LAN: LAN management.

In switching from a stand-alone microcomputer environment to a LAN, it is essential to have two or more people designated as LAN managers. If the LAN is large, several people may be actively involved as LAN managers; if the LAN is small, one person may be the principal manager and the second the alternate. (What constitutes a small, medium, or large LAN is difficult to define. For our purposes, small LANs are those with fewer than 50 workstations and only 1 server; a medium-size LAN will have from 50 to 150 nodes and 3 or fewer servers. Large LANs will be all other LANs. Be aware that some small LANs can be as complex to manage as a large one.) The alternate

LAN manager assists the primary manager as necessary and fills in when the primary is absent.

During installation, LAN management is a full-time job. After the LAN is in operation, management tasks are less time-consuming. For a small LAN, management tasks may take less than one hour a day; for a large LAN, management may be a full-time position and may even require more than one full-time person. It is easy for a business to overlook the costs of LAN management.

LAN Management Tasks

Before the LAN is installed, LAN managers should be hired or existing personnel trained. The amount of training varies according to the complexity of the system. At a minimum, managers should know the fundamentals of data communications and how to:

- connect and disconnect workstations
- diagnose and correct medium problems
- add and delete users
- create the users' environments
- implement security
- create, modify, and manage the printing environment
- install and modify applications
- take system backups
- recover from system failures
- monitor and evaluate performance
- add new resources, such as a new server
- maintain LAN documentation and procedures
- assist in setting up LAN interconnections
- detect and remove viruses

Connecting and Disconnecting Workstations   A LAN often is not static. New workstations need to be added and existing ones moved or removed, particularly during LAN installation and the initial stages of operation. The procedures for installing a new workstation vary from one implementation to another, but usually the following steps are required:

1. Install the LAN adapter in the workstation.
2. Establish a connection on the medium for the new workstation. This may require a new port on an MAU or wiring hub, a new BNC connection on a coaxial cable, or simply a tap into a cable.
3. Connect the workstation to the medium by establishing a connection between the LAN adapter and the medium.
4. Install network software in the workstation.

5. Boot the new workstation and test its ability to communicate over the network.

Once the new workstation is working, the network documentation ought to be updated to reflect the new address and wiring circumstances.

Diagnosing and Correcting Problems   In some LANs, the most common problems are medium faults—wiring breaks, loose connectors, and unterminated cables. Being able to locate and correct these faults is critical to the success of the LAN. A host of other problems can occur as well. Some of these include:

- improperly installed network software
- improperly installed application software
- user errors
- broken equipment
- improper security settings

Solving these problems requires diagnostic skills and the right set of tools. These tools are discussed in the following chapter.

Adding and Deleting Users   Each LAN user must identify himself or herself when logging onto the LAN. Each user is authorized to run certain applications and perform a set of actions on selected files. These privileges are described in the following section on security. The network manager must assign user IDs to individuals and delete or modify user IDs when a user leaves or changes job functions. Users are usually associated with a group, for example, one for personnel administration, one for payroll administration, and so on. Like users, groups have assigned privileges on the LAN. Again, it is the responsibility of the LAN manager to define the required groups and to assign individuals to one or more groups. Sometimes, the LAN manager will pass user and group administration functions to unit managers.

For each new user, the LAN administrator typically will create or assist in creating the user's environment. Some of the tasks that might be completed are:

- create a home directory for the user
- add the user to the network mail system
- create a **user login script**—a set of actions to be taken when the user logs in, such as setting search paths and initial menus
- set default security parameters
- set limits on resource utilization, such as the maximum amount of server disk that the user can consume
- set printer mappings

user login script   A set of actions to be taken when the user logs in, such as setting search paths and initial menus.

Creating the Users' Environments   The LAN administrator must assist in creating the proper environment for each user. This includes providing access to the proper applications, setting up user menus as called for, setting up the proper printing environment, and providing access to the necessary servers. Much of this is accomplished via batch command files and user login scripts. The key to setting up these environments is to make LAN use transparent, so the user has access to the necessary LAN facilities without being made aware of the details of the LAN itself.

Implementing Security   In making the transition from a stand-alone to a LAN environment, resources that were once private may become shared. A file that resided on a stand-alone system may be placed on a file server, a program that existed on one or two microcomputers may be placed on a file server, or a printer available to only one micro might be attached to a printer server. Being placed in a shared circumstance does not mean, however, that any user should to be able to read or modify the file, run the application, or use the printer. Instead, the LAN manager must create an access profile for each user, group, file, application, and hardware device. Some attributes thus defined are given in Table 13-2.

There may be more or fewer capabilities depending on the particular implementation. Additional utilities frequently can be purchased to enhance the capabilities provided with the LAN software. For example, most LANs do not provide the ability to view what is displayed on a workstation's monitor or to take control of the keyboard, but several utilities exist that can be added to do this.

Creating, Modifying, and Managing the Printing Environment   There can be two types of printers on a LAN: dedicated and shared. **Dedicated printers** are attached to workstations and can be used only by a person at that workstation. **Shared printers** are those controlled by a server and available to designated users. The latter type of printer is discussed in this section.

The general layout for a LAN printing system, a **spooler**, is illustrated in Figure 13-6. An application might go through the following steps to print a document on a shared printer:

1. The application opens a printer port, such as LPT1 in a DOS system, and begins writing to that device.

2. The LAN printer software intercepts the print stream and routes it over the network to the server.

3. The server print collector accepts the print stream and stores it in a file.

4. Steps 2–3 continue until the application closes the connection to the printer port or until a time-out limit of no print output is reached. In either case, the workstation software sends an end-of-job designater to the server.

5. The server closes that print job and schedules the job to be printed.

6. The printer driver looks at the scheduled jobs, selects the one with the highest priority, and prints it on the printer.

7. On completion of printing a job, the printer driver selects the next available job and prints it, and so on.

dedicated printer   A printer that can be used only by a person at the workstation to which the printer is attached.

shared printer   A printer controlled by a server and available to designated users.

spooler   A software system that collects printer output (typically on disk) and schedules the data for printing. Spool is an acronym for simultaneous peripheral operation online.

TABLE 13-2   Security Attributes

File Capabilities

    Ability to examine a directory listing

    Ability to read or write a file

    Ability to delete, rename, or create a file

    Ability to execute an application

    Ability for several users to simultaneously use a file

    Ability to restrict a file to one user at a time

    Ability to define file ownership

    Ability to pass privileges on to another user

User and Group Capabilities

    Allow file access according to the capabilities just described by user and group

    Require a password

    Require passwords to have a minimum number of characters

    Require passwords to be changed at certain intervals

    Allow logins only during specified times

    Allow a user to login only from selected workstations

    Inclusion of users in a group

    Specify account expiration date

    Restrict amount of disk space used

    Detect multiple login attempts and deactivate workstation or account

Monitoring Capabilities

    Identify users logged on to system

    View information about users

    View information about jobs

    View a user's activity on servers

    View what is displayed on a workstation

    Take control of a workstation's keyboard

From each user's perspective, the needed printer is always available and dedicated to that user. It is the spooler that provides this virtual printer capability. The spooler can also provide other functions such as:

- printing multiple copies
- printing a document on several printers
- holding a document on disk after printing or instead of printing
- printing selected portions of a document
- printing banners before each print job

Figure 13-6

Spooler Configuration

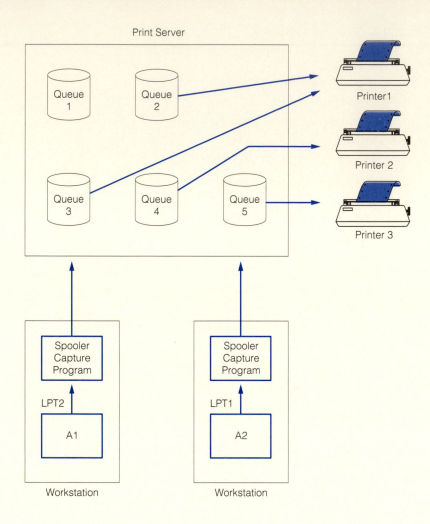

At the more detailed level, there are many factors to consider and parameters to set when installing and controlling a printing subsystem. The factors are too many to cover in detail here, and the ways in which they are established vary from one LAN to another. In essence, the LAN administrator carries out the following tasks:

- mapping printer ports on workstations to a print queue
- mapping print queues to one or more printers
- associating a printer with one or more print queues
- changing the configuration described in the three preceding steps
- assigning a printer priority scheme, such as printing small jobs before large jobs
- monitoring the print jobs on disk
- removing print jobs from disk
- starting or stopping print jobs or printers
- adding or deleting printers

Being able to obtain printed output is one of the basic needs of a LAN system. With all the configuration options typically available, the LAN administrator can provide an environment that meets or exceeds the needs of the LAN users; on the other hand, a poorly designed configuration can hinder printing effectiveness.

Installing and Modifying Applications   When installing a new application, the LAN manager must plan how the application will be used, which users will need it, and on which server(s) the application will reside. Applications not designed for shared use must be installed in a way that prohibits concurrent usage. Applications that can be used concurrently need to be installed in a manner that maximizes their capabilities for each user. Most important, the LAN administrator must understand and comply with the application vendor's **software license agreements**. License agreements vary considerably. Some software programs are licensed for only one workstation; some are licensed for a specific number of concurrent users, such as four concurrent users; some are licensed to allow access for all users on a specific server; and some are licensed to allow access for all users on all servers. Obviously, understanding the license agreements is important for both application selection and installation.

Each application user ideally will be able to match his or her hardware with the application's features. Accordingly, a user with a color monitor ought to be able to tailor the application and have it display that user's preferred foreground and background colors. A user with a monochrome monitor will have a different user profile that runs correctly on his or her workstation. Other features that might be accounted for include the type of graphics adapter, display size, amount of memory available, and so on. Once the application is operational, the LAN administrator is responsible for installing application upgrades. A major application release sometimes will provide significant changes in how the system works and the user interface to the system. The LAN manager must plan for the transition from the old system to the new one. In such cases, it is usually prudent to have both application versions available to make the transition to the new application easier.

Taking System Backups   Recall that in the stand-alone microcomputer environment, each user is responsible for backing up his or her data files. On a LAN, this responsibility is assumed by the LAN administrator. The administrator must design a backup policy that will allow data files and programs to be recovered. A variety of backup devices are available. The main options are given in Table 13-3. Associated with the backup devices is backup software. Most LAN systems provide this software. Some companies choose to purchase separate backup software that provides a more robust set of capabilities than the LAN version. Table 13-4 lists common backup capabilities.

Recovering from System Failures   The main purpose of taking backups is to recover from failures. The LAN administrator must prepare procedures that will be implemented if the LAN fails. Because some failures do not affect files, the recovery procedures must encompass more than file recovery. For example, a workstation may fail in the middle of an application. The LAN

software license agreement
A document provided by the software vendor that specifies the rights and restrictions of using the software.

TABLE 13-3 Backup Device Alternatives

Diskette	Hard Disk	Magnetic Tape (several different technologies)
Optical Drive	Digital Audiotape	Digital Videocassette

TABLE 13-4 Common Backup Options

Timed backups where the backup is scheduled to start at a specific time	Only backup files that have been modified since the last backup	Ability to specify a list of files or directories to backup
Ability to specify a list of files to exclude from the backup	Ability to back up files for a specific user	Ability to back up hidden and system files
Ability to change the directories of the files being backed up	Ability to preserve or change file ownership and attributes during backup and restore	Data compression to reduce the number of bits stored on the backup medium
Allow wildcard naming conventions	Ability to back up open files	Ability to back up local drives on a workstation
Data verification during backup	Ability to resume backup after interruption	Ability to create and review backup audit and error logs

administrator ought to have a procedure for recovering the application and lost work.

Monitoring and Evaluating Performance   LAN usage is likely to change over time. New users might be added, some workstations deleted, and applications added or deleted. The LAN administrator must monitor the LAN usage and plan necessary changes. If usage increases, a new server may be needed or, if multiple servers exist, the usage may need to be better balanced among them. Things the LAN administrator may monitor include:

printing environment	disk usage
number of active users	application usage
transmission faults	server-busy statistics

Based on the performance statistics, the LAN administrator will plan corrective action as necessary.

Adding Resources   The LAN administrator must plan the acquisition and integration of any new LAN resources into the system. If a file server is added, the LAN administration must decide which files are to be placed on the new server and which users the file server will primarily serve. After integrating the new server, the administrator will monitor the LAN activities to ensure that service is satisfactory and that all components are used effectively.

Maintaining LAN Documentation and Procedures   Much of the success of data-processing administration stems from having good, current documentation and procedures. The LAN administrator is responsible for creating and updating this documentation.

Assisting in Setting Up LAN Interconnections   In Chapter 12 you read about the ways in which one network can be connected to another network. The LAN administrator is involved in setting up the proper hardware and software interfaces on the LAN side of the connection. If two LANs are being connected, the administrator may be responsible for all of the interconnection details.

Deleting and Removing Viruses   One concern of network administrators at all levels is the proliferation of computer viruses and similar disruptive programs or code modules. Today's network administrators must have up-to-date virus detection and removal software and procedures. There are several sources of software for virus detection, and many of them can stay memory resident and provide continuous scanning. All network administrators need to include computer viruses in their planning and procedures.

WAN Management Tasks

The responsibilities of WAN managers differ somewhat from those of a LAN manager. A LAN administrator is an integral part of the network management team; however, in this section the term *WAN management team* refers to the group of network managers whose responsibilities include WAN management. Some LAN management tasks typically *not* carried out by a WAN manager are:

- creating user environments, a task typically carried out by programming personnel
- creating, modifying, and managing the printing environment, a task typically carried out by operations personnel
- installing and modifying applications, a task typically carried out by programming and operations personnel
- taking backups, a task typically carried out by operations personnel

A representative list of WAN management tasks is given below:

- connect and disconnect workstations
- diagnose and correct medium problems
- add and delete users
- implement security

- recover from system failures
- monitor and evaluate performance
- add resources, such as a new server
- maintain LAN documentation and procedures
- assist in setting up LAN interconnections
- detect and remove viruses
- interface with a common carrier
- estimate equipment and media costs
- configure network components to meet transmission and cost requirements
- interface with corporate and vendor personnel in devising network solutions
- resolve problems regarding international telecommunications
- develop and maintain network software
- coordinate and consolidate network management

Items in this list up to and including detecting and removing viruses are tasks common to LANs and WANs and have been discussed above. Let us look at those management tasks that are unique to WANs.

Interfacing with a Common Carrier   As technology advances, we may see increasing instances of LANs being implemented using a medium provided by a common carrier. Currently, the use of common carrier media in LANs is uncommon whereas in WANs it is commonplace. In the United States, a company can choose from among several common carriers. Each common carrier will have characteristics that sets it apart from its competitors. Differences among common carriers may include rates, types of media and services, locations serviced, and quality of service and support. The WAN management team must be familiar with the advantages and disadvantages of each common carrier and choose the most cost-effective alternatives.

Network problems can be caused by a company's equipment, by a common carrier's equipment, or by the interface between the two. When problems occur that cannot be isolated to the company's equipment, the network management team must work with the common carrier in diagnosing and correcting the problem.

Estimating Equipment and Media Costs   A LAN administrator will also carry out this task; however, the number of options and range of prices are much greater in a WAN. In configuring portions of a WAN, the management team must evaluate several common carriers, perhaps several services per common carrier, and data communications equipment from a variety of vendors. Often the number of possible solutions will be large. If a company considers three common carriers, two services per carrier, and five different data communications providers each of which has three pieces of equipment to consider, the number of combinations of vendors, services, and equipment is 150. Choosing the best one requires considerable analysis and expertise.

Configuring Network Components   Like estimating equipment and media costs, configuring network components is a process of evaluating a large number of alternatives. A LAN's standard and topology limits the ways in which network components can be added. In a WAN there are usually fewer restrictions, the configuration task is much more complex, and the cost of solutions is often greater than for LAN configuration solutions. For example, adding a node to a LAN usually means finding the closest wiring hub or cable and attaching the node to it. Adding a node to a WAN often requires obtaining one or more communications lines from a common carrier, deciding which existing nodes the new node is to be linked to, procuring the hardware and software for the new node, preparing the site for installation of the new node, and training personnel to manage the new equipment.

Resolving Problems Regarding International Telecommunications

In Chapter 11 you read about issues regarding international networks. LAN administrators need not be concerned with international issues. Managers of international WANs must address the issues raised in Chapter 11. These issues are:

- politics
- regulations
- hardware
- language
- tariffs

The WAN management team must consider these issues in estimating network costs, use, and configuration.

Developing and Maintaining Network Software   A LAN administrator is responsible for setting up a user's application environment but seldom gets involved in fixing or writing network software. The WAN management team may need to customize some characteristics of the network or install corrections to faulty network programs. If a company has a unique device that needs to be attached to the network, the WAN management team may need to write the network interface code or modify an existing interface. When errors are detected in network software, the software vendor may distribute patches to the code. The WAN management team will be responsible for inserting the patches and testing the system to ensure it works properly.

Coordinating and Consolidating Network Management   A LAN administrator is usually responsible for one or more LANs in a specific location. The WAN management team is responsible for the coordination and consolidation of all aspects of network management to include the operations and interconnections of subnets. The knowledge and responsibilities of the WAN management team are far beyond those of the LAN manager. Problems that cannot be solved by local operations or LAN management personnel become the responsibility of the WAN management team. WAN managers must remain aware of problems in all segments of the network to avoid duplicating diagnosis and correction of problems that have already been encountered and resolved.

SUMMARY

As the use of data communications expands, so will the role and importance of network management. The keys to effective network management are: personnel who are competent and knowledgeable and who can work well with a broad spectrum of users; planning; and the effective use of network management tools. Network management is involved in the design, testing, and operations of a system. A certain amount of implementation or development is also required in some installations.

Network management is both a function and an application. The application portion should be designed and implemented like any other business application. The primary functions for computerized implementation are problem-reporting systems, tools, network management software that reacts automatically to problems in the network, and diagnostic systems. With careful management, the network can be a valuable asset to a company; with poor or no management, even the best designed application system can fail. If the network is incorrectly designed, is not modified to meet changing demands, or is frequently inoperable, and if problems are not readily resolved, users will lose confidence in the system, and the network's effectiveness will be diminished.

KEY TERMS

availability, *426*

control center, *435*

dedicated printer, *442*

effectiveness, *429*

LAN administrator, *424*

modular expansion, *432*

network administrator, *424*

network manager, *424*

network statistics, *435*

problem-reporting system, *436*

release control, *437*

reliability, *428*

shared printer, *442*

software license agreement, *445*

spooler, *442*

user login script, *441*

REVIEW QUESTIONS

1. What are the two main objectives of network management?

2. Why is user satisfaction an important network management objective?

3. Describe the functions performed by the network management team.

4. How do problems get reported and resolved? What documents are generated as a result of the problem-reporting system? Who receives copies of these documents?

5. How are statistics used in network management?

6. Describe the documentation created and maintained by the network management team.

7. List ten LAN management tasks.

8. What must a LAN manager do when installing a new workstation?

PROBLEMS AND EXERCISES

1. Identify and describe five sub-objectives of network management. Match each sub-objective with a main network management objective.

2. Design a problem-reporting form. What are the essential elements of a problem-reporting form?

3. If you were assigned to recruit a LAN manager, what experience would you require of qualified candidates? What salary can a LAN manager expect?

4. A personnel file contains data regarding an employee's name, address, date of birth, date of hire, performance rating, and salary. You have been assigned the task of setting security for this file for all employees and employees in the personnel and payroll departments. Suppose that you can set security attributes on each data item. What attributes would you assign to:

   a. all employees?

   b. employees in the personnel department?

   c. employees in the payroll department?

   Explain your decisions.

5. How are backup files used in recovering from a disk head crash that destroys both the disk and the data stored thereon?

6. A company has decided to install a local area network and has collected data from two vendors regarding their equipment reliability. The figures the company obtained are as follows:

Device	Vendor A		Vendor B	
	MTBF	MTTR	MTBF	MTTR
Workstation	4000	2.5	3500	1.5
LAN adapter	8000	1.0	8500	1.0
File server	3500	4.5	3500	4.0

Which vendor has the best availability? Which vendor has the best reliability? Which vendor has the best effectiveness?

REFERENCES

Brambert, Dave. "The Layered Look." *LAN*, Volume 7, Number 10, October 1992.

Bruno, Charles. "Taking the Work Out of Virus Detection." *Network World*, Volume 9, Number 43, October 26, 1992.

Conliffe, Alison. "Inoculating the LAN." *Network World*, Volume 9, Number 48, November 30, 1992.

Didio, Laura. "Security Breaches." *LAN Times*, Volume 8, Issue 23, December 9, 1991.

Duffy, Jim. "Seeking Network Management Harmony." *Network World*, Volume 9, Number 39, September 28, 1992.

Gupta, Uma G. "Global Networks: Promises and Challenges." *Information Systems Management*, Fall 1992.

Korzeniowski, Paul. "LANs a Weak Link in Security Chain." *Software Magazine*, Volume 12, Number 14, October 1992.

Muller, Nathan J. "Integrated Network Management: With Complexity Comes a Need for Control." *Information Systems Management*, Fall 1992.

Nickel, Wallace E. "Determining Network Effectiveness." *Mini-Micro Systems*, November 1978.

Niden, Howard. "Framework for Network Planning: A Corporate Model." *Information Systems Management*, Fall 1992.

Radding, Alan. "System Management." *InfoWorld*, Volume 14, Issue 50, December 14, 1992.

Vacca, John. "Masters of Disasters." *Network World*, Volume 9, Number 40, October 5, 1992.

14

Network Management Systems

CHAPTER OBJECTIVES

After studying this chapter you should be able to:

- Discuss the general workings of a network management system
- Compare the SNMP and CMIP standards
- Explain the capabilities of IBM's Netview network management system
- Explain the capabilities of Novell's Network Management System
- Compare and contrast network management tools

This chapter begins with a discussion of a generic Network Management System (NMS) and NMS protocols, and concludes with a brief look at two NMS implementations: IBM's Netview and Novell's Network Management System. The chapter concludes with an overview of tools used in managing a network.

453

NETWORK MANAGEMENT SYSTEM SOFTWARE

A network should be under continuous scrutiny to ensure that the objectives of customer satisfaction and cost-effectiveness are met. Too often, network problems surface through user complaints. This is usually not the way a network manager wants to learn about problems. A far better way is to have potential problems detected and reported by a network management system, so problems may be corrected before users become aware of them.

Network Management System (NMS) A combination of hardware and software used by network supervisors to monitor and administer a network.

A **Network Management System (NMS)** is a combination of hardware and software used by network supervisors to monitor and administer the network. The NMS must be able to determine the status of network components such as modems, lines, terminals, multiplexers, and so on. If a device's status indicates that malfunctions are occurring, the NMS will either take automatic corrective action or alert a network supervisor of the condition. The network supervisor may then use network control functions of the NMS to take corrective action. An NMS also gathers network statistics, such as line utilization information, together with capabilities for evaluating those statistics. The information produced assists network supervisors in capacity planning.

In the past, most network software vendors neglected the area of network management. With few exceptions, the network software and hardware were built and installed with little support for managing them. Although management of small networks is not difficult, the composition of networks has changed as more businesses made the move to online systems. Two of these changes have had a significant impact on the ability to manage networks. First, the number and complexity of network nodes have increased. Early networks may have consisted of one central processor with communications controllers and terminal devices. The host assumed a supervisory role and provided a centralized point of control and management. Often the communications links were point-to-point leased or switched lines. In contrast, many of today's networks have multiple processing nodes and hundreds or thousands of connected devices. The network may consist of LANs, X.25 networks, leased lines, satellite and microwave links, switched lines, and PBX systems. Numerous interfaces between different types of equipment and networks are relatively common.

Second, many of today's networks are a hybrid of processors, terminals, controllers, modems, and other components from different vendors. Just managing a homogeneous network in which all the components are provided by one vendor is difficult. In the past, effectively managing a large network with components from multiple vendors approached the impossible. This problem fortunately is being recognized by network managers and vendors alike, and NMSs are being sold from both network vendors and independent software companies. We first consider the requirements of a generic NMS and then discuss the specific capabilities provided by IBM's Netview, Netview/PC, and Netview/6000. These products were chosen for two reasons: their applicability to a large body of users and functionality. The reader should be aware that other products exist, some of which provide more comprehensive management features.

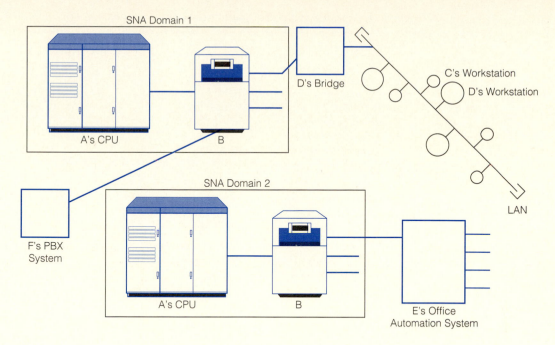

SNA Domain 1

A's CPU

B

D's Bridge

C's Workstation

D's Workstation

LAN

F's PBX
System

SNA Domain 2

A's CPU

B

E's Office
Automation System

Figure 14-1

Integrated Network

A Generic Network Management System

To understand an NMS, consider a hypothetical network of a large, international manufacturing firm. This company has processing nodes in many locations throughout the world. A small portion of this network from one manufacturing location is depicted in Figure 14-1. The backbone network is an SNA network (see Chapter 11), and there are two domains. The major components of the system come from seven different vendors. The host processors in both domains are from Company A. The communications controllers were purchased from Company B, but run IBM NCP (Network Control Program) software. The Engineering and Development Department has an IEEE 802.3-compatible LAN to support its design efforts. The workstations are special purpose and were provided by two companies, C and D. A bridge to the SNA network is provided using Company D's equipment. The interface to the SNA network is via LU 6.2. The office automation system uses equipment from Vendor E and interfaces to the SNA system in the same way as the engineering bridge. The PBX system obtained from Vendor F is also tied into the network. Modems and multiplexers were all obtained from Vendor G. What will the network management team need to know to keep this network running efficiently? A summary of this information appears in Table 14-1.

In a large network, if all of the data being gathered is sent to the network managers, both the network and the network managers would have a difficult time keeping up with it. Simply receiving the data is not enough; it must be received in a usable format. The NMS is responsible for ensuring that the correct data is received and that it is in a usable format. The network segment illustrated in Figure 14-2 shows a network component, a portion of the NMS,

TABLE 14-1   Network Management Information

A. Host processors
    1. Status
    2. CPU busy rates
    3. Internal queues, such as on TCP
    4. Transaction turnaround time in the CPU
    5. Buffer utilization
    6. Peak activity times
    7. Performance during peak activity

B. Communications controllers
    1. Status
    2. Processor busy rates
    3. Buffer utilization
    4. Queues
    5. Peak activity time
    6. Performance during peak activity

C. Lines
    1. Status
    2. Number of failures
    3. Number of retries
    4. Aggregate data rate
    5. Peak activity time
    6. Performance during peak activity
    7. Active devices on the line
    8. Line quality
    9. Changes in line quality

D. Modems
    1. Status
    2. Errors

E. Terminals
    1. Status
    2. Number of failures
    3. Failure types
    4. Number of transactions
    5. Type of transactions
    6. Transaction response time

F. Processing nodes
    1. Status
    2. Number of transactions
    3. Response time
    4. Type of transactions

and the connection to the control center. The NMS will continually obtain status and operational data from the component(s) it is monitoring. Ordinarily the data will be routine, and either ignored or logged for later evaluation. Specifically, if the component being monitored is a communications line, some of the information the NMS will receive could be the number of errors

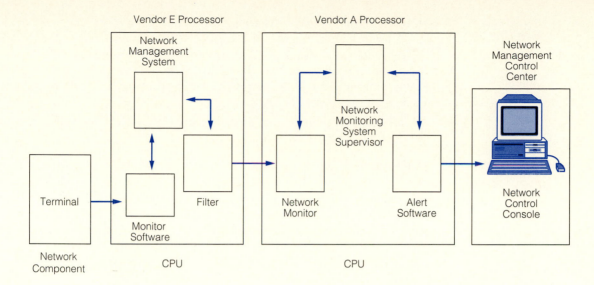

Figure 14-2

Network Management
System

encountered since the last status report, current status, line quality, number of retries on the line, and number of characters transmitted or received. When some statistic changes, it must be brought to the attention of the network managers, which is called an **alert** or **alarm**. If a problem has occurred, the NMS should also assist the managers in solving the problem by indicating the potential causes and perhaps even solutions.

If the values received are within tolerance, and if data collection is enabled, the data will be logged. Later it may be evaluated for trend analysis and capacity planning. If the data is not within accepted tolerance levels, this must be brought to the attention of the network managers. An alert is necessary for a data communications line if the line is down, the error rates have exceeded some threshold, the number of retries is excessive, or the line is congested. A change in service level also may be cause for an alert for a component that is being closely monitored. For example, if a line has been operating between 20% and 25% capacity and suddenly experiences 50% load capacity, an alert may signal this change.

When an alert condition has been detected, it must be forwarded to the network management center. Steps that may be taken in this process include:

1. Identification of probable causes of the alert condition.

2. Formatting the message for the NMS presentation services. Component addresses, status, and probable causes must be identified. In Figure 14-2 this function is performed by the software component identified as a **filter**, which is used to screen and format data sent to the management center. A filter can perform many functions, one of which is to control the flow of data to the center. Flow control avoids flooding the control center with repetitious status messages.

3. Transmission of the data to the control center for display.

alert A signal given by the network management system that a statistic, such as current line status, line quality, or number of retries on the line, has changed since the last status report. Also known as an alarm.

filter A software component used to screen and format data sent to the management center.

4. Passing the message through a formatter at the control center, which determines where and how the message is to be displayed. Many NMS presentation services utilize color monitors to present the data. Warnings may be displayed in yellow, outages in red, and major catastrophes in blinking red with an audio signal. The message will also usually be logged to an alert history file.

5. The network management team acting on the alert as necessary and documenting the event and its solution.

As mentioned earlier, obtaining the proper information to manage a network is difficult enough in a homogeneous network environment. In a mixed-vendor configuration, additional complexities must be resolved. In Figure 14-2 the network management control center is attached to one of the host processors and uses software provided by that vendor, Vendor A. Vendor A's network management tools are designed to monitor only its own equipment and to present messages in a specific format. In the configuration shown, terminals attached to Vendor E's processors may be involved in a session with a host logical unit. This terminal also may not be supported by the host system.

The problems that must be resolved in this type of environment include obtaining status information from each vendor's equipment, formatting the alerts in a manner consistent with the host's requirements, and routing alerts and their associated data to the host node for display. Once the alert has been raised, the system managers must react to it. For example, if a device is malfunctioning and disrupting the network, the device needs to be deactivated until the problem is fixed. The NMS will provide an interface that allows the network managers to deactivate the device and later bring it back online. If several vendors are represented, each vendor is likely to have different peripheral control utilities and different command languages. In Vendor A's environment the command to bring a failed terminal, such as the terminal known to the system as TERMINAL-X, back online may be RESTORE TERMINAL-X, whereas in Vendor E's system the same command may be DEVICE TERMINAL-X UP. Thus, once the alert has been received, correction in a mixed-vendor network may not be simple. One cannot expect network managers to know the command languages required to remedy faults on several different vendor systems. Even on one system there may be several interfaces for fault correction. One interface may be used for physical devices and another for logical devices and connections. If a terminal has failed and needs to be restored, it may be necessary to activate the terminal on the line via a peripheral utility program and, using a different utility, notify application programs that the terminal is again available.

To reduce the complexities of dealing with multiple-vendor equipment, and sometimes even a variety of interfaces from one vendor, the NMS may provide a command mapping function. This allows the network managers to work with one command language that has a consistent interface. The command mapping function will select the proper interface program(s) to receive the message and translate the command into a format acceptable to these programs.

Simple Network Management Protocol (SNMP)
SNMP provides a guideline for creating network management software products. SNMP has four key components: the SNMP protocol, structure of management information (SMI), management information base (MIB), and the network management system (NMS).

NETWORK MANAGEMENT PROTOCOLS

Network interconnection raises an additional network management problem. The problem is how to monitor nodes on one subnetwork from a node on a different subnetwork, such as monitoring a node on a token ring from a network management console attached to an IBM SNA network. To facilitate the exchange of management data among network nodes, a network management standard or protocol is essential. If such standards exist, network designers can build their networks with the ability to exchange management and control data. Two such standards have evolved: the **Simple Network Management Protocol (SNMP)** and the **Common Management Information Protocol (CMIP)**. CMIP is also sometimes referred to as the **Communications Management Information Protocol**.

Simple Network Management Protocol

The SNMP is a part of the TCP/IP suite described in Chapter 12. Originally the protocol was implemented on UNIX systems. Since the first SNMP products appeared in 1988, they have rapidly gained in acceptance and popularity. The protocol is endorsed by companies such as IBM, Hewlett-Packard, and Sun Microsystems and is implemented on most microcomputer, minicomputer, and mainframe computers under a variety of operating systems. As the protocol has spread, its capabilities also have been expanded to accommodate new needs. Currently, the SNMP standard is called SNMP Version 2 (SNMPv2).

SNMP has four key components: the protocol itself, the **Structure of Management Information (SMI)**, the **Management Information Base (MIB)**, and the Network Management System (NMS). The SNMP is an application layer protocol that outlines the formal structure for communication among network devices. The SMI details how every piece of information regarding managed devices is represented in the MIB. The MIB is a database that defines the hardware and software elements to be monitored. SNMPv2 expanded the capabilities of the original MIB and this new version is referred to as MIB II. The NMS is the control console to which network monitoring and management information are reported. The components of the SNMP are shown in Figure 14-3.

Each SNMP device has an **agent** that collects data for that device. The data is stored in the device's MIB. A vendor that creates a device adhering to the SNMP standard will include an agent as one of the device components. Thus, there are agents for routers, servers, workstations, bridges, terminal servers, multiplexers, hubs, repeaters, and concentrators. An SNMP **management component** interfaces with agents to provide network control. The management component uses three basic commands, GET, SET, and TRAPS, to control a device. The **GET** command allows the management component to retrieve data stored in the device's MIB, and the **SET** command allows data fields stored in the device's MIB to be reset. **TRAPS** allows an SNMP device to trap and forward unsolicited data; for example, a trap would be used to

Common Management Information Protocol (CMIP) Guidelines issued by the International Standards Organization for creating network management products. Also known as the Communications Management Information Protocol.

Structure of Management Information (SMI) A component of the SNMP that details how information is represented in the management information base (MIB).

Management Information Base (MIB) A database that defines the hardware and software elements to be monitored in the SNMP.

agent A device component that collects data for the device, which is then stored in the management information base (MIB).

management component A component that interfaces with the SNMP agent to provide network control.

GET An SNMP command that allows the management component to retrieve data stored in a device's management information base (MIB).

SET An SNMP command that allows data fields stored in a device's management information base (MIB) to be reset.

TRAPS An SNMP command that allows a device to trap and forward unsolicited data, such as an alert condition.

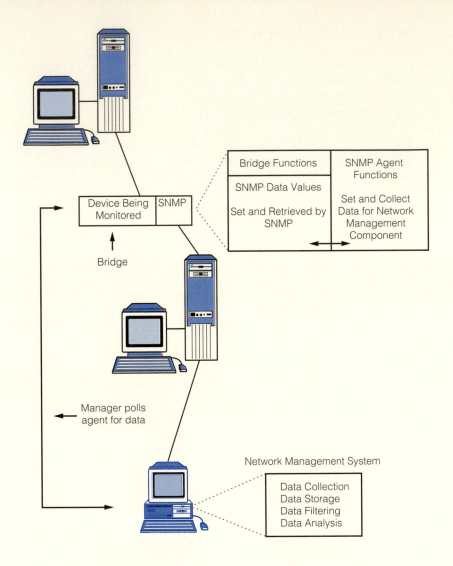

Figure 14-3

Details of the SNMP
Environment

Bridge Functions

SNMP Agent
Functions

SNMP Data Values

Set and Retrieved by
SNMP

Set and Collect
Data for Network
Management
Component

Device Being
Monitored   SNMP

Bridge

Manager polls
agent for data

Network Management System

Data Collection
Data Storage
Data Filtering
Data Analysis

notify the management component of an alert condition. One example of a
trap is a cold-start trap that notifies the management component when a
device has been powered up.

The MIB contains information that the network administrator needs to
monitor and control the network. Each device being monitored has its own
individual MIB that contains data relative only to that device. A device MIB
has two parts, a proprietary part in which data defined by the device vendor
is saved and the part in which data common to all MIBs are stored. The data
stored in device MIBs can be collected in a network management MIB that
contains data for multiple network components. A new SNMP standard also
provides for a **Remote Monitoring MIB (RMON MIB)**, which describes nine
different device groups. A vendor must choose an appropriate group for a
device and is required to support all of the data objects defined for that group.
There is also an ability to support devices that do not directly support SNMP.

**Remote Monitoring MIB
(RMON MIB)**   An SNMP
standard that describes nine
different device groups. A
vendor must choose an ap-
propriate group for a device
adhering to this standard
and is required to support
all the data objects defined
for that group.

SNMP allows network managers to get the status of devices and set or initialize devices. If problems occur, an event mechanism generates a message that is displayed on the network monitoring console. Being a simple protocol, SNMP has a few shortcomings. Its command set is limited; there are limited provisions for security; and, because it lacks a strict standard, there is some inconsistency among different vendors' implementations.

Common Management Information Protocol

In competition with SNMP is the International Standards Organization's (ISO) Common Management Information Protocol (CMIP). CMIP has a more complex protocol for exchanging messages among network components and has the potential for better control and the ability to overcome the limitations of SNMP. Unfortunately, there currently are no provisions for direct interoperability of SNMP and CMIP; however, some NMSs communicate with SNMP agents as well as CMIP agents concurrently. Thus interoperability may arise through specific NMS implementations. Because CMIP was developed more recently than SNMP, operational systems are just beginning to emerge. It will take some time for CMIP to overcome the market penetration of SNMP. CMIP has been endorsed by AT&T and Digital Equipment Corporation, and its capabilities are being implemented in each vendor's product line.

With this general overview of network management, we now look at a specific implementation of an NMS system, IBM's Netview, Netview/PC, and Netview/6000 products. Netview/6000 supports SNMP and it is realistic to assume that CMIP support will also be implemented.

IBM'S NETWORK MANAGEMENT SYSTEM

Netview and Netview/PC were introduced by IBM in 1986, and another version, Netview/6000, was introduced in 1992. The original Netview consolidated and extended several network management packages that had been used to monitor and control SNA networks. Netview is thus oriented to managing the host SNA environment. Netview/PC contains logic for monitoring IBM's token-ring network, PBX systems, and other vendors' equipment. Netview/6000 runs on IBM's UNIX-based systems and provides support for multivendor networks with no centralized host system.

Netview

Netview runs on an IBM host system and is the NMS for monitoring and controlling an SNA network. The functions it provides include control services and diagnostic control capabilities, such as hardware monitoring, session monitoring, and status monitoring. Hardware monitoring collects status information from physical devices, and session monitoring provides information on SNA sessions. Status monitoring provides display information regarding system components and assists in restarting system elements following a failure. The control function provides the ability to activate and deactivate devices. In addition to the management and control functions, Netview provides two other basic facilities: help and a user interface. The help function provides users with online assistance as well as an operator tutorial. The user interface allows scripts, called Clists, to be prepared by users to monitor devices and/or to automate startup and shutdown sequences.

Netview/PC

Netview/PC, as the name indicates, runs on a microcomputer. Netview/PC is an important component in IBM's open communications architecture (OCA). IBM recognizes that networks tend to have a mixture of vendor equipment. OCA opens an IBM network from a management perspective by providing other vendors with interface specifications. Through these, other vendors can have their equipment integrated more completely into the network. Within Netview/PC this integration is effected through an Application Program Interface (API).

API allows users to write applications that can interface to non-IBM devices. The API applications can be written to have device-specific interfaces as well as a Netview interface; this allows the application to establish the management connection between the device and IBM's network management tools. Within Netview/PC, IBM provides this interface to its token-ring LAN and to Rolm computerized PBX systems. Status information collected by the microcomputer running Netview/PC may be stored on the microcomputer's local disk and/or forwarded to Netview, which runs on the host system. If alerts are received, they either may be handled at the microcomputer or may be forwarded to the host for operator intervention and resolution. The interface between the host and the microcomputer is either via an SNA 3270 terminal or as an LU 6.2 session type.

Netview/6000

Netview/6000 represents IBM's NMS for decentralized networks and networks using the SNMP. Netview/6000 requires fewer system resources than Netview and can run on smaller platforms. Netview/6000 has the ability to monitor up to 30,000 different objects and will support SNA capabilities such as LU 6.2, the Virtual Terminal Access Method (VTAM), and Advanced Peer-to-Peer Networking (APPN). Netview/6000 also provides support for managing LANs and devices such as bridges, wiring hubs, and routers.

Netview Architecture

The Netview architecture identifies three types of control points: focal points, entry points, and service points. A focal point is a central point for network management and monitoring functions. Focal points provide host-oriented functions including functions related to billing, line optimization, and performance analysis. Entry points relate to IBM or IBM-compatible network elements. Entry point functions include remote management and control modules, which allow the element to be controlled remotely from the control center and to communicate with Netview. Service points are gateways into the Netview system from non-SNA devices. Service points are characterized by Netview/PC and the devices it monitors and controls.

To summarize, through Netview and Netview/PC, IBM has created a system that allows centralized control of a distributed system that consists of IBM, IBM-compatible, and non-IBM equipment. Netview provides the ability to monitor and control the SNA network, and Netview/PC provides the same function for other network components. With Netview/6000, the management and control functions have been extended to include decentralized networks and multivendor networks.

NOVELL'S NETWORK MANAGEMENT SYSTEM

The acronym *NMS* is used to represent both a generic term for a network management system and Novell Corporation's specific system, also called Network Management System. Novell's NMS contains a collection of tools oriented toward managing LANs using Novell's network operating system. The main functions managed by NMS are network faults, performance, configuration, security, and accounting.

NMS consists of several components including Network Management Map, Network Services Manager, and Netware Management Agents. The Network Management Map (NMM) is essentially a database that represents all LAN components, such as details about servers, workstations, LAN adapters, wiring hubs, bridges, and routers. The NMM is a resource for other NMS components. In addition to collecting network configuration data, the NMM can graphically display the complete or partial network configurations.

The Network Services Manager (NSM) and the Netware Management Agents (NMAs) components work together to provide statistics and alerts to the NMS console. The NMS polls NMAs for statistics similar to the way in which SNMP collects data from device agents. The NSM can organize and report on data collected. A dedicated or nondedicated workstation is used as the LAN administrator's interface to the NMS. Other features found in Novell's NMS include:

- application program interfaces to give third-party vendors access to NMS functions
- modules for monitoring packets, protocols, and media
- modules to track wiring hub performance
- automatic server fault detection and alert notification
- an interface to IBM's Netview
- graphical and text reporting
- setting of thresholds for devices

Table 14-2 lists several NMSs and their vendors.

TABLE 14-2   Network Management Systems

Company	Product
Applied Computing Devices, Inc.	Network Knowledge Systems
AT&T	Accumaster Integrator
Cabletron Systems, Inc.	Spectrum
Cheyenne Software, Inc.	Monitrix Network Manager
Digital Equipment Corporation	DECmcc
D&G Infosystems, Inc.	LANWatchMan
Hewlett-Packard Company	HP Open View Network Node Manager
Hughes LAN Systems, Inc.	Monet Network Manager
Intel Corporation	LANDesk Manager
MAXM Systems Corporation	MAXM
MCI Corporation	FocusNet
NCR Corporation	NetWare Management Systems
Nynex Allink Company	Allink Operations Coordinator
Objective Systems Integrators, Inc.	NetExpert Toolkit
SunConnect	SunNet Manager
Systems Center, Inc.	Net/Master
Unisys Corporation	CNMS
Visisoft, Inc.	VisiNet Enterprise

NETWORK MANAGEMENT TOOLS

To carry out its various duties, the network management team frequently employs a variety of tools. In addition to the tools previously described for managing a LAN, a variety of other tools exist. These can be divided according to their function: diagnostic tools, monitoring tools, and management tools. They differ from the LAN tools discussed in Chapter 13 because they can be used for both LANs and WANs.

LAN analyzer   A diagnostic tool that monitors network traffic, captures and displays data sent over the network, generates network traffic to simulate load or error conditions, tests cables for faults, and provides data helpful for system configuration and management.

Diagnostic Tools

LAN Analyzers   **LAN analyzers** are similar to digital line monitors (discussed in Chapter 8). A LAN analyzer monitors network traffic, captures and displays data sent over the network, generates network traffic to simulate load or error conditions, tests cables for faults, and provides data helpful for system configuration and management.

Analog Line Monitors   An **analog line monitor** measures and displays the analog signals on the communications circuit or on the data communications side of the modem, enabling the user to check for noise and proper modulation. Analog line monitors are primarily used by a common carrier to evaluate their circuits and are seldom used in a user's environment.

Cable Testers   **Cable testers** are used to detect faults in cables by generating and monitoring a signal along the cable. By monitoring the signal, a cable tester not only can detect faults in the medium itself, or in medium connections, but also can identify the location of the fault.

Emulators   An **emulator** is a diagnostic tool that enables the user to check for adherence to a specific protocol. For example, a vendor must have its X.25 software certified by a packet distribution network before being allowed to connect to the system to avoid disrupting other system users; one way the software can be tested is with an emulator. The emulator acts like an X.25 node, generating both correct and incorrect messages to ensure that the system reacts according to the X.25 specifications. Emulators of this type usually allow the user to specify the types of messages to be transmitted. Emulators also can be used during the development process to ensure that the interfaces between software levels are correct.

Remote Control Software   **Remote control software** tools allow a LAN administrator to remotely view a user's monitor and take control of the user's keyboard. This capability is helpful during initial diagnostic work because it allows the network administrator to experience the problem firsthand. Sometimes the problem can be resolved remotely, thus providing more immediate correction and a reduction in the diagnostic time required by hands-on diagnostics.

Current Documentation   One of the best diagnostic tools is current documentation, including software listings that reflect the correct release and patch levels, logic diagrams, internal documentation, maintenance manuals, and any other supporting documents. Although documentation may seem obvious as a diagnostic tool, its importance cannot be overstated.

Diagnostic tools help *locate* problems in the network, whereas monitoring and management tools are used to *avoid* problems in the network. Monitoring and management functions include capacity planning, general project management, performance, and configuration. Several of these tools have been developed for microcomputers and are affordable for many users. Capacity planning is an extremely important function of network managers, who must recognize when resources are approaching full capacity and plan for expansion or reconfiguration to avoid saturation and decreased service. Project management tools allow a manager to plan and monitor the progress of projects. System performance and configuration address how well the system is working and the location and types of network components.

Four tools that are very effective in planning for capacity are metering software, performance monitors, simulation models, and workload generators.

---

analog line monitor   A diagnositc tool that monitors and displays the analog signals on the communications circuit or on the data communications side of the modem, enabling the user to check for noise and proper modulation.

cable tester   A diagnostic tool used to detect faults in cables by generating and monitoring a signal along the cable.

emulator   A diagnostic tool that enables the user to check for adherence to a specific protocol.

remote control software   A diagnostic tool that allows a LAN administrator to remotely view a user's monitor and take control of the user's keyboard.

Monitoring Tools

metering software   A monitoring tool used on LANs to enforce adherence to software license agreements by keeping track of the number of times an application is executed.

Metering Software   Metering software is used on LANs to enforce adherence to software license agreements. Metering software runs on a LAN server and keeps track of the number of times an application is executed. If an organization has a license to concurrently run 25 copies of a word processing program, the LAN administrator will set the metering count to 25 for that application. Whenever a user starts the application, the counter is incremented by 1, and when a user exits the application, the counter is decremented by 1. If the usage counter is at 25 and a user attempts to start the application, the metering software denies the request.

performance monitor   A monitoring tool that provides snapshots of how a system is actually functioning, which helps the network management team identify trends in the use or misuse of the network.

Performance Monitors   Performance monitors provide snapshots of how a system is actually functioning, typically capturing such information as number of transactions, type of transaction, transaction response times, transaction processing times, queue depths, number of characters per request/response, buffer utilization, number of I/Os, and processing time by process or process subprogram. When collected over time, information of this nature enables the management team to identify trends in the use or misuse of the network, such as whether the number of a specific type of transaction is steadily increasing and whether the capacity for handling that transaction type is being reached, or whether users are playing Star Trek or Adventure during lunch hour when the peak processing load occurs.

simulation model   A monitoring tool that allows the user to describe network and system activities and to receive an analysis of how the system can be expected to perform under the described conditions.

Simulation Models   Simulation models allow the user to describe network and system activities and to receive an analysis of how the system can be expected to perform under the described conditions. This service is especially useful during the development stage to predict response times, processor utilization, and potential bottlenecks. During operational situations, simulation models help determine what size transaction load will likely reach or exceed full capacity as well as the effect of adding transactions, applications, and terminals to the existing system.

A good simulation model in the development stage can avert performance issues during the design stage. Simulation models vary significantly with respect to the amount of information provided and the manner in which the user defines the workload. A simple model for line utilization and polling overhead might interactively prompt the user for the speed of the line, data link protocol, number of polling characters, modem turnaround time, and number of stations on the line, resulting in a report indicating the processing and line overheads of the polling and the maximum and average wait times a device might expect between polls. A comprehensive model, on the other hand, uses a network configuration file and a transaction file as input. The configuration file will contain the complete hardware configuration, including disk drives, disk-drive performance characteristics, line types, data link protocols, terminal types, database files and their locations, and access methods. The transaction file will contain a list of transaction types and the activities each transaction type performs, such as number of I/Os to each disk, the access method used, number of instructions executed, and number of characters input from and output to a terminal.

In addition to the two user-supplied files, the simulation model is driven by software performance characteristics such as polling overhead, instruction execution times, and disk access times. This type of model outputs information similar to that provided by a performance monitor, including expected response times, line utilization, processor utilization, and disk utilization. The simulation model essentially enables the user to see how an application will run without ever writing it. If the model predicts that a particular communications line will have 300% utilization and a response time of 10 minutes, either a faster circuit or more circuits will be needed to support the workload.

The time required to set up a simulation run varies with the amount of detail needed. The comprehensive model just described requires a considerable amount of information regarding the application. Usually it is not necessary to have the correct initial configuration, as the model will indicate areas of over- and underutilization. If the processor is 150% busy, either a larger or an additional processor is needed.

Workload Generators   Whereas the simulation model predicts system utilization, a **workload generator** actually generates the transaction loads and pseudo-application processes for execution on the proposed configuration. If the model and the workload generator were perfect, the results would be identical; in actual practice, however, some variation between the two is likely to occur. A workload generator together with a performance monitor can illustrate how the system will actually function in the proposed configuration. It also can be used for stress testing. As with any model, the above models are only as good as the inputs, the people who use and interpret them, and the closeness of the models to actual use. Their value decreases with the amount of time required to utilize them and increases with their ability to portray an application accurately. This means they should be used carefully and the results interpreted sensibly.

workload generator   A monitoring tool that generates transaction loads and pseudo-application processes for execution on a proposed configuration to illustrate how a system will actually function.

Log Files   Log files are another tool valuable in monitoring a system. Certain logs—such as a system log or network messages—should be maintained continually, whereas others can be used only when necessary. A line trace, for example, is a log of the activity on a particular line that is normally used only when a problem has been detected. Some software has been designed to log its activities on demand; the network manager would enable or disable the logging, depending on what information is required. Log files are used for both diagnostic functions and predictive or management functions.

log file   A monitoring tool used for both diagnostic functions and predictive or management functions.

Network Configuration Tools   Network configuration tools are used to plan the optimum network configuration with respect to sources and types of circuits. In the past these have been relatively expensive to purchase or use, and some were limited to one common carrier's facilities or geographical locations. These systems are now available both on microcomputers and at more affordable prices.

network configuration tool   A monitoring tool used to plan the optimum network configuration with respect to sources and types of circuits.

Management Tools

Menuing and Inventory Software   **Menuing software** is used in both LANs and WANs to provide users options via a menu of choices. On LANs, menu software allows a network administrator to quickly implement a set of choices and the actions associated with those choices. **Inventory software** is capable of interrogating many components of a LAN and collecting information on those components. Examples of the data collected include network addresses, CPU types, operating systems, disk utilization on servers and workstations, and workstation and server memory configurations. Many of the statistics needed by a network administrator in managing and fixing a network are automatically provided and reported by inventory software.

Project Planning Tools   **Project planning tools** are beneficial in the administration of the network, in planning the activities of the team members, in the installation of new equipment and software, and in numerous other management activities. Many of these tools are now available on microcomputers, bringing them to more users at a relatively low cost.

Database Management Systems and Report Generators   Database management systems and report generators are also useful management tools. The database can be used to store statistical and operational information, which a good query/report writer can select, synthesize, and summarize. These systems can schedule members of the network management team, store and retrieve error and trouble report information, and produce reports on modeling. Database management systems are available on most systems today and can be very useful in storing, modifying, and retrieving data about the network management function. State-of-the-art systems enable users to define a database; enter, modify, and delete information; and generate reports without having to write any or much code. Many of the microcomputer relational-model database systems provide all these features and are oriented toward users with little expertise in programming or systems.

SUMMARY

Managing a network can be a complex task requiring a wide range of information and tools. NMSs and utilities assist the administrator in managing the network and correcting network problems. An NMS collects statistics on network components, provides alerts when proper operation is threatened, and generates standard reports to allow the network manager to monitor performance and take corrective actions before problems develop. Two network management protocols, Simple Network Management Protocol (SNMP) and Common Management Information Protocol (CMIP), have been defined to assist vendors in creating software and hardware that can be monitored. The SNMP is part of the TCP/IP suite and is widely used in a variety of hardware and software platforms. The CMIP is an International Standards

Organization recommendation for collection and reporting of management information. Although more comprehensive than the SNMP, CMIP is not yet widely implemented.

A number of vendors provide NMSs. IBM's Netview has three variations, Netview, Netview/PC, and Netview/6000. Each is designed to support different network configurations. Netview is designed to support SNA networks, Netview/PC provides interfaces to non-IBM devices in an SNA network, and Netview/6000 is designed for noncentralized networks using a variety of vendor platforms. Novell Corporation's NMS is called Network Management System and provides management capabilities for LANs running under Novell's NetWare LAN operating system. NMS services are also provided by a variety of other vendors.

In addition to a comprehensive NMS, a variety of tools and utilities are available to assist network managers in performing their duties.

KEY TERMS

agent, *459*

alert (alarm), *457*

analog line monitor, *465*

cable tester, *465*

Common Management Information Protocol (CMIP), or Communications Management Information Protocol, *459*

emulator, *465*

filter, *457*

GET, *459*

inventory software, *468*

LAN analyzer, *464*

log file, *467*

management component, *459*

Management Information Base (MIB), *459*

menuing software, *468*

metering software, *466*

network configuration tool, *467*

Network Management System (NMS), *454*

performance monitor, *466*

project planning tool, *468*

remote control software, *465*

Remote Monitoring MIB (RMON MIB), *460*

SET, *459*

Simple Network Management Protocol (SNMP), *459*

simulation model, *466*

Structure of Management Information (SMI), *459*

TRAPS, *459*

workload generator, *467*

REVIEW QUESTIONS

1. How are statistics used in network management?

2. What functions are performed by network management systems?

3. Describe how IBM's Netview and Netview/PC interact with each other.

4. Compare and contrast Netview and Netview/6000.

5. Describe the capabilities of Novell's Network Management System.

6. Describe the function and use of four LAN management tools.

7. Describe the function and use of:

   a. analog line monitor

   b. emulator

   c. simulation model

   d. log files

   e. metering software

   f. menuing software

   g. remote control software

8. How are project management tools used in network management?

9. Compare the Simple Network Management Protocol (SNMP) and the Common Management Information Protocol (CMIP).

10. Why are SNMP and CMIP necessary?

PROBLEMS AND EXERCISES

1. Investigate a network management system other than IBM's Netview. How does it compare to the features provided by Netview?

2. Explain how five of the statistics listed in Table 14-1 might be used in managing the network.

3. Describe two situations in which it would be beneficial to have a LAN utility that allows the network manager to view what is displayed on a workstation's monitor. As a workstation user, would you have any concerns regarding the use of such a tool? If so, what are your concerns?

4. Describe a situation in which it would be beneficial for a network manager to take control of a workstation's keyboard.

5. Find two software applications that perform the functions described in Exercises 3 and 4. What features do these applications provide? What do they cost?

REFERENCES

Carleton, Russ. "Distributed Protocol Analyzers." *InfoWorld*, October 5, 1992.

Cashin, Jerry. "Standards the Key Note in Network Management." *Software Magazine*, Volume 12, Number 15, November 1992.

Dolan, Tom. "SNMP Streamlines Multi-Vendor Network Management." *LAN Technology*, Volume 7, Number 2, February 1991.

Hurwicz, Michael. "Network Management Tools." *Computerworld*, May 1, 1989.

Jander, Mary. "SNMP 2: Coming Soon to a Network Near You." *Data Communications*, Volume 21, Number 16, November 1992.

O'Connell, Brian. "Simplify, Simplify, Simplify." *DEC Professional*, Volume 11, Number 10, October 1992.

Stephenson, Peter. "Network Monitoring: Don't Launch a LAN without It." *MIS Week*, June 4, 1990.

Takeuchi, Naomi. "A Day in the Life of a Protocol Analyzer." *LAN Technology*, Volume 7, Number 2, February 1991.

Treece, Terry. "Control from the Console." *LAN Technology*, Volume 8, Number 10, October 1992.

Security, Recovery, and Network Applications

· ·

CHAPTER OBJECTIVES

After studying this chapter you should be able to:

- Compare the three major classes of security: physical, data access, and encryption
- Describe the functions of the OSI presentation and application layers
- Discuss error detection and recovery capabilities
- Describe data-compression techniques and the role of data compression in networks
- Discuss the types and capabilities of groupware

*I*n this chapter we discuss some of the functions found in the OSI reference model's application and presentation layers. Two important functions found at these layers are providing security and recovering from failures. Security helps protect network resources by limiting access by unauthorized users and preventing authorized users from making mistakes and making unauthorized data accesses. Networking, particularly LANs, has given rise to a new class of applications called groupware. In this chapter you will read about several varieties of groupware applications and how they support the interaction of individuals in a workgroup. In providing users access to network applications and utilities, the network administrator must ensure that the software is used in accordance with provisions stipulated by the software vendor. Failure to adhere to these provisions may result in legal action and associated penalties. We begin with a short review of the functions of the application and presentation layers.

THE PRESENTATION LAYER

The presentation layer accepts the data from the application layer and provides generalized formatting of the data. Thus, if there are data preparation functions common to a number of applications, rather than being embedded in each application, these functions can be resolved by the presentation services. The types of functions that can be performed at this level are encryption, compression, terminal-screen formatting, and conversion from one transmission code to another (e.g., EBCDIC to ASCII).

THE APPLICATION LAYER

The application layer is functionally defined by the user. Application programs sometimes must communicate with each other. The content and format of the data being exchanged are dictated by the needs of the organization. The application determines which data is to be transmitted, the message or record format for the data, and the transaction codes that identify the data to the receiver. An order entry transaction started on a sales node may need to pass product shipping information to a warehouse node. This message will contain the ship-to address, part identifiers, quantities to be shipped, and a message code indicating the action to be taken by the receiving application.

OSI LAYER FORMATTING

At each OSI level above the physical level, headers and control characters can be added to a message. Header information would include transaction identification, originating terminal, time stamp, transaction type, destination information, routing information, and sequence numbers.

Application Layer Formatting   The basic concern of the application level is to establish and maintain a connection that allows two applications to communicate. Formatting by the application layer is meant to organize the data into fields and to order the fields into records. Some systems, such as the U.S. bankwire system, use variable-length fields with separators as field delimiters. Most business systems use fixed-length fields organized into records of variable or fixed length, like those in a COBOL program. The only requirement is that the sending and receiving applications agree on the message format. The application can also attach a descriptive header to the message, possibly containing a transaction identification, date and time stamp, originating terminal or application, and an identifier telling the receiving application what to do with the message — for instance, add to database, modify a database record, or database inquiry. Figure 15-1 gives an example of a message built by the application level.

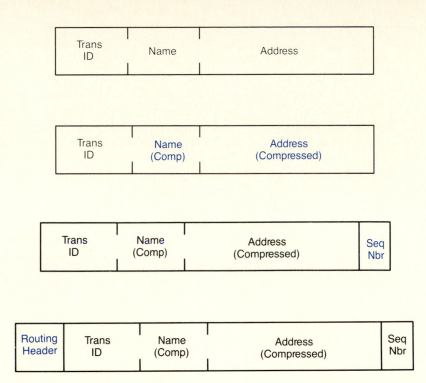

Figure 15-1

Application Formatted
Message

Figure 15-2

Presentation Layer —
Compression

Figure 15-3

Transport Layer — Sequence
Number

Figure 15-4

Network Layer — Destination
Header

Presentation Layer Formatting   The application layer passes the message to the presentation layer. In Figure 15-2, the only change made by the presentation layer is compression.

Session Layer Formatting   The next layer is the session layer, responsible for establishing the connection, recovery (should the session be disrupted), flow control, and dialogue rules. The session layer adds nothing to the message in our example.

Transport Layer Formatting   The transport layer in this example helps provide end-to-end message accountability. The transport layer breaks a long message into smaller transmission blocks, if necessary, and enables its peer on the receiving side to reconstruct the message. For the message in Figure 15-3, the transport layer has appended a message sequence number, which can be used for recovery if one of several packets that form the message is lost. This is not the same sequence number as the data link control sequencing for HDLC.

Network Layer Formatting   One function of the network layer is routing. In performing this function it can append the routing information to the message, as illustrated in Figure 15-4.

Data Link Layer Formatting   At the data link layer, the control information is included in the message. This includes the headers, block check char-

HDLC Header	Routing Header	Trans ID	Name (Comp)	Address (Compressed)	Seq Nbr	HDLC Trailer

Figure 15-5

Final Message Format with HDLC Protocol

acters, and, if needed, transparency control characters. The changes that would be made to the messages at this level are described in Chapter 9.

device formatting   Formatting a message for display on a specific type of terminal, printer, log file, or similar output device.

Device Formatting   Message formatting is only one part of the formatting that must be done. **Device formatting** prepares the message for display on a specific type of terminal, printer, log file, or similar output device. For page mode terminals, the message and data fields within the message must be defined by control or escape sequences. Field alignment, page numbering, titles, subtitles, column headings, and carriage control must be inserted for printed output. Record blocking and message formatting must be implemented for log files. Figure 15-5 shows the message in its final transmission format.

SECURITY

Security does not prevent unauthorized access to a system, but only makes such access more difficult. The delay to access the system should be long enough either to make unauthorized access cost prohibitive or to give the system manager time to detect and apprehend the perpetrator, or both. In the first case, the rewards of unauthorized access would be less than the cost of breaking into the system. In the second, the attempted penetration would be detected and further attempts suppressed. From the system owner's perspective, the cost of security should be no more than the potential loss from unauthorized system access.

Note also that levels of security may exist. No security means that any user can access and use anything on the system. On a system with no security, a user could give himself or herself a raise or a good performance rating. On the other hand, total security means no one can access or use anything on the system. Obviously, selecting the proper security level for each user is important. Imposing tighter security makes the system more difficult to use and increases the system overhead. Security should protect data from intentional or accidental loss or disclosure, without adversely affecting employees' ability to perform their jobs.

Vendor-Provided Security

Security needs are as various as the number of users. Each organization has its own security objectives, and it is therefore difficult to provide one security system that meets everyone's needs. Vendors of hardware or systems software tend to provide only basic security features. This security is generally found only in vendor-provided user interfaces, such as command interpreters and operator- or programmer-level interfaces. When provided, such facilities are generally limited to user identification and authentication. At the data level, additional protection includes layered security for access to files and operating system safeguards, such as prohibiting one process from interfering with the data of another process and viewing the data of an active or recently terminated process.

This section addresses security concerns more directly affecting the data communications network, and does not include operating system security.

Physical Security

Physical security means using techniques such as door locks, safes, and security guards to deny physical access to areas containing sensitive information. Because physical security is independent of hardware or software, it can be planned long before the installation of a network and hardware. If access is prevented to physical components of the system such as terminals, communications circuits, processors, and modems, the likelihood of unauthorized access is significantly decreased. Physical security will not prevent an authorized user from accidentally or intentionally misusing the system. This is significant because studies have shown that the biggest security risk companies face is the accidental or intentional destruction or misuse of data by employees.

Because of the notoriety given to hackers, for some people security is associated with issues such as user IDs and passwords to protect against unauthorized remote access. However, security was a requirement for some applications before remote access was common and in some current systems that do not provide remote access. Enforcement of security in these systems is easier than it is in most of today's networks. A batch processing system is an example of a system that might not allow remote access. Consider the security implications of such a system. All the computerized data and devices that can access that data can be contained within a single computer room. Paperwork used for generating batch inputs and printed outputs are the only forms of data that need to leave the computer facility. Security for this system can be primarily satisfied by physical security.

Because gaining access to computerized data in a pure batch facility requires gaining access to the computer room, security locks on computer room doors and proper staff training regarding computer room access provide a security level adequate for many installations. While the computer staff is on duty, they control computer facility access; during off-shift hours, security guards can take over. The hard-copy documents that are removed from the computer room can be controlled through corporate policies for dissemination and protection of paperwork.

A common physical security measure is a surveillance system. Security personnel can use this system to screen entry to the premises. The premises may be the property on which the facility is located, individual buildings,

physical security   Measures such as door locks, safes, and security guards, taken to deny physical access to restricted areas.

rooms within a building, or combinations of these. Additional security can be provided for sensitive areas with closed-circuit television monitors, motion sensors, alarms, and other such intrusion-detection devices. Many installations can justify features such as closed-circuit television and motion sensors because they provide for equipment protection as well as data protection. Use of these devices may result in reduced insurance rates and partially offset their cost.

Other physical security measures that may be used include:

- All equipment should be located in secure areas with controlled personnel access.

- Nonsecure transmission media, such as broadcast radio, should be avoided where possible because such transmissions are easier to intercept. Use a conducted medium rather than a radiated one for such transmissions.

- If broadcast radio must be used, all transmitted data should be encrypted (encrypting only sensitive data identifies it as such to a potential penetrator and makes his or her work easier).

- Switched lines should be avoided, if possible. Recall that switched lines are those that can be accessed through the telephone company's switching equipment. If you have a switched line, any person with a computer and a modem has the ability to access your system. When they are used, switched lines should be physically disconnected during the hours they are not required, thus limiting the potential for unauthorized use.

- Computers being used for highly sensitive applications should be disconnected from networks whenever possible, placing an additional barrier to access from other network nodes. For example, some U.S. military computers are connected to a national network, except those that are used for highly classified data.

In most current processing environments, protecting computer rooms from physical access is not sufficient to protect data. Access to data is available via terminals distributed throughout the organization. Many online systems also have the ability to access the system remotely via switched circuits. Because physical security is not enough, other security levels—encryption and access security—must be added.

Encryption

encryption   A process in which transmitted data is scrambled at the sending location and reconstructed into readable data at the receiving end.

Encryption should be used with all media carrying sensitive data. The particular encryption algorithm chosen should be capable of deterring unwarranted use by making it too costly or time-consuming to decipher the message.

Data Encryption Standard (DES)   An algorithm that uses an encryption key to transform data, called plaintext, into an encoded form, called encrypted or ciphertext.

Data Encryption Standard   One of the most common yet controversial encryption algorithms is the **Data Encryption Standard (DES)** adopted by the National Bureau of Standards. DES is an algorithm that uses an encryption key to transform data, called **plaintext**, into an encoded form called encrypted text or **ciphertext**; likewise, someone who knows the encryption key can retransform the encrypted data to its original plaintext. Making the transformation from encrypted text to plaintext without the encryption key is a laborious and time-consuming process. The controversy surrounds the effectiveness of the standard. In 1976 it was estimated that it would take an average of 91–2000 years to break the DES code. Opponents of the algorithm countered that the code could be broken in 6 minutes to 12 hours at a cost of $20–$5000. The primary criticism of the DES is that only 56 bits are used for the encryption key. Critics believe this allows for too few different possible data permutations because systematic attempts to decrypt the message would allow message decryption within a reasonable time. With the increasing speed and lower cost of computer hardware, most critics and proponents agreed that the algorithm had an effective life of approximately 10 years, meaning it should now be at the end of its effectiveness.

Encryption introduces overhead to a network and has the potential of slowing communication. This is particularly true if the encryption is done with software. Therefore, most DES algorithms make use of integrated circuits designed for encrypting and decrypting data. The chips may be integrated onto processor or controller boards or used in stand-alone external boxes. The encryption devices can be placed between individual nodes or at the origin and destination of the message. Figure 15-6 illustrates several configuration options. If the encryption devices are placed at each node, the message must be decrypted at each intermediate node, which increases the likelihood of interception. In end-to-end encryption, only the text body can be encrypted and end-to-end addressing must remain clear so intermediate nodes can perform the routing correctly.

Other encryption algorithms have been proposed, although none has gained the acceptance of the DES. One of the more promising, referred to as

plaintext   The unencrypted or properly decrypted version of a message or data. Plaintext is intelligible. Also known as clear text.

ciphertext   The encrypted version of a message or data.

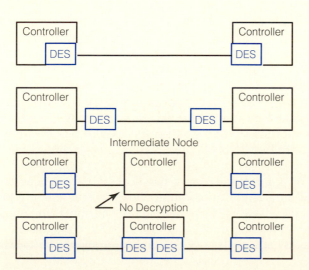

Figure 15-6

Encryption Configurations

trapdoor encryption   An encryption algorithm that utilizes large prime numbers and two keys, one key made public and the other kept secret by the message recipient. The public key encrypts the data, and the private key decrypts the ciphertext. Also known as the public key method.

the **trapdoor encryption** or the **public key method**, utilizes large prime numbers and two keys, one key made public and the other kept secret by the message recipient. The public key encrypts the data; the private key decrypts the ciphertext. A new encryption chip called the Clipper chip is being proposed by the U.S. government for encrypting data on networks and telephone lines. If this chip is installed in telephone and computer equipment, the U.S. government also wants to reserve the right to tap communications lines and decode messages that may pertain to criminal investigations. Most practitioners agree that secure communications is a good idea but have concerns over abuses that might arise if the government has the ability to decrypt all messages.

Key administration is an important function in an effective encryption program. Administration includes:

- key creation
- key distribution
- key storage/safeguarding/restoration
- setting standards for frequency of changing keys

Standards organizations have recognized the critical nature of key management and have adopted several standards to guide key administrators. Among these are ANSI X9.17, which addresses key management for financial institutions, and U.S. Federal Standard 1027, for security requirements of equipment using the DES standard. An organization that is serious about security and encryption should have one or more persons designated as security administrators whose function is to implement security and detect attempts to breach security. Security measures that might be implemented are given in Table 15-1.

User Identification and Authentication

identification   Information assigned to a specific user of a system for security and control purposes. User identification ranges from simple user names to high-security measures such as voice print and fingerprint identification.

authentication   A process in which a system user is required to provide and/or verify his or her user identification to gain system access.

password   A secret expression used by authorized persons to prove their right to access a system.

Encryption is only one aspect of security. In most systems the first level of security is user identification and authentication. User **identification** runs the gamut from simply providing a user name to biological measures such as retina scans, voice prints, palm prints, or fingerprint identification, which are usually employed only in high-security systems such as those of the intelligence and military communities. In business applications, identification is generally supplied by user name or electronic badge. After identification comes **authentication**, which requires the user to provide additional information unique to that particular user, such as a password or a fingerprint.

Passwords   A **password** is the most common form of authentication. It is maintained in a file of information about system users, which typically includes user ID, password, defaulted security attributes for any files created, and possibly an access profile. Because this file contains the information needed to access any portion of the system, it should be carefully secured and encrypted. Passwords should be changed frequently, either centrally by

TABLE 15-1 Sample Security Measures

All users must have a password.

Passwords must be at least six characters long.

Passwords must be changed at least monthly.

Passwords will be changed immediately if there is suspicion that a password has been compromised.

Passwords will not contain users' initials, month abbreviations, or other obvious character strings.

Passwords must not be written down.

Passwords must be created randomly so they do not contain sequence numbers or other instances of succession.

Unsuccessful attempts to logon to the system will be recorded. Data recorded will include the time, terminal from which the attempt is made, and the user ID for which the login is attempted.

All unsuccessful login attempts will be investigated.

All sensitive data will be encrypted.

Encryption keys will be changed regularly.

Two people will be responsible for encryption key administration.

No single individual can change the encryption key.

Switched (dial-up) lines will be disconnected when not in use.

Manual answer and user verification must be used for all switched connections or call-back units will be used.

the network administrators or in a decentralized manner by the users. If centrally managed, passwords are assured of being changed regularly and assigned on a random basis. The major flaw of centralized management is the timing of distribution to users: Dissemination of new passwords must be timely and well coordinated. The logistics in a large, distributed network are considerable. The distribution process also is likely to be the weakest element in the security system: Because passwords are usually distributed in written form via mail or courier, ample opportunity exists for unauthorized users to obtain them. Personal Identification Numbers (PINs) are passwords associated with automatic terminal machine (ATM) cards. The card distributor usually mails the card to the user and mails the PIN in a separate envelope. This reduces the risk of an unauthorized person obtaining both the card and the password, but it is not a very secure method. Consequently, some banks now allow users to select their own PIN, which avoids the need to send the password through the mail.

Decentralized password changes rely on users to change their passwords regularly, either by themselves or through their managers. Individual users can change their passwords without leaving any written record of the password, and they can make changes as often as they like. The password file can be centrally examined periodically, and if users have not changed their passwords within a specified time, they can be so notified or their access privileges can be revoked. Some systems contain provisions for password aging. In this case, the security administrator can specify that users must change passwords at least monthly, and users who have not changed their passwords in the allotted time are warned during their login. The security administrator may allow the user several such "grace" logins. If the user still fails to make a password change under the established rules, his or her account is deactivated. The user will then need to see the security administrator to have the account reactivated. The biggest problem with user-assigned passwords is that they are typically nonrandom, because users like to select a password that is easy to remember, such as their initials, birth date, or names of family members. Unfortunately, this type of password is also more easily guessed by a potential intruder. Some dos and don'ts regarding password selection are included in Table 15-1.

Ultrasensitive Applications

Identification and authentication are usually insufficient for sensitive applications, as we must also identify what functions a given user may or may not perform. The two most common ways of controlling user access are by adding layers of identification and authentication, or by employing user or application profiles.

Layered IDs Layers of identification and authentication help to screen access to sensitive transactions. Once users have been logged onto the system via the initial identification procedures, they can be asked to provide additional identification and authentication information every time they attempt to access a new application or a sensitive transaction within an application. In a banking application, an operator might be required to provide another password or authorization code to transfer funds from one account to another. The operator will use one user ID and password to gain access to the system. This level of access will allow the operator to check account balances and make changes to data other than account balances. If the operator needs to run a transaction that will change an account balance, he or she must first provide another password. If the transaction exceeds a certain limit, an additional password may be required. The advantage of layered IDs is that each application or transaction can have its own level of security, so applications that are not sensitive can be made available to everyone and those that are very sensitive can be protected with one or more levels of security. The disadvantage of layered IDs is that the user must remember several different authentication codes, thus increasing the probability of the codes being written down and thereby made accessible to others.

user profile Information needed to define the applications and transactions a user is authorized to execute.

User Profiles A **user profile** contains all the information needed to define the applications and transactions a user is authorized to execute, such as a user in a personnel application who is authorized to add employees, delete employee records, and modify all employee data fields except salary. The profiles maintained in a user file can be very detailed, covering each application or transaction, or relatively simple, including only a brief profile. With a brief profile, a user might be assigned an access level to the system for each of four functions: read, write, execute, and purge. Specifically, suppose a user has been given Level 8 read access, Level 6 write access, Level 8 execute access, and Level 2 purge access. Each file and transaction are also given an access profile. A user is granted access to the file or transaction only if his or her access number is equal to or greater than that of the file or transaction. Thus, if the payroll file has access attributes of 8, 8, 10, and 10 for read, write, execute, and purge, respectively, the user just described will only be able to read the information in the file. This is because the user's read access meets or exceeds the file's security profile. A write access of 6 is insufficient to allow the user to write to the file.

The advantage of the brief profile is its simplicity. Its disadvantage is the difficulty in stratifying all users across all applications and files in this manner. Of course, this type of profile could be provided for all files or applications, which then becomes a complex profile that is difficult to maintain and administer. Another effective aspect of user profiles is the restriction of logins to specific days and times. In some systems, the security administrator can define a calendar specifying when a given user is allowed to be logged in. Thus, most workers can be given a profile restricting their access to the system to normal working days and hours. Attempts to login during times outside this profile will be unsuccessful.

Menu Selection and User Profiles   User profiles can be very effective when used in combination with a menu selection system that displays user options on the terminal so the user can select the transactions or applications to perform. If a user profile is available, the menu can be tailored to the individual user, and the only transactions the user will see are those to which he or she has access. In the example above, the user who could only read the payroll file would see only that option displayed on the menu, whereas the payroll manager would likely have all options displayed. The security of the system is enhanced by denying users visibility to transactions and files that they are not permitted to access.

Time and Location Restrictions

Time and location restrictions play an important part in system security. In a stock trading application, for instance, buying and selling stock on the exchange is limited to a specific period, so any attempt to trade stock outside of that period will be rejected. In a personnel application, it would be prudent to restrict those transactions that affect employee salary or status to normal working hours. This kind of security can be further enhanced by making sensitive portions of the application system unavailable during nonworking hours.

Transactions can also be restricted by location. A money transfer transaction would be denied to a bank teller terminal if such transactions had to be initiated by a bank officer. Also, money transfer transactions will always be denied if the terminal is attached to a switched or dial-up communication line. In a manufacturing plant, a shop-floor terminal would be unable to start an accounts receivable or payable transaction, because those transactions are limited to terminals in the accounting department. This can be implemented either by attaching applications to specific terminals or by terminal identification coupled with its location and a transaction profile. A terminal profile could list the location of the terminal and the transactions valid from that terminal. Time and location restrictions with user controls provide a hierarchy of security precautions.

Switched Ports with Dial-In Access

Perhaps the most vulnerable security point of any system is a switched port that allows dial-in access. The dangers of this should be evident: It enables any person with a telephone and a terminal to access the system. For that reason, extra security precautions should be taken. The switched line should be operational only during the periods when transactions are allowed. In an order entry application, this would likely be between 8:00 A.M. and 8:00 P.M.; in a university environment this might be 24 hours a day. During the period when transactions are disallowed, the line should be disabled. A call-back unit as described in Chapter 8 can be used to ensure that only calls from authorized locations are received.

When switched lines are used, user identification and authentication procedures and restricting transactions are very important to maintain system security. The telephone numbers of the switched lines should be safeguarded as carefully as possible. A manual answer arrangement should be used in high-security installations, thus allowing person-to-person authentication as well as the usual application-based authorization. Another method used to stall unauthorized users of switched lines is to hide the carrier tone until an authentication procedure has been provided, a solution that is most practical when telephones are manually answered. This method is meant to foil hackers who try to gain access to systems by randomly dialing business telephone numbers until a computer installation is reached.

Recognizing Unauthorized Access Attempts

All the security techniques discussed are simply delaying tactics, and thus their implementation alone may not provide adequate security. A tight security system should recognize that an unauthorized access attempt may be occurring and should provide methods to suppress such attempts. In the movie *Wargames*, a computer was used to generate passwords until a correct one was found. Even relatively unsecured systems would discourage this type of activity. A very simple way to counter such attempts is to temporarily retire the affected terminal, meaning that the system would not accept input from that terminal for a specified period. Such an algorithm might work as follows: After three unsuccessful access attempts, no input from that terminal would be accepted for 5 minutes. Assuming a 6-character password of only letters and numbers, which gives more than 2 billion possible passwords, if 1 billion of these were tried, with a 5-minute delay between each try, more than 9500 years would be needed to gain access. Alternatively, the security system might deactivate the account, disallowing its use to both authorized and unauthorized users. This method is included in a security feature called intruder detection in Novell's NetWare operating systems.

A second algorithm employed in some systems simulates a successful logon. After a certain number of unsuccessful logon attempts, the user receives a successful logon message. Rather than actually being granted access to the system, however, the user is provided with a fake session. While this session is being conducted, security personnel can determine the terminal from which access is being made and the types of transactions the user is attempting to run. This type of simulated session can also help keep the penetrator busy while security personnel are dispatched to the location for investigation. Again, switched connections make such an activity more difficult, especially with respect to apprehension. Stoll, 1989, provides insight regarding an actual case of security violations and detection.

Automatic Logoff

People are often the weakest link in security. All too frequently, operators write their passwords on or near the workstation or they leave the area with their workstation still logged on, allowing anyone to perform transactions on their behalf. This not only jeopardizes the security of the system but also can place the employee's job in jeopardy. The system can assist operators by logging off any user who has not entered a transaction within a certain amount of time, such as 2 minutes. Operators who leave their terminals for more than 2 minutes will have to go through the identification and authentication procedures upon returning. Alternatively, the user can be required to go through an authentication procedure for every transaction. Unfortunately, this adversely affects operator performance. The first alternative is relatively simple to implement on most systems, and in most cases operator efficiency will be unimpeded.

Transaction Logs

Transaction logs are an important adjunct to security. Every logon attempt should be logged, including date and time, user identification, unsuccessful authentication attempts (with passwords used), terminal identification and location, and all transactions initiated from the terminal by that particular user. If several unsuccessful logon attempts are made, the information could also be written on the console of the operator or security personnel so other actions — such as investigation — can be initiated. Transaction logs are also beneficial to electronic data-processing (EDP) auditors and diagnostic personnel.

Computer Viruses, Worms, and Trojan Horses

The need for a new type of security surfaced in the latter part of the 1980s with the introduction of computer viruses, worms, and Trojan horses. Most security countermeasures until that time were oriented toward individuals actively attempting to breach security for personal gain, revenge, or gratification. During this type of security violation, the perpetrator of the breach or the perpetrator's system was actively connected to the network. In contrast, computer viruses, worms, and Trojan horses operate independently of the person who implanted them. A virus infection can be implanted intentionally or accidentally.

A variety of viruses have been discovered and although their implementation differs, there is usually a common objective: to bring down a system or disrupt users. A virus is typically a fragment of code that attaches itself to a legitimate program or file. The virus has the ability to duplicate itself to other programs and files. Once attached, the virus may attack a variety of resources. Some have destroyed or altered disk files, some simply display annoying messages, and others have caused system failures.

Detection and correction of viruses or viral equivalents can be time-consuming and expensive. Special antiviral software often is purchased to eliminate and detect viruses. Viruses can be introduced intentionally or accidentally. An unintentional infection can occur when an employee uses an infected disk, unaware that the disk carries a virus. Within a short time the entire network might be infected. Detection may be made more difficult because some viruses remain dormant for a period of time, propagating themselves before becoming active. New virus strains called **stealth viruses** or **polymorphic viruses** also change their appearance by encrypting themselves, which makes them quite difficult to identify.

Antidote programs exist for most known viruses, and using these antiviral programs can help keep a system healthy. Additional measures also should be taken to prevent infections, including procedures to prevent employees from using personal disks in workstations, checking new software on a virus-free system separate from a production system before installing the software for general use, and closely monitoring the source of all new files. Using diskless workstations is another excellent way to limit exposure.

A worm is a self-replicating, self-propagating program. Original worm programs were benign. They were designed to replicate themselves on network nodes that were relatively idle and carry out useful work. However, the most famous worm program was a rogue known as the Internet worm. The Internet worm surfaced in 1988 on the Internet. It replicated itself primarily on computers using the UNIX operating system. Once established on such a computer, the worm began replicating itself on other network nodes. Eventually, some of the network nodes became saturated with copies of the worm program, reducing the amount of useful work and in some instances causing the computers to fail. Although the worm was not released intentionally, the consequences were far-reaching and the Internet worm illustrated the disruption that can be caused by such programs.

A Trojan horse program contains code intended to disrupt a system. Trojan horse programs are code segments hidden inside a useful program.

stealth virus   A computer virus that has the ability to change its signature of identity, thus making the virus more difficult to detect and eradicate. Also known as a polymorphic virus.

Trojan horse programs have been created by disgruntled programmers. In one such instance, a programmer inserted code that would periodically activate and erase accounting and personnel records. A Trojan horse program differs from viruses and worms in that it does not attempt to replicate itself.

Although the implementation of viruses, worms, and Trojan horses differs, their consequences are often the same—system disruption. A comprehensive security system must guard against each.

ERROR DETECTION AND RECOVERY

Error detection and recovery, specifically redundancy checks and message sequence numbers at the data link and transport layers, have already been discussed in Chapters 2 and 9. Recall that these checks provide detection of lost or garbled messages, and the recovery technique is usually to retransmit the message or messages that are in error. Another level of recovery in data communications systems is the recovery of the system once a message has arrived and before it is processed. This type of recovery ideally is coordinated with the database recovery system. Although individual implementations may differ in their approach, the basic elements of such a recovery system are outlined in this section.

When a message arrives at a node, a certain amount of processing must be accomplished to satisfy the message requirements. For example, the message is forwarded to the next node and stored. After the message has been stored, it can be delivered to a local application or transmitted to the next node on the path to its destination. During this processing cycle the application(s) processing the message, or the system itself, may fail. This section discusses one option for recovery of a lost message or a failed system.

When a node receives a message and acknowledges receipt to the sender, responsibility for the message is transferred from the sender to the receiver. This means the receiving node must be able to re-create the message and ensure its correct processing in the event of any possible failure. Designers of simple terminal systems sometimes maintain that it is the responsibility of the terminal operator to resubmit any possibly lost messages in the event of a failure. This approach can be justified only on the grounds that it is easier than implementing more sophisticated software that would resolve most of the problems automatically. Although such recovery systems slow the system and increase processor utilization, these resources still usually cost less than relying on an operator to recover transactions.

Message Logging

Message logging, also called **safe storing**, means writing the message to a file so it can be reviewed or recovered. To be sure that a message can be re-created, the message should be logged before being acknowledged. The object of the recovery process is to close all windows of vulnerability and create

message logging   Also referred to as safe storing, this recovery system writes the message to a file prior to acknowledgment so the message may be reviewed or recovered later if necessary.

a system in which no messages are lost and all are processed only once. If message receipt is acknowledged and then the message is logged to an audit file, there is a small window of time—perhaps 50 milliseconds—during which a system failure could prevent the message from being re-created. If failure occurs after acknowledgment has been returned but before the write to the log file has been completed, the message will have been lost. Furthermore, it is not enough to initiate the write to the log file and acknowledge the message before the log write is successfully completed. In this case queues on the log device might delay the write, or a file error could occur that prevents the write from being completed. Thus, the acknowledgment will have already been sent and a failure could again cause the message to be lost. As it is typically the responsibility of the receiver to re-create a message once the message has been acknowledged, it is important to design the system so reception acknowledgment is sent only after the message is logged.

Database-System Consistency

In addition to message logging, a transaction must be started for update transactions. A transaction is a logical collection of processing activities that either will be completely accomplished or will leave the database in the same state as it was prior to the start of the transaction. Though this may sound complicated, it is actually quite simple as shown by the following example.

Consider a banking application in which a customer wants to transfer money from her checking account to her savings account. We will call the record in the checking account Record C and the record in the savings account Record S. At the beginning of this transaction, Record C has a balance of $1000 and Record S has a balance of $3000.

A transaction will be started indicating that $500 is to be deducted from the checking account (Record C) and deposited into the savings account (Record S). After attempting to process the transaction, the database can be in only two possible states: Records C and S contain either $500 and $3500 or $1000 and $3000. The combination of $500 and $3000 and the combination of $1000 and $3500 are inconsistent states. If a failure should occur when Record C has attained the value $500 and Record S still has the value $3000, recovery must be invoked. The recovery process must either roll the value of Record C back to $1000 or roll the value of Record S forward to $3500. This transaction is used in the following discussion. Figure 15-7 illustrates the various states of the database for this transaction.

Message Processing

Once the message has been written to the log file, the acknowledgment returned to the sender, the data edited, and a transaction started, the message can be processed. The transaction is forwarded to an application process. The unique transaction ID created when the transaction began is passed along with the message.

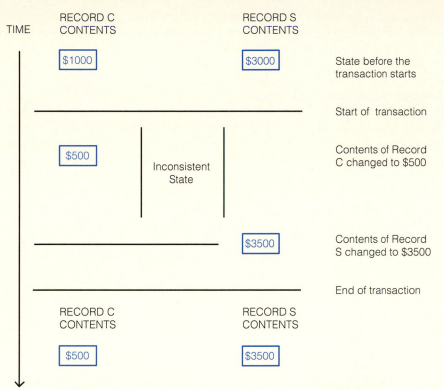

Figure 15-7

Database States during Transaction

TIME

RECORD C CONTENTS | RECORD S CONTENTS

$1000 | $3000 — State before the transaction starts

Start of transaction

$500 | Inconsistent State — Contents of Record C changed to $500

$3500 — Contents of Record S changed to $3500

End of transaction

RECORD C CONTENTS | RECORD S CONTENTS

$500 | $3500

*The database must be left in a consistent state — either the state at the beginning of the transaction or the state at the end of the transaction.

Database Update   The application accesses the two records to be updated in the database and issues a database write request for both records. Before the updates are posted to the database, the database management system writes the before- and after-images to an audit file. The **before-images** are balances of $1000 and $3000 for Records C and S, respectively. The **after-images** for those records are $500 and $3500. After the audit writes have been completed, the writes to the database can be initiated. Just as it was incorrect to acknowledge the message before completing the write to the log file, it is incorrect to write to the database prior to completing the before- and after-image writes—to do so would create a small time window that would make recovery impossible. If a failure occurs before the audit images are captured on disk or tape, the transaction might be unrecoverable. In some systems both the database and the audit writes may be deferred until a later time, with the records held in memory for some time to expedite processing. Deferring the writes does not alter the fact that writes to the audit trail must be completed before the writes to the database.

before-image   The status of a record before it has been processed.

after-image   The status of a record after it has been processed.

Response Message   Having completed the database updates, the application prepares a response and returns it to the TCP. The TCP then ends the transaction by writing an end transaction record to the transaction log and ensuring that all audit buffers have been written to the audit file. After both events have occurred, the transaction is completed and the response message can be sent back to the originating terminal.

Recovery After Safe Storing

Recovery following failure is a joint effort between database and data communications systems. At any point after the safe storing of the original message, recovery to a consistent state is possible. Suppose a failure occurs after the application has received the message and modified the first but not the second database record. The database system begins the recovery process first. When the system is restored to operational status, the transaction will be labeled incomplete. The database management recovery system will use the before-images it captured to restore the database to its state prior to the beginning of the transaction. The before-image of the updated record is written back to the database, thus erasing the update. Next, the database recovery process sends a message to the TCP advising that the transaction was unsuccessful and the before-images have been posted. The TCP retrieves the message associated with that transaction, starts a new transaction, and forwards the message to the application.

Retry Limit   It is possible that the same transaction could fail again, which is often a problem due to database files being full, access method tables being full, or unusual data conditions, such as division by zero. To protect against an infinite recovery loop, the recovery system should have a retry limit that prevents a transaction from being restarted indefinitely. If the retry limit is exceeded, the failed transaction must be handled differently. One outcome is to display an appropriate error message on the computer operator's console and to notify the initiator of the transaction that the transaction cannot be completed. The computer operator must then follow the necessary procedures to have the problem corrected. When the cause of the failure has been removed, the transaction can be resubmitted from the transaction log or from the user. In some cases it is not appropriate to restart from the transaction log. For example, the transaction may have been to book a traveler on a flight. If the system were unable to process the transaction, the traveler may have booked the flight with another carrier.

Audit Trails   Like security systems, recovery systems are not completely reliable. If system failure includes failure of the device (tape or disk) containing the transaction and database audit logs, automatic recovery becomes impossible. In such instances a database backup version is reloaded and as many after-images as possible are reposted to the database to bring it forward in time. Those images on the medium that failed are not available, of course, so some processing is lost. To limit the exposure due to failure of the audit media, many systems allow the user to have multiple copies of the audit trails. Having audit trails on a disk drive is preferable because of the disk's random access capability; a magnetic tape could be used if no disk is accessible.

Chapter 16 contains further discussion regarding transaction design in an online system.

WORKGROUP SOFTWARE

Most LAN implementations have the potential for effectively using **workgroup software**, often referred to as **groupware**. In this section, you will learn what a workgroup is and some of the application tools used to increase the group's productivity.

Before you can fully appreciate the functions of workgroup software, you must understand what we mean by a workgroup and the functions needed by the group. First, a group consists of two or more workers. In doing their jobs, these workers must share information, communicate with each other, and coordinate their activities. Specific work tasks that are group activities include meetings, office correspondence, and group decision making. Groupware is designed to make arranging and carrying out these tasks easier and less time-consuming.

The functions performed by groupware are not new. For years they have been done manually or with limited degrees of computer support. Networked systems in general and LANs in particular provide the communication link that was previously missing in computerizing many of these tasks. The groupware applications that have been created thus far fall into the following broad categories:

electronic mail	conferencing
work-flow automation	document coauthoring and document
decision support	management

> **workgroup software** Often referred to as groupware, this software facilitates the activities of a group of two or more workers by reducing the time and effort needed to perform group tasks such as meetings, office correspondence, and group decision making.

Electronic Mail Systems

One of the earliest workgroup applications was electronic mail (E-mail). An E-mail system has many of the capabilities of a conventional postal system such as collecting and distributing correspondence. An E-mail system also should be able to accept correspondence of various sizes and types and route the correspondence to its recipients in a timely manner. We have, however, come to expect many more capabilities from an E-mail system. Before we discuss these, we first consider how an E-mail system might operate on a LAN by tracing a piece of correspondence through a hypothetical system. For specifics, suppose a LAN user, Maria, must send a mail message announcing a meeting to five other department heads; Alice, Mike, Tom, Shelly, and Chen.

Creating the Message   Before a message can be sent, it must be created. In general, there are two ways to create a message: through the facilities of the mail system or through an external word processing, desktop publishing, or other text/graphics system. If an external message creation facility is used, Maria can start that application, create the message, and save it on disk. Following that, she starts the mail application and imports the message into the mail system. Alternatively, most of today's E-mail systems allow users to designate their message creation software. Thus, the message can be composed from within the mail system itself (i.e., the word processor is invoked from the mail system and essentially becomes a mail job).

Sending the Message   Once the message has been created, it can be scheduled for delivery. The mail administrator, the person responsible for installation and management of the E-mail application, will have identified all eligible E-mail users and their associated mail addresses. In sending her message, Maria gives either the name of each user or the name of a predefined **distribution list** containing those names or perhaps a combination of these two alternatives. A distribution list contains the names of individual users or the names of other distribution lists, and thus provides a simple mechanism to send messages to workgroups. Maria may have defined a distribution list called DEPT-HEADS that includes the names of the other five department heads. The E-mail system takes care of breaking the distribution list into its individual components so each name on the list receives the message.

When the delivery system gets the message and a list of the recipients, it can route the message to the proper destinations. For each recipient, the mail message is delivered into a disk file called the user's "mailbox." The message is available to each recipient almost immediately.

Reading the Message   A message is available for reading once it has been delivered. Suppose Chen has just logged onto the LAN. If mail is waiting, he receives a message that he has mail. If a mail message arrives while he is working at his workstation, he receives a mail-waiting message. To read his mail, Chen starts the mail application and receives a list of his mail headlines. After viewing the available messages, usually identified with the sender's identification and a subject line, Chen has several available options including, but not limited to, the following:

1. He can ignore Maria's message altogether.
2. He can leave the message in his mailbox for later viewing.
3. He can delete the message without reading it.
4. He can read the message and delete it.
5. He can read the message and file it in an electronic folder.
6. He can read the message and forward it to other mail users.
7. He can read the message and send his response to the originator, Maria.

Responding to the Message   If Chen decides to read and respond to Maria's message, he can enter his comments on the message and choose the message response option. He also may send his comments to other recipients

> **distribution list**   A predefined list of individual users, represented by a single E-mail address, that replaces the need to enter each user's individual address when sending a message to them collectively as a workgroup.

and to a third party. After responding, Chen may delete the message, print it, or file it in an electronic folder.

Other E-mail Features

Other capabilities you may find in an E-mail system are described in this section.

Expiration Dates and Certified Mail   If the message is not read within a designated time limit, it can be automatically deleted from the user's mailbox. A sender can also send "certified mail." When a recipient reads the message, the sender receives a notice that the message has been read. A notice is also sent if the message expires without being read.

Mail Classes and Mail Agents   There may be several classes of mail, such as first, second, and third classes. First class can be used for individual correspondence and second class for business news such as company stock quotes and product announcements. Third class can be used for junk mail such as garage sales, want ads, and social-group announcements. A **mail agent** is a software module that can automatically act on behalf of a user. For example, if a user goes on vacation, a vacation agent can forward the user's mail to another user or file the mail in an electronic folder. The vacation agent might also send each correspondent a message stating that the user is on vacation and nominate an alternative recipient.

mail agent A software module that can automatically act on behalf of a user to forward mail or alert other users that the recipient is unavailable.

Broadcast Messages and Message Attachment   A **broadcast message** is one sent to all users (or all but a few users) on the network. Broadcast capability is convenient for sending messages of general interest to all network users. Sometimes this correspondence is an assemblage of several discrete components. For example, a mail message may consist of text created by a word processor, graphic images created by a graphics or spreadsheet application, fax images, and digitized voice. The mail service may maintain an electronic bulletin board. Users can be notified that there are general-interest messages posted to the bulletin board. This keeps user mailboxes from being filled with messages while giving users an opportunity to both read and post general-interest messages.

broadcast message A message sent to all users on a network E-mail system.

Miscellaneous Capabilities   Mail systems seem to be constantly expanding in capabilities as software vendors strive to surpass their competition or just remain competitive. Capabilities offered include:

spelling checker	notification of mail arrival
search messages for keywords	message priorities
voice overlay	carbon copies
security and message	notification of failure to deliver a
encryption	message
ability to create user profiles	interactive mail

Mail Administration

Administering a mail system can be a time-consuming responsibility. User lists and distribution lists must be established and maintained. Periodically old mail messages may need to be manually removed from the system. There is also the potential for mail to be misused, which may include sending a high volume of broadcast junk mail, hate/love letters, and advertisements for personal gain. One responsibility of mail administration is to set corporate policy for acceptable and unacceptable use of the mail system.

Electronic mail is becoming a significant communication tool for many companies. It has become the fundamental means of communication for some corporations. In a private mail system where the communications network already exists, an electronic mail system can help reduce telephone and postage charges. It allows messages to be quickly composed and delivered. Recipients can review their mail at their own convenience, eliminating some of the interruptions of telephone communications.

Some disadvantages also arise from the use of electronic mail. Earlier we discussed the importance of security, and mail system security is one responsibility of mail administration. A secure mail system will provide options for controlling mail messages, such as the ability to encrypt messages. Without such safeguards, one employee may be able to access another's mail file and read his or her correspondence. One of the corporate policies should describe penalties for such unauthorized access. On the other hand, in some cases employees have been fired because their mail messages fell into the wrong hands. Like any tool, a mail system can be misused.

Electronic Mail Interchange Standard — X.400

One of the first standards for the application layer of the OSI model pertains to the interface of electronic mail systems. The **X.400 standard**, developed by the Consultative Committee on International Telegraph and Telephony (CCITT), provides a platform for the implementation of a worldwide electronic message-handling service. Because a wide variety of electronic mail systems are in use today, connecting these systems to provide message exchange between heterogeneous mail systems is the focus of the X.400 standard. X.400 is to mail systems as the OSI reference model is to the interconnection of different networks.

X.400 standard   A standard developed by the CCITT that provides a platform for the implementation of a worldwide electronic message-handling service.

The implementation of X.400 is based on a hierarchy of entities. The hierarchy is used for implementing worldwide message distribution and for addressing. At the top of the hierarchy is a country, followed by a public administration agency or private regulated operating agency, a company, and a user. Addresses for the senders and recipients of a mail message are generated from this hierarchy. An address consists of a country name, a public utility name, a company name, and a user name.

An X.400 system allows users to exchange electronic messages. The users can be in the same or different companies, can be using the same or different mail systems, and can be in the same or different countries. Mail transfer is accomplished via mail agent processes. Each user has a mail agent called a **User Agent (UA)**. A user agent allows a user to compose a message, provides recipient addresses, and receives messages. The interface between UAs is accomplished by **Message Transfer Agents (MTAs)**. An MTA can service none, one, or several UAs. The network of MTAs is responsible for taking a message from a sender's UA and delivering it to the recipient's UA. This environment is depicted in Figure 15-8, which shows a U.S. user communicating with an Australian user.

The X.400 standard describes two different domains: a private domain, which represents a private electronic mail system corresponding to a company in the above hierarchy, and a public domain, which represents a delivery and interconnection network corresponding to the public administration agency in the hierarchy. In some ways the public domain provides a function similar to that provided by an X.25 network—the ability to provide connections and message routing among systems. The public domain is called an **Administrative Management Domain (ADMD)** and the private domain is called a **Private Management Domain (PRMD)**. An interdomain interface is defined to establish protocols for passing messages among different domains. Protocols are defined for communicating among ADMDs and between PRMDs and ADMDs, and for the contents of the message itself. X.400 is significant because it establishes a standard for user communication. It has been implemented in several systems. If the standard is universally followed,

User Agent (UA)   A mail agent that allows a user to compose a message, provides recipient addresses, and receives messages.

Message Transfer Agent (MTA)   An interface between user agents.

Private Management Domain (PRMD)   A domain that represents a private electronic mail system corresponding to a company in the X.400 standard hierarchy.

Administrative Management Domain (ADMD)   A domain that represents a delivery and interconnection network corresponding to a public agency in the X.400 standard hierarchy.

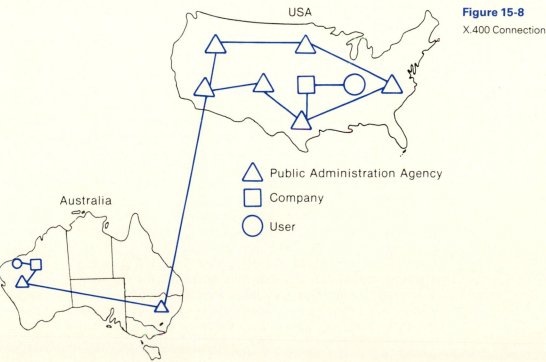

Figure 15-8

X.400 Connection

computer users anywhere will be able to communicate with each other electronically.

The CCITT X.500 Standard

Imagine the complexities of managing a worldwide X.400 electronic mail system. Currently, there are more than 15 million E-mail users in private companies who account for 6 billion messages. Experts predict that by 1997 there will be 30 million business E-mail users who will send 12 billion mail messages. Keeping track of all these users and their mail addresses is a complex task that is addressed by the **X.500 standard**. The X.500 standard specifies how to create a directory system to maintain electronic mail user names and their network addresses. Thus, a user who needs to send a mail message to another user but does not know that user's mail address can search the X.500 directory for the necessary information. The directory will contain the addresses of mail users worldwide.

Electronic Conferencing Applications

Electronic conferencing applications range from simply arranging meetings to conducting the meetings themselves. Arranging a meeting or conference requires that the participants be notified and that a mutually agreeable meeting date and time be set. Conferencing applications provide assistance with one or more of these tasks. If each attendee has an electronic calendar, groupware can book the meeting at the best time. Given an interval during which the meeting must take place, the groupware application consults the calendars of the attendees. It notes the date and time that all attendees are available and schedules the meeting on their electronic calendars. If scheduling conflicts arise, the application can help resolve them. Some schedulers even double-book participants and allow them to choose which appointment to keep. Others report the conflicts and suggest alternative meeting times with no or reduced conflicts, allowing the person calling the meeting to find the best possible time. Once a meeting is scheduled, the electronic calendar software can issue an RSVP notice to the participants. Like personal calendars, groupware calendars can issue reminders of forthcoming events. The reminder might be a mail message or an audio tone. Some groupware allows users to declare meetings to be recurring, such as weekly, monthly, biweekly, and so on. The scheduler then automatically books these meetings for the attendees.

If the meeting is held with participants in different locations, teleconferencing groupware can also assist with communications among the attendees. Some teleconferencing applications allow images displayed on one computer monitor to be displayed on remote monitors. Individuals at all locations can modify the screen image and have the changes immediately reflected on the screens of the other participants. Thus, conference attendees can both view and modify computer-generated data and graphs. Viewing and modifying

---

X.500 standard   A standard that specifies the procedure for creating a directory system to maintain electronic mail user names and their network addresses, as well as the names and addresses of other network resources such as printers and servers.

electronic conferencing An application that assists users in arranging and conducting meetings electronically.

data coupled with audio transmission and freeze-frame or full-motion video allows geographically distributed conferences to be held, saving both travel costs and personnel time. Another conference or meeting communications aid is the creation and distribution of electronic minutes.

Work-Flow Automation

Attendees at a meeting may accept action items they must complete, or a workgroup manager may assign tasks to workgroup members. One responsibility of a workgroup manager is monitoring the progress of such tasks. Progress monitoring is not a new concept. For many years, managers have used **Program Evaluation and Review Technique (PERT)** charts or similar methods to track a project's progress and determine its **critical path**. The critical path of a project is the sequence of events that takes the longest to complete. Often, a project can be divided into several tasks. Some tasks can be done in parallel, while other tasks cannot start until one or more tasks have been completed. For example, when building a house, the roof cannot be put on until the building is framed. Plumbing and electrical wiring can possibly be done concurrently. The project cannot be completed until the path with the longest duration is completed. Thus, project managers pay close attention to the project's critical path(s) to avoid delays. Although some project management work has been computerized for many years, much of the monitoring work was done by people. Groupware has extended the abilities of earlier systems by automating the tracking function.

Figure 15-9 is a PERT chart for selecting a LAN vendor. The critical path for the selection process is indicated by the heavier line. It is the critical path because it has the longest elapsed time between the start and the end points. Groupware helps in monitoring the critical path and keeps the group working together. Through the groupware application, group members can also keep aware of the status of other tasks that may affect their work.

Program Evaluation and Review Technique (PERT) A technique that tracks a project's progress to determine its critical path and to monitor personnel, schedules, and project resources.

critical path The sequence of events that takes the longest to complete.

Figure 15-9

PERT Chart for Selecting a LAN Vendor

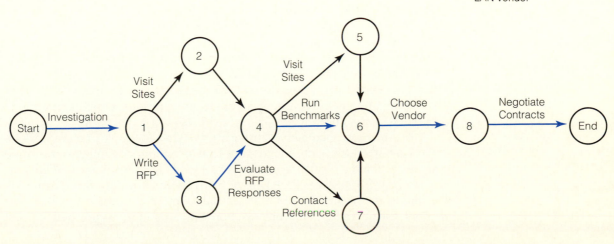

With work-flow automation groupware, a manager can assign tasks to individuals or groups (through the group leader). The individual can either accept the task, negotiate a change, or refuse the task. Once a task is accepted, a completion date is set. The worker uses the groupware application to record his or her progress and to signal the completion of the task. The manager can then either agree that the task is complete and close it out or reach the decision that the task has not been satisfactorily completed and refuse to accept the work. In the latter case, the worker is notified and must rework the task until the result is acceptable. The groupware work-flow application tracks all tasks and evaluates progress. The group manager can query the system and obtain reports of each task's status. If several tasks are in progress at once and other tasks are awaiting the outcome of those tasks, the groupware monitors the progress of the critical paths and helps the manager keep the project on schedule.

Other functions that may be simplified with work-flow automation software include:

- establishing and monitoring to-do lists
- task delegation
- holding completed tasks until released by a manager
- task deletion
- preventing a worker from modifying an accepted task
- setting or resetting task start and stop times
- adding, deleting, or changing the people responsible for tasks
- providing task and group reports

Document Coauthoring and Document Management

Word processing, text editors, and document exchange software were among the early computer applications. Most of these systems, however, were designed to allow only one person to manipulate a document at one time. If you have ever worked on a team to write a program, a report, or a manual, you are probably aware of the limitations inherent in these systems. If you and one of your team members wanted to work on the document at the same time, you found either that it could not be done or that concurrent document updates created contention problems. In a workgroup, it is often desirable and sometimes necessary to have several workers actively working on one document simultaneously. Document coauthoring and management applications provide this capability.

document coauthoring system   A system that allows two or more workers to work on one document concurrently.

A full-function **document coauthoring system** allows two or more workers to work on one document concurrently. Concurrent processing presents some complex problems regarding posting changes to the same pages. Some current coauthoring systems do not provide this ability; however, they do provide the management and control abilities that allow a document to be shared without risk of contention problems. Some document managers help control the flow of documents through the production cycle. Group users are identified as the principal document author, coauthors, or editors. The document manager assists in the production of the document by controlling the flow of the document from one designated user to another.

Document management software can control access to the document by a checkout mechanism. Workers can check out all or portions of the document. Once a portion is checked out, update access to that portion of the document by other users is typically restricted because the worker checking it out may change it. If a worker changes the document, the document management software monitors the changes and records the identity of the person making the change. When the document is ready for review, the application can route the document to the proper reviewers and editors. The reviewers and editors then can make notations and suggestions, with or without changing the document itself, and the application will keep track of the person making those remarks.

Other document management features include document organization, archiving, location, and full file searches. Imagine the number of documents generated per year by a large law office. Some law offices generate more than 50,000 documents per year including wills, contracts, legal briefs, and trial notes. Keeping track of this volume almost necessitates the use of a system that allows documents to be stored, archived to backup media, and retrieved when needed. For such large systems, standard directory and filenaming conventions are often severely limited. A document management system allows users to store a single document under a variety of different subjects. As in a library card catalog, the document can then be found by attorney, client, subject, date created, last date accessed, project, department, author, and a variety of other descriptive categories. Some systems allow users to specify combinations of these attributes as well. Full file searches systematically search files stored on disk or archival directories looking for user-defined text strings.

Group Decision Support

Group decision support software on LANs facilitates the communication of ideas among the members of a group. Each participant has a workstation from which to make comments and suggestions, which are exchanged among the users in an anonymous way. This allows the lowest member in the organizational hierarchy to feel free to criticize suggestions made by the highest member. The key to making this work is protecting the source of ideas and comments. Included in the software are tools to gather and manipulate data from a variety of sources, such as a database, a spreadsheet, and graphic images. Companies that have used decision support technology have found that better decisions are reached in a shorter period of time.

It is important to emphasize that groupware is not intended to replace person-to-person interactions. Our future should not be one in which we get assignments via computers, are computer graded, and are fired or promoted

group decision support software LAN software that facilitates the communication of ideas among members of a group.

via the computer. Instead, groupware complements person-to-person interactions. Groupware provides a tool for assigning and monitoring the group's
tasks with the objective of making the group more productive.

Time-Staged Delivery Systems

**time-staged delivery
system** Software that allows users to identify a
transmission package, designate one or more recipients of the package, and
specify a delivery priority.

Time-staged delivery systems have some characteristics of a mail system.
Time-staged delivery software allows users to identify a transmission package, designate one or more recipients of the package, initiate the delivery of
the package, and specify a delivery priority. If we relate time-staged delivery
and electronic mail to regular mail service, electronic mail is like express mail
service whereas time-staged delivery is equivalent to parcel post or surface
mail. Electronic mail is usually oriented toward short messages of several
pages or less. Time-staged delivery systems may be used for short messages,
for transaction routing, or to transmit entire files.

   With time-staged delivery, the user specifies a required delivery time. The
system then schedules the message transmission to meet the requested goal.
Suppose a user needs to send a lengthy report from New York City to each of
five manufacturing plants, and that the message must be available at each
plant by 9:00 A.M. local time. The report to London needs to arrive several
hours before the one destined for California, so it will have a higher priority
in transmission than the California-bound package. The delivery system also
can use the delivery time to defer transmission until a more convenient time.
Rather than sending data in real time, when the system may be quite busy, it
can delay transmission until a less busy time, such as early morning hours.
In distributed processing environments, the ability to designate transmission
packages and delivery times can be an important capability. An example of a
time-staged delivery system is IBM's SNA delivery system (SNADS).

SUMMARY

Security is a delaying tactic used to deter unauthorized personnel from gaining access to a system and to provide time to catch those who attempt such
access. Security of systems and networks is of growing concern to system
managers. Security can be implemented at multiple levels within a system.
There is an overhead to implementing security precautions, and the cost of
the security system should not exceed the potential loss from unauthorized
use of the system.

   Reliability and presentation of data are very important to the success of
any system. Many software functions in a data communications network
handle these requirements. Data is encrypted to prevent unauthorized disclosure, compressed to economize online time and disk storage, edited to eliminate as many errors as possible, and formatted to make it understandable
and presentable. Data is formatted for output as well as for exchange between
processes and media.

The error detection and recovery discussed in this chapter are different from the error checks made by VRC, LRC, and CRC discussed earlier. This chapter discussed error detection and recovery in connection with system and application recovery. The data communications and database systems should work together to provide a comprehensive recovery that leaves the system in a consistent state, with no transactions lost or processed more than once. The recovery system should also assist with user recovery and establish or help establish users' restart points.

Two network applications that are becoming commonplace in networks are electronic mail and time-staged message delivery systems. These provide communication among network users and move data from one node to another in an orderly, timely manner.

KEY TERMS

Administrative Management Domain (ADMD), *495*

after-image, *489*

authentication, *480*

before-image, *489*

broadcast message, *493*

ciphertext, *479*

critical path, *497*

Data Encryption Standard (DES), *478*

device formatting, *476*

distribution list, *492*

document coauthoring system, *498*

electronic conferencing, *496*

encryption, *478*

group decision support software, *499*

identification, *480*

mail agent, *493*

message logging (safe storing), *487*

Message Transfer Agent (MTA), *495*

password, *480*

physical security, *477*

plaintext, *479*

Private Management Domain (PRMD), *495*

Program Evaluation and Review Technique (PERT), *497*

stealth virus (polymorphic virus), *486*

time-staged delivery system, *500*

trapdoor encryption (public key method), *480*

User Agent (UA), *495*

user profile, *482*

workgroup software (groupware), *491*

X.400 standard, *494*

X.500 standard, *496*

REVIEW QUESTIONS

1. What is the greatest security risk a company faces? Why is this so?

2. How has data communications complicated the ability to provide security of data?

3. Describe a number of physical security features and how they protect unauthorized access.

4. What is data encryption? What benefits does it provide?

5. What are user identification and authentication? Describe three methods for accomplishing identification and authentication.

6. How can you recognize and overcome unauthorized access attempts?

7. What is a computer virus? How can you protect against computer viruses?

8. Why are error detection and recovery important?

9. Describe the steps a system might take to provide a good recovery environment.

10. What is a workgroup?

11. Describe four classes of groupware.

12. Describe eight features that might be found in an electronic mail system.

13. Describe the motivation behind the X.400 and X.500 standards.

14. What is work-flow automation? How does it help promote workgroup productivity?

15. How does a document coauthoring and document management system differ from a word processing application?

16. What are the benefits or uses of a time-staged message delivery system?

PROBLEMS AND EXERCISES

1. Investigate the security features of a system to which you have access. Describe the strong and weak points of the security provided.

2. Research the security capabilities of a current version of Novell Corporation's NetWare. Describe how users and groups are managed. What file security attributes are there? What provisions exist for password administration (requiring users to change passwords, time and location restrictions, and so on)?

3. Research the literature and find three incidents of virus or viral-like infections. What problems were caused and how were the problems corrected? Were the perpetrators apprehended? If so, what happened to them?

4. Computer crime can result from a lack of security. Find three instances of computer crimes (including intentional destruction of data) and describe the nature of each. What security measures could have prevented these crimes?

5. Investigate an electronic mail system and determine which of the features described earlier in the chapter it provides. Does it provide any capabilities not listed in the chapter? If so, what are they?

6. Find a company that uses electronic mail (LAN or WAN based). Interview several mail users to determine how frequently they use the mail, their likes or dislikes of electronic mail, and the overall impact of the mail system on how they do business. How would their work be different if electronic mail were not available?

7. Some people feel that work-flow management, electronic calendars, and E-mail are intrusive systems because they automatically schedule people for a meeting, mon-

itor their work progress, report back to the originator of a message that the message has been read, and so on. Discuss why people might feel this way. What are your personal viewpoints on these groupware applications?

REFERENCES

Becker, Pat. "Down or Out?" *LAN*, Volume 7, Number 10, October 1992.

Black, David. "The Squeaky Wheel." *LAN*, Volume 8, Number 1, January 1993.

Carr, Grace M. "Share and Share Alike." *LAN Technology*, Volume 9, Number 12, November 1992.

Hellman, Martin E. "Commercial Encryption." *IEEE Network*, Volume 1, Number 2, April 1987.

Naecker, Philip A. "Security: Security Checklist." *DEC Professional*, Volume 8, Number 4, April 1989.

Nunamaker, Jay F., Jr. "Teamwork Tools Lead the Way to Creative Collaboration." *Corporate Computing*, Volume 1, Number 2, August 1992.

Rochlis, Jon A., and Mark W. Eichin. "With Microscope and Tweezers: The Worm from MIT's Perspective." *Communications of the ACM*, Volume 32, Number 6, June 1989.

Seeley, Donn. "Password Cracking: A Game of Wits." *Communications of the ACM*, Volume 32, Number 6, June 1989.

Spafford, Eugene H. "Crisis and Aftermath." *Communications of the ACM*, Volume 32, Number 6, June 1989.

Stoll, Clifford. *The Cuckoo's Egg: Inside the World of Computer Espionage*. New York: Doubleday, 1989.

Vaughan-Nichols, Steven J. "Transparent Data Exchange." *Byte*, Volume 16, Number 12, November 1991.

Whitten, David. "X.400: Breaking Vendor Boundaries for Enterprise-Wide E-Mail." *Telecommunications*, Volume 23, Number 7, July 1989.

Systems Analysis

CHAPTER OBJECTIVES

After studying this chapter you should be able to:

- List and briefly describe the phases in the product life cycle
- Describe the characteristics of good transaction design
- Discuss the ways of acquiring hardware and software

*S*ystems analysis is the process of designing systems. The system being designed may be an applications system, a data communications system, or a database system. In application each of these systems must be integrated successfully to create the data-processing system. Because this is a text about data communications, we focus on issues involved in analysis of the data communications system, but we cannot do this without considering the needs of other parts of the data-processing system. For example, an airlines reservation system may have the objective of confirming a reservation within two seconds. The time for this transaction will be divided between the data communications system for message transfer, the application system for processing, and the database management system for data access. Only by looking at all aspects of this transaction are we able to configure the data communications system that, in concert with the other subsystems, is able to meet the transaction requirements. In this chapter we discuss some aspects of data communications analysis and design that are essential to configuring components of the data communications system. The Syncrasy case study at the conclusion of this chapter shows how the chapter material can be applied.

THE DESIGN PROCESS

All design processes are oriented toward one goal: producing a product. In building a product, designers need a plan that takes them from the point of conceptualization through implementation. The plan must have a progression of steps for defining the problem, proposing and evaluating solutions, selecting an approach, identifying constraints, designing the solution, and then implementing the solution. Typical criteria that must be satisfied are cost-effectiveness, good performance, ease of maintenance, and ease of use.

THE PRODUCT LIFE CYCLE

The product life cycle recognizes that a product goes through several well-defined stages during its life. Designers identify four to six major product life-cycle phases. Five phases are listed in Table 16-1, and the characteristics of each are defined below. Other design approaches may use different descriptions for the phases or a different number of phases. Even though approaches may differ, the objectives and items produced are essentially the same. If a network manager must set up a new network or expand an existing one, he or she will need to go through an analysis and design process like that described in the system life cycle.

　　Feedback loops to previous steps occur throughout all phases of the design. The design phases and feedback loops are illustrated in Figure 16-1. The significance of feedback loops is twofold. First, they recognize that designers must sometimes make design changes. For instance, designers may find in the design phase that one of the product requirements cannot be met within established cost constraints. In this event, there are four alternatives: (1) the cost constraints in the product requirements can be revised; (2) the product requirements can be revised to meet the cost constraints; (3) the problem definition can be changed to eliminate the need for the particular product requirement; or (4) the entire project can be canceled because none of the above is practical, meaning the problem cannot be satisfactorily solved within the established parameters and no viable alternative parameters can be found. Feedback loops are used when evaluating and making these changes. Second, at the completion of each phase, a review is conducted to ensure that

TABLE 16-1　**Product Life-Cycle Phases**

1. Investigation
2. Analysis
3. Design
4. Implementation
5. Operation and Maintenance

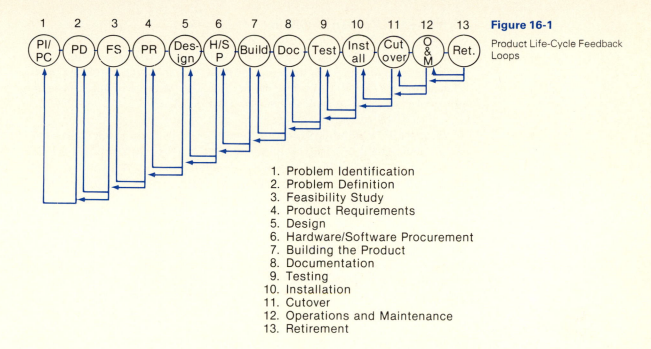

Figure 16-1

Product Life-Cycle Feedback
Loops

1. Problem Identification
2. Problem Definition
3. Feasibility Study
4. Product Requirements
5. Design
6. Hardware/Software Procurement
7. Building the Product
8. Documentation
9. Testing
10. Installation
11. Cutover
12. Operations and Maintenance
13. Retirement

the results are consistent with the outputs of previous phases. Management approval is usually necessary before design proceeds to the next phase. Feedback loops provide a self-checking mechanism to ensure that the project is staying on track.

LIFE CYCLE PHASES

Investigation

The first phase of the product life cycle is oriented toward identifying and defining the problem the product will solve. It consists of three subphases: problem identification/product conceptualization, problem definition, and the feasibility study. We use a two-tiered numbering system in defining the phases. The first number represents one of the five major phases given in Table 16-1, and the second number represents a subphase.

Phase 1.1: Problem Identification/Product Conceptualization Products start from a need or problem, which can be real or anticipated. Once a problem has been identified, it must receive management attention. Management then allocates resources to investigate the problem. This phase is the only one of the 13 life-cycle phases that may not have formal output. If there is a product, it is a problem statement.

Phase 1.2: Problem Definition   The first formal step in the design process is to fully define the problem being solved. It is very important at this point to distinguish between a problem to be resolved and solutions to the problem. If solutions work their way into the problem statement, the ability to examine all possible solutions is limited. The product of this phase is a document that fully identifies all facets of the problem.

Phase 1.3: Feasibility Study   When the problem being solved is understood and defined, a feasibility study begins. A feasibility study is the first step in solving the problem. The objective of the feasibility study is to examine all possible solutions, identify the best ones, and determine whether they are realistic. The product of this phase is a document detailing all solutions considered, their strengths and weaknesses, and why they were rejected or accepted. At the conclusion of this phase, the best solutions — those that solve the problem cost-effectively — are examined in considerable detail before starting the process of developing or acquiring the solution. In addition to documenting the alternatives considered and determining which will be the best approach, the feasibility study contains a recommendation for proceeding to the next phase, for abandoning the project because no realistic solutions can be found, or for revising the problem definition to permit a feasible solution (a feedback loop).

Analysis

The product investigation stage provides an organization with a basic understanding of the problem being solved. The analysis phase has one subphase, the purpose of which is to identify the requirements of the product.

Phase 2.1: Product Requirements   This phase is sometimes referred to as preliminary design or the design objectives phase. The outcome of this step is a statement of both the design objectives and the design constraints. Essentially this document is a contract between management and the designers determining what is to be produced, in what time frame, and at what cost. This document is sometimes called a **functional specification** because it specifies the functions that must be included in the product.

Design

The design phase is sometimes divided into two subphases, preliminary or systems-level design and detailed design. A two-tiered approach is usually preferred for large projects, whereas a one-level approach is often suitable for smaller designs. Only one subphase is described below.

Phase 3.1: Design   This is one of the longest phases in the life cycle. There are many outcomes from this phase, and depending upon the specific design approach, the outcomes may vary. Minimum outcomes will include an

functional specification
An agreement between management and designers outlining design objectives, such as the product to be produced, and design constraints, such as time and cost.

internal specification, an external specification, and a database design. Other deliverables typically include prototypes, product models, and logic and data-flow diagrams. For a software system, the **internal specification** details how the developers view the system. It describes the modules and algorithms for building the system. You can think of the internal specification as the product's blueprints. The **external specification** details end-user interfaces to the system and the information users can get from the system. One item in an external specification may be a terminal screen layout and the functions it provides. The external specification is somewhat similar to a user's manual.

Implementation

The implementation phase consists of six subphases, some of which may not be required. The product and its supporting components are built and installed during the implementation phase.

Phase 4.1: Hardware/Software Procurement   If all of the equipment needed to solve the problem is already available, this phase will not exist. If additional hardware or software is necessary to implement the design, it must be selected, ordered, and installed. This may require a detailed investigation of vendor capabilities and a formal bidding process. One tool used in the formal bidding process is a request for proposal (RFP). The RFP is discussed in a later section. Following vendor selection, site inspections and preparations may be necessary. The equipment required should be completely installed and operable by the beginning of the final testing phase.

Phase 4.2: Building the Product   The system can be created once the design specifications have been completed. The products of this step are a variety of documents, prototypes, functional test results, and the (almost) completed product. We define **functional testing** as the testing of individual modules to ensure that they produce the correct results. This is different from integrated and stress testing, which come later.

Phase 4.3: Documentation   Documentation is an integral part of each phase. It is also identified as a separate phase to emphasize its importance and to identify some of the documents that need to be produced. The products of this phase are the formal documents that must accompany the finished product, including reference manuals, maintenance manuals, users' manuals, and operators' manuals.

Phase 4.4: Testing   Functional testing is completed during the building phase. The formal testing phase is for integration and stress testing. The products of this phase are a test plan, a test bank, test reports, and eventually the formal acceptance of the product by the operations group. **Integrated testing** ensures that all parts of the system function well together. If the outputs of one program are the inputs to another, integration testing determines whether the interface between the two programs works correctly. Like-

internal specification Specifications or "blueprints" for developing a software system.

external specification Specifications detailing end-user interfaces to a system and information available to the user.

functional testing   Testing individual modules to ensure that they produce the desired results.

integrated testing   A procedure that ensures that all parts of a system are functionally compatible.

wise, if two processes exchange messages in processing a transaction,
integrated testing checks the compatibility of their message formats. **Stress
testing** ensures that the system can sustain the designated workload. This
may include the ability to process a specific number of transactions per unit
of time, provide a stated response time to a set of transactions, or complete a
given set of work, such as a batch job, within a specified amount of time.

Phase 4.5: Installation   The system is ready to be installed upon successful completion of the testing phase. The results of this phase are an
installation plan and an operational system.

Phase 4.6: Cutover   The cutover phase consists of phasing out the old
system and making the new one fully operational. The eventual result of this
phase is an active working system. Preliminary outputs are a plan for how
cutover will be accomplished and contingency plans if the new system does
not meet expectations.

Operations and Maintenance

The last phase in the life cycle of a product is the operations and maintenance
phase. It consists of two subphases: (1) operations and maintenance and (2)
retirement.

Phase 5.1: Operations and Maintenance   During this phase the product is enhanced to provide new capabilities, the system is monitored and
tuned to maintain adequate performance levels, and system bugs are fixed.
The products are change requests, updates to the existing documentation to
reflect changes, and a myriad of statistics and reports necessary for the monitoring and control functions.

Phase 5.2: Retirement   At some time the product will be replaced. The
results of this phase are utilities to assist in transforming to the replacement
system and archiving the retired one.

TRANSACTION DESIGN

A **transaction** is defined as a user-specified group of processing activities
either that are completed or, if not completed, that leave the database and
processing system in the same state as before the transaction started. Thus, a
transaction always leaves the database and the system in a consistent state. A
transaction is also a unit of recovery, an entity that the recovery system
manages. Recovery and contention have a great influence on transaction design. From the perspective of an application, it makes little difference how or
when the transaction begins, ends, or is recovered. From a systems design
and system recovery perspective, good transaction design is very important.

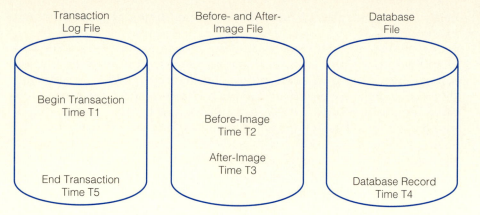

Figure 16-2

Records Written for a Simple Transaction

Review of Transaction Activities

Before discussing transaction design, it is useful to discuss the activities needed to start, end, and process a transaction. A generic recovery system is assumed; details vary with implementations. Beginning and ending a transaction require a certain amount of work, and additional work is required when processing a transaction. Starting a transaction demands that a unique transaction identifier be generated. A beginning transaction record is then written to the transaction log. Each record updated by the transaction must be locked to avoid concurrent update problems. Some records that are read but not updated also may have to be locked. All updates must be posted to the before- and after-image audit trail before being written to the database. At the end of the transaction all audit buffers must be flushed to disk and end-of-transaction markers written to the audit trail.

A simple transaction that updates one record may therefore result in five writes: the begin-transaction record, the end-transaction record, the before-image, the after-image, and the record itself, as illustrated in Figure 16-2. This may appear to be a rather high overhead, but it is not. The cost of inconsistent data can be much greater, and many systems use techniques to optimize the capturing of audit images. Audit images are like insurance policies — they cost a small amount over time but pay large dividends when needed.

Grouping Activities into a Single Transaction

Transaction design covers two areas: the grouping of activities into one transaction and how that transaction is implemented within the system. The need for a transaction to leave the system in a consistent state often dictates the transaction's composition. In other cases the composition is not quite so obvious. In transferring funds from one bank account to another, for instance, it is clear that the deposit and withdrawal must be placed together in one transaction, for to do otherwise would make the database inconsistent. A trial balance would not balance if funds are taken from one place but not deposited in another.

An example of a transaction with less obvious boundaries is adding an employee to a company database. This statement assumes that the transaction activities required are selection and assignment of an employee number, addition of an employee record, and addition of zero to several associated records — employee history, payroll, dependents, and benefits. The employee number is selected so that employee numbers form an increasing numeric sequence with no gaps. This requires reading a control record that contains the next number in the sequence, incrementing the sequence number on the control record, and rewriting the control record.

Although the employee will not be fully entered into the system until all these activities have been completed, it may be unnecessary to group all activities in a single transaction. The selection and assignment of an employee number and the creation of an employee record are tightly coupled events. Thus, if an employee number has been removed from the control sequence, there should be an employee record with that number, which number should be available for reuse if adding the employee to the file fails. However, adding a dependent record, which requires only that an employee record exist, is not so tightly linked with the process of creating the employee record. Indeed, dependent records are frequently added long after an employee has been hired. The same can be said for payroll records, benefits, and work history. In this example, there might be one or several transactions.

Advantages and Disadvantages of Single Versus Multiple Transactions

What would be the advantages and disadvantages of making the employee transaction a single or multiple transaction?

Brief Versus Long Transactions   A single transaction requires only one begin-and-end transaction activity. Although not an overriding consideration, there is an overhead to starting and ending a transaction that a careful designer will attempt to minimize. On the other hand, a long transaction has a greater risk — albeit very slight — of a failure that would involve a recovery. Long transactions also require that records be locked for a longer period, which both increases the likelihood of deadlock and increases the time the records are unavailable. When record locking is used to resolve the multiple update problems of contention (which arise when two or more users attempt to access the same records), deadlock can occur. As discussed in Chapter 6, deadlock results when two different users (in this case, transactions) have controls over records and attempt to access records the other user has already locked, as illustrated in Table 16-2.

Multiple Sessions with One Operator   The major consideration in whether to group multiple updates into one transaction is none of the above, however. Because the weakest link in a transaction is perhaps the operator, good transaction design avoids multiple sessions with the terminal operator

TABLE 16-2 **Deadlock Situation**

	Transaction 1	Transaction 2
T	Read and lock Record A.	Read and lock Record B.
I	Attempt to read Record B.	Attempt to read Record A.
M		
E	Wait.	Wait.

whenever possible. If it is decided when adding a new employee to treat all activities as one transaction, complications could arise, as follows: The terminal operator begins the transaction by entering the employee data, triggering updates to the employee number assignment file, the employee file, and perhaps a number of access method files. All these updates are accomplished by one interaction with the terminal. Having been updated, the employee number assignment record and the new employee record are locked. The operator next enters job history information. If the operator takes a lunch break at this point, putting the transaction on hold with its records locked, then, because the employee number assignment record must be used every time an employee is added, no employees can be added during this interval.

The problem with having a transaction span sessions with one operator is not just the operator's potential absence; it is also the amount of time that a transaction must be held in limbo while the operator enters more information. Compared to the milliseconds required to update databases and process transactions, the minutes required to enter the data are rather long. This situation is further complicated when records are locked across sessions with the operator. Fortunately, techniques exist for avoiding such delays.

How to Avoid Multiple Sessions   If system design requires all the activities described for adding an employee to be a single transaction, the transaction should be planned to avoid multiple sessions with the operator once the transaction begins. Essentially the solution is to gather all necessary information before beginning the transaction. One way this could be accomplished is described here. The operator enters the information for the new employee. The data is edited, and if there are no inconsistencies the record is safe stored. The operator is then prompted for job history data. Again, edit checks are performed and the record is safe stored. The same is done for dependent, payroll, and benefits data. If a failure occurs during this process, the data already input will be available, so the operator will not need to enter it again. Once all of the data has been entered, the transaction is initiated. The database locks are kept for the minimum required time, because no additional sessions with the operator are required. Upon completion, the result is returned to the operator. Should the operator leave the terminal in the midst of the transaction, no records are left locked during the period.

To summarize, transactions should be designed to be as brief as possible and to avoid multiple interactions with an operator. The overriding consideration is to design transactions so the database is always left in a consistent state and so recovery can be assured. The participation of a terminal operator in the recovery process should be kept to a minimum. Operators should be notified of the last activity completed on their behalf so they can continue from the correct place.

SELECTING HARDWARE AND SOFTWARE

When implementing an online application, it is sometimes necessary to acquire additional hardware and software to support the application, especially if the online application is the first break from the more traditional batch operating environment. In addition to the hardware and software, new services such as communications media, support personnel, and education may be needed. If the new application fits the existing equipment as is or with minor enhancements, selection of hardware and software is a relatively simple task. In those situations where major acquisitions are necessary, the prudent systems group should evaluate the offerings of several vendors. In the remainder of this section we assume that support of the new application requires a major upgrade of hardware and software. Selecting a hardware or software system involves selecting more than just a system: A vendor is also being selected. The vendor's ability to maintain, enhance, and expand the components may well determine the selection's overall success. Therefore, the components and the vendor must be evaluated with equal care.

Request for Information

Request For Information (RFI) An informal method of investigating hardware and software solutions by presenting a brief statement of a problem to be solved and a list of questions soliciting solutions to the problem.

Sometimes a company may want to simply investigate hardware and software solutions to a problem. One way to do this is a **Request For Information (RFI)**. An RFI consists of a brief statement of a problem to be solved and a list of questions regarding solutions to the problem. Vendors are asked to respond to the RFI and propose solutions. For example, a company intending to install a local area network might release an RFI asking vendors to describe the type of network they would propose to support 150 workstations. Some of the questions that might be included in this RFI are:

- What media access control is recommended?
- How many file servers are necessary?
- What type of hardware is used for file servers?
- How many printers can be supported in the recommended configuration?
- What type of wiring is required?
- What is the cost of the configured equipment?
- What are the names of three references with comparable systems?

The RFI may be a preliminary step for the more formal equipment procurement process discussed below, or it may form the basis for the selection itself.

The advantages of an RFI are the ease of creation and response. In general, it is not as detailed as the request for proposal discussed in the next section, and it does not usually entail benchmark tests or other time-consuming analyses such as detailed system sizing and transaction analysis. In some cases where the problem is innovative and unique, the RFI may be aimed at developing a partnership with another company to develop a new product or research new features to add to the existing system.

Request for Proposal

Most smaller companies and private companies can use the rather informal approach of the RFI or alternate methods for system selection. In larger corporations and most government implementations, equipment selection involving a large cash outlay must be based on a competitive bid process and fair appraisal. This is accomplished when the user creates and issues a **Request For Proposal (RFP)**, sometimes referred to as a **Request For Quotation (RFQ)**. In some countries this is called a request for a tender offering. Regardless of the name, the process yields a document describing the problem to be resolved and requesting qualified vendors to submit plans and costs for solving the problem. Henceforth, the term *RFP* refers to the document describing the problem to be solved. An RFP, which has no well-defined format, is used to procure a broad range of equipment from low-cost items such as terminals and multiplexers to large-scale processing systems and software. The RFP for the first category of equipment might consist of fewer than 20 pages, whereas the latter might require several hundred pages of description. It is up to the user to determine what is pertinent to the proposal.

Request For Proposal (RFP) Sometimes referred to as a Request for Quotation (RFQ), a formal document describing the problem to be solved and requesting qualified vendors to submit plans and costs for solving the problem.

Format and Content of the RFP

The arrangement of the following topics in an RFP is not set, except that within a document the ordering should be logical (for example, descriptions of how responses are to be delivered should not be placed between descriptions of the hardware and software components).

Table of Contents   A table of contents should be included for any lengthy RFP document and for some shorter ones. Because the RFP is usually aimed at a team of specialists from several disciplines, a table of contents gives the responders a quick reference to specific topics.

Introduction   The first section of the RFP should be a brief introduction. It can include overviews of the company, the problem to be solved, and the anticipated schedule for completion of the proposal, evaluation, selection, installation, and live operation.

Response Ground Rules   The ground rules for responding to a proposal are ordinarily placed at the beginning or end of the RFP. This establishes the schedule for the selection process, how responders interact with the user during the process, the format for a proposal, the manner in which proposals are evaluated, and how multiple-vendor responses are to be treated. The schedule should include:

- the date proposals are to be submitted
- the place, date, and time for submission of all proposals
- the dates during which vendor presentations can be made
- the date the winning proposal will be selected
- the anticipated delivery dates of the equipment being procured
- the anticipated date the system will be operational

The time and place of proposal submission are quite important. Most RFPs specify a date and time after which proposals will no longer be accepted. RFP responders often are allowed to make a presentation to the selection committee. The presentation enables the vendor to provide additional technical information and to answer any questions the selection committee may have. As such presentations tend to be time-consuming, it is usually a good practice to narrow the field of candidates to a small number of final presenters, perhaps five.

The date of selection tells vendors when they will be notified of success or failure. All responders to the RFP should receive a minimum of two notifications, the first an acknowledgment of proposal receipt and the second a notification of proposal acceptance or rejection. Although the equipment delivery date applies only to the winning proposals, it is important to all responders, because companies frequently need considerable lead time to manufacture or obtain equipment. If the specified delivery date is too soon for a particular vendor, the vendor can suggest a more realistic date in the proposal. The anticipated date to commence operations is important in helping the vendor to determine the number of employees needed for development and installation and to evaluate the costs and risks involved. Some vendors may have the needed equipment in stock, whereas others might require a significant development investment. As with delivery date, responders might wish to propose their own operational date.

Fair Appraisal   If the appraisal process is to be conducted fairly, all responders should be treated equally. This can be difficult if one responder is the incumbent vendor and because personal associations frequently exist between vendor personnel and the selection committee. Furthermore, vendors' sales representatives like to use the selection period to practice their sales skills—with lunches, dinners, entertainment, and an increased presence. One common practice during submission and evaluation is to require all communications between a vendor and the selection committee to be made through a small group of user personnel, thus providing each vendor with consistent intermediaries and response. While evaluating the RFP, vendors frequently need to ask questions of the user. The user can distribute to all vendors a list of relevant questions and answers, which is especially helpful to clarify points in the RFP. However, distribution of questions that disclose information regarding a particular vendor's solution should be avoided.

Response Format   The format of the response is a user option. It is customary to have the response submitted in two volumes, one consisting of technical responses and the other for the financial and contractual response. Each section might be evaluated by a different group, thereby preventing the technical evaluation from being biased by price. In the final analysis a combination of the two reports determines the winner. Providing an outline for responders to follow in their proposals makes for consistency in content and format that decreases the work of evaluation. Question sheets and checklists also provide a quick means of obtaining information.

Evaluation Criteria   The RFP should contain information regarding how the proposal is to be evaluated. Otherwise it is like giving an examination without saying how it will be graded or giving the relative point values for each question. A complete description is usually impossible, but, as a minimum, features should be defined as "mandatory," "highly desirable," or "optional but influential." The more influential features should be pointed out so the responder can more completely describe these critical aspects of the system. This also assists the vendors to determine whether their solution is viable and describes the key points to make in the response. In the final analysis, a grading of key requirements plus a weighting applied to each requirement usually makes the overall evaluation easier. For example, 5 points could be assigned for meeting a requirement completely, 3 for meeting it partially, and 0 for deficiencies. Weights that reflect relative importance can then be assigned to each requirement. For a communications system, being able to interface with IBM's SNA network might carry a weight of 10, and an interactive screen design feature might carry a weight of 2, which implies that an SNA interface is 5 times as important as interactive screen-design aids. Table 16-3 illustrates a portion of a sample evaluation sheet. The technical winner would be the responder with the highest number of points. If a point value is given to the pricing as well, the technical and financial evaluations can be combined to make the overall best response even more obvious.

TABLE 16-3   Sample RFP Evaluation Sheet

Item	Weight	Vendor 1		Vendor 2		Vendor 3	
		Score	*Total*	*Score*	*Total*	*Score*	*Total*
Cost	10	5	50	7	70	6.3	63
Documentation	6	3	18	9	54	6	36
Support	5	2	10	8	40	7	35
Education	5	4	20	8	40	5	25
Page Total			98		204		159

Multiple-Vendor Bids   Several vendors can cooperate in proposing a solution for very large projects, one vendor providing the hardware and system-level software while another contracts for custom application software. In other instances, one vendor might supply the processors, another the terminal subsystems, and a third the software. Users should specify any special rules regarding multiple-vendor bids. As a minimum, users generally prefer to have one vendor as prime contractor with overall responsibility for the entire proposal. Of course, as long as the implementation goes smoothly, multiple independent vendors pose no problems. But when delays occur, it is much easier for the user to contact one responsible vendor for resolution. Having one vendor as the primary contractor simplifies problem resolution for the user and eliminates finger pointing among vendors.

User Characteristics   It often helps a vendor to be provided with a description of the user's company, personnel, and current processing environment. This perspective enables the responder to address the proposal more appropriately. For instance, because there are a multitude of payroll and accounts receivables applications, a section describing the user's company would give insight into how the company works and how the payroll or accounts receivable applications differ from those of other companies.

Problem Description   The major portion of the RFP is devoted to a description of the problem to be solved. This should not include any perceived solutions because such solutions are usually biased by a particular hardware and software environment. An RFP that states that a processor is "capable of executing 2 million instructions per second (MIPS) and supports line speeds in excess of 56 Kbps" is presenting the vendor with a perceived solution to the problem. What is preferable is a problem described in sufficient detail to allow responders to configure a system based on their own hardware and software capabilities. In actuality, many RFPs are released with the anticipation of only one or a few viable contenders. The RFP sometimes is written in such a way that only one or two vendors even stand a chance of successfully competing. In these cases it is up to the vendors to determine their chances of success and weigh the risk of losing their investment in preparing a response.

ADDITIONAL EVALUATION CONSIDERATIONS

MIPS Rates

The quoted MIPS rates represent the perceived processing power, most likely based on the amount of work accomplished by one or several processors with which the committee has experience. MIPS rates are a measure of instructions executed per unit of time, but not necessarily of throughput. Operating systems, database systems, and data communications systems all consume processing resources while providing varying levels of function. A system that provides complete recovery of database and data communications networks can be expected to execute more instructions than one without those capabilities. The application software also can vary significantly in the number of instructions required, depending on the efficiency of the written code as well as the efficiency of the code generated by the compilers. Higher-level languages such as database query languages and interpreters also can consume more machine cycles.

More on Problem Description

The statement of the problem should be a description of the applications to be run, together with the type of transactions expected to be executed. A transaction might be described as being local to one node or requiring communication between nodes and might also define the number of input and output characters, transaction frequency, peak transaction rate, and work performed by the transaction. This type of definition is covered in more detail in the section on system configuration. The amount of work necessary to provide such information may be significant. However, it is impossible to derive the solution without doing this analysis. There are benefits to be derived from this type of problem statement as well: The vendor's response might come up with a novel and economical solution, or it might provide some preliminary design solutions. Regardless, the vendor is allowed to configure the system in a manner fitting their hardware and software rather than some preconceived solution.

Subrequirements

If the system to be procured is large, the requirements can be broken into subsections dealing with data communications, terminals, hardware, and software. Sufficient transaction and batch processing detail should be provided to enable the vendor to size and price the system.

Benchmarks

A **benchmark** test is one or more programs that are run on a proposed hardware configuration to verify the ability of the hardware to meet the application requirements. Benchmark programs usually simulate the activity required by the proposed application. Thus, benchmark testing is useful in assuring that the proposed configuration will actually solve the problems. However, care must be taken when using a benchmark. Benchmarks are also a measure of how well a group of experts can run benchmark programs. A far better measure of performance is the analysis of an already operational

benchmark   A test in which one or more programs are run on a proposed hardware configuration to verify the ability of the hardware to meet a system's application requirements.

system that supports a processing load similar to that of the anticipated system. If benchmark programs are necessary, they should not be required of all responders. Instead, the field of candidates should be narrowed to a small number, such as five, and these finalists should run the tests. This does not preclude other responders from eventually running the benchmark as well. For instance, the five finalists might fail to perform the benchmark as expected on the proposed configuration, thereby elevating the responses of other vendors. The rationale behind having only a selected group run the benchmark test is that such tests are expensive for both vendor and user. Equipment must be allocated and configured, tests written, systems tuned to maximum performance, results evaluated, and reports written. The user should be involved in the testing as a monitor at least and ideally as a partici-pant. A great deal of information can be gained by such participation.

Other Points in the RFP

Other factors that should be addressed in the RFP include education offered, including cost and location; maintenance costs and hours; extended mainte-nance coverage; software license; microcode; maintenance and user fees for the software; location of maintenance offices; escalation procedures for main-tenance; locations of spare parts and the time required for delivery; number, location, and type of available support personnel; national and international support policies where applicable; and the availability of backup systems in the event of a prolonged failure for whatever reason.

References

Every vendor should be asked to submit at least three reference accounts for contact; those unable to supply three good reference accounts should be scrutinized very carefully. The requester should also attempt to contact three additional accounts not listed as references; this can prove very informative. Sometimes the references themselves can provide names of other accounts. If the vendor's customer base is large, references in a similar business or with a similar transaction load as that of the user should be contacted.

Final Selection Considerations

Once the responses to the RFP have been evaluated, the field should be narrowed to three to five finalists. These are the vendors who can be expected to run a benchmark. These vendors' references should be contacted at this time, and contract negotiations should begin. The vendor's standard contract should be reviewed by the user's attorneys. If nonstandard components are to be used, the user should attempt to make contractual agreements about when the components are to be delivered, what constitutes acceptance of the components, and what penalties, if any, will apply for nonconformance. Support and maintenance issues should be resolved. The user should know from which office their support is coming, what the expected response time will be, what charges are involved, what the escalation procedures are, and whether the vendor is willing to provide backup systems should the purchased system malfunction for any significant length of time. The user should ascertain how frequently new releases are made and what the policy is for fixing bugs of various levels of severity, and distributing the solutions, and what this service costs. The user should determine whether enhancements to the product are planned, how frequently they will be made, and the costs involved in receiving them.

Unfortunately, the history of user-vendor relationships is full of well-intentioned but unfulfilled promises of things to be delivered and services to be provided. There is also a history of hidden costs and support problems. For a sizable purchase, the purchaser should make every attempt to protect the investment. Standard contracts provided by a vendor are designed to protect the vendor. In many instances this does not adequately protect the purchaser. Attorneys representing the purchaser should review and modify the standard vendor contracts for any significant purchase. A thorough analysis of a number of vendor's solutions to a processing problem provides a user with a higher probability of success in selecting the equipment best suited to an application. The time invested in this activity is frequently regained several times over in project implementation.

SYSTEM CONFIGURATION

Sizing is the analysis conducted to determine the amount of hardware required to support a system. Sizing must consider the system throughput and the required transaction response times during peak processing periods. Sizing and configuring a system are ongoing activities. Over time, the manner in which an online system is used tends to vary. New transactions may be introduced and existing ones changed or discontinued, or the frequency with which they are invoked might change. Changes in batch processing requirements and hardware also can alter the response characteristics of a system. For example, in a virtual memory system, memory pages are swapped to disk. So long as sufficient real memory is available, paging does not seriously affect response times. As more applications are added to the system, the paging rate increases and performance decreases. Eventually a point will be reached where the system spends more time satisfying memory management requests than it does processing data. This is just one of a number of potential system bottlenecks. Sizing and configuring a network requires a comprehensive knowledge of the application, system, and performance objectives. In this section the focus is on the information that must be collected to make an educated estimate of the resources required to meet the response time requirements of the online system. Batch processing and the transfer of large amounts of data are not considered.

sizing The analysis conducted to determine the amount of hardware required to support a system. Sizing must consider the system throughput and the required transaction response times during peak processing periods.

Response Time

Good response times are important to the success of an online system. During the design process, response times are set for each transaction, the response times for critical transactions are included in the RFP, and response times are measured during benchmark tests. Response time consists of two components: data communications and processing. The data communications component is the time required to transmit a message from source to destination and receive any necessary response. The processing component consists of the activity required by one or more processors in satisfying the request, including field editing, message routing, message formatting, data manipulation and calculation, recovery overhead, and database access. All of these factors must be known to properly size and configure a system. One can start to analyze response time at either the processing or the data communications component. It is usually easier to begin with the processing component and then determine the required line speeds needed to meet the data communications component.

Processing Time Requirements   Processing time requirements start with a detailed definition of the transaction. Because input-output access time is almost always the most time-consuming factor in the processing component of a transaction, the number and type of accesses must be determined. A banking transaction in which the account record must be retrieved using the customer's name may have a higher overhead than the same transaction using the account number. This would occur if the account number were the primary key of retrieval and the customer name were a secondary key. Account numbers also are unique, whereas the name may not be. Thus, the transaction using customer name requires the retrieval and search of an index and multiple accesses to the account file if duplicate names exist. The transaction using account number may require only one access to the account file.

Disk Access Time   For each transaction the number of database or file accesses must be counted, including in the count auxiliary accesses for indices. If optimization features such as cache memory (which reduces disk accesses) or storage of indices on the same cylinder as related data are available, they should be considered in determining the required access times. Being able to complete this step requires a knowledge of the database design, the manner in which records are accessed, and how the transaction requests records from the database management system.

CPU Time   Another component of transaction processing is the amount of CPU time required. This is difficult to approximate unless the transaction has been measured by a performance monitor. A very rough estimate based on the number of instructions executed or just the processing time itself often is sufficient. For the majority of transactions the amount of time spent executing instructions is minor compared to the amount of time waiting for I/O completions. CPU time becomes a concern only when transactions are CPU-intensive or when CPU time is in short supply. Thus, CPU times become a critical element in a statistical transaction where the solution requires iterative techniques and little or no I/O. In the banking situation mentioned above, CPU time is negligible when compared to the I/O time.

Data Communications Time Requirements　A transaction's I/O time and processing time make up the processing component of response time. The data communications component consists of line time plus time to handle the message at any intermediate nodes. Line time is a function of the type of line used, the transmission speed of the line, and the total number of characters transmitted.

The preceding considerations will result in the minimum expected response time. A number of other factors — all dealing with contention for system resources — will potentially add to the minimum response time. If the communications links are shared by a number of devices through multidrop, multiplexing, or similar techniques, the links may not be immediately available or the terminal's apparent line speed may be slower than that of the link. In such cases the average time spent waiting in the transmit queue must be included in the total response time. It is beneficial to determine the worst-case response time as well. Queuing at the TCP, the application, and the disk are other places where delays can occur. The TCP ordinarily handles multiple terminals, but only one terminal receives the attention of a TCP at a given time. The same is true of the application and disk processes. The service times for these potential delays are derived by calculating the expected transaction arrival rates and mean service times.

Example Computation of Transaction Response Time

This example assumes that disk access time has three components: seek time, latency, and transfer time. **Seek time** is the time it takes to move the read/write heads to the proper cylinder. A seek time of 20 milliseconds (ms), which is typical of a number of disk drives, is used in this example. **Latency** is the average time required for the requested data to revolve under the read/write heads. After the seek, the data may have just passed under the heads, thus requiring a full revolution of the disk, or it could be just arriving at the heads, thus requiring no latency. Some disks revolve at 3600 rpm, resulting in a full latency of 16.6 ms and an average latency of 8.3 ms. **Transfer time**, usually negligible compared to the other two components, is the amount of time required for the data to be sent over the channel to the CPU's memory. If the channel speed is 5 million characters per second and the block size being transferred is 500 characters, then the transfer time is approximately 0.1 ms (approximately because a small amount of processing time is also required). These figures represent the amount of time required for random access to the disk.

In the following library transaction, a patron wants to renew two books but does not have a library card available. The transaction requires the following processing:

1. Read the patron record using the name as a key. This requires an index record. On the average three names will qualify. These three records, with address and library card number, are displayed on the operator's

seek time　The time it takes to move the read/write heads to the proper cylinder.

latency　The average time required for the requested data to revolve under the read/write heads.

transfer time　The amount of time required for the data to be sent over the channel to the CPU's memory.

terminal. This requires reading one index record and three data records.

2. Select the proper patron and retrieve the books-checked-out records, one for each book borrowed. Two records are retrieved using the library card number and requiring an index record search of one index record and two data records.

3. Update both book records to reflect the new due date. This requires two writes to the book file and no updates to the index file.

Processing Time   Total disk activity for this transaction involves seven reads and two writes. The system also uses transaction auditing, which requires writes to the before- and after-image audit files and two writes to the audit trail for the beginning and ending of the transaction. An efficient audit system is assumed, so the two before-images and two after-images are written with one disk write each. Thus, a total of 13 disk accesses occur, 9 for the transaction and 4 for the audits. Disk time is therefore:

13 seeks @ 20 ms each	260.0 ms
13 latencies @ 8.3 ms each	107.9
Total disk time	367.9 ms

Approximately 20 ms of processing or CPU time and approximately 100 ms of queuing time are used within the system (waiting for disk and application). Total processing time, then, is:

Disk access time	367.9 ms
Processing time	20.0
Queue wait time	100.0
Total processing time	487.9 ms

Data Communications Time   The number of characters transmitted to the terminal is:

Input last name	10
Output three records	150
Input selected record	10
Output two records	100
Input updated data	100
Output completion status	10
Protocol, formatting	190
Total no. of transmitted characters	570

If the expected response time is 2 seconds, then (without considering the overhead of the data link protocol) approximately 4560 bits must be transferred in 1.512 seconds, requiring a transmission speed of at least 3015 bps. This equates to a standard speed of 4800 bps and represents the minimum line speed. A higher speed link may be needed. If asynchronous transmission is used, 10 bits per character will be required and the minimum line speed will be 3770 bits per second. With a multipoint line, polling overhead and possible modem turnaround times must be factored in. This example, however, assumes a point-to-point line.

Sizing exercises almost always make numerous assumptions. The previous example assumed an average number of disk accesses and average queue times and processing time. With a multipoint line, assumptions would have to be made regarding the number and size of messages transmitted before a particular terminal's poll was received. Prediction of performance becomes easier once the system has been installed and is operational, when variables such as queue time can be more readily determined. Sizing in the case of an already operational system helps determine the impact of changing the transaction load, adding transactions, or changing the batch component of the processing load. Even though sizing analysis is partly an imprecise estimate, it is still valuable in predicting initial system sizing and components, as well as in anticipating the growth of an established system.

Network Modeling   The larger the network, the more difficult it is to conduct sizing and performance estimates. The use of formal modeling tools in these instances is often required. Modeling tools run the gamut from simple spreadsheet templates to formal simulation and modeling systems, which allow components to be described and connected, different forms of arrival rates to be generated, transactions to be described, and critical system factors to be calculated. These factors will include items such as:

response times
   best
   average
   percentile, such as 95% will be under 3 seconds
disk accesses
disk access times
number of characters transmitted
line times
line speeds
processing time
peak performance characteristics

Some modeling systems, in addition to producing the performance figures, also generate software to measure the results on a live system. Transaction scripts are prepared and run on the proposed hardware to find the actual performance information. Live terminals can also be used to input transactions and give prospective users a feel for system performance.

Network Configuration Tools   Design aids also exist to help configure the optimal network links. These tools allow users to indicate the nodes that must be connected and the expected traffic between nodes. Using this information and existing tariff data, the configurator will recommend the lowest cost network connections to connect all of the nodes. Again, if the system being designed is complex, this type of design aid can help economize on the recurring communication costs of network links.

Case Study

Having installed their network, the Syncrasy Corporation has begun development of a distributed order-processing system. A number of transactions have been identified for the system, one of the most complex of which is the order entry transaction. The analysis that went into the design of this transaction follows.

Order Entry Design Requirements

The order entry transaction is to serve the customers in North America. Orders will be filled from the closest warehouses in New York City, Chicago, Kansas City, or Los Angeles. Each warehouse location maintains its own computer system and inventory. The network configuration is depicted in Figure 16-3. Placing an order involves the following activities.

Customer Identification   The operator enters the customer's name. If the name is already in the database, order entry commences; if the name is not on file, a customer entry screen is presented and the required information, such as billing and shipping address, is entered. A credit limit is established for the customer. When the customer records have been set up, the order can be entered.

Order Entry   Order line items are entered, consisting of part numbers together with the quantity for each part. Any number of line items can make up an order. It has been determined that the average Syncrasy order has 8 line items, 10% of all orders have more than 20 line items, and 2% have more than 30 line items.

Figure 16-3

The Syncrasy Order Entry Network

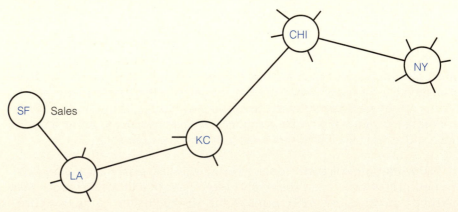

San Francisco searches Los Angeles, then Kansas City, then Chicago, and then New York City.

Total Order Value/Credit Limit Check   The total value of the order is computed by summing the products of line item price and quantity. This value is then compared with the customer credit limit; if the limit is exceeded, the customer is advised and credit can be extended by manual authorization procedures if necessary.

Inventory Check   Inventory is checked to determine which ordered parts are in stock, with the closest warehouse checked first. If the entire order cannot be filled from the nearest warehouse, the others are checked. The operator is notified of any line items unavailable from inventory. The customer then has the options of canceling all or part of the order or entering the entire order and back-ordering the out-of-stock items. It has been determined that 5% of all transactions encounter the out-of-stock condition and that in only 10% of these situations (0.5% of all situations) are ordered items canceled as a result of insufficient stock.

Inventory/Credit Update   If an order is placed, the inventory in each shipping warehouse is updated, and if it is not a cash transaction, the customer's credit limit is adjusted.

Receipt and Order Confirmation   A receipt and order confirmation are printed at the order entry location.

Packing Lists/Shipping Labels   Packing lists and shipping labels are printed at each of the affected warehouses.

Billing

Billing information is generated and accounts receivable files are updated. If the customer pays cash, no invoice is generated, but the general ledger files are updated.

Transaction Design Selected

Syncrasy wants the transaction designed so records can be locked for update as briefly as possible and remain unlocked while awaiting operator inputs. If the entire logical transaction is to be decomposed into multiple database transactions, the subtransactions must be individual elements; for recovery to be consistent, it would be improper to debit the accounting files without a corresponding credit entry. However, the primary design consideration is to provide the best possible response for the customer, meaning that customer identification and order verification must be performed in the minimum possible time. Page mode terminals were selected for this application. They have no local processing capabilities. A number of transaction designs can meet the above criteria. The design selected by the Syncrasy analysts and the rationale behind their decisions are described below.

Customer ID/Credit Check   The operator first enters the customer identification, either customer number or name. This information is transmitted to the local host and the database is searched to determine whether the customer has already been defined. If the customer is on file, the customer's billing and shipping address are displayed on the operator's terminal. If the customer is not on file, a customer definition form is displayed on the operator's terminal. When the customer data has been entered, it is edited for consistency; if the edit checks are successful, a credit check is performed. If the credit check is positive, the transaction to add a new customer record is started, the customer data is added to the database, the transaction is completed, and the information is displayed on the operator's terminal together with the order entry line item screen. The new customer who fails to pass the credit check is asked to pay cash or is referred to the credit department for approval.

Customer Order   Once the customer has been properly identified, the operator enters order line items. This part of order entry can be quite complex, because orders can be open-ended. A virtually unlimited number of line items is allowed and the customer can cancel any or all of the order on an out-of-stock condition or insufficient credit condition. Ten line items can be entered on the first screen; subsequent screens allow 20 line items. Because orders are open-ended, a design decision must be made regarding long orders. The first design alternative basically consists of limiting the number of items per order, and the second allows any number of items and makes a special case of extremely long orders. The problem with long orders is essentially that the transaction control process (TCP) buffers line items as they are received; however, a maximum buffer size is set for storing them. If more line items are ordered than can fit in the buffer, either a buffer overflow algorithm must be employed or the transaction must be limited to a specific number of line items.

In Syncrasy's case, optimization is meant to favor the customer, not the programmer. Because a customer may decide to cancel all or part of an order if a line item is unavailable, dividing a logical transaction into two or more separate recovery transactions was considered impractical. If an order for 40 items were divided into two transactions of 20 items each, the customer could find a line item unavailable in the second transaction and cancel the entire order. This would present a number of problems for the system. Once the first transaction was completed, picking and packing lists would have been printed at warehouse locations. These actions then would have to be reversed. A completed transaction also would need to be backed out, requiring an interface with the audit logs or necessitating that the application keep track of all line items. The first case is usually too difficult in vendor-supplied recovery systems, which are designed to back out a particular uncompleted transaction or to roll all or a group of transactions forward. Very seldom is the recovery system able to back out one particular transaction that has already been completed.

Backing Out a Transaction   Indeed, backing out one completed transaction could affect other already completed transactions. If a part were ordered in both transactions A and B, with B starting after A, then to back out A it would be insufficient to replace A's before-images in the file because that would erase B's update. All transactions completing after A would have to be examined to determine whether they affected A's records, or A's order quantity would have to be added back into the inventory. Even this could create problems if automatic reordering is used. B's transaction could have precipitated a reorder, and adding A's quantity back in could place the quantity back over the reorder point. Subsequent orders could again trigger a reorder. In either case, if the item is expensive, then an overstock condition could be reached, which might adversely affect profits. Syncrasy has decided that for transactions in excess of 30 line items (the first two screens), those items over 30 will be written to an overflow disk file. Experience has indicated that only 2% of all transactions fall into this category. Thus, the operator enters line items until all have been completed. All line items are held in the TCP, with some records possibly in the overflow disk file. The number of line items is maintained in the data entry record, so it is known whether overflow has been used.

Inventory Check   The next stage of the transaction is to determine whether sufficient inventory is available to fill the order. The goods can be shipped from four warehouse locations in North America, so the application uses a search priority, with the first search being at the closest warehouse. Two alternatives were considered in doing the database searches. The first involves locking records as the search progresses and the second involves scanning all items without locking them and then rereading the records for update. In the first case, when out-of-stock conditions are encountered, locks must be either released or held across the operator sessions. In the second case extra reads are required, and the record could be changed by other transactions in the interval between the initial read and the subsequent update read, which could create an out-of-stock condition that was not identified in the initial read.

Inventory Check/Update Alternatives   Analysis of orders indicates that in only 5% of the transactions is there insufficient stock in all warehouse locations and that in only 10% of those situations are one or more line items canceled as a result. The first of these numbers is the more significant, for in 5% of all transactions the operator must be prompted to determine whether any line items should be canceled. This portion of the overall transaction presented the most significant dilemma for the analysts. The five basic approaches considered follow. In each of them, the customer record is read and locked unless it is a cash transaction, thus prohibiting the same customer from placing orders concurrently and exceeding the credit limit.

1. Read records without locking them: If all stock levels could be met then the records would have to be reread, locked, and updated. In 5% of the cases, the operator would be consulted before proceeding. In 95% of the circumstances the records would be read twice and updated once. In rare situations, the stock levels could be decreased by other transactions. In this case, an insufficient stock level would be recognized, thus defeating the intent of deferring the updates.

2. Lock records as they are read and defer updates until the entire order can be completed: If an item is out of stock, the records can be unlocked and the operator informed of the out-of-stock items. Then the transaction can be started again if the order is placed.

3. Same as Transaction 2, except do not unlock the records during the operator session: This ensures that other transactions will not decrease stock levels already checked.

4. Read the records with lock, update them as read, and back out all updated records when an insufficient stock level is encountered: The database management system being used can support this situation. A transaction can be started and, if an insufficient stock level is encountered, the transaction can be aborted, which automatically reverses all updates.

5. Lock records and update them as read: If an out-of-stock condition is encountered, all locks can be maintained across the session with the operator. This option has the problem of potentially locking a large number of records and keeping them locked over a session with the operator. It is possible that the customer will take a long time to decide about canceling line items.

The design team considered options 2 and 4 as the best approaches. Option 4 was selected because the number of exceptions is low and because transaction backout creates less overhead than locking and releasing locks, rereading records, or spanning sessions with an operator. Option 4 optimizes the transaction for the typical situation; the atypical situation results in more overhead. (If the number of exceptions increases, however, one of the other approaches might be preferable.) As an integral part of the transaction, an order record is written to a log file. This record is important with respect to completing the rest of the transaction. Rather than having the customer wait while picking list algorithms are processed, packing lists written, shipping labels created, accounting records updated, and so on, the order confirmation is returned to the order location as promptly as possible. The log entry is used to activate the rest of the transaction after customer notification. In all of the above scenarios, the transaction would be defined for the updating of the inventory records and the entering of the log file record.

Customer Order Confirmation   Once the inventory has been updated, the order is confirmed with the customer. The order, together with shipping information, is printed at the order point. A background process used to complete the order reads the transaction log record and produces the packing lists, shipping labels, and accounting entries. While this background activity is occurring, other order entry transactions can be started. Because this design separates the noncustomer portions of order processing from those directly affecting customer wait time, the customer is delayed for the minimum amount of time and the order is divided into recoverable, indivisible components: customer identification, order entry and verification, and background processing. ❖

SUMMARY

The acquisition of hardware, software, and services is a time-consuming process. For potential vendors to adequately size and price a system, a significant amount of information must be collected, organized, and presented to them. The information should be in the form of a statement of a problem to be solved rather than a response to a solution. This request for proposal (RFP) allows vendors to configure their systems in the way in which they work best. The evaluation of responses is also time-consuming. Careful preparation of the RFP can simplify the evaluation process. The field of viable vendors should be narrowed to a small number who can best solve the problem. This select group can then be evaluated in depth and can be required to make presentations and run benchmarks. System configuration and sizing is an ongoing process. It also requires a good knowledge of the equipment and application involved. By modeling a developing system or monitoring an existing system, performance problems can be anticipated and avoided.

KEY TERMS

benchmark, *519*

external specification, *509*

functional specification, *508*

functional testing, *509*

integrated testing, *509*

internal specification, *509*

latency, *523*

Request For Information (RFI), *514*

Request For Proposal (RFP), *515*

Request For Quotation (RFQ), *515*

seek time, *523*

sizing, *521*

stress testing, *510*

transaction, *510*

transfer time, *523*

REVIEW QUESTIONS

1. What problems might result if you eliminated the feasibility study phase in the product life cycle and proceeded directly into designing a solution?

2. What are the implications of having transactions involve multiple sessions with a terminal operator? Are there any benefits to having multiple sessions with an operator?

3. What impact will long transactions have on a system?

4. Why is transfer time considered insignificant in sizing a system?

5. When a request for proposal (RFP) is released to vendors, why should a single contact point for questions be established?

6. Why should an RFP focus on problem definition rather than problem solutions?

7. Compare and contrast an RFI and an RFP. Give an example where an RFP will likely be required.

PROBLEMS AND EXERCISES

1. Are there any applications where long transactions are necessary? If so, what are some examples?

2. Write a request for information to solicit information about statistical time division multiplexers.

3. A banking application is defined below. Calculate the response time for each transaction.

Banking Application Parameters

   A banking application is designed to provide ATM and teller services. During the peak application period, 20 ATM transactions and 10 teller transactions must be processed per second. These 30 transactions are of three types: cash withdrawal, account balance inquiry, and account transfer. Cash withdrawals account for 15 of the transactions, 10 are account balance inquiries, and 5 are account transfers. A description of each transaction is given in Table 16-4.

4. A hospital patient admission transaction generates a large number of database updates. Some of the files updated include:

   a. patient file

   b. room file

   c. several records in an inventory file for patient supplies

   d. insurance coverage file

   e. multiple records in the patient fee file for room costs, supplies, and so on

   How would you define the transaction for these activities: Would you define one transaction or multiple short transactions? Justify your decision.

TABLE 16-4   Transaction Activity

Cash Withdrawal Transaction

> Data communications input: 50 characters
>
> Disk accesses: 10
>
> Data communications output: 100 characters
>
> Line speed: 4800 bits per second

Account Balance Inquiry Transaction

> Data communications input: 20 characters
>
> Disk accesses: 4
>
> Data communications output: 50 characters
>
> Line speed: 4800 bits per second

Account Transfer Transaction

> Data communications input: 50 characters
>
> Disk accesses: 12
>
> Data communications output: 50 characters
>
> Line speed: 4800 bits per second

Distributed Systems

CHAPTER OBJECTIVES

After studying this chapter you should be able to:

- Define the concept of a distributed system
- Trace the evolution of distributed systems
- Explain the concepts of client/server computing
- Describe the functions of a remote file system
- List the advantages and disadvantages of distributed systems
- Discuss the use and problems of database management in distributed systems
- Describe the requirements of distributed systems and distributed databases

*T*hus far, we have looked at networked systems primarily from the perspective of using them for their communications capabilities. Another application of networking is distributing and sharing resources. One direction of network technology has been creating the ability to effectively distribute processing resources such as hardware, software, and data, as well as the use, management, and control of these resources.

DISTRIBUTED SYSTEMS DEFINITIONS

Systems can be distributed in a variety of ways. In Chapters 3 through 11 you read about LANs and WANs, and although it was not explicitly stated, many of those networks' resources were distributed. For example, a LAN's processing load is split among servers and workstations, both acting in concert to help workers attain their objectives. In this use of the system, processing is distributed. Data also can be distributed over two or more nodes, such as on file servers, SQL servers, and workstations. However, although data is distributed, there is not always a distributed data management capability. In these instances, the distributed data is treated as "islands of data" without the benefit of the comprehensive, coordinated management of a distributed database management system. The same may be said for WANs.

The ultimate goal of distributed processing and databases is to essentially make the network the computer. In early computing systems, all data and processing were confined to one computer. In early networks, we were able to distribute the computing load among several computers by essentially replicating what was done on individual computers. If a network had three nodes, processing was taking place simultaneously on all three computers, but most of the processing entailed a single program on one system accessing and processing data on the same system. The network was used primarily to transport completed reports, for data input on terminals attached to a remote computer, and so on. Ideally, we would like to have the aggregate resources of a network applied as appropriate to cooperatively work on problems. In this context, a single transaction might use processing resources of several computers, access and update data in a database distributed over multiple disk drives on multiple computer nodes, and perhaps output data in several geographically distributed places. Such distributed collaboration of hardware and software naturally will be transparent to users of the system. Before we introduce the technology of distributed processing and distributed databases, we first more precisely define the various aspects of distributed systems.

First, there is a distinction between distributed processing and distributed databases. From the preceding paragraph, you may have an intuitive idea about these distinctions. **Distributed processing** refers to the geographic distribution of hardware, software, processing, data, and control. The data communications system is the glue that holds the distributed system together and makes it workable. Geographic distribution does not mean great distances. As stated earlier, a LAN is a distributed processing system and, by definition, serves a limited area. A company also can have a distributed system contained in a single computer room. The key factor in having a distributed processing system is networking two or more independent computing systems where there is an interdependence among the nodes thus connected. The dependence can be for processing power, data, application software, or use of peripherals.

Often distributed systems also are characterized by distribution of control. If the nodes are placed in different locations, there is local responsibility for each node. A manufacturing organization may have processing nodes in

distributed processing
The geographic distribution of hardware, software, processing, data, and control.

the headquarters offices, regional offices, and warehouses. In each of these locations, there will be an operations staff responsible for running the systems. There may also be a local support and development organization responsible for developing, installing, and maintaining applications and databases.

Data is often one of the objects distributed in a network. Frequently people refer to data distribution as a **distributed database**. Simple data distribution, however, is not sufficient for having a distributed database. To have a true distributed database, there must be a comprehensive, coordinated system that manages the data. Later in this chapter, you learn about the requirements of a distributed database management system and how it differs from distributed file systems. Because distributed data and databases are an important aspect of distributed systems, a large portion of this chapter addresses the issues surrounding this topic.

One objective of distributed processing is to move data and processing functions closer to the users who need those services and thereby to improve the system's responsiveness and reliability. A second objective is to make remote access transparent to the system user, so the user has little or nothing special to do when accessing the other nodes of the system. How these objectives are met is explained below. First, however, we review how distributed systems evolved.

> **distributed database** A database wherein data is located on two or more computing systems connected via a data communications network. The fact that data is distributed should be transparent to database users.

EVOLUTION OF DISTRIBUTED SYSTEMS

At the dawn of the computer age, computers were big and expensive, and operating systems were either nonexistent or incapable of supporting multiple job streams. As a result, for the organizations that could afford it, computer systems were acquired for every department needing computational power. In a manufacturing organization, one computer would be dedicated to inventory, one to accounting, and one to manufacturing control. These were decentralized processing systems, but they were considerably different from the current concept of distributed systems in one important respect, the sharing of resources.

Duplicated Databases and Inconsistent Data

Processors in those early systems usually were not connected via communications links. As a result each maintained its own database, often with duplicated data. Both the warehouse database and the accounting department database contained the same customer information, the former for shipping and the latter for invoicing. When a customer moved, the address change was not likely to be reflected in both databases at once, and in some instances not before a considerable amount of time had elapsed. Such redundant storage of data, with the attendant update problems, created data inconsistencies. Data

Figure 17-1

Early Distributed Processing
System

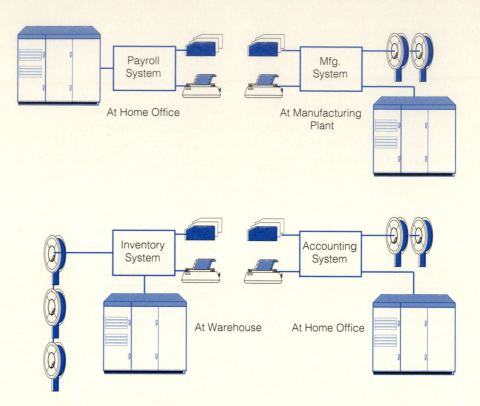

At Home Office

At Manufacturing
Plant

At Warehouse   At Home Office

inconsistencies often are manifested by conflicts in reports. Managers are
generally intolerant of such conflicting reports. Perhaps more important,
shipments or invoices could be sent to the incorrect address and perhaps be
lost. Because each department was essentially the proprietor of its own system, there was little sharing of computer resources. This meant that one
system might be completely inundated with work while another was relatively idle. One possible early decentralized processing system is depicted in
Figure 17-1.

Centralization

centralized system   A
single system capable of
supporting multiple job
functions using shared
resources.

The early decentralized systems were far from ideal. In addition to data
inconsistencies, there were extra costs for hardware, operations, maintenance, and programming. As systems grew larger and operating systems
more comprehensive, there was a movement to large, **centralized systems**, as
illustrated in Figure 17-2. Large, centralized systems had the benefits of a
single operations center, control, and — according to some — economies of
scale, as a single large system was likely to cost less than several smaller
decentralized systems. In many organizations having centralized systems, a
single programming department was established for all application develop-

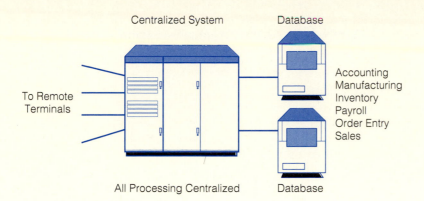

Figure 17-2

A Centralized System

Centralized System   Database

To Remote
Terminals

Accounting
Manufacturing
Inventory
Payroll
Order Entry
Sales

All Processing Centralized   Database

ment and maintenance. To reduce data redundancy and promote data sharing among users, centralized databases also were established.

Disadvantages of Centralization

It was later found that large centralized systems also have inherent problems. First, if the large central system fails, the entire system fails, and if a component fails, all or part of the application system also may be unavailable. In the decentralized approach, failure of one node results in part of the overall system being lost, but many processing functions can be continued. In this respect, decentralized systems are more reliable than the single centralized system.

Many end users of centralized systems — the accounting department, warehouse, and so forth — found their needs inadequately met by a centralized system. Because the system was shared, users often found it unresponsive, particularly regarding when jobs would be run and getting resources for new development. With a departmental system in a distributed or decentralized environment, a user contends only with other users in the department, so it was relatively easy to establish priorities. Setting interdepartment priorities, however, sometimes was not easy. The same held true for programming. In the centralized environment, a programming team may have been assigned to develop an application or a new report for a department. Because developers were not under the direct control of the department, it was sometimes difficult for the department to change priorities and directions.

Expansion and growth of the large centralized system posed another problem for some companies, that of controlling system growth. Too often growth was not in small, manageable increments but in giant steps, such as conversion to a larger processor with a different operating system. This conversion meant down time while the new system was being installed. Sometimes programs had to be revised and new program bugs were encountered. The change was usually disruptive to all users. In contrast, when upgrading a distributed system, growth was generally in smaller, more manageable increments. In addition, if a new processor became necessary, only those using that node were affected, not the entire user community.

Networked Systems

Networking provides some of the benefits of both centralized and distributed environments: more localized processing and control with shared data, processing power, and equipment. We again use a LAN as an example; these comments generally apply to wide area networks as well. In a LAN, end users have a workstation capable of performing a variety of application functions such as word processing, working with spreadsheets, and so on. Each workstation is also able to call on the processing power and database capabilities of a larger system—a server or host processor—to accomplish more complex and time-consuming processing tasks. Some of the data required frequently by a user at a workstation may be resident on the workstation's local disk drives. This may include documents in process and budget data for spreadsheets. Data that either is infrequently used or is too big for the workstation's local disks can be maintained at a larger host. Despite this data being maintained by another node, the workstation can access that data as though it was stored locally. Workstations are also able to share other network resources such as printers and magnetic tape drives. The key to a distributed system is making resource distribution transparent to the users of the system. When the resources being distributed are data, sophisticated network software is necessary. The software responsible for doing this is called a **Distributed File System (DFS)**.

Distributed File System (DFS)   Network software responsible for making network resources available to multiple users regardless of their location in the network.

DISTRIBUTED FILE SYSTEMS

In distributed systems, users must have the ability to locate and use remote files as though those files were locally resident. The objectives of a DFS are given in Table 17-1 and are described below. Again, do not confuse a DFS with a distributed database management system. Although there are similarities between the two, distributed database systems significantly extend the capabilities of a DFS.

transparent access   The ability of a user to access distributed files as though they were located on the user's local node.

Transparent Access   **Transparent access** means that a user at one node must be able to access distributed files as though they were located on the user's local node. This means a user should be able to use the file system commands of the local system to access remote files—even if the remote file is located on a node with a different operating and file system.

Operating System Independence   In building a distributed system, a user should be able to configure heterogeneous systems. This may mean that different operating systems and file systems are involved. Not only should

TABLE 17-1 **Distributed File System Objectives**

Provide transparent access to distributed files

Provide operating system independence

Provide file system independence

Provide architecture independence

Provide contention resolution

Provide security

Provide file directory information

Provide location independence

designers be able to build a system composed of different hardware and software, but also they must make these differences transparent to users.

File System Independence With file system independence, different file systems, such as DOS, UNIX, and VMS, may be used in one network. Just as important, the differences among the file systems should be transparent to users. For example, the local file system commands should be functional when accessing a file on a remote node having a different file system.

Architecture Independence The DFS should allow any network configuration — star, bus, ring, interconnected, and so on. Neither the architecture nor the network software should limit the ability to distribute files.

Contention Resolution The DFS ought to provide a mechanism that prevents data corruption due to contention. Such corruption can result when two or more users try to access and update the same file or record.

Security A DFS must provide the requisite level of security. Files should be able to be secured for local access only or for remote access. When remote access to a file is allowed, the DFS must be able to grant or deny requests based upon the requester's ID. Inherent in this requirement is the ability (1) to provide user identities for users on a node that does not support user IDs, such as a single-user microcomputer, and (2) to reconcile network differences among user IDs.

File Directory Information The DFS is responsible for transparently satisfying user requests. This means it must maintain a directory of remote files and their locations. When a user requests access to a file, the directory is consulted to find the node(s) that houses the file.

Location Independence Location independence means a file can be located at any node in the network. A file also must be able to be moved from one node to another without disrupting applications or end-user access to that file.

Network File System (NFS)
A distributed file system developed by Sun Microsystems that is also compatible with DOS- and UNIX-based systems.

Remote File Sharing (RFS)
A distributed file system that is only supported by UNIX-based systems.

Several DFS implementations exist. The one most often used for networks with equipment from a variety of vendors is the **Network File System (NFS)**, developed by Sun Microsystems. It is implemented not only on Sun systems but also on a variety of UNIX-, VMS-, and DOS-based systems. Sun Microsystems has placed the NFS protocol specifications in the public domain to allow other vendors to implement it. The objective of publishing the protocol was to spread its use and establish NFS as a standard.

A UNIX operating system DFS, **Remote File Sharing (RFS)**, currently runs only on UNIX-based systems. This protocol is supported by the American Telephone and Telegraph Company (AT&T), the originator of the UNIX operating system. One current limitation of RFS is its restriction to UNIX-based systems. With RFS, files that physically exist on one node can appear as though they are resident on other nodes. Thus, a user can access the remote file as though it were a local file.

CLIENT/SERVER COMPUTING

client/server (C/S)   A data-processing architecture in which one or more processes called servers provide processing services for other processes called clients. The server and client can be running in the same network node or in different network nodes.

Networks are changing the way we view computing and how we design application systems. Data processing has evolved from batch oriented systems on stand-alone computers, to online transaction processing with terminals and a host computer, to distributed application processing using several computers in a network. One of the distributed software architectures on networks is called client/server computing. Recall from our discussion in the Introduction that **client/server (C/S)** computing divides the work an application performs among several computers. In C/S computing one application called the client requests processing services from another application called the server. In LAN systems, the client and the server processes typically run in different computers. Some of the more common server functions are database services in which a database server processes database requests and mail services that route and store mail messages. A client process may use the services of several different server applications in carrying out its work.

The concept of C/S computing is a technology developed neither for LANs nor even for networking; however, networks in general and LANs specifically have created an environment endemic to C/S technology. Perhaps looking at the precursors of today's C/S environment will make it easier to understand the LAN implementations. Figure 17-3 depicts a large computer to which many terminals are connected. Terminal users each have a set of applications and transactions they are allowed to run, and different users may have different sets of capabilities. A person's job needs determine which applications and transactions may be used. Figure 17-3 shows three classes of software components in the host processor: a transaction control process (TCP), applications, and database management system.

Let us consider the needs of Kim, a specific terminal user. Kim works in the personnel department. Some of the functions she can do are adding employees, updating employee records, and deleting the records of employees who left the company more than three years ago. The add-employee transaction requires the services of three different applications, one each for

A Processor

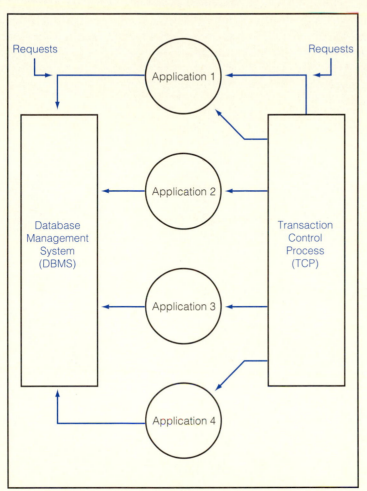

TCP has a role as a client with applications as servers.
Applications have roles as clients with DBMS as a server.

Figure 17-3

Requester/Server
Computing in a Mainframe
Computer

employee, insurance, and payroll updates. When Kim requests that a certain transaction, such as adding an employee, be run, her request is received by the TCP. The TCP is responsible for routing the transaction to the appropriate applications. In this case, three applications will need to work on the transaction, a capability we can call **cooperative computing**. In this scenario, the TCP requests each application to perform a service. In some systems, the TCP is called a requester and the applications are called servers. In today's terminology the TCP could be called a client. The **client** makes requests that are carried out in whole or in part by other processes called **servers**. In this example, the applications in turn make requests of the database management system and the operating system for services they perform. Thus, a server can also become a client.

cooperative computing A data-processing model in which two or more processes collaborate on the processing necessary for a single transaction or application. The cooperating processes may reside in different computers.

client A software application that requests services from the server in a client/server computing environment. Some systems may refer to the client as a requester.

server In client/server computing, the software application that provides clients with the services they request.

In WANs, some companies have extended the notion of this type of C/S technology by allowing the server processes to be on nodes different from the one on which the client is running. This provides a distributed processing environment in which the hardware, software, and data resources of several computers combine to solve a problem. In essence, with C/S computing *the network becomes the computer*. We can also talk about server classes. A server class is represented by one or more applications, all of which can carry out

Figure 17-4

A LAN Client/Server
Computing Environment

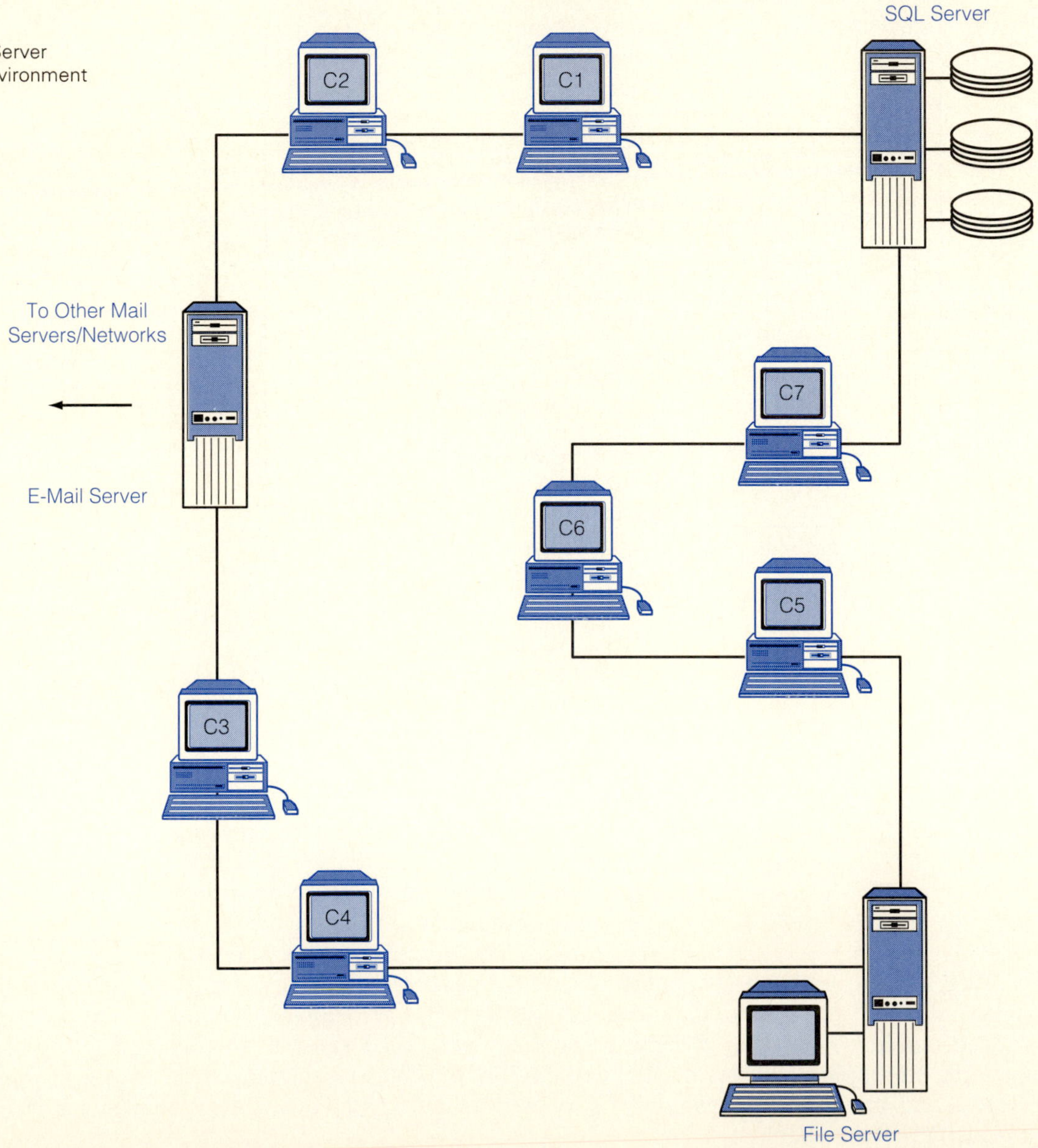

certain tasks. With server classes, a client does not need the services of a particular server process because any process in the class can perform the requested service.

A C/S LAN configuration is illustrated in Figure 17-4. This figure shows two instances of C/S computing; a database or SQL server and an electronic mail (E-mail) server. (SQL is an abbreviation for structured query language, a standard database language.) Earlier we described how a database server works. An E-mail server operates like a post office for its clients. An E-mail server will perform functions such as supplying mail addresses given a user's name, distributing mail, and providing mail agent functions. There are several types of mail agents, one of which is a vacation agent. An E-mail vacation agent can provide services such as collecting incoming mail in an electronic folder or rerouting mail to another designated user while the original recipient is away.

In LAN C/S technology, clients typically run in workstations and request services from microcomputer, minicomputer, or mainframe nodes that operate exclusively as servers. Alternatively, C/S computing can be implemented in a peer-to-peer LAN. In a peer-to-peer C/S environment, server and client processes can be running in the same node. In Figure 17-5, both Client A and Server 1 are running in Node 1.

Figure 17-5

A Peer-to-Peer Client/Server Environment

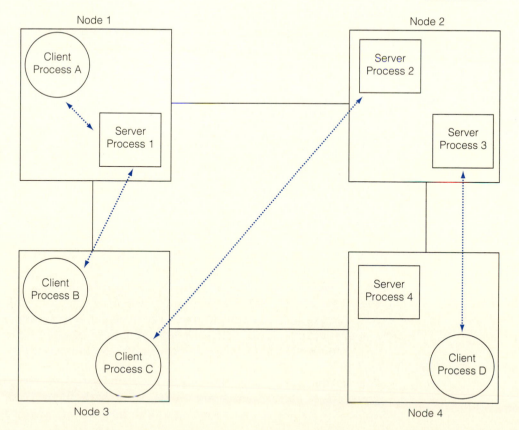

Advantages of C/S Computing

System Expansion   Growth is one objective of many companies, and it is often accompanied by the need for additional computing power. With C/S computing the computing power is distributed over multiple processors. Because the computer is the network, in C/S computing we can expand the computer by adding hardware and software components to the network. Adding to the network can be done in small, manageable increments. This means the computer can be scaled up (or down) without incurring large expenses and major hardware upgrades. Applications also can be easily expanded. Once the C/S environment is set up, new applications can be quickly installed and can immediately take advantage of the services available. This growth is made easier because the application functions provided by the server processes are already in place, and the work of the applications programmers is reduced.

Modular Applications   C/S applications are generally improved because applications are modular. Modularity can reduce the memory required for client applications and provide optimization for server processes. Part of the application logic is contained in the servers and hence does not need to be replicated in the client portion of the code. An analogy may be helpful here. If you are building a house, you would not be likely to do all of the jobs yourself because it will be difficult for you to learn all of the necessary carpentry, plumbing, electrical, and landscaping skills. However, if you become a client and use the services of those who already know how to do these things, you will likely get the job done faster and better. This analogy applies directly to the concept of C/S computing. Server modules are optimized to perform their function on behalf of their clients, and the clients do not need to be burdened with the logic essential to performing those tasks.

Portability   Some computer systems are better able to perform certain jobs than others. For example, some platforms are noted for their ability to do high-resolution graphics applications, such as computer-aided design and drafting (CAD), whereas other hardware and software combinations are well suited for office automation applications. The combination of hardware and software of an SQL server also makes the server able to manage data more effectively than a general-purpose computer and operating system. As new technologies emerge, the C/S environment provides a relatively easy way to integrate such technologies into the network. A company can switch among hardware and software vendors to find its ideal computing system. Ordinarily, these changes will not affect the remaining components. Using an SQL server as an example, if a new, more powerful server engine becomes available, it should be easy to install the new engine in place of existing SQL servers or to simply add the new server to augment existing servers.

Standards   As C/S develops we will likely see new standards for the way in which clients and servers communicate. Some of these are already being developed by leaders in C/S technology. With interface standards available, software and hardware from many vendors can be integrated to create a modular, flexible, extendable computing environment.

Disadvantages of C/S Computing

One disadvantage of C/S technology on WANs is reduced performance because of the slowness of the communications links. With high-speed LANs, the communication link does not become an obstacle to performance. Another disadvantage of C/S computing on networks is the complexity of creating the optimum C/S environment. This disadvantage is common to WAN and LAN implementations. Once these problems are overcome, several advantages are afforded by C/S computing.

C/S Technology

C/S technology on LANs is in its infancy, but its direction has already begun to take shape. In this section we look at some of the technology that underlies C/S computing, the interfaces that exist between clients and servers, and standards that are being developed.

Clients and servers must have a way to communicate with each other. There are two basic ways in which this is done: remote procedure calls and messages. You may be familiar with programming languages that support **local procedure calls**. With local procedure calls, one segment of a program invokes logic in another program segment called a procedure. The procedure does its work, and then the results and processing control are passed back to the point in the program from which the procedure was called. You can think of the procedure as performing a service for the program. **Remote procedure calls** extend this concept to allow an application on one computer to call on the services of another process. The process being called could be running in the same computer or, as is typically the case in C/S computing, the process being called could be running in another computer. Moreover, the process being called may not be running at the time of the call. The remote procedure call in this instance initiates the server process on the other computer.

Message exchange is a more flexible method of communication. The client and the server enter into a session (recall the OSI session layer) and exchange information. The client sends a request and the server responds with the answer to the request.

One issue to be resolved with C/S computing is how to find the server or servers that perform the needed functions. Today, we are looking primarily at clients and servers that are attached to the same LAN. It is logical to extend this to having servers and clients on different LANs. To maintain the modularity and flexibility of C/S computing, we would like to be able to add servers, delete existing ones, and perhaps move an existing server from one LAN to another. Changes of this nature also should be transparent to the clients, which means the clients should not have to be reprogrammed. This problem can be solved by having servers "advertise" themselves. For example, they

local procedure call In programming one procedure in a program can call another procedure in the same program. The called procedure carries out a processing task for the calling procedure. Generally, the two procedures exchange information through a list of parameters that are passed between the calling and the called procedure.

remote procedure call A remote procedure call is similar to a local procedure call except that the calling and called procedures are not a part of the same program. The called and calling procedures may be located in the same computer or in different networked computers.

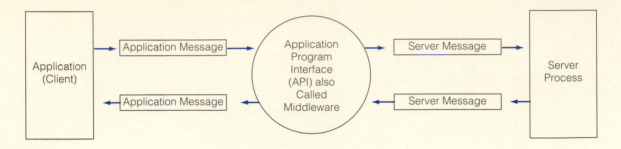

Figure 17-6

Client/Server Application
Program Interface

middleware A software
interface that functions as
an intermediary between
clients and servers.

**Distributed Computing En-
vironment (DCE)** A stan-
dardization for middleware
established by the Open
Software Foundation that
specifies the use of remote
procedure calls, security,
name services, and mes-
sages for client/server
computing.

**Object Request Broker
(ORB)** A standardization
for middleware established
by the Object Management
Group that assures hard-
ware and software independence by locating a server
that is capable of satisfying
a client's request.

might place an entry into a network directory or send messages to all nodes
registering their presence.

Clients communicate with servers through an application program interface as illustrated in Figure 17-6. Standards are being developed that will
make forming C/S interfaces easier. Having many different C/S interfaces
should be avoided to maintain flexibility. It is better to have one or a few
standard interfaces so a company can develop client applications that will be
able to access servers created by other companies. These interfaces have come
to be called **middleware**. The objective of middleware is to serve as an intermediary between clients and servers, which means the middleware is responsible for making the connection between clients and servers. This is similar
to the function performed by the logical link control layer, which, you may
recall, is the interface between the network layer and media access control.

One example of middleware and its standardization efforts is the **Distributed Computing Environment (DCE)** specifications established by the Open
Software Foundation. DCE addresses the use of remote procedure calls, security, name services, and messages for C/S computing. Another example is
the **Object Request Broker (ORB)** established by the Object Management
Group. A client will communicate with a server through the services of the
ORB. The ORB will receive a client's request, find a server capable of satisfying
that request, send the message to that server, and return the response to the
client. The ORB thus provides client and server independence. Any client that
can communicate with the ORB is then able to communicate with any server
that can communicate with the ORB. This provides both hardware and software independence.

We can use three models to represent the distribution of functions in a
C/S environment. First, the majority of the application logic can reside in the
client system with only the specialized server logic residing in the server
system, as illustrated in Figure 17-7(a). In this model, the server is less burdened and can be more responsive to volumes of client requests. This is
usually the model used for database servers. In a database server, the server
responds to a client's request for data and data meeting the constraints of the
request are returned to the client for processing. This model is sometimes
called the data management model.

A second model uses the client primarily to display or print data, and the
data management and application logic are resident on the server, as illustrated in Figure 17-7(b). This approach could be used for graphics applications

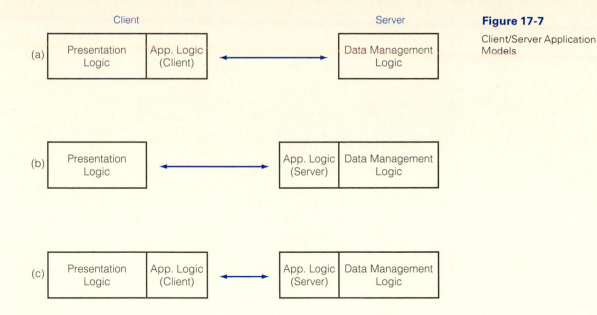

Figure 17-7

Client/Server Application
Models

wherein a high-speed server processor is used to generate the drawing details and the workstation is responsible for displaying the details on the monitor. This model can be called the presentation model.

The third possibility embeds application logic in both the client and the server, as illustrated in Figure 17-7(c). This model might be used in a transaction processing system where the application contains logic about customers and the server contains the application logic for banking accounts.

ADVANTAGES AND DISADVANTAGES OF DISTRIBUTED SYSTEMS

Advantages

Each distributed system just described has numerous advantages. For one, storing data close to the location that uses it most in a network situation minimizes the amount of data that must be transmitted between nodes and provides better response times. Because maintenance of the data is a local responsibility, there is more of a vested interest in keeping the data current. Third, nonlocal transactions are still possible, as are transactions that must span several nodes, the only penalty being slower response times due to slow transmission speeds on the communications links. Distributed systems also give local users more control over their data-processing system. This provides users with the flexibility to tailor changes to their own particular needs without disrupting other network nodes. Reliability also is higher than with a centralized system, for the failure of one node does not mean the entire system is down. Each node has most of the data it needs to continue local processing, so applications can continue with only a slight degradation in service.

Disadvantages

There are also disadvantages to the distributed approach.

Multiple-Node Transactions Are Slower   Whenever a transaction must span more than one node, response time is longer than if the transaction ran on one node only. Suppose a salesperson for a computer vendor enters an order for a new system consisting of processors, disks, and terminals. The response time for placing the order will be faster if all the equipment is available in the local warehouse than if each component must come from a different location. In the latter case, a message would have to be sent to the other warehouses in sequence until the order was filled.

Maintaining Transaction Integrity   You have already read in Chapter 16 that a transaction is an atomic piece of work. In a centralized database, this atomic property is guaranteed by the database management system's recovery system. However, when a transaction updates files on several nodes, several independent database management systems are involved. Each may be capable of guaranteeing the integrity of the *portion* of the transaction processed on its system, but there is no coordination among the various database management systems. In fact, it may be difficult to even establish a consistent, unique transaction identifier for node-spanning transactions.

Contention and Deadlock   Update transactions on multiple nodes increase the risk of contention and deadlock. As discussed in previous chapters, a record being updated is locked until the end of the transaction, to avoid the problems of concurrent updates. Because a transaction that spans several nodes is slower than one on a single node (due to data communications transmission time), affected records remain locked longer. Thus, the probability increases that the records will be needed by another transaction, and hence the amount of contention and the potential for deadlock increase.

Potential for Failure   The longer response time for transactions that span multiple nodes also increases the probability of a failure that will produce an unsuccessful transaction.

Determining Participating Nodes

Most database management systems available today were not designed for distributing data over several nodes. With a transaction that accesses and updates records on multiple nodes, the system must determine which other nodes must be involved. It is unthinkable to require the user to do this, because one of the objectives is to make the distributed nature of the system transparent to the user. It is also desirable to reserve the ability to redistribute data and processes without disrupting users.

One approach to identifying the location of resources is to programmatically define the nodes that are to participate by coding the locations into the programs. This requires that the programming staff know the location of data their programs are using. As nodes are added or data is relocated, it is likely that program changes also will be required. This approach is preferable to relying on the user to decide the location of files, but it presents considerable problems with respect to maintaining the system, extending the system, and redistributing system resources.

Network Dictionary of Locations   A better way to identify resource locations is to have a network dictionary that describes the locations of all distributed data and processing entities referenced in the system. The application or transaction control process can access the dictionary to learn where the required resources are located. Redistribution of files requires a simple update to the dictionary and programs are unaffected by such changes.

Central Versus Distributed Dictionary   The dictionary can be either centrally located and maintained or replicated at all nodes. The centralized approach, with several weaknesses, is the less desirable. First, when the central node becomes unavailable, the distributed system is inoperable. Local operations could continue, but finding remote resources would be impossible. The centralized dictionary approach could be augmented by establishing one or more alternate nodes with backup dictionary capability. The backup nodes are used if the primary fails.

A second problem with a centralized dictionary is that additional access time is required to obtain the information, and the possibility exists that the central node will become a performance bottleneck. In a local area network with high-speed links, communication time might not be significant. But accessing data via a slow communications link with several hops through intermediate nodes can significantly slow the application response time, especially if the dictionary must be consulted several times for each transaction.

A distributed dictionary resides on all nodes or strategically located nodes. This provides faster access to the dictionary than in the centralized approach. The disadvantage of distributed dictionaries is the need to keep all dictionaries properly updated, particularly if the contents change frequently. Despite this shortcoming, a distributed dictionary usually gives better performance than a centralized one.

Routing, Transmission, and Processing

Once the locations of the distributed resources have been determined, a strategy must be developed for accessing and processing the data. Designers of distributed systems have several options in determining how the remote processing and accesses will be handled. In general, the strategy selected depends on the type of transaction.

Remote Access and Local Processing   One method for processing with distributed data is remote access and local processing. This type of transaction is used effectively when most of the data being accessed is needed at the local node. Consider a system for a state's highway patrol force. If a state trooper stops a car and inquires regarding the driver's record, the application on a local node will issue a read request for the driver's files on a remote node. The set of records for the driver is transmitted to the local node and from there to the display device in the trooper's car. In this case, there was a local request for remote access, and all data satisfying that request was sent to the local node for processing. It is possible that the driver is cited for a violation as a consequence of the trooper's work. In this case, the driver's record might be modified locally and then a local request for updating the record in the remote file will be made. The revised record will be transmitted over the network and the database updated as a consequence of the remote update request. The characteristics of the police transaction are that every record accessed was transmitted over the network to the local node, all processing was done locally, and all updates were brought about via local requests. This is similar to the way in which a LAN file server operates.

Partial Remote Processing   A second method for handling distributed processing requires that the remote node perform some amount of application processing. Consider a transaction to list all employees having more than 10 years of service and a salary less than $20,000: For a company with 100,000 employees, all 100,000 records will need to be accessed to satisfy the query. To pass each of the 100,000 records to the requesting node for selection would place a large load on the communications subsystem and take considerable extra time. A much better alternative is to have a server process on each remote node access the records, perform the selection, and then transmit only the results to the requesting node, where the list will be consolidated.

Total Remote Processing   Consider a transaction that updates records at a remote node. When the record is required locally, the remote record is transmitted to the local node, an update is made, and the record is sent back to the remote node for updating in the database. In some instances the entire update can be performed remotely, as in giving an across-the-board pay raise to employees.

Suppose a company has decided to distribute the personnel and payroll applications and maintains that data in each of five regional processing centers. A manager in the corporate headquarters may have the responsibility for administering a 6% pay raise for all 100,000 employees. If the first strategy is used, each of the 100,000 records must be read remotely, transmitted over the network, updated, sent back over the network, and updated in the database. For this transaction, however, there is no need to transmit any data to the local node. A better alternative is to send the request to a server process on the remote node and have all the work done there. You should recognize this type of processing as being equivalent to the capabilities of the local area network's SQL server described in Chapter 4.

Many other examples of the division of activity among nodes could be cited. In essence, there are only the three basic methods just discussed: (1) access remote records, pass them to the local node, process the records locally, and then return them to the remote node(s) for updating as necessary; (2) send messages to remote application servers that accept and process data and then return only the required information to the requesting nodes; or (3) a combination of the two approaches, which is sometimes the best alternative. The design objective is always to make the transaction as efficient as possible, which means minimizing the transmission of many records between nodes.

DATABASE MANAGEMENT IN DISTRIBUTED SYSTEMS

Having discussed how data can be manipulated with remote file systems, we now look at the more complex problem of distributed databases. Most current database management systems were designed to operate on only one node. There was no need to keep track of files or databases on another node or to manage transactions that span multiple nodes. In some instances the problem of distributed transactions is compounded by having two different database systems involved. One example is when one node uses one vendor's hardware and software and another node uses a different vendor's hardware and database management system. In such cases, it is not likely that the database management systems will cooperate with each other except through user-written programs or routines.

Rules for a Distributed Database

You have already read about the objectives of distributed file systems. A similar set of objectives or rules has been established for distributed databases (Date, 1987). These rules, given in Table 17-2, are explained below. Note that in some instances the rules are comparable to those for distributed file systems and that the rules extend the capabilities of remote file systems.

Rule 1   **Local autonomy** means that users at a given node are responsible for data management and system operation at that node. A local node has a certain amount of independence regarding these local operations. This independence is not unrestrained, however. As with individuals in a free society who have individual independence, the independence extends only where it does not adversely affect another member of the society. Thus, a local node does not typically have the independence to arbitrarily remove its node from the network if that action is detrimental to operating the distributed system. Another implication of local autonomy is that users at a node accessing only data local to that node should neither experience performance degradations

local autonomy   A condition in which users at a given node are responsible for data management and system operation at that node.

TABLE 17-2   Date's 12 Rules for Distributed Databases

1. Local autonomy
2. No reliance on a central site
3. Continuous operation
4. Location independence
5. Fragmentation independence
6. Replication independence
7. Distributed query processing
8. Distributed transaction management
9. Hardware independence
10. Operating system independence
11. Network independence
12. DBMS independence

nor need to interact with the system differently as a result of being part of a distributed system.

Rule 2   No reliance on a central site means that all nodes in the distributed system shall be considered as peer nodes with no node identified as a supervisor. Furthermore, there shall not be one node upon which other nodes must rely, such as a single node that contains a centralized data dictionary or directory.

continuous operation   A condition in which adding nodes to the network, removing network nodes, or having one node fail will not discontinue availability of other nodes.

Rule 3   **Continuous operation** means that adding nodes to the network, removing network nodes, or having one node fail will not discontinue availability of other nodes. Naturally, a single node failure will likely disrupt access for the users local to that node; however, users at other nodes can continue to use the distributed database, and their disruption will be limited to an inability to access data stored only at the failed node.

Rule 4   Location independence means that data can be placed anywhere in the network and that its location is transparent to those needing access to it. Data can be moved from one node to another, and users or programs needing access to that data will not be disrupted.

Rule 5   In the personnel and payroll example cited earlier in this chapter, each regional node had personnel and payroll files for the employees in that region. Physically these were separate files, but logically their combination formed the corporate personnel file and payroll file. Fragmentation independence means that data that appears to users as one logical file can be transparently partitioned over multiple nodes. Thus, the personnel file is fragmented over several regional nodes. The corporate personnel director must be able to make inquiries regarding all employees, such as finding the average salary of all employees, and receive the answer consolidated from all fragments. The manager also must be able to initiate the query in the same way he or she would have if the table had not been fragmented. The distributed database management system is responsible for making the various fragments appear as a single file.

Rule 6 Storing the same file in multiple locations is called replication. Replication independence means that any file can be replicated on two or more nodes and that such replication is transparent to both users and applications. Replication is desirable for files that need to be accessed by several nodes, such as a network directory. Replication can enhance performance and availability. The distributed database management system is responsible for managing updates to replicated data and keeping the replicated data consistent.

Rule 7 When we discussed access strategies for distributed files, three alternatives were given: remote access and local processing, partial remote processing, and total remote processing. The alternative used depended on the application program's logic. **Distributed query processing** means that a user at one node can start a query involving data on other nodes. Access and processing strategies such as those discussed earlier must be supported. The location of the data must be transparent to the user and the application. The query also must be completed in an optimum way. This might mean that database servers on several nodes cooperatively work on a portion of the query. In this way, the minimum amount of data will be transmitted over the network to the requesting node. The database management system is responsible for determining the access strategy and carrying it out.

distributed query processing A condition in which a user at one node can start a query involving data on other nodes.

Rule 8 **Distributed transaction management** means that node-spanning transactions must be allowed. Moreover, transactions that update data on several nodes must be recoverable. This requires that a transaction started on one node can update records on other nodes and that the database management systems on those other nodes coordinate their activities regarding locking records and effecting transaction backout and recovery.

distributed transaction management In a distributed database, a transaction may be operated on by several processes in different computer nodes. Transactions of this type must be managed by the distributed database system to ensure database integrity either by completing the transaction or by reversing any updates done by a transaction that cannot be completed.

Rule 9 Hardware independence means that the distributed network can consist of hardware from a variety of vendors. Nodes in the distributed system can come from a variety of vendors, such as IBM, DEC, and Tandem.

Rule 10 When different hardware vendors supply network nodes, it is likely that different operating systems will be used. This capability is known as operating system independence.

Rule 11 Another consequence of Rule 9, hardware independence, might be that different network architectures, software, and protocols are used. If the vendors designed their network systems according to the OSI reference model and related standards, such interconnection will be easier. Network independence means that multiple kinds of network software may be used in connecting the nodes together. Some network nodes may be part of an SNA network, others may be members of a DECNET network, and still others may be nodes on an Ethernet local area network. Using disparate network systems must not adversely affect distributed database capabilities.

Rule 12   Database management system independence means that a variety of database management systems may be used in the distributed database. One node might use an IMS database, another might use DB2, and a third might use Oracle. Each database management system has a different data access and manipulation language, has different recovery mechanisms, and stores data in different formats. The distributed database management system must make these differences transparent to both users and applications. A user also should be able to access data managed by such a variety of database management systems without learning a variety of data access languages. Specifically, the user should be able to access distributed data using the same interface he or she uses to access data stored locally. This rule implies that database recovery systems be coordinated and database language differences accommodated. Implementation of this rule is very complex.

Currently, there is no system that adheres to all of these rules. Creating a distributed environment that encompasses all 12 rules will require a considerable investment. Until then, those who want to implement distributed databases will need to settle for less than the capabilities implied by these rules. The best way to implement distributed databases today is to use hardware and software from one vendor only and to choose a vendor having a database system that supports distributed capabilities.

SUMMARY

Distributed systems are becoming viable processing systems. They are currently at the frontier of database management systems and data communications systems. Many of the problems that impede their widespread use are in the area of database technology rather than data communications. Distributed data and distributed transactions may have a significant impact on the utilization of network resources. Specifically, data transfers, message transfers, and recovery messages can cause increased media traffic. Development in the problem areas should be spurred by potential advantages of distributing data to where it is most often used, by sharing of processing and data resources, and by providing more control to end users.

KEY TERMS

centralized system, *536*   client/server (C/S), *540*
client (requester), *541*   continuous operation, *552*

REVIEW QUESTIONS

1. What are the disadvantages of replicating data on multiple nodes?

2. What types of files are candidates for replication?

3. Describe three methods for keeping replicated files current.

4. What benefits do relational model database management systems provide in distributed database applications?

5. List four current problems in distributed processing.

6. List four applications that are good candidates for distributed processing.

7. Distinguish between distributed processing and distributed databases.

8. Describe the objectives of a distributed file system.

9. What are the advantages and disadvantages of distributed systems?

10. List and describe the 12 rules for distributed databases.

PROBLEMS AND EXERCISES

1. Research the literature for database management systems that are or claim to be distributed. Determine how well these systems conform to Date's 12 rules for a distributed database.

2. You have been asked to design the placement of files for a personnel database. Your company has four regions, each of which has a personnel office, and there is a personnel office in a separate world headquarters complex. The files in the system are: employee, benefits, job history, payroll, department, skills, insurance, and insurance claims. Devise a plan for placing each of these files assuming each location has computer facilities. Would you recommend a distributed database solution? If so, would you replicate any files? Would you partition any files? Document your decisions.

3. Research Digital Equipment Corporation's implementation of the remote file system. Describe how files are distributed and how users are able to access them.

REFERENCES

Date, C. J. "Twelve Rules for a Distributed Database." *Computerworld*, June 8, 1987.

Hubley, Mary. "Distributed Open Environments." *Byte*, Volume 16, Number 12, November 1991.

Manson, Carl, and J. Scott Haugdahl. "Dynamic and Distributed." *Byte*, Volume 16, Number 3, March 1991.

Nitzsche, Kyle. "The Elusive Illusion." *Network World*, Volume 9, Number 48, November 30, 1992.

Asynchronous Transmission

This appendix supplements the discussion of asynchronous transmission protocols in Chapter 10. You may wish to refer to that material before continuing. Asynchronous transmission occurs one character at a time. Sending and receiving stations are not synchronized with each other, which means a sending station can send a character at any time, with no prescribed interval to the next character. Of course, the receiving station must also be ready to accept a character at any time. In the discussion that follows, an asynchronous point-to-point line with a transmission speed of 1200 bps is assumed.

THE UART

At the heart of asynchronous transmission is a processing chip called the **Universal Asynchronous Receiver/Transmitter (UART)**. The UART accepts characters via parallel transmission from the terminal or host and places them on the circuit serially. It also accepts bit serial transmissions from the communications line and passes the characters to the data terminal equipment in bit parallel fashion.

DETECTING INCOMING CHARACTERS

To detect an incoming character, the UART samples the state of the communications circuit at a rate 16 times the expected bit rate. On a 1200-bps line, one bit passes every $1/1200 = 0.000833 = 0.833$ milliseconds, so a sampling of the line is taken every 52 microseconds. Figure A-1 illustrates this situation. The line is sampled so frequently to identify immediately when the state of the line has changed from the mark condition to the space condition. When a line transition is detected, the sampling interval is changed to ensure that the line is always being sampled in the middle of a bit interval. This is far safer than attempting to interrogate the line at the beginning or ending of a bit, when a slight timing error could cause the bit to be missed. Thus, when it appears that a start bit has arrived, there is a delay of 7/16 of a bit interval (0.364 milliseconds in the current example) before the line is sampled again, so that the sample is taken approximately in the middle of the bit interval. If the line is in the space condition, it is assumed this represents a start bit. Line sampling timing is adjusted to sample the line during every bit interval (every 0.83 milliseconds), and the line is sampled once for each bit and nearly in the center of the bit interval. As discussed in Chapter 9, four items must be agreed on by sender and receiver before asynchronous communications can begin: line speed, number of bits per character, presence of a parity bit, and message termination characters. Line sampling makes use of the agreed-on line speed.

RECEIVING INCOMING CHARACTERS AND PARITY CHECK

Knowledge of the number of bits expected per character is used to receive the bits making up each character. This discussion assumes 7 bits per character plus 1 parity bit. Having detected the start bit, the UART then assembles the next 7 bits that should make up the character. The ninth bit, the parity bit, follows the start bit and the 7 data bits. The parity bit is received and checked against the 7 data bits already received. If parity does not check, then a parity error message is sent to the transmitter so the character can be retransmitted. If parity checks, the next bit is examined to see whether it is a stop bit or a

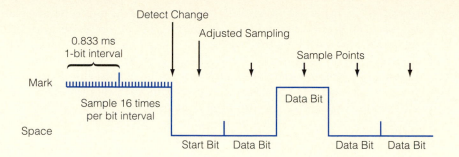

Figure A-1

Asynchronous Line
Sampling

mark condition. If a stop bit or mark condition is not detected, a transmission error is assumed to have occurred. If everything is correct, the UART returns to sampling the line. It is necessary to know how many bits compose a character, as well as whether parity is being transmitted and checked, to know when to expect the stop bit.

MESSAGE TERMINATION

If termination characters have been specified, the communications process driving the line must examine the character to determine whether it matches any of the defined termination characters. If there is no match, the character is placed in memory awaiting the rest of the message. If an interrupt character is detected, appropriate action is taken, depending upon the interrupt character.

Suppose two interrupt characters have been designated, a backspace and a carriage return. The backspace is used to cancel a character just received, and a carriage return, to signal the end of the message. If a backspace character is received, it causes the end-of-buffer pointer to be decreased by one, meaning it essentially erases the previously received character. The next character transmitted (if not another backspace) is placed in the buffer over the previously received character. Because every keystroke in asynchronous transmission is transmitted immediately to the host (with dumb terminals, anyway), hitting an incorrect character followed by backspace transmits two characters to the host: the incorrect character and the backspace character. On the other hand, if the carriage return character is received, the end of the message has been indicated. On receiving this interrupt character, the system makes the data available to the application program.

DATA OVERRUNS

A UART usually has two registers available for receiving data from the line and two for receiving data from the data terminal equipment (DTE). This allows a received character to be checked for parity and placed into memory while another character is being received. Even so, **data overruns** are still possible, especially when an intelligent or smart terminal is transmitting data from its buffer. At such a time the data may be transmitted at intervals much faster than operator typing speeds. Even when the line speed is not exceeded, the receiving hardware or software may be incapable of receiving a continuous stream of characters at that speed. One solution to this problem is to increase the interval between transmitting characters.

Binary Synchronous Transmission

Binary synchronous (BISYNC) protocols transmit data a block at a time. This requires that the sender and receiver be in sync with each other. To achieve this timing, synchronous modems contain clocks synchronized with each other during transmission. This timing can be compared to joggers and their watches: The jogging watch can be set to a pace related to the length of the runner's stride and the distance to be run. The watch determines the necessary number of strides per minute and emits a beep every time the jogger's foot strikes the ground. There must be synchronization between the watch's beeping tone and the runner's feet. Likewise, the clocks in the synchronous modems must be in time with each other so the receiving modem will look for an arriving character at the correct time.

ESTABLISHING SYNCHRONIZATION

To establish this timing ordinarily requires two or more synchronization (SYN) characters. The sending station prefixes all transmissions with a number of SYN characters. If the modems are not in sync when the first SYN character arrives, the entire character will not be received correctly, although the receiving modem will be aware that a character stream is arriving. The second SYN character assures synchronization. Additional SYN characters are transmitted with equipment that requires more than two characters for synchronization. SYN characters are hexadecimal 32 in EBCDIC, hexadecimal 16 in ASCII, and hexadecimal 3A in SBT; these are the three codes supported by BISYNC.

In BISYNC transmission, the line is continuously monitored, awaiting the SYN character that signals the beginning of a message. A copy of the SYN character is maintained in a register and compared with the data received. When the first SYN character has arrived, the next character is checked to determine whether it is also a SYN character. The first SYN character sets bit synchronization; the second sets character synchronization. Once synchronization is established, individual characters can be received and processed.

TRANSMISSION CONTROL CHARACTERS

BISYNC uses a number of special transmission control characters to indicate the beginning of the data or header information, the end of the data or transmission block, the end of transmission, acknowledgments of data received, and so on. A list of these characters follows.

SYN   The SYN character establishes synchronization. It precedes all message blocks and may be inserted in long messages to maintain synchronization.

STX   STX indicates start-of-text; what follows is data.

SOH   SOH means start-of-header. The optional header field follows. Headers may contain application-dependent data such as transaction codes and terminal ID.

ETX   ETX indicates end-of-text. It tells when a complete text message has been received. If lengthy text is broken into blocks for transmission, only the final block will contain the ETX character.

ETB   ETB signals the end of the transmission block and requires an acknowledgment (see ETX, above).

ITB   ITB marks the end of an intermediate transmission block. In some cases a number of blocks may be transmitted without being acknowledged. An ITB character is used to signal the end of these blocks. The actual character used to represent the ITB is IUS in EBCDIC and US (unit separator) in ASCII and SBT.

EOT   EOT means end-of-transmission and is used to terminate a transmission. It differs from ETX in that ETX signals the end of a logical message. Multiple messages may comprise one transmission; EOT signals this condition. Following the transmission of EOT, the transmitting station relinquishes control of the link. All stations are reset following EOT. EOT can also be used as a response to a poll and to signal an error condition that precludes message completion.

ACK0   Positive acknowledgment is signaled by ACK0, which is actually a two-character sequence consisting of a DLE character (see below) plus a character that is code dependent. In ASCII, 0 is the second character. BISYNC uses ACK0 and ACK1 in an alternating acknowledgment scheme.

ACK1   Positive acknowledgment. See ACK0, above. ACK1 is a two-character sequence consisting of DLE (see below) and a second code-dependent character, a 1 in ASCII.

NAK   NAK, meaning **negative acknowledgment**, is used to indicate that the previous block was received in error and should be retransmitted. It is also used as a negative response to a poll message.

ENQ   ENQ, meaning **inquiry**, is used to bid for the line in contention mode, to initiate a poll or select message, or to ask that a response to a previous transmission be resent.

DLE   DLE, **data link escape**, is used to implement transparency. It is also used to form other control characters such as ACK0.

WACK, TTD, RVI   These are used for special control situations defined later. Each represents a special kind of positive acknowledgment.

Control for Long Messages   Messages, particularly long ones, can be broken into blocks for transmission to minimize the amount of data that might have to be retransmitted in case of errors and to accommodate buffer sizes in the receiving equipment. In the case when all intermediate blocks can be transmitted before acknowledgment is required, the ITB control character is used to terminate the block. If ETB is used instead, each block must be acknowledged. Alternating acknowledgments—ACK0 and ACK1—are used to provide a small amount of error control. ACK0 is always a positive response to a line bid or to selection.

TRANSMISSION SEQUENCES

In the examples that follow, the character sequences should be read from left to right, with the first character transmitted appearing on the left. BCC represents the block check character, either LRC or CRC.

Point-to-Point Contention Mode   In point-to-point contention, a station must first bid for and be granted access to the line. This sequence is given in Table B-1. At this point the line is available for either station to issue a bid. A negative response to the line bid would be NAK. If a station were unable to receive data for some reason, it would NAK the line bid.

Multipoint Mode   A polling sequence with positive and negative responses is shown in Table B-2. A selection sequence is portrayed in Table B-3. In the selection sequence in Table B-3, the station being selected at first gave a negative acknowledgment to the selection, or a NAK. A printer would respond in this manner if its buffer was not empty and it was unable to accept more data. A positive acknowledgment was given to the subsequent selection, and the data was transmitted. EOT in the selection stream ensures the status of the link.

WACK   On occasion a station may wish to positively acknowledge receipt of a block and also advise the sender that it is not ready to receive the next block, such as when a printer with limited buffer size is out of paper or otherwise unable to empty its buffer. The WACK character is used both to positively acknowledge receipt of a block and also to tell the sending station to wait before transmitting further. WACK is a two-character sequence — DLE followed by a code-dependent character (a semicolon in ASCII and a comma in EBCDIC). The message sequence for WACK is presented in Table B-4. The WACK response in Table B-4 delays the sender from transmitting the remainder of the text block. The sender would continue prompting the station with ENQs until the receiver is able to receive. A positive response to ENQ will allow the sender to continue with the message.

TTD   Sometimes a sending station becomes temporarily busy and so is unable to continue sending its message. If the sender wants to maintain

TABLE B-1   **A BISYNC Contention Mode Line Bid**

Line Bidder		Responder	Comment
SYN SYN ENQ	⟶		Line bid
	⟵	SYN SYN ACK0	Positive response
SYN SYN STX text ETB BCC	⟶		Message block 1
	⟵	SYN SYN ACK1	Positive response
SYN SYN STX text EOT BCC	⟶		Last block
	⟵	SYN SYN ACK0	Positive response

control of the communications circuit during such an interval, it can do so with the temporary text delay (TTD) control sequence. TTD consists of STX followed by ENQ. The transmitting sequence for this is given in Table B-5. The TTD sequence must be repeated within 2 seconds to avoid time-out. The

TABLE B-2   **BISYNC Polling**

Supervisor		Secondary	Comment
SYN SYN address1 ENQ	$\longrightarrow$		Poll to Station 1
	$\longleftarrow$	SYN SYN EOT	No data to send
SYN SYN address2 ENQ	$\longrightarrow$		Poll to Station 2
	$\longleftarrow$	SYN SYN STX data EOT BCC	Data sent
SYN SYN ACK0	$\longrightarrow$		Positive response
SYN SYN address3 ENQ	$\longrightarrow$		Poll to Station 3

TABLE B-3   **A BISYNC Selection**

Supervisor		Secondary	Comment
SYN SYN EOT SYN SYN address ENQ	$\longrightarrow$		Selection
	$\longleftarrow$	SYN SYN NAK	Negative response; unable to receive
SYN SYN EOT SYN SYN address ENQ	$\longrightarrow$		Retry
	$\longleftarrow$	SYN SYN ACK0	Positive response
SYN SYN STX text ETX BCC	$\longrightarrow$		Data sent
	$\longleftarrow$	SYN SYN ACK1	Positive response
SYN SYN EOT	$\longrightarrow$		End of data

TABLE B-4   **BISYNC WACK**

Sender		Receiver	Comment
SYN SYN ENQ	$\longrightarrow$		Line bid
	$\longleftarrow$	SYN SYN ACK0	Positive response
SYN SYN STX text ETB BCC	$\longrightarrow$		Data
	$\longleftarrow$	SYN SYN WACK	WACK
SYN SYN ENQ	$\longrightarrow$		Line bid
	$\longleftarrow$	SYN SYN ACK0	Positive response
SYN SYN STX text EOT BCC	$\longrightarrow$		Data
	$\longleftarrow$	SYN SYN ACK0	Positive response

usual time-out value of 3 seconds avoids a long wait for a station that is not online.

RVI   When a receiving station has a high-priority message to transmit to a sending station, the receiver can indicate this by acknowledging a message with a reverse interrupt (RVI) character sequence. RVI is a two-character sequence — DLE plus a code-dependent second character (< in ASCII and @ in EBCDIC). RVI acknowledges the message received and alerts the sender to relinquish the line as soon as possible, so the station that has been receiving can assume control of the link. An RVI sequence is illustrated in Table B-6. RVI does not cause the sender to immediately discontinue transmission; rather, the sender continues transmitting until its buffers are empty and it is capable of receiving data.

TABLE B-5   **BISYNC TTD**

Sender		Receiver	Comment
SYN SYN ENQ	⟶		Line bid
	⟵	SYN SYN ACK0	Positive response
SYN SYN STX ENQ	⟶		TTD
	⟵	SYN SYN NAK	Response to TDD
(within 2 seconds)			Avoid time-out
SYN SYN STX ENQ	⟶		TTD
	⟵	SYN SYN NAK	Response to TDD
SYN SYN STX text ETB BCC	⟶		Data
	⟵	SYN SYN ACK1	Acknowledgment

TABLE B-6   **BISYNC RVI**

Sender		Receiver	Comment
SYN SYN ENQ	⟶		Line bid
	⟵	SYN SYN ACK0	Positive response
SYN SYN STX text ETB BCC	⟶		Data
	⟵	SYN SYN RVI	Reverse interrupt
SYN SYN STX text ETX BCC	⟶		Empty buffer
	⟵	SYN SYN ACK1	Acknowledgment
SYN SYN EOT	⟶		Transmit end
	⟵	SYN SYN ENQ	Line bid
SYN SYN ACK0	⟶		Positive response
	⟵	SYN SYN STX text ETB BCC	Priority message

TRANSPARENCY

Transparency means that any bit sequences can be included in the text, even those that are also used as control characters. In its original use with RJE, the only BISYNC characters that needed to be transmitted were the control characters and displayable characters. As BISYNC's functions were expanded to include the transfer of binary data, transparency was added. Unfortunately, this add-on solution was inelegant. Without transparency, a data byte that looks like an ETX character would prematurely terminate the message. Because the link protocol would interpret the two characters following the phony ETX as CRC, the CRC check would probably fail, and the block would be negatively acknowledged, thus causing the block to be retransmitted over and over until a retry limit was reached. The data link escape (DLE) character is employed to provide transparency, and essentially is inserted before any control characters. DLE STX initiates transparent mode, and DLE ETX, DLE ETB, DLE ITB, or a like sequence terminates the block. The DLE character can be used in this manner with the STX, ETB, ITB, ETX, ENQ, DLE, and SYN control characters.

This all seems straightforward, as though all that was needed was to frame the message with DLE STX and DLE ETX. Unfortunately, it is still possible to have within the text two adjacent characters that form a DLE ETX sequence, which would prematurely terminate the message. The solution to this problem is to insert DLE before each DLE in the text. Thus, what has happened is that one character has been picked to represent transparency. Because this character also may appear in the text, it has to be accommodated within the text. The text is scanned for any DLE characters; for each one found, an additional DLE is inserted. The data stream is scanned on the receiving side as well; whenever two DLE characters are encountered next to each other, one is discarded, thus ensuring that the only DLE ETX sequence is at the end of the block. The insertion of DLE will, of course, change a DLE ETX data sequence into a DLE DLE ETX sequence. DLE ETX in this case is not construed as a termination. The DLE DLE grouping indicates that DLE is for data and not control. Before- and after-images of a sample text message are given in Figure B-1.

Text Before Transparency

```
    E           D               D  E           S
    T           L               L  T           Y
    X           E               E  X           N
```

Text After Transparency

```
D  S    E           D  D     D  D  E    S      D  S     D  E
L  T    T           L  L     L  L  T    Y      L  Y     L  T
E  X    X           E  E     E  E  X    N      E  N     E  X
```

Start of Text   Inserted for   Inserted for   End of
                       Transparency   Synchronization   Text

Figure B-1

A Sample Text Message

Synchronous Data Link Control

This appendix supplements the discussion of IBM's Synchronous Data Link Control (SDLC) protocol given in Chapter 9. You may wish to review that material prior to continuing. This SDLC discussion is focused on the control field functions and the Ns and Nr message sequencing concept. The control field provides the abilities to designate the type of the frame — unnumbered, supervisory, or informational — and to acknowledge receipt of frames.

UNNUMBERED FRAMES

Unnumbered frames are used for control functions such as resetting a station's Ns and Nr counts to zero, causing stations on switched lines to disconnect, rejecting a frame received in error, and transmitting data such as broadcast or status messages that do not need a sequence check. The general format of the unnumbered control field is given in Figure C-1. The first two bits — 11 — identify the frame as unnumbered. The code bits are used to identify the frame function, initialize station, reject frame, disconnect, and so on. The 5 bits allow for 32 different functions. The existing control functions for unnumbered frames are given in Table C-1.

P/F Bit   The P/F (poll/final) bit, which is common to all control fields, is set when a station is being polled and when the final frame for a message is sent. Just as in BISYNC, messages can be broken into blocks for transmission; all but the last such block will have the P/F bit set to zero. The P/F bit also is used in loop configurations to specify optional and mandatory responses to polling.

Figure C-1

Control Field Format:
Unnumbered Frame

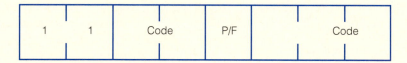

| 1 | 1 | Code | P/F | | | Code |

TABLE C-1   Unnumbered Control Functions

Code for Unnumbered Control	Function
UI	Identifies an information frame as unnumbered.
SNRM	Sets normal response mode. Resets Ns and Nr count fields.
DISC	Places secondary station in disconnect mode.
RD	Indicates a secondary station request to disconnect.
UA	Signals a positive acknowledgment to an SNRM, DISC, or SIM command.
RIM	Indicates a secondary station request for initialization.
SIM	Primary initializes secondary. Ns and Nr counts are set to 0.
DM	Indicates that a secondary station is in disconnect mode.
FRMR	Signals that an invalid frame has been received.
TEST	Means that a test frame has been sent to a secondary station, which will respond with a test frame.
XID	Requests an ID exchange.

SUPERVISORY FRAMES

The control field format for the supervisory frame is given in Figure C-2. The first two bits (10) designate the frame as supervisory. The P/F bit is as described above. The receive count field (explained below) is used to acknowledge receipt of frames. The code field is 2 bits wide and therefore can represent only four different control functions, three of which have been specified thus far. Two control functions are used to indicate whether the station is Ready to Receive (RR) or Not Ready to Receive (RNR) data. The third control function (REJ) is used to reject a frame.

INFORMATION FRAMES

The information frame is used primarily to send data; its control field format is given in Figure C-3. Unlike the other two types of frames, only the first bit (0) is used to designate the frame as informational. The P/F bit is as described above. The send count (Ns) and receive count (Nr) fields are each made up of 3 bits. As discussed in Chapter 9, the Ns field is used by a station to count the number of messages sent to another station. The Nr field is a count kept by a receiving station of the number of messages received from another station. Each station maintains separate Ns and Nr count fields for each station with which it communicates. When a station is initialized by the supervisor, the Ns and Nr counts are set to zero, so the Nr count becomes the message number the receiving station expects next. The first message sent is message number 0. After either count reaches 7, the next increment rolls the count over to zero, meaning that, at most, seven messages can be sent before an acknowledgment is necessary.

EXAMPLE: HOW Ns AND Nr COUNTS ARE USED

This example, illustrated in Table C-2, shows the values of the address field, the frame type, the Ns and Nr counts, and the P/F bit, in that order. The supervisor station polls the secondary stations. The supervisor uses a super-

1	0	Code	P/F	Receive Count (Nr)

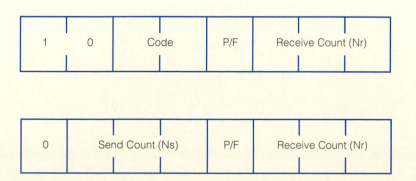

Figure C-2

Control Field Format: Supervisory Frame

0	Send Count (Ns)	P/F	Receive Count (Nr)

Figure C-3

Control Field Format: Information Frame

TABLE C-2   **Example of the Use of Ns and Nr Subfields**

	Supervisor					Secondary Station				
Address	Frame Type	Ns Count	Nr Count	P/F Bit		Address	Frame Type	Ns Count	Nr Count	P/F Bit
A	RR	0	0	1	$\longrightarrow$					
					$\longleftarrow$	A	RR	0	0	1
B	RR	0	0	1	$\longrightarrow$					
					$\longleftarrow$	B	I	0	0	0 data
		0	1		$\longleftarrow$	B	I	1	0	0 data
		0	2		$\longleftarrow$	B	I	2	0	0 data
		0	3		$\longleftarrow$	B	I	3	0	1 data
B	RR	0	4	0	$\longrightarrow$					
C	RR	0	0	1	$\longrightarrow$					

visory frame to indicate that it is ready to receive. The P/F bit is set to 1 to indicate that Station A is being polled. The Nr count is set to zero, indicating that the next frame expected from Station A is frame number 0. Station A has no data to send and thus responds with a supervisory frame indicating that it is ready to receive and that the next frame expected from the supervisor is frame number 0. The final bit is set to 1 in this instance to indicate that there is no data to send.

Station B is then polled. Station B does have data to transmit and uses the information frame to do so. Four frames are required to transmit the entire message. For the first three frames the P/F bit is set to 0 to indicate that more frames will follow. The last frame in the message has the P/F bit set to 1. The Ns count for Station B is incremented with each frame. The Nr count is incremented following the receipt of each frame, although the supervisor sends no acknowledgment in this case until the final frame is received. On receiving the final frame, the supervisor acknowledges receipt of all messages at once with a supervisory frame. The P/F bit is not set on this frame, because Station B is not being polled. Much of the efficiency of bit-oriented data link protocols stems from their ability to transmit multiple frames without acknowledgment and to transmit in full duplex mode. This avoids the wait times required by other protocols such as BISYNC, which require that each message be acknowledged before another may be sent.

....

Packet Distribution Networks

....

This appendix supplements the discussion of packet distribution networks in Chapter 11. You may wish to review that material prior to continuing. This appendix covers CCITT standards X.3, X.28, and X.25 and omits discussing standards X.75 and X.29. CCITT standards X.28, X.29, X.3, and X.25 cover the interface between Data Terminal Equipment (DTE) and Data Circuit-Terminating Equipment (DCE) in a single packet distribution network. Standard X.75 covers the interface between two different PDNs. Standards X.28 and X.29 are quite similar: X.28 concerns the interface between the Packet Assembly/Disassembly (PAD) and a start-stop (asynchronous) terminal; X.29 covers the same situation for a packet mode terminal (a terminal capable of performing PAD functions). In general, X.29 refers to the network-host interface; it covers the PAD-PAD interface as well. Because of the similarity between X.28 and X.29, only X.28 is discussed.

The X.3 STANDARD

The PAD interfaces to start-stop terminals, packet mode terminals, or other PADs.

Basic Functions of the PAD   When a PAD interfaces with a start-stop terminal, the message characters arrive at the PAD one character at a time and must be grouped together into a packet for transmission over the network. While building the buffer for the data terminal equipment (DTE), the PAD can also perform a limited amount of editing on the data, restricted to deleting characters from the buffer or deleting the buffer's entire contents. Editing is enabled by the user and is done on receiving the proper editing control signals. The PAD knows to transmit a packet whenever the packet reaches the designated packet size, a message termination character is received, or after no characters have been received for a specified amount of time. The receiving PAD must take the data from the user data field and send it one character at a time to the receiver, including framing the character with start and stop bits as necessary and adding a parity bit if required by the DTE. In addition to the handling of packet assembly/disassembly functions, the PAD is also involved in control and error functions: It is responsible for a portion of the setup and clearing of virtual calls, pacing of data to the DTE, and reacting to reset and interrupt conditions.

PAD Operations Parameters   PAD operations are controlled by a set of PAD parameters, which in most cases the user can tailor to the operations of the particular terminal and application. The parameters of significance to business applications follow. They show the flexibility available with a PAD.

Echo   The PAD can optionally echo a transmitted character back to the DTE. Some terminals require this feature in order to display the character on the terminal's output device.

Termination Characters   The user can specify virtually any character as a termination character. Termination characters signal the PAD to end a message and to forward the packet to the network.

Timer Delay Interval   Another way that a message can be terminated is via timer delay, which can be specified at values from 0 to 255, in twentieths of a second. When no characters have arrived within the delay interval, the PAD assumes the message is complete and transmits the packet. A timer delay value of 0 means there can be no delay interval in completing the message. The maximum specifiable delay is 12.75 seconds.

XON/XOFF Capability   Some DTE equipment can announce its readiness to accept data via XON and XOFF signals. XON means the device is able to receive a certain number of characters, related to the device's buffer size. When the buffer is filled to a certain threshold, the device transmits the XOFF signal to the sender, which holds the sender off until the buffer is emptied below the threshold. The PAD allows this capability of the device to be enabled or disabled.

Break Signal   The DTE can transmit a break signal to the PAD, which is a sequence of 0 bits over a designated time interval. The user can specify the action the PAD is to take on receiving such a signal: do nothing, transmit an interrupt packet to the host, reset itself, transmit a break message to the host, remove itself from the data transfer state, or discard the output to the DTE.

Padding   On receipt of a carriage return character, some devices — especially the mechanical ones, such as printers — require a certain amount of time to move the printing mechanism to the beginning of the line. To provide sufficient time for carriage return, pad characters are sometimes inserted after the carriage return. The PAD allows from 0 to 7 pad characters to be transmitted to the DTE after a carriage return. Padding can also be specified to follow a line-feed character.

Line Speed   Nineteen different speeds are available, ranging from 50 bps to 64 Kbps. Once set, the line speed may not be changed. This read-only parameter allows a host to ascertain the speed of the device with which it is communicating.

Line Feed After Carriage Return   The PAD can be instructed to always insert a line-feed character following a carriage return. This option provides output line-spacing for the receiving device.

Folding   This parameter allows the length of the output to be adjusted to the device. The folding parameter can be any value from 0 to 255. A zero value means no folding is to take place; any other value represents the number of characters to transmit to the receiving device before automatically inserting the formatting characters, such as carriage return or line feed.

Editing   The PAD can perform the limited editing functions of character deletion and line deletion. One parameter enables this capability, and there is one parameter to store each of the line and character delete codes. If the PAD is editing-enabled and receives a character that matches the character delete parameter, the last character in the edit buffer is deleted. This works just like the backspace on most terminals. Similarly, if a line delete character is received, the entire contents of the edit buffer are deleted. The edit buffer can also be displayed.

THE X.28 STANDARD

The X.28 specifications define the manner in which a start-stop terminal interfaces with a PAD, whose functions and options have just been defined. The data terminal equipment can access a PAD via a switched or a leased connection. The speed of the connection is determined by the capability of the DTE and by the PDN administrators. The PAD expects eight-bit characters from the DTE and transmits eight-bit characters to the DTE. When looking at the characters for control purposes, the PAD looks at only the first seven bits. The eighth bit may either be parity or data; if data, then the first seven bits should not match any of the control functions, such as editing. The major portion of the X.28 standard defines the signals exchanged between DTE and PAD, including how to interrogate and alter the PAD parameters, the definition of the break signal, call establishment sequences, network user identification procedures, call clearing, and fault conditions.

THE X.25 STANDARD

The X.25 specification defines the interface between data terminal equipment and the network for terminals operating in the packet mode, including the interface between the PAD and the network. The specification first briefly discusses the X.21 and X.21bis interfaces, the general interfaces between synchronous and asynchronous devices, respectively. That is followed by a brief discussion of the LAPB data link protocol, which is very similar to HDLC and SDLC. Frames are formatted as described for SDLC. For information regarding this portion of the X.25 recommendation, the reader is referred to the SDLC descriptions in Chapter 9 and Appendix C. At the network level, the objective is end-to-end routing. To provide the information necessary for end-to-end routing, a portion of the data or information field is used by the PDN. The shortest message that can be transferred is three characters in length, because at least three characters of the information field are required by the PDN for routing and control. These three characters contain fields for general format identification, logical channel identification, and packet-type identification. Additional fields are defined in some packets, particularly those used for control. A representative sample of these fields is given in Figure D-1.

General Format Identification (GFI)   The **General Format Identification (GFI)** is the first field of the data field of the frame. The GFI indicates the format of the remainder of the data field. The four bits of the GFI designate the sequence number modulus for the packet and also indicate whether the packet is a datagram, information packet, call setup packet, or control packet. The sequence number modulus operates like the Ns and Nr fields in HDLC.

Logical Channel Identification   The **logical channel identification** field consists of two parts, the logical channel group number and the logical channel number. The group number occupies the four bits following the GFI. With four bits, 16 different channel groups can be specified. The eight bits following the channel group identification constitute the logical channel address. There may thus be 256 different logical addresses per channel, providing a total of 4096 different circuits or logical addresses in the network.

Octet

1	General Format Identifier | Logical Channel Group Number
2	Logical Channel Number
3	Packet Type Identifier
4	Calling DTE Address Length | Calling DTE Address Length
	DTE Address
	Facility Length
	Facilities
	Call User Data

Packet Type   The third octet designates the packet type, in six broad categories: call setup and clearing, data and interrupt, datagram, flow control and reset, restart, and diagnostic. Each category except diagnostic is further broken down into subtypes, such as the call setup and clearing subtypes of incoming call, call connected, clear indication, DCE clear confirmation, call request, call accepted, clear request, and DTE clear confirmation.

Information Field   The defaulted recommended length of the information field is 128 octets, but X.25 provides for optional lengths of 16, 32, 64, 128, 256, 512, and 1024 octets. Message sequence numbers are used to account for packets. By default, the modulus for sequence numbers is 8, with 128 a suggested alternative. The sequence numbers work like those in the Ns and Nr fields of SDLC. A window size n is set that restricts a sender to transmitting at most n messages without acknowledgment. The default window size is 2 for a modulus of 8. The window size can be changed if the user has been given the option of flow control parameter negotiation, which enables the user to change the packet size, sequence number modulus, window size, and circuit speed.

Optional Parameters   Network administrators may optionally put a number of other parameters under user control, such as the barring of all incoming calls. In this case, DTE will be allowed only to initiate calls. By the same token DTE can be barred from initiating calls and allowed only to receive calls. A user also can elect to reverse charges so the recipient of the call becomes responsible for the packets transmitted. The user might be allowed to alter the datagram queue length, which determines the number of incoming datagrams that can queue up before datagrams begin to be discarded. If queue depth is set at 16, then 16 datagrams will be allowed in the inbound queue. If 16 datagrams are waiting when another arrives, the late arrival will be discarded. Finally, the user is able to specify whether a closed or bilateral closed user group should be established. Closed user group members are allowed to communicate only with each other. In a bilateral closed user group, two DTEs that agree to communicate can do so, but communication with all other DTEs is prohibited. Options added to these closed groups allow for incoming and outgoing communications with the rest of the user community.

Datagrams   The X.25 specification also covers the use of datagrams. The datagram message is restricted to 128 octets. The user can elect to receive acknowledgment of datagrams in three instances: if the datagram is rejected, discarded, or accepted, result conditions that are returned to the user only when requested by the user. The user optionally may receive the capability to specify whether notification be given on nondelivery or delivery of a datagram. Datagrams are given sequence numbers, and there is an acknowledgment window that operates the same as with virtual circuits.

Acronym Glossary

For a more thorough definition, please refer to the Key Terms Glossary.

ACU   Auto-Call Unit

ADCCP   Advanced Data Communications Control Procedure

ADMD   Administrative Management Domain

AM   Amplitude Modulation

ANSI   American National Standards Institute

API   Application Program Interface

ASCII   American Standard Code for Information Interchange

API   Application Program Interface

ATM   Asynchronous Transfer Mode

BCC   Block Check Character

BCD   Binary Coded Decimal

BISYNC or BSC   Binary Synchronous Communications

BIU   Bus Interface Unit

BPS   Bits Per Second

CAD   Computer-Aided Design

CAI   Computer-Aided Instruction

CAM   Computer-Aided Manufacturing

CCITT   Consultative Committee on International Telegraph and Telephony

CDDI   Cooper Distributed Data Interface

CICS   Customer Information Control System

CIU   Communications Interface Unit

CLNP   Connectionless Network Protocol

CMIP   Common Management Information Protocol

CPU   Central Processing Unit

CRC   Cyclic Redundancy Check

CRT   Cathode Ray Tube

C/S   Client/Server

CSMA/CA   Carrier Sense with Multiple Access and Collision Avoidance

CSMA/CD   Carrier Sense with Multiple Access and Collision Detection

DBMS   Database Management System

DCE   Data Communications Equipment

DCE   Distributed Computing Environment

DES   Data Encryption Standard

DFS   Distributed File System

DPSK   Differential Phase Shift Keying

DTE   Data Terminal Equipment

EBCDIC   Extended Binary-Coded Decimal Interchange Code

E-mail   Electronic Mail

FDDI   Fiber Distributed Data Interface

FDM   Frequency Division Multiplexing

FEP   Front End Processor

FM   Frequency Modulation

FMS   File Management System

FQDN   Fully Qualified Domain Name

FSK   Frequency Shift Keying

GDSS   Group Decision Support System

HDLC   High-Level Data Link Control

IEEE   Institute of Electrical and Electronic Engineers

IP   Internet Protocol

ISDN   Integrated Services Digital Network

ISO   International Standards Organization

LAN   Local Area Network

LAPB   Link Access Procedure, Balanced

LATA   Local Access and Transport Area

LLC   Logical Link Control

LRC   Longitudinal Redundancy Check

LU   Logical Unit

MAC   Media Access Control protocol

MAU   Multistation Access Unit
MIB   Management Information Base
MNP   Microcomputer Network Protocols
MTA   Message Transfer Agent
MTBF   Mean Time Between Failures
MTTR   Mean Time To Repair
MUX   Multiplexing
NAU   Network Addressable Unit
NCP   Network Control Program
NFS   Network File System
NMS   Network Management System
ORB   Object Request Broker
OS   Operating System
OSI   Open Systems Interconnection reference model
PAD   Packet Assembly/Disassembly
PBX   Private Branch Exchange
PCM   Pulse Code Modulation
PDN   Packet Distribution Network
PERT   Program Evaluation and Review Technique
POP   Point Of Presence
PRMD   Private Management Domain
PSE   Packet-Switching Equipment
PSK   Phase Shift Keying
PU   Physical Unit
PUCP   Physical Unit Control Point
PVC   Permanent Virtual Circuit
QAM   Quadrature Amplitude Modulation
RAID   Redundant Arrays of Independant Disks
RBOC   Regional Bell Operation Company
RFI   Request For Information
RFP   Request For Proposal
RFQ   Request For Quotation
RFS   Remote File Sharing

RJE   Remote Job Entry
RMON MIB   Remote Monitoring Management Information Base
SBT   Six-Bit Transcode
SDLC   Synchronous Data Link Control
SMDS   Switched Megabit Data Services
SMDS   Switched Multimegabit Data Service
SMI   Structure of Management Information
SNA   Systems Network Architecture
SNADS   SNA Distribution Services
SNMP   Simple Network Management Protocol
SQL   Structured Query Language
SSCP   Systems Services Control Point
SSR   Spread Spectrum Radio
STDM   Statistical Time Division Multiplexing
STE   Signaling Terminal Equipment
SVC   Switched Virtual Circuit
TCP   Transaction Control Process
TCP/IP   Transaction Control Protocol/Internet Protocol
TDM   Time Division Multiplexing
TSAP   Transport Service Access Point
UA   User Agent
UPS   Uninterruptible Power Supply
VDT   Video Display Terminal
VDU   Video Display Unit
VHF   Very-High-Frequency radio waves
VRC   Vertical Redundancy Check
VTAM   Virtual Telecommunications Access Method
WAN   Wide Area Network
WATS   Wide Area Telecommunications or Telephone Service
XTP   Xpress Transfer Protocol

Key Terms Glossary

access time   The total time required in accessing a disk, including seek time, latency, and transfer time.

access method   A software subsystem that provides input and output services as interface between an application and its associated devices. It eliminates device dependencies for an application programmer.

access security   Security that controls a user's access to data. The controls may regulate a user's ability to read and update data, to delete files, and to run programs.

access server   An interconnection utility that allows microcomputers to access LAN resources from remote locations.

active hub   A node connection hub used in an ARCnet LAN that provides signal regeneration and allows nodes to be located up to 2000 feet from the hub.

active node   A node capable of sending or receiving network messages.

active port   The status of a bridge port that will accept packets from the LAN end of the port.

acoustic coupler   An acoustic coupler converts digital signals to analog and analog to digital. It is used mostly in switched communications and uses the telephone handset to pass data between a terminal or computer and the acoustic coupler.

adaptive routing   A routing algorithm that evaluates the existing paths and chooses the one that will provide the best path for a message. Routes may change due to congestion and path failures.

Administrative Management Domain (ADMD)   A domain that represents a private electronic mail system corresponding to a public delivery network in the X.400 standard hierarchy.

Advanced Data Communications Control Procedure (ADCCP)   An ANSI standard bit-oriented data link control. Pronounced "add-cap."

after-image   The status of a record after it has been processed.

agent   A device component that collects data for the device, which is then stored in the management information base (MIB).

aggregate data rate   The amount of information that can be transmitted per unit of time.

alert   A signal given by the network management system that a statistic, such as current line status, line quality, or number of retries on the line, has changed since the last status report. Also known as an alarm.

American National Standards Institute (ANSI)   A U.S. standards-making agency.

American Standard Code for Information Interchange (ASCII)   A code that uses seven or eight bits to represent characters. One of the two common computer codes. See also EBCDIC.

Amplitude Modulation (AM)   One method of changing the properties of a wave to represent data.

analog line monitor   A diagnostic tool that monitors and displays the analog signals on the communications circuit or on the data communications side of the modem, enabling the user to check for noise and proper modulation.

analog transmission   Refers to measureable physical quantities, which in data communications take the form of voltage and variations in the properties of waves. Data is represented in analog form by varying the amplitude, frequency, and/or phase of a wave or by changing current on a line.

application layer   One of the layers of the International Standards Organization's (OSI) reference model. The functions of this layer are application dependent.

Application Program Interface (API)   In LANs, the interface between application programs and the network software.

ARCnet   Local area network implementation based on Datapoint's attached resource computer network.

Asynchronous Transfer Mode (ATM) A high-speed transmission protocol in which data blocks are broken into small cells that are transmitted individually and possibly via different routes in a manner similar to packet-switching technology.

asynchronous transmission (Async) The oldest and one of the most common data link protocols. Each character is transmitted individually with its own error detection scheme, usually a parity bit. The sender and receiver are not synchronized with each other. Also known as start-stop protocol.

attenuation A weakening of a signal as a result of distance and characteristics of the medium.

AT&T divestiture In 1984, AT&T was broken up into independent RBOCs and a separate AT&T company. The divestiture ended the regulated monopoly of AT&T as well as freeing AT&T and the RBOCs to enter into business areas previously denied to them.

authentication A process in which a system user is required to provide and/or verify his or her user identification to gain system access.

Auto-Call Unit (ACU) A device used to place a telephone call automatically without manual intervention.

availability All necessary components of a network are operable and accessible when a user requires them.

backbone network A network used to interconnect other networks or to connect a cluster of network nodes.

backup software Software that is responsible for reading the files being backed up and writing them to the backup device.

baluns Adapters that change coaxial cable connectors into twisted-pair wire connectors, allowing transfer from one medium to another or from a connector for one medium to a different medium.

bandwidth The difference between the minimum and the maximum frequencies allowed. Bandwidth is a measure of the amount of data that can be transmitted per unit of time. The greater the bandwidth, the higher the possible data transmission rate.

baseband transmission Sends the data along the channel by means of voltage fluctuations. The entire bandwidth of the cable is used to carry data.

baud rate A measure of the number of discrete signals that can be observed per unit of time.

Baudot A code obtained from the telegraph industry that is used in data communications with telegraph lines or equipment originally designed for telegraphy. It is limited in its number of representable characters.

before-image The status of a record before it has been processed.

benchmark A test in which one or more programs are run on a proposed hardware configuration to verify the ability of the hardware to meet a system's application requirements.

Binary Coded Decimal (BCD) A coding scheme for the storage of data in digital computers. The code may either be four-bit or six-bit.

Binary Synchronous Communications (BISYNC or BSC) protocol A transmission protocol introduced by IBM as the data link protocol for remote job entry. It later became a de facto standard for many types of data transmission, particularly between two computers. Data is transmitted a block at a time, and the sender and receiver need to be in time with each other. Specific control characters are used to indicate beginning of text, end of text, start of header, and so on.

bit parallel transmission The simultaneous transmission of bits over a wire medium.

bit rate One method of measuring data transmission speed—bits per second.

Bits Per Second (BPS) The number of bits that can be transferred over a medium in one second. Bps is a measure of data transmission speed.

bit stuffing The implementation of transparency in SDLC through bit insertion.

bit-oriented synchronous data link protocol A data link protocol in which one or more bits are used to control the communications link. Bit synchronous protocols are commonly used on both LANs and WANs.

Block Check Character (BCC) In the error detection methods of longitudinal redundancy check (LRC) or cyclic redundancy check (CRC), an error detection character or characters, called the BCC, is appended to a block of transmitted characters, typically at the end of the block.

block mode A mode in which data is entered and transmitted in one or more sets or blocks.

breakout box A passive, multipurpose diagnostic device that is patched or temporarily inserted into a circuit at an interface.

bridge The interface used to connect networks using similar data link protocols.

broadband transmission A form of data transmission where data is carried on high-frequency carrier waves; the carrying capacity of the medium is divided into a number of subchannels, such as video, low-speed data, high-speed data, voice, and so on, allowing the medium to satisfy several communication needs.

broadcast message A message sent to all users on a network.

broadcast radio Employs AM, FM, and shortwave radio frequencies, with a total frequency range from 500,000 to 108 million cycles per second. Its primary applications include paging terminals, cellular radio telephones, and wireless local area networks.

broadcast routing Routing in which the message is broadcast to all stations. Only the stations to which the message is addressed accept it.

brouter A term used to describe bridges that are able to connect two LANs using different data link protocols.

buffer overflow/overrun A situation that arises when the buffer is either too small or too full to receive the transmitted data. In either case there is no place to store the arriving characters, and the data is lost.

bus A communications medium for transmitting data or power. A local area network topology.

Bus Interface Unit (BIU) In a local area network, the bus interface unit provides the physical connection to the computer's I/O bus.

byte count protocol A type of synchronous protocol that delineates data by including the number of characters being transmitted within the message.

cable tester A diagnostic tool used to detect faults in cables by generating and monitoring a signal along the cable.

cache memory High-speed memory that improves a computer's performance.

call clearing The process that dissolves a switched virtual circuit.

call-back unit A security device for switched connections. It operates by receiving a call, verifying the user, severing the call, and calling the user back.

Carrier Sense with Multiple Access and Collision Avoidance (CSMA/CA) A media access control technique that attempts to avoid collisions.

Carrier Sense with Multiple Access and Collision Detection (CSMA/CD) A media access control technique that attempts to detect collisions and is the most common of the access strategies for bus architectures.

carrier signal A wave that continues without change. The carrier signal can be modulated by a modem so a receiver can interpret the information.

Carterphone case A U.S. case regarding attaching devices to a telephone company's network.

CCITT V.10 and V.11 Electrical interfaces for data transmission.

CCITT V.24 A functional interface similar to RS-232-C.

CCITT V.25 A specification for establishing and terminating sesssions with an auto-call unit.

CCITT V.28 A specification for electrical interface similar to that of RS-232-C.

CCITT V.35 A standard for data transmission at speeds up to 48,000 bits per second using a 34-pin connection.

CCITT X.20 and X.21 Standards that cover the interface between DCE and DTE for packet distribution networks.

CCITT X.24 A functional interface for packet distribution networks.

Centrex service A telephone company service that provides PBX capabilities to a company. With the Centrex service, the PBX equipment is located on the telephone company's premises.

character count termination A transmission termination technique where a transmission is complete when a specified number of characters have been received. Allows the computer to save the data in blocks and avoid buffer overflow.

character synchronous protocol A type of synchronous protocol oriented toward specific data codes and specific characters within those codes.

checksum A technique used to check for errors in data. The sending application generates the checksum from the data being transmitted. The receiving application computes the checksum and compares it to the value computed and sent by the sending station.

ciphertext The encrypted version of a message or data.

circuit Either the medium connecting two communicating devices or a path between a sender and a receiver where there may be one or more intermediary nodes. The exact meaning depends on the context.

client A software application that requests services from the server in a client/server computing environment. Some systems may refer to the client as a requester.

client/server protocol An application framework in which the processing load is divided among several processes called clients and servers. Clients issue requests to servers, which provide specialized services such as database processing and mail distribution. Within this framework, clients are able to concentrate on business logic while servers can use specialized hardware and software that allows them to provide their services more efficiently. When clients and servers are located in different computers, application processing is distributed over multiple computers and, in effect, the network becomes the computer.

cluster controller A device that manages multiple terminals by buffering data transmitted to and from the terminals and performing error detection and correction.

coaxial cable A transmission medium consisting of one or two central data transmission wires surrounded by an insulating layer, a shielding layer, and an outer jacket. Coaxial cable has a high data-carrying capacity and low error rates.

code independence The ability to sucessfully transmit data regardless of the data code, such as ASCII or EBCDIC.

collision In a CSMA/CD media access control protocol, a collision occurs when two stations attempt to send a message at the same time. The messages interfere with each other, so correct communication is not possible.

common carrier A public utility that provides public transmission media, such as the telephone companies and satellite companies.

Common Management Information Protocol (CMIP) Guidelines issued by the International Standards Organization for creating network management software products. Also known as the Communications Management Information Protocol.

Communications Interface Unit (CIU) In a local area network, the communications interface unit provides the physical connection to the transmission medium.

communications server A server that monitors connections to the host by determining whether there is a free port to make the connection and granting or denying the request accordingly.

Computer-Aided Design (CAD) An application of computers in the design process. One component is computer drafting.

Computer-Aided Instruction (CAI) The use of computers to facilitate the education process.

Computer-Aided Manufacturing (CAM) The use of computers to solve manufacturing problems. CAM includes robotic control, machine control, and process control components.

concentrator A computer that provides line-sharing capabilities, data editing, polling, error handling, code conversion, compression, and encryption.

conditioning A service provided by telephone companies for leased lines. It reduces the amount of noise on a line, providing lower error rates and increased speed.

conducted media Media that use a conductor such as a wire or fiber optic cable to move a signal from sender to receiver.

congestion control The reduction of transmission delays.

Connectionless Network Protocol (CLNP) The counterpart to the Internet Protocol (IP), this protocol provides message services such as message priorities, route selection parameters, and security parameters.

connector Establishes the physical connection between the computer and the medium.

consistency A consistent system is one that works predictably with respect both to the people who use the system and to response times.

Consultative Committee on International Telegraph and Telephony (CCITT) An international standards organization.

contention A convention whereby devices obtain control of a communications link. In contention mode, devices compete for control of the line either by transmitting directly on an idle line or by issuing a request for line control.

contention mode A mode in which the host and the terminal contend for control of the medium by issuing a bid for the channel.

context data A requirement of multithreaded processes that entails unifying the work by keeping track of the completed parts as well as the parts yet to be worked on, and ensuring that an interrupted transaction is restarted at the correct point.

control center A network component responsible for monitoring the network and taking corrective action when necessary.

conversational mode A mode in which the terminal and the host exchange messages.

cooperative computing A data-processing model in which two or more processes collaborate on the processing necessary for a single transaction or application. The cooperating processes may reside in different computers.

Cooper Distributed Data Interface (CDDI) An ANSI LAN standard for twisted-pair-wire LANs spanning a distance of approximately 200 kilometers and providing speeds of 100 Mbps. An extension of the fiber distributed interface LAN.

corporate license A license that gives a corporation unlimited use of software at all locations.

CPU time The amount of time required for the CPU to execute the processing instructions, including those executed by the database management system, operating system, data communications software, and applications programs.

critical path The sequence of events in a project that takes the longest to complete.

crosstalk When the signals from one channel distort or interfere with the signals of a different channel.

current loop A transmission technique that uses changes in current flow to represent data. Does not require a modem and operates at speeds up to 19.2K bits per second.

Customer Information Control System (CICS) A TCP provided by IBM. Its primary function is as an interface between terminal users on one side and application programs or the database on the other.

Cyclic Redundancy Check (CRC) An error detection algorithm that uses a polynomial function to generate the block check characters. CRC is a very efficient error detection method.

daisy chain A connection arrangement in which each device is connected directly to the next device. For example, a daisy chain of devices A, B, C, and D might have A connected to B, B connected to C, and C connected to D. Also known as cascading.

Database Management System (DBMS) A system that organizes data into records, organizes records into files, provides access to the data based on one or more access keys, and provides the mechanism for relating one file to another.

database server A computer that allows microcomputers on a network to request database processing of records, returning a single figure answer rather than the set of records essential to determining the answer.

data communications   The transmission of data to and from computers and components of computer systems.

Data Communications Equipment (DCE)   One class of equipment in data communications, including modems, media, and media support facilities.

Data Encryption Standard (DES)   An algorithm that uses an encryption key to transform data, called plaintext, into an encoded form, called encrypted or ciphertext.

datagram   One type of connection option for a PDN. The message fits into the data field on one packet. There is less accountability for packet delivery than for other connection types.

data link layer   One of the layers of the International Standards Organization's OSI reference model. The data link layer is responsible for node-to-node-message transfers.

data link protocol   Convention that governs the flow of data between a sending and a receiving station.

data switch   A device implemented on sub-LANs to provide connections between microcomputers.

Data Terminal Equipment (DTE)   The second class of equipment in data communications, including terminals, computers, concentrators, and multiplexers.

dataset/modem   Short for modulator-demodulator. A device that changes digital signals to analog signals for transmitting data over telephone circuits. Also used for some fiber optic transmission (digital fiber optics do not require a modem) and any transmission mode requiring a change from one form of signal to another.

deadlock   A state that exists when two or more processes are unable to proceed. It occurs when two or more transactions have locked a resource and request resources that other involved processes already have locked.

dedicated printer   A printer that can be used only by a person at the workstation to which the printer is attached.

dedicated server   One or more computers that operate only as designated file, database, or other types of servers.

dibits   A transmission mode in which each signal conveys two bits of data.

Differential Phase Shift Keying (DPSK)   A modulation technique that uses phase modulation. DPSK changes phase each time a 1 bit is transmitted and does not change phase for 0 bits.

digital transmission   A transmission mode in which data is represented by binary digits rather than by an analog signal.

direct sequencing   Sends data out over several different frequencies simultaneously to increase the probability of success.

discovery packet   A packet sent by the sending station on all available routes to evaluate and determine the best route from the information collected by the packet.

disk drive interface/controller   Sets the standards for connecting the disk drive to the microprocessor and the software commands used to access the drive.

disk caching   Similar in function to cache memory except that main memory serves as a high-speed buffer for slower disk drives.

disk seek enhancement   An I/O optimization technique that reduces the head movement during seeks and improves performance.

diskless workstation   A workstation that has no local disk drives, reducing the ways in which a virus can be introduced.

Distributed Computing Environment (DCE)   A standardization for middleware established by the Open Software Foundation that specifies the use of remote procedure calls, security, name services, and messages for client/server computing.

distributed database   A database wherein data is located on two or more computing systems connected via a data communications network. The fact that data is distributed should be transparent to database users.

Distributed File System (DFS)   Network software responsible for making network resources available to multiple users regardless of their location in the network.

distributed processing   The geographic distribution of hardware, software, processing, data, and control.

distributed query processing   A condition in which a user at one node can start a query involving data on other nodes.

distributed routing determination   A routing algorithm in which each node calculates its own routing table based on status information periodically received from other nodes.

distributed transaction management   In a distributed database, a transaction may be operated on by several processes in different computer nodes. Transactions of this type must be managed by the distributed database system to ensure database integrity either by completing the transaction or by reversing any updates done by a transaction that cannot be completed.

distribution list   A predefined list of individual users, represented by a single E-mail address, that replaces the need to enter each user's individual address when sending a message to them collectively as a workgroup.

document co-authoring system   A system that allows two or more workers to work on one document concurrently.

document management system   A system that helps an organization manage and control its documents.

domain   In IBM's SNA, the network components managed by a systems services control point.

dotted quad   The four-octet address representation on the Internet.

double buffering   Used when buffer overflow/overrun occurs to avoid losing characters.

downloaded   The process of transferring data or an application from the server to the workstation.

DS1/T1 through T4/DS4   High-speed data transmission circuits from a common carrier.

dumb terminal   A terminal that passively serves for input and/or output but performs no local processing.

duplexed servers   The fault-tolerance technique in which one server can fail and another is available to continue working.

echo   The reflection or reversal of the signal being transmitted. Also used to define a transmission convention in which the receiver of data sends the data back to the sender to assist in error detection.

echo supressor   A device that allows a transmitted signal to pass in one direction only, thus minimizing the echo effect.

effectiveness   A measure of how well a system serves users' needs.

electronic appointment calendar   A work-group productivity tool that is stored on the network, so that users can consult each other's appointment calendars.

electronic conferencing   An application that assists users in arranging and conducting meetings electronically.

electronic mail (E-mail)   An online service equivalent to the postal system which allows users to send and receive messages from other users electronically.

electronic meeting systems   Network software that allows participants to exchange machine readable information in the form of graphics, text, audio, and full-motion video.

emulator   A diagnostic tool that enables the user to check for adherence to a specific protocol.

encryption   A process in which transmitted data is scrambled at the sending location and reconstructed into readable data at the receiving end.

end office   A telephone company office to which a subscriber is connected. Also called a class 5 office.

enterprise network   A network of two or more LANs connected to each other, or one or more LANs connected to a WAN.

ergonomics   The science of designing equipment to maximize worker productivity by reducing operator fatigue and discomfort while improving safety.

Ethernet   A local area network implementation using the CSMA/CD protocol on a bus. The IEEE 802.3 standard is based on Ethernet. One of the popular local area network implementations.

exclusive open mode   A file open mode in which an open request is granted only if no other user has the file opened already.

Extended Binary-Coded Decimal Interchange Code (EBCDIC)   A code that uses eight bits to represent a character of information. One of the most common computer codes. *See also* ASCII.

external specification   Specifications detailing end-user interfaces to a system and information available to the user.

fault tolerance   A combination of hardware and software techniques that improve the reliability of a system.

Fiber Distributed Data Interface (FDDI)   An ANSI LAN standard for fiber optic LANs spanning a distance of approximately 200 kilometers and providing speeds of 100 Mbps.

fiber optic cable   A transmission medium that provides high data rates and low errors. One or more glass or plastic fibers are woven together to form the core of the cable. This core is surrounded by a glass or plastic layer called the cladding. The cladding in turn is covered with plastic or other material for protection. The cable requires a light source, most commonly laser and light-emitting diodes.

file exchange utilities   A work-group productivity tool that allows files to be easily copied from one network node to another.

File Management System (FMS)   A system that provides a subset of a database management system's capabilities. An FMS provides functions such as storage allocation and file access methods for a single file.

file server   A computer that allows microcomputers on a network to share resources such as data, programs, and printers. The file server's software controls access to shared files, as opposed to the operating system of the microcomputer.

file transfer utility   An intrinsic part of many routers, this utility allows files to be moved between network nodes.

filter   A software component used to screen and format data sent to the management center.

flooding   A technique used by a bridge to locate a destination address not present in the bridge's routing table by sending a packet out on all possible paths. An acknowledgment from the receiving station will contain the destination address of the packet, which can then be added to the bridge's routing table.

Fractional T-1   A T-1 service that fills the void of high speed transmission options between 64 Kbps and 1.5 Mbps by providing a portion of T-1 line to customers.

frame   A term used to describe a transmission packet in bit-oriented protocols.

framing protocol   A type of synchronous protocol that uses reserved characters or bit patterns to delineate data and control fields within the message.

frequency division multiplexing (FDM)   A technique that divides the available bandwidth of the circuit into subchannels of different frequency ranges, each of which is assigned to one device.

frequency hopping Data is transmitted at one frequency, the frequency changes, and the data is transmitted at the new frequency. Each piece of data is transmitted over several frequencies to increase the probability that the data will be successfully received.

Frequency Modulation (FM)/Frequency Shift Keying (FSK) One method of changing the characteristics of a signal to represent data. The frequency of the carrier signal is changed. Often used by lower speed modems.

Front-End Processor (FEP) A communications component placed at the host end of a circuit to take over a portion of the line management work from the host. Also referred to as a communications controller or a message switch.

full duplex A data transmission mode in which data is transmitted over a link in both directions simultaneously.

Fully Qualified Domain Name (FQDN) The computer.domain notation used to specify addresses in the Internet.

functional specification An agreement between management and designers outlining design objectives, such as the product to be produced, and design constraints, such as time and cost.

functional testing Testing individual modules to ensure that they produce the desired results.

gateway The interface used to connect two dissimilar networks or systems by providing conversion from one network to another.

geosynchronous orbit A satellite orbit in which the satellite is stationary with respect to the earth. The satellite is always positioned over the same location.

Group Decision Support System (GDSS) System that assists individuals and groups in the decision-making process and helps them set objectives.

groupware A collective of work-group productivity tools that allows a group of users to communicate and to coordinate activities.

guardbands Subchannel separators that are implemented in frequency division multiplexing to avoid crosstalk.

half duplex A data transmission mode in which data can travel in both directions over a link but in only one direction at a time.

half-session layer Represents a single layer (transmission control, flow control, and presentation service) in the four-layer definition of SNA functional layers.

Hertz (Hz) The term used to denote frequency; one hertz is one cycle per second.

hierarchical topology A network topology in which the nodes are arranged hierarchically. Also known as a tree structure.

High-Level Data Link Control (HDLC) A positional synchronous protocol that operates in full duplex mode in both point-to-point and multipoint configurations. Data is transmitted in fixed-format frames consisting of start flag, address, control information, block check character (CRC), an end-of-frame flag. HDLC is an International Standards Organization standard similar to IBM's SDLC.

Hush-a-Phone Case A U.S. case that set a precedent regarding attaching equipment to telephone networks.

I/O optimization A variety of ways to optimize the task of file access which increases the performance of the server.

I/O driver The part of the operating system that manages the input/output subsystem by providing low-level access to devices.

identification Information assigned to a specific user of a system for security and control purposes. User identification ranges from simple user names to high-security measures such as voice print and fingerprint identification.

IEEE 802.3 standard A standard that covers a variety of CSMA/CD architectures that are generally based on the Ethernet.

IEEE 802.4 standard A subcommittee that sets standards for token bus networks.

IEEE 802.5 standard A subcommittee that sets standards for token-ring networks.

impulse noise A noise characterized by signal "spikes." In telephone circuits it can be caused by switching equipment or by lightning strikes and in other situations by transient electrical impulses such as those occurring on a shop floor. Impulse noise is a common cause of transmission errors.

inactive node A node that may be powered down and is incapable of sending or receiving messages.

inactive port The status of a bridge port that will not accept packets from the LAN end of the port.

information superhighway A national information system geared toward moving the raw materials (data) and finished goods (information and ideas) of information to their needed locations.

infrared transmission Uses electromagnetic radiation of wavelengths between visible light and radio waves. It is a line-of-sight technology used to provide local area connections between buildings and is also the medium used in some wireless local area networks.

Institute of Electrical and Electronic Engineers (IEEE) A professional society that establishes and publishes documents and standards for data communications. IEEE has established several standards for local area networks, including the IEEE 802.3 and IEEE 802.5 standards for LAN technology.

Integrated Services Digital Network (ISDN) The integration of voice and data transmission (and other formats such as video and graphics images) over a digital transmission network. This network configuration is proposed by numerous common carriers.

integrated testing A procedure which ensures that all parts of a system are functionally compatible.

intelligent terminal   A terminal that has both memory and data processing capabilities.

interconnected (plex or mesh) network   A network topology in which any node can be directly connected to any other node.

intermodulation noise   A special form of crosstalk, which is the result of two or more signals combining to produce a distorted signal.

internal specification   Specifications or "blueprints" for developing a software system.

International Standards Organization (ISO)   An organization that is active in setting communications standards.

Internet   A specific collection of interconnected networks spanning more than 40 countries throughout the world.

interoperability   The ability of all network components to connect to the network and to communicate with shared network resources.

interrupt   A signal issued by hardware or an application requesting a service from the operating system.

interrupt characters   A set of characters that terminate a message or cause an interruption in transmission to perform a special action, such as a backspace.

inventory software   A management tool used to collect LAN component data, such as network addresses and CPU types, that will assist a network administrator in managing and fixing a network.

inverse multiplexer   A mux that provides a high-speed data path between two devices by separating data onto multiple lower-speed communications circuits.

key disk   A security system in which a flexible disk must be in the disk drive when the application is run.

LAN analyzer   A diagnostic tool that monitors network traffic, captures and displays data sent over the network, generates network traffic to simulate load or error conditions, tests cables for faults, and provides data helpful for system configuration and management.

LAN Server (IBM)   An example of LAN software that runs under an existing OS, OS/2.

latency   The average time required for the requested data to revolve under the read/write heads.

leased lines   Lines leased from common carriers. Lines are leased when the connection time between locations is long enough to cover the cost of leasing or if speeds higher than those available with switched lines must be attained.

learning bridge   Bridge that builds its own routing table from the messages it receives, rather than having a predefined routing table. Also known as a transparent bridge.

license agreement   An agreement that covers the rules under which you are allowed to use a product.

line monitor   A device used to diagnose problems on a communications link. Also known as a protocol analyzer.

link   The circuit established beween two adjacent nodes, with no intervening nodes.

Link Access Procedure, Balanced (LAPB)   A bit synchronous protocol similar to high-level data link control. LAPB is the protocol specified for X.25 networks.

Local Access and Transport Areas (LATA)   The region served by a regional Bell operating company(RBOC). Following the divestiture of AT&T the U.S. was divided into local access and transport areas. LATAs are not rigidly defined, but calls within a LATA are handled exclusively by the RBOC (the call is not handled by a long-distance carrier but still may be a toll call).

Local Area Network (LAN)   A communications network in which all of the components are located within several kilometers of each other and that uses high transmission speeds—generally one million bits per second or higher.

local procedure calls   In programming, one procedure in a program can call another procedure in the same program. The called procedure carries out a processing task for the calling procedure. Generally, the two procedures exchange information through a list of parameters that are passed between the calling and the called procedure.

locks   Record or file-level control that overcomes the problem with file open contention.

log file   A monitoring tool used for both diagnostic functions and predictive or management functions.

Logical Link Control (LLC)   A sublayer of the OSI reference model data link layer. The logical link control forms the interface between the network layer and the media access control protocols.

Logical Unit (LU)   In IBM's SNA, a unit that represents a system user. Sessions exist between LUs or between an LU and the SSCP. Several types of LUs have been defined.

Longitudinal Redundancy Check (LRC)   An error-checking technique in which a block check character is appended to a block of transmitted characters, typically at the end of the block. The block check character checks parity on a row of bits.

LU 6.2   An SNA logical unit type representing a program-to-program session.

mail agent   A software module that can automatically act on behalf of a user to forward mail or alert other users that the recipient is unavailable.

Management Information Base (MIB)   A database that defines the hardware and software elements to be monitored in the SNMP.

matrix switch   A device that allows terminal connections to be switched among the available processors.

Mean Time Between Failures (MTBF)   A measure of

the average amount of time a given component may be expected to operate before failing.

Mean Time To Repair (MTTR)   The average amount of time required to repair a broken piece of equipment and restore it to service.

Media Access Control (MAC) protocol   A sub layer of the OSI reference model's data link layer. The media access control protocol defines how a station gains access to the media for data transmission. Common MAC protocols are carrier sense with multiple access and collision detection (CSMA/CD) and token-passing.

medium   In data communications, the carrier of data signals. Twisted-pair wires, coaxial cables, and fiber optic cables are the most common LAN media.

menuing software   A management tool used to provide users options via a menu of choices.

message logging   Also referred to as safe storing, this recovery system writes the message to a file prior to acknowledgment so the message may be reviewed or recovered later if necessary.

message sequence numbers   A system in which each transmitted message is given a sequential number, allowing multiple messages to be transmitted without acknowledgment.

Message Transfer Agent (MTA)   An interface between E-mail user agents.

metering software   A monitoring tool used on LANs to enforce adherence to software license agreements by keeping track of the number of times an application is executed.

Microcomputer Network Protocols (MNP)   A set of modem protocols providing for data compression and error checking, such as MNP Level 4 and MNP Level 5.

microwave radio   A method of transmitting data using high-frequency radio waves. It requires a line of sight between sending and receiving stations. Capable of high data rates, microwave is used for wide area networks and wireless LANs.

middleware   A software interface that functions as an intermediary between clients and servers.

mirrored disks   A fault tolerance technique in which two disks containing the same data are provided so that if one fails, the other is available, allowing processing to continue.

mobile computing   Has expanded the role of broadcast radio in data communications. It requires a wireless medium such as cellular radio, radio nets, and low orbit satellites.

modular expansion   A system that allows the user to upgrade from a small system to a more powerful system by adding more of the same type of processor to the existing system.

modem eliminator   A device that allows data transmission over short distances without a modem. Provides for signal timing as well as data transmission.

modem turnaround time   The time required for a modem to make the transition from sender to receiver on half duplex links. It includes the time for the old sender to drop the carrier signal, for the new sender to recognize that the carrier signal has been dropped, and for the new sender to raise the carrier signal that must be detected by the new receiver.

multipoint connection   A connection in which several terminals share one communications link.

multimedia technology   Technology that extends a computer's capabilities by adding audio and video to data.

multimode graded-index fiber   Acts to refract the light toward the center of the fiber by variations in the density of the core.

multimode step-index fiber   The oldest of the fiber optic technologies, in which the reflective walls of the fiber move the light pulses to the receiver.

multiple access   The ability for nodes to access a medium that is not carrying a message.

multiplexer   A hardware device that allows several devices to share one communications channel.

multiplexing   A line-sharing technology that allows multiple signals to be transmitted over a single link.

Multistation Access Unit (MAU)   In an IBM token ting LAN, a MAU is used to interconnect workstations.

multithreading   The capacity a process has to work on multiple requests at once.

NetWare   A leading example of the integrated LAN operating system software approach by Novell.

network   Two or more computers connected by a communications medium, together with all communications, hardware and software components. Alternatively, a host processor together with its attached terminal, workstations, and communications equipment, such as transmission media, modems, and so on.

Network Addressable Unit (NAU)   In IBM's SNA, any device that has a network address, such as logical units and physical units.

network architecture   The way in which media, hardware, and software are integrated to form a network

network configuration tool   A monitoring tool used to plan the optimum network configuration with respect to sources and types of circuits.

network control   Involves the sending and receiving of node status information to other nodes to determine the best routing for messages.

Network Control Program (NCP)   A data communications program that helps manage a communications network. Specifically, a program that runs in IBM's 37xx line of communications controllers.

network directory services   A database that contains the names, types, and network addresses of network resources. Examples of resource types include users, printers, and servers. The directory database may be replicated on several network nodes, thus allowing users and processes to locate resources they need to complete their work.

Network File System (NFS)   A distributed file system developed by Sun Microsystems that is also compatible with DOS and UNIX-based systems.

network layer   One of the layers of the International Standards Organization's OSI reference model. The network layer is responsible for end-to-end message routing.

Network Management System (NMS)   A combination of hardware and software used by network supervisors to monitor and administer a network.

network manager   An individual or management team responsible for configuring, planning, tuning, and establishing standards and procedures for a network.

network routing manager   A designated node that has an overview of network functioning, location of any bottlenecks, and location of utilized facilities.

network routing table   In the process of message transmission, a table in which the network layer looks up the destination address to find the next address along the path.

network statistics   Information, such as error rates, data rates, and the number of retransmission attempts resulting from errors, that is collected to analyze network performance trends.

network topology   A model for the way in which network nodes are connected. Network topologies include bus, ring, and star.

neutral working   A method of transmitting data in a current loop where current represents a 1 bit and the absence of current indicates a 0 bit.

node   A processor in a network, either a LAN or a WAN.

non-dedicated server   A computer that can operate as both a server and a workstation.

number received (Nr) subfield   In bit synchronous transmission such as HDLC, a field on the transmission frame and on the receiver's system used to represent the frame sequence number the receiving station expects to receive next.

number sent (Ns) subfield   In bit synchronous transmission such as HDLC, a field on the transmission frame and on the sender's system used to represent the frame sequence number being transmitted.

Object Request Broker (ORB)   A standardization for middleware established by the Object Management Group that assures hardware and software independence by locating a server that is capable of satisfying a client's request.

octet   A group of eight bits used in bit synchronous protocols. Data, regardless of its code, is treated as octets.

office automation systems   A special case of a distributed system, with both data and processing distributed among several different components.

open architecture   Architecture whose network specifications are available to any company. This allows a variety of companies to design hardware and software components that can be easily integrated into new and existing networks.

Open Systems Interconnection (OSI) reference model   A seven-layered set of functions for transmitting data from one user to another. Specified by the International Standards Organization.

Operating System (OS)   The overall manager of the computing system that performs all of its functions transparent to the applications program and the programmer.

Packet Assembly/Disassembly (PAD)   A function in a packet-switching network that breaks messages into packets for transmission and reassembles packets into messages at the message's destination.

packet switching   The transmission of a message by dividing the message into fixed length packets and then routing the packets to the recipient. Packets may be sent over different paths and arrive out of order. At the receiving end, the packets are reordered. Routing is determined during transmission of the packet. Also known as packet distribution network (PDN), public data network, X.25 network, or value-added network.

Packet-Switching Equipment (PSE)   Equipment that accepts and forwards messages in a packet distribution network.

path   A group of links that allows a message to move from its point of origin to its destination.

parity check/Vertical Redundancy Check (VRC)   The same as parity error checking. For each character transmitted, an additional bit, the parity bit, is attached to help detect errors. The bit is chosen so that the number of 1 bits is even (even parity) or odd (odd parity).

parity data   In RAID technology, additional data that provides the ability to reconstruct data that has been corrupted.

passive hub   A node connection hub used in an ARCnet LAN that does not provide signal regeneration, so nodes can be located no farther than 100 feet from the hub.

password   A secret expression used by authorized persons to prove their right to access a system.

performance monitor   A monitoring tool that provides snapshots of how a system is actually functioning, which helps the network management team identify trends in the use or misuse of the network.

Permanent Virtual Circuit (PVC)   One of three types of connection for a packet distribution network. A PVC provides a permanent link (like a leased line) between two nodes. It is usually selected when two nodes require continual transmission.

phase jitter   A variation in the phase of a continued signal from cycle to cycle.

phase modulation   A change in the phase of a carrier signal. Commonly used alone or in conjunction with amplitude modulation to provide high-speed transmission (4800 bits per second and higher).

Phase Shift Keying (PSK)   A form of phase modulation.

physical layer   One of the layers of the International Standards Organization's OSI reference model. The physical layer specifies the electrical connections between the transmission medium and the computing system.

physical security   Measures, such as door locks, safes, and security guards, taken to deny physical access to restricted areas.

Physical Unit (PU)   In SNA, a hardware unit. Four physical units have been defined: Type 5, host processor; Type 4, communications controller; Type 2, cluster or programmable controller; and Type 1, a terminal or controller that is not programmable.

Physical Unit Control Point (PUCP)   In IBM's systems network architecture (SNA), a physical unit control point resides in nodes that do not contain a systems services control point (SSCP). The PUCP is responsible for connecting the node to and disconnecting the node from the network.

plain text   The unencrypted or properly decrypted version of a message or data. Plain text is intelligible. Also known as clear text.

Point Of Presence (POP)   A point of presence in the U.S. public telephone network. A point of presence is a point at which a transfer is made from a local telephone company to the long-distance carrier.

point-to-point connection   A connection using a communication line to connect one terminal or computer to a host computer.

polar working   One method used to implement current loop transmission.

polling   The process of asking terminals whether they have data to transmit.

port concentrator   A device that allows multiple input streams from a multiplexer to be passed to the host through a single communications port.

port selector   A device that helps determine which users are granted access to applications where the number of potential terminal users far exceeds the number of available lines. Also known as a data switch.

positional protocol   A type of synchronous protocol that delineates fields by the use of fixed-length fields on the message, by indicating the size of the message with a character count embedded in the message, or both.

presentation layer   One of the layers of the International Standards Organization's OSI reference model. The presentation layer addresses message formats.

primary center   A telephone company class 3 station. A primary center is one station higher than a toll center.

print server   A computer that allows several users to direct their printed output to the same printer.

printer driver   A software module that determines how to format data for proper printing on a specific type of printer.

Private Branch Exchange (PBX)   Telephone switching equipment located on corporate premises and owned by the corporation. A PBX allows telephone calls within an office to be connected locally without using the telephone company's end office or transmission circuits.

Private Management Domain (PRMD)   A domain that represents a delivery and interconnection network corresponding to a company in the X.400 standard hierarchy.

Program Evaluation and Review Technique (PERT)   A technique that tracks a project's progress to determine its critical path and to monitor personnel, schedules and project resources.

project management system   A management tool that assists in planning projects and allocating resources.

propagation delay   The amount of time it takes for a signal to travel from its source to its destination.

protected open mode   A file open mode that is granted only if no other user has already been granted exclusive or protected mode.

protocol   Convention used for establishing transmission rules. Protocols are used to establish rules for delineation of data, error detection, control sequences, message lengths, media access, and so on.

protocol converter   A special-purpose device that allows a terminal to look like a different type of terminal in order to facilitate interconnection between different computer systems.

Pulse Code Modulation (PCM)   A method for transmitting data in digital format.

quadbits   A technique in which each signal carries four bits of data. Requires 16 different signals.

Quadrature Amplitude Modulation (QAM)   A modulation technique using both phase and amplitude modulation.

queuing time   The amount of time the transaction must wait in queues for service.

radiated media   Media that use radio waves of different frequencies or infrared light to broadcast through air or space and accordingly do not need a wire or cable conductor to transmit signals.

recovery   The act of restoring a system to operational status following a failure.

redirector   A software module that intercepts and re-routes network application I/O requests before they get to the workstation's OS.

Redundant Arrays of Independent Disks (RAID)   A fault-tolerance disk storage technique that spreads one file plus the file's checksum information over several disk drives. If any single disk drive fails, the data stored thereon can be reconstructed from data stored on the remaining drives.

Regional Bell Operating Company (RBOC)   The AT&T divestiture resulted in the formation of RBOCs and a separate AT&T company. An RBOC is responsible for local telephone services within a region of the United States.

regional center   A class 1 telephone station.

reliability   The probability that the system will continue to function over a given time period.

remote control software   A diagnostic tool that allows a LAN administrator to remotely view a user's monitor and take control of the user's keyboard.

Remote File Sharing (RFS)   A distributed file system that is only supported by UNIX-based systems.

Remote Job Entry (RJE)   An application of data communications. Batches of data are collected at a remote site and transmitted to a host for processing. In early implementations the input was card format and the output was printer format (between the remote terminals and the host processor).

remote login facility   A network utility that allows users to log onto a remote system thereby establishing the user as a local user on the remote node.

Remote Monitoring MIB (RMON MIB)   An SNMP standard that describes nine different device groups. A vendor must choose an appropriate group for a device adhering to this standard and is required to support all the data objects defined for that group.

remote procedure call   A remote procedure call is similar to a local procedure call except that the calling and called procedures are not a part of the same program. The called and calling procedures may be located in the same computer or in different networked computers.

repeater   A device used to amplify signals on a network. Repeaters allow the medium distance to be extended.

response time   The amount of time required for a user to receive a reply to a request. Usually the time elapsed between the user pressing the Enter key to send the request (or the equivalent) and the return of the first character of the response.

Request For Information (RFI)   An informal method of investigating hardware and software solutions by presenting a brief statement of a problem to be solved and a list of questions soliciting solutions to the problem.

Request For Proposal (RFP)   Sometimes referred to as

a Request For Quotation (RFQ), a formal document describing the problem to be solved and requesting qualified vendors to submit plans and costs for solving the problem.

reverse channel   Allows transmission in both directions on a line that is essentially half duplex. The reverse channel generally has a lower transmission rate than the forward channel and is used to acknowledge receipt of data. Reverse channels help reduce the need for modem turnaround.

ring topology   A network configuration commonly used to implement local area networks. The medium forms a loop to which workstations are attached. Data is transmitted from one station to the next around the ring. Generally the access protocol is token-passing.

root bridge   The bridge assigned the highest priority.

router   A network interconnection device and associated software that links two networks. The networks being linked can be different, but they must use a common routing protocol.

routing   An algorithm used to determine how to move a message from its source to its destination. Several algorithms are used.

routing table   An information source containing node addresses and the identification of the path to be used in transmitting data to those nodes.

RS-232-C standard   An Electronic Industries Association (EIA) standard for asynchronous transmission.

RS-366 standard   An Electronic Industries Association (EIA) standard for automatic-call unit interface.

RS-449 standard   An Electronic Industries Association (EIA) standard that improves on the capabilities of RS-232-C.

satellite radio transmission   Transmits data via very-high-frequency (VHF) radio waves and requires line-of-sight transmission between stations.

sectional center   In the telephone network, a class 2 station.

security   Controls implemented by network management to delay unauthorized access to a system.

seek time   In disk accessing, the time it takes to move the read/write heads to the proper cylinder.

serial binary transmission   The successive transmission of bits over a wire medium.

server   In client/server computing, the software application that provides clients with the services they request. A computer that provides LAN services.

server license   A license that allows an application to be installed on one server.

session   The dialog between two system users.

session layer   One of the layers of the International Standards Organization's OSI reference model. The session layer is responsible for establishing a dialogue between applications.

shared open mode   A file open mode that allows several users to have a file open concurrently.

shared printer   A printer controlled by a server and available to designated users.

Signaling Terminal Equipment (STE)   Node used to provide an interface between two different packet-switching networks.

Simple Network Management Protocol (SNMP) SNMP provides a guideline for creating network management software products. SNMP has four key components: the SNMP protocol, structure of management information (SMI), management information base (MIB), and the network management system (NMS).

simplex transmission   A mode of data transmission in which data may flow in only one direction. One station is always a sender and another is always a receiver over a simplex link.

simulation model   A monitoring tool that allows the user to describe network and system activities and to receive an analysis of how the system can be expected to perform under the described conditions.

single mode transmission   The fastest fiber optic technique, in which the light is guided down the center of an extremely narrow core.

single threading   A technique in which only one operation is processed at a time.

site license   A license that gives the user unlimited rights to use the software at a given site.

sizing   The analysis conducted to determine the amount of hardware required to support a system. Sizing must consider the system throughout and the required transaction response times during peak processing periods.

Six-Bit Transcode (SBT)   A six-bit computer code developed by IBM primarily for RJE.

smart terminal   A terminal that can save data entered by the operator into memory.

SNA Distribution Services (SNADS)   An SNA facility that provides asynchronous distribution of documents throughout a network.

software license agreement   A document provided by the software vendor that specifies the rights and restrictions of using the software.

source routing   A learning bridge algorithm in which the sending node is responsible for determining the route to the destination node. The routing information is appended to the message and the bridges along the route use the routing information to move the message from the source to destination.

spanning tree   A method by which learning bridges build their own routing table.

spanning tree algorithm   A learning bridge algorithm in which bridges exchange routing information with one another. Based on the routing information thus received, each bridge maintains a routing table that shows how to route messages to other LANs.

spooler   A software system that collects printer output (typically on disk) and schedules the data for printing. SPOOL is an acronym for Simultaneous Peripheral Operation On Line.

Spread Spectrum Radio (SSR)   The primary application for data communications is for use with wireless LANs. It has a characteristic reliability in environments where signal interference is likely.

starLAN   A configuration similar to the basic star topology in that each workstation is connected to a wiring hub. The primary medium used for implementations is twisted-pair wires.

star topology   A network topology using a central system to which all other nodes are connected. All data are transmitted to or through the central system. Also known as star network.

star-wired LAN   A variation of star topology in which a wiring hub is used to form the connection between network nodes.

static routing   A form of routing in which one particular path between two nodes is always used.

Statistical Time Division Multiplexing (STDM)   A technique that provides improved time-sharing efficiency by transmitting data only for those lines with data to send, rather than allowing idle lines to occupy carrying capacity of the communications circuit. Also known as a stat mux.

stealth virus   A computer virus that has the ability to change its signature or identity, thus making the virus more difficult to detect and eradicate. Also known as a polymorphic virus.

store-and-forward system   When transmitting data between two nodes, the messages are logged at intermediate nodes, which then forward them to the next node.

StreetTalk (Banyan)   A database that provides network directory services.

stress testing   A procedure that ensures that the system can sustain the designated workload.

Structure of Management Information (SMI)   A component of the SNMP that details how information is represented in the management information base (MIB).

Structured Query Language (SQL)   A relational database language developed by IBM and later standardized by the American National Standards Institute (ANSI).

sub-LAN   A network that provides a subset of LAN capabilities, primarily peripheral sharing and file transfer, but has lower data transfer rates and diminished transparency than a LAN.

subnet   The first set of numbers in an Internet address representing the network identification of a node's network.

switched connection   A communications link established when one station dials a telephone number to connect to another station. A switched connection uses voice circuits. The circuit exists for the duration of the session.

Switched Multimegabit Data Services (SMDS)   A high-speed connectionless digital transmission service.

Switched Virtual Circuit (SVC)   One of three types of circuits in a packet distribution network. When a session is required between two users, an end-to-end circuit is determined and allocated for the duration of the session. Similar to a switched connection.

synchronous   A transmission protocol where the sender and receiver are synchronized. Data is generally transmitted in blocks, rather than a character at a time as in asynchronous transmission.

Synchronous Data Link Control (SDLC)   An IBM positional synchronous protocol that operates in full duplex or half duplex mode in both point-to-point and multipoint configurations. Data is transmitted in fixed-format frames consisting of start flag, address, control information, block check character (BCC) and end-of-frame flag.

Systems Network Architecture (SNA)   IBM's architecture for building a computer network. Encompasses hardware and software components, establishing sessions between users, and capabilities such as office and message/file distribution services.

Systems Services Control Point (SSCP)   In IBM's SNA, the process that controls a domain. It is responsible for initiating network components, establishing sessions, and maintaining unit status.

terminal   An input/output device that can be connected to a local or remote computer called a host computer.

terminal emulation   A software program and a hardware interface that allow one microcomputer to function as a variety of terminals in support of changing requirements.

terminator   A resistor at a cable end that absorbs the signal and prevents echo or other signal noise.

think/wait time   The amount of time an operator will wait or think while entering data for each transaction.

throughput   The amount of work performed by a system per unit of time.

Time Division Multiplexing (TDM)   A technique that divides transmission time by allotting to each device a time slot during which it can send or receive data.

time-out interval   A period of time allowed for an event to occur. If the event does not happen, the time-out expires and the process initiating the event is notified.

time-staged delivery system   Software that allows users to identify a transmission package, designate one or more recipients of the package, and specify a delivery priority.

token-passing   A media access control protocol in which a string of bits called the token is distributed among the network nodes. A computer that receives the token is allowed to transmit data onto the network. Only the stations receiving a token can transmit. Token-passing is implemented on ring and bus LANs.

token-passing bus   A LAN architecture using a bus topology and token passing media access control protocol.

token-passing ring   A LAN architecture using a ring topology and token passing media access control protocol.

toll center   In the telephone network, a toll center is a class 4 switching office. Also called a class 4 station.

transaction   A user-specified group of processing activities that either are entirely completed or leave the database and processing system in the same state as before the transaction was initiated.

Transaction Control Process (TCP)   A process that receives inputs from terminals and routes them to the proper application processes. TCPs also may edit input data, format data to and from a terminal, log messages, and provide terminal job sequencing. Examples include IBM's CICS and Tandem's Pathway. Also called a teleprocessing monitor or message control system.

Transmission Control Protocol/Internet Protocol (TCP/IP)   A suite of internetwork protocols developed by the U.S. Department of Defense for internetwork file transfers, electronic mail transfer, remote logons, and terminal services.

transaction log   Records all of the data received and is used in recovering from failures and in system auditing.

transaction routing   The routing of a transaction received from a terminal to one or more application programs.

transfer time   The amount of time required for the data to be sent over the channel to the CPU's memory.

transparency   The ability to send any bit string as data in a message. The data bits are not interpreted as control characters.

transparent access   The ability of a user to access distributed files as though they were located on the user's local node.

transponder   In satellite communications, a transponder receives the transmission from earth (uplink), amplifies the signal, changes frequency, and retransmits the data to a receiving earth station (downlink).

transport layer   One layer of the International Standards Organization's OSI reference model. The transport layer is responsible for generating the end user's address and for the integrity of the receipt of message blocks.

Transport Service Access Point (TSAP) An address used by the transport layer to uniquely identify session entities.

trapdoor encryption An encryption algorithm that utilizes large prime numbers and two keys, one key made public and the other kept secret by the message recipient. The public key encrypts the data, and the private key decrypts the ciphertext. Also known as the public key method.

transceiver A device that receives and sends signals. A transceiver helps form the interface between a network node and the medium.

tribits A method of modulation that allows three bits to be represented by each signal.

Uninterruptible Power Supply (UPS) A backup power unit that continues to provide power to a computer system during the failure of the normal power supply. A UPS is frequently used to protect LAN servers from power failures.

uploading The transfer of files or programs from the terminal to the host.

User Agent (UA) A mail agent that allows a user to compose a message, provides recipient addresses, and receives messages.

user login script A set of actions to be taken when the user logs in, such as setting search paths and initial menus.

user profile Information needed to define the applications and transactions a user is authorized to execute.

Video Display Unit (VDU) A terminal that uses a technique such as a cathode ray tube or a liquid crystal display to represent data. Also referred to as a Video Display Terminal (VDT) or Cathode Ray Tube (CRT).

Vines (Banyan) An example of LAN software that runs under an existing OS, UNIX.

virtual circuit A connection, established when setting up a communications session, between a sender and a receiver in which all messages are sent over the same path.

virtual routing No permanently established path exists; instead each node consults its routing table to determine which node should next receive the message.

Virtual Telecommunications Access Method (VTAM) One of IBM's telecommunications access methods.

virus detection software Software that analyzes a system and attempts to discover and remove any viruses that have infected the system.

weighted routing When multiple paths exist, each is given a weight according to perceived utilization. A random number is generated to determine which of the available paths to use based upon their weights.

white noise One source of data communication errors. It results from the normal movements of electrons and is present in all transmission media at temperatures above absolute zero. Also known as thermal noise and Gaussian noise.

Wide Area Network (WAN) A network that typically covers a wide geographical area and operates at speeds lower than LAN speeds.

Wide Area Telecommunications or Telephone Service (WATS) An inbound or outbound telephone service that allows long-distance telephone service. In the United States the inbound service is associated with the 800 area code toll-free numbers.

Windows NT A leading example of the integrated LAN operating software approach by Microsoft.

wiring hub Used by some LAN implementations to provide node-to-node connection.

workgroup software Often referred to as groupware, this software facilitates the activities of a group of two or more workers by reducing the time and effort needed to perform group tasks such as meetings, office correspondence, and group decision making.

workload generator A monitoring tool that generates transaction loads and pseudo-application processes for execution on a proposed configuration to illustrate how a system will actually function.

X.400 standard A standard developed by the CCITT that provides a platform for the implementation of a worldwide electronic message-handling service.

X.500 standard A standard that specifies the procedure for creating a directory system to maintain electronic mail user names and their network addresses as well as the names and addresses of other network resources such as printers and servers.

Xpress Transfer Protocol (XTP) An extension of TCP/IP that enhances performance by reducing the amount of processing and allowing some functions to be worked on simultaneously.

zero-slot LAN A low-speed LAN using "standard" microcomputer components that do not require an additional slot on the motherboard for a LAN adapter.

Index